SIMONE WEIL

JOHN XXIII

JANANI LUWUM

BLACK ELK

FLORENCE
NIGHTINGALE

FRANCIS OF ASSISI

SOJOURNER TRUTH

ANNE FRANK

MARIA SKOBTSOVA

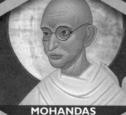

MOHANDAS
GANDHI

CESAR CHAVEZ

Every single day I read Robert Ellsberg's concise, fascinating, and inspiring lives of the saints in my copy of *Give Us This Day*. And every single day I am amazed by the astounding lives that have been lived out of love for Christ. Happily, many of these wonderful stories are now gathered together in this marvelous new book, which will guide you through the year with the help of these patrons and companions.

—James Martin, SJ, author of *Jesus: A Pilgrimage*

This delightful book reminds us how blessed we are, in every age, to have people of good faith who are called to love and serve people in need. They call us all to a greater purpose.

—Kathleen Norris, author of *The Cloister Walk* and *Acedia and Me*

The diversity of these holy men and women calls out my own gifts, and their total dedication alerts me to put my "yes" into motion for the day. Thank you for being a companion and inspiration for my faith journey!

—Carolyn Y. Woo, President and CEO of Catholic Relief Services and author of *Working for a Better World*

This is not only a classic collection of lives of the saints but also an introduction to many un-canonized holy lives, producing such delightful juxtapositions as St. Nicholas and Mozart, St. Mary Magdalene and Albert Luthuli, St. Monica and Helder Camara. As a reader of *Give Us This Day*, from which these are drawn, I've enjoyed meeting new holy men and women and am now delighted to have them alongside traditional saints of the day. Thank you for this literary treat.

—Christopher Jamison, OSB, Director of the National Office for Vocation, London, and author of *Finding Sanctuary*

Robert Ellsberg is way up there in my pantheon of spiritual writers. He's especially good at connecting us with the divine spark in practitioners of every spiritual tradition. These very human stories of the holy ones among us have a special knack of enlivening my spirit.

—Helen Prejean, CSJ, author of *Dead Man Walking*

Saints are the living Word of God, the Word made flesh, but their biographies are often too encrusted within sentimentality and piety to serve as an inspiration for us. Ellsberg gives us their essence in this treasure of a book. Nobody writes better about the lives of the saints than Robert Ellsberg!

—Ronald Rolheiser, OMI, President of the Oblate School of Theology and author of *The Holy Longing* and *Sacred Fire*

It is a challenge to provide inspiration in a brief and daily format. Robert Ellsberg's writing does so, exposing us to numerous little-known saints, with a generous sprinkling of contemporary saintly lives, his signature contribution. This book is a keeper.

—Pat Farrell, OSF, Past President of the Leadership Conference of Women Religious

Blessed Among Us

Day by Day
with Saintly Witnesses

Robert Ellsberg

A *Give Us This Day* Book

LITURGICAL PRESS
Collegeville, Minnesota

www.litpress.org

A *Give Us This Day* Book
published by Liturgical Press

Cover design by Ann Blattner

About the cover: The holy people featured on the dust jacket and end sheets of this volume are details from the *Dancing Saints* icon at Saint Gregory of Nyssa Episcopal Church, San Francisco, California. The *Dancing Saints* is a monumental icon created by iconographer Mark Dukes and the people of Saint Gregory's. Visit saintgregorys.org to learn more. Images used by permission.

1	2	3	4	5	6	7	8	9

Library of Congress Cataloging-in-Publication Data

Names: Ellsberg, Robert, 1955–, author.
Title: Blessed among us / Robert Ellsberg.
Description: Collegeville, Minnesota : Liturgical Press, 2016.
Identifiers: LCCN 2016007536 (print) | LCCN 2016014574 (ebook) |
    ISBN 9780814647219 | ISBN 9780814647455
Subjects: LCSH: Christian saints—Biography. | Christian biography. |
    Devotional calendars.
Classification: LCC BR1710 .E45 2016 (print) | LCC BR1710 (ebook) |
    DDC 270.092/2—dc23
LC record available at http://lccn.loc.gov/2016007536

To Mary Stommes,
Sue Kuefler,
and Peter Dwyer.

*"It all happened while we sat there talking,
and it is still going on."*

—Dorothy Day

CONTENTS

FEBRUARY

MARCH

APRIL

MAY

JUNE

JULY

AUGUST

SEPTEMBER

OCTOBER

NOVEMBER

DECEMBER

INTRODUCTION

From the early days of Christianity it was understood that a Christian was someone who strived to imitate or follow Christ. This was not simply a matter of believing in certain doctrines but of allowing one's identity and way of life to be shaped by Jesus and his example of self-giving love. One was not born this way; in some way or another it involved a process of conversion, of "putting off the old person and putting on Christ," as St. Paul put it. All Christians were called to this conversion—the work of a lifetime, even if it might begin, as it did for Paul, with a dramatic turning point.

As Jesus foretold of his disciples, those who followed this path were liable to share his own fate: misunderstanding, persecution, and even death. For that reason, in the early Church, martyrdom became a particular proof of authentic discipleship. Beginning with the first martyr, St. Stephen, such witnesses (the literal meaning of martyr) were seen as reenacting the passion of Christ. It was said of St. Polycarp, an early bishop who was martyred in 155, that his very death was "conformable to the gospel." The early Christians venerated the stories of such witnesses, preserving their relics and memorializing the anniversaries of their deaths—their *dies natalis,* or birth to eternal life. This was the origin of the cult of saints.

As the era of persecution waned, it became clear that there were other ways, no less heroic, of bearing witness to Christ—through ascetical lives of prayer, service to the Church, or the practice of charity. New models of holiness emerged in the form of desert monastics, missionaries, bishops, and other teachers of the Christian faith. Regardless of the form, there were certain individuals who set a standard for Christian practice; their witness inspired the faith of their contemporaries, even evoking a sense of wonder. Such individuals seemed a living link with the Gospel itself. As Alban Butler, one of the great English compilers of saints' lives, put it, they were "the Gospel clothed, as it were, in a body."

In the early days, saints were recognized more or less by public acclamation. Their memory was preserved through the ongoing prayers of the faithful. To the extent that such devotion was reinforced by reports of miracles, attention often shifted from the actual lives of the saints to their role as heavenly patrons. *The Golden Legend*, a collection of saints' lives by Jacobus de Voragine (d. 1298), was one of the most popular books of the Middle Ages. It emphasized the fabulous and miraculous deeds of the saints—helping to boost the popularity of such figures as St. George (who battled a dragon) or St. Christopher (who carried the Christ child on his back) over much better-attested, if more prosaic, figures as St. Augustine or St. Ambrose.

Over time, the Vatican assumed responsibility for the naming of saints, introducing the much more complicated process of canonization. Among the minimal criteria was the reasonable confidence that such a person in fact existed. But there were many other considerations and factors to be examined— so many that the process could take centuries. In recent years Pope John Paul II streamlined the procedure considerably. Moved by a belief that the Church needed more examples of holiness from our own time and from many diverse cultures, he beatified and canonized over a thousand men and women— far more than in previous centuries combined.

Nevertheless, the process still remains complicated. Saints are usually proposed for canonization in the diocese in which they lived. If their "cause" is accepted in Rome, they are declared Servants of God. At that point a lengthy investigation of their life and writings is conducted; witnesses, if still living, must be interviewed; records attesting to the candidate's orthodoxy and heroic virtues are submitted to Rome. If all this is accepted, the candidate is named Venerable. And then a very particular condition comes into play: certified miracles must be attributed to the candidate's intercession, one to be beatified, or declared Blessed, another to be canonized and declared a Saint. (In the case of a martyr—such as Oscar Romero, recently beatified—the first miracle is waived.)

Needless to say, such an extensive and prolonged process tends to be quite selective. It favors those with an enduring community—such as a religious order—willing to invest the time and resources, often over a span of generations. For that reason, even among the list of contemporary saints, a great number are founders or members of religious congregations. Unfortunately, this tends to perpetuate a narrow understanding of holiness as primarily the attribute of celibate priests and members of religious orders—a relatively small number of the faithful.

And yet, as the Church clearly teaches, holiness is the universal vocation of every Christian. In the Second Vatican Council's Constitution on the Church we read: "In the Church not everyone marches along the same path, yet all are called to sanctity" (Lumen Gentium 32). As the document explains, the paths to holiness are without number. Regardless of whether we are priests, nuns, or laypeople, regardless of whether we are celibate or married, of exceptional abilities, or completely average, there is a path to holiness that takes account of our particular gifts and duties in life, a path that is different for each one of us. All Christians are called to walk that path, its goal none other than the fullness of love.

It is holiness, and not canonization, that is the goal of Christian life. And yet the veneration of canonized saints can foster a very different impression. It may also lead us to suppose that saints are a relatively small number of exceptional figures (usually men, almost never laypeople), as remote from the experience of most ordinary Christians as the figures in a stained-glass window. In fact, the actual number of saints is infinitely wider. It includes all those holy men and women, many known only to a few or to God alone, who are memorialized collectively on November 1, the feast of All Saints. It is to be in *that* number (as the old hymn puts it) that we place our hopes when the "saints go marching in."

*

The present volume is drawn from entries I have written over the past five years for *Give Us This Day*, a resource for daily prayer, published monthly by Liturgical Press. In selecting entries the editors encouraged me to draw widely from the annals of historical saints, as well as those currently on the road to canonization. But they also urged me to include men and women beyond the official list, including some who clearly fall outside the official criteria for sainthood. I needed little encouragement in this direction. This expansive spirit reflects the approach of my previous books, *All Saints: Daily Reflections on Saints, Prophets, and Witnesses for Our Time* and *Blessed Among All Women: Reflections on Women Saints, Prophets, and Witnesses for Our Time*. (Readers interested in more comprehensive treatments of many of the figures in this volume may well be interested in consulting those works.) While most readers of *Give Us This Day* have welcomed this approach, it may call for some further explanation.

I believe the underlying spirit is reflected in the title chosen for both the daily column as well as the present volume: "Blessed Among Us." While generally guided by the official calendar of saints, I have tried to invoke a more inclusive "cloud of witnesses" (Hebrews 12:1)—an eclectic company of men and women whose example may expand our moral imaginations and thus inspire us to answer more faithfully our own call to holiness.

The example of saints and holy people has always served this function. The conversion of St. Augustine was prompted in part by his reading the life of St. Antony, one of the early Desert Fathers. St. Ignatius Loyola was inspired in his vocation by *The Golden Legend*—the only reading material at hand as he was recovering from a war injury. St. Edith Stein converted to Catholicism after staying up all night reading the life of St. Teresa of Avila. There is a contagious effect to such stories, as one lamp lights another.

But the influence of great minds and souls is not restricted to those who pass the rigorous test of canonization. Pope Francis offered his own suggestive opening, in his address to the U.S. Congress in 2015, when he pointed to the example of four "great Americans": Abraham Lincoln, Martin Luther King Jr., Dorothy Day, and Thomas Merton. Such figures, he noted, "offer us a way of seeing and interpreting reality."

Among the canonized saints we find many who struggled to respond in the spirit of Christ to the needs of their time and thereby opened a path for others to follow. But there are many other men and women who challenge us to see and interpret the reality of our own time: an era of globalization and religious pluralism, of new scientific awareness as well as massive violence, an era marked, among other things, by unprecedented threats to the well-being of the earth, our home. Among saints of the past, rooted in very different cultural contexts, many are distinctly unhelpful in responding to our present needs. All the more reason to take a broader view.

At the same time this brings us back to the teachings of Jesus. Long before the official process of canonization with its criteria of orthodoxy, the evidence of an enduring cult, and the certification of miracles, he set the conditions for our salvation: "I was hungry and you fed me . . . naked and you clothed me. . . . Insofar as you did these things for the least of my brothers and sisters, you did them to me." We have his story of the Good Samaritan—the very definition of an outsider—who served to demonstrate what it truly means to love our neighbor as ourselves. We have his recital of the Beatitudes: "Blessed are the poor in spirit . . . the merciful . . . the pure of heart . . . the peacemakers . . ." These are not exactly the traditional criteria for naming saints. But they come closer to characterizing the qualities that unify the diverse men and women whose stories are recounted here, all these "blessed among us."

ROBERT ELLSBERG

JANUARY

1 Mary, Mother of Jesus • St. Zdislava Berka

2 St. Basil the Great • Blessed Marie Anne Blondin

3 St. Genevieve • Lanza del Vasto

4 St. Syncletica • St. Elizabeth Ann Seton

5 St. John Neumann • St. Genevieve Torres Morales

6 St. Gertrude of Delft • St. André Bessette

7 St. Angela of Foligno • St. Raphaela Mary

8 Giotto • Galileo Galilei

9 Blessed Alix le Clercq • Venerable Pauline Jaricot

10 St. Leonie Aviat • Blessed Maria Dolores Rodriguez Sopena

11 Lambert Beauduin • Mev Puleo

12 St. Aelred of Rievaulx • St. Marguerite Bourgeoys

13 Blessed Jutta of Huy • George Fox

14 Blessed Odoric of Pordenone • Anthony Brouwers

15 St. Ita • St. Arnold Janssen

16 St. Joseph Vaz • Blessed Juana Maria Lluch

17 St. Antony of Egypt • Roberto de Nobili

18 St. Prisca • St. Margaret of Hungary

19 St. Paula • Mother Joseph of the Sacred Heart

20 Alessandro Valignano • Blessed Cyprian Michael Iwene Tansi

21 St. Agnes • Venerable Mary Angeline McCrory

22 Blessed William Joseph Chaminade • Venerable Satoko Kitahara

23 Blessed James the Almsgiver • St. Marianne Cope

24 St. Francis de Sales • Blessed Nikolaus Gross

25 Dorothy Hennessey • Samuel Ruiz

26 Saints Timothy and Titus • Blessed Michael Kozal

27 St. Angela Merici • Mahalia Jackson

28 St. Thomas Aquinas • Fyodor Dostoevsky

29 St. Andrei Rublev • Maisie Ward

30 Venerable Mary Ward • Mohandas Gandhi

31 St. Marcella • St. John Bosco

JANUARY

Mary, Mother of Jesus
(First Century)

Mary, a young Galilean woman of Nazareth, was betrothed to a carpenter named Joseph. One day, according to the Gospel of Luke, she was visited by the angel Gabriel, who proclaimed that she would bear a son named Jesus, who would be called "the Son of the Most High." How could this be, she asked, since she was as yet unmarried? The angel told her she would conceive by the power of the Spirit and assured her, "With God nothing will be impossible." And so she responded, "Let it be done to me according to your word."

It was in the space created by Mary's faith—and not simply in her womb—that the Word became flesh. For this reason she has been called not only the Mother of Jesus but Mother of the Church. In subsequent centuries, Mary's status and her distinctive nature would be the subject of dogmatic pronouncements and learned tomes. In the Gospels Jesus frequently rejected the claims of blood or natural kinship in favor of discipleship. In this perspective, Mary's preeminence is due to her having exemplified the spirit of true discipleship: attention, reverence, and obedience to the word and will of God.

The Gospel of John places Mary at the foot of the cross. According to Luke she was among the disciples who gathered in Jerusalem after Jesus' ascension (Acts 1:14). She was in effect the first and paradigmatic disciple. She is thus the first to be honored among the saints.

"My soul magnifies the Lord, and my spirit rejoices in God my Savior, for he has regarded the lowliness of his handmaiden. For behold, henceforth all generations will call me blessed; for he who is mighty has done great things for me, and holy is his name."

—Luke 1:46-49

St. Zdislava Berka
Dominican Tertiary (1220–1252)

St. Zdislava was born to a noble family in Bohemia. A precociously pious child, at the age of seven she tried running off to the forest to pursue the life of a hermit. Her parents restrained her. Eventually, they also compelled her to marry Count Havel of Lemberk, with whom she bore four children. Together they occupied a fortified castle in a frontier area subject to the incursion of Mongol invaders. While Havel engaged in frequent battles, Zdislava generously opened the doors of the castle to homeless refugees. She obliged her husband's insistence that she wear costly garments, befitting her station; he, in turn, tolerated her extravagant charity. According to one story, when Havel tried to evict a sick beggar from their bed, he found the man transformed into the figure of Christ crucified. (According to a more prosaic version of the story, Zdislava gave away their bed and replaced it with a crucifix.)

At some point, when Zdislava learned of the Dominican Order, she hastened to become one of the earliest Tertiaries. She endowed hospitals, helped build churches with her own hands, and established a Dominican convent, where she was eventually buried.

St. Zdislava was canonized in 1995. She is the patron of those in difficult marriages and those ridiculed for their piety.

"Faithful God, by her married life and works of charity you taught Saint Zdislava to pursue the way of perfection. By her prayers, may family life be strengthened and be a witness to Christian virtue."

—General Calendar of the Order of Preachers

St. Basil the Great
Bishop and Doctor of the Church (ca. 330–379)

St. Basil was raised in a family of saints (his parents, three siblings, as well as his grandmother would all be canonized). Yet there was nothing inevitable about his vocation. Only at the age of thirty did he experience a deep conversion—like "waking from a profound sleep"—and renounce all worldly ambitions to devote his life to God. After touring the monastic world, Basil established a monastery in his hometown of Caesarea. Rather than stressing individual feats of asceticism, Basil's rule emphasized the importance of community. The monastery, he believed, should be an ideal society in which love of God and love of neighbor would be cultivated in tandem. He believed the monastery should be at the service of society. Guests were welcome. The monastery included both an orphanage and a school and became a center for the works of mercy.

Eventually Basil became the bishop of Caesarea. Aside from his role as a champion of theological orthodoxy (along with his brother Gregory of Nyssa he helped to define Church teaching on the Trinity), he was a persistent advocate for social justice, going beyond the usual exhortation to charity. The needs of the poor, he taught, held a social mortgage on the superfluous holdings of the rich. Basil died on January 1, 379.

"Are you not a robber, you who consider your own that which has been given you solely to distribute to others? This bread which you have set aside is the bread of the hungry . . . those riches you have hoarded are the riches of the poor."

—St. Basil the Great

Blessed Marie Anne Blondin
Founder, Sisters of St. Anne (1809–1890)

Esther Blondin, the daughter of poor farmers, was born in Lower Canada. At twenty, she entered domestic service, eventually finding work with a teaching order in Montreal. There she learned to read and write, managing eventually to be hired as a teacher and even to serve as principal of a parochial school.

In 1848 she proposed to the bishop of Montreal to found a congregation dedicated to the "education of poor country children, both boys and girls in the same schools" (a daring proposal for the time). With his approval, a novitiate was established for the new congregation, the Sisters of St. Anne. In 1850, Blondin, who had taken the religious name Marie Anne, was selected to serve as superior.

While the order quickly grew and spread, a new chaplain, appointed by the bishop, began to exert dictatorial control. When Mother Marie Anne resisted, he compelled her to resign as superior. Although she complied without protest, he was not satisfied until she had been relegated to a position of complete obscurity. She spent the rest of her life performing domestic chores in the laundry and kitchen. When a novice asked why the foundress was assigned to such lowly work, she replied, "The deeper a tree sinks its roots into the soil, the greater are its chances of growing and producing fruit."

Blondin died on January 2, 1890. A generation would pass before her memory was restored to honor in her congregation. She was beatified in 2001.

"May Holy Eucharist and perfect abandonment to God's Will be your heaven on earth."

—Spiritual testament of Blessed Marie Anne Blondin to her sisters

St. Genevieve
Patron of Paris (ca. 442–ca. 500)

When St. Genevieve was only seven, a traveling bishop, visiting her village outside of Paris, asked her whether she wished to dedicate her life to God. The young girl heartily assented. Eight years later she confirmed this intention by formally putting on a veil and consecrating herself to Christ.

Genevieve lived in a time of war, famine, and social conflict. Clovis, king of the Franks, often sought her counsel and also responded to her entreaties on behalf of prisoners and the poor. She earned her reputation as a protector of Paris when her prayers successfully averted a siege by Attila the Hun.

Devotion to St. Genevieve steadily increased following her death. Centuries later her relics were credited with ending an epidemic in Paris. Though her shrine was desecrated during the French Revolution, her protection continued to be invoked in times of disaster or national crisis. In 1962 Pope John XXIII declared her a patron of the French security forces.

"When she was brought again on the morn, [Bishop] Germain saw in her a sign celestial, I know not what, and said to her: God salute thee, Genevieve. Daughter, rememberest thou what thou promised to me yesterday of the virginity of thy body? Holy father, said the maid, I remember well that, and by the help of God I desire and think to accomplish my purpose."

—From *The Golden Legend* by Jacobus de Voragine

Lanza del Vasto
Peacemaker (1901–1981)

Lanza del Vasto was born into a noble family in Italy in 1901. His study of philosophy left him searching for some deeper wisdom, perhaps lost in the West. In 1936 he traveled to India, where he met Mahatma Gandhi, who dubbed him "Shantidas"—Servant of Peace. It was an encounter that utterly changed his life.

In 1948, he and his wife formed the Community of the Ark in France, a community of families united by a rule, vows, and common prayer. Living off the land, raising their own food, all without electricity or modern machines, they took their inspiration from Noah's Ark—joining together to preserve certain values from the deluge of violence, ugliness, and efficiency that threatened to make the planet uninhabitable. With his long white beard, his staff, and homespun clothes, del Vasto easily looked the part of a modern Noah.

Although the community was open to persons of all religious faiths, del Vasto remained rooted in his Catholic tradition, and many of his most personal initiatives focused on efforts to remind the Church of the message of peace. In 1963 he fasted in Rome for forty days, appealing to the pope to issue a statement on the arms race. In return he was rewarded with an advance copy of Pope John XXIII's encyclical *Pacem in Terris*.

Until his death on January 5, 1981, he offered a consistent witness to peace and the possibility of a healthy, whole, and joyful life.

"The future must be a future of nonviolence, or else there will be no future."
—Lanza del Vasto

St. Syncletica
Desert Mother (d. ca. 350)

The fourth-century ascetics who drifted into the desert included many women as well as men. St. Syncletica was among the most renowned of these Desert Mothers. She was born in Alexandria to a wealthy family. When her parents died she gave away all her property, retreated with her blind sister to a remote crypt, and devoted herself to a life of prayer. Gradually other women were attracted by her reputation for spiritual wisdom. They formed a community over which she presided as abbess.

A gifted preacher, Syncletica had a special gift for discerning people's readiness for monastic life. Many of her homilies have been preserved. In one of them, she said: "Oh, how happy should we be did we but take as much pain to gain Heaven and pleased God as worldlings do to heap up riches and perishable goods! By land they venture among thieves and robbers; at sea they expose themselves to winds and waves; they suffer shipwrecks and perils; they attempt all, dare all, hazard all; but we, in serving so great a Master, for so immense a good, are afraid of every contradiction."

Syncletica lived to the age of eighty-four. Toward the end of her life she suffered from a painful cancer. Unable to speak, she continued to preach by her example of fortitude and faith. Her feast day is January 5.

"I think that for those living in community obedience is a greater virtue than chastity, however perfect. Chastity carries within it the danger of pride, but obedience has within it the promise of humility."

—St. Syncletica

St. Elizabeth Ann Seton
Founder, Sisters of Charity of St. Joseph (1774–1821)

Born two years before the American Revolution, Elizabeth Ann Bayley was raised in a prosperous and staunchly Episcopalian family in New York City. At the age of twenty she married a successful merchant named William Seton, with whom she bore five children. Her fortunes underwent a drastic change, however, when her husband's business failed and he was then stricken with tuberculosis. Desperate to improve his health, she accompanied him and their daughter on a voyage to Italy. But William did not survive the journey.

Accepting hospitality from Italian friends, Elizabeth prolonged her stay for some months. So touched and consoled was she by her hosts' faith that she determined to become a Catholic. Upon her return, however, she confronted severe anti-Catholic prejudices among her family and their social circle and soon found herself isolated and penniless.

A priest in Baltimore provided Seton a way out when he invited her to start a school in his parish. Accepting this mission, she gradually attracted other women to join her. In 1809 they took religious vows and formed the Sisters of Charity of St. Joseph—the first native-born congregation in the United States. Mother Seton was their first superior.

Before long, schools and orphanages under her direction opened in several cities. By the time of her death on January 4, 1821, there were twenty such houses across the country. With her canonization in 1975, she became the first native-born saint of the United States.

"The first end I propose in our daily work is to do the will of God; secondly, to do it in the manner he wills it; and thirdly, to do it because it is his will."
—St. Elizabeth Ann Seton

9

St. John Neumann
Bishop (1811–1860)

John Neumann was born in Bohemia to Czech and German parents. Though he wished to study for the priesthood, his local diocese already had a surfeit of priests. He therefore departed for America, where he was accepted at a seminary in New York and was ordained in 1836. Specially gifted with languages, he was well suited for work among the various immigrant populations. After some years working with German immigrants in the Rochester area, he applied to join the newly arrived Redemptorist missionary order, whose novitiate was in Pittsburgh. There he would remain for eight years, eventually becoming the Redemptorist Provincial for North America.

In 1852, four years after becoming a naturalized citizen, Neumann was named the fourth bishop of Philadelphia. Among his principal accomplishments was the establishment of a thriving network of parochial schools—the first in the country. He also completed construction of a cathedral, founded a congregation of teaching sisters, and introduced the Forty Hours Devotion to America. Exhausted by his labors, he collapsed and died on January 5, 1860. He was canonized by Pope Paul VI in 1977.

"Everyone who breathes . . . has a mission, has a work. We are not sent into this world for nothing; we are not born at random. . . . God sees every one of us; He creates every soul . . . for a purpose. As Christ has His work, we too have ours; as He rejoiced to do His work, we must rejoice in ours also."

—St. John Neumann

St. Genevieve Torres Morales
Founder, Congregation of the Sacred Heart of Jesus
and the Holy Angels (1870–1956)

Genevieve Torres Morales, who was born in eastern Spain, survived a truly terrible childhood. Following the death of her parents when she was eight, she quit school to work and help support her brother. At thirteen a gangrenous tumor required the amputation of her leg—without the benefit of anesthesia. As a result she walked on crutches and suffered recurrent pain for the rest of her life. This disability would thwart her desire to enter the Carmelites.

Nevertheless, her own sufferings opened her heart to the needs of others. Along with two other women, with whom she shared a house in Valencia, she began to take in homeless women. Her spiritual director encouraged her to pursue this work of mercy, and by 1911 it had become a full-time occupation. Other women began to arrive—some to help, others in need—and Genevieve was inspired to form the Congregation of the Sacred Heart of Jesus and the Holy Angels. The sisters, who initially took private vows, were known as *Angèlicas*.

The growing congregation, devoted to helping poor, homeless, and abandoned women, received papal recognition in 1953. Genevieve, the first mother superior, died on January 5, 1956. She was canonized in 2003 by Pope John Paul II, who described her as "an instrument of God's tender love for lonely people in need of love, comfort, and physical and spiritual care."

"Self-love is horrible, for it conceals itself in the tissues of our heart under the seductive guise of well-being."

—St. Genevieve Torres Morales

11

St. Gertrude of Delft
Beguine Mystic (d. 1358)

St. Gertrude, a Dutch peasant girl, supported herself in domestic service. Betrothed at one point, she was devastated when her fiancé chose instead to marry another. In this rejection, however, she discerned the hand of Providence guiding her to a different life. She was accepted into a Beguine community in Delft, where she spent the rest of her life. The Beguines were then flourishing in the Lowlands. In this remarkable network of communities, unmarried laywomen devoted themselves to prayer, study of Scripture, and charitable works, while supporting themselves through needlework or other crafts.

For some years Gertrude led an unremarkable life. Then on Good Friday in 1340 she received the five marks of Christ's wounds on her body. These wounds would bleed seven times a day. When Gertrude confided this news to one of her fellow Beguines, the story quickly spread, and she was soon besieged by curious onlookers. This attention proved a severe mortification, and when she prayed to Christ to withdraw the favor the bleeding stopped. But she remained a gifted spiritual counselor, skilled at reading the souls of others and even prophesying the future.

After uttering her last words—"I am longing to go home"—she died on the feast of the Epiphany in 1358.

"Draw and unite me entirely to yourself. May I remain inseparably attached to you even when I am obliged to perform external duties for my neighbor's good. And afterwards may I return to seek you within me when I have accomplished them."

—St. Gertrude of Delft

St. André Bessette
Holy Cross Brother (1845–1937)

André Bessette was born in 1845 to a working-class family in Quebec. Orphaned at the age of twelve and lacking any trade or education, he was forced to support himself through various manual occupations. In time his intense spirituality—particularly his devotion to St. Joseph—attracted the attention of his pastor, who recommended that he enter the Holy Cross Order as a lay brother. (His pastor even sent a letter to the superior, reading, "I am sending you a saint.") Upon his acceptance, Bessette was assigned the post of doorman at Notre Dame College near Montreal. (He liked to joke that on completing his novitiate he was shown the door and remained there for forty years.)

Despite his lowly station, Brother André's reputation for holiness began to grow. He spent much of his spare time visiting the sick, and he was eventually credited with many healing miracles (which he was always quick to credit to St. Joseph and the mercy of God). Eventually, huge numbers flocked to the school for his blessing, and it required a team of secretaries to answer the 80,000 letters he received each year. Despite the fragile health of his youth, he lived to the age of ninety-one. After his death on January 6, 1937, a million people filed by his coffin.

Brother André was beatified in 1982; his canonization by Pope Benedict XVI followed in 2010.

"God chose the most ignorant one. If there was anyone more ignorant than I am, God would have chosen him instead of me."

—St. André Bessette

13

St. Angela of Foligno
Franciscan Mystic (1248–1309)

St. Angela came from a wealthy family in Foligno, Italy, where her early life was given over to frivolity and pleasure seeking. She married a rich man and bore three sons. But her existence lacked a higher purpose. By the time she was thirty-seven she desperately prayed to St. Francis for some relief. The next day, while sitting in church, she vowed to transform her life.

The opportunity for radical change came through tragic circumstances: the death of her entire family during an outbreak of plague. Yet, in her loss, Angela discerned the hand of God leading her to a life of penance and prayer. During a subsequent pilgrimage to Assisi she was overwhelmed by the love of God. After giving away all her property, she joined the Third Order of St. Francis and resolved to live on alms.

In time Angela gathered around herself a family of Franciscan tertiaries, both men and women, for whom she served as spiritual mother. In her extensive writings, she described her intimacy with God and her vivid contemplation of Christ's passion. Her intense mystical experiences, however, did not distract her from concern for others. With her companions she nursed the sick and waited on the poor. "The world," she said, "is great with God."

Angela died on January 4, 1309. She was canonized by Pope Francis in 2013. Her feast is celebrated in the United States on January 7.

"In an excess of wonder I cried out: 'This world is pregnant with God!' Wherefore I understood how small is the whole of creation . . . but the power of God fills it all to overflowing."

—St. Angela of Foligno

St. Raphaela Mary
Founder, Handmaids of the Sacred Heart (1850–1925)

Raphaela Porras was born in a small Spanish town near Cordoba. Her father, the local mayor, died when she was four; her mother's death followed when she was nineteen. At that point she and her sister entered a convent of the nuns of Mary Reparatrix. This community had been invited to Cordoba by a priest who had failed to secure the prior permission of his bishop. The bishop responded by expelling the community, allowing only the novices, including Raphaela and her sister, to remain. Raphaela was put in charge. It was not an auspicious beginning.

When it came time for them to pronounce final vows, the bishop presented them with a new Rule of his own composition. Rather than comply, the whole community chose to flee the city in the middle of the night. The bishop tried to enlist the civil authorities to pursue them, but he actually had no authority, since they were not yet a canonically approved community.

The sisters eventually settled in Madrid, where they secured recognition as Handmaids of the Sacred Heart. Their mission: educating children and assisting with retreats. In 1893 Raphaela resigned as Mother General. She spent the last thirty-two years of her life in obscurity within the congregation she had founded. She died on January 6, 1925. She was canonized in 1977.

"God wants me to submit to all that happens to me as if I saw him there commanding it."
—St. Raphaela Mary

Giotto
Artist (ca. 1266–1337)

Giotto di Bondone, known simply as Giotto, was one of the greatest religious artists of the late Middle Ages. Most of the details of his biography are subject to question—whether he was born in Florence or elsewhere, whether he was the son of a shepherd or a blacksmith, whether there is any truth to the story that he was taken on as an apprentice by the great artist Cimabue who was impressed to see the boy drawing remarkably lifelike pictures of sheep on a rock. But there is no doubting his extraordinary talent. One time the pope is said to have sent a messenger to request a demonstration of his reputed skill. Giotto picked up a brush, and with it painted a red circle so exact that it appeared to be the work of a compass. When the pope received this he "instantly recognized that Giotto surpassed all the painters of his time."

Giotto accompanied Cimabue to Assisi, where the master had been commissioned to paint several frescoes. Giotto has been credited with the great fresco cycle of the life of St. Francis that covers the walls of the Basilica of St. Francis. These images, as much as the written stories of the saint's life, offer the best early commentary on the life of St. Francis and his spirituality.

Giotto died on January 8, 1337, and was buried in the Cathedral of Florence.

"Once Cimabue thought to hold the field as painter; Giotto now is all the rage, dimming the luster of the other's fame."

—Dante, *The Divine Comedy*

Galileo Galilei
Scientist (1564–1642)

The Italian scientist Galileo achieved his original fame through his invention of one of the early thermometers, his experiments in physics, and his refinement of the telescope. It was his passion for astronomy—specifically his determination to prove Copernicus's theory that the earth revolves around the sun—that led him into trouble with the Church.

A number of theologians were sympathetic to Galileo's efforts, including Cardinal Baronius, who noted, "The Holy Ghost intended to teach us how to go to heaven, not how the heavens go." Nevertheless, Galileo was instructed to desist from his work. When he persisted, he was summoned to Rome by the Holy Office.

Galileo's trial occurred in 1633. Though he was treated with reasonable courtesy, the pope had issued a document threatening him with torture if he did not cheerfully submit to the findings of the court. In the end he was condemned as "vehemently suspect of heresy" for maintaining the doctrine "which is false and contrary to the Sacred and Divine Scriptures, that . . . the earth moves and is not the center of the world."

Galileo fell to his knees and abjured any heretical opinions he may have held. Convinced of his sincere repentance, the court sentenced him to house arrest in Florence for the rest of his life. There he continued his scientific work, though by 1638, the man who had first seen mountains on the moon was completely blind. He died on January 8, 1642. In 1992 Pope John Paul II declared that the Church had erred in the condemnation of Galileo as a heretic.

"Since no two truths can contradict one another, [the Copernican position] and the Bible would be seen to be of necessity perfectly harmonious."
—Galileo Galilei

Blessed Alix le Clercq
Cofounder, Augustinian Canonesses of Our Lady
(1576–1622)

Alix le Clercq was born to a wealthy family in the Duchy of Lorraine. At the age of seventeen she began to feel the tug of a higher purpose. When she described this to her pastor, Fr. Peter Fourier, he urged her to join a convent. But conventional religious life, she believed, was not for her. This intuition was confirmed by a vision of Our Lady, clothed in an unfamiliar habit, who spoke to her: "Come, daughter, and I will welcome you." She believed herself called to something new—an "active foundation." It took some years and many frustrating sidetracks before she determined her true mission: "to teach children to read and write and sew, and especially to love and serve God."

Eventually, with other women she had found to join her, along with Fr. Fourier's support, she won approval from Rome for her congregation: the Augustinian Canonesses of Our Lady. In later years it became common for religious sisters to work in teaching and other active ministries. But in Alix's time this was still a novelty, and her community faced constant pressure to adapt to a more conventional mold. She herself suffered unrelenting criticism. Meanwhile, Fr. Fourier, following an all-too-common pattern in such partnerships, tried to suppress the history of her own role as cofounder of the congregation. But she knew she had fulfilled her mission. She died on January 9, 1622, at the age of forty-five, and was beatified in 1947.

"I value one act of humility more than a hundred ecstasies."

—Blessed Alix le Clercq

Venerable Pauline Jaricot
Founder, Society for the Propagation of the Faith
(1799–1862)

Though born to a wealthy family in France, Pauline Jaricot felt called from an early age to give everything to the cause of Christ. She proved adept at translating her pious impulses into successful organizations, beginning at nineteen when she formed the girls working in her father's factory into a network of prayer. The next year she organized the Society for the Propagation of the Faith to support overseas missions through prayer and fund-raising. Her third great project was a "Living Rosary," a network of groups of fifteen persons, each of them assigned to pray a single mystery of the rosary for an entire month.

Despite her accomplishments, Pauline was beset by detractors and other setbacks. The last years of her life were spent in poverty as she struggled to repay debts incurred by a swindler. In her will she wrote, "My only treasure is the cross. . . . What difference does it make to me . . . that You take away from me earthly goods, reputation, honor, health, life, so that You lead me to descend through humiliation into the deepest pit of the abyss . . . for it is in this deep abyss that I find the hidden fire of Your love."

She died a pauper on January 9, 1862. Her cause for canonization is in process.

"Oh! I'd love to have a well of gold to give some to all the unfortunate so there would not be any more poor people at all and that no one would cry anymore."

—Venerable Pauline Jaricot

19

St. Leonie Aviat
Founder, Oblate Sisters of St. Francis de Sales
(1844–1914)

Leonie Aviat, the daughter of French shopkeepers, was educated in the Visitation convent in Troyes. There she experienced the first stirrings of a religious vocation that would only grow over time. Her path was revealed one day when she took her mother's eyeglasses to a factory for repair and found herself deeply moved by the condition of the young women working there.

In this era of industrialization, many young rural women were being drawn to the city, lured by the glamour of factory work, only to face homelessness and every kind of exploitation. The chaplain at Leonie's school, Fr. Louis Brisson, had some years earlier established a center in Troyes to house and educate such women. Leonie volunteered to join him and soon became the administrator of the house. With other volunteers, she and Fr. Brisson eventually formed a new congregation, the Oblate Sisters of St. Francis de Sales. Taking their inspiration from "Jesus the Worker," they sought to form young workingwomen into apostles who would spread the spirit of God's love in their workplaces. As she instructed her sisters, "Let us be God's little tools and allow Him to use us according to His wishes."

The congregation was approved in 1911, by which time communities had spread to South Africa and Ecuador. Mother Leonie, who served as superior, died on January 10, 1914. She was canonized in 2001.

"You must not wish to live outside the 'present moment.' It contains the light that you must follow and the help necessary for each circumstance."

—St. Leonie Aviat

Blessed Maria Dolores Rodriguez Sopena
Founder, Ladies of the Catechetical Institutes
(1848–1918)

Dolores Rodriguez Sopena was the daughter of a lawyer whose work caused the family to move throughout Spain, and even for some years to Puerto Rico and Cuba. Dolores had little interest in high society. She was irresistibly drawn to those on the margins—the poor, the sick, and prisoners. While living in Cuba she established "Centers of Instruction" to help poor children with their religious education.

After returning to Madrid she submitted to the spiritual direction of a Jesuit priest. She tried to comply with his urging that she enter a Salesian convent, but this lasted only ten days. Formal religious life was not for her.

In 1885 she opened a sort of settlement house—a place that could attend to both the material and spiritual needs of her poor neighbors. With friends she established "Centers for Workers"—a name that would not offend the anticlerical sentiment of the time. Eventually she won support in Rome for a religious institute, the Ladies of the Catechetical Institutes, to organize these centers. She and her companions lived together in a religious community, but they did not wear a habit or display any outward sign of religion. Their aim was to enter into friendship with the workers, to offer material support, while also affirming moral and spiritual values.

She died on January 10, 1918, and was beatified by Pope John Paul II in 2002.

"Make of all one family in Christ."
—The motto of Blessed Maria Dolores Rodriguez Sopena

Lambert Beauduin
Monk and Liturgist (1873–1960)

In 1906 Octave Beauduin, a Belgian diocesan priest, entered the Benedictine monastery of Mont César and took the name Lambert. In the monastery he fell in love with liturgy, and before long began to write essays on the importance of liturgical renewal. He stressed, in particular, the active participation by laity in the Mass, the center of Catholic life. Not only would this deepen the sense of Catholic identity, he believed, but it would foster broad social renewal. Beauduin was sent to teach at Sant'Anselmo in Rome. There he influenced an American Benedictine, Dom Virgil Michel, who would return to become a leading figure in the American liturgical movement.

In the meantime, Beauduin had also been drawn to Eastern forms of Christianity. With permission, he started a monastery in Belgium devoted to healing the ancient division between Christianity of the East and West. He also promoted dialogue toward reunion with the Anglican Church. This particular enthusiasm provoked a furious backlash, which extended to Rome. In 1931 he was ordered to leave Belgium for an "exile" lasting twenty years. Part of that time he spent in France, where he befriended the papal nuncio—the future Pope John XXIII.

In 1951 he was permitted at last to return to his monastery in Belgium, where he lived quietly until his death on January 11, 1960. By that time Pope John had called for the Second Vatican Council, where many of Beauduin's views on ecumenism and liturgical renewal would find vindication.

"Liturgy is theology . . . the theology of the people."

—Lambert Beauduin, OSB

Mev Puleo
Witness to Solidarity (1963–1996)

When she was fourteen, Mev Puleo, a young American, accompanied her parents on a trip to Brazil. While riding a bus up a steep hill to view the famous statue of Christ the Redeemer that overlooks Rio de Janeiro, she could see on one side the opulent homes and immaculate beaches enjoyed by the rich. On the other side she saw "ramshackle homes, children in rags, young and old begging for our coins." These contradictions laid the foundation for her vocation: to create a bridge between the different worlds she had viewed from that bus.

Photography was her special vehicle. She traveled throughout the Third World, documenting the life, struggles, and humanity of the poor. Her aim was "to revere the human spirit and bridge the distance between persons." In Latin America she interviewed activists, prophetic bishops, and liberation theologians, sharing in writings and presentations a vision of a Church and a world renewed in the light of God's reign.

Two years after her marriage in 1992 she was diagnosed with a malignant brain tumor. Still she continued her work. In 1995 she received the U.S. Catholic Award for furthering the cause of women in the Church. She died on January 12, 1996, at the age of thirty-two.

"Jesus didn't die to save us from suffering—he died to teach us how to suffer. Sometimes I actually mean it. I'd rather die young, having lived a life crammed with meaning, than to die old, even in security, but without meaning."

—Mev Puleo, writing as a college student

St. Aelred of Rievaulx
Abbot (1110–1167)

St. Aelred, who was born in northern England, spent his life within the penitential atmosphere of a Cistercian monastery. Yet it might be said of him, as he said of one of his monks, that he was "friendship's child," for he spent all his energy "in seeking to be loved and to love."

In his early life, Aelred served in the court of the kings of Scotland. He might well have enjoyed a successful career in this service had an errand not brought him to Yorkshire to visit the new Cistercian monastery of Rievaulx. There, feeling that he had found his true home, he immediately applied for entry.

Aelred's rise within the monastic community was rapid, culminating in his election as abbot, an office he retained until his death at the age of fifty-seven. During his term the monastery grew to include over six hundred monks, making it the largest religious community in England.

Aelred called the monastery a school of love. He encouraged the cultivation of true friendship among his monks as a reflection of their friendship with and love for Christ. As he wrote in his treatise *Spiritual Friendship*, "I call them more beasts than men who say life should be led so that they need not console anyone nor occasion distress or sorrow to anyone . . . seeking to love no one and be loved by none."

Aelred died on January 12, 1167.

"God is friendship. . . He who dwells in friendship dwells in God, and God in him."
                                        —St. Aelred of Rievaulx

St. Marguerite Bourgeoys
Founder, Congregation of Notre Dame of Montreal
(1620–1700)

In 1653 Marguerite Bourgeoys arrived in the French colony in Montreal to serve as schoolmistress. Though she had always felt a religious calling, she had found no community in France willing to accept her. Thus, when she heard the call for volunteers in Montreal, she eagerly responded to an opportunity to help implant the Gospel in New France. Montreal, at the time, was no more than a primitive fort, enclosing a settlement of about two hundred souls. Initially, as she found, there were actually no children to teach, and it would be several years before the first school was constructed. In the meantime, Marguerite occupied herself with a range of charitable activities and worked hard to promote religious life in the colony.

In her early years on the frontier she endured poverty, hunger, and the persistent perils of war. But as Montreal steadily expanded, so too did Marguerite's sense of vocation. In the course of several trips to France she recruited women to help her start a new missionary congregation dedicated to education. In 1676 she succeeded in winning recognition for the Congregation of Notre Dame—the first non-enclosed foreign-missionary community for women in the Church.

Marguerite served as superior of the congregation until her retirement at the age of seventy-three. She died on January 12, 1700, and was canonized in 1982.

"God is not satisfied if we preserve the love we owe our neighbor; we must preserve our neighbor in the love he ought to have for us."

—St. Marguerite Bourgeoys

Blessed Jutta of Huy
Mystic (ca. 1160–1228)

As a young girl Jutta had no wish to marry, but the decision was not in her hands. Her parents arranged her marriage when she was thirteen, and she bore three children. But when her husband died, leaving her a widow at eighteen, she refused to remarry. One night on a dark street she was confronted by a potential rapist. Her biographer, Hugh of Florette, records her feelings: "What should she do? To whom could she turn? If she wished to escape there was nowhere to go. If she tried to resist the man was stronger." At that moment they were surprised by the appearance of a woman—Jutta believed it was the Blessed Mother—and her assailant fled.

Afterward, Jutta went to work in the local leprosarium, caring for the sick and dying whom society shunned. Some years later, when she was thirty-three, she received permission from her bishop to be enclosed in a cell attached to the hospital. There she spent the rest of her life, receiving visitors, food, and communion through a small opening in the wall. Jutta enjoyed frequent colloquies with Christ, the Blessed Mother, and other saints, and she became widely known as a wise and gifted reader of souls. Her reputation enabled her to upbraid even clergy and prominent citizens for their secret sins, and they learned at their peril not to ignore her spiritual counsel.

She died on January 13, 1228.

"Mother, behold your daughter. I entrust her to you as your own daughter, as your own special servant forever; preserve and protect her and guide her as your own child."

—Words spoken by Christ in one of Blessed Jutta's visions

George Fox
Quaker (1624–1691)

George Fox, the son of a weaver, was born in Leicestershire in the time of the Puritan revival. Despite the stern atmosphere of religious fervor, Fox found no priests or preachers who "spoke to his condition." Eventually, after much searching, he received an experiential sense of the "Seed of God" present in his own soul. His mission in life would be to attend to that seed, to heed the "inner voice," and to awaken others to a similar consciousness.

Fox felt impelled to share his vision with other "Friends," often earning scorn and persecution. He was frequently beaten by his fellow Christians, put in stocks, or cast in jail. In 1656 he spent months in a windowless dungeon, confined in the mire of his own filth. His message was taken as a sweeping rebuke to the institutional Christianity of his time—as so it was. At the same time he adopted social attitudes at odds with his "worldly" contemporaries.

Fox wore plain clothes and paid no respect to social hierarchy. He spoke plainly without any deference for rich or poor. He would swear no oath. He opposed war and violence and constantly warned the rich to "take heed of oppressing the poor."

It was a magistrate who first coined the term "Quaker," after Fox enjoined him to "tremble before the Lord." Yet within a decade tens of thousands had joined the "Society of Friends." Fox died on January 13, 1691.

"Be patterns, be examples . . . wherever you go, so that your carriage and life may preach among all sorts of people, and to them. Then you will come to walk cheerfully over the world, answering that of God in every one."
—George Fox

Blessed Odoric of Pordenone
Franciscan Missionary (ca. 1285–1331)

O doric of Pordenone passed his early life as a conventional Franciscan friar, a vocation he embraced at the age of fifteen. In 1317, however, some impulse inspired him to embark on a fantastic journey that took him to the ends of the known world and back again.

Starting in Venice he sailed east, traveling overland from Constantinople to Baghdad and the Persian Gulf. From there he sailed to Malabar and southern India where he spent time with the ancient Christian community. Still, he pushed on, to Ceylon, Sumatra, and Java, then north to Canton and the great ports of China. He spent several years in Beijing before turning homeward through Tibet, on to Persia, and eventually back to Italy.

The reasons for his travel are mysterious. As for his decision to spend his final years in seclusion, he is said to have complied with a vision from St. Francis, who ordered him to stay put. He did dictate an account of his journeys, and it was widely circulated. While providing little information about his activities or the motive for his grand tour, his travelogue offered an eyewitness account of the extraordinary things he had witnessed, including the curious customs, the prodigious sights, and the religious practices of the people he encountered.

Odoric died on January 14, 1331. He was beatified in 1755.

"As I, friar Odoric, have travelled among the remote nations of the unbelievers, where I saw and heard many great and wonderful things, I have thought fit to relate all these things truly."

—Blessed Odoric of Pordenone

Anthony Brouwers
Promoter of the Lay Mission Movement (1912–1964)

In 1955 Monsignor Anthony Brouwers, a priest from Los Angeles, made a tour of Catholic missions in East Africa. As director of the diocesan office of the Society for the Propagation of the Faith, Brouwers had tried zealously to promote interest in the theme of mission and to raise funds for overseas missionaries. But what he learned in his three-month tour caused him to change his focus. Among all the priests, religious, and bishops he met he heard a constant refrain—that all too much of their time was spent on work that could be performed by lay helpers. "Everywhere I saw priests and religious trying their human best to be doctors, dentists, nurses, builders, mechanics, plumbers, and electricians, and scores of other craftsmen."

For Brouwers this pointed to an obvious need for laypeople with practical skills to join as helpers in mission. Returning to Los Angeles he resolved to recruit and train laypeople to serve as short-term missionary volunteers. It was an advanced idea for the time and Brouwers faced opposition from many corners. But he found his willing volunteers. By 1957 the first of these Lay Mission-Helpers were on their way to Africa. In the decades that followed, they were joined by more than seven hundred others.

Brouwers was a tireless promoter of the movement. After a long struggle with multiple myeloma, he died on January 14, 1964.

"Quick minds and keen eyes will be watching you constantly in the mission. You are a witness, someone showing others what they can or should be."
—Monsignor Anthony Brouwers

St. Ita
Abbess (d. ca. 570)

Though St. Ita is one of the most popular of Irish saints, it is difficult to disentangle history from legend. Perhaps of royal descent, Ita spurned noble suitors and proclaimed her determination to become a nun. Eventually, with her father's consent, she traveled to Killeedy in Limerick, where she attracted other young women to join her in a monastic community. There is some evidence that she presided over a "double monastery" that included both men and women—a practice not uncommon in the Celtic Church. Among other things she ran a school for young boys, some of whom, including the great St. Brendan, would become famous saints in their own right.

Fabulous stories surround the life of St. Ita, attesting to her charity, her healing powers, and her gifts of prophecy. According to one story she once reunited a man's body with his head—decapitated in battle—and restored him to life. Other stories recount feats of asceticism, such as the report that she subsisted for some years entirely on food provided from heaven. Though wealthy lords offered her abundant land, she spurned any temptation to worldly power and insisted on confining her monastery holdings to just four acres.

Ita died and was buried in the monastery she had founded.

"Three things that please God most are true faith in God with a pure heart, a simple life with a grateful spirit, and generosity inspired by charity. The three things that most displease God are a mouth that hates people, a heart harboring resentments, and confidence in wealth."

—St. Ita

St. Arnold Janssen
Founder, Society of the Divine Word (1837–1909)

Arnold Janssen, the son of a farmer, was born in Germany in 1837. He was ordained a priest in 1861 and spent twelve years teaching science and mathematics. But all the while his heart was stirred by the missionary imperative—to "go and make disciples of all nations." In response he launched a popular magazine, *The Little Messenger of the Sacred Heart*, aimed at stimulating mission consciousness. He followed this with the idea of forming a missionary seminary. The Church in Germany at that time was suffering a wave of anti-Catholic legislation. A bishop with whom he discussed his plan was dismissive, remarking: "He wants to found a mission house and he is penniless. He is either a fool or a saint." Janssen was no fool. He moved across the border to Holland and started his seminary in a run-down inn. It was the seed of the Society of the Divine Word (SVD), the mission order he would direct for over thirty years.

Fr. Janssen himself never served overseas. But before long he was sending mission priests to China, Papua New Guinea, and other parts of the world. He also founded an order of lay brothers and two congregations of women before his death on January 15, 1909. Today the members of his SVD family number over ten thousand and serve in more than seventy countries. Janssen was canonized in 2003.

"What you cannot accomplish is not the will of God."

—St. Arnold Janssen

St. Joseph Vaz
Apostle of Sri Lanka (1651–1711)

Joseph Vaz was born in Portuguese Goa to a Catholic family of Brahmin background. The Church in Goa had produced a number of native vocations, and Joseph was ordained a priest in 1676. After hearing of the sufferings of Catholics in Ceylon (now Sri Lanka), deprived by their Dutch rulers of an opportunity to practice their faith, Joseph contrived to sneak onto the island in the guise of a coolie laborer. Once ashore, he made contact with Catholic families and carried out a clandestine ministry.

Eventually he traveled to the Sinhalese Buddhist kingdom of Kandy, where he was able to work in relative freedom. Other Goan priests joined him. They lived in complete poverty, subsisting on alms and dressing like the poorest of their flock. Vaz and his companions studied the Buddhist classics, engaged in respectful dialogue, and made no distinction between Christians and non-Christians in their care for the sick and other humanitarian work.

Having declined the wish of Pope Clement XI to make him a bishop, Vaz died in Kandy on January 16, 1711. He left behind a vibrant Catholic community, which continues in the present. He was canonized by Pope Francis during his visit to Sri Lanka in 2015.

"Let it be known to all that I sell and offer myself as a perpetual slave of the Virgin Mother of God. This I do through a free, spontaneous and perfect act of devotion which in law is known as an irrevocable act among the living."
—St. Joseph Vaz

Blessed Juana Maria Lluch
Founder, Congregation of the Handmaids
of the Immaculate Conception, Protectress of Workers
(1862–1916)

Juana Maria Lluch was born to a wealthy family in Valencia, Spain. While deeply religious, she did not embrace an "otherworldly" piety but "lived the ordinary in an extraordinary way." As a teenager she became concerned with the plight of factory workers. In this era of industrialization, rural farmworkers were increasingly drawn to the city to work on assembly lines. Without the protection of unions, they were vulnerable to every form of exploitation. At the age of eighteen Juana approached her archbishop with the idea of launching a congregation to serve the workers. Perhaps not surprisingly, given her youth and inexperience, her proposal was rejected.

Nevertheless, in 1884 she established a shelter for factory workers that combined religious instruction with various forms of material support. In time, this included a school for the workers' children. In 1892, joined by other women and with eventual support from the Church, she launched the Congregation of the Handmaids of the Immaculate Conception, Protectress of Workers. Her goal was to be like Mary, a "handmaid of the Lord," available in any way to do God's will.

By the time Juana Maria died on January 16, 1916, her congregation had spread to many cities. She was beatified in 2003.

To be "holy in heaven, without any ostentation on earth."

—Blessed Juana Maria Lluch, describing her goal

St. Antony of Egypt
Abbot (251–356)

St. Antony was an early and celebrated champion of the ascetic life as well as a pioneer of Christian monasticism. Born in Egypt to wealthy Christian parents, he was transformed one day after hearing the Gospel text in which Jesus instructed a rich young man to sell all he had, give to the poor, and find treasure in heaven. To Antony it seemed this message was addressed personally to him.

After selling his property, Antony set out for the desert, where he embraced a solitary and ascetic life. Aside from hunger and lack of sleep, he contended with many psychological and spiritual ordeals. Constantly assailed by demons, which appeared in various guises—some hideous and others alluring—he sought to still his passions and tap into the source of life. After twenty years of isolation he eventually welcomed a community of monks, who were drawn by his magnetic example. He served as abbot of this early monastery and eventually established a network of similar communities.

Despite his deprivations, Antony remained a picture of health, and lived to the age of 105. Soon after his death an account of his life by St. Athanasius, bishop of Alexandria, became hugely popular, serving as a prototype for later saints' lives. Aside from dramatizing Antony's adventures in self-denial, it emphasized his humanity, his psychological insight, his capacity for compassion and joy.

"Let us not look back upon the world and fancy we have given up gross things. For the whole of earth is a very little thing compared with the whole of heaven."
—St. Antony

Roberto de Nobili
Jesuit Missionary (1577–1656)

Roberto de Nobili, an Italian Jesuit who served in India, was one of the grand pioneers of "inculturation." Settling in the Portuguese colony of Goa in southern India, he soon traveled inland to Madurai, a center of Tamil culture effectively beyond the range of colonial penetration. Nobili was determined to shed all European trappings and to present the Gospel in terms of Indian religion and culture. He was probably the first Westerner to master Sanskrit and to read the Hindu classics in their original language. With permission from his superiors, he moved into a simple hut, put aside his black soutane, and draped himself in the red-ochre robe of an Indian holy man, or *sanyasi*. Having made it clear that he had no wish to impose Western culture, Nobili found Hindu scholars quite receptive to philosophical and religious debate, and many were drawn to explore his faith.

Nobili's methods, however, drew criticism from the local Church in Goa. He was accused of dressing like a heathen and tolerating pagan idolatry. He defended himself by documenting the many ways the early Church had "baptized" and absorbed various pagan customs and rituals. Though condemned by a local Church conference, he was vindicated on appeal to Pope Gregory XV. He died on January 16, 1656.

"Let others struggle for the good things in life. . . . As for me, I have decided to spend my days unknown in some obscure corner to sacrifice my wretched life for the salvation of souls."

—Roberto de Nobili

St. Prisca
Evangelist and Martyr (First Century)

St. Prisca was one of a number of women who played prominent roles in the early Church—not simply as "helpers" to the male apostles but as evangelists and Church administrators in their own right. Prisca and her husband Aquila were Jewish tentmakers in Corinth. Though originally from Rome they had, along with all Jews, been expelled from the imperial capital by order of the emperor Claudius. St. Paul met them soon after his own arrival in Corinth. Their common trade—Paul too was a tentmaker—provided the basis for their acquaintance. But soon, through Paul's influence, they also shared a common zeal for the Gospel. Their home served as Paul's base of operations in the city. Before long they were also serving as evangelists, preaching the Gospel to their fellow Jews.

Prisca and Aquila followed Paul to Ephesus, where they again established a church in their home that included both Gentile and Jewish Christians. Later they returned to Rome and there too established a home church. Paul addressed them in his letter to the Romans as his "co-workers in Christ Jesus."

If, in returning to Rome, they had hoped to find greater tolerance under the emperor Nero, they were sorely disappointed. According to tradition, Prisca and Aquila perished in the general persecution around the year 64.

"Greet Prisca and Aquila, my co-workers in Christ Jesus, who risked their necks for my life, to whom not only I am grateful but also all the churches of the Gentiles; greet also the church at their house."

—St. Paul (Rom 16:3-5)

St. Margaret of Hungary
Nun (1242–1271)

St. Margaret did not initially have much say about her religious vocation. Her father, King Bela IV of Hungary, offered her to a Dominican convent when she was only three, thereby fulfilling an oath to God in return for protection from Tartar invaders. When Margaret was ten, her parents built her a convent of her own on an island on the Danube. There she was professed at the age of thirteen, and there she remained for the rest of her life. When King Ottokar of Bohemia sought her hand, her father urged her to accept this proposal, but by this time she claimed her own destiny. In fact, she said she would sooner cut off her nose than leave the convent.

Perhaps in rebellion against her noble birth or the deference of her fellow nuns, Margaret went to extremes of self-abnegation. *Butler's Lives of the Saints* reports, with some delicacy, "Her charity and tenderness in rendering the most nauseating services to the sick were marvelous, but many of the details are such as cannot be set out before the fastidious modern reader." She also received visions of Christ, with whom she often shared ecstatic conversations. But the extent of her austerities undoubtedly shortened her life. She died on January 18, 1271, at twenty-eight. Her canonization in 1943 boosted the spirits of her compatriots under Nazi occupation.

"I esteem infinitely more the King of Heaven and the inconceivable happiness of possessing Jesus Christ than the crown offered me by the king of Bohemia."

—St. Margaret of Hungary

St. Paula
Widow and Scholar (347–404)

St. Paula, who was born to an aristocratic family in Rome, enjoyed a happy marriage and bore several children. After being widowed at thirty-two, however, she committed herself to Christ and adopted a life of severe austerity. A turning point came with her introduction to St. Jerome, a priest and scholar, who became her spiritual director and lifelong friend.

Jerome was better known for his pugnacious personality than for his human warmth. Nevertheless, when Jerome left Rome for the Holy Land in 385, Paula and one of her daughters elected to accompany him. With Jerome, she used her wealth to establish two monasteries in Bethlehem, one for men and another for women. Though she personally oversaw the women's community, Paula's principal work was to look after Jerome and assist him in his scholarly projects. As a child she had learned Greek, and now, with Jerome, she undertook the study of Hebrew. Thus she provided invaluable assistance with his masterwork, the Vulgate Bible—a Latin translation from the original languages, which became the official text of the Church for over 1,500 years.

Paula died on January 26, 404, and was buried in the Church of the Nativity, the site of her Savior's birth. Having successfully exhausted her fortune, she died penniless.

"God is my witness that what I do I do for His sake. My prayer is that I may die a beggar, not leaving a penny to my daughter and indebted to strangers for my winding-sheet."
—St. Paula

Mother Joseph of the Sacred Heart
Sister of Providence (1823–1902)

Esther Pariseau was born in Quebec in 1823. At twenty she entered the Sisters of Charity of Providence in Montreal and took the name Joseph of the Sacred Heart. In 1856 her superior received a request from the bishop of Nisqually (now Seattle) seeking missionaries to work in his diocese in the Pacific Northwest territory. Sr. Joseph was appointed to answer this call, joined by four other sisters. After settling in Vancouver, they quickly established an infirmary, an orphanage, a home for the mentally ill, and an academy. "Schools are needed first of all," she noted to her sisters. "Americans do not count the cost where education is concerned [and] their generosity will help us to maintain our establishments for the poor." She personally designed the buildings and oversaw their construction.

In all, Mother Joseph, as she was known, established eleven hospitals, seven academies, five schools for Native American children, and two orphanages in an area that encompassed Washington, Oregon, Idaho, Montana, and southern British Columbia. When she died on January 19, 1902, she was widely recognized for her contributions in settling the Northwest. Among other honors, she was inducted into the National Cowgirl Hall of Fame.

"My dear sisters, allow me to recommend to you the care of the poor in our houses, as well as those without. Take good care of them; have no fear of them; assist them and receive them. Then, you will have no regrets. Do not say: ah! this does not concern me, let others see to them. My sisters, whatever concerns the poor is always our affair."
—Mother Joseph of the Sacred Heart

Alessandro Valignano
Jesuit Missionary (1539–1606)

Alessandro Valignano, who was born to an aristocratic family in Italy, entered the Jesuits in 1566. In 1573, only two years after his ordination, he was entrusted with an extraordinary task. He was appointed Jesuit Visitor to the East, the highest authority over a territory stretching from Mozambique to Japan.

At the time a papal decree granted the Portuguese and Spanish crowns authority for establishing and administering the Church in the territories. The Far East fell under Portuguese control. Valignano, however, was determined to disengage the Jesuit missions from the colonial project. In part he accomplished this by selecting Jesuits from only Spain and Italy.

Valignano believed the conquest model of evangelization, as pursued in Latin America, would be absolutely fruitless in penetrating the ancient civilizations of Japan and China. He rejected the idea of Christendom—the assumption that there was an essential identity between Christianity and European society. The Gospel, according to Valignano, must be rooted in the culture of the people.

Thus, the Jesuits in Japan set about mastering the language and adopting Japanese customs and dietary standards. Nevertheless, despite promising beginnings, this strategy ran aground—in Japan, because of persecution, and in China, because of Roman hostility to the practice of inculturation. Valignano died in Macao on January 20, 1606.

"As a result of our not adapting ourselves to their customs, two serious evils followed. . . . First, we forfeited the respect and esteem of the Japanese, and second, we remained strangers, so to speak, to the Christians."
—Alessandro Valignano

Blessed Cyprian Michael Iwene Tansi
Monk (1903–1964)

I wene Tansi was born in a village in Nigeria and raised in the traditional religion of the Ibo people. When his father died, his mother sent him to a Catholic school where he was baptized in 1912 and took the name Michael. After entering the seminary, he became one of the first native Nigerians ordained to the priesthood.

Fr. Tansi proved a hardworking priest, and he radiated a deep and compelling faith that won the affection of his flock. But increasingly his heart was set on a different goal: to become a Trappist monk. There being no such communities in Nigeria, he applied for admission to a Trappist monastery in Leicester, England, where he was accepted in 1950 and became Brother Cyprian. When another Nigerian priest joined the community, he floated the idea of founding a daughter community in Nigeria. Eventually, permission came to launch a community in Africa—though not in Nigeria, as he had hoped, but in Cameroon. Before he could implement this plan, however, he fell ill and died on January 20, 1964, without ever leaving England.

Believing that his example might nourish the faith of his people, the Trappists returned his remains to Nigeria. There his story did indeed inspire fervent devotion and prayers for his intercession. Support for his cause was joined by Cardinal Francis Arinze, an important Vatican official, who as a boy had received his catechism and baptism from Fr. Tansi. In 1998 Cyprian Michael Iwene Tansi became the first West African to be beatified.

"God will give you double what you give him."

—Blessed Cyprian Michael Iwene Tansi

41

St. Agnes
Martyr (ca. 304)

According to legend, Agnes was born to a rich and noble family of Rome. Though her beauty attracted the interest of many prosperous suitors, she rebuffed them all, insisting that she had consecrated herself to her true spouse, Jesus Christ. Her suitors denounced her as a Christian, and she was brought before a magistrate. He in turn employed various forms of persuasion, ranging from mild entreaty to the display of instruments of torture. None of these efforts could induce her to offer incense to the gods. When she remained adamant, she was consigned to a brothel. Yet even there she exuded such an aura of purity that no man could touch her. At this point the frustrated judge ordered her to be beheaded. Agnes greeted the sentence joyfully and, according to St. Ambrose, "went to the place of her execution more cheerfully than others go to their wedding."

At the time of her death Agnes was thirteen years old.

The stories of such "virgin martyrs" have often been used in Christian history to valorize the virgin state. The story of St. Agnes does not so much depict a vindication of sexual purity as the struggle of a young woman, empowered by Christ to define her own identity against the culture's claim to identify her in terms of her sexuality. The God she worshiped set an altogether different value on her body and her human worth.

"Christ made my soul beautiful with the jewels of grace and virtue. I belong to Him whom the angels serve."
—St. Agnes

Venerable Mary Angeline McCrory
Founder, Carmelite Sisters for the Aged and Infirm
(1893–1984)

Mary Angeline McCrory was born in Northern Ireland in 1893. At the age of nineteen she joined the Little Sisters of the Poor, a French congregation dedicated to care for the destitute aged. After completing her novitiate in France she was sent to the United States, where she was eventually put in charge of a nursing home in the Bronx.

Over time, however, she felt increasingly constrained by her congregation's exclusive focus on the destitute aged. After all, she reasoned, the ordeals of old age—loneliness, fear, disability—applied to people of all social classes. After consulting with Cardinal Hayes, the archbishop of New York, she received support to start a new congregation. This congregation, the Carmelite Sisters for the Aged and Infirm, was recognized in 1931. Explaining their mission, Mother Mary said, "Our Apostolate is not only to staff and operate up-to-date Homes for the Aged. As religious, it is to bring Christ to every old person under our care. Bringing Christ means giving them His compassion, His interest, His loving care, His warmth—morning, noon, and night!"

The work of the sisters spread to eighteen elder-care facilities around the country, plus one in Ireland. Mother Mary died on January 21, 1984, her ninety-first birthday. The cause for her canonization was introduced, and she was declared venerable in 2012.

"If you have to fail, let it be on the side of kindness. Be kinder than kindness itself to the old people."

—Venerable Mary Angeline McCrory

Blessed William Joseph Chaminade
Founder, Marianists (1761–1850)

William Joseph Chaminade was ordained a priest in France in 1785. Following the Revolution of 1789 he refused to take the oath of allegiance to the Civil Constitution of the Clergy. As a consequence he was forced to go underground. During these years, while carrying on his clandestine mission, often at great risk, he cultivated a deep devotion to Mary, "the way that leads to the Son." "Jesus," he later wrote, "made Mary the companion of his labors, of his joy, of his preaching, of his death. Mary had a part to play in all the glorious, joyful, and sorrowful mysteries of Jesus."

After his return to Bordeaux in 1800, he drew on this spiritual vision to build what became the Marianist Family. It started with sodalities to promote a deeper spiritual life among the laity and to promote "the spectacle of a people of saints." At a time when the main business of the bishops was rebuilding the institutional structures of the Church, Chaminade was counseled against focusing so much effort on lay spirituality. But he persisted, eventually adding a clerical order and religious institutes to his "family." In this he drew inspiration from the early Church community in Jerusalem. The foundation of the Church, he believed, was not a hierarchical structure but a new spirituality.

The Marianists spread beyond France, coming to America in 1849, the year before Chaminade's death on January 22, 1850. He was beatified in 2000.

"The levers that move the moral world somehow need a new fulcrum."
—Blessed William Joseph Chaminade

Venerable Satoko Kitahara
"The Mary of Ants Town" (1929–1958)

Despite her upbringing in an affluent Tokyo suburb, Satoko Kitahara shared with other Japanese the trauma of war. In the wake of the firebombing of Tokyo, her country's defeat, and the disillusioning exposure of militarist lies, she suffered a profound crisis of faith. Her spiritual journey led her to seek baptism as a Catholic. From then on, she wrote, "I experienced a desire amounting almost to a necessity to 'serve,' which seemed to be a natural accompaniment to being a follower of Christ."

After reading an article about a shantytown of homeless squatters not far from her home, she found her opportunity. The residents of this so-called Ants Town supported themselves by collecting recyclable rubbish. Satoko began to volunteer her time among them, offering lessons to the children and organizing excursions. But eventually she was challenged by one of the community leaders. He mocked the "charity" of Christians who simply offer handouts or donate their extra time. Had not Christ emptied himself to take on the life of a slave? Stunned by these words, Satoko determined to become one with the ragpickers, living among them and joining them in begging for trash.

She was revered as "the Mary of Ants Town." But such loving service carried a heavy price. Already weakened by tuberculosis, Satoko died on January 23, 1958, at the age of twenty-nine. In 2015 she was declared venerable.

"I feel my path to Heaven will be a long and painful one. I do not intend to work just for my own eternal salvation, closing my eyes to the people around me."
—Venerable Satoko Kitahara

Blessed James the Almsgiver
Priest and Martyr (d. 1304)

James of Pieve was born in a small town near Chiusi in Lombardy. Though he studied for the law he was inspired one day, after hearing a sermon on the cost of discipleship, to become a priest and devote himself to the poor. (There is some uncertainty about whether he was a Franciscan or a Servite—both have claimed him.)

Nearby there was an abandoned hospital with an attached chapel. At his own expense and labor he restored the buildings and soon made them available for care of the sick. For all this, and for sharing his legal knowledge with the poor of the land, he became a popular local figure.

In researching the history of the hospital, James discovered evidence that its revenues had been unjustly appropriated by previous bishops of Chiusi. He brought his findings to the current bishop, but found him unwilling to acknowledge or rectify the injustice. Consequently James brought a suit in both civil and ecclesiastical court.

The case was decided in James's favor. Afterward, the bishop invited James to dinner, having prearranged for brigands to ambush and assassinate him on the way home.

James was killed on January 15, 1304. The townspeople gave him the name "the Almsgiver," and he was beatified in 1806.

"The conscientious student of Italian (and other) history has often regretfully to confess that the social and ecclesiastical life of the 'ages of faith' was not always so ideal as certain apologists are inclined to represent it."
—*Butler's Lives of the Saints*

St. Marianne Cope
Servant of the Lepers (1838–1918)

Barbara Koob, who was born in Germany, immigrated with her family to the United States, where their name became Cope. In 1862 she entered the Third Order Regular of Franciscans and received her religious name. Her early years were spent teaching in her order's schools and later serving as administrator of a hospital. In 1883, now the superior general of her congregation, she received a request from King Kalakaua in Hawaii for help in caring for leprosy patients. Though fifty other congregations had already declined the king's plea, Mother Marianne responded at once: "I am hungry for the work and I wish with all my heart to be one of the chosen Ones, whose privilege it will be, to sacrifice themselves for the salvation of the souls of the poor Islanders."

That year she and six sisters sailed for Hawaii and immediately set to work establishing a hospital in Maui. Given the general fear of contagion and the social stigma attached to those suffering from Hansen's disease, the sisters' dedication to their patients won wide respect. Eventually Mother Marianne consented to move to the island of Molokai, where the most serious cases were confined. There, one of her first tasks was to care for Fr. Damien de Veuster, the famous "Apostle to the Lepers," who had succumbed to the disease during his long years of service.

Sr. Marianne died of natural causes on August 9, 1918. She was canonized in 2012. Her feast day is January 23, the day of her birth.

"Let us make best use of the fleeting moments. They will not return."
—St. Marianne Cope

St. Francis de Sales
Doctor of the Church (1567–1622)

Francis de Sales was born in Savoy to a wealthy family. Soon after his ordination in 1593 he volunteered for a dangerous mission: to serve as a priest in the region around Lake Geneva, a bastion of Calvinism. For years he trudged through the region on foot, enduring poverty and harsh winters, and many times barely escaping assassination. Rather than simply denouncing Calvinism, he chose instead to proclaim the positive message of the Gospel in a way that would overcome negative stereotypes of Catholicism. As a result of his mission, hundreds of families were reconciled with the Catholic faith.

In 1602 Francis was named bishop of Geneva. Unable to enter his see, he administered the diocese from a town fifty miles to the south. Nevertheless, he achieved fame as a preacher and spiritual director. With one of his directees, a wealthy widow named Jeanne de Chantal, he founded the Order of the Visitation. It was Francis's goal to rejuvenate the Church by raising the level of spiritual devotion. In his book *An Introduction to the Devout Life*, he taught a way of holiness that could be adapted to the strengths, life-situation, and duties of any person. It was a matter of weaning oneself from sin and enlarging one's capacity for love and the practice of virtue. "Genuine devotion," he wrote, "is simply true love of God."

Francis died in 1622. He was named by Pope Pius XI the patron saint of writers.

"The measure of love is to love without measure."

—St. Francis de Sales

Blessed Nikolaus Gross
Martyr (1898–1945)

Nikolaus Gross was born to a working-class family in Essen, Germany. In 1917, after years of work as a coal miner, he joined the Christian Miner's Trade Union and afterward threw himself into union work, ultimately becoming editor of the union newspaper. He married and had seven children.

An early foe of the Nazis, he used the paper to resist their pernicious ideology. "If something is demanded of us that goes against God or the Faith," he wrote, "then not only may we, but we must, refuse obedience." Statements like this caused the paper to be suppressed. Though Gross was repeatedly interrogated, he evaded arrest, even while serving as a courier for the underground resistance.

In a 1943 pamphlet he wrote, "We never know what problems are waiting to test the power and strength of our souls. . . . But even darkness is not without light. Hope and faith, which always hasten ahead of us, already have a presentiment of the breaking of a new dawn. If we know that the best thing in us, the soul, is immortal, then we also know that we shall meet each other again."

Gross was arrested on August 12, 1944, and hanged on January 23, 1945. The chaplain who witnessed his death observed, "Gross bowed his head silently during the blessing. His face already seemed illuminated by the glory into which he was getting ready to enter." Gross was beatified in 2001.

"If we do not risk our life today, how do we want then to justify ourselves before God and our people?"

—Blessed Nikolaus Gross

Dorothy Hennessey
Franciscan, Witness for Peace (1913–2008)

In 2001, Sr. Dorothy Hennessey, then eighty-eight, made headlines when she was arrested with her younger sister Gwen Hennessey for trespassing at the School of the Americas in Fort Benning, Georgia. They were part of a large contingent of human rights protesters waging a campaign to close the school, whose alumni included the perpetrators of torture, massacres, and military coups in Latin America. Dorothy and Gwen were sentenced to six months in prison. When their judge offered to commute Dorothy's sentence to "motherhouse arrest," she replied, "I'd rather not be singled out. If you wouldn't mind, I would just as soon have the same sentence as the others."

Dorothy had entered the Franciscan Order at nineteen and spent many years teaching. But over time her sense of global responsibility was awakened through letters from her brother Ron Hennessey, a Maryknoll priest in Guatemala, who reported on the violence and atrocities occurring at the hands of the military. In the early 1980s she went to Nicaragua during the time of the "Contra" war to serve as a "Witness for Peace." In 1986, now in her seventies, she took part in a continental walk for peace across the entire United States.

In 2002 she and her sister Gwen received the Pacem in Terris award from the diocese of Davenport, an award previously won by Mother Teresa, Dorothy Day, and Martin Luther King Jr.

Dorothy died on January 24, 2008, at the age of ninety-four.

"We can't protest everything, but we can pick out some of the worst things to protest, and that's what I've tried to do."

—Sr. Dorothy Hennessey

Samuel Ruiz
Bishop of Chiapas (1924–2011)

In 1960 Don Samuel Ruiz was installed as bishop of the diocese of San Cristobal de Las Casas in Chiapas. The impoverished diocese in southern Mexico was named after Bartolomé de Las Casas, a prophetic Dominican of the sixteenth century who served there as the first bishop. Don Samuel proved a worthy successor.

He had started out as a staunch conservative, but the experience of Vatican II and the subsequent awakening of social consciousness in the Latin American Church had changed him profoundly. He became an outspoken champion of the marginalized Mayan Indians, affirming their culture and defending their rights. His stand put him in frequent conflict with the government and with wealthy landowners, who accused him of being a dangerous radical. He withstood an investigation by the Vatican in 1993 and later survived an ambush by gunmen. Nevertheless, when an armed insurrection led by Zapatista rebels erupted in Chiapas, the government asked him to serve as a mediator. Though he helped to broker a lasting cease-fire, he emphasized that there could be no peace without justice. "Justice means bringing down from their throne those who are privileged and elevating those who are humble to the same heights."

In 2000, on reaching the mandatory retirement age of seventy-five, Ruiz stepped down as bishop. He died on January 24, 2011.

"I can tell you that I am the same person, but that I am not the same. The bishop that arrived here has been left behind, has evolved."
—Bishop Samuel Ruiz on his retirement

Saints Timothy and Titus
Bishops (First Century)

Both Timothy and Titus were companions of St. Paul, whom they joined on his missionary journeys. What little we know of their lives is gleaned from the Acts of the Apostles and a few epistles that Paul addressed to them from the road.

Though Timothy had a Jewish mother and a Gentile father, he was evidently uncircumcised. Upon his conversion, however, St. Paul insisted that he rectify this state, thus easing his acceptance among the Jews. However, in the case of Titus, whose two parents were both Gentiles, Paul determined that no circumcision was necessary: the Gospel required only faith, rather than submission to the law.

Timothy accompanied Paul on many of his travels and went in his place to visit the churches in Thessalonica and Corinth. According to tradition, he became the first bishop of Ephesus. Paul's letters to Timothy—one of them written from his imprisonment in Rome—are heartfelt and personal. In one of them he encouraged Timothy, who apparently drank only water, to "take a little wine" (1 Tim 5:23).

St. Titus also accompanied Paul on his mission journeys and served as his secretary and occasional emissary. According to tradition, Paul appointed him bishop of Crete, where he served until his peaceful death at an advanced age.

"To Timothy, my beloved child . . ." (1 and 2 Tim 1:2)

"To Titus, my true child in a common faith: Grace and peace from God the Father and Christ Jesus our Savior." (Titus 1:4)

—St. Paul

Blessed Michael Kozal
Bishop and Martyr (1893–1943)

Michael Kozal was born in a small village in Poland. After entering the seminary he was ordained a priest in 1918. In the following years he undertook a number of assignments, concluding with his appointment as rector of the major seminary of Gniezno. In 1939 he was named auxiliary bishop of Wloclawek, where he was consecrated in the cathedral on August 13.

His episcopal service was short-lived. Two weeks later, on September 1, the Nazis invaded Poland and immediately launched a campaign against the Church and other symbols of national identity. German troops arrived in Wloclawek on September 14 and proceeded to suppress religious publications, seize church buildings, and arrest hundreds of clergy. Bishop Kozal protested, but to no avail. Refusing the opportunity to flee, he insisted on remaining with his people.

On November 7 he was arrested along with other priests and imprisoned in the city jail. He was confined in a convent for over a year, then transported in 1941 to Dachau, where thousands of clergy were already held captive. During his imprisonment he continued to exercise his priestly mission, offering spiritual guidance to his fellow priests and, when possible, celebrating Mass. He said, "I give you the greatest gift, Jesus in the Eucharist. God is with us. God will never abandon us." On January 30, 1943, he was executed by a fatal injection and incinerated in the camp crematorium.

Kozal was beatified by Pope John Paul II during one of his first pilgrimages to his native Poland.

"Now is the easiest way to eternity."

—Last words of Bishop Michael Kozal

St. Angela Merici
Founder, Ursulines (1474–1540)

Born in Lombardy and orphaned at an early age, Angela Merici became a Franciscan tertiary and embraced a life of prayerful simplicity. After spending many years in almost continuous pilgrimage, she had a vision one day in which she beheld a company of angels and maidens descending from a ladder in the heavens. A voice revealed that she would found a community whose members would be as numerous as the maidens thus revealed to her.

For some years Angela offered religious instruction to the children of her poor neighbors. Other women were gradually inspired to join her. Finally, Angela had a group of twenty-eight women prepared to consecrate themselves to God's service. They chose as their patron St. Ursula, a legendary fourth-century martyr widely venerated as a protector of women.

Although she devised a simple rule for her Ursuline community, Angela did not initially conceive of them as a religious order. While dedicating themselves to the education of poor girls, the members wore no habits and took no vows.

By the time of her death on January 27, 1540, Angela was revered as a living saint. Four years after her death Rome approved a constitution for her congregation, which would in time come to number many tens of thousands. Angela was canonized in 1807.

"Do now what you'll wish you had done when your moment comes to die."
—St. Angela Merici

Mahalia Jackson
Gospel Singer (1911–1972)

Mahalia Jackson, known as the "Queen of Gospel," was born to a poor family in New Orleans. She found her calling at Mount Mariah Baptist Church, where she began singing in the choir. After moving to Chicago she met the famous Gospel choir leader Thomas Dorsey and began to tour. Gradually her reputation spread throughout the country, and indeed the world. She became the first Gospel singer to perform at Carnegie Hall.

Despite her fame, she constantly confronted prejudice. In the 1950s Martin Luther King Jr. invited her to help raise money for the Montgomery Bus Boycott. From that time on she was always available whenever King called. Sometimes, when feeling low, he would ask her to sing his favorite song, "Take My Hand, Precious Lord," a song she would later sing at his funeral. She hoped her music would "break down some of the hate and fear that divide the white and black people of this country."

In fact, Jackson played a significant role in King's most famous oration. She was at his side, performing on the steps of the Lincoln Memorial on the famous March on Washington. As King approached the conclusion of his written speech, Jackson called out, "Tell them about the dream, Martin." At this point, King departed from his speech to deliver the historic lines that became a signature of his legacy.

Mahalia Jackson died on January 27, 1972.

"After you sing the blues, you still have the blues. I sing God's music because it makes me feel free."
—Mahalia Jackson

St. Thomas Aquinas
Theologian and Doctor of the Church (1225–1274)

Thomas desired from his youth to become a Dominican friar. After he declared this intention, his family kidnapped him and locked him in their castle in southern Italy. Eventually, when his will proved resolute, they set him free to pursue his vocation.

Thomas's initial studies gave no promise of his later eminence. While studying in Cologne he rarely spoke, thus earning the nickname "the Dumb Ox." Only his teacher, Albert the Great, recognized his abilities and predicted that the lowing of this "dumb ox" would eventually be heard around the world.

By the time he received his doctorate in Paris, Thomas was recognized as an unrivaled genius, and his services were in wide demand, both by the Dominicans and the papal court. In 1266 he began his masterpiece, the *Summa Theologiae*, a vastly ambitious exposition of the Catholic faith in which he brilliantly adapted the philosophy of Aristotle in the service of Christian theology.

The project was never completed. During Mass one day Thomas had a mysterious experience that caused him to hang up his writing instruments, never to resume. When asked about his silence, he replied, "All that I have written seems to me like so much straw compared to what I have seen and what has been revealed to me."

Thomas died three months later on March 7, 1274, at the age of forty-nine. His feast day is January 28, the day of his birth.

"Three things are necessary for the salvation of man: to know what he ought to believe; to know what he ought to desire; and to know what he ought to do."
—St. Thomas Aquinas

Fyodor Dostoevsky
Novelist (1821–1881)

Fyodor Dostoevsky, the great Russian novelist, studied engineering before deciding to pursue a literary career. His first story, "Poor People," published in 1846, reflected his lifelong concern for the sufferings of common people.

In 1849 Dostoevsky was arrested for his role in a socialist study circle. Sentenced to death, he was actually reprieved within minutes of his scheduled execution. He spent the next four years in hard labor in a Siberian prison camp—an experience that provided him with much material for his later work. Through this ordeal, with only the New Testament as his companion, he found the themes that would dominate his novels: the common human solidarity in the sin of the world, the redemptive meaning of suffering, and the power of Christ's love.

Dostoevsky's life was marked by deep anguish. He suffered from epileptic seizures; his compulsive gambling contributed to lifelong penury. Two of his children died, and he was wracked with guilt over the early death of his first wife, whom he had neglected.

His brilliant novels, *Crime and Punishment, The Idiot, The Brothers Karamazov*, were marked by an acute understanding of psychology and an obsession with the nature of evil, the condition of human rebellion against God, and the quest for salvation. Though his work was honored in the Soviet era for its realism, he had prophesied the oppressive nature of any effort to achieve utopia apart from God. For Dostoevsky, authentic community and human fellowship could be founded only on a living faith in Christ.

He died on January 28, 1881.

"The world will be saved by beauty."

—Fyodor Dostoevsky

St. Andrei Rublev
Russian Monk and Iconographer (d. 1430)

The use of icons—highly spiritualized depictions of Christ, Mary, and the saints—became one of the earliest and most distinctive elements of Byzantine spirituality. Intended for use in worship, icons were not meant to serve as realistic portraits but as windows linking earthly and heavenly realities. The production of icons was itself a spiritual work, generally in the hands of monks, and accompanied by intense prayer. The artist's identity was seldom known. Nevertheless certain iconographers became known for their distinctive style.

Andrei Rublev, a Russian monk of the fifteenth century, is among the most widely revered. He brought the icon to a new level of artistic and spiritual depth and inspired a school of faithful imitators. Little is known of his life, and very few of his works have survived. One of his greatest icons, "The Savior of Zvenigorod," was found in 1918 on a board used as the stairway of a barn.

Rublev's work is characterized by a lightness and delicacy of style and an unusually creative representation of theological mysteries. His most famous work is his icon of the Holy Trinity, inspired by the biblical story of three mysterious angels who visited the tent of Abraham at the oak of Mamre. Seated around a table, set for a meal, the three angelic figures show the differentiation, and at the same time the identity and interrelationship, between the persons of the Trinity.

Rublev has been canonized by the Russian Orthodox Church.

"He who venerates the icon . . . venerates in it the person of the one so depicted."
—Second Council of Nicaea, 787

Maisie Ward
Publisher and Writer (1889–1975)

Maisie Ward was raised in one of the most distinguished Catholic families in England. Yet she wished to do more for her faith. She joined the Catholic Evidence Guild, a group that published apologetic tracts and engaged in street-corner preaching on behalf of the faith. The success of a Catholic street-corner preacher in Hyde Park required a mastery of Church history, theology, and a knowledge of all the standard arsenal of anti-Catholic arguments. Ward was a natural. In this enterprise she met Frank Sheed, her future husband, and the two of them went on to found a publishing house that featured the best Catholic writers of the day. For many decades Sheed & Ward was a singular force in elevating the intellectual standards of the English-speaking Catholic world.

Maisie Ward was herself a prolific author of dozens of books, including biographies of her friends G. K. Chesterton and Caryll Houselander, lives of the saints, histories of the Church, and countless works on Scripture and spirituality—all marked by great learning, a zeal for the Church, and a joyous zest for living. She and Frank, who eventually moved to the United States, did as much as anyone to open the windows of the Church, exemplifying the apostolate of the laity and preparing the way for Vatican II. She died on January 28, 1975.

"It is the chief character of a life lived for God that there is time in it for everything that matters."

—Maisie Ward

Venerable Mary Ward
Founder, Institute of the Blessed Virgin Mary
(1585–1645)

The life of Mary Ward was set against the anti-Catholic persecution of the Elizabethan era. Though her family was among the landed gentry whose status afforded some free space to practice their faith, Mary insisted that she was called to become a nun. As there was not, at the time, a single convent in England, she departed for Belgium to pursue her calling. Once there, inspired by the Jesuits, she determined that her true mission was to found an institute of women, living in a non-enclosed community, who would be free to carry out apostolic work in the world. It was an idea ahead of its time.

Mary made a series of perilous visits to England to find recruits. But in the labyrinthine quest for official approval of her Institute, she faced the greater ordeal. Her plan departed significantly from the prescribed place for women in the Church. She and her companions were mocked as "Lady Jesuits." At one point she was arrested by Church officials and charged with heresy. Though her imprisonment was brief, she remained under a cloud of ecclesial disapprobation.

Finally, in broken health, Mary returned to England, where she died on January 30, 1645, at the age of sixty. Fifty-eight years later the rule of her Institute was confirmed by Pope Clement XI. She was declared venerable by Pope Benedict XVI in 2009.

"The trouble and the long loneliness is not far from me, which, whensoever it is, happy success follows. . . . The pain is great, but very endurable, because He who lays on the burden also carries it."

—Mary Ward

Mohandas Gandhi
"Great Soul" of India (1869–1948)

Mohandas Gandhi, who led the Indian movement for independence, did more than any person in history to advance the theory and practice of nonviolence. His influence in world history is incalculable. Yet he always posed a special challenge for Christians. Here was a Hindu who politely rejected the dogmatic claims of Christianity while embracing, with extraordinary consistency, the ethical claims of Christ.

Gandhi remained a devoted Hindu throughout his life. His experience of the conduct of Christian missionaries in India and their general alliance with colonialism made him doubtful that their religion had any unique claim to the truth. Yet in the Sermon on the Mount and the "law of love" he found what he called the "true message of Jesus." In Jesus' teaching and his practice of redemptive suffering he found the exemplification of nonviolence and the essence of true religion.

For Gandhi, the nonviolent struggle for independence was a deeply spiritual, and not simply political, cause. Believing in the identity between means and ends, he approached each campaign as an "experiment in truth," an effort to realize God's will on earth. He was assassinated on January 30, 1948, by Hindu fanatics who opposed his efforts to overcome Hindu-Muslim conflict in the aftermath of Independence.

His influence is felt not only in movements for peace and justice but in the lives of many Christians who, thanks to his witness, have learned to read the Gospel with new eyes and to become more faithful followers of Jesus.

"Living Christ means a living Cross; without it life is a living death."

—Mohandas Gandhi

61

St. Marcella
Widow (325–410)

Marcella was born to a wealthy family in Rome. Upon her father's death she was urged to marry, and she did so. Her husband was also a wealthy man, but his death left her a widow after only seven months of marriage. Afterward she resisted all invitations to remarry, happily dedicating herself to a life of prayer.

She gave away all her fortune, "preferring to store her money in the stomachs of the needy rather than hide it in a purse." After reading the life of St. Antony she was inspired to emulate his monastic life. Thus she began to gather a community of like-spirited women, both widows and unmarried maidens, who shared her appetite for holiness. Though they followed no formal rule, this was perhaps one of the earliest of such communities of Christian women.

When St. Jerome arrived in Rome he was introduced to this community and consented to serve as its spiritual director. So impressed was he by their learning and piety that he compared them to the holy women who surrounded Jesus. Marcella, he said, was another Mary Magdalene.

In 410 Rome was sacked. Invading hordes broke into Marcella's house, seeking hidden treasure, and beat her savagely. Her brave composure put her assailants to shame. But at eighty-five she found it hard to recover from such trauma. She died within a few months.

"By heaven's grace, captivity has found me a poor woman, not made me one. Now I shall go in want of daily bread, but I shall not feel hunger since I am full of Christ."
—St. Marcella

St. John Bosco
Founder, Salesians of Don Bosco (1815–1888)

John Bosco was born to a peasant family in Piedmont. Following his father's death he was raised by his mother, an especially devout woman. The seeds of John's vocation were evident in early life. At the age of nine he had a dream in which he managed to tame a crowd of unruly boys after receiving encouragement from a mysterious lady. "Softly, softly," she told him. "If you wish to win them! Take your shepherd's staff and lead them to pasture." Gradually, even as an adolescent, he discerned his calling: to care for poor boys, to help them with their religious instruction, and inspire them to lead healthy, moral lives.

After pursuing ordination, John set about to implement his mission. He established an oratory to house hundreds of homeless boys. He went on to organize workshops to impart practical skills and employment. His dedication drew wide admiration and support and eventually a band of dedicated assistants. With them he formed a new religious congregation named after St. Francis de Sales.

The Salesians grew in number, and eventually their communities spread throughout Italy and across the world. Don Bosco died on January 31, 1888. He was canonized in 1934.

"I have promised God that until my last breath I shall have lived for my poor young people. I study for you, I work for you, I am also ready to give my life for you. Take note that whatever I am, I have been so entirely for you."
—St. John Bosco

FEBRUARY

1 St. Brigid of Ireland • Alfred Delp

2 St. Cornelius the Centurion • Blessed Mary Catherine Kasper

3 St. Claudine Thévenet • Servant of God Mary Elizabeth Lange

4 St. Joan of Valois • St. John de Britto

5 St. Agatha • Pedro Arrupe

6 St. Paul Miki and Companions • Venerable Thecla Merlo

7 Blessed Rosalie Rendu • Blessed Mary of Providence
(Eugénie Smet)

8 Blessed Jacoba of Settesoli • St. Josephine Bakhita

9 St. Apollonia • Blessed Marianus Scotus

10 St. Scholastica • Daniel Egan

11 St. Evagrius Ponticus • Muriel Lester

12 Brother Lawrence of the Resurrection • Dorothy Stang

13 St. Catherine dei Ricci • Georges Rouault

14 Saints Cyril and Methodius • Brother James Miller

15 St. Claude de la Colombière • Ben Salmon

16 St. Verdiana • Walter Burghardt

17 Martyrs of China • Janani Luwum

18 Blessed Fra Angelico • Michelangelo

19 St. Conrad of Piacenza • St. Philothea of Athens

20 Servant of God Francis X. Ford • Dorothy Gauchat

21 St. Robert Southwell • Blessed Maria Enrica Dominici

22 St. Margaret of Cortona • Hans and Sophie Scholl

23 St. Polycarp • Blessed Rafaela Ybarra de Vilallonga

24 Blessed Margaret Ebner • Blessed Josefa Naval Girbés

25 St. Walburga • Venerable Felix Varela

26 Blessed Isabel of France • Antonio Valdivieso

27 St. Gregory of Narek • St. Gabriel Possenti

28 Martyrs of the Plague of Alexandria • St. John Cassian

FEBRUARY

St. Brigid of Ireland
Abbess of Kildare (ca. 450–525)

St. Brigid lived in the era when traditional Irish religion was giving way to the formal institution of Christianity. Her very name was that of a Celtic sun goddess in ancient times. As best as can be known, Brigid was born into slavery and was baptized in her childhood by St. Patrick. She was granted her freedom when it proved impossible to curb her enthusiasm for giving alms.

Brigid became a nun and ultimately abbess of Kildare, a double monastery consisting of both men and women. Through her fame as a spiritual teacher the abbey became a center for pilgrims. So great was her authority that she even induced a bishop to join her community and to share her leadership.

The themes of generosity and compassion feature in many miracles attributed to Brigid, whose only desire was "to satisfy the poor, to expel every hardship, to spare every miserable man." One time "she supplied beer out of one barrel to eighteen churches." On another occasion she encountered a leprous woman asking for milk, but "there being none at hand she gave her cold water, but the water was turned into milk, and when she had drunk it the woman was healed."

In St. Brigid, the Irish people found a repository for primeval religious memories of the maternal face of God. She became known as "The Mary of the Gael."

"I would like a great lake of beer for the King of the kings; I would like the people of heaven to be drinking it through time eternal."

—St. Brigid

Alfred Delp
Jesuit Martyr (1907–1945)

Alfred Delp, who was born in Mannheim, Germany, entered the Jesuits in 1926. During the Second World War he joined a secret anti-Nazi group that was planning to build a new Christian social order after the war. When the group was exposed in the summer of 1944, Delp was arrested and charged with treason. The Gestapo tried unsuccessfully to link him with a plot against Hitler's life but settled instead for demonstrating his "defeatist" attitude, evidenced in part by his membership in the Society of Jesus.

Confined to a dark cell and held in chains, Delp passed his time in the Advent season of 1944 writing a series of meditations. "Others have you in their power now; they torture and frighten you, hound you from pillar to post. But the inner law of freedom sings that no death can kill us; life is eternal." In a final testament to his friends, he reminded them that he was "sacrificed, not conquered." Writing with manacled hands, he noted, "If through one man's life there is a little more love and kindness, a little more light and truth in the world, then he will not have lived in vain."

Fr. Delp was hanged on February 2, 1945.

"The conditions of happiness have nothing whatever to do with outward evidence. They are exclusively dependent on man's inner attitude and steadfastness, which enable him, even in the most trying circumstances, to form at least a notion of what life is about."

—Fr. Alfred Delp

St. Cornelius the Centurion
Convert (First Century)

Cornelius was a Roman centurion in Caesarea—that is, an officer in the occupying army that had only recently crucified the Lord. Nevertheless, he is described in Acts as "a devout man who feared God with all his household, gave alms liberally to the people, and prayed constantly to God."

One day he received a vision of an angel who instructed him to send for the disciple Peter in Joppa. Peter, meanwhile, received a dream in which he was presented with a feast consisting of every kind of animal, both clean and unclean. A voice instructed him, "What God has cleansed, you must not call common." As he pondered the meaning of this dream, Peter learned that a cohort of soldiers was waiting to escort him to the home of Cornelius in Caesarea. Though ordinarily he would have balked at entering the home of a Gentile, he now discerned the meaning of his dream—that he should "not call any man common or unclean."

Peter proceeded to preach the Gospel to Cornelius and his household. Perceiving that the Holy Spirit had poured down on this Gentile gathering, he baptized them in the name of Jesus Christ.

This baptism of the first Gentile convert was a significant turning point for the Church. When Peter recounted this story to the otherwise skeptical disciples they were persuaded: "Then to the Gentiles also God has granted repentance unto life."

"Now we are all here present in the sight of God, to hear all that you have been commanded by the Lord."

—St. Cornelius (Acts 10:33)

Blessed Mary Catherine Kasper
Founder, Poor Handmaids of Jesus Christ (1820–1898)

Catherine Kasper, who was born in 1820 to a poor peasant family in Germany, turned to hard manual labor—even breaking rocks for road building—to help support her family. One day at work she had a vision of a new congregation: "Sisters!" she exclaimed. "What a large number of Sisters!"

She persuaded the bishop of Limburg to allow her to build a small house where she could invite other women to join her in charitable work. In time this would become the seed of a new congregation. Mother Mary, as she was now known, chose the name: "We should like to be called Poor Handmaids of Jesus Christ, and have for our patroness Mary, the first Handmaid of the Lord."

As the order grew, small communities spun off from the motherhouse. They would consist of four sisters: two engaged in nursing, one to run a kindergarten, and another to tend to the homeless. But eventually, in response to demand, the sisters' work extended to schools and even hospitals. In 1859 Mother Mary opened a new mission in Holland, and in 1869, responding to an invitation from the bishop of Fort Wayne, Indiana, she sent her sisters to the United States.

Mother Mary urged her sisters to be saints: "but hidden saints." She died on February 2, 1898, and was beatified in 1978. Thousands of her sisters continue to work around the world.

"God's divine will shall and must be accomplished in me, by me, and for me."
—Blessed Mary Catherine Kasper

St. Claudine Thévenet
Founder, Congregation of the Religious
of Jesus and Mary (1774–1837)

In Lyons, the city where Claudine Thévenet was born in 1774, the Terror of the French Revolution was particularly ferocious. When she was nineteen, she witnessed two of her brothers being led to the guillotine and heard them, in their last words, call out to her to forgive their executioners. The trauma of this experience remained with her. But in the bitter years that followed, she tried her best to honor this pledge.

For some while this took the form of charitable work in her parish, where her priest recognized and encouraged her special gifts. Eventually, in 1816, she founded the Congregation of the Religious of Jesus and Mary, which focused on the education of young—especially poor—women. This expanded to care for orphans and homeless children. She died on February 3, 1837.

In pronouncing her canonization in 1993, Pope John Paul II observed, "In the frailty of a child Claudine Thévenet discerned the power of God the Creator; in the child's poverty, the glory of the Almighty, who does not cease calling and who calls us to share the fullness of life; in the child's abandonment, Christ crucified and risen, who is ever present in his brothers and sisters, the least of people. . . . She ceaselessly invoked God's goodness."

"Be disposed to suffer everything from others and to not make anyone suffer anything."
—St. Claudine Thévenet

Servant of God Mary Elizabeth Lange
Founder, Oblate Sisters of Providence (ca. 1784–1882)

There is uncertainty surrounding Elizabeth Lange's origins. Most likely she was an emancipated Haitian slave who came to the United States in 1791 and settled in Baltimore, a city swollen with other refugees of the Haitian revolution. Observing that there was no public education available for black children in the city, Elizabeth opened a school in her own home. Later, with the support of the Sulpician Fathers, she established an academy for black girls. Though her confessor encouraged her to enter religious life, there were no white orders that would accept black members. Hence, she decided to start her own congregation, the Oblate Sisters of Providence—the first religious congregation for women of African descent. In 1829, with support from the archbishop, she and three others pronounced their vows. Taking the name Mary, she became the order's first superior.

Eventually, the sisters also opened an orphanage and a home for elderly widows, and they nursed the sick during an outbreak of cholera. They faced constant financial insecurity. At one point, shocked by the sisters' poverty, the archbishop ordered them to close their home, but Mother Lange refused. Aside from hard work and hardship, the sisters also endured various expressions of overt racism—even from fellow Catholics, who did not believe black women should be clothed in religious habits.

Mother Lange died on February 3, 1882.

"We believe the suffering that has been intrinsic to our Congregation from its beginning enables us to reach out to others with tenderness and compassion."

—Creedal statement of the Oblate Sisters of Providence

St. Joan of Valois
Founder, Annonciades of Bourges (1464–1505)

S t. Joan, daughter of King Louis XI of France, was apparently misshapen from birth, a fact that aroused her father's contempt. When she was eight weeks old he arranged her betrothal to her two-year-old cousin Louis, duke of Orleans. The marriage transpired when Joan was twelve. Though her husband accepted the arrangement, he felt no more affection for his bride than had her father. Joan was subjected to constant abuse and ridicule in the court. She accepted all without shame or complaint. But when Louis, after becoming king, sought to have the marriage annulled on the grounds of Joan's deformity, she resisted as best she could. Nevertheless, Pope Alexander VI, judging that the marriage was not entered freely, decided in Louis's favor. Joan accepted this decision as the will of God and retired to Bourges to devote herself to a life of prayer and charity. Louis bestowed on her the title Duchess of Berry.

With the support of her Franciscan confessor, Joan established a religious foundation devoted to "the ten virtues of Our Lady." The first postulants were eleven girls from the local school—some of them not yet ten. Under a rule that eventually received papal approval, they became the Annonciades of Bourges. Publicly renouncing her title and her property, Joan embraced a life of voluntary poverty. She died within a year. Her canonization followed in 1950.

"If so it is to be, praised be the Lord."

—St. Joan's response to the annulment of her marriage

St. John de Britto
Jesuit Martyr of Goa (1647–1693)

John de Britto was born to a noble family in Lisbon in 1647. From childhood his imagination was aroused by tales of the early Jesuit missionaries. His sole desire was to be one of them, a wish he fulfilled at fifteen when he was admitted to the Society of Jesus.

After ordination in 1673, de Britto was sent on mission to Goa, a Portuguese colony in southern India. There he sought to conform as much as possible to the appearance of an Indian holy man, dressing appropriately, abstaining from meat, and translating the Gospel message into terms comprehensible to a high-caste Hindu audience.

In 1686 he and a group of Indian catechists were seized and subjected to excruciating tortures over a period of days. Upon his release and recovery he was recalled to Lisbon. His superiors tried to persuade him to remain in Europe, but he insisted on returning to his mission in India. Three years later he was arrested by a local prince and sentenced to death. In a letter to his superior he wrote: "The only crime with which I am charged is that I teach the religion of the true God and do not worship idols. It is indeed glorious to suffer death for such a crime."

On February 4, 1693, he was beheaded before a large crowd. John de Britto was canonized in 1947.

"I await death and I await it with impatience. It has always been the object of my prayers. It forms today the most precious reward of my labors and my suffering."
—St. John de Britto

St. Agatha
Martyr (Dates Unknown)

St. Agatha is one of the so-called Virgin Martyrs—young women who, finding in Christ an identity that freed them from cultural mores, provoked their enemies to heights of sadistic cruelty. Little is known of the life of St. Agatha, though echoes of her cult can be traced to the early Church.

According to a biography written in the sixth century, Agatha was a wealthy young woman in Sicily who dedicated her virginity to Christ. Invoking the prohibition against Christianity, a consul named Quintianus tried to extort her hand in marriage. When she refused, he consigned her to a brothel, where she successfully deflected all threats to her virtue. Enraged, Quintianus then put her in prison, where she was subjected to hideous tortures, culminating in the amputation of her breasts. Afterward Agatha received a vision of St. Peter, who not only consoled her in her sufferings but healed her wounds. But this was not the end of her ordeal. She was next forced to roll naked over live coals. Still, she prayed, "Lord, my Creator, thou hast always protected me from the cradle; thou hast taken me from the love of the world and given me patience to suffer. Receive now my soul." Having uttered her last words, she died in peace.

One of the most venerated of the Virgin Martyrs, Agatha is invoked by those suffering from breast cancer and by victims of sexual assault.

"Jesus Christ, Lord of all things! You see my heart, you know my desires. Possess all that I am—you alone. I am your sheep; make me worthy to overcome the devil."
—St. Agatha

Pedro Arrupe
Superior General of the Society of Jesus (1907–1991)

edro Arrupe, who was elected superior general of the Jesuits in 1965, oversaw a renewal of the Society so profound that he is revered by many Jesuits as a "second founder." Specifically, he was instrumental in defining the modern mission of the Jesuits in terms of "faith that does justice."

Arrupe's sense of solidarity with a suffering world had roots in his early years as a priest. Assigned to Japan in 1936, he was serving only four miles from the center of Hiroshima on August 6, 1945, when he was nearly blinded by the flash of the first atomic bomb. The memory of that day and of the survivors whom he tended was present to him in each Mass he celebrated for the rest of his life.

His compassion developed over time into a conviction that ministry to oppressed and suffering peoples must not remain on the personal level alone but should also promote structural changes in the world. Under his leadership Jesuits around the world took up the promotion of justice as an essential aspect of evangelization.

In 1981 Arrupe suffered a disabling stroke. He spent his final years mute and dependent on others. Now, after years of prophetic leadership, he served God through prayer and patient suffering. Thus he exemplified the Ignatian discipline of "finding God in all things." He died on February 5, 1991.

"More than ever I find myself in the hands of God. This is what I have wanted all my life from my youth. But now there is a difference; the initiative is entirely with God."

—Pedro Arrupe, SJ, after suffering a stroke

St. Paul Miki and Companions
Martyrs of Japan (d. 1597)

St. Francis Xavier and the first Jesuit missionaries arrived in Japan in 1549. By the end of the century the number of Christians numbered as many as 300,000. But this trend was soon reversed; indeed, as rapidly as it had spread, the Christian religion would be all but eradicated.

The reasons for the persecution were complex. A major cause was fear on the part of powerful rulers that the missionaries were advance agents for foreign colonialism, or that foreign cultural influences would interfere with the cause of national unification. In 1587 Hideyoshi, a powerful feudal lord, ordered the expulsion of all foreign missionaries. In 1597 he condemned twenty-six Christians to death. These included three Japanese Jesuits, of whom the best known was Paul Miki, a convert from a wealthy family, who had achieved renown as a popular preacher. On February 5 these martyrs were publicly crucified in Nagasaki.

Later waves of savage persecution virtually swept Christianity out of sight. Through such experience Japanese Christians acquired a distinctive spirituality. Refined in the crucible of martyrdom and suffering, the Japanese Church promoted a fervent devotion to the crucified Savior. This was joined by a commitment to the cross as a symbol of endurance and the hope of final victory. Such a spirit helped to sustain a faithful remnant during a long underground existence.

"My religion teaches me to pardon my enemies and all who have offended me. I do gladly pardon the emperor and all who have sought my death. I beg them to seek baptism and be Christians themselves."
—St. Paul Miki

Venerable Thecla Merlo
Cofounder, Daughters of St. Paul (1894–1964)

Teresa Merlo was born in 1894 to an Italian peasant family. When she was twenty-one she was introduced to Fr. James Alberione, founder of the Society of St. Paul, an order dedicated to evangelization through Catholic media. He recruited Merlo to help start a female branch of the Pauline family, the Daughters of St. Paul. Taking the religious name Thecla (after St. Paul's helper), she became the first superior general, a position she occupied until her death.

The first assignment for the Daughters was to put out a newspaper. Quickly, they mastered the skills of editing and typography and learned how to operate printing presses—hardly typical work for women religious at that time. As Mother Thecla noted, "Our Congregation will always be young, because it will make use of every new means to do good." This included publishing magazines and books and eventually operating bookstores in which to sell them. They took to television, radio, and any other media that would help spread the Gospel.

Mother Thecla became a mother to the ever-growing Pauline family as it spread throughout the world—to Africa, Asia, Latin America, and the United States. She died on February 5, 1964. Her cause for canonization is in process.

"The powerful idea that must animate us is the thought of souls. This thought must spur us on. We must be concerned about how we are to reach people and bring them the word of truth and salvation. How many souls never hear of God! Who will help them?"

—Venerable Thecla Merlo

Blessed Rosalie Rendu
Daughter of Charity (1786–1856)

Rosalie Rendu was raised on a farm in southern France. During the Terror of the Revolution her parents sheltered priests on the run, and it was from one of them that Rosalie received her First Communion. In 1802, after religious houses reopened in France, she entered the Daughters of Charity in their motherhouse in Paris. In 1815 she was named superior.

In these early years of the industrial era the poor of Paris inhabited a world of terrible squalor. These were the people Victor Hugo immortalized as "Les Misérables"—eking out a miserable existence in overcrowded, disease-ridden slums. The Daughters of Charity served the poor in every way. In time their motherhouse became a gathering place for intellectuals and others concerned with social questions—among them, Frederic Ozanam, who sought Mother Rosalie's advice in launching the Society of St. Vincent de Paul.

Eventually violence erupted in Paris. In the Revolutions of 1830 and 1848 Mother Rosalie found her life imperiled when she protected victims of violence, regardless of their side in the conflict. On one occasion she intervened on behalf of an officer about to be shot at the barricades: "We do not kill here," she insisted.

Mother Rosalie died on February 7, 1856. She was beatified in 2003.

"In an era troubled by social conflicts, Rosalie Rendu joyfully became a servant to the poorest, restoring dignity to each one. . . . Her secret was simple: to see the face of Christ in every man and woman."
—Pope John Paul II

Blessed Mary of Providence (Eugénie Smet)
Founder, Helpers of the Holy Souls (1825–1871)

ugénie Smet was born in 1825 to a wealthy family in Lille, France. After attending a Jesuit retreat in boarding school she experienced a surge of religious devotion, inspiring her, in particular, to pray for the rescue of souls from purgatory. Eventually, she managed to launch a new order, the Helpers of the Holy Souls, dedicated to this mission: "Through constant prayer and the practice of the works of mercy to relieve and deliver the souls who are completing their expiation before being admitted to the bliss of heaven."

At the time, Mother Mary, as she was known, seemed hardly aware of the purgatorial sufferings of the poor in her midst. This was to change with a knock on the door by someone who asked if "one of the ladies" would visit a poor woman who would not receive a priest or nun. In this request Mother Mary heard the voice of Providence: "This is how you will love me." From this point the mission of the Helpers changed. She asked the pope to approve a "fourth vow" for her Institute: "To consecrate ourselves to the relief of the Church suffering" by the practice of charity.

The Constitution of the Institute was approved in 1859. Mother Mary died on February 7, 1871, and was beatified in 1957.

"We believe that there are no boundaries to love and that we are in solidarity with all those who follow Jesus Christ in his Paschal Mystery, whether they are on earth or have already passed through death."

—Constitution of the Helpers of the Holy Souls

Blessed Jacoba of Settesoli
Franciscan (1190–1273)

Jacoba of Settesoli was a young widow in Rome. From the moment she first learned about Francis of Assisi she longed to meet him. The opportunity arose when Francis and his companions came to Rome seeking the pope's approval for their new order. After hearing him preach, Jacoba approached and asked how she might also follow him. Because she still had children to raise, he advised her not to give up her home. "A perfect life can be lived anywhere," he said. "Poverty is everywhere. Charity is everywhere."

Following this counsel, Jacoba joined the Third Order of St. Francis, turned over administration of her property to her sons, and devoted herself to prayer and charitable works. She remained close to Francis. He gave her a pet lamb, which used to follow her about. As Francis was nearing death he sent Jacoba a message, urging her to come quickly and to bring a shroud for his body and wax candles for his burial.

She hastened to Assisi, doing as he had asked. She also brought him a batch of his favorite almond cookies. At first there was consternation about allowing a woman into the friary, but Francis interceded and welcomed her as "Brother Jacoba." There she remained at his side until his death. Afterward he was buried in her shroud.

Jacoba remained in Assisi until her own death on February 8, 1273. She was buried near the tomb of St. Francis.

"While I was praying a voice within me said, 'Go, visit your father, blessed Francis, without delay, and hurry, because if you delay long you will not find him alive.'"

—Blessed Jacoba of Settesoli

St. Josephine Bakhita
Ex-slave and Nun (1869–1947)

Bakhita was born in southern Sudan in 1869. When she was nine she was kidnapped and sold into slavery. Transferred from one master to another over a period of years, she was finally sold to an Italian family who brought her back to Italy to work as a servant and nursemaid to their baby. When this child was old enough to be sent to a boarding school run by the Daughters of Charity, Bakhita accompanied her. It was there that she first heard the Gospel and divined God's will that she be free.

When Bakhita's mistress announced plans to return to Sudan, Bakhita expressed her intention to remain. When pleading did not change her mind, the Signora sued in court for the return of her "property." Only then did Bakhita discover what no one had bothered to inform her: that slavery was illegal in Italy. She had been free all along.

By this time Bakhita heard a voice urging her to consecrate herself to God. She was baptized with the name Josephine Bakhita and accepted into the novitiate of the congregation that had sheltered her.

She lived to the age of seventy-eight, mostly engaged in simple tasks, cooking, sewing, serving as doorkeeper. No work was unimportant when done for "the Master"—her favorite word for God. Living through two world wars, she earned a growing reputation for holiness. She died on February 8, 1947, and was canonized in 2000.

"What do I do? Exactly what you are doing—the will of God."

—St. Josephine Bakhita to a visiting bishop

St. Apollonia
Martyr (d. 249)

St. Apollonia is described variously as a deaconess or a consecrated virgin in the city of Alexandria. She was among a number of Christians martyred during a frenzy of persecution. According to the account in Eusebius's history of the Church, a mob seized Apollonia, "battered her till they knocked out all her teeth, built a pyre in front of the city, and threatened to burn her alive unless she repeated after them their heathen incantations." When she was released momentarily to consider her options, Apollonia startled her assailants by jumping into the fire.

St. Augustine, for one, was troubled by the thought that Apollonia's impulsive action hovered uncomfortably close to suicide. He proposed that she may have been directly inspired in her gesture by the Holy Spirit. In any case, her defiance in the face of death showed the power of her faith and the futility of her captors' threats.

"Oh, great and wondrous struggle of this virgin, who, by the grace of a compassionate God, went to the fire so as not to be burned and was burned so as not to be consumed, as if neither fire nor torture could touch her! . . . By her love of heaven she expelled every earthly fear and grasped the trophy of the cross of Christ."

—Blessed Jacobus de Voragine (*The Golden Legend*)
on St. Apollonia

Blessed Marianus Scotus
Monk (d. ca. 1080)

Marianus Scotus, an Irish monk whose Gaelic name was Muiredach, set off with several companions on a pilgrimage to Rome. They never made it farther than southern Germany. In Regensburg they stopped to enjoy the hospitality of a double monastery (of men and women) under the governance of Abbess Emma. Marianus being a gifted scribe, the abbess persuaded him to remain for some time and make her a copy of the Bible. One Bible became many Bibles, which Marianus faithfully copied by hand.

While his brothers laboriously supplied him with vellum sheets, Marianus worked virtually nonstop. One night, the nun whose job it was to light his lamps neglected her duty and went to sleep. Waking some hours later, she hastened to his cell and found him busily writing with one hand, while from the other, which he held upright, three bright rays of light emanated. This wonder was related to the abbess, and the fame of Marianus spread.

During his many years working for the nuns, he copied many other manuscripts and also produced a comprehensive "chronicle" of the world. Eventually the time came to resume his pilgrimage to Rome. But instead he received a revelation that he should remain in Regensburg. There Abbess Emma provided land on which to establish his own monastery. The fame of this monastery attracted many fellow Irish monks, and there Marianus remained until his death.

"The holy man wrote the Holy Scriptures not once or twice but repeatedly—all the while clad in sorry garb, living on slender diet."

—From an early biography of Blessed Marianus

St. Scholastica
Nun (d. 543)

St. Scholastica was the twin sister of St. Benedict, founder of Western monasticism. Our knowledge of her story depends on two chapters in the *Life of Benedict* by St. Gregory the Great. There we learn that she entered religious life at an early age and apparently rose to the office of abbess in a convent near her brother's monastery at Monte Cassino. Gregory's account of her last days illustrates the affectionate and yet somewhat competitive relationship between the siblings. It also provides a monastic parable about the power and virtue of love versus a rigid devotion to rules.

Benedict and Scholastica had the custom of meeting once a year in a house between their respective monasteries to spend the day talking of spiritual matters. One year, as dusk began to fall, Scholastica begged Benedict to spend the night that they might continue to discuss the joys of life in heaven. Benedict refused, citing the monastic rules, from which it was "impossible" to deviate. Scholastica began to pray, whereupon the heavens erupted in a thunderous downpour that made travel impossible. "What have you done?" Benedict asked in alarm. Scholastica answered simply, "I asked you, but you were unwilling to listen to me. I asked my Lord and He listened to me." And so they passed the night, and "had their fill of spiritual talk."

It was their last meeting. Scholastica died three days later.

"[Benedict] had them place [her body] in the tomb he had prepared for himself. In that way it came about that those who had always been of one mind in the Lord were not even bodily separated in the tomb."

—Commentary of St. Gregory the Great

Daniel Egan
"The Junkie Priest" (1915–2000)

Daniel Egan, a Bronx native, joined the Franciscan Friars of the Atonement in 1935 and was ordained a priest. A turning point in his life came in 1952, as he was preaching in a church and noticed a woman in grave distress. She confessed that she was a drug addict struggling to kick her habit. Though Egan called every hospital in town, none would admit her: "She was shrugged off as a criminal." He decided at that moment that he must open a home for women like this. That was the inspiration for Village Haven, a halfway house for women addicts, located across the street from the women's house of detention.

The location was no accident. As Egan discovered, most of the women in the city jail were drug addicts. And yet few resources at the time were dedicated to recovery from addiction. Most authorities, even medical professionals, wrote off such addicts as hopeless cases. Fr. Egan believed otherwise.

Egan received permission from his order to dedicate himself full time to working with addicts, and he became such an expert in the field that he was dubbed "the Junkie Priest"—a name he happily adopted.

Fr. Egan died on February 10, 2000.

"If we had the vision of faith, we would see beneath every behavior—no matter how repulsive—beneath every bodily appearance—no matter how dirty or deformed—a priceless dignity and value that makes all material facts and scientific technologies fade into insignificance."
—Fr. Daniel Egan

St. Evagrius Ponticus
Desert Father (345–399)

Evagrius was born in 345 in a small town in Pontus (in present-day Turkey) and became a deacon in the church of Constantinople. His life took a turn when he fell in love with the wife of a prominent official. Unsettled by his conflicting desires, he fell into a profound spiritual crisis. In a dream he vowed to leave Constantinople and "watch after his soul." The very next day he boarded a ship for the Holy Land, and thence to the Egyptian desert, where he took up the ascetic life of the early monks and spent the rest of his life.

Evagrius believed that prayer was the foundation of all Christian knowledge. As he noted, "If you are a theologian, you truly pray; if you truly pray, you are a theologian." His handbook on prayer played an enormous role in the foundation of monastic spirituality. With keen sensitivity for human psychology, Evagrius studied the various "demons" which assail the monk. Along with gluttony, lust, anger, sloth, and pride, he examined the demon of "acedia"—the spirit of dryness and depression, or as he called it, "the noonday demon." His main defense against such demons was the practice of contemplative prayer—a state of pure openness to God without words or mental images.

In time Evagrius attracted many disciples. He was in their midst when he became seriously ill. He asked to receive Holy Communion and died soon afterward.

"By true prayer a monk becomes another angel, for he ardently longs to see the face of the Father in heaven."

—St. Evagrius Ponticus

Muriel Lester
Peacemaker (1883–1968)

As a young child of privilege growing up in England, Muriel Lester had an experience that changed her life. While traveling by train in her first-class carriage, she glanced out the window at a rabbit warren of unsavory houses in London's East End. "Do people live there?" she asked. "Yes," her nanny said. "But you needn't worry about them. They don't mind it. They're not like you." Years later, she found opportunities to visit and know the people who lived there and to discover that they were, in fact, just like her—though thinner, paler, and destined to live short lives of worry and want. Muriel left her privileged life behind to devote herself to befriending these people, to sharing their lives and enlarging their hopes.

She established a community center called Kingsley Hall. Though rooted in the Gospels, the community was independent; it was simply "a fellowship based on the attempt to practice the presence of God." She became a tireless promoter of her causes—whether for the poor, the rights of women, the message of nonviolence, or the cause of Indian Independence. She befriended Gandhi, who insisted on staying with her while in London negotiating with the Crown.

She maintained her balance through a practice of contemplative prayer, yielding to "the rhythmic flow of the Eternal Spirit." Lester died on February 11, 1968.

"We should stop praying the Lord's Prayer until we can see that we are tied to the same living tether not only with our fellow countrymen but with everybody on the planet."

—Muriel Lester

Brother Lawrence of the Resurrection
Carmelite Lay Brother (1611–1691)

Little is known of the early life of Brother Lawrence. Born in French Lorraine, he served briefly in the army and saw action in the Hundred Years' War. One cold midwinter day in the presence of a leafless tree, he suddenly thought that soon this tree would be covered again with leaves. This thought filled him with "a high view of the providence and power of God." Eventually he found his way to the Carmelites in Paris and was admitted as a lay brother.

He spent the next forty years in the monastery kitchen and died at the age of eighty. He accomplished no great deeds and left no writings aside from a few letters. But he happened to make a great impression on a Church official who visited the monastery and was astonished by the depth of the lay brother's spiritual wisdom. A record of their conversations and letters was later published as *The Practice of the Presence of God*. Through this book, Brother Lawrence emerged as a great spiritual master. His method was to cultivate at all times a consciousness of the presence of God. In this spirit, our circumstances didn't matter; we could find ourselves in a constant state of prayer or conversation with God. "Our sanctification," he believed, "did not depend upon *changing* our works, but in doing for God's sake that which we commonly do for our own."

Brother Lawrence died on February 12, 1691.

"God regards not the greatness of the work, but the love with which it is performed."
—Brother Lawrence

Dorothy Stang
Martyr of the Amazon (1931–2005)

On the morning of February 12, 2005, Sr. Dorothy Stang, an American-born nun who had spent forty years in Brazil, set off for a meeting of landless farmers. Along the muddy trail her way was blocked by two hired gunmen who asked whether she carried any weapon. In reply she produced her Bible and began to read the Beatitudes: "Blessed are the poor in spirit. . . Blessed are the peacemakers." And then they shot her.

Sr. Dorothy, born in Dayton, Ohio, joined the Sisters of Notre Dame de Namur out of high school and volunteered in 1966 to work in Brazil. Eventually she was drawn to the remote regions of the Amazon and the cause of poor farmers who were exploited and robbed by rich loggers and cattle barons. She had come to see the connections between defending the rights of the poor and protecting the ecological balance of the rain forest itself.

Well into her seventies, she trudged through mud and thick forests to attend prayer services and labor meetings. Her efforts on behalf of the farmers and the imperiled rain forest marked her as an enemy by those who hired her assassins.

Her death aroused the government of Brazil and the whole world to the cause of ecology and justice for which she offered her life.

"I light a candle and look at Jesus on the cross and ask for the strength to carry the suffering of the people. Don't worry about my safety. The safety of the people is what's important."

—Sr. Dorothy Stang

St. Catherine dei Ricci
Mystic (1522–1590)

Catherine dei Ricci, who was born in Florence, entered the Dominican convent when she was thirteen. She rose in prominence in her community, and by the age of thirty she was elected prioress for life. Her reputation for wisdom and holiness traveled far beyond the convent, and she corresponded with many members of the clergy, including three future popes. It was for her ecstatic visions, however, that she attracted the most attention (quite contrary to her desires). At the age of twenty Catherine received the first of a series of extended visions in which she not only beheld but reenacted scenes from Christ's passion: holding out her hands to be bound, standing to be scourged, bending her head to receive a crown of thorns. These visions, which lasted from midday each Thursday until noon on Friday, were repeated every week for twelve years. In the midst of these experiences she would often address her fellow sisters with unusual eloquence and conviction.

Catherine also received the stigmata—the wounds of Christ on her feet, hands, and side—as well as a mysterious ring around her finger. This sign of her betrothal to Christ appeared differently, depending on the witness. Far from taking pride in these supernatural gifts, which aroused the wonder and skepticism of curiosity seekers, Catherine accepted them as a form of mortification. Her greatest happiness, she said, was simply in caring for the sick.

She died on February 2, 1590, and was canonized in 1746. Her feast day is February 13.

"We must look to life not death as our goal."

—St. Catherine dei Ricci

Georges Rouault
Artist (1871–1958)

The French artist Georges Rouault began his career as an apprentice in a studio for stained-glass restoration, an experience that influenced his painting style—easily recognized by the use of color and the distinctive black outlines on his figures. At the age of thirty, moved by his discovery of Christ, he underwent a deep conversion. Filled with disdain for the hypocrisy of bourgeois religion, he was determined to celebrate Christ's presence among the poor, the suffering, and sinners.

Aside from explicitly religious themes, Rouault constantly returned to three settings: the brothel, the circus, and the courtroom. Each offered an opportunity to reflect on the themes of sin, hypocrisy, and judgment, and thus, in the pathos of the human condition, to suggest a symbolic link with the passion of Christ. "All of my work is religious," he said, "for those who know how to look at it."

For Rouault painting was itself a form of prayer. In 1948 he shared with the public his most personal work, "Miserere," the fruit of twenty years of labor. A series of fifty-eight engravings based on the passion and death of Christ, it is one of the great christological statements of the century. Though recognition of Rouault's importance as a religious artist was slow in coming, in 1953 he was named a papal knight by Pope Pius XII. He died on February 13, 1958.

"My only ambition is to be able one day to paint Christ so movingly that those who see Him will be converted."

—Georges Rouault

Saints Cyril and Methodius
Apostles to the Slavs (d. 869, 885)

Cyril and Methodius were brothers born in Thessalonica in the early ninth century. Cyril, the younger, studied philosophy at the imperial university in Constantinople, where he was ordained a priest. His older brother Methodius remained a monk in Greece. Both had participated in cultural and diplomatic missions among the Slavs and had some knowledge of their language. When, therefore, the emperor received a request for Christian missionaries from the ruler of Moravia, he commissioned the two Greek brothers. They set off in 863.

Though German missionaries had been operating in the East for some while, they were hampered by their refusal to instruct the people in any language but Latin. Cyril and Methodius, in contrast, preached in the vernacular. What is more, they invented a Slavonic alphabet into which they translated the Scriptures, with the result that they are remembered among other things as founders of Slavonic literature. They also introduced the Slavonic language into the liturgy (to this day the official liturgical language of many churches of the East).

Though their innovations led to conflict with the German bishops, their mission was a huge success. They are honored in the calendars of both the East and the West, remembered not only as apostles to the Slavic peoples but as innovative missionaries and pioneers of inculturation.

"They desired to become similar in every aspect to those to whom they were bringing the Gospel; they wished to become part of those peoples and to share their lot in everything."

—Pope John Paul II on Saints Cyril and Methodius

Brother James Miller
Missionary, Martyr (1944–1982)

James Miller, a Christian Brother from Wisconsin, spent nearly ten years teaching in his order's schools in Nicaragua. Though committed to improving the lot of the poor, he was decidedly nonpolitical. He left the country in 1979, just as the Sandinista Revolution was toppling the dictatorship of Anastasio Somoza.

Two years later, in 1981, he was sent to Huehuetenango, Guatemala, to teach in the Colegio De La Salle. He also served as an assistant administrator of the Casa Indigena De La Salle, a special program to form educated leaders among the poor Indian population. During these years a fierce wave of government-sponsored violence struck the rural indigenous peoples as well as their allies. Aware of this violence, Miller's friends and family had tried to dissuade him from accepting this assignment. Though he acknowledged their concerns, he accepted the risks.

On February 13, 1982, Miller was shot and killed by masked men in a speeding car. His killers were never identified, nor was there a clear motive. Some speculated that it was a warning to the Christian Brothers to cease interfering with the army's practice of rounding up Indian boys—including students from the Casa—to serve in the army.

"I am personally weary of violence, but I continue to feel a strong commitment to the suffering poor of Central America. . . . I pray to God for the grace and strength to serve Him faithfully by my presence among the poor and oppressed of Guatemala. I place my life in His Providence and place my trust in Him."

—Brother James Miller

St. Claude de la Colombière
Jesuit (1641–1682)

As a young Jesuit, Claude de la Colombière cultivated a deep devotion to the Sacred Heart of Jesus. This prepared him well when he was appointed superior of the Jesuit house at Paray-le-Monial in Burgundy. There, at the local Visitation convent, was a nun named Margaret Mary Alacoque (later canonized), who claimed to have received a series of mysterious revelations directing her to promote devotion to the Sacred Heart. She had encountered nothing but discouragement from her superior and her confessor. Then she happened to hear Claude preach. Immediately she "heard in her soul" the words, "He it is I send you." After he agreed to become her confessor, she found great consolation in her mission: "He taught me to cherish the gifts of God and to receive his communications with faith and humility."

In 1676 Claude was sent to London to serve as a preacher to the Duchess of York at the Queen's Chapel at St. James' Palace. Though he traveled incognito, it was a perilous assignment. In the wake of the "Popish Plot" of Titus Oates, Claude was seized and imprisoned. Tried before the House of Commons, he was spared execution by the personal intervention of King Louis XIV. After returning to France, his health broken by his ordeal, he lived on for only three years.

He died on February 15, 1682. He was canonized in 1992.

"It is one of the most firmly established and consoling of truths that have been revealed to us that nothing happens to us in life unless God wills it so."
—St. Claude de la Colombière

Ben Salmon
Catholic Conscientious Objector (1889–1932)

Of the many conscientious objectors imprisoned during World War I, Ben Salmon stood apart. He was the only imprisoned conscientious objector who attributed his resistance to war to his Roman Catholic faith.

Salmon was raised in Denver in a working-class Catholic family. Though known as something of a rebel for his activities as a union organizer, he remained a devout Catholic who took pride in his membership in the Knights of Columbus.

When war was declared in 1917, Salmon, who was newly married, applied for conscientious objector status. While the government made provision for members of historic "peace churches," there was no precedent at the time for recognizing Catholic conscientious objectors, and he received no support from his Church. Salmon was tried in a military court and sentenced to death—a sentence subsequently reduced to twenty-five years in prison. His stand won him general contempt—even from fellow Catholics, who called him a heretic and a coward. In prison, he was placed in solitary confinement. After going on a hunger strike, he was force-fed and finally confined to a mental asylum. There he wrote a two-hundred-page manuscript offering a lucid critique of the Church's just war teaching—possibly the first of its kind by an American Catholic.

Upon his release in 1920 Salmon led a quiet life, raising three children, but he never fully recovered from his ordeal and died at the age of forty-three on February 15, 1932.

"The justice of man cannot dethrone the justice of God. There is no such animal as a 'just war.'"
—Ben Salmon

St. Verdiana
Anchoress (1182–1242)

Verdiana served as a housekeeper for relatives in Castelfiorentino, a town outside Florence. With the permission of her employers she joined a pilgrimage to the shrine of St. James of Compostela, during which she made such a tremendous impression on her fellow pilgrims that they begged her to remain among them. She agreed, on the condition that she might live as a hermit, and so they gladly built her a small cell attached to the wall of St. Antony's oratory. There, at the age of twenty-six, following a solemn procession accompanied by her confessor and a large crowd, she entered her cell. The entrance was sealed behind her. In this room, with only a small window opening onto the oratory, she spent the following thirty-four years of her life.

Many people came to seek her prayers and spiritual counsel. The story circulated that Verdiana was joined in her cell by two snakes, which ate from her bowl. Among her human visitors, apparently, was St. Francis of Assisi, who is said to have admitted her to his Third Order.

When she died on February 10, 1242, the bells of Castelfiorentino spontaneously rang. Her cell became a famous site of pilgrimage. Her feast is observed by the Franciscans on February 16.

"She had a very great love for the poor, to whom she gave everything which the piety of visitors brought to her, and she only cared to receive the poor and the afflicted."

—*Butler's Lives of the Saints*

Walter Burghardt
Jesuit (1914–2008)

Through years of teaching, scores of books, and his forty-four years as editor of *Theological Studies*, Walter Burghardt helped to invigorate the life of the American Catholic Church. Perhaps his greatest passion lay in preaching: "wrestling with a Lord who reveals and conceals; God's word issuing from these all too human lips." (A university study named him—the only Catholic—among a list of the twelve best preachers in the U.S.) In every way he could, he tried to inspire this passion in others. "All too frequently," he wrote, "our people are not confronted with a word that nourishes while it challenges, heals while it bruises." An increasingly educated populace, he noted, "is no longer silent before homiletic pap and bromides."

In 1991 Burghardt embarked on a new crusade—"Preaching the Just Word"—to combine homiletics with a passion for social justice. "I agonize because in this land of milk and honey, one of every five children grows up beneath the poverty line—and our pulpits are silent."

At the age of eighty-five, in a combination memoir/love letter to the Church entitled *Long Have I Loved You*, he traced the great figures and movements that had shaped him, and the challenges facing the Church. If he acknowledged his "reluctance in dying," it was a reflection, he said, of his great joy in the life he had lived.

Fr. Burghardt died on February 16, 2008, at the age of ninety-three.

"Courage is not *the absence of fear. It is feeling afraid to do something but finding the strength to do it."*

—Walter Burghardt, SJ

Martyrs of China
(d. 1748–1900)

The earliest Christian missionaries found a hospitable welcome in China. In the 18th and 19th centuries, however, as Chinese rulers grew wary of foreign intrusion, Christian missionaries were subjected to periodic waves of persecution. The earliest martyrs originally commemorated on this date were five Spanish Dominicans, including a bishop, killed in 1748.

A larger number of martyrs come from the Boxer Rebellion in 1900. The Boxers were a nationalist secret society whose uprising targeted Europeans and Chinese converts to Christianity. The roots of the rebellion lay in resentment against the European powers and the exploitative treaties they had imposed following the Opium Wars of the mid-nineteenth century. The Boxers rode a wave of resentment against foreign imperialism, but they were animated by special hatred of Christianity. Their uprising claimed among its victims several hundred missionaries, most of them Protestants, and nearly thirty thousand Chinese Christians, mostly Catholics. On July 9, 1900, a large group of Franciscan priests as well as a community of Franciscan Missionaries of Mary were seized along with their bishop, Gregory Grassi, and condemned to death. Though Bishop Grassi had urged the nuns to dress in Chinese clothes so they might escape, they had refused. "Don't stop us from dying with you," they replied. Bishop Grassi gave the group absolution, after which the priests were beheaded, while the nuns had their throats slit.

These martyrs were canonized in 2000. Their original feast day on February 17 is now celebrated on July 9.

"If it be God's will that we should be martyred, then we must accept it."
—St. Francis Fogolla

Janani Luwum
Anglican Archbishop and Martyr (1924–1977)

Janani Luwum was the Anglican primate of Uganda. By all accounts he was a traditional prelate, not naturally suited to the role of prophet. But this was the era of General Idi Amin, whose reign of terror claimed tens of thousands of victims. Amin was famous for his paranoid wrath, and there were few who dared to provoke him.

Though Luwum tried to steer clear of politics, by 1977 a neutral course had become impossible. After Amin circulated rumors that the Anglican bishops were plotting violence against him, Luwum issued an angry denial and a demand for proof. In early February government troops surrounded his residence and held the archbishop at gunpoint while they conducted a search for "incriminating evidence." The bishops responded with their most outspoken denunciation of conditions in the country. If this was how an archbishop was treated, no one was safe.

On February 16 the bishops were summoned to the presidential palace where Amin unveiled a cache of weapons supposedly confiscated from the archbishop. Eventually he dismissed them all—except for Archbishop Luwum. The next morning it was announced that the archbishop had died while trying to escape. Only after some weeks was his bullet-riddled body released. According to later testimony, Luwum had refused Amin's order that he sign a confession. Realizing that his fate was sealed, he had begun to pray, thus provoking Amin's murderous rage. The president himself fired the fatal shots.

"Even if I have to die for my convictions, I can never lower the standards God has set me."
—Archbishop Janani Luwum

Blessed Fra Angelico
Dominican Artist (ca. 1395–1455)

Fra Angelico, born Guido di Pietro, was a Dominican friar and artist who lived in a community near Florence. His religious name was Fra Giovanni, but he became better known to his brothers as Fra Angelico—a tribute both to his angelic piety and to his artistic talents. Though he filled various offices within the community, it was in painting that he found the deepest expression of his religious vocation.

As an early precursor of the Florentine Renaissance, Fra Angelico's frescoes and paintings featured vivid color, startlingly lifelike portraits, an ingenious use of perspective, and realistic backgrounds. But his primary end was not the aesthetic but the religious impact of his work. His frescoes include scenes from the lives of Mary and Christ. Nearly all of them include Dominican saints—dressed identically to the friars who would be viewing the paintings. The message was plain. The viewer was to place himself imaginatively in the scene before him and identify with the attitude of devotion as displayed in the painting itself.

For Fra Angelico the religious life was a life lived in the presence of Christ and emotionally engaged in the ongoing drama of redemption. It was this mystical vision that was communicated in his paintings with such angelic purity.

Fra Angelico was beatified in 1982 by Pope John Paul II, who also named him patron of artists.

"He who occupies himself with the things of Christ should live with Christ."
—Blessed Fra Angelico

Michelangelo
Artist (1475–1564)

Michelangelo Buonarroti, one of the greatest artists of all time, found his vocation while still a child in Florence. His talents blossomed early. When he was twenty-two he produced his *Pietà*, a depiction of Mary cradling in her lap the body of her crucified son. The pathos of this work contrasts with his colossal statue of David, commissioned by a Florentine guild.

As an artist, Michelangelo naturally relied on commissions from wealthy patrons; for many of his greatest works, this meant the Church. Through his religious works he conveyed a visual theology as vivid and influential as Dante's *Divine Comedy*. His masterwork, the ceiling of the Sistine Chapel, commissioned by Pope Julius II, depicts the drama of the book of Genesis, from the Creation to the Flood. For this work he spent four years lying on his back, painting by candlelight atop the massive scaffolding. Such images as the outstretched hand of God imparting life to Adam, or his later epic vision of the Last Judgment, have left an indelible impression on the religious imagination of the West.

Toward the end of his life he designed the dome of St. Peter's Basilica—refusing any payment—and returned to the theme of the *Pietà*, in some ways even more moving for its rough-hewn, unpolished quality. He included himself as an old man in the guise of Joseph of Arimathea. He died just short of his eighty-ninth birthday on February 18, 1564.

"True painting is only the image of the perfection of God, a shadow of the pencil with which he paints, a melody, a striving after harmony."
—Michelangelo

St. Conrad of Piacenza
Franciscan Tertiary (ca. 1290–1351)

St. Conrad, a young nobleman from Piacenza, was out hunting one day when he ordered his servants to set fire to brushwood to drive out his game. Following a sudden turn in the wind, Conrad watched in horror as the fire consumed the neighboring fields. After returning quietly to town, he said nothing about his part in this disaster. But when a peasant was subsequently charged with the crime and sentenced to death, Conrad was filled with remorse. Stepping forward, he accepted the blame and paid for the damages, though this left him nearly ruined. In this misfortune, however, Conrad saw the hand of God. Consequently, he and his wife decided to give up all their property and pursue religious life. While his wife entered a convent of Poor Clares, Conrad entered the Third Order of St. Francis, joining a group of hermits in the Valley of Noto.

Contrary to his intentions, Conrad's sacrifice caused him to be widely admired. To escape the throng of visitors he retired to a remote grotto. But when his prayers were credited with ending a famine, he felt he had no choice but to welcome the stream of suffering pilgrims who came seeking his intervention. Many other miracles were credited to Conrad; birds fluttered over his head whenever he exited his hermitage. When he discerned that his final hour had arrived, he lay on the ground in front of a crucifix and died on February 19, 1351.

"If the sinner do penance for his sins, and do judgment and justice, and restore the pledge and render what he has robbed, he shall surely live and shall not die."
—Ezekiel 33:14-15

St. Philothea of Athens
Monastic Martyr (1522–1589)

Revoula Venizelos was born to a wealthy family in Athens. At the age of twelve, much against her will, she was betrothed to a much older man who treated her with contempt. For three years she endured this abuse. When he eventually died she gave away her property, adopted a monastic life, and took the name Philothea—"friend of God." She founded a monastic complex dedicated to St. Andrew, which included a hospital, a home for the aged, workshops, and a school for girls and boys. While her reputation for holiness attracted many women to her monastery, her charitable activities earned the admiration of all the Christians of Athens.

In this time of Turkish occupation, Philothea got into trouble for rescuing and sheltering women who had been abducted and enslaved by the occupiers. Her actions enraged the Turkish rulers, who had her dragged from her convent and savagely beaten. Several days later, she died from her wounds. Recognized as a martyr by the Eastern Orthodox Church, she was declared the patron of Athens.

"The Faithful of Athens and all the world honor Philothea the martyred nun and rejoice in her holy relics. For she has exchanged this passing life for the life that knows no end through her struggle and martyrdom; and she begs the Savior to have mercy on us all."

—Troparion to St. Philothea

Servant of God Francis X. Ford
Bishop and Martyr (1892–1952)

I n 1912, Francis Ford, straight out of high school in Brooklyn, became the first recruit to join the new Maryknoll Fathers and Brothers, a missionary society founded the previous year. In 1918, following his ordination, he joined the first group of four Maryknoll priests to embark on a mission to China.

In Kaying, in southern China, where he spent more than twenty years, he saw the Catholic population increase to twenty thousand. Eventually he would be appointed as its first bishop. He loved his flock and reminded fellow clergy to encounter the Chinese in a spirit of "reverence, respect, and love, a meeting of brothers." He especially welcomed the Maryknoll Sisters, recognizing their facility in entering the world of Chinese women. "Hours spent in the chapel are not the only means of entertaining the Beloved Guest of the soul. We can often please Him better when we are out in the highways and byways of China, offering to needy souls the hospitality of our Christian love."

Ford remained in China throughout the war. But in 1950, following the Communist Revolution, he was placed under house arrest and charged with espionage. Though never tried, he was starved, beaten, and regularly paraded before mocking crowds. He died in prison on February 21, 1952. His cause for canonization is in process.

"Grant us . . . to be the doorstep by which the multitudes may come to Thee. And if . . . we are ground underfoot and spat upon and worn out, at least we . . . shall become the King's Highway in pathless China."
—Bishop Francis X. Ford

Dorothy Gauchat
Cofounder, Our Lady of the Wayside (1921–2000)

Dorothy Gauchat and her husband Bill were literally drawn together by the spirit of Dorothy Day. Their marriage and their mission in life was shaped by the message of the Catholic Worker, that Christ comes to us in the disguise of our neighbor. Dorothy first met Bill in the 1930s when he operated a Catholic Worker house of hospitality in Cleveland. After their marriage they settled on a farm in Avon, where they raised three children and continued to practice the works of mercy. A turning point came with a call from a Catholic hospital asking if they would care for a severely disabled infant, not expected to live. At first Dorothy resisted—but then she was overwhelmed by the thought that this was "one of God's immortal creations: hurt, yes; sick, yes; hopelessly handicapped, yes; but immortal." They took in the child and cared for him. From this small beginning they found their lifelong vocation as foster parents to a stream of other children, most often labeled as hopeless cases. In the case of one boy, severely disabled with cerebral palsy, they adopted him as their own son.

When Bill was seemingly healed of terminal cancer following a pilgrimage to the shrine of Our Lady of Guadalupe, the Gauchats undertook a new ambitious plan, opening a home large enough to care for dozens of severely disabled children: "Our Lady of the Wayside." Long after her husband's death, Dorothy carried on with this mission. In 1987 she also founded a hospice for infants with HIV/AIDS, where she worked until her own death on February 20, 2000.

"Our faith supported our actions: If one does not love his neighbor, he cannot love God. These unwanted waifs are our neighbors."

—Dorothy Gauchat

St. Robert Southwell
Jesuit Poet and Martyr (ca. 1561–1595)

In the late sixteenth century Jesuit missionaries spanned the globe, facing every type of peril. Yet for English Jesuits there was nowhere they faced any greater danger than when they traveled in their own country—England under the reign of Queen Elizabeth. Still, despite persecution, a Catholic remnant in England remained, sustained by a network of underground priests and a stream of missionaries smuggled in from the Continent.

Robert Southwell was born in Norfolk and studied at the English college in Douai, France. At eighteen he was accepted by the Jesuits. Five years later he stole into England and embarked on a clandestine ministry that lasted six years. During this time he achieved both notoriety and literary fame through the publication of religious poems and a number of tracts defending the loyalty of his fellow Catholics.

Inevitably, he was captured. For three years he was held without charge in the Tower, subjected repeatedly to torture. Many of his greatest poems were written in prison, including "The Burning Babe." In this poem Southwell describes a vision on Christmas Day, in which Christ—as a "babe all burning bright"—appears to the poet, revealing his mission of redeeming love.

Eventually Southwell was tried and sentenced to death. Before mounting the gallows he addressed the crowd: "I am come hither to play out the last act of this poor life . . ." Quoting St. Paul, he said, "Whether we live or die, we belong to the Lord."

"Not where I breathe, but where I love, I live; / Not where I love, but where I am, I die."
—St. Robert Southwell

Blessed Maria Enrica Dominici
Sister of St. Anne and Providence (1829–1894)

Maria Enrica Domenici was born in Turin. From an early age she felt irresistibly drawn to religious life. "Only God could fill and satisfy my poor heart," she reflected. "As for everything else, I did not care." In 1850 she entered the Sisters of St. Anne and Providence, an institute devoted to the education of poor girls.

As Pope Paul VI noted in the homily at her beatification, she was in many ways a typical religious of her time, and yet, he said, her life proclaimed at once the "essential fragility of the human and the absolute greatness and transcendence of God." Though she had hoped to be sent as a missionary to India, she was told her talents were needed at home. In 1861 she was elected superior of her community, a post she occupied for thirty-three years, until her death.

She showed great skill in administration and personal courage in her care for victims during an epidemic of cholera. Eventually she was able to send sisters on the mission to India she had wished for herself. Her letters reflect her deep and intimate relationship with God: "I seemed to rest on the bosom of God, like a little girl sleeping peacefully at her mother's breast; I loved God and would almost say, were it not for fear of exaggerating, that I tasted his goodness."

She died on February 21, 1894, and was beatified in 1978.

"To will what God wills, as God wills it and as far as he wills it."

—Blessed Maria Enrica Dominici

St. Margaret of Cortona
Penitent (1247–1297)

St. Margaret was raised in a poor family in Tuscany. Following the death of her mother when she was eleven, Margaret's new stepmother turned her out of the house. Eventually, with few apparent options, she eloped with a young nobleman, who kept her as his mistress. Though she bore him a son, he would not marry her. Eventually, when he was murdered, Margaret took this as a sign of God's judgment. Penniless, she returned to her father's house, but he would not take her in. She made her way to Cortona, where she had heard of the compassion of the Franciscan friars. There she introduced herself by walking through town with a rope around her neck, a sign of her penitence. The friars urged her to quit this spectacle and also curbed her proclivity to extremes of asceticism. Eventually she was accepted as a Franciscan tertiary. With other women she formed a nursing community, caring for the sick and the poor.

Over time, as stories spread of her holiness and her purported miracles, as well as her private colloquies with Christ, Margaret attracted wide attention. The Franciscans urged her to embark on a public crusade to call sinners to conversion. Penitents from all over Italy, and as far away as France and Spain, made their way to Cortona to hear her spiritual discourses.

She died on February 22, 1297. She was canonized in 1728.

"Show now that thou art converted; call others to repentance. . . . The graces I have bestowed on thee are not meant for thee alone."

—A message from the Lord to St. Margaret of Cortona

Hans and Sophie Scholl
Martyrs of the White Rose (d. 1943)

I n the fall of 1942 the citizens of Munich were astonished by a series of leaflets that circulated throughout the city. They contained a sweeping indictment of the Nazi regime and enjoined readers to work for their nation's defeat. At a time when the merest hint of dissent was a treasonable offense, the audacity of this call to resistance threw the Gestapo into a rage.

Calling themselves "The White Rose," the authors of these leaflets were in fact a few dozen university students who had been inspired by Christian faith and the idealism of youth to challenge the Nazi regime. At the center of the group were a brother and sister, Hans and Sophie Scholl, only twenty-four and twenty-one. Hans was a medical student who had served on the Russian front. Sophie studied philosophy. Discerning with uncommon clarity the depth of Nazi depravity, they had decided to wage a spiritual war against the system, armed with no other weapons than courage, the power of truth, and an illegal duplicating machine. By proclaiming the truth they hoped they might help break the Nazi spell and inspire others, who were experiencing doubts, to take up active resistance.

Hans and Sophie were caught on February 18, 1943. Quickly convicted of treason they were sentenced to death and beheaded on February 22.

"Life is always on the edge of death; narrow streets lead to the same place as wide avenues, and a little candle burns itself out just like a flaming torch does. I choose my own way to burn."

—Sophie Scholl

St. Polycarp
Bishop and Martyr (ca. 69–155)

Polycarp was one of the most revered of the apostolic fathers—that generation of bishops who received their faith from the original apostles. According to tradition, Polycarp had been a disciple of St. John the Evangelist. As a young man he met St. Ignatius of Antioch and kissed his chains as he passed through Smyrna on his way to martyrdom in Rome. Years later, as an old man, Polycarp met his own death as a martyr. The account of his death, circulated in a letter from Smyrna, is the oldest account of Christian martyrdom outside the New Testament. As this text affirmed, martyrs were not simply those who suffered for their beliefs. Polycarp's death was "a martyrdom conformable to the gospel." In other words, the death of the holy bishop was a mystical reenactment of the passion of Christ.

At the time of his arrest in 155, Polycarp was eighty-six, having served as bishop for many decades. When ordered to worship Caesar, he replied, "How can I blaspheme my King who saved me?" He was sentenced to be burned. But the narrator records a miraculous sign: "For the fire made the shape of a vaulted chamber like a ship's sail filled by the wind, and made a wall around the body of the martyr. And he was in the midst, not as burning flesh, but as bread baking or as gold and silver refined in a furnace." The whole crowd marveled.

"He who has given me strength to face the flames will also enable me to stay unflinching at the stake."
—St. Polycarp

Blessed Rafaela Ybarra de Vilallonga
Founder, Congregation of the Guardian Angels
(1843–1900)

Rafaela Ybarra represents the unusual case of a founder of a religious congregation who yet remained a laywoman, responsible for a large extended family, while also dedicating herself fully to the needs of the wider community.

Born in Bilbao, Spain, to a wealthy family, Rafaela was married at eighteen and bore seven children. Following her sister's death, she adopted her five children as well. After reading *The Introduction to the Devout Life* by St. Francis de Sales—a book that indicates the path to holiness available to people in all stations of life—she determined to embrace a life of charity and service. In her own domestic life, she might well have found sufficient opportunities for a life of devotion. Instead, Rafaela set out for the hospitals and the streets of Bilbao to find others—particularly poor and unprotected young women and children—in need of her maternal attention. After founding soup kitchens, orphanages, and support centers for unmarried women, she founded the Institute of the Guardian Angels to manage her various charities.

In 1898 her husband died. Rather than enter her own congregation she took in her six grandchildren after her daughter-in-law died. When she herself died on February 23, 1900, she was mourned as the beloved Mother of Bilbao. Thousands thronged to her funeral, many of them direct recipients of her care. She was beatified in 1984.

"From the Cross and prayer she was able to draw strength to offer herself on the altars of Christian love."
—Pope John Paul II

Blessed Margaret Ebner
Mystic (1291–1351)

From the age of fifteen until her death forty-five years later, Margaret Ebner lived as a Dominican nun in present-day Germany. Yet for many years after entering religious life, as she would later recall, she lived without any true "awareness of herself." In 1312 she was overcome by a mysterious illness that became so serious that she could scarcely leave her bed. This condition, accompanied by a deep depression, lasted fourteen years, only to be lifted with her introduction to a new confessor, a priest named Henry, the leader of a pious fellowship called the "Friends of God." Not only did she recover from her illness but her personality was deeply transformed. "Sorrow became non-sorrow," and she seemed to live each day in the presence of the heavenly life. She emerged as a prophet and visionary whose pronouncements and counsel were heeded far beyond the walls of her monastery.

Henry, at first her spiritual teacher, then her friend, and ultimately her devoted pupil, was left to wonder. She had "mastered the steps of the dance of a true life to the sweet piping" of Christ, he wrote. Her "prophetic voice makes me speechless." Margaret wrote down her visions and spiritual adventures, in which she saw the world in its ultimate dimension—suffused by the divine presence.

In 1979 she became the first saint beatified by Pope John Paul II.

"I ask you, my Lord, to feed me with your sweet grace, strengthen me with your pure love, surround me with your boundless mercy, and embrace me with your pure truth."

—Blessed Margaret Ebner

Blessed Josefa Naval Girbés
Lay Apostle (1820–1893)

Josefa Naval Girbés was born in a town near Valencia in Spain. Though she never sought to enter a religious order, at eighteen she took a vow of perpetual virginity and devoted herself to the service of God and her neighbors. At the suggestion of her parish priest, she opened an embroidery workshop in her home, where young women could learn a trade, while also engaging in prayer and Bible study.

Her quiet faith and undramatic ministry left no great record on the world. Yet she made a great impression on her neighbors, especially when she risked her life to care for the sick during an outbreak of cholera. She died on February 24, 1893, and was buried, according to her wishes, in the habit of a Third Order Carmelite. Fifty years after her death, devotion to her memory was sufficient to inspire the diocese of Valencia to promote her cause for canonization. She was finally beatified in 1988. In his homily, Pope John Paul II recognized her as an example of the apostolate of the laity, citing the words of Vatican II: "Sharers in the priestly, prophetic, and kingly functions of Christ . . . they carry out their own part in the mission of the whole Christian people with respect to the Church and the world."

"A woman simple and docile to the Spirit, she reached the pinnacle in her long life of Christian perfection, dedicated to the service of others."
—Pope John Paul II

St. Walburga
Abbess and Missionary (ca. 710–ca. 779)

S t. Walburga, an Anglo-Saxon nun in Dorset, was the niece of St. Boniface, the renowned English monk who launched a successful mission to Germany in the eighth century. Two of Walburga's brothers joined Boniface in his journey, and soon they appealed to England for additional volunteers. Walburga made the journey in 750. Her brother Winnebald presided over a large "double-monastery" near Stuttgart. He asked Walburga to preside over the women, while he would oversee the men. After his death in 761 she assumed the office of superior over both the monks and nuns.

By this time she had become skilled in the medical arts, and she acquired a reputation as a gifted healer. This reputation continued after her death, when an aromatic fluid, of supposed healing properties, flowed from a fissure in the rock on which her tomb rested. Among the deeds ascribed to her in life was the cure of a young girl who suffered from an uncontrollable appetite. As a result, Walburga is often depicted as holding three ears of corn—though some have claimed that this symbol owes more to the association of her name with the earth goddess Walborg.

"O holy St. Walburga, glorious servant of God, after you had lived holily in peaceful obscurity, you were united by your blessed death to your Divine Spouse, Jesus Christ, in order to receive from Him the reward of your virtues. Forget not those who still have to struggle amid the stormy sea of life, and obtain for them the prize of victory. Amen."
—Prayer to St. Walburga

Venerable Felix Varela
Priest (1788–1853)

Felix Varela, a Catholic priest and theologian, was one of the most remarkable figures of the early nineteenth-century Church. Born in Havana, Cuba, he was ordained a priest at the age of twenty-three and served for many years as a professor of philosophy. In 1821 he was elected a delegate to the Spanish Cortes in Madrid. There he introduced bills calling for Cuban independence from Spain and another for the abolition of slavery. As a result of such seditious talk he was forced to flee Spain and go into exile. He never returned to Cuba.

Settling in New York City, he spent many years in pastoral work among the city's poor Irish immigrants. Still passionately loyal to his homeland, he began a Spanish-language newspaper, which became a voice for Cuban independence. His activities posed such a threat to Spain that the government mounted an assassination plot. Meanwhile he earned a doctorate in theology and served as vicar general of the archdiocese of New York. Varela wrote a book—far in advance of its time—promoting the value of religion as a guardian of liberty, while at the same time challenging the Church to embrace the spirit of liberty and democracy. "Where the Spirit is," he proclaimed, "there is liberty."

Varela died on February 25, 1853, in St. Augustine, Florida. In 1911 his remains were removed to Cuba, where his grave was honored by Cuban patriots of all political tendencies. His cause for canonization is currently in process.

"I have always concluded that Christianity and liberty are inseparable."
—Venerable Felix Varela

Blessed Isabel of France
Franciscan Princess (1225–1270)

Beautiful, clever, and the daughter of Louis VIII, King of France, Princess Isabel was destined for a life of pomp and luxury. But her heart was drawn elsewhere. When her frequent fasts and austerity caused her to fall ill, her mother consulted a holy woman. She said that when Isabel recovered she should be considered as dead to the world. So it was. Isabel refused all proposals of marriage—even when urged on by Pope Innocent IV, who told her that marriage would serve the good of Christendom. She insisted on serving God before all else.

Increasingly, Isabel felt attracted to the Franciscan movement, which was sweeping Europe. At dinner each day she would welcome a number of poor people, whom she waited on personally. In the evenings she would leave the palace to visit the sick. When her brother Louis ascended the throne, he agreed to support her plan to establish a Franciscan convent. St. Bonaventure himself helped to devise its rule. It was called the Monastery of the Humility of the Virgin Mary.

Isabel did not formally join the enclosed community. Instead, she lived in quarters separate from the nuns and continued to wear secular clothing, while devoting herself to prayer and contemplation. She died in 1270.

"We beheld in her a mirror of innocence, and at the same time an admirable model of penance, a lily of purity, a fragrant rose of patience and self-renunciation, an endless fountain of goodness and mercy."
—From the "Life of Isabel of France"

Antonio Valdivieso
Bishop and Martyr (1495–1550)

Antonio Valdivieso, a Spanish Dominican assigned to Nicaragua, was the first bishop in the Americas to die for the cause of justice and the defense of the Indians.

From the moment he arrived in Nicaragua in 1544, Valdivieso vigorously opposed the cruel oppression of the native Indians by the Spanish, including the governor and his family. Departing for Spain, he presented his complaints directly to King Charles V. The king in turn named him bishop of Nicaragua. Afterward, Valdivieso returned with trepidation, convinced that his new appointment was the equivalent of a death sentence.

When he landed in Central America, Spanish soldiers tried unsuccessfully to prevent his return to the capital in Leon. Once in the cathedral he resumed his prophetic preaching. Before long, plans for his assassination were being openly discussed. On February 26, 1550, the governor's son and several of his henchmen forced their way into the bishop's home and stabbed him, along with two other Dominicans.

"I write these letters hurriedly in order that Your Majesty might be aware . . . of the great need that exists in these parts for justice."

—Bishop Antonio Valdivieso

St. Gregory of Narek
Doctor of the Church (ca. 951–1003)

In April 2015, in a Mass commemorating the Armenian genocide, Pope Francis declared St. Gregory of Narek a Doctor of the Church. Though little known in the West, Gregory was much better known in the Armenian Catholic Church, where he was long venerated as a saint and a master of mystical prayer.

Gregory was born in the city of Narek. At a young age he entered the local monastery, where he remained for the rest of his life. A prolific writer, Gregory's reputation rests especially on his Book of Lamentations, a collection of ninety-five prayers, which he subtitled "Conversations with God from the depth of the heart." He worked on this book, "an encyclopedia of prayer for all nations," over many years, finishing it just prior to his death—"Its letters like my body, its message like my soul."

Posing the question as to what gift one might offer to God, he answered, "the sighs of the heart." Thus, his first prayer begins, "The voice of a sighing heart, its sobs and mournful cries, / I offer up to you, O Seer of Secrets, / placing the fruits of my wavering mind / as a savory sacrifice on the fire of my grieving soul / to be delivered to you in the censer of my will."

Gregory died in 1003.

"And though my body die in sin, with your grace and compassion, may I be strengthened in you, cleansed of sin through you, and renewed by you with life everlasting, and at the resurrection of the righteous be deemed worthy of your Father's blessing."

—St. Gregory of Narek

St. Gabriel Possenti
Passionist Priest (1838–1862)

Gabriel Possenti, who was born to a large family in Assisi, surprised his friends and family when, at the age of sixteen, he announced his intention to join the Passionist order. Hardly a model of piety, he was known among his friends as a lighthearted prankster and something of a dandy. Unbeknownst to others, however, he had made a vow, during a serious illness, that if he recovered he would enter religious life. Afterward he could not be dissuaded.

Gabriel applied himself avidly to his spiritual formation, seeking in all things to find the way of holiness. "I will attempt day by day to break my will into pieces," he wrote. "I want to do God's Holy Will, not my own." His spiritual director continuously rejected Gabriel's pleas to practice more severe mortifications. Finally, to provide a lesson in humility, he ordered Gabriel to wear a barbed chain outside his clothing, "so that all may see what a man of great mortification you are." Gabriel complied cheerfully.

After only four years in religious life Gabriel showed the first signs of tuberculosis. As his condition worsened, all were struck by his ability to maintain his good cheer and gentleness. He died on February 27, 1862.

Canonized in 1920, he was declared a patron of Catholic youth.

"[Mary] does not look to see what kind of person you have been. She simply comes to a heart that wants to love her. She will even be at hand to accompany you on the trip to eternity."

—St. Gabriel Possenti

119

Martyrs of the Plague of Alexandria
(d. 261)

This day commemorates the heroic charity of Christians during an outbreak of plague in the Egyptian city of Alexandria in 261. So virulent was the disease that every house in the city was affected. The bodies of the dead and even the dying—a source of general dread—were cast into the streets, contributing to the stench of pestilence.

At this point a wonderful thing happened. Christians of the city, who had been forced by persecution to hide themselves and conduct their meetings in secret, now emerged from their homes to attend to the dead and dying. At great risk to themselves—both from infection and from the possibility of arrest—they nursed the sick, washed the bodies of the dead, and saw to their burial. For many of these Christians, this service literally entailed the laying down of their own lives for their neighbors. Those who died were recognized by the Church as true martyrs of charity, and they were added to the calendar of the saints.

"Many who had healed others fell victims themselves. The best of our brethren have been taken from us in this manner: some were priests, others deacons, and some laity of great worth. This death, with the faith which accompanied it, appeared to be little inferior to martyrdom itself."
—St. Dionysius, bishop of Alexandria

St. John Cassian
Abbot (ca. 360–ca. 435)

John Cassian was born somewhere in what is now Romania around the year 360. As a young man he embarked on a great quest for spiritual wisdom. At first he visited the holy places in Palestine and lived there for a time as a monk. Eventually he was drawn to Egypt, home of the great and mysterious Desert Fathers. For ten years he traveled about interviewing these spiritual athletes. His later account helped popularize the ascetic spirituality of these monks and hermits throughout the West. His *Conferences* became one of the most influential handbooks of monastic spirituality.

The world delighted in hearing of the Desert Fathers, of their feats of heroic self-denial, their miracles, and their combat with demons. Cassian was less interested in these exploits. The Desert Fathers whom he interviewed spoke rather as masters of the spiritual life, experts in human psychology, whose wisdom was born of years of spiritual practice and disciplined introspection. The purpose of asceticism, as Cassian learned, was not self-denial for its own sake. The final goal was love. As one of the monks put it, "Solitude, watches in the night, manual labor . . . and the other disciplines. . . . They are the rungs of a ladder up which the heart may climb to perfect charity."

Sometime after his travels Cassian was ordained a priest, and he later founded monasteries in the area of Marseilles.

"It is the bigger miracle to eject passion from your own body than it is to eject an evil spirit from another's body."

—St. John Cassian

MARCH

1 George Herbert • Venerable Engelmar Unzeitig

2 St. Agnes of Bohemia • John Wesley

3 Venerable Concepción Cabrera de Armida • St. Katharine Drexel

4 Blessed Placide Viel • Martin Niemoeller

5 St. Gerasimus • St. Kieran of Saighir

6 St. Colette • Jean-Pierre de Caussade

7 Saints Perpetua and Felicity • St. Catherine of Bologna

8 St. John of God • St. Marie-Eugenie Milleret

9 St. Gregory of Nyssa • St. Frances of Rome

10 The Forty Martyrs of Sebastea • Harriet Tubman

11 St. Teresa Margaret Redi • James Reeb

12 Blessed Angela Salawa • Rutilio Grande

13 St. Matilda • Blessed Dulce Pontes

14 Fannie Lou Hamer • Chiara Lubich

15 St. Louise de Marillac • Mother Benedicta Riepp

16 St. John de Brebeuf • Eusebio Kino

17 St. Patrick • St. Gertrude of Nivelles

18 St. Cyril of Jerusalem • Antonio de Andrade

19 St. Joseph • Blessed Marcel Callo

20 Mother Catherine Spalding • St. Maria Josefa de Guerra

21 St. Benedetta Frassinello • Viola Liuzzo

22 Blessed Clemens August van Galen • Luis Espinal Camps

23 Blessed Sibyllina of Pavia • St. Rebecca Ar-Rayès

24 St. Catherine of Vadstena • Blessed Oscar Romero

25 St. Dismas • Ida B. Wells

26 Anne Frank • Raoul Wallenberg

27 St. John of Egypt • *The Cloud of Unknowing* Author

28 Moses • Marc Chagall

29 Micah • Karl Rahner

30 St. John Climacus • Thea Bowman

31 John Donne • St. Maria Skobtsova

MARCH

George Herbert
Anglican Vicar and Poet (1593–1633)

George Herbert was born to a distinguished Welsh family. He received a superb education, served a term in Parliament, and seemed well launched on a path of worldly success. At the age of thirty-three, however, he announced that he had decided to seek holy orders in the Anglican Church. After ordination he accepted a position as rector of a church in Bemerton, a tiny rural parish that was half in ruins. His ministry lasted only three years, as he died of consumption on March 1, 1633. So his name might have vanished in obscurity, except for a manuscript of poems, published after his death, which established his reputation as one of the greatest poets in the English language.

All his poems deal with the religious life, written in a simple, fresh style that reflects the virtues of balance and moderation prized in Anglican spirituality. One poem, "Prayer," consists of nothing but concise images piled one upon another: "Prayer the Churches banquet, Angels age / God's breath in man returning to his birth / The soul in paraphrase, heart in pilgrimage." Each image constitutes a sermon in itself—"Reversed thunder," "Heaven in ordinarie"—until the poem rises to a breathless whisper: "The land of spices; something understood."

Writing verse for Herbert was a form of prayer, a way of contemplating God, offering praise, but also questioning his Creator. In short, it was the path to "heaven in ordinarie."

"Love bade me welcome: yet my soul drew back / . . . 'You must sit down,' says Love, 'and taste my meat': / So I did sit and eat."

—George Herbert

Venerable Engelmar Unzeitig
Priest and Martyr (1911–1945)

As a boy growing up in Germany, Engelmar Unzeitig dreamed of becoming a missionary priest—to travel to foreign lands and dedicate his life to saving souls, perhaps by the laying down of his life. At the age of eighteen he entered the seminary of the Mariannhill Missionaries and was ordained just weeks before the outbreak of World War II. Two years later, after preaching in defense of the Jews, he was arrested by the Gestapo; in June 1941 he was conveyed to Dachau, a notorious concentration camp.

Dachau's wartime population had swelled to 200,000 inmates, including nearly 3,000 members of the clergy. Housed in a special "priest's barracks," these clergy were held in particular contempt by the SS guards. Yet despite the hellish conditions, Fr. Unzeitig considered it a school for holiness.

He survived nearly four years of starvation, beatings, and exposure to the freezing elements. Then in January 1945 the camp was hit by an outbreak of typhoid. Those who were infected were confined to a special barracks and left to die in horrible squalor. Fr. Unzeitig was one of twenty priests who volunteered to join them. Here at last was his mission. For six weeks he cared for and consoled the sick and dying—washing their fevered bodies, cleaning their filthy pallets, but also hearing confessions and offering the last rites. Inevitably, he succumbed to the disease himself, dying on March 2, 1945. He was declared venerable by Pope Benedict XVI in 2009.

"One sees again and again that the human heart is attuned to love, and it cannot withstand its power in the long run."

—Venerable Engelmar Unzeitig, in a letter days before his death

St. Agnes of Bohemia
Princess and Abbess (ca. 1203–1280)

Agnes, who was born in Prague, was the daughter of the king of Bohemia. Despite the privileges of her station, she enjoyed no freedom to decide her own destiny. She was simply a commodity to be invested wherever she might bring the highest return for her family and its dynastic interests. Starting at the age of three she was shipped to various kingdoms and betrothed to strangers she had never met. Through chance or providence, all these engagements came to naught. Finally, when she was to be paired with King Henry III of England, she wrote to the pope asking him to prevent the marriage on the grounds that she wished to consecrate herself to Christ. Surprisingly, Henry yielded, granting that, "I cannot take offense if she prefers the King of Heaven to me."

What inspired this bold intention? Agnes had been deeply affected by the arrival in Prague of the first Franciscan friars, followed shortly by the arrival of five Poor Clare sisters. In 1236, her royal life behind her, she formally joined them. Agnes received a number of personal letters from St. Clare, who called Agnes her "half-self," holding her "more than any other in the greatest affection."

Agnes spent forty-four years as a Poor Clare and inspired many other noble women in Europe to follow her example. She died in 1280 and was canonized in 1989.

"You have chosen with your whole heart and soul a life of holy poverty and destitution. Thus you took a spouse of a more noble lineage."
—St. Clare to St. Agnes

John Wesley
Founder of Methodism (1703–1791)

John Wesley, the son of devout Anglicans, received holy orders following his studies at Oxford. Rather than serve in a parish, Wesley felt called to become a missionary preacher. He tried this out in Georgia, but his efforts were singularly unfruitful, and he was virtually booted out of the colony.

In 1783 he returned to England with a sense of failure—a feeling that he, "who went to America to convert others, was never really converted to God." The turning point came during a mission on Aldersgate Street in London where, as he said, he suddenly "felt my heart strangely warmed." For the first time he trusted that Christ had indeed saved him from the law of sin and death. He found his voice as an evangelist and preacher, imparting to the crowds—particularly the poor and working class who flocked to his sermons—a conviction that the essence of Christianity was love.

The spirit of Methodism, as it became known, combined an affective piety with earnest morality. Wesley himself was an ardent opponent of slavery and a champion of prison reform. Though he separated from the Anglican Church, he was a proponent of what would later be termed ecumenism. In meeting other Christians his first question was not about doctrine but only this: "Is thine heart right, as my heart is with thy heart? . . . If it be, give me thy hand."

He died on March 2, 1791.

"How far is love, even with many wrong opinions, to be preferred before truth itself without love?"
—John Wesley

Venerable Concepción Cabrera de Armida
Mystic (1862–1937)

Concepción Cabrera de Armida was born in San Luis Potosi, Mexico. She married at the age of twenty-two and bore nine children. When she was thirty-nine her husband died, leaving her alone to care for her children. Despite her trials, she maintained a disciplined life of prayer and enjoyed frequent mystical colloquies with Jesus and Mary. These she recorded in handwritten notes that eventually totaled 60,000 pages, resulting in 200 books. This fulfilled a message reportedly received from God: "Ask me for a long suffering life and to write a lot. . . . That's your mission on earth."

Her writings on the Eucharist, prayer, and the spiritual life were examined and viewed favorably by Church authorities. Some of them were distributed, inspiring the foundation of five apostolates of the "Work of the Cross," including religious and priestly congregations.

Conchita, as she was known, died on March 3, 1937, in Mexico City. Her cause for canonization was introduced in 1959, and in 1999 she was declared venerable.

"I carry within me three lives, all very strong: family life with its multiple sorrows of a thousand kinds, that is, the life of a mother; the life of the Works of the Cross with all its sorrows and weight, which at times crushes me until I have no strength left; and the life of the spirit or interior life, which is the heaviest of all, with its highs and lows, its tempests and struggles, its light and darkness. Blessed be God for everything!"

—Venerable Concepción Cabrera de Armida

St. Katharine Drexel
Founder, Sisters of the Blessed Sacrament (1858–1955)

Katharine Drexel was born into one of the wealthiest families in America. Before her father died he established a trust for his three daughters worth fourteen million dollars. Devout Catholics, they all three regarded their fortune as an opportunity to glorify God through the service of others.

There were certainly plenty of claims on the generosity of a young Catholic heiress. But Katharine felt a special dedication to those ignored by the Church—especially Indians and blacks. She endowed scores of schools on Indian reservations. In 1878 during a private audience with Pope Leo XIII she begged the pope to send priests to serve the Indians. He responded, "Why not become a missionary yourself?"

Finding no existing religious order corresponding to her sense of mission, Katharine founded her own: The Sisters of the Blessed Sacrament for Indians and Colored People. She insisted that her sisters rely on alms, while she reserved her trust money to fund such initiatives as the Bureau of Catholic Indian Missions and the founding of Xavier University in New Orleans, the first Catholic college established for African American students.

Mother Drexel, whose life spanned the era of slavery and the dawn of the civil rights movement, died on March 3, 1955. She was canonized in 2000.

"Often in my desire to work for others . . . some hostile influence renders me powerless. My prayers seem to avail nothing. . . . In such cases I must not grieve. I am only treading in my Master's steps."
—St. Katharine Drexel

Blessed Placide Viel
Nun (1815–1877)

Victoire Eulalie Jacqueline Viel was born in a small village in Normandy to a family of poor farmers. When she was seventeen she went to visit an older cousin who had entered the community of St. Mary Magdalen Postel, founder of the Sisters of the Christian Schools. The sisters were living in poverty in a ruined abbey at Saint-Sauveur-le-Vicomte. Victoire's heart was immediately won, and she begged to be admitted. Clothed as a novice, she received the name Placide.

Mother Postel was then nearly eighty, yet she recognized extraordinary qualities in the young novice and began grooming her for leadership. She arranged for Placide to complete her education, taught her the skills of administration, and entrusted her with ever-widening responsibilities. This aroused the resentment of her cousin, Sr. Marie, who constantly tried to sabotage Placide's assignments. Nevertheless, when Mother Postel died in 1846, Placide—only thirty-one—was elected to replace her. She tried to assuage Sr. Marie by putting her in charge of daily administration, while she went about establishing new houses and raising funds. Whenever Placide returned she would sleep in an attic garret, her cousin having claimed the superior's quarters. This unpleasantness lasted ten years, until Sr. Marie's death.

Justifying the foundress's confidence in her, Placide directed the Institute for thirty-one years, overseeing a fantastic expansion of the community, including 105 convents and scores of orphanages and schools for girls. She died on March 4, 1877, and was beatified in 1951.

"I would like a house full of children, in which God would be well-served."
—Blessed Placide Viel

Martin Niemoeller
Confessing Pastor (1892–1984)

Martin Niemoeller served as a highly decorated German U-boat commander in World War I. Though he became a Lutheran pastor, he continued to dream of national glory, and he supported the cause of National Socialism. Nevertheless, within months of Hitler's rise to power he felt uneasy with the Nazis' hateful extremism. He further rejected the "German Christian movement," which identified the Gospel with Nazi ideology. When anti-Jewish legislation was applied to Christian pastors of "non-Aryan" extraction, he organized a petition of protest. This later became the seed of the so-called Confessing Church.

On July 1, 1937, Niemoeller was arrested and imprisoned, his confinement lasting until the end of the war. As he learned of the extent of the Nazi crimes, he felt shame for not having spoken out earlier—especially on behalf of the Jews. Parting company with many Germans who refused to acknowledge any complicity with Hitler, he drafted a confession of guilt for the churches, which emphasized the Christian role in fostering a climate of anti-Semitism.

In later years, in light of the threat of nuclear war, Niemoeller realized that he could no longer justify any use of violence. As he described the key to his ethical principles, he simply asked, "What would Jesus do?" He died on March 6, 1984, at ninety-two.

"When the Nazis came for the Communists, I was silent, because I was not a Communist. . . . When they came for the Jews, I was silent. And when they came to get me, there was no one left to speak."
—Pastor Martin Niemoeller

St. Gerasimus
Hermit (d. 475)

Born in Lycia in Asia Minor, St. Gerasimus was moved to abandon his wealthy life and live as a hermit in Palestine. Settling on the Jordan, he attracted many disciples, whom he organized into a community of hermitages. Their rule was extremely severe. The hermits lived on dates, bread, and water, dividing their time between prayer and manual labor (basket weaving). They slept on reed mats and were allowed no fire in their cells. Despite this austerity, the fame of Gerasimus's community extended throughout the Eastern Church. He is said to have attended the Fourth Ecumenical Council of Chalcedon in 451.

One day Gerasimus came upon a lion in terrible pain. Examining the animal, he discovered and extracted a thorn from its paw. After he had nursed the lion back to health, the creature became his devoted companion. When, many years later, Gerasimus died, his lion could not be consoled. Stretching himself over the grave of his beloved master, he remained there for several days until he too expired.

Among the lives of the saints, there are many examples of such special friendships with animal companions. In art, St. Jerome, who also settled in Palestine, is often depicted with a lion. But this is surely a confusion based on the Latin spelling of his name, Geronimus. The lion belonged to St. Gerasimus.

"Our friend has left us orphans and has gone to join the Master whom he served, but do thou take thy food and eat."

—St. Gerasimus's successor, comforting the disconsolate lion

St. Kieran of Saighir
Abbot and Bishop (Sixth Century)

The life of St. Kieran, said to be the first native-born saint of Ireland, is steeped in legend. Did his conversion precede the arrival of St. Patrick? Did he travel to Rome where he was ordained a bishop, or was he one of the first twelve bishops appointed by St. Patrick? It is impossible to answer with any certainty. According to one story Patrick sent him to found a monastery in a certain place. Kieran asked how he would know the right place, and Patrick gave him a bell that would ring when he had found the location.

According to other stories, Kieran began his life as a holy hermit who gathered about him a community of animals. These became his first disciples: Brother Boar, Brother Badger, Brother Fox, Brother Wolf. Later, when they were joined by human disciples, the animals stayed on to assist in building a monastery. From the huts of this community the town of Saighir arose, and Kieran served both as abbot and bishop.

The extravagant lore surrounding St. Kieran includes many miracles, such as his raising the dead, feeding vast multitudes, adjudicating disputes through his clairvoyant powers, the ability to travel vast distances in no time, and exercising other seemingly magical powers. But he was also revered for his learning and his godly character.

"From his youth 'he never drank by which he might be drunken, never wrapped himself in downy raiment, never partook of a banquet, never slept his fill, nor for love of carousing rushed off anywhither.'"
—From one of Kieran's early biographers

St. Colette
Reformer of the Poor Clares (1381–1447)

St. Colette was born to a poor family in Picardy, France. Upon the death of her parents, she was cared for by the local abbey where her father had worked. Naturally drawn to contemplative life, she became a Third Order Franciscan and afterward received permission to enter an enclosed cell attached to the church. There she spent four years in solitude and prayer, until one day, on the feast of St. Francis, she received an extraordinary vision. She saw Francis and the Blessed Mother begging Christ to put her in charge of reforming the Franciscan Order. In an audience with Peter de Luna—recognized by the French, in this time of papal schism, as Pope Benedict XIII—he endorsed her mission and appointed her superior of any convent she might found or reform.

At once this uneducated young maid of twenty-four set off on a tour of all the Poor Clare houses in France. She was met with wide scorn and even violent opposition. Nevertheless, she founded seventeen new convents and restored to many others the strict poverty of the primitive rule of St. Clare. Her reform also spread to a number of friaries, and many noble families sought her wisdom and counsel. Like her master, St. Francis, she was drawn to animals, especially lambs and birds, which she easily tamed. She died in 1447 and was canonized in 1807.

"Blessed be the hour in which our Lord Jesus Christ, God and Man was born. Blessed be the Holy Spirit by whom he was conceived. Blessed be the glorious Virgin Mary of whom the Incarnate Word was born."
—St. Colette

Jean-Pierre de Caussade
Jesuit and Spiritual Director (1675–1751)

L ittle is known of this French Jesuit, whose priestly life was spent in a series of relatively obscure assignments. For one year he served as spiritual director to a community of Visitation nuns. To them he addressed a series of letters and conferences, published a century after his death as *Abandonment to Divine Providence*. It was quickly recognized as a spiritual classic, and on this work his reputation rests.

The theme of the book is easily summarized. In brief, it outlines the path to holiness that lies in the performance of our everyday tasks and duties. Every moment, according to Caussade, is given to us from God and thus bears the stamp of God's will for us. When we "accept what we cannot avoid and endure with love and resignation things which could cause us weariness and disgust," we are following the path to sanctification.

The key words in Caussade's work are "the present moment." It is even possible, he claims, to speak of "the sacrament of the present moment." Just as Christ, in the Eucharist, is visible to the eyes of faith, so to the faithful Christian it should be evident that God's will is truly present, though disguised, in what otherwise might be dismissed as the ordinary and everyday. By living in this spirit of mindfulness and abandonment, our own lives become holy texts, a "living gospel."

Father de Caussade died on March 6, 1751.

"Every moment we live through is like an ambassador who declares the will of God."
—Jean-Pierre de Caussade, SJ

Saints Perpetua and Felicity
Martyrs (d. 203)

The Passion of Perpetua and Felicity," an account of the martyrdom of a prosperous young woman and her servant in Carthage, is one of the most powerful and poignant documents of the early Church. Perpetua was twenty-two when she was arrested with her servant Felicity for violating a prohibition against conversion to Christianity. "The Passion," written largely in the voice of Perpetua herself, depicts the struggle of a woman to claim her own identity and vocation against the claims of society. To the consul who appeals to her status as a wife, daughter, and mother, she simply names herself: "I am a Christian."

In a series of prophetic visions Perpetua is comforted by the assurance that her fate is ordained and her brief suffering will lead to eternal reward. She is consoled to be able to entrust her infant son to safe hands, and so receives the grace to bear whatever may come. Felicity, meanwhile, who is eight months pregnant at the time, goes into premature labor in her prison cell and is able to hand over her newborn daughter to Christian friends.

The next day the prisoners go forth from the darkness of the prison into the glaring amphitheater, "as it were to heaven, cheerful and bright of countenance." They are stripped before the jeering crowd, and after exchanging a kiss of peace, are exposed to wild beasts and finally put to the sword.

"This is what the Lord promised us. We have received his promise."

—St. Perpetua

St. Catherine of Bologna
Abbess (1413–1463)

St. Catherine was born into a noble family in Bologna and raised in luxury. Yet at fourteen she persuaded her family to let her join a community of Franciscan tertiaries. From an early age she had experienced visions of Jesus, "who would enter into her soul like a radiant sunshine to establish there the profoundest peace." But there were also demonic thoughts that sometimes plunged her into despair. Through constant prayer she vanquished such doubts, and one night during the Christmas vigil she was rewarded by an encounter with the Blessed Mother, who offered her the great privilege of holding her infant Son.

After some years Catherine was directed to take charge of a convent of Poor Clares in Bologna. Her reputed gifts of healing and prophecy—as well as her deep kindness—attracted many novices. Whenever she had to correct a young sister, she would insist on sharing her punishment. When one of the novices was tempted to leave, Catherine pledged to take her place in purgatory until the end of time if only she would remain. (The novice stayed.)

Catherine died on March 9, 1463. Among her last instructions, she said, "If you would have all, you must give all."

"It means little to wear a worn habit and walk with bowed head; to be truly humble one has to know how to bear humiliation. It is the touchstone of Christian discipleship."

—St. Catherine of Bologna

St. John of God
Founder, Brothers Hospitallers (1495–1550)

The early life of John of God is cloaked in mystery. He served in the Spanish army until the age of forty and then resolved to live a life of penance. For some years he roamed the streets of Grenada proclaiming the sins of the world and was taken for a lunatic. Eventually he was persuaded by a famous preacher to express his love for God in a more constructive fashion.

He began at once to offer shelter and hospitality to poor and homeless people gathered from the streets. Eventually this hospitality became a full-time occupation. With the assistance of interested benefactors, he supported a household of ex-prisoners, prostitutes, the sick, crippled, and dying outcasts of the town. In time the bishop conferred his approbation by clothing John in a religious habit and giving him the name John of God. The town expressed its appreciation by providing him with a hospital.

John frequently enjoyed mystical visions. Once, while washing the feet of a beggar, he was astonished to see the man transfigured and bathed in a radiant light. A celestial voice spoke: "John, all you do for the poor in my name is done for me. It is my hand that receives your alms; it is my body that you clothe, my feet that you wash."

John died on March 8, 1550. Many of his helpers later joined to become the Brothers Hospitallers.

"I know of no bad person in my hospital except myself alone, who am indeed unworthy to eat the bread of the poor."

—St. John of God

St. Marie-Eugenie Milleret
Founder, Religious of the Assumption (1817–1898)

Marie-Eugenie Milleret was raised in a nominally Catholic, middle-class home. Her parents separated when she was thirteen, and she lived with her mother until the latter's death two years later. Placed with relatives in high society, she felt a great emptiness in her life. This changed when she attended a series of Lenten sermons by the famous Dominican preacher Henri Lacordaire in the Cathedral of Notre Dame. It was "an appointment with grace." From that point she believed herself consecrated for some great purpose.

Another priest, Abbé Theodore Combalet, convinced her that she would be the instrument of his dream to found a contemplative congregation devoted to the education of young women. Accordingly, Marie-Eugenie prepared for this project by rigorous study and spiritual formation until 1839, when, only twenty-two, she launched the Religious of the Assumption.

In the years that followed, as the Congregation grew, she found herself negotiating a complicated series of challenges, first with her spiritual director, Abbé Combalet, which ultimately led to a parting of the ways, and then with the archbishop of Paris, who constantly interfered with her plans—objecting to the sisters' poverty, their engagement in social issues, their combination of contemplative life and engagement in the world. Nevertheless, her Congregation grew and prospered. She died on March 10, 1898. She was canonized in 2007.

"The more I go on, the less sympathy I feel for priests or pious laypeople. . . . Nothing that is big and broadminded resonates within them. Must I modify our own way of life so as to suppress everything in it that shocks their narrow minds?"

—St. Marie-Eugenie Milleret

St. Gregory of Nyssa
Bishop (ca. 330–ca. 395)

St. Gregory was one of ten children born in Cappadocia to a remarkable family: his parents, his sister, and two brothers were canonized as saints. At first Gregory pursued a secular path, studying philosophy in Athens. But eventually he was persuaded to renounce "the ignoble glory" of secular knowledge and to seek ordination. In 372 he was named bishop of the small outpost of Nyssa. It was a time of bitter rivalry between orthodox bishops and the proponents of Arianism, a heresy that denied the full divinity of Christ. Through his prolific writing, preaching, and contributions at the Council of Constantinople (381), Gregory emerged as one of the most effective champions of orthodoxy. He helped provide the language that affirmed the unity of being among the Persons of the Trinity, while also defending the unity of divine and human wills in Christ.

Aside from doctrinal questions, Gregory was highly influential in the area of mystical theology. He prepared many texts on the theme of the soul's journey to union with God, including a "Life of Moses," which presents the story of Moses, his communion with God in the burning bush, and his wanderings in the desert as a symbolic account of the spiritual life.

"If, by life rightly led, you wash away the mud that has been put on your heart, the Godlike beauty will again shine out in you."

—St. Gregory of Nyssa

St. Frances of Rome
Widow (1384–1440)

Frances, who was born to a noble family of Rome, married a wealthy young man at the age of thirteen. Though a dedicated wife and mother, she yearned to be of wider service and spent her free time nursing the sick in the local hospital. Later, as outbreaks of plague and the violence of civil war encroached on her world, she emptied the family storehouse, sold all her jewels, and turned part of her house into a hospital. When her children died, her husband released her from the obligations of married life, freeing her to form a society of women dedicated to serving God and the poor.

Frances's practical skills in managing a household and her attention to the needs of others were combined with a deep life of prayer. For the last twenty years of her life, so she reported, an archangel—visible only to her—accompanied her at all times, withdrawing when she committed a fault and then returning when she made her confession. Her last years, when she was no longer capable of nursing, were dedicated entirely to prayer.

On the evening of March 9, 1440, sensing that her end was near, she said, "The angel has finished his task; he beckons me to follow him." All of Rome turned out to mourn the passing of a saint. She was canonized in 1608.

"God's will is mine."

—St. Frances of Rome

The Forty Martyrs of Sebastea
(d. 320)

I n 320 the Emperor Licinius, reversing a previous edict of toleration, authorized a fresh wave of persecution. A decree published in Cappadocia charged that all Christians must renounce their faith, upon pain of death. When this decree was pronounced to the army stationed in Sebastea (in present-day Turkey), forty soldiers refused to comply. Consigned to prison, they sang aloud from the Psalms, "He that dwelleth in the aid of the most High shall abide under the protection of the God of Heaven."

Eventually the governor devised a creative punishment. He ordered the soldiers to strip and stand on a frozen pond to endure the freezing wind and cold. Meanwhile, on the edge of the pond he provided a fire and a warm bath for anyone who would defect. For three days and nights an ever-dwindling number endured. When one of the cohort abandoned the cold, another soldier, moved by the witness of the shivering survivors, stripped off his uniform and took his place with his brothers on the ice.

After all the martyrs had eventually succumbed, their bodies were burned. Local Christians secretly gathered their ashes, and these relics were widely distributed throughout Cappadocia. Some were obtained by the holy brothers, St. Basil and St. Gregory of Nyssa, who established a church upon them and buried the rest with their parents.

"Lord, we are forty who are engaged in this conflict: grant that forty may be crowned and that we may not fall short of the sacred number."
—The Martyrs of Sebastea

Harriet Tubman
Ex-Slave, Abolitionist (ca. 1820–1913)

Harriet Tubman was born into slavery on a plantation in Maryland. While growing up she experienced the typical cruelties of slave life, the beatings and daily indignities. Like other slaves she became skilled in the art of passive resistance while struggling to maintain an inner conviction that she was worth more than a piece of property. But she was not content merely to survive with her inner dignity intact. She was convinced that God intended her to be free.

From the time she was a child Tubman was subject to deep trances in which she heard the voice of the Lord. In one of these experiences in 1849 she perceived that the time for her escape had come. Traveling by night, following the North Star, she passed through swamps and forests until she crossed into the free state of Pennsylvania. She looked at her hands "to see if I was the same person. There was such a glory over everything and I felt like I was in heaven." But she perceived a wider mission. She could not be truly free while others remained in bondage.

And so over the next twelve years she made nineteen perilous trips to "Pharaoh's Land," rescuing at least three hundred slaves, including her parents. Each time she risked death. Despised by the slave owners, she was known among the slaves as "Moses."

After the Civil War she retired to a house in Auburn, New York, supporting herself with a small garden. She lived to her nineties and died on March 10, 1913.

"I said to de Lord, 'I'm goin' to hold steady on to you, an' I know you'll see me through.'"
—Harriet Tubman

St. Teresa Margaret Redi
Carmelite (1747–1770)

St. Teresa Margaret Redi, who lived six short years in the Carmelite convent of Florence before her death at twenty-two, has been compared to the later, and better-known, St. Thérèse of Lisieux. Born to a noble family in Tuscany, Teresa was educated in a convent in Florence before determining that she was called to the Carmelites. Though her father tried desperately to dissuade her, he eventually relented, convinced of the genuineness of her vocation.

As a novice Teresa eagerly embraced the ascetic discipline of the rule—while comprehending that God desired love and not merely outward obedience. For the sake of love, she was willing to exceed anything required of her. As she wrote, "Nothing will seem difficult when we realize that the loved one wants only love for love. He has given himself completely to us; let us give him our whole heart and we shall live in joy."

After taking her vows, Sr. Teresa served as infirmarian—delighting in the opportunity to care for her ailing sisters, even when, unbeknownst to them, she had her own private sufferings. On Pentecost 1767 she was struck deeply by the verse, "God is love." Afterward, in every action, every form of service, every act of devotion, she endeavored to return God's love. The power of this intention took a toll. After a sudden illness, she died of peritonitis on March 7, 1770. She was canonized in 1934.

"Love does not want a divided heart; he wants all or nothing."

—St. Teresa Margaret Redi

James Reeb
Civil Rights Martyr (1927–1965)

everend James Reeb, a white Unitarian minister from Boston with a wife and four children, had long been committed to racial justice. When a call for volunteers came from the civil rights movement for a march from Selma to Montgomery, Alabama, Reeb was among the first of hundreds of northern clergy who responded. A previous march, on March 7, had been blocked in Selma by mounted state troopers who charged the demonstrators with whips and clubs as they tried to cross the Edmund Pettus Bridge—a day known as Bloody Sunday.

Reeb arrived in Selma two days later on March 9. His stay was short. That very night, as he and two other ministers left a diner, they were accosted by a gang of white men with clubs. One of them struck Reeb in the head, cracking his skull. He died two days later.

President Johnson invoked Reverend Reeb in his speech before a joint session of Congress: "At times history and fate meet in a single time in a single place to shape a turning point in man's unending search for freedom. . . . So it was last week in Selma, Alabama."

Soon after, Congress passed the Voting Rights Act. Later that year three men charged with Reeb's murder were acquitted by an all-white jury.

"James Reeb symbolizes the forces of good will in our nation. He demonstrated the conscience of the nation. He was an attorney for the defense of the innocent in the court of world opinion. He was a witness to the truth that men of different races and classes might live, eat, and work together as brothers."

—Martin Luther King Jr.

Blessed Angela Salawa
Franciscan Tertiary (1881–1922)

Angela Salawa was born to a poor family in Krakow, Poland. At the age of sixteen she found work as a maid and lived a carefree and worldly life. A turning point came as she was dancing during a wedding reception and suddenly perceived that Christ was standing in the room, seeming to hold her in a gaze of loving reproach. Immediately she went to a nearby church where she prayed for the courage to amend her life. Rather than enter a religious order, she decided to pursue a life of prayer and service in the world. In 1912 she became a Third Order Franciscan.

With the outbreak of World War I, Krakow was evacuated, but Angela chose to remain, nursing soldiers and prisoners of war, and offering comfort to all those touched by suffering. In her diary she wrote to Christ: "I want you to be adored as much as you were destroyed." Her own health suffered, but no one noticed. In 1916 she was fired by her employer, who accused her of stealing. Penniless and without other resources, she lived out her last years in a basement room, where she died alone on March 12, 1922, at the age of forty.

Despite her obscurity, her reputation for holiness endured beyond her death. She was beatified in 1991 by Pope John Paul II.

"Lord, I live by your will. I shall die when you desire; save me because you can."
—Blessed Angela Salawa

Rutilio Grande
Jesuit Martyr of El Salvador (1928–1977)

Rutilio Grande, who was born into a poor family in El Salvador, entered the Jesuits at seventeen. His early years as a priest were undistinguished. Only in the mid-1960s did he undergo a second conversion, acquiring a new sense of vocation. The role of the priest, he determined, was not to set an example of perfection, but an example of self-sacrifice and loving service.

Increasingly, Grande exemplified a new Church in El Salvador, committed to awakening in the poor a sense of their dignity and rights. Before long, he acquired a reputation as a "radical," an enemy of the system. Under pressure, he resigned as director of social action projects for the seminary and took up a post as pastor of the small town of Aguilares. There he established a vigorous social ministry. Once again, his sermons became infamous among the town's elite. In one he proclaimed that if Jesus Christ were to come to El Salvador he would be condemned as a dangerous rabble-rouser and crucified again.

On March 12, 1977, his van was sprayed with gunfire, killing him along with an old peasant and a teenage boy who were traveling with him. His death marked a turning point for El Salvador—the first but not the last time a priest would face violence. In particular, Grande's death touched the new archbishop, Oscar Romero, prompting his own journey on the road to Calvary.

"Very soon the Bible won't be allowed to cross our borders. We'll get only the bindings, because all the pages are subversive."

—Fr. Rutilio Grande

St. Matilda
Widow (ca. 895–968)

St. Matilda, who was born to a noble family in Germany, was raised by her grandmother, an abbess in the local convent. In time she was betrothed to Henry, son of the duke of Saxony, who would become the king of Germany. He was known as "the Fowler," for his favorite pastime. Though Matilda lived in royal luxury, wealth held no interest. While Henry was off engaged in almost constant warfare, Matilda was left to her ardent prayers and her many charities. When in 936 Matilda learned that her husband had died, she immediately stripped off her jewels and pledged that she was done with the cares of the world and the privileges of office.

Matilda had raised five children. Otto, her eldest, inherited his father's throne, but he was challenged by his embittered brother Henry (known as "the Quarrelsome"), and the two siblings engaged in many years of intrigue and sometimes bloody conflict. Though Matilda had dispensed with all her wealth, her children believed she had secret reserves. At one point this suspicion caused her sons to form an alliance to spy on their mother and investigate her accounts. She remarked, "I would willingly endure all they could do against me if it would keep them together—provided that they could do it without sin."

In later years she retired to one of the convents she had founded and lived there until her death on March 14, 968.

"My very dear one . . . how many times have you changed iniquity to justice."
　　　　　　　　—Tribute to St. Matilda by her son Henry

Blessed Dulce Pontes
Servant of the Poor (1914–1992)

rmã Pontes was born in Salvador, Brazil, to a well-to-do family. As a child, the sight of homeless beggars in her neighborhood inspired her to devote her life to the poor. At eighteen she joined the Congregation of Missionary Sisters of the Immaculate Conception, a Franciscan community founded in Brazil in 1910. She took the religious name Dulce, after her mother, who had died when she was three.

Within a year of entering religious life she had formed the Workers Union of St. Francis, the first Christian worker's movement in Brazil. Meanwhile she took to sheltering homeless sick people in abandoned houses, begging for food and medicine. As their numbers steadily increased, Dulce begged permission from her superior to house them in the chicken sheds of the convent. Eventually this gave rise to St. Anthony's Hospital, a complex of medical, educational, and social services. She could never pass a person in need without seeing the face of Christ: "We may be the last door, and for this reason we cannot close it." In 1959 Sr. Dulce's various programs were consolidated as the Charitable Works Foundation of Sister Dulce (OSID).

Twice nominated for the Nobel Prize, Sr. Dulce became one of the most beloved figures in Brazil. She died on March 13, 1992, and was beatified in 2011.

"There is nothing better that you can do in this world than to totally give yourself to God in the person of the poor and our needy brother."
—Blessed Dulce Pontes

Fannie Lou Hamer
Civil Rights Leader (1917–1977)

Until 1962 the life of Fannie Lou Hamer was little different from that of her parents or other poor blacks living in the Mississippi Delta. One of twenty children, she was educated to the fourth grade and then took up the sharecropping life to which she was seemingly destined. Her life changed suddenly after she attended a civil rights rally and was inspired to register to vote. As a consequence, she and her family were evicted from their home. She took this as a sign to work full time as a field secretary for the Student Nonviolent Coordinating Committee, where she quickly rose to a position of leadership.

In 1963 she was arrested while trying to desegregate a bus terminal in Charleston, South Carolina. In jail she was savagely beaten, emerging with a damaged kidney and her eyesight permanently impaired. In 1964 she led a "Freedom Delegation" from Mississippi to the Democratic National Convention in Atlantic City. Though the delegation was evicted by the party bosses, Hamer touched the conscience of the nation with her eloquent account of the oppression of blacks in the segregated South and their nonviolent struggle to affirm their dignity and human rights.

She continued in that struggle, battling injustice, war, and poverty, sustained by her deep faith in the God of the oppressed. She died on March 14, 1977.

"Christianity is being concerned about your fellow man, not building a million-dollar church while people are starving right around the corner. Christ was a revolutionary person, out there where it was happening. That's what God is all about, and that's where I get my strength."

—Fannie Lou Hamer

Chiara Lubich
Founder of the Focolare Movement (1920–2008)

Chiara Lubich, a schoolteacher and Third Order Franciscan, was born in Trent, Italy. Her true vocation took form in 1943 under the Allied bombing of her city when she and a number of other women determined that love was the fundamental reality of life and the purpose of their existence. In the next months, while caring for victims of the war, Lubich conceived of a new movement, the Focolare (meaning "hearth"), to promote unity, reconciliation, and the spirit of love.

The message of Focolare was simple, but it spread quickly in Italy and elsewhere in war-torn Europe. With its joyful spirit, its emphasis on the laity, the promotion of Scripture, liturgical renewal, and ecumenism, it fostered the spirit of renewal that took shape in Vatican II. Based in small communities of both married families and single people, the Focolare eventually spread to 180 countries, promoting a unity across all borders of religion, race, and nation. Lubich was embraced by Pope John Paul II and always remained rooted in her Catholic faith, but she gladly accepted invitations to speak to Buddhist, Muslim, and Jewish audiences around the world. She died on March 14, 2008.

"What is the secret? It is that we risked our life at the beginning for a great Ideal, the greatest: God. It is that we believed in His love and then we abandoned ourselves moment by moment to His will. If we had done our own will there would have been nothing of all this today. Instead we plunged ourselves into the divine adventure."
—Chiara Lubich

St. Louise de Marillac
Cofounder, Daughters of Charity (1591–1660)

Louise de Marillac enjoyed a happy marriage to a wealthy courtier to the queen of France. But when her husband died she vowed to devote the rest of her life to the service of God. After some years searching for her vocation, she was introduced to Fr. Vincent de Paul, who became her spiritual director and with whom she went on to form one of the great partnerships in the history of religious life.

Monsieur Vincent, as he was called, was widely known for the extraordinary range of his charitable projects. Among other things, he had recruited a circle of aristocratic ladies who joined him in working among the sick and destitute of the Parisian slums. Louise gladly joined them. But soon she and Vincent conceived the notion of a community of women completely committed to loving service among the poor. From this seed developed the Daughters of Charity. Their plan for a congregation of women living outside an enclosed convent and engaged in apostolic work in the world was a novel concept for its time. Nevertheless, they obtained Rome's consent. In their spiritual formation the Daughters were instructed that they should never hesitate to leave off other spiritual obligations should they be summoned by those in need. As they were ever reminded, the poor were their masters, in whom they should seek the face of Christ.

Louise died on March 15, 1660. By the time of her canonization in 1934, the Daughters of Charity numbered more than 50,000 worldwide.

"[A Daughter of Charity] is well aware that we are leaving God for God if we leave one of our spiritual exercises for the service of the poor."

—St. Louise de Marillac

Mother Benedicta Riepp
Benedictine Founder (1825–1862)

Benedicta Riepp spent eight years as a nun in the ancient Benedictine Abbey of St. Walburg in Bavaria. In 1852, she responded to an appeal from Abbot Boniface Wimmer of St. Vincent's Abbey in Latrobe, Pennsylvania, for nuns to teach the children of German immigrants in this frontier settlement. Sr. Benedicta exchanged the splendor of her 900-year-old monastery for a log cabin in the wilderness. She eagerly set about establishing the earliest Benedictine women's communities in America.

Unfortunately, she quickly ran into a complex conflict with the abbot, who believed the sisters were canonically under his jurisdiction. Benedicta appealed to her superior at St. Walburg and returned to Europe, hoping for an audience with the pope. Rebuffed in these efforts, she returned to America only to find that she was no longer recognized by Rome as superior and that all the Benedictine sisters in the United States were now under the authority of the bishops in their respective dioceses.

Happily, a Benedictine monastery in St. Cloud, Minnesota, an offshoot of her first foundation, welcomed Benedicta. With the blessing of Abbot Wimmer and the permission of Rome, she remained there until her death from tuberculosis on March 15, 1862. Four years later the St. Cloud community moved to nearby St. Joseph, and by the mid-twentieth century it had become the largest Benedictine community in the world.

"It would be my consolation and joy . . . if one spirit and one life could be preserved in the hearts of all. . . . Then one way of life and one love would obtain among all."

—Mother Benedicta Riepp, OSB

St. John de Brebeuf
Jesuit Martyr (1593–1649)

In 1625 John de Brebeuf, a French Jesuit missionary, arrived in the young colony of Quebec. His aim was not to serve the French community, but to evangelize the Native Americans. To that end he settled among the Hurons, mastering their language, sharing their privations and the terrible conditions of life in the wilderness. Though his presence was tolerated, the Indians regarded him with suspicion, often blaming him for epidemics or bad weather. At one point he and his companions learned a council had decided on their death. De Brebeuf hosted a farewell banquet in which he spoke so eloquently of God and the rewards of heaven that his life was spared. In later years he could boast of having conducted almost two hundred baptisms.

Increasingly, however, the Jesuit missions were imperiled by intense inter-tribal warfare. On March 16, 1649, the Huron village where de Brebeuf and another priest lived was overrun by a party of Iroquois, and its inhabitants were massacred. The priests were subjected to grotesque tortures. For Fr. de Brebeuf this lasted for three hours, until he was finally executed with a fatal blow. He was canonized in 1930. With the other North American martyrs his feast is commemorated on October 19.

"I vow . . . never to shirk the grace of martyrdom if, in your mercy, you offer it some day to your unworthy servant . . . and when I am about to receive the stroke of death, I bind myself to accept it from your hand in the joy of my heart."

—St. John de Brebeuf

Eusebio Kino
Jesuit Missionary (1645–1711)

Eusebio Kino was born in 1645 in the principality of Trent. At the age of twenty he joined the Jesuits, hoping to be sent to Asia. Instead, he was sent to New Spain, where he was assigned to the region of Pimería Alta—"the outskirts of Christendom"— an area comprising present-day Sonora in Mexico and Arizona. For twenty-four years, on horseback and on foot, he covered this vast territory—almost twenty thousand square miles. Kino was a skilled astronomer and mapmaker. Armed with an astrolabe, he drew remarkably detailed and accurate maps. Among other things, he was able to prove that Baja California was not, as was supposed, an enormous island.

Kino's style of mission proved highly successful. Among the Pima Indians of the Southwest he tried to enter into friendly dialogue, sitting and conversing with them before ever attempting to preach. In the end he established two dozen missions and performed thousands of baptisms. He strenuously opposed the enslavement of Indians to work in silver mines, and his outspokenness resulted in complaints and efforts to have him expelled. Among other things, Kino successfully introduced cattle ranching into the territory; the success of his own ranch covered the costs of his mission work. In the midst of all his labors, he found time to write twenty books on astronomy, cartography, and religion.

Kino died on March 15, 1711.

"The adversities of this world, and rightly so, have to do with the celestial favors done for us by God."

—Eusebio Kino, SJ

St. Patrick
Apostle to Ireland (389–461)

St. Patrick is remembered for his role in implanting the Church in Ireland. But his first introduction to Ireland was involuntary. At the age of sixteen he was kidnapped from his village in Roman Britain and taken to Ireland as a slave. Sold to a local king, he spent six years in menial occupations. His life was not valued more highly than the beasts he tended.

All the while he clung to his Christian faith and dreamed of home. Eventually, an opportunity arose for him to escape. He made his way back to his home. But he had changed. Apart from the scars of his ordeal, he bore the zeal of a profound faith. He believed his sufferings and deliverance had been ordained for some purpose.

After studying for the priesthood in Gaul he had a dream in which Irish voices, the voices of those who had stolen his youth, cried out for him to return. In 432, by now a bishop, he returned to the land of his oppressors to devote himself to their salvation.

Patrick's thirty years as a wandering bishop are the stuff of legend. He is justly honored as the patron of Ireland. But it is well to remember that Patrick was the victim of Irish injustice before he became the symbol of Irish pride. His spiritual conquest of Ireland followed the prior victory of love over the anger and bitterness in his own heart.

"Christ be with me, Christ before me, Christ behind me, Christ in the heart of everyone who thinks of me."
—St. Patrick

St. Gertrude of Nivelles
Abbess (ca. 626–659)

St. Gertrude was the daughter of a nobleman in present-day Belgium. When she was ten, at a feast hosted by her father, she was brought in to meet King Dagobert. The king pointed out a handsome knight and asked whether she wouldn't like to be his wife. Recoiling, she replied that she would only accept Jesus Christ as her lord and master.

When her father died, her mother Itta endowed a double monastery (for men and women) in Nivelles. She shaved Gertrude's hair in a tonsure, consecrating her to Christ, and appointed her as superior.

Gertrude revealed deft skills in managing the growing community, and she was widely admired for her knowledge of Scripture and holy texts. She welcomed pilgrims, including two Irish monks who settled on her property and there, with her consent, established a monastery. She sent for one of them when she was close to death. He told her that she would die the next day but should have no fear, because St. Patrick himself would welcome her soul. As foretold, she did indeed die on his feast day, March 17.

St. Gertrude is often depicted with mice running up her crozier. She is a patron of travelers, gardeners, and lovers of cats, and she is invoked against rats and pestilence.

"When she was in her parents' home . . . God's holy maid Gertrude grew by day and night in word and wisdom. She was dear to God and more loveable to men than all her generation."

—From *The Life of St. Gertrude*

St. Cyril of Jerusalem
Doctor of the Church (ca. 315–386)

S t. Cyril was born in Jerusalem, where he was later ordained a priest and became bishop in 350. Almost immediately he found himself embroiled in controversies inherited from his predecessor. Jurisdictional disputes with the bishop of Caesarea resulted in a formal investigation by the local synod. Among the gravest accusations was that Cyril had sold church property— namely, gifts from the emperor—to give alms to the famine-stricken poor. Cyril was condemned and forced into exile. He returned after some years to find himself caught in new battles over the Arian heresy. Cyril was accused by members of each side of being too sympathetic to the other. He died in 386 at the age of about seventy. Of his thirty-five years as a bishop, nearly sixteen were spent in exile.

In 1882 Cyril was named a Doctor of the Church, largely on the basis of his work *The Catechetical Lectures*. These talks, delivered to adult catechumens in the Catholic faith, represent one of the first systematic accounts of Christian theology, centered on the articles of the creed. They underline Cyril's determination to present the faith in a positive light and to maintain a balance between correct belief and holy action.

"Let us, then, endure in hope. Let us devote ourselves, side by side with our hoping, so that the God of all the universe, as he beholds our intention, may cleanse us from our sins, fill us with high hopes from what we have in hand, and grant us the change of heart that saves."
—St. Cyril of Jerusalem

Antonio de Andrade
Jesuit Missionary and Explorer (1580–1634)

Antonio de Andrade was born in Portugal. After entering the Jesuits he set out for the Portuguese colony of Goa in southern India, where he was ordained. Eventually, a new mission took him to the Moghul city of Agra in the north. There he learned Persian, the language of traders, and heard intriguing rumors of a lost community of Christians in the land of Tibet. Disguised as Hindus, he and a Jesuit brother joined a caravan of pilgrims and made their way north up the Ganges and through the Himalayas. Braving hunger, snow blindness, and frostbite, they crossed the pass at an altitude of 18,000 feet and became the first Westerners in Tibet.

Andrade settled in the town of Tsaparang in the kingdom of Guge. The local king was intrigued by the foreigner's story and his exotic religion. Though not moved to convert, the king begged Andrade to remain and allowed him to build a small "house of prayer." Andrade, realizing there were no Christians in Tibet, was anxious to return to Goa and issue a report, but he promised to return. And so he did, with other Jesuits, making several journeys back and forth. An account of his adventures, published in Lisbon, quickly became an international "best seller." Ultimately, Andrade was assigned to other missions. A new king in Tibet was less friendly to Christianity, and the mission dissolved. Andrade never returned. He died on March 19, 1634.

"It was all dazzling whiteness to our eyes, and we could make out no sign of the route we were to follow."

—Antonio de Andrade, SJ

St. Joseph
(First Century)

St. Joseph's part in the nativity story is a familiar feature of every Christmas pageant. But for many centuries the Church paid him scant attention. Only in the sixteenth century did the Church officially encourage his cult, as St. Joseph began to figure as an ideal "provider and protector" of the Holy Family. In 1870 Pius IX declared him Patron of the Universal Church. Besides his feast day on March 19, an additional feast for St. Joseph the Worker was assigned by Pope Pius XII on May 1.

Joseph and Mary were betrothed when she was discovered to be pregnant. Matthew's Gospel relates the story from Joseph's perspective. Here, the discovery of Mary's pregnancy precedes any divine reassurance, thus presenting Joseph with a terrible dilemma. According to the law Mary should be stoned to death. But Joseph, "being a just man and unwilling to put her to shame," resolves to divorce her quietly. Fortunately, an angel appears in Joseph's sleep to explain the source of Mary's condition, and he is apparently satisfied.

Aside from his virtues as a father and man of faith, Joseph is also a poor working man—a detail not without significance in the Gospels. Though linked to the house of David, he remains a carpenter from a Galilean town so miniscule that it serves as the butt of jokes. Thus, while Joseph recedes from the Gospel story, he remains a reminder of Jesus' humble origins—and an enduring reminder of his humanity.

"Is this not the carpenter's son?"

—Matthew 13:55

Blessed Marcel Callo
Martyr (1921–1945)

Marcel Callo was born in Brittany in 1921. At fourteen he joined the Young Christian Workers, a movement to promote Catholic values among the working class, and he soon became one of its most dedicated activists. In 1943 Marcel was among the many Frenchmen rounded up for forced labor in Germany. Though he might have gone into hiding, he accepted his deportation as a kind of missionary assignment.

Sure enough, in Germany he connected with other members of the movement to organize religious services and maintain the faith of their comrades in exile. The Gestapo became suspicious of their activities, and Callo was arrested and subjected to hard labor. Still, in a letter home, he observed, "How grateful I am to Christ for having marked out for me the way in which I now am. . . . Yes, it is good and a source of strength to be suffering for those one loves."

In October 1944 he was transferred to Mauthausen concentration camp. There he was starved and whipped, but he did not lose faith. After his death from typhus on March 19, 1945, a fellow prisoner spoke of his supernatural expression: "It expressed a profound conviction that he was going toward a blissful end. It was an act of faith and hope in a better life. Never have I seen in a dying man an expression such as this. . . . He had the face of a saint."

Marcel Callo was beatified in 1987.

"Christ is with us. We must not give in. God is looking after us."

—Blessed Marcel Callo

Mother Catherine Spalding
Cofounder, Sisters of Charity of Nazareth (1793–1858)

Catherine Spalding was born and raised in Maryland. At the age of nineteen, accompanied by the uncle who had raised her, she traveled to Kentucky to present herself to Bishop John Baptist David of the new diocese of Bardstown. Inspired by the success of the Sisters of Charity in Baltimore, he had issued a call for young women willing to start a similar congregation in Kentucky to educate the children of families flocking to the frontier. Catherine was one of three women who answered this call. Together, they formed a new community, the Sisters of Charity of Nazareth. Though she was the youngest, Catherine was elected superior—a post to which she was regularly reelected for successive six-year terms.

Although the original motive of the congregation was education, the sisters, inspired by the Rule of St. Vincent de Paul, extended their charitable work to include nursing and care for widows and orphans. During an outbreak of cholera the sisters demonstrated great heroism in their care for the sick. Mother Spalding was particularly devoted to the orphanage—"the only place on earth to which my heart clings." She poured herself out in service to her sisters, those in her care, and to the wider community, thereby fulfilling the motto of her congregation: "The charity of Christ impels us." She died on March 20, 1858.

"Our Community must be the center from which all our good works must emanate and in the name of the Community all must be done. Then let none of us be ambitious as to who does more or who does less. God will judge it all hereafter."

—Mother Catherine Spalding

St. Maria Josefa de Guerra
Founder, Institute of the Servants of Jesus (1842–1912)

Maria Josefa de Guerra was born in Vitoria, Spain, the daughter of a chair maker who died when she was seven. As she later liked to say, she was "born with a religious vocation." But she struggled for some time to find her way, trying one congregation and then another. Before taking vows with the Handmaids of Mary Serving the Sick she experienced doubts. After months of consultation with her archbishop and other spiritual advisors, she decided to found her own institute, the Servants of Jesus.

The mission of the Institute was to offer care for the sick and dying, whether in hospitals or in their homes. The Servant of Jesus was instructed to "provide for the sick, whom she accompanies unto the door of eternity, a blessing better than that of a missionary, who, with his preaching, calls those who are lost to the right path of life." The Institute made its first foundation in Bilbao in 1871. Maria remained the superior for the next forty years, during which time she founded forty-three houses and welcomed over one thousand sisters.

She died on March 20, 1912. With her canonization in 2000 she became the first Basque woman saint.

"Don't believe sisters that assistance consists only in giving medicines and food to the sick. There is another type of assistance . . . the assistance of the heart that enters in sympathy with the person who suffers and goes to meet his necessities."

—St. Maria Josefa de Guerra

St. Benedetta Frassinello
Founder, Benedictine Sisters of Providence
of Rocco Scriva (1791–1858)

Benedetta Cambiagio grew up in Pavia, Italy. Though as a child she dreamed of a life given to prayer, she complied with her parents' desire that she marry a good Christian man—Giovanni Frassinello. As it turned out, Giovanni agreed with her desire that they live as brother and sister, and that they should care for Benedetta's sister, Maria, who suffered from cancer. When Maria died in 1825 the Frassinellos felt they were now free to pursue the vocations they both desired. With permission from the Church, Giovanni joined the Somaschi Canons, while Benedetta entered a Capuchin convent.

Her time in the convent did not last long. As a result of ill health she was asked to return to her family. But then, in a deep vision, she received the conviction that she must dedicate herself to the rescue of young girls, whose poverty put them in danger of prostitution. The bishop endorsed her plan, and even encouraged Giovanni to leave his own community to help Benedetta with her mission. And so they resumed their chaste, and unusual, partnership.

Together they organized orphanages, schools, and workshops where poor girls could receive education, skills, and formation in Christian values. Eventually Benedetta founded a new Congregation, the Benedictine Sisters of Providence of Rocco Scriva. She died on March 21, 1858, and was canonized in 2002.

"With boundless confidence in the Lord's goodness, she abandoned herself to his 'loving Providence,' deeply convinced, as she liked to repeat, that one must 'do everything for love of God and to please him.'"

—Pope John Paul II

Viola Liuzzo
Civil Rights Martyr (1925–1965)

Selma, Alabama, was the site of one of the great campaigns of the civil rights struggle, a place where white supremacists had drawn a line, determined to suppress the growing cry for freedom. In February 1965 a march from Selma to the state capital was blocked on the Edmund Pettus Bridge by a phalanx of state troopers, who rushed into the crowd wildly swinging their clubs and whips. On March 21 another march was scheduled—this time under the protection of the National Guard. A call went out to the nation for volunteers. Among those who responded was Viola Liuzzo, a white, thirty-nine-year-old housewife, mother of five, and Catholic convert. Fearing her family would try to dissuade her, she didn't tell anyone in advance of her plans. Instead she set off from Detroit in her Oldsmobile sedan and called her family from the road, begging them to understand that this was something she had to do. They never saw her again.

The march was a great success. But that night, as Viola was ferrying a young black civil rights worker, Leroy Moton, on the road back to Selma, a car full of Klansmen sped up beside them and fired a fusillade of bullets into her car. Viola was killed instantly.

Not everyone honored her actions. But for another America, those who shared Martin Luther King's vision of justice and dignity for all, Viola's sacrifice would be remembered as a milestone on the long march to freedom.

"It's everybody's fight. There are too many people who just stand around talking."
—Viola Liuzzo

Blessed Clemens August van Galen
Bishop (1878–1946)

Clemens van Galen, scion of an aristocratic family in West-phalia, was ordained a priest in 1904. In September 1933, in the early months of the Third Reich, he was consecrated as bishop of Munster. From the beginning, Bishop van Galen regarded the Nazis as an idolatrous cult, and he used his pulpit to issue a series of defiant sermons: "Not one of us is certain that he will not any day be dragged from his house and carried off to the cells of some concentration camp. I know full well that this may happen to me, perhaps now or on some future day."

As details emerged of the Nazi euthanasia program—which ultimately claimed 100,000 lives—Bishop van Galen spoke out courageously: "Once [we] admit the right to kill unproductive persons, then none of us can be sure of his life. A curse on men and on the German people if we break the holy commandment 'Thou shalt not kill.' . . . Woe to us German people if we not only license this heinous offence but allow it to be committed with impunity."

Though he incurred the Fuhrer's wrath and was subject to constant harassment, his international reputation probably spared his life. He survived the destruction of his cathedral by Allied bombing, and then the war. In 1946 he was named a cardinal but died only a few days later. He was beatified in 2005.

"I call aloud as a German man, as an honorable citizen, as representative of the Christian religion, as a Catholic bishop: We demand Justice!"
—Blessed Clement August van Galen

Luis Espinal Camps
Jesuit Martyr (1932–1980)

uis Espinal Camps was born in Barcelona, Spain, and entered the Jesuits at the age of seventeen. Early on he became interested in film, videography, and journalism, both as a way of documenting social reality and as a means of promoting human values. In 1968, frustrated by censorship under the Franco dictatorship in Spain, he accepted an invitation to work with the Church in Bolivia. There he quickly embraced his new homeland, immersing himself in its diverse cultures and learning everything he could about social conditions.

Through radio and television programs, and his writing in books and magazines, Espinal aligned himself with the poor and victims of human rights abuses. He was also outspoken in denouncing the narco-traffickers who were responsible for much violence. He aimed to be "the voice of those who have no voice, the voice to cry out those things that others keep silent about." Inevitably, he made enemies. He was repeatedly detained, his broadcasts were censored, and he received numerous death threats. But he was not deterred.

Espinal was abducted on the night of March 21, 1980. The next day his body was found, bearing the marks of terrible torture and riddled with seventeen bullets. Seventy thousand people reportedly attended his funeral. His tomb bears the inscription, "Assassinated for helping the people."

"Whosoever does not have the courage to speak on behalf of other people does not have the right to speak with God."

—Luis Espinal Camps, SJ

Blessed Sibyllina of Pavia
Anchoress (1287–1367)

Orphaned as a young child, Sibyllina was forced to work as a maid. She suffered from failing eyesight, and by the time she was twelve she had gone completely blind. No longer able to support herself, she was fortunate to find a community of Dominican tertiaries in Pavia who agreed to take her in. They taught her to chant and to pray the Office, and Sibyllina was delighted with her new life. But she prayed intensely to St. Dominic that she might regain her eyesight and thus contribute more usefully to the community.

One night she had a dream in which St. Dominic took her by the hand and led her through a dark passageway that emerged into a field of sunshine. "In eternity, dear child," he said. "Here, you must suffer darkness so that you may one day behold eternal light." When she awoke Sibyllina discerned that she was not meant to recover her eyesight—but that her life was no less meaningful for her disability. She asked to be enclosed as an anchoress in a cell attached to the church in Pavia where she could devote herself to prayer.

Thus, at the age of fifteen she entered the cell where she would remain alone for the next sixty-five years. Through a small opening in the wall she could attend to the worship inside the church. And through a window on the street she could receive the pilgrims and penitents who came to her for prayers and spiritual counsel.

Sibyllina died in 1367. She was beatified in 1854.

"O Lord, enkindle our hearts with the fire of the Spirit, who wonderfully renewed Blessed Sibyllina. Filled with that heavenly light may we come to know Jesus Christ crucified and always grow in your love."

—*General Calendar of the Order of Preachers*

St. Rebecca Ar-Rayès
Nun (1832–1914)

Rebecca Ar-Rayès (Rafqa Butrusia) was born in 1832 to a Maronite Christian family in Lebanon. In 1855 she entered a convent in Ghazir—the same year that Druze militia unleashed a savage wave of violence against the Christian population. While thousands of Christians were massacred, Rebecca and the other sisters were hidden by friendly Arabs. When her congregation dissolved, she entered a new convent of the Baladiya Order. She cheerfully took to contemplative life, eagerly performing any assignment and even volunteering to share the punishment for the infractions by other sisters.

So privileged did Rebecca feel in her new life that she feared she would become spoiled. She prayed to God that she might experience some of Christ's suffering and so relieve the suffering of others. Soon after this prayer she lost her vision; this was followed by increasing paralysis that allowed her only to knit and pray the rosary. She accepted these ordeals without a murmur. Her sufferings, she said, were nothing compared to Christ's agony. "I have sins to expiate, but he, in his love for us, has borne an infinite degree of opprobrium and so much suffering, and we think so little of it."

She died on March 23, 1914, at eighty-one. She was canonized in 2001.

"May the sick, the afflicted, the war refugees, and all victims of hatred, yesterday and today, find in St. Rafqa a companion on the road, so that, through her intercession, they will continue to search in the night for reasons to hope again and build peace."

—Pope John Paul II

St. Catherine of Vadstena
Abbess (ca. 1331–1381)

Catherine was one of eight children born to St. Bridget of Sweden—one of the most extraordinary and charismatic women of her age. While her parents engaged in continuous pilgrimage, Catherine was raised in a convent. After marrying a young nobleman, she persuaded him to adopt a chaste relationship. By this time her mother Bridget, now a widow, had returned to Sweden and established a convent at Vadstena. Catherine was overjoyed to be reunited with her mother, but this happiness was soon dispelled when Bridget embarked on yet another mission, this time to persuade the pope to return from Avignon to Rome. Catherine said that on that day she "forgot how to smile." At the age of nineteen she won her husband's consent to join her mother in Rome. Once there, in the hot and dissolute city, she longed for Sweden. But when word arrived of her husband's death, she received a vision of Mary who instructed her to remain beside her mother. So she did— for twenty-five years.

Bridget eventually died while making a pilgrimage to the Holy Land, and it fell to Catherine to accompany her remains back to Sweden. By now she had assumed much of her mother's eloquence and charisma. The nuns at Vadstena happily welcomed her as their abbess. Her final years were spent promoting her mother's cause for canonization, as well as her mission: to reform the papacy, by this time in schism. She died on March 22, 1381.

"You ask me to help you, but how can I when all you want is to go back to Sweden?"

—Words of the Blessed Mother, spoken in a dream to St. Catherine

Blessed Oscar Romero
Archbishop and Martyr (1917–1980)

The selection of Oscar Romero as archbishop of San Salvador in 1977 delighted the country's oligarchs. Previously known as a traditional and conservative prelate, there was nothing in Romero's background to suggest he was a man to challenge the status quo. No one could have predicted that in three short years he would be recognized throughout the world as a "voice for the voiceless." Nor could one foresee that he would arouse such hatred on the part of the rich and powerful that he would be targeted for assassination.

What caused this change? Within weeks of his installation Romero was shaken by the assassination of his friend Rutilio Grande, a Jesuit dedicated to social justice. In the following weeks, Romero increasingly took on the cause of justice. His weekly sermons cast the glaring light of the Gospel on the realities of the day. He came to embody the Church's "option for the poor." As he said, "A church that does not unite itself to the poor . . . is not truly the Church of Jesus Christ."

On March 23, 1980, he appealed to members of the military to refuse illegal orders. "I beseech you, I beg you, I command you, stop the repression!" He was shot the next day, while saying Mass—the first bishop slain at the altar since Thomas Becket in the twelfth century.

In May 2015, following a belated decree from the Vatican that he had died as a martyr "in hatred of the faith" (and not, as his critics charged, because he had mixed himself up in politics), Oscar Romero was beatified in a ceremony in San Salvador.

"If God accepts the sacrifice of my life then may my blood be the seed of liberty. . . . A bishop will die, but the church of God— the people—will never die."
—Blessed Oscar Romero

St. Dismas
The Good Thief (First Century)

St. Dismas is the name traditionally assigned to one of the two criminals—most likely insurrectionists—who were crucified on either side of Jesus on Golgotha. According to the Gospel of Luke (chapter 23), one of these criminals joined in the general mockery of the crowd: "Are you not the Christ? Save yourself and us." The other criminal, however, rebuked him: "Do you not fear God, since you are under the same sentence of condemnation? And we indeed justly, for we are receiving the due reward of our deeds; but this man has done nothing wrong." Addressing the Lord, he said: "Jesus, remember me when you come into your kingdom."

These words elicited from Jesus one of the most poignant lines in Scripture: "Truly, I say to you, today you will be with me in Paradise."

Many apocryphal legends of St. Dismas circulated in the early Church, and his name was added to the Roman martyrology. His story is a reminder that physical proximity to Jesus was no guarantee of salvation. Those who taunted him on the cross or pounded the nails in his hands were just as close. But words of true faith—even uttered in the last moments of a wretched life—could open the doors of paradise.

"Jesus, remember me when you come into your kingdom."

—St. Dismas (Luke 23:42)

Ida B. Wells
Reformer (1862–1931)

Ida B. Wells was born into slavery in Mississippi in 1862. Her struggle against racial injustice began in 1884 when a train conductor tried to evict her from her first-class seat to make room for a white man. She sued the train company and in the process acquired a national reputation. On that basis, she became editor of a black newspaper in Memphis called *The Free Speech and Headlight*.

When, in 1892, three black men were lynched in Memphis, Wells was galvanized to action. In the years since Emancipation, lynching had become the ultimate form of white terrorism in the South. Though the pretext was often some alleged "outrage" against (white) womanhood, Wells conducted exhaustive research documenting the actual causes: failure to show proper deference to whites, registering to vote, "talking back," complaining about work, or sheer bad luck . . . Whatever the reasons, it was a reminder that the underlying code of slavery lived on. Christian ministers, meanwhile, were generally oblivious to the parallels between this public violence and the death of Jesus on a cross.

Following her editorials, an outraged mob destroyed her press and would have lynched her too if she had been present. Settling in Chicago, she became a "journalist in exile," tirelessly carrying on the fight against lynching. She did not live to see success, but her courageous witness lit a torch that others carried in the struggle for freedom and dignity.

"We submit all to the sober judgment of the Nation, confident that, in this cause, as well as all others, 'Truth is mighty and will prevail.'"

—Ida B. Wells

Anne Frank
Witness (1929–1945)

Anne Frank was born on June 12, 1929. The date of her death is unknown. She died at fifteen of typhoid sometime in March 1945 in a German concentration camp—her death one small contribution to the Nazi dream of a world without Jews. But through the discovery and publication of her diary, her small flame has continued to burn, fulfilling her own dream: "I want to go on living after my death."

The story of Anne's survival for two years with her family in a "secret annex" during the Nazi occupation of Amsterdam is well known. In her diary she recorded the mundane details of daily life. But she also tried to record the movements of her own heart, her hopes and dreams, her moral determination to maintain the virtues that might contribute someday to a better world.

Her story bears witness to a recent time in the heart of Western "civilization" when children were hunted down like vermin for extermination. At the same time she bears witness to a power stronger than her tormentors—the sacred core of a human soul that refuses to yield to darkness. As she wrote, "In spite of everything I still believe that people are really good at heart. . . . I must uphold my ideals, for perhaps the time will come when I shall be able to carry them out." The diary of this young girl, composed in her own "little piece of blue heaven, surrounded by heavy black rain clouds," has been acclaimed as one of the great moral documents of the twentieth century.

"I know what I want. I have a goal, an opinion, I have a religion and love. Let me be myself and then I am satisfied. I know that I'm a woman, a woman with inward strength and plenty of courage. If God lets me live . . . I shall not remain insignificant, I shall work in the world and for mankind! And now I know that first and foremost I shall require courage and cheerfulness."

—Anne Frank

Raoul Wallenberg
Righteous Gentile (1912–Unknown)

Among the list of Righteous Gentiles—Christians who undertook the rescue of Jews from Nazi extermination— the name Raoul Wallenberg is highly honored. Born to a life of privilege, a member of one of Sweden's most distinguished families, he volunteered in the midst of the war for a hazardous diplomatic mission in Budapest with the intention of rescuing Hungarian Jews. By the time he arrived in Budapest in July 1944 half a million Jews had already been deported to death camps. Additional transports were leaving every day. Under the cover of his diplomatic status, Wallenberg went to work distributing Swedish passports to Hungarian Jews, then browbeat the Hungarian authorities to respect the protected status of these "subjects" of a neutral state.

That fall the Nazis swept away the fiction of Hungarian autonomy and took charge of the deportations under the direction of Adolf Eichmann. As the Soviet Red Army approached, it became a race to see whether the Nazi's passion for killing would triumph over the Swede's passion for life. Wallenberg's efforts probably saved 100,000 lives. As the Red Army arrived in Budapest, Eichmann fled and Wallenberg remained. There he disappeared into the mists of the Soviet Gulag, his exact fate unknown. Though the Soviets claimed he died in custody in 1947, for many years, into the 1960s, there were reported sightings and chance encounters with the missing Swede.

"I will never be able to go back to Sweden without knowing inside myself that I'd done all a man could do to save as many Jews as possible."
—Raoul Wallenberg

St. John of Egypt
Hermit (ca. 304–394)

St. John was among the most famous of the early Desert Fathers; his ascetic exploits were celebrated by a number of saints, including Augustine, Jerome, and John Cassian. After spending his early life as a carpenter, John received a call to a life of prayer and solitude. He apprenticed himself to an elderly monk who tested his capacity for obedience by forcing him to perform seemingly ridiculous exercises, like faithfully watering a dead twig or moving heavy rocks from place to place. Upon his master's death, he set out for the desert wilderness. In a remote cave he constructed a cell in which he walled himself in, allowing only a single window through which he received donations of food. John received visitors only on Saturdays and Sundays. The other days he spent in prayer. Nevertheless, pilgrims flocked to see him, drawn by his renowned gifts for prophecy, healing, and the ability to read people's souls. Even the emperor sent messengers to receive his wisdom.

John spent over forty years in this life. At the age of ninety, sensing that his end was near, he closed his window, leaving instructions that no one should disturb him for three days. At the conclusion of that period he was found to have expired while kneeling in prayer.

"Am I a saint, or a prophet like God's true servants? I am a sinful and weak man. . . . Live always in the fear of God, and never forget his benefits."

—St. John of Egypt

The Cloud of Unknowing Author
Mystic (Fourteenth Century)

Nothing is known of the English mystic identified simply as the author of *The Cloud of Unknowing*. This classic text was written in the late fourteenth century—the time of Chaucer—in a vernacular English. The identity of its author—whether a priest, religious, or hermit—has eluded discovery. Not even the author's gender can be definitively ascertained. Nevertheless, it can safely be asserted that the author of *The Cloud* was one of the great spiritual masters of all time.

Intended for those called to the contemplative life, *The Cloud* reflects the tradition of the *via negativa*, the idea that we can more reliably say what God *is not* than what God *is*. The hidden nature of God is shielded from human understanding by "a sort of cloud of unknowing." Because God is not a concept, God cannot be known by the intellect. But what cannot be *thought* may yet be *known* by love. Through the sharp arrows of love directed toward God in contemplative prayer, it is possible to pierce the "cloud of unknowing" and attain blessed union with God. This requires that we wrap ourselves in a "cloud of forgetting," abandoning all images and concepts of the divinity and overcoming our attachment to the world.

Though the fate of its author remains unknown, *The Cloud of Unknowing* continues to inspire and instruct.

"'Well,' you will say, 'where am I to be? Nowhere, according to you!' And you will be quite right! 'Nowhere' is where I want you! Why, when you are 'nowhere' physically, you are 'everywhere' spiritually."

—The Cloud of Unknowing

Moses
Liberator and Mystic

At the heart of the Exodus, the foundational story of Israel, lies the figure of Moses, one of the great and mysterious characters in the Bible. In his *Life of Moses*, St. Gregory of Nyssa reads this story as a symbolic treatise on mystical prayer. More recently, liberation theologians have fastened on the social and political dimensions of the Exodus. Moses is the paradigmatic liberator, the human agent of God's desire to bring people out of bondage. Perhaps he was both—mystic and liberator.

What is certain is that Moses' role in the Exodus is rooted in his unique relationship with God. In their first encounter, God speaks to him from the midst of a burning bush and reveals himself as one who hears the cry of the oppressed. Moses' mission is inseparable from his intimate communion with the Lord, with whom he would speak "face to face, as a man speaks to his friend." Later mystics were fascinated by the information that Moses entered into a cloud to speak with God—an image familiar in the annals of mystical literature. But in the end, the significant issue is not that God spoke to Moses; it matters what was said. The topic was not simply God's glory but the liberation of the oppressed. Thus, Moses reflects the essential fusion of the mystical and the political.

After forty years in the wilderness, Moses lived only to look over the Promised Land from the heights of Mt. Nebo. There he died alone, and there the Lord performed the last rites of friendship by burying Moses in a secret place.

"Thus says the Lord, the God of Israel, 'Let my people go.'"

—Moses, speaking to Pharaoh (Exodus 5:1)

Marc Chagall
Artist (1887–1985)

Marc Chagall was born to a Hasidic Jewish family in a town in Belarus, part of the Russian Empire. Determined to become an artist, he moved to Paris, where his distinctive style drew on various modernist influences. His work was marked by recurring dreamlike images of his homeland—rural villages filled with floating cows, fiddlers, roosters, and weddings. After travels in Palestine, biblical images also entered his work. In 1938, following the Kristallnacht pogrom in Germany, Chagall painted his "White Crucifixion," depicting Jesus on the cross, clothed with a Jewish prayer shawl as a loincloth, and surrounded by scenes of Jewish persecution. This painting, which Pope Francis has named as a personal favorite, not only emphasizes the Jewishness of Jesus but relates the crucifixion to the contemporary passion of the Jews and the ongoing suffering of humanity. Christ, for Chagall, symbolized "the true type of the Jewish martyr." And as the Holocaust unfolded, the number of martyrs swelled beyond imagination.

Chagall managed to escape with his wife to New York in 1941. She died there two years later. After the war he returned to France, where he became one of the most celebrated and beloved artists of his time. The visual symbols of his lost village in Belarus—of suffering, love, work, and hope—became the common treasury of humanity. He died on March 28, 1985.

"For me Christ is a great poet, the master whose poetry is already forgotten by the modern world."

—Marc Chagall

Micah
Prophet (Eighth Century BC)

The prophet Micah was a younger contemporary—perhaps even a disciple—of the prophet Isaiah. Like Isaiah he operated in the southern kingdom of Judah in the eighth century BC. Unlike Isaiah, who sprang from the priestly elite, Micah came from a small village in the countryside. He identified with the poor of the land, those who bore the burden of the city folk with their privilege and their greed. The rich, he said, were like cannibals feeding off "the flesh of my people." In harsh tones he denounced those who "abhor justice and pervert all equity." The northern kingdom of Israel had fallen to Assyria. Micah warned that the same fate awaited Judah. He did not even spare Jerusalem from the heat of divine judgment to come. The corruption had gone too far; the wound was "incurable."

And yet what God sought from Judah was correction, not destruction. Micah proclaimed the preservation of a saving "remnant" from which a new nation would emerge. There would be a lasting era of peace and justice, war would be no more, and justice would reign. What in return did God require? Not burnt offerings, lavish sacrifices, or elaborate worship: "but to do justice, and to love kindness, and to walk humbly with your God."

"They shall beat their swords into plowshares, and their spears into pruning hooks; nation shall not lift up sword against nation, neither shall they learn war any more."

—Micah 4:3

Karl Rahner
Jesuit Priest and Theologian (1904–1984)

Karl Rahner, a German Jesuit, passed his life in a routine of teaching and writing. But in his quiet and methodical way he did more than any other theologian to overcome the gulf between Catholic theology and the modern world. His chief aim was to make Christian faith intelligible to people living in a world marked by doubt, pluralism, science, and historical consciousness. Though most of his work was addressed to theologians, he remained first of all a priest concerned with the pastoral needs of the Christian people and the opportunity for dialogue with all people of good will.

Rahner believed that all human existence is rooted in the holy and infinite mystery of God. Therefore religious experience was not so much a separate category of existence as it was the potential for a certain quality or depth available in everyday life. By nature, human beings are created with an openness to God. To the extent that we accept this gift—that is the way of salvation. The Gospel names this truth, which is embodied in the person of Christ.

For much of his life Rahner was subject to severe censorship. But Pope John XXIII appointed him an expert at Vatican II, where he left his mark on almost every declaration of the Council. His only sadness, in later years, was that the promise of the Council remained to be fulfilled. Yet he remained hopeful. He died on March 30, 1984.

"The Christian of the future will be a mystic or he will not exist at all."

—Karl Rahner, SJ

St. John Climacus
Monk (Seventh Century)

St. John Climacus, a Byzantine monk, is remembered for having popularized the image of the ladder as a symbol of the spiritual life. His treatise, *The Ladder* [Greek = *Klimax*] *to Paradise*, became a classic work of monastic spirituality, and it also supplied the name by which he is remembered.

John was born in Palestine and entered the monastery on Mt. Sinai when he was sixteen. For forty years, from the age of thirty-five to seventy-five, he lived the solitary life of a hermit, before serving as abbot for the final four years of his life. John's great humility was a veil that disguised his ardent prayer and his many spiritual gifts. When his fellow monks once chided him for being too talkative, he resolved to maintain complete silence for an entire year.

In his famous book John outlined a sequence of thirty steps that begin with renunciation and ascend up the spiritual ladder to the perfection of faith, hope, and charity. Despite his desire for obscurity, his reputation for holiness extended far beyond the monastery. Even Pope St. Gregory the Great wrote to ask for his prayers.

His work inspired a famous icon that shows a group of monks climbing a ladder with Christ at the top, waiting to greet them. While angels urge them on, demons attempt to derail and pull them down. At the bottom of the icon, pointing to the ladder for his fellow monks, is St. John Climacus.

His feast is celebrated on March 30.

"Let the remembrance of Jesus be present with your every breath, and you will then understand the meaning of stillness."

—St. John Climacus

Thea Bowman
African American Franciscan (1937–1990)

Thea Bowman was one of the great treasures of the American Catholic Church. Ablaze with the spirit of love, the memory of struggle, and a faith in God's promises, she impressed her audiences not just with her message but with the nobility of her spirit.

Born in rural Mississippi, she converted to Catholicism while attending parochial school. Later, as a Franciscan nun, she found herself the only African American in a white religious order. But she had no desire to "blend in." She believed her identity as a black woman entailed a special vocation. She believed the Church must make room for the spiritual traditions of African Americans, including the memory of slavery, but also the spirit of hope and resistance reflected in the spirituals, the importance of family, community, celebration, and remembrance.

Bowman was a spellbinding speaker who preached the Gospel to audiences across the land, including the U.S. bishops. After being diagnosed with incurable cancer she bore a different kind of witness. She continued to travel and speak, even from her wheelchair. To her other gifts to the Church she added the witness of her courage and trust in God. "I don't make sense of suffering. I try to make sense of life," she said. "I try each day to see God's will." She died on March 30, 1990, at the age of fifty-two.

"What does it mean to be black and Catholic? It means that I come to my church fully functioning. I bring myself, my black self, all that I am, all that I have, all that I hope to become."

—Sr. Thea Bowman

John Donne
Anglican Priest and Poet (1572–1631)

John Donne, an Anglican priest, is remembered as one of the greatest of the English metaphysical poets. Unlike his contemporary George Herbert, whose poetry is marked by lightness and balance, Donne's work is marked by stress and strain, a fit commentary on his preoccupation with death and the struggle for salvation. *"Batter my heart, three person'ed God; for, you / as yet but knocke, breathe, shine, and seeke to mend / that I may rise, and stand, o'erthrow mee, and bend / Your force, to breake, blow, burn and make me new."*

If for Herbert the encounter with God is a gentle caress, in Donne it is a wrestling match such as Jacob experienced in his encounter with the angel—a match one must pray to lose. Donne experienced much hardship and sorrow—particularly the death of his beloved wife, a crushing loss from which he never recovered. And yet he clung to the assurance that by sharing the cross of Christ we might also have a share in his resurrection: *"Be this my Text, my Sermon to mine owne, / Therefore, that he may raise the Lord throws down."* His own death came on March 31, 1631.

"Death be not proud, though some have called thee / Mighty and dreadful, for thou art not soe, / For, those, whom thou think'st thou dost overthrow, / Die not, poore death, nor yet canst thou kill me . . . / One short sleep past, wee wake eternally, / And death shall be no more; death, thou shalt die."
—John Donne

St. Maria Skobtsova
Orthodox Nun and Martyr (1891–1945)

Lisa Pilenko, as she was born, began her life in a prosperous aristocratic family in Russia. A political activist in her youth, twice married and the mother of three, she joined the throng of refugees uprooted by the revolution in 1923 and made her way to Paris. There, after the death of her youngest daughter, she experienced a profound conversion. She emerged with a determination to seek "a more authentic and purified life" and with a new calling: "to be a mother for all, for all who need care, assistance, or protection."

In Paris she immersed herself in social work among the destitute Russian refugees. Each person, she believed, "is the very icon of God incarnate in the world." With the encouragement of her bishop she became a nun, but she wished to pioneer a new form of monasticism, engaged in the world, avoiding "even the subtlest barrier which might separate the heart from the world and its wounds." In 1932 she made her monastic profession and became Mother Maria. In a house in Paris she established a soup kitchen, with her "cell" consisting of a cot in the basement beside the boiler.

After the German occupation of Paris she worked with her chaplain to hide and rescue Jews, leading eventually to her arrest along with her son. She survived two years in Ravensbruck concentration camp before perishing in the gas chamber on the eve of Easter, March 31, 1945.

In 2004 she was canonized by the Russian Orthodox Church.

"At the Last Judgment, I shall not be asked whether I was successful in my ascetic exercises. . . . Instead I shall be asked, Did I feed the hungry, clothe the naked, visit the sick and the prisoners."

—Mother Maria Skobtsova

APRIL

1 Blessed Giuseppe Girotti • Ignatia Gavin

2 St. Francis of Paola • Venerable Carla Ronci

3 C. F. Andrews • Jean Goss

4 St. Benedict the Black • Martin Luther King Jr.

5 St. Juliana of Liège • Pandita Ramabai

6 St. Mary Crescentia • Blessed Michael Rua

7 St. John Baptist de la Salle • Blessed Maria Assunta Pallotta

8 St. Julie Billiart • Martyrs of the Rwandan Genocide

9 Mother Mary Demetrias Cunningham • Dietrich Bonhoeffer

10 Pierre Teilhard de Chardin • Howard Thurman

11 St. Guthlac • St. Stanislaus

12 Peter Waldo • St. Teresa of Los Andes

13 St. Martin I • Blessed Margaret of Citta-di-Castello

14 St. Lydwina of Schiedam • Bishop James A. Walsh

15 Mother Lurana White • Corrie ten Boom

16 St. Benedict Joseph Labre • St. Bernadette Soubirous

17 Sor Juana Inés de la Cruz • Anna Dengel

18 Venerable Cornelia Connelly • Blessed Savina Petrilli

19 St. Alphege • Blessed Bernard the Penitent

20 St. Hildegund of Schonau • St. Agnes of Montepulciano

21 St. Apollonius • St. Anselm

22 Käthe Kollwitz • Engelbert Mveng

23 Blessed Maria Gabriella Sagheddu • Cesar Chavez

24 St. Mary Euphrasia Pelletier • Blessed Mary Elizabeth Hesselblad

25 St. Mark • St. Pedro de San José Betancur

26 Venerable Nano Nagle • Juan Gerardi

27 St. Zita • Niall O'Brien

28 Blessed Luchesio and Buonadonna • Jacques Maritain

29 Blessed Pauline von Mallinckrodt • St. Catherine of Siena

30 St. Marie of the Incarnation • Daniel Berrigan

APRIL

Blessed Giuseppe Girotti
Dominican Priest and Martyr (1905–1945)

Giuseppe Girotti was born in northern Italy in 1905. At the age of thirteen he entered the Dominican seminary and was ordained in 1930. A brilliant student, he was sent for Scripture studies to the Angelicum University in Rome and later to the École Biblique in Jerusalem, where he studied under the great Dominican scholar Marie-Joseph Lagrange. Returning to Italy, he taught in the Dominican Theological Seminary of Turin.

In September 1943 the Nazis occupied Italy and commenced an intense campaign of persecution against the Jews. Suddenly the lessons of Scripture took on a different urgency. Through his study of the Hebrew Scriptures, Fr. Girotti had come to feel a deep affinity with the Jewish people, his "elder brothers" in faith. From the seminary he conducted an effective support network for endangered Jews, offering shelter, safe transport, and false baptismal certificates. Following the Gestapo's discovery of his activities, he was arrested on August 29, 1944. After passing through a series of jails he ended up in Dachau, along with 2,500 Catholic priests and other clergy. With 1,000 of these priests he shared a barracks designed for 180 inmates. In these filthy conditions, disease was rampant. Yet throughout this ordeal he impressed his companions with his joy and his radiant faith.

Eventually falling ill, he was transferred to the hospital—hardly a place of healing. There on April 1, 1945—Easter Sunday—he was dispatched by lethal injection. He was beatified in 2014.

"Everything I do is out of love."
—Blessed Giuseppe Girotti

Ignatia Gavin
"Angel of Alcoholics Anonymous" (1889–1966)

I rish-born Sr. Ignatia Gavin immigrated to the United States in 1914 and later entered the Sisters of Charity of St. Augustine. In 1934 she was assigned to oversee admissions at St. Thomas Hospital in Akron, Ohio. Hospital policy did not allow the admission of alcoholics. But at the urging of Dr. Bob Smith, later a cofounder with Bill W. of Alcoholics Anonymous, she began admitting alcoholics under such diagnoses as "acute gastritis." Eventually the hospital agreed to open a wing dedicated to the care of alcoholics—a first for the country. Dr. Smith attended to their physical needs, while Sr. Ignatia focused on moral and spiritual support.

The principles of AA required that an alcoholic have a sincere commitment to sobriety; there was no point in pressuring people to join the program before they were ready. With support from a sponsor and ongoing meetings with fellow alcoholics, those submitting to the "12-Step Program" of AA showed remarkable success. Sr. Ignatia presented patients on their discharge with a Sacred Heart medallion—insisting that they return it before taking another drink.

It is estimated that before her retirement in 1965 Sr. Ignatia assisted in the treatment of 10,000 alcoholics. The number who have benefited from AA is incalculable.

She died on April 1, 1966.

"The alcoholic is deserving of sympathy. Christ-like charity and intelligent care are needed so that with God's grace he or she may be given the opportunity to accept a new philosophy of life."

—Sr. Ignatia Gavin

St. Francis of Paola
Founder, Minim Friars (1416–1507)

The long-childless parents of this saint had prayed to St. Francis of Assisi for a son. In time their prayers were answered. They named their son Francis, and no doubt their intentions exerted a powerful influence on his later vocation. At twelve, he spent a year in a Franciscan house, receiving there a basic education and acquiring a taste for asceticism. Eventually, he left to take up the life of a hermit, living in a cave near his hometown of Paola.

In time, Francis attracted disciples, the foundation of a religious order he called the Minim Friars—a name reflecting the desire that they be counted the least in the household of God. Along with traditional religious vows, Francis added a fourth: that his followers abstain not only from meat but also from any animal products whatsoever. Beyond a spirit of penance, this strict diet also reflected the saint's determination to extend the spirit of nonviolence to all God's creatures. Among the miraculous legends associated with Francis are many involving the restoration of life to assorted animals, including a favorite trout, which a hapless cleric had caught and cooked.

In 1481, King Louis XI of France, facing death, begged Francis to come and heal him. Francis made the trip, traveling barefoot the whole way. Though he told the king that life and death were in God's hands, he managed to reconcile the king to his fate and remained by his side until the end.

Francis died on Good Friday in 1507 at the age of ninety-one.

"All creatures obey those who serve God with a perfect heart."

—St. Francis of Paola

Venerable Carla Ronci
Lay Apostle (1936–1970)

Carla Ronci was born in Rimini, Italy. As a child, she termed herself "neither very good nor very naughty." She dated her "conversion," at fourteen, to her encounter with a group of Ursuline nuns working with abandoned children; they instilled in her a desire to serve God through other people. While working as a tailor, Carla threw herself into Catholic Action—a movement popular with young people seeking to live out their faith. With her vivacious personality, she soon became a leader. Happily scooting about on her Vespa motorbike, she visited the sick, organized religious education programs, and worked with children, helping them to know and love God. "I began to see Jesus in others," she wrote. "I felt I could meet Jesus in the poor, the suffering, and little."

Confirmed in her vocation to pursue sanctity in the world, in 1962 she joined a secular institute, *Mater Misericordiae*, which allowed her to live a prayerful life while living at home. She felt a special mission to pray for priests, for their perseverance and faith.

In 1969 she contracted lung cancer. "Lord," she prayed, "you can no longer suffer in your own body, so take mine to continue your Passion and Redemption." Her death followed on April 2, 1970. She whispered to her confessor, "Here he comes . . . Jesus smiles on me." She was declared venerable in 1997.

"I am happy to exist. I am content with everything that surrounds me because in everything I detect a gift of God. All the peace which fills and pervades my heart comes from possessing Jesus."

—Venerable Carla Ronci

C. F. Andrews
Missionary (1871–1940)

Charles Freer Andrews was born in Birmingham, England. While studying at Cambridge he underwent a deep conversion and was ordained in the Anglican Church. From that moment his faith was infused with a commitment to service. Eventually this led him to volunteer to teach in India. His arrival there in 1904 was a great turning point in his life.

So deeply did Andrews identify with the culture and aspirations of the Indians that he quickly identified with their struggle for independence. This drew him to South Africa, where an obscure Indian lawyer named Mohandas Gandhi was waging a campaign for civil rights. The intimate rapport between Gandhi and Andrews was immediate. As Gandhi put it, "It was an unbreakable bond between two seekers and servants."

Andrews was one of the first Westerners to recognize Gandhi's greatness as a spiritual leader and the significance of his experiments in nonviolence. To Andrews, the Hindu Gandhi embodied the spirit of Christian love in a way that put other Christians to shame. Gandhi in turn recognized in Andrews the best type of missionary—not proselytizing but bearing witness to the Gospel through deeds.

Andrews returned to India with Gandhi and remained at his side until his death. Scandalized by racial divisions in the Church, and feeling that his priestly identity set him apart from ordinary humanity, he resigned his holy orders. Still, he continued his prophetic ministry, seeking to encounter Christ "in the faces of those I met," especially the poor. Andrews died on April 5, 1940. He was mourned throughout India.

"Christ seeks from us deeds not words."
—C. F. Andrews

Jean Goss
Peacemaker (1912–1991)

As a teenager in Paris, working in the railway union, Jean Goss first learned how to struggle for justice without violence. Nevertheless, he joined the army at the start of World War II and fought bravely. But at a certain point a mystical experience convinced him that he could not kill other human beings. Though he was subsequently captured by the Germans and spent the rest of the war as a POW, by this time "the old Jean Goss was gone. I don't know where he went. I couldn't hate anymore."

In 1958 he married an Austrian pacifist, Hildegard Mayr, and together they traveled the globe promoting the practice of nonviolence. Their outreach extended to the Vatican. After literally bursting into the office of Cardinal Ottaviani of the Holy Office, they lobbied tirelessly for the cause of peace. At Vatican II their efforts were largely responsible for a declaration affirming the right of conscientious objection as well as a condemnation of nuclear war.

In Latin America, they helped establish *Servicio Paz y Justicia* (Service, Peace, and Justice), whose director, Adolfo Perez Esquivel, later won the Nobel Prize. In the Philippines in the 1980s they offered training that contributed to the People's Power Revolution and the overthrow of the dictator Ferdinand Marcos. Planting seeds of peace throughout the world, they worked together until April 3, 1991, when Jean died. Hildegard carried on alone.

"Structures that are not inhabited by justice and love have no liberating or reconciling force, and are never sources of life."

—Jean Goss

St. Benedict the Black
Franciscan (ca. 1526–1589)

St. Benedict was the son of African slaves owned by a rich family in Sicily. Set free as a child, Benedict attracted attention, even as a youth, for his patience and charity. Once, as he was being taunted on account of his color, a passing Franciscan noticed him and invited him to join his community of hermits. Benedict did this. Eventually, so evident was his holiness that he was chosen to be the superior of the community.

In time this informal group was directed by the pope to affiliate with a regular order. They joined the Friars Minor of the Observance. Benedict was accepted as a lay brother and put to work as a cook. Once again, however, his special gifts drew wonder and respect. Though he was illiterate, he had an extraordinary knowledge of Scripture and theology. His gift for reading souls put him in great demand as a spiritual director. Eventually his fame became a form of penance, as the sick flocked to him for healing and pilgrims of every station sought his counsel.

Benedict died in 1589 at the age of sixty-three. He was canonized in 1807. Apart from widespread veneration in Latin America, St. Benedict was claimed as a patron saint of African Americans.

"There's a sweet, sweet Spirit in this place."

—From the cornerstone of St. Benedict
the African Parish in Chicago

Martin Luther King Jr.
Apostle of Freedom (1929–1968)

In December 1955 Martin Luther King Jr., a young Baptist minister only twenty-six at the time, stepped forward to lead a protest committee in Montgomery, Alabama. The arrest of a black seamstress, Rosa Parks, for refusing to yield her seat on a bus to a white man had sparked a bus boycott by the city's black population, galvanizing a new civil rights movement and launching King's public mission. The tactics of nonviolent resistance, tested in Montgomery, were later extended throughout the South, and King emerged not only as a brilliant strategist and orator but as a true prophet who proclaimed to his generation the justice and mercy of God.

He faced constant threats. His house was bombed. He was repeatedly jailed. But he was never tempted by despair. In 1963 he delivered his famous speech, "I Have a Dream," in which he envisioned an America redeemed by the transforming power of love and the promise of equality. His popularity was never higher. But rather than bask in recognition, he continued to delve deeper into the roots of American racism and violence and the challenge of his vocation as a minister of God.

When he spoke out against the Vietnam War and tried to forge the bonds of an alliance to overcome poverty, he was denounced by the head of the FBI as the most dangerous man in America. In Memphis, where he had gone to support a strike by sanitation workers, he was assassinated on April 4, 1968.

"Darkness cannot drive out darkness; only light can do that. Hate cannot drive out hate; only love can do that."

—Martin Luther King Jr.

St. Juliana of Liège
Visionary (ca. 1192–1258)

St. Juliana is largely remembered for her role in promoting the Feast of Corpus Christi—an accomplishment she did not live to witness. Born in Liège, Belgium, Juliana was orphaned at the age of five and raised in an Augustinian monastery. For many years she received a strange vision of the moon marked by a black spot. She feared, at first, that this was a demonic apparition. But then one night, in a dream, Christ explained that the moon represented the Church calendar and the black spot signified the absence of a feast dedicated to the Blessed Sacrament. In later years, when she became a Premonstratensian nun and later prioress of a convent at Mount Cornillon, she spoke of her vision and enlisted the help of learned canons to advance her mission.

Otherwise, Juliana's life was marked by many trials and tribulations. Accused falsely of mishandling funds, she was expelled from her convent. Though later vindicated, she never found a secure home, wandering from one community to another. She spent her final years as an impoverished recluse and died on April 5, 1258. Years later, one of her patrons, James Pantaleon, now Pope Urban IV, remembered her vision. By his decree the Feast of Corpus Christi was added to the Church calendar.

"Word made Flesh, by word he maketh / Very bread his Flesh to be; / Man in wine Christ's Blood partaketh; / And if senses fail to see, / Faith alone the true heart waketh / To behold the mystery."

—Hymn composed by St. Thomas Aquinas
for the Feast of Corpus Christi

Pandita Ramabai
Indian Christian and Reformer (1858–1922)

Pandita Ramabai, the daughter of a wealthy Brahmin scholar and his much younger wife, was born in Karnataka, India. Having been instructed by her father to read Sanskrit, at the age of sixteen she walked across India, winning fame by reciting classic poetry and acquiring an honorific title: "Pandita," mistress of wisdom.

Married at twenty-two, she was widowed only a year later. Her own experience and her travels in India had sensitized her to the plight of widows and orphans, inspiring her to establish centers for their care in Poona and Bombay. Soon she became the leading advocate for the rights and welfare of women in India.

In 1883, while visiting England, she studied the Bible and asked to be baptized. News of her conversion provoked angry controversy in India, where she was accused of betraying her culture. She insisted that in the Gospel of Christ she had found the expression of her own spiritual intuition: her growing belief that to serve women and the poor was a religious, and not simply a social, work. Ironically, her fellow Christians also criticized her for making no effort to seek converts, pressing her for proof of her doctrinal orthodoxy. In reply she said that her creed was to love God and her neighbor as herself. To this end, she said, she prayed not for the conversion of Hindus but of her fellow Christians.

"People must not only hear about the kingdom of God but must see it in actual operation, on a small scale perhaps . . . but a real demonstration nevertheless."
—Pandita Ramabai

St. Mary Crescentia
Franciscan Contemplative (1682–1744)

Anna Höss, the daughter of poor weavers, was born in a small town in Bavaria. While praying in the chapel of a local convent of Third Order Franciscans she seemed to hear a voice from the crucifix saying, "This shall be your home." Though her father tried to get the convent to accept her, they refused, for she lacked the required dowry. Nevertheless, when she was twenty-one, the Protestant mayor of the town, who had done favors for the convent, interceded with the nuns to accept her as a postulant. She took the name Mary Crescentia.

Her first years in the convent were filled with trials. The other nuns resented Mary, calling her a beggar, assigning her the most menial tasks, and forcing her to sleep in a corner on the floor. She accepted these ordeals with humility. In time, under a new superior, her virtues were recognized. She was accepted as a full member of the community and steadily entrusted with positions of increasing responsibility: portress, novice mistress, and eventually mother superior of the community. Through her wisdom and prayer she carried the community to new heights of devotion, and her reputation spread beyond the convent.

After her death on April 5, 1744, her tomb became a site of pilgrimage. She was beatified in 1900 and canonized by Pope John Paul II in 2001.

"The practices most pleasing to God are those which He himself imposes—to bear meekly and patiently the adversities He sends or which our neighbors inflict on us."
—St. Mary Crescentia

Blessed Michael Rua
"Second Father of the Salesian Family" (1837–1910)

For Michael Rua, who played a key role in founding the Salesians, the decisive moment of his life occurred when he first encountered Don John Bosco, the charismatic chaplain of his school in Turin. Already Bosco was envisioning a mission to rescue and educate poor and unwanted boys. Rua became the first member of the Society of St. Francis de Sales, taking his religious vows at the age of eighteen. Four years later, though only a subdeacon, he was appointed the society's first spiritual director.

Ordained a priest in 1860, he accompanied Don Bosco as his closest aide, traveling with him and serving as vicar of the society. Before his death in 1888, Bosco petitioned the pope to name Rua as his successor, declaring, "If God said to me, 'Imagine a young man with all the virtues and an ability greater than you could even hope for, then ask me and I will give him to you,' I still never could have imagined a Don Rua."

Rua oversaw the rapid expansion of the Society from 64 houses to 341 in 23 countries, maintaining the founder's vision to care for the poor through high schools, orphanages, and vocational schools. Because of his fidelity to the founder's memory he was known as "the Living Rule." He died on April 6, 1910, and was beatified in 1972.

"I have seen poverty everywhere, and yet, thank God, I have also seen thousands of children taken off the streets and changed into honest citizens and good Christians."
—Blessed Michael Rua

St. John Baptist de la Salle
Founder, Institute of the Brothers
of the Christian Schools (1651–1719)

John Baptist de la Salle was born into a noble family in Rheims. Ordained in 1678, he shortly earned a doctorate in theology and seemed comfortably on track for a successful career in the Church. Yet, his life took a different, unexpected direction. It began when he took an interest in the struggles of schoolteachers in Rheims, whom he often invited to dine with him. Eventually this became an invitation to share his home, and later a house that he established for them. He was committed to helping them see their work as a true religious vocation. Not all accepted his influence, but as others were attracted, he conceived the formation of a religious congregation of consecrated laymen: the Institute of the Brothers of the Christian Schools.

He might have endowed the order with his own wealth but chose instead to give away his fortune and to rely on providence. His schools soon spread throughout France and eventually beyond. In his Rule for the Brothers, he outlined their mission to serve as "ambassadors of Christ to the young"—not just imparting education but promoting through their own example the spirit of the Gospel.

He died on April 7, 1719. Canonized in 1900, he was named patron of schoolteachers.

"I will often consider myself as an instrument which is of no use except in the hands of the workman."

—St. John Baptist de la Salle

Blessed Maria Assunta Pallotta
Missionary Sister (1878–1905)

aria Assunta Pallotta was born to a working-class family in Italy. By the time she was eleven she was helping to support her siblings. But all the while she dreamed of a religious vocation. When she was in her late teens, with support from her parish priest, she entered the Franciscan Missionaries of Mary, traveling to the motherhouse in Rome. There, and in subsequent assignments, she joyfully embraced all duties, no matter how menial. She was especially happy to be assigned to farmwork, caring for chickens, goats, and pigs. In a letter to her parents she explained her sense of mission: "I ask the Lord for the grace to make known to the world purity of intention— which consists in doing everything for the love of God, even the most ordinary actions."

Eventually, she would travel to the far side of the earth. It was only a few years since several members of her order had endured martyrdom during the Boxer uprising in China. Maria was eager to replace them. In February 1904, soon after taking her final vows, she received the joyous confirmation of her new assignment. Almost immediately she departed for China, arriving during a particularly extreme winter. Only a year later she was stricken with typhus. She died on April 7, 1905. In 1954 she became the first non-martyr missionary sister to be beatified.

"What God wills, as He wills, and may His Will be done."

—Blessed Maria Assunta Pallotta

St. Julie Billiart
Cofounder, Institute of Notre Dame de Namur
(1751–1816)

Julie Billiart was born to a peasant family in Picardy, France. By the time she was seven she was teaching the catechism to other small children of the town. At fourteen she took a vow of chastity and devoted herself to works of mercy and the religious instruction of her poor neighbors. Her spiritual authority was widely recognized in her hometown. During the French Revolution she got into trouble for harboring illegal priests and had to be smuggled out of her house and go into hiding. When her persecutors pursued her she exclaimed, "Dear Lord, will you not find me a corner in paradise, since there is no room for me on earth?"

Eventually, however, it became safe for her to resume catechetical work, and with the support of her confessor she undertook the foundation of a new congregation, the Institute of Notre Dame, devoted to the Christian education of the poor and the training of religious teachers.

Julie was afflicted over many years by strange maladies that left her at various times paralyzed and unable to speak. Nevertheless, she made as many as 120 journeys on behalf of her mission. Fifteen new convents were established during her lifetime, including the motherhouse in Namur.

She died on April 8, 1816, at the age of sixty-four. She was canonized in 1969.

"Let us always go on sowing the good seed; then live in the peace of God."

—St. Julie Billiart

Martyrs of the Rwandan Genocide
(April 1994)

On April 7, 1994, radio stations in Rwanda transmitted a fearsome message: it was time to "cut the tall trees" and eliminate the "cockroaches." Upon this signal, Hutu militia began the wholesale extermination of their Tutsi neighbors and moderate Hutus. In the course of a hundred days nearly a million people were killed—mostly by machetes and other primitive weapons. Many of the massacres occurred in churches, where Tutsis had sought refuge. That such horror could occur in a predominantly Catholic country raised troubling questions about the meaning of evangelization. Nuns, priests, and catechists were among the victims. (In other cases, shockingly, they collaborated with the killers.) Church leaders, whether Catholic or Protestant, were largely mute.

But the shame was not confined to the Church. European colonists had propagated the notion that Hutus and Tutsis—traditional social castes—were actually separate races. After Independence, under the banner of "Hutu Power," Tutsis had become scapegoats and frequent victims of persecution. Now, in the midst of a systematic genocide, the international community largely stood by and watched. Armed UN peacekeepers were under orders not to intervene except to protect Europeans.

If there were many perpetrators as well as guilty bystanders, there were also many individuals who showed immense courage in their efforts to save others, whether neighbors or strangers. And among those labeled "cockroaches," there were many who bravely asserted their humanity and died proclaiming the name of God.

"If you really knew me, and you really knew yourself, you would not have killed me."
—From a poem by a genocide survivor

Mother Mary Demetrias Cunningham
Founder, Mission Helper Sisters (1859–1940)

Mary Demetrias Cunningham, the daughter of Irish immigrants—one of thirteen children—was born in Washington, DC. At the age of ten, her family moved to Baltimore. It was only a few years after the Civil War, and Mary was disturbed to witness the blatant discrimination against African Americans—even in her parish church, where black children were not permitted to receive religious instruction. Eventually, she began to teach them herself on the church stairs until she was finally given the use of an unoccupied classroom.

In time, with other interested women, she leased a house, intending to form a community dedicated to the religious instruction of African American children. Despite repeated entreaties, she could not win the support of her pastor. Finally she threw herself on the ground before him and begged, "For the love of God, let me go." The priest agreed to put the matter to Cardinal Gibbons, who replied, "Let her go; something may come of it." This was the origin in 1890 of the Mission Helper Sisters.

Aside from religious education, the sisters opened centers for vocational training. In time their services extended beyond the original focus on African Americans to the needs of the poor in general, including day-care centers for immigrants and schools for the deaf. They spread throughout the United States as well as Puerto Rico and Venezuela.

Mother Mary Demetrias died on April 9, 1940.

"God's will is the holiest thing on earth."

—Mother Mary Demetrias Cunningham

Dietrich Bonhoeffer
Theologian and Confessor (1906–1945)

Dietrich Bonhoeffer, a Lutheran theologian, was among those Christians in Germany who recognized early on the enormity of the evil posed by Hitler's regime. The claims of the Nazi state, he believed, posed a confessional challenge— ultimately a question about whether the Church worshiped God or a national idol. Bonhoeffer was a leader in the so-called Confessing Church, organized to oppose efforts by the state to co-opt and control the churches in Germany. In 1939, he accepted an opportunity to escape the country and teach in New York. Almost immediately he regretted the decision. "I will have no right to participate in the reconstruction of Christian life in Germany after the war if I do not share in the tribulations of this time with my people."

Upon his return, he joined in a conspiracy to overthrow Hitler. When the plot eventually unraveled, Bonhoeffer and his fellow conspirators were arrested. After two years in a military prison he was hanged on April 9, 1945.

In his early theology Bonhoeffer had written about the "cost of discipleship" and the need to reject "cheap grace"—"the grace we confer on ourselves." In his life and witness he offered a poignant model of a form of contemporary holiness—not withdrawn from the world but fully engaged "in life's duties, problems, successes and failures."

"The church's task is not simply to bind the wounds of the victim beneath the wheel, but also to put a spoke in the wheel itself."

—Dietrich Bonhoeffer

Pierre Teilhard de Chardin
Mystic and Scientist (1881–1955)

The work of the French Jesuit Pierre Teilhard de Chardin underlies many of the most creative movements in contemporary theology and spirituality. A scientist of the first rank, he published scores of scholarly articles and took part in anthropological excavations on three continents. All the while he worked out a profound theological synthesis, integrating the theory of evolution with his own cosmic vision of Christianity.

And yet throughout his career he was denied permission by Rome to publish any of his theological writings, to lecture publicly, or to accept any academic appointments. This treatment caused him severe frustration, yet he submitted in obedience, convinced that he served Christ best by faithfulness to his vocation.

Teilhard's spirituality was marked by a strong apprehension of the incarnation. With a mystic's eye he perceived the face of the divine in all of creation: "I want to teach people how to see God everywhere, to see Him in all that is most hidden, most solid, and most ultimate in the world."

He spent his final years in New York, where he died on Easter Sunday, April 10, 1955. After his death, the publication of his writings—previously passed from hand to hand among a select few—found a wide and devoted audience that continues to grow.

"The day will come when, after harnessing the ether, the winds, the tides, and gravitation, we shall harness for God the energies of love. And on that day, for the second time in the history of the world, man will have discovered fire."

—Pierre Teilhard de Chardin, SJ

Howard Thurman
Theologian and Mystic (1899–1981)

Howard Thurman was born in segregated Daytona Beach, Florida. He was raised by his mother and his grandmother—the latter, a former slave. From her, he said, he learned "more about the genius of the religion of Jesus than from all the men who taught me Greek. Because she moved inside the experience and lived out of that kind of center."

After studies at Morehouse College in Atlanta, Thurman studied for ministry at Rochester Theological Seminary in Rochester. A turning point in his life came in 1935 when he traveled for six months in India and met Mohandas Gandhi. On his return he became an early link between Gandhi's idea of nonviolence and the later civil rights movement. (Martin Luther King later cited Thurman as an inspiration.) But his travels also caused him to think more critically about Christianity and its compromises with social injustice. From this came his book *Jesus and the Disinherited*, which examined the ministry of Jesus as a resource for resolving the race crisis. Thurman saw Jesus as a member of an oppressed people, living under occupation, united with all the disinherited people of the world.

In his later books Thurman explored the nature of religious experience: "the finding of man by God and the finding of God by man." Thurman's brand of mysticism was an intense awareness of "a conscious and direct exposure" to God, a relationship in which "we find our true dignity and the sacred core of our being."

"There must be always remaining in every man's life some place for the singing of angels."
—Howard Thurman

St. Guthlac
Hermit (d. 714)

This Anglo-Saxon saint was born of a noble family and spent his early life as a warrior, engaging in battle against Welsh enemies. When he was twenty-four, however, "a spiritual flame began to kindle his heart." Reflecting on the vanity of human existence, he vowed to become "Christ's man." The next day he laid down his arms, bade farewell to his comrades, and set off on a new life.

Guthlac spent two years in a monastery in Repton, where his austerity—especially his disdain for liquor—provoked resentment from his brothers. By the time he won their affection, he was already dreaming of new adventures. With the consent of his community he set out for a deserted country in East Anglia, so forlorn and (by rumor) populated by monsters that it was considered uninhabitable. In this marshy "desert," he made his abode.

Like St. Antony of old, he was beset by "arrows of despair" and other temptations. Guthlac battled with legions of spirits who assaulted him in terrifying forms. Protected by the armor of faith, he ultimately won the day and was troubled no more.

Guthlac enjoyed great friendship with the creatures around him. Birds would land on his shoulders and sing, and he was reported to converse with angels. On the day of his death his hermitage was illuminated by a dazzling light "compared with whose brilliance the sun seemed pale as a lamp in daylight."

"My spirit has run the course in the race of this life and is impatient to be borne to those joys whose course has no ending."

—St. Guthlac

St. Stanislaus
Bishop and Martyr (1030–1079)

The role of the Polish Church in hastening the downfall of communism has been widely told. But in their stand against tyranny and injustice, the recent generation of Polish Catholics upheld an ancient tradition. One of the most revered saints in Poland is St. Stanislaus, a bishop of Cracow, who died as a martyr in the eleventh century.

Among the Polish bishops of his day, Stanislaus was the only one with the courage to stand up to the tyrannical king Boleslaus II and to denounce his cruelty and abuse of power. The last straw came when Boleslaus abducted the beautiful wife of one of his noblemen and carried her away to his castle. Upon hearing of this outrage, Stanislaus went to rebuke the king and to threaten him with excommunication if he did not amend his ways. When all other methods of persuasion failed, Stanislaus carried through on his threat. Thus, when Boleslaus and his retinue arrived at the cathedral for Mass, he was turned away at the door.

Enraged, Boleslaus ordered his guards to kill the bishop. When they balked at his command, Boleslaus drew his own sword and performed the bloody deed himself. Stanislaus was immediately acclaimed as a martyr. Pope Gregory VII put the country under an interdict, which endured until the death of the unrepentant Boleslaus. St. Stanislaus was canonized in 1253.

"If the world hates you, realize that it hated me first."

—John 15:18

Peter Waldo
Poor Man of Lyons (ca. 1140–ca. 1218)

Peter Waldo, a wealthy merchant of Lyons, amassed his fortune by lending money at interest. In about 1170, concerned for the welfare of his soul, he asked a priest to tell him the most perfect way of attaining God. He was amazed to hear the words from Scripture: "If thou wilt be perfect, go sell what thou hast . . ." He had never heard this text before. After paying a couple of priests to translate the Gospels into the vernacular, he undertook a serious study of Scripture. He then turned over part of his property to his wife and daughters and distributed the rest to the poor. He took to the streets, proclaiming his deliverance from the bondage of money and preaching the Gospel to all who would listen.

As followers joined him, he sought Vatican approval for his movement. In 1179 Pope Alexander approved his vow of poverty but forbade his preaching. Waldo tried to comply, but he could not put from his mind the command of Christ, "Preach the gospel to all creatures. . . ." The Poor Men of Lyons, or Waldensians, based their life on the Sermon on the Mount. They embraced poverty, refused to take oaths, and rejected all violence. Otherwise, in all doctrinal matters they were quite orthodox. Nevertheless, for violating the papal decree, Waldo was charged with heresy and excommunicated.

The Waldensians managed to survive persecution. Waldo himself faded from history around the same time another poor man from Assisi—with happier results—was petitioning the pope to approve his mendicant brotherhood.

"No man can serve two masters, God and Mammon."

—Matthew 6:24

St. Teresa of Los Andes
Carmelite (1900–1920)

This St. Teresa, the first canonized saint of Chile, has been likened to her patron St. Thérèse of Lisieux. Indeed, it was her reading of St. Thérèse's autobiography, *The Story of a Soul*, that inspired her vocation at the age of fifteen. As she noted in her diary, "I am God's, He created me and is my beginning and my end. If I am to become entirely His, I must do His will. . . . From now on I put myself in Your divine hands: do what You like with me."

When she was nineteen she entered the Carmelite convent in Los Andes and took the name Teresa. Though the convent was quite poor, Teresa found it to be "heaven on earth." As she wrote, "I believe holiness consists in love. I wish to be holy; therefore I will give myself to love. . . . Whoever loves has no will except that of the Beloved. . . . I wish to offer myself constantly as a victim so that I become like the one who suffered for me and loves me."

Teresa died of typhus on April 12, 1920. Though not yet twenty, she was allowed to make her final vows while on her deathbed. Her canonization followed in 1993, and her shrine in Chile continues to draw crowds of pilgrims.

"My vocation becomes more dear to me the more I penetrate it. The true Carmelite, as I understand it, does not live. God is the one who lives in her."

—St. Teresa of Los Andes

St. Martin I
Pope and Martyr (d. 655)

St. Martin, a native of Umbria, became pope in 649. He presided over a council that condemned the doctrine of "Monothelitism," the claim that in Christ there is only one divine will. Martin and the orthodox bishops believed this teaching departed from the teaching of the Council of Chalcedon (451), which affirmed the full co-presence of human and divine natures in Christ.

So divisive were these issues that the emperor had issued an edict banning any further discussion of the matter. Enraged to learn that the council had ignored his edict, he dispatched troops to Rome to arrest the pope. Martin was seized and transported in chains on a long voyage to Constantinople. There, after three months of solitary confinement and suffering from dysentery, he was tried and convicted of treason against the emperor. Deposed from office, he was flogged and received a sentence of death—subsequently commuted to exile in the Crimea.

In his place of exile Martin experienced great physical hardship but suffered more from the sense of having been forgotten by the Church of Rome. He felt truly alone. He died in 655. The Church that had quickly abandoned him was also quick to venerate him as a martyr, the last pope, so far, to have earned this crown.

"As for this wretched body of mine, God will look after it; he is near at hand, so why should I be anxious? I hope that in his mercy he will not prolong my course."
　　　　　　　　　　　　　　　　　　　　　—St. Martin I

Blessed Margaret of Citta-di-Castello
Third Order Dominican (1286–1320)

Blessed Margaret was born blind and deformed. Her wealthy parents, ashamed of their daughter, kept her locked in a cell, lest anyone learn of her existence. When she was six they took her to a shrine, hoping for a miraculous cure; when this failed to occur, they abandoned her. Fortunately, kindly strangers rescued her and took her home.

Despite the harshness of her early childhood, Margaret had a sweet disposition and easily charmed everyone she encountered. Eventually a convent offered to take her in. Margaret was delighted and adapted eagerly to the austerities of religious life. This being a rather lax convent, Margaret's zealous devotion affronted other members of the community, who eventually tired of her presence and kicked her out. Once again, friendly souls came to her rescue. She became a Dominican tertiary, spending much of her time in prayer. She knew the Psalter by heart and achieved such ecstasies, it is said, that she sometimes levitated a foot off the ground. She also cared for young children in the town and formed a little school, earning the grateful devotion of her neighbors. She died at the age of thirty-three. Miraculous cures were reported at her tomb, which became a popular pilgrimage site.

"Oh, if you only knew what I have in my heart!"

—Blessed Margaret of Citta-di-Castello

St. Lydwina of Schiedam
Patron of Sufferers (1380–1433)

Lydwina was born in 1380 to a poor family in the small Dutch town of Schiedam. On a winter's day when she was fifteen she had an accident while skating on the frozen canal. At first she seemed to have suffered a few broken ribs. But her condition rapidly deteriorated, inaugurating an illness that would leave her an invalid for the next forty years.

In time, at the urging of her confessor, Lydwina began to meditate on the sufferings of Christ, striving to unite her own sufferings with his. Through this reflection she gradually perceived a wider meaning in her suffering. This was her vocation: to bear her sufferings with courage and faith as a loving sacrifice for the sins of others.

Before long, word of Lydwina's suffering and faith spread widely. Pilgrims came from great distances to witness someone so intimately united with the passion of Christ. For her part, Lydwina experienced visions in which she visited the Holy Land and held conversations with Christ and his Mother.

She had her detractors, even a parish priest who at one point thought she was a fraud. A Church inquiry upheld her good faith and confirmed the miraculous sign that she subsisted on the Eucharist alone for the last nineteen years of her life.

At last her sufferings came to an end. She died on April 14, 1433. She was beatified in 1890.

"Meditation on the Passion and reception of the Eucharist became, as it were, the two arms with which Lydwina embraced her Beloved."
                                        —St. Lydwina's first biographer

Bishop James A. Walsh
Cofounder, Maryknoll Fathers and Brothers
(1867–1936)

James A. Walsh, a Boston-born priest, was educated by French seminary professors who inspired him with tales of St. Theophane Venard and other missionary martyrs. He imbibed the conviction that mission—the call to make disciples of all nations—was an essential expression of the Church's life. Soon after his ordination he became director of the Society of the Propagation of the Faith in Boston, raising money for overseas mission. At a time when the Church in America was itself considered a mission field, the SPF's work did not generate great enthusiasm; missionaries were considered foreign types, laboring among cannibals and exotic heathens. Fr. Walsh wanted to modernize this view of mission and translate it into the American idiom, so that American Catholics might claim their role in the universal Church.

At a Eucharistic Congress in 1910 he met Thomas F. Price, a like-minded priest from North Carolina. Together they conceived the idea of an American Catholic missionary society. With backing from the bishops, their project was recognized in Rome in 1911, and thus was born the Catholic Foreign Mission Society of America, better known as Maryknoll.

While Price departed with the first mission group to China in 1918, Walsh remained at home to serve as superior general, mission promoter, and spiritual father of the growing Society. Named a bishop in 1933, he died on April 14, 1936.

"What we priests and laymen can do by effort and prayer to win the world to Christ, this we should do."

—Bishop James A. Walsh

Mother Lurana White
Founder, Franciscan Sisters of the Atonement
(1870–1935)

L urana White was raised in New York by a wealthy family of High Church Episcopalians. While attending a boarding school run by an order of Episcopal sisters she felt a strong attraction to religious life. With her family's permission she entered the order as a postulant. She was pained, however, that her Episcopal order did not take a corporate vow of poverty. At this time she heard about an Episcopal priest, Paul Watson, who was promoting reunion between the Anglican Communion and Rome. Eventually they met and vowed to found a new Episcopal order in the spirit of St. Francis: the Society of the Atonement. Watson understood atonement both in the sense of redemption as well as *at-one-ment*—the cause of Christian unity. As founder of the Sisters of the Atonement, White became Mother Lurana. She and Watson established a new home on a site named Graymoor in Garrison, New York.

Fr. Watson's enthusiasm for Rome faced increasing opposition within the Episcopal Church. Eventually, in 1909, he and Mother Lurana successfully petitioned the Vatican to accept their community into the Catholic Church.

The community grew rapidly. Graymoor became a center not only for retreats but for hospitality to indigents and the down-and-out. On one occasion a priest came seeking the superior of the sisters. Dubious when Mother Lurana introduced herself, he protested that surely she was too young. She replied, "That is one fault of mine which will be remedied in time." She died on April 15, 1935.

"I wished to do and suffer something worthwhile for God and for others."
                                        —Mother Lurana White

Corrie ten Boom
Rescuer and Witness (1892–1983)

Corrie ten Boom lived in Haarlem, Holland, with her older sister Betsie and their widowed father. They were devout Christians who measured their quiet lives by the plain values of the Gospel. With the Nazi occupation of Holland, that faith was put to a terrible test.

While the occupation brought hardship for everyone, for the Jews it meant something infinitely worse. Corrie prayed that some way would open for her to be of help. The opportunity came quickly, when a Jewish woman knocked on her door one night, having heard that the ten Booms might offer shelter. Immediately Corrie invited her in. Others began to arrive. Corrie sought help from members of the underground who provided stolen ration cards and constructed an ingenious hiding space in an upstairs bedroom. Eventually, their luck ran out. They were seized by the Gestapo. Corrie and Betsie were sent to Ravensbruck concentration camp.

Betsie convinced Corrie that God was with them in the camp and that they had a mission to bear witness there to God's love. "We must tell people what we have learned here," she said. "We must tell them that there is no pit so deep that he is not deeper still." Soon after, Betsie died. Corrie, however, through some mysterious fluke, found herself released. Returning home to wait out the war, she lived on for nearly forty years, traveling the world to bear witness to God's love. She died on April 15, 1983.

"You can never learn that Christ is all you need, until Christ is all you have."
—Corrie ten Boom

St. Benedict Joseph Labre
Poor Man of God (1748–1783)

Benedict Joseph Labre was born to a large family in a village in northern France. At the age of twelve his family sent him to live with an uncle, a parish priest. There he received some rudimentary education. When his uncle died Benedict decided to devote his life to God. He was turned away from the Trappists and a series of other religious communities. Discouraged, he divined that his true vocation was to seek a cloister within the world. Accordingly he set off on foot on a pilgrimage lasting several years, wandering thousands of miles across Europe, all the while praying and visiting shrines.

Benedict dressed in rags and never bathed, a habit that discouraged human contact. He declined to beg but accepted alms. When no food was offered he lived off what was discarded on the road. His appearance evoked as much contempt as pity. But those who were able to see beneath his appearance—including, eventually, his confessor—recognized the saint in their midst.

In time Benedict settled in Rome, where he spent his nights in the ruins of the Colosseum and his days praying in the churches of the city. At the age of thirty-five he collapsed and died on April 16, 1783. His reputation quickly spread. Biographies were published. One of these made its way to his village, where his astonished parents learned what had become of their long-lost son. He was canonized in 1883.

"I am only a poor, ignorant beggar."

—St. Benedict Joseph Labre

St. Bernadette Soubirous
Visionary of Lourdes (1844–1879)

St. Bernadette was born in Lourdes, a small town on the northern slopes of the Pyrenees. A sickly child, she lived with her family in a basement hovel. One morning in 1858, when she was fourteen, Bernadette and two other children were gathering firewood near a remote cave. Passing the grotto, Bernadette looked up to see a beautiful young woman holding a rosary. The other children saw nothing. But as word spread of the apparition, crowds began to follow Bernadette as she returned and conversed with the Lady, who identified herself as "the Immaculate Conception." In one of her encounters, the Lady instructed Bernadette to drink from the waters in the cave. Although there was no visible sign of water, when Bernadette scratched in the ground she unearthed a growing stream. Before long it became a gushing spring, which continues to the present.

Far from rushing to embrace these miraculous events, Church officials were initially reserved, subjecting Bernadette to interminable interviews and cross-examinations. To escape the attention, both positive and negative, Bernadette entered an order of nursing sisters and was sent to a convent in Nevers. There her health deteriorated, and she died after great suffering in 1879 at the age of thirty-five. By that time Lourdes had become the most popular pilgrimage site in Europe, famous for its healing miracles. The Church embraced this cult, erecting a Basilica. Bernadette was canonized in 1933.

"I shall spend every moment loving. One who loves does not notice her trials; or perhaps more accurately, she is able to love them."

—St. Bernadette

Sor Juana Inés de la Cruz
Poet and Scholar (1651–1695)

Sor (Sister) Juana was born in a small town not far from Mexico City. From her earliest childhood she displayed an extraordinary passion for knowledge, learning to read by the age of four and quickly mastering Latin. Her wit and beauty won her a position as a lady-in-waiting in the vice-regal court. But then suddenly, at the age of nineteen, she turned her back on the court and entered the Convent of St. Jerome.

She was not motivated by great piety. In light of her "total antipathy" for marriage, she simply deemed convent life "the least unsuitable" alternative. Within the cloister she was free to indulge her voracious appetite for learning of every sort, and she produced many volumes of poetry—one of the great literary outputs of the baroque era.

The watershed in her life occurred in 1690 when she ventured to write on theology. The bishop of Pueblo praised her orthodoxy but condescendingly urged her to restrict herself to activities more becoming a woman. She responded with a lengthy treatise championing the equal rights of women to learning: "You foolish men, accusing women for lacking reason when you yourselves are the reason for the lack."

Her letter caused an uproar. Soon after, she made a public renewal of her vows, dispersed her famous library, and wrote no more. In 1695, while nursing her sister nuns during an outbreak of plague, she fell ill and died on April 17.

"There is no creature, however lowly, in which one cannot recognize that God made me."
—Sor Juana Inés de la Cruz

Anna Dengel
Founder, Medical Mission Sisters (1892–1980)

Anna Dengel was born in Austria. From an early age she felt called to some service and responded eagerly to a notice appealing for medical doctors in India. She completed medical studies, and in the early 1920s traveled to North India. Muslim women there would not be seen by male doctors, and so there was enormous demand for her services. This experience inspired her to envision a congregation of women trained in medicine: "to live for God . . . to dedicate themselves to the service of the sick for the love of God and . . . to be properly trained according to the knowledge and standards of the time."

Traveling to the United States, Dengel began recruiting vocations, and in 1925 she established the Medical Mission Sisters—the first Roman Catholic congregation to provide doctors for mission work. In her book *Mission for Samaritans* Dengel offered several motives for her work: the example of Christ the Healer, the example of the Good Samaritan, and restitution for the debt owed by the white race "to the peoples subjugated and exploited by our forefathers." Healing, for Dengel, was not just a work of mercy but a work of justice.

Anna Dengel died on April 17, 1980. Today her sisters number 650, operating in nineteen countries on five continents and sharing one mission, "To be a healing presence at the heart of a wounded world."

"Be optimistic no matter what comes. We don't have to be afraid; we are in God's hands."

—Anna Dengel

Venerable Cornelia Connelly
Founder, Society of the Holy Child Jesus (1809–1879)

Cornelia Connelly was born in 1809 to a wealthy Philadelphia family. In 1831 she married an Episcopal priest, Pierce Connelly, who subsequently renounced his Anglican orders and, joined by Cornelia, entered the Catholic Church. In 1839 Pierce confided his wish to seek ordination as a Catholic priest. Cornelia was stricken. Still, the dutiful wife, she tried to believe in the coincidence between her husband's wishes and the will of God. She remained behind, pregnant with her fifth child (two had died), while Pierce went to Rome to pursue his vocation. Eventually he summoned his family. The pope had approved his ordination, provided that Cornelia would make a vow of chastity.

Several bishops urged Cornelia to go to England to establish a religious congregation for the education of girls. She accepted the challenge, taking her children with her, and within a few years she had achieved some eminence in the English Catholic Church. But her trials were not over. Pierce renounced his priesthood and wished her to resume her marital duties. When Cornelia refused, he brought a suit against her in Anglican court. The court decided in Cornelia's favor, and Pierce, enraged, kidnapped her children and took them back to America. She never saw them again.

Cornelia remained superior of her congregation for over thirty years, winning admiration for all she did to advance the education of young women. But she always bore the weight of her sorrows. She died on April 18, 1879.

"Is not our faith a sword of strength? I feel it so, my Lord."

—Venerable Cornelia Connelly

Blessed Savina Petrilli
Founder, Sisters of the Poor of St. Catherine of Siena
(1851–1923)

Savina Petrilli was born in Siena in 1851. When she was ten she read a biography of St. Catherine of Siena, the great patron of her city, and found herself tremendously inspired. At eighteen, while on a pilgrimage to Rome, she had occasion to meet Pope Pius IX. When he learned that she was from Siena he told her that she must learn to walk in the footsteps of St. Catherine. Perhaps he said this to all the girls from Siena. But for Savina it was a sign!

Returning home, where she had for some years taught catechism to young children, she approached the archbishop and told him of her dream to found a new congregation. With his permission she took religious vows and drew up the rules for a community called the Sisters of the Poor of St. Catherine of Siena. Willing companions arrived, and in 1877 they received formal approbation from Rome. Initially they focused their care on abandoned children. But in time their mission expanded to include hospitals and homes for the elderly, always retaining a focus on the poor.

Savina died of cancer on April 18, 1923. By that time her congregation, which numbered five hundred sisters, had spread to the United States, South America, India, the Philippines, and elsewhere. She was beatified in 1988.

"Whoever looks at us must see Jesus in us, for charity is the virtue above all others that makes God present."

—Blessed Savina Petrilli

St. Alphege
Archbishop of Canterbury, Martyr (953–1012)

Alphege was a monk and later bishop of Winchester. He lived in a time when England was subject to the periodic terror of Danish marauders. In 994 he undertook a peacemaking mission to several Danish warlords. In the process he converted them to Christianity while winning assurance of their peaceful intentions.

In 1005 Alphege was named archbishop of Canterbury. But in the meantime the Danish terror had returned to southern England. In 1010 the Danes laid siege to Canterbury. Despite the payment of tribute, the invaders overran the city and held the archbishop and many other prominent citizens hostage. The others were released on the payment of ransom, but when an exorbitant sum was demanded for the release of Alphege, he forbade his people to pay. In retaliation he was brutally murdered.

Alphege was afterward revered as a martyr as well as a national hero. A later archbishop of Canterbury, Lanfranc, came to question whether, given the circumstances of his death, the sainted Alphege should properly be regarded as a martyr. But he was satisfied by the answer of his protégé, St. Anselm, who said that to die for justice was martyrdom indeed.

"Then was he captive who had been the head of the English race and of Christendom. There was misery to be seen where bliss had been before in that unhappy city whence came to us first Christendom and happiness in the sight of God and man."

—Anglo-Saxon Chronicle

Blessed Bernard the Penitent
Monk (d. 1182)

Before embarking on his life as a penitent (for sins which remain mysterious) Blessed Bernard of Maguelone in Provence obtained from his bishop a letter stating that "in expiation of the horrible crimes committed by him," he was to go barefoot for seven years, to observe a Lenten fast in the forty days before Christmas, along with other dietary austerities, and that he was not to wear a shirt for the rest of his life. The letter is dated October 1170.

Bernard kept and exceeded this penance, carrying heavy chains as he walked on pilgrimage over great distances. These included three trips to Jerusalem, and even, it was said, to India. At last, when he arrived at the monastery of Saint-Omer in northern France he discerned that the time of his travels had passed. He was given a small house next door to the monastery, where he devoted himself to prayer and works of mercy, nursing the sick and cleaning churches. He continued to stand out with his ascetical practices, such as walking barefoot even in the winter.

Eventually he asked to be admitted to the monastery, and he was given a habit. By now he was widely regarded as a saint, with a gift for prophecy and a reputation for many miracles. When he died his funeral was thronged by a huge crowd.

"God grants us all a good end."

—Blessed Bernard the Penitent

St. Hildegund of Schonau
Monk and Virgin (d. 1188)

St. Hildegund was the daughter of a German knight. After the death of her mother she accompanied her father on a pilgrimage to the Holy Land. She was about twelve at the time, and for protection on the journey she was disguised as a boy called Joseph. On the way home her father died, leaving Hildegund/"Joseph" to undergo a series of extraordinary adventures before making it back to Germany.

All the while and over many years, she maintained her identity as a boy and then a man. Finally, back home, she was admitted to the Cistercian monastery in Schonau, where she remained until her death, still a novice, never having taken vows. Only at that point was the secret of her sex discovered.

Despite its fabulous qualities, the story of St. Hildegund is attested by many contemporary sources. It is interesting to note that such stories of women passing as men in religious life are far from uncommon in the annals of the saints. Though some of these are undoubtedly apocryphal, still several remain in the official calendar of saints, perhaps serving as parabolic reminders of the ideal that "in Christ"—if seldom elsewhere—"there is no male or female."

"If I were to dress as a woman they would think of me as a woman, and then what would become of me?"

—St. Joan of Arc

St. Agnes of Montepulciano
Dominican (ca. 1268–1317)

St. Agnes was born in a Tuscan village near Montepulciano. Precociously devout, she persuaded her parents at the age of nine to allow her to enter a local convent. There the community was similarly struck by her wisdom and piety. Soon after she transferred to a community in Proceno, where, within a few years, she was elected abbess, although—in light of her youth, only fifteen—a special papal dispensation was required. Her reputation for holiness quickly spread, and stories of healings, visions, and miracles were widely reported.

Eventually, the people of Montepulciano were eager to reclaim their spiritual prodigy. Agnes agreed to take over a new convent, which she put under the Rule of St. Dominic. Toward the end of her life she received a vision in which an angel offered her a cup, saying, "Drink this chalice, spouse of Christ; the Lord Jesus drank it for you." Some days later she was struck by a painful illness.

Agnes died on April 20, 1317, at forty-nine. Her tomb became a popular shrine, visited by St. Catherine of Siena, one of many who venerated her memory. She was canonized in 1726.

"If you loved me, you would be glad because I am about to enter the glory of my Spouse. Do not grieve over much at my departure; I shall not lose sight of you. You will find that I have not abandoned you and you will possess me forever."

—St. Agnes of Montepulciano, parting words to her sisters

St. Apollonius
Martyr (d. 185)

Apollonius, a philosopher and member of the Roman Senate, found that his status offered no protection when he was denounced as a secret Christian. Brought before the Senate for judgment, he was interviewed by the proconsul Perennis.

The account of his trial is marked by surprising civility. It apparently pained Perennis to apply the law to someone so learned and highborn. Apollonius, for his part, responded to his interrogation with poise and eloquence, willing to pay respect to the emperor in all things permissible, withholding only that ultimate deference due to God alone.

When Perennis advised him that he should honor the gods and he would live, Apollonius answered, "The decree of man does not prevail over the decree of God. The more you kill these innocent faithful, mocking justice and the laws, the more God will increase their number." Death, as he noted, must come for all, "but the ways of dying are not the same." Christians, he observed, prepare for death each day by controlling their passions and living in conformity with God's laws.

After listening to his eloquent summary of Christian teaching, Perennis confessed that he would like to release him, but the emperor's decree forbade it. "At least I want your death to be gentle," he said. In accordance with this wish Apollonius was spared any torture and was swiftly beheaded.

"Yes, I am a Christian. I worship and I fear the God who made heaven, earth, the sea and all that is in them."

—St. Apollonius

St. Anselm
Doctor of the Church (1033–1109)

St. Anselm spent the better part of his life, until the age of fifty-nine, in a Benedictine abbey in Normandy, where he attained the office of abbot. In 1092, however, during a visit to England, he was compelled, much against his desires, to accept the vacant see of Canterbury. As archbishop of Canterbury and primate of the British Isles, Anselm displayed the same gifts for leadership and pastoral discernment he had displayed in his years as abbot. His tenure was marked, however, by continuous tensions with the monarchy over the independence of the Church from lay political control. Twice he was compelled to go into exile. He returned to England for a final time in 1106 and was reconciled with King Henry I, but his death followed three years later.

It is less for his ecclesiastical accomplishments than for his contributions as a theologian that Anselm is remembered. Known as the "father of scholasticism," Anselm is famous for defining the task of theology as "faith seeking understanding," and for trying to present logical proofs for the existence of God. In his masterpiece, *Why God Became Human*, Anselm provided an explanation of the incarnation: Humanity, having infinitely offended God in the sin of Adam, had to make an infinite satisfaction. Only a Redeemer who combined the natures of God and humanity could perform such a function. Though his reasoning owed more to the code of feudal honor than Scripture, it proved compelling for many centuries.

"To what was I aspiring, for what do I sigh? I sought after good things and, behold, [here is] turmoil. I was striving unto God but collided with myself."

—St. Anselm

Käthe Kollwitz
Artist (1867–1945)

Käthe Kollwitz, one of the great artists of the twentieth century, lived most of her life in Berlin. Her husband was a doctor who practiced in a working-class section of the city, and his patients served as models for many of her drawings and lithographs. Few artists were ever so committed to representing the private struggles and suffering of the poor. Her depictions of hunger, unemployment, domestic violence, and the oppressive burden of despair are among the most poignant images in all modern art.

Kollwitz was particularly sensitive to the experience of women, especially the aspects of maternal love. She depicted a mother's delight in the presence of her children as well as her fierce determination to protect her young. She herself was no stranger to loss. In World War I her youngest son, Peter, was killed at the front. His death was a "thunderbolt." Peter, she wrote, "was seed for the planting that should not have been ground." Eventually she transformed her grief into a passionate commitment to peace. In 1932 she unveiled a commissioned war memorial entitled "The Mourning Parents," its figures modeled after herself and her husband.

With the rise of the Nazis her work was banned. Somehow she survived the years that followed, the terror, the hunger, the devastation of war, all the while holding intact her faith in a new world. She died on April 22, 1945, days before the Armistice.

"One day, a new idea will arise and there will be an end to all wars. I die convinced of this."
—Käthe Kollwitz

Engelbert Mveng
Jesuit Theologian and Artist (1930–1995)

Engelbert Mveng, the first Cameroonian Jesuit, was trained in the Belgian Congo and studied in Belgium and France before returning to his homeland following his ordination in 1963. Drawing on his African cultural roots, Mveng developed a unique theological voice, combining art, anthropology, and history. He believed that art was "essentially a cosmic liturgy and a religious language," which imparted a vision of human destiny and its relation to God. Through his own work, which included altarpieces, Stations of the Cross, and other paintings, he translated the divine mysteries into a distinctively African visual idiom of signs and symbols. "Every rite, dance, piece of music and work of art," he wrote, "is a cosmic celebration of life's victory over death."

Mveng was a key promoter of inculturation—the incarnation of the Gospel into the language, culture, and worldview of African peoples. Through this "de-Europeanizing" of the Gospel, the African Church not only found its own voice but contributed to making the Church more truly "catholic."

He was also a theologian of liberation, which for him involved aligning oneself with the Kingdom of God—the forces of truth, freedom, justice, and love—against the kingdom of this world, which breeds poverty, injustice, tears, and discord. "It is from this kingdom that we must free ourselves."

While inspiring a generation of African theologians, Mveng also had his enemies. On April 23, 1995, he was murdered by unknown assailants.

"The vocation of human beings on earth is to ensure the victory of life over death."
—Fr. Engelbert Mveng

231

Blessed Maria Gabriella Sagheddu
Trappistine Nun (1914–1939)

Born to a poor family in Sardinia, Maria Gabriella's move toward religious life began at fourteen, following the death of a beloved sister. Afterward she became active in Young Catholic Action and then, at the age of twenty, entered a Trappistine abbey near Rome.

Her spiritual life was regulated by the disciplines of Trappist life. But in one respect she felt an unusual and distinctive mission: to dedicate her prayer and sacrifices for the cause of Christian unity. Though her abbess shared her commitment to ecumenism, this was not a popular cause among Catholics of the time. Maria felt a special conviction that division among Christians was a wound in the very heart of Christ. She wished that everyone might "turn to God and for his kingdom to be established in every heart."

Falling ill at the age of twenty-three, she offered her life for the cause of unity, inspired by the prayer of Jesus in the Gospel of John, "that they all might be one." She died on April 23, 1939. She was beatified in 1983.

"Sister Maria Gabriella, called by her vocation to be apart from the world, devoted her life to meditation and prayer centered on chapter seventeen of Saint John's Gospel, and offered her life for Christian unity. . . . The example of Sister Maria Gabriella is instructive; it helps us to understand that there are no special times, situations or places of prayer for unity. Christ's prayer to the Father is offered as a model for everyone, always and everywhere."

—Pope John Paul II, *Ut Unum Sint*

Cesar Chavez
Farmworker, Labor Organizer (1927–1993)

In the early 1960s Cesar Chavez wrote a new chapter in the history of the American labor movement by organizing the first successful union of farmworkers. Through his commitment to nonviolence and his deep faith in the justice of his cause, he transformed a local labor struggle into a moral crusade that brought hope to the hopeless and aroused the conscience of the nation.

Cesar Chavez was born in 1927 to a Mexican-American family in the Southwest. As a child he performed stoop labor in the fields as his family followed the crops up and down the West Coast. As a young man with a family he was eager to move away from the poverty of his upbringing. But he was influenced by a priest who instilled in him a passion for social justice and later by community activists who trained him in the techniques of organization. After moving to Delano, California, he founded the United Farmworkers Union (UFW).

The union was built on principles of sacrifice and solidarity and a commitment to nonviolence. Marches by the UFW often had a religious character, reinforced by public prayer, banners of Our Lady of Guadalupe, and public fasting. Along with strikes and picket lines, the UFW added consumer boycotts that appealed for public support. The strikers faced arrests and beatings, and the movement had its martyrs. And yet, whenever the cause faced defeat, Chavez breathed life into the struggle through his personal commitment and charisma.

He died on April 23, 1993.

"It is my deepest belief that only by giving our lives do we find life."

—Cesar Chavez

St. Mary Euphrasia Pelletier
Founder, Good Shepherd Sisters (1796–1868)

Rose Virginie Pelletier was born in Brittany, France. At the age of twenty-four she joined the Refuge of Our Lady of Charity of Tours, a community dedicated to the rescue of prostitutes. Though she was eventually elected superior, she was soon persuaded to take over management of another refuge for "fallen women" in Angers. She approached her charges with compassion and charity: "Love them, console and strengthen these wounded sheep; make them happy, very happy, by God's grace; this is your duty." She added: "It is better not to preach too much; it only wearies them." Eventually she founded a new congregation, the Institute of Our Lady of Charity of the Good Shepherd. She urged her sisters to approach troubled women and girls with the tenderness that Veronica showed Christ when she wiped his brow. As Mother Euphrasia, she saw her order grow and spread across the globe. "Having brought to birth all our young sisters in the Cross," she wrote, "I love them more than life itself. And the root of that love is in God and in the knowledge of my own unworthiness."

Mother Euphrasia died of cancer in 1868. At that time her sisters numbered nearly 3,000 in 110 convents. As she had said, "The habit we wear must be zeal, and that zeal must embrace the whole world." She was canonized in 1940.

"Go after the lost sheep without other rest than the cross, other consolation than work, other thirst than for justice."

—St. Mary Euphrasia Pelletier

Blessed Mary Elizabeth Hesselblad
Founder, Brigittines in Rome (1870–1957)

Mary Elizabeth Hesselblad, who was born to a poor Lutheran family in Sweden, immigrated to the United States in 1888 and enrolled in nursing school in New York City. There, among her patients, she encountered her first Catholics. An ardent Protestant, she was initially repelled by their devotion to Mary and the saints. But at the same time she felt a mysterious attraction. Later, on witnessing a Corpus Christi procession, she heard an inner voice say, "I am the one whom you seek." In 1902 she asked to be received into the Catholic Church.

On a pilgrimage to Rome she visited the house where St. Bridget, Sweden's great medieval patron, had lived. The house was occupied by Carmelites, and she asked to be admitted. Yet a greater dream propelled her: to reestablish St. Bridget's order, the Brigittines, in Rome. In 1906, with the support of Pope Pius X, her dream was realized; she recited the ancient vows and was clothed in the old Brigittine habit. The mission of the order would be "Contemplation, adoration, and reparation." During World War II she offered refuge to many Jews, for which she was later honored in Israel as one of the Righteous Among the Nations.

Hesselblad died on April 24, 1957. She was beatified in 2000.

"Dear Lord, I do not ask to see the path. . . . I will hang on tightly to your hand and I will close my eyes, so that you know how much trust I place in you, Spouse of my soul."

—Blessed Mary Elizabeth Hesselblad

St. Mark
Evangelist (First Century)

Who was St. Mark? A disciple of Jesus and thus a witness to the story recounted in his Gospel? Perhaps the John Mark who appears in the book of Acts as a companion to Paul in his missionary journey? Regardless of his sources or his identity there is no doubt that in writing the first Gospel narrative, sometime around the year 70, Mark had a decisive influence on the subsequent shape of Christianity. Previously the teachings of Jesus circulated in the form of sayings. Paul's letters contain almost no reference to the actual life story of Jesus. But for Mark, the authority of Jesus' message was rooted in his paradoxical identity as the suffering and crucified Messiah. For Mark, this was best communicated in the form of a story.

His Gospel ends on a curiously dynamic and open-ended note. In place of an explicit account of the resurrection, he ends with the discovery of an empty tomb and the words of an angel: "Go tell his disciples and Peter that he is going before you to Galilee. There you will see him, as he told you." Thus Mark addresses contemporary disciples. Jesus is no longer in the past or confined to Mark's story. He has gone ahead to Galilee. Mark's readers must write their own conclusion by taking up the cross of discipleship and going forth to meet him for themselves.

"'But what about you?' he asked. 'Who do you say I am?' Peter answered, 'You are the Messiah.'"
—Mark 8:29

St. Pedro de San José Betancur
Founder, Hospitaler Bethlemites (1619–1667)

St. Pedro de San José Betancur, who with his canonization in 2002 became the first saint of Guatemala, is sometimes called "the Saint Francis of the Americas." He was born in the Canary Islands and there spent his youth as a shepherd. At thirty-one he traveled to Guatemala but arrived so impoverished that he relied for subsistence on a Franciscan breadline. Hoping to become a priest, he enrolled in a Jesuit college, yet he found that academic studies did not suit him. He soon withdrew and became instead a Franciscan Tertiary.

Pedro devoted himself to the works of mercy, establishing a hospital—Our Lady of Bethlehem—as well as a hostel, a school, chapels, and other charitable institutes, which he supported by begging in the streets. When young men sought to join him he founded a new order, the Hospitaler Bethlemites.

Devotion to the Holy Family played a central role in his spirituality. He is credited with having originated the *Posada* celebrations that remain popular to this day in Mexico and Central America. On Christmas Eve a man and woman, representing Mary and Joseph, lead a procession in search of shelter in Bethlehem. Wherever this custom is observed, it offers a reminder that the best way to honor the Holy Family and the birth of Christ is to extend charity and hospitality toward those in need.

St. Pedro died on April 25, 1667.

"Brother Pedro was a man of deep prayer who sought assiduously the will of God in each moment."
—Pope John Paul II

Venerable Nano Nagle
Founder, Presentation Sisters (1718–1784)

Honora Nagle, known as Nano, was born in a small town in County Cork, Ireland. Though she came from a wealthy family, like all Irish Catholics she felt the repressive burden of England's penal laws—a set of punitive restrictions on the faith and liberties of Irish Catholics designed to demoralize and weaken a defeated people. Apart from banishing all bishops and religious orders from Ireland, the laws abolished all Catholic schools.

Nano's early education was in one of the illegal "hedge schools" that proliferated in the countryside. Eventually she found the means to travel to Paris, where she quickly adapted to the pleasures of high society. But upon the death of her parents she returned to Ireland and felt called to address the misery of her people. In Cork she established a network of clandestine schools. As more women came to join her she chose to establish a religious order devoted to serving the poor in every way. In 1775 she founded the Presentation Order, which eventually numbered many thousands, not only in Ireland but also in the West Indies and North America.

By the time of her death on April 26, 1784, her work was known and revered throughout Ireland and beyond. Her life is best summed up in her own motto: "Not words, but deeds."

She was declared venerable by Pope Francis in 2013.

"Love one another as you have hitherto done. Spend yourselves for the poor."
—Venerable Nano Nagle

Juan Gerardi
Bishop and Martyr (1922–1998)

I n 1996 the United Nations brokered an end to thirty-six years of civil war in Guatemala. Although the military had insisted on immunity for war crimes, including scorched-earth policies resulting in the destruction of over four hundred Indian villages, the peace agreement called for an investigation of human rights abuses. Bishop Juan Gerardi, auxiliary bishop of Guatemala City and head of the archdiocesan office of human rights, initiated the Recovery of Historical Memory (REMHI) project to conduct an exhaustive investigation.

Two years later Gerardi presented the findings in a 1,400-page work, *Guatemala: Never Again!* It outlined four decades of assassination, torture, and massacres, including the death of hundreds of lay catechists. The conclusion: almost 90 percent of the 200,000 noncombatant deaths and disappearances were caused by the Guatemalan military.

Issuing the report, Bishop Gerardi said, "We are collecting the people's memories because we want to contribute to the construction of a different country. This path was and continues to be full of risks, but the construction of the Kingdom of God entails risks, and only those who have the strength to confront these risks can be its builders."

Two days later, on April 26, 1998, military assassins ambushed Bishop Gerardi in his home and smashed in his skull with a slab of cement.

"Years of terror and death have reduced the majority of Guatemalans to fear and silence. Truth is the primary word that makes it possible for us to break this cycle of death and violence and to open ourselves to a future of hope and light for all."

—Bishop Juan Gerardi

St. Zita
Domestic Worker (ca. 1218–1278)

St. Zita is the patron of servants and domestic workers. Such was her own station for forty-seven years of service—from the age of twelve to the time of her death—with a wealthy family in Lucca, Italy. Early on, Zita was recognized for her unusual piety—a source of contempt among many of the household staff. She rose in the night for prayer and always attended the first Mass of the morning. But apart from such devotions, Zita considered her work itself to be an expression of her spiritual life: "A servant is not good if she is not industrious; work-shy piety in people of our position is sham piety." Gradually her qualities won respect and admiration. Her employer even overlooked her profligate generosity to the poor and sick. In her later years she spent increasing time visiting the sick and prisoners. She had a special devotion to those facing sentences of death; for these, she prayed without ceasing.

She died on April 27, 1278. Among other things, St. Zita is often invoked for the finding of lost keys.

"Notwithstanding her extreme attention to her exterior employments, she acquired a wonderful facility of joining with them almost continual mental prayer and of keeping her soul constantly attentive to the divine presence. Who would not imagine that such a person should have been esteemed and beloved by all who knew her?"
—Rev. Alban Butler

Niall O'Brien
Missionary (1939–2004)

Fr. Niall O'Brien, an Irish Columban priest, arrived in the Philippines in 1964, soon after his ordination in Dublin. Eventually he settled in Negroes, one of the larger islands of the Philippines and essentially an enormous sugarcane plantation in which workers labored in appalling poverty. Fr. O'Brien immersed himself in the world of these workers, hoping to bring them the solace of faith. But before long he determined that true charity required social justice. With the purchase of land, he formed a worker's cooperative, modeled on the kibbutzim of Israel; he organized base Christian communities in which workers might come to a deeper understanding of their dignity as children of God; he began to promote a nonviolent "revolution from the heart." Before long he was branded as a communist.

In 1983 O'Brien along with two other foreign priests and six lay workers were arrested on trumped-up murder charges. They faced the death penalty. After most of a year in prison—where the bishop appointed them as chaplains—an international campaign helped secure their release on the condition that they leave the country. Three years later the People's Power Revolution of 1986 drove Ferdinand Marcos from power, and O'Brien returned to Negroes to resume his work for nonviolent social change.

He died on April 27, 2004.

"The Church's teaching is unambiguous with regard to the pursuit of justice. Christianity is grotesque when it turns its back on justice. It's not Christianity, it's something else."

—Fr. Niall O'Brien

Blessed Luchesio and Buonadonna
Franciscan Tertiaries (d. 1260)

This married couple lived in the Italian town of Poggibonsi, where Luchesio worked as a merchant and moneylender. His life was not marked by any special motive beyond making money. Sometime in his thirties, however, a change came over him, prompted perhaps by the death of his children. He gave up his business and distributed his wealth, keeping only a small plot of land to farm. He and his wife, Buonadonna, began to serve the sick and poor, sharing their food with those less fortunate and entrusting themselves to Providence.

At this point, St. Francis of Assisi happened to visit their town on one of his preaching tours. The couple were taken by his message and asked him if there was not some way for them to follow his path without separating and entering religious life. Francis had longed to establish a Third Order in the Franciscan family for laypeople living in the world. Happily, he clothed Luchesio and Buonadonna in the plain habit and cord of the order. By tradition they became the first Franciscan tertiaries.

The couple lived on for many years. As Luchesio approached the end of his life, Buonadonna prayed that they might not be separated by death. Her prayer was answered; both husband and wife died on the same day, April 28, 1260.

Luchesio was later officially beatified; Buonadonna was also remembered, at least locally, as blessed.

"Implore God, who gave us to each other as companions in life, to permit us also to die together."
　　　　　　　　　　　　　　　　　　　—Blessed Buonadonna

Jacques Maritain
Philosopher (1882–1973)

Jacques Maritain, the foremost Catholic philosopher of the twentieth century, was born in Paris and raised in a Protestant home. By the time he entered the Sorbonne he had succumbed to the pervasive attitude of agnosticism. Still, something within him could not be reconciled to the possibility of a world without transcendent meaning. Among his fellow students he found a soul mate in a young Russian student, Raissa, who would become his wife and lifelong companion. Together they pledged themselves to see if within one year they could "find meaning for the word 'truth.'" Their journey led them both into the Catholic Church.

From that time on they regarded themselves as living at the service of God and the Church. Jacques became a professor at the Institut Catholique in Paris. He devised a creative way of applying the thought of Thomas Aquinas to the modern world, addressing such topics as art and culture, democracy, and human rights.

With the war, they immigrated to the United States. Jacques was widely regarded as the world's preeminent Catholic lay intellectual. He served at one point as French ambassador to the Vatican. He contributed to the development of the United Nations and helped draft the UN declaration on human rights. When Raissa died in 1960 he surprised the world by resigning from his teaching to become a novice of the Little Brothers of Jesus. He lived out his remaining days in a slum neighborhood in Toulouse. He died on April 28, 1973.

"Christianity taught men that love is worth more than intelligence."

—Jacques Maritain

Blessed Pauline von Mallinckrodt
Founder, Sisters of Christian Charity (1817–1881)

Pauline von Mallinckrodt was the daughter of a German politician. Though raised in comfort, even as a child she felt a deep bond with the poor. After the family moved to Paderborn, she was particularly moved by the hardship of slum dwellers and other victims of the Industrial Revolution. With other young women she began to care for the sick and dying. In 1840 she conceived the idea of forming kindergartens for young children whose working parents could not care for them. Two years later, she extended her work to care for the blind.

In 1849 Pauline and her companions formed the Sisters of Christian Charity. The Congregation grew quickly, and by 1871 there were 244 sisters. At this point, however, a program of anti-Catholic legislation under Otto von Bismarck struck all religious communities in Prussia. In 1876 the sisters' house in Paderborn was seized. Pauline accepted these events with equanimity: "The Lord gives and the Lord takes away," she said. The community moved to Belgium.

Meanwhile, requests came from the United States for sisters to work with German immigrants. Mother Pauline herself made the voyage and established a motherhouse for the order in Wilkes-Barre, Pennsylvania. When the persecution in her homeland lifted she returned to Paderborn. There she died on April 30, 1881. She was beatified in 1985.

"We must confidently look for God in our suffering brethren."

—Blessed Pauline von Mallinckrodt

St. Catherine of Siena
Doctor of the Church (1347–1380)

St. Catherine of Siena was one of the greatest saints of a tumultuous era. Like other great mystics, she enjoyed an intimate relationship with Christ. What was distinctive about Catherine was the way she mediated through her own heart the burning love of Christ and the needs of her time.

Early in life she declared her betrothal to Christ. When her parents retaliated by forcing her to work as a household servant, she responded by erecting within her heart "a secret cell" of "self-knowledge" to which she could retreat from her daily drudgery. Eventually, while still living at home, she was permitted to put on the habit of a Dominican tertiary. But after three years she experienced a mystical marriage with Christ. This launched her on a new public career, as she cared for the poor and sick and attracted a large band of disciples.

In 1374 she received a divine commission to help heal the world and the Church. She wrote hundreds of letters to the pope, monarchs, and other powerful men, counseling them on their duties to make peace and restore unity in the Church. She even traveled to Avignon on a mission to persuade the pope to return to his see in Rome.

After a final vision in which she saw the Church, as if like a mighty ship, placed on her back, she collapsed in pain. She died soon after on April 29, 1380, at the age of thirty-three.

"To the servant of God every place is the right place, and every time is the right time."
—St. Catherine of Siena

St. Marie of the Incarnation
Ursuline Mystic and Missionary (1599–1672)

Marie Guyart was born in Tours, France. From an early age she experienced a strong attraction to religious life. At the age of seven, she received a vision of Christ as a young child who asked her, "Do you want to be with me?" And yet, at seventeen, under strong pressure from her family, she agreed to marry a young silk worker. When he died a year later, leaving her with an infant son, she vowed that she would not remarry. In 1625 she began to receive a series of visions of the Trinity, culminating in the sensation of "spiritual marriage" to Jesus. In 1632, leaving her son in the care of her sister, she entered the Ursuline convent in Tours, taking the name Marie of the Incarnation.

In 1639 she volunteered for the new mission in Quebec, becoming the first French missionary sister in Canada. While facing cold, fires, illness, and war, she set about studying the native languages and compiling dictionaries and catechisms. Her convent became a center for missionary work in Canada. All the while, she experienced the mystical presence of Christ and his Mother. By the Spirit of Jesus, she felt her own spirit transported to the Indies, Japan, among the Huron, "to everywhere in the inhabited world where there were human beings whom I could see belonged to Jesus Christ."

She died on April 30, 1672. Honored as one of the founders of Canada, she was canonized in 2014.

"[God] has never led me by feelings of fear, but always by a spirit of love and trust."
—St. Marie of the Incarnation

Daniel Berrigan
Jesuit, Peacemaker (1921–2016)

Daniel Berrigan, one of the great prophets and peacemakers of his time, died on April 30, 2016, just shy of his 95th birthday. Along with his friends Dorothy Day and Thomas Merton, he charted a course of uncommon faithfulness to the way of Jesus, standing with the victims of violence and bearing witness to the God of Peace.

Ordained a Jesuit priest in 1952, Fr. Berrigan found his distinctive vocation amidst the horrendous death toll of the Vietnam War. In 1968, along with his brother Philip, a Josephite priest, and seven others, he seized files from a draft board in Catonsville, Maryland, and burned them with homemade napalm. From the courtroom transcripts he produced a classic play, *The Trial of the Catonsville Nine*, which included his words: "We have chosen to say / with the gift of our liberty / if necessary our lives: the violence stops here / the death stops here . . . / this war stops here." Eventually he served two years in prison for this action—one of innumerable arrests over the years. Much less public was his service in a home for cancer patients, and later with AIDS patients during the height of the deadly epidemic of the 1980s. "Peacemaking is hard," he wrote, "hard almost as war. / The difference being one / we can stake life upon / and limb, and thought, and love."

"Our apologies, good friends, for the fracture of good order, the burning of paper instead of children. . . . We could not, so help us God, do otherwise. For we are sick at heart, our hearts give us no rest for thinking of the Land of Burning Children."

—Daniel Berrigan, SJ

MAY

1 Thomas à Kempis • Ade Bethune

2 St. Athanasius • Takashi Nagai

3 Saints Philip and James • Servant of God Elisabeth Leseur

4 Anna • Mother Mary Ignatius Hayes

5 St. Jutta • Henry David Thoreau

6 Blessed Mary Catherine of Cairo • Blessed Anna Rosa Gattorno

7 St. Rosa Venerini • Servant of God Demetrius Gallitzin

8 Blessed Mary Catherine of St. Augustine • Blessed Miriam Teresa
Demjanovich

9 St. Pachomius • Blessed Theresa of Jesus Gerhardinger

10 St. Damien of Molokai • Walker Percy

11 St. Magdalene of Canossa • Horace McKenna

12 Venerable Edel Quinn • Vincent Donovan

13 St. Mary Mazzarello • René Voillaume

14 St. Matthias • The Syrophoenician Mother

15 St. Isidore • Peter Maurin

16 St. Brendan • Julian of Norwich

17 Jeremiah • Emily Dickinson

18 St. Dymphna • Larry Rosebaugh

19 St. Alcuin • St. Celestine V

20 Blessed Columba of Rieti • St. Toribio Romo González

21 Blessed Franz Jägerstätter • Christian de Chergé
and Companions

22 The Baal Shem Tov • St. Joachima de Vedruna

23 Girolamo Savonarola • Servant of God Emil Kapaun

24 St. Joanna the Myrrhbearer • Venerable Maria of Jesus of Agreda

25 St. Mary Magdalene de' Pazzi • St. Madeleine Sophie Barat

26 St. Bede the Venerable • St. Philip Neri

27 St. Augustine of Canterbury • St. Melangell of Wales

28 St. Mariana of Quito • Marc Sangnier

29 Noah • St. Ursula Ledóchowska

30 St. Joan of Arc • Cardinal Emmanuel Suhard

31 Saints Mary and Elizabeth • St. Baptista Varano

MAY

Thomas à Kempis
Spiritual Master (1380–1471)

Thomas à Kempis was born in the town of Kempen, near Düsseldorf. His early formation came in the Brethren of the Common Life, a society that gathered laypeople and clergy in a religious brotherhood committed to living in the spirit of the Gospel. In 1399 he entered an Augustinian monastery in Zwolle and was ordained a priest. Though his life as a monk was unremarkable, he is remembered for his book *The Imitation of Christ*—probably the most influential handbook of spiritual devotion ever written. Although addressed chiefly to his brother monks, it epitomized the spirituality of the Brethren, showing how a life of religious devotion could be lived in the world and not just in a monastery or convent.

For Thomas, the imitation of Christ does not mean emulating his external deeds but adopting the inner pattern of his piety: humility, detachment from the world, prayer, and obedience to the will of God. The path to holiness is available to everyone, requiring no particular setting, occupation, or station in life. The spiritual life is concerned not with one's outward activities but with the spirit that underlies them. The world judges according to appearances; God sees what is in the heart. Thus, "God regards the greatness of the love that prompts a man, rather than the greatness of his achievement."

Thomas died in 1471 at the age of ninety-one.

"A humble knowledge of yourself is a surer way to God than a deep search after learning."

—Thomas à Kempis

Ade Bethune
Liturgical Artist (1914–2002)

I n 1934 Ade Bethune, a nineteen-year-old art student in New York, was intrigued when friends told her about a new movement called the Catholic Worker that sought to relate the Gospel to social issues. When she saw their newspaper she was attracted by its message but found it visually drab. On her own initiative she sent a series of illustrations. One depicted Joseph and Mary being evicted from the inn in Bethlehem. Others depicted saints in modern clothes going about their everyday business. A few days later she visited the Worker headquarters and encountered Dorothy Day, who mistook her for a homeless woman seeking shelter. Shyly, she introduced herself: "I'm the girl who sent the pictures." Immediately Day set her to work on illustrations of more saints, and Bethune saw a great program open for her.

In later years Bethune would redefine the character of modern religious art. She worked in virtually every medium. But whatever the medium, her vocation as an artist always served her religious vision. As Day put it, her work reflected "a sense of the sacramentality of life, the goodness of things." It was a lesson she derived from the saints, who showed that there is a road to holiness in everything we do, provided we do it with love.

Bethune died on May 1, 2002, at the age of eighty-eight.

"The saints are Christ. In their heroic deeds shines Christ's example, reflected and multiplied through time and space."

—Ade Bethune

St. Athanasius
Archbishop and Doctor of the Church (ca. 297–373)

St. Athanasius was born in Alexandria, Egypt. As a young man he served as secretary to the local archbishop, whom he succeeded upon the latter's death. The Church at this time was divided by the teachings of Arius, an Alexandrian priest who denied that Christ was one in being with God the Father. Though his teachings were condemned in a local synod, the influence of Arius quickly spread throughout the empire.

Athanasius devoted himself to combatting this influential heresy, though at times he fought an uphill battle. As his enemies grew in power they resorted to calumny and false charges against the archbishop that ranged from theft and subversion to murder. Though Athanasius repeatedly proved his innocence, he was five times banished from Alexandria. Altogether, he spent seventeen years in exile, including several years hiding in the desert. (During this period he wrote a classic life of the desert ascetic St. Antony.)

Happily, Athanasius was able to spend the last seven years of his life in relative peace in Alexandria, where he died in 373. He had lived to see the tide at last turn against the Arians and the triumph of orthodoxy. Cardinal Newman would later describe him as "a principal instrument after the Apostles by which the sacred truths of Christianity have been conveyed and secured to the world."

"For the Son of God became man so that we might become God."

—St. Athanasius

Takashi Nagai
Mystic of Nagasaki (1908–1951)

On the morning of August 9, 1945, Dr. Takashi Nagai was working at the medical center in Nagasaki, Japan, when he saw a flash of blinding light, followed by darkness, and heard a crashing roar as his concrete building, and his world, collapsed around him. After escaping from the rubble, he joined the hospital staff in treating dazed and dying survivors. Only gradually did the extent of the destruction become clear. An atomic bomb had killed nearly 80,000 people.

In the days to follow, he witnessed scenes of horrifying suffering. But Nagai, a devout Catholic, struggled to find in the cross some meaning to this event. In this light he expressed gratitude to God that his own Catholic city had been chosen to atone for the sins of humanity.

He found it remarkable that by chance, Nagasaki, principal home of Japan's Catholic population, had been chosen that day as an alternate target and that the pilot had fixed his target on the Urakami Cathedral. The war ended on August 15, feast of the Assumption of Mary, to whom the cathedral was dedicated. In all this, Nagai saw the mysterious hand of Providence. Nagasaki, he came to believe, had been chosen to bear witness to the cause of international peace.

Radiation sickness left him an invalid, and he spent his remaining years as a contemplative in a small hut near the cathedral ruins. He died on May 1, 1951, at the age of forty-three.

"Grant that Nagasaki may be the last atomic wilderness in the history of the world."
—Dr. Takashi Nagai

Saints Philip and James
Apostles (First Century)

Relatively little is recorded of the apostle Philip, though he figures in several stories in the Gospel of John. It is Philip who reports to Jesus on the scant resources available to feed a multitude of five thousand. At the Last Supper he asks Jesus, "Show us the Father and we shall be satisfied," eliciting the reply: "Have I been with you so long, and yet you do not know me, Philip? He who has seen me has seen the Father."

St. James—not to be confused with the other James, the brother of John—is identified as the son of Alphaeus. Some believe that he is the same one known as "the brother of the Lord," who saw the risen Christ and became the first bishop of Jerusalem. At the Council of Jerusalem he agrees with Peter that Gentile Christians need not be circumcised.

This apostle is traditionally credited with the Epistle of James, which expresses concern about the intrusion of class divisions within the community of faith and stresses the importance of works of mercy toward the poor and justice for the oppressed. This James insists that Christians must be "doers and not simply hearers of the word." According to the chronicles of Josephus, he was stoned to death in the year 61.

A dedicatory inscription to these two saints on a basilica in Rome is the reason for their joint commemoration on this day.

"As the body apart from the spirit is dead, so faith apart from works is dead."
—Epistle of James 2:26

Servant of God Elisabeth Leseur
Faithful Witness (1866–1914)

Elisabeth, who was born in Paris, married Dr. Felix Leseur when she was twenty-two. While she was a devout Catholic, her husband was a determined atheist. Over time, as his convictions hardened, he became the editor of a militantly anti-Catholic newspaper. Yet his efforts to shake Elisabeth's beliefs only strengthened her resolve to study and deepen her faith. Though these tensions in her marriage caused her bitter suffering, Elisabeth came to believe the salvation of her husband was her actual life's mission.

When she confided to him the firm belief that he would one day become a priest, her husband ridiculed the notion. But two years later, as she was dying of breast cancer, he became increasingly impressed by her courage and equanimity, and the realization that she drew this strength from her faith.

Elisabeth died on May 3, 1914. She had for years been corresponding with a wide array of spiritual seekers, who thronged to her funeral. Felix was overcome to discover a note in his wife's spiritual diary in which she offered her sufferings and her life for his conversion. He went on to edit and publish her spiritual writings. In 1923 he was ordained as a Dominican priest.

"Silence is sometimes an act of energy, and smiling, too."

—Servant of God Elisabeth Leseur

Anna
Prophetess (First Century)

A few verses in the Gospel of Luke supply all that is known of Anna, "a prophetess, the daughter of Phanuel of the tribe of Asher." This old woman, a widow of eighty-four, hung about the temple of Jerusalem, worshiping "with fasting and prayer night and day," while anxiously awaiting some sign of Israel's Redeemer.

Her long years of patient vigil were rewarded one day when Mary and Joseph brought their infant son to the temple for his ritual presentation to the Lord. Anna's story follows the longer account of Simeon, an old man who had been assured by the Holy Spirit that he would not die before he had seen the Messiah. Upon witnessing the child Jesus accompanied by his parents Simeon blessed God and said, "Lord now lettest thou thy servant depart in peace . . . for mine eyes have seen thy salvation, which thou hast prepared in the presence of all peoples."

Although no words are attributed to Anna, there is a similar sense of fulfillment in her story. Beyond Jesus' immediate family, she is the first woman to be granted such insight into the divine mystery concealed in these humble beginnings. And she is the first to proclaim this good news to those like herself—poor and of no account—who lived by faith and waited in hope.

"And coming up at that very hour she gave thanks to God, and spoke of him to all who were looking for the redemption of Israel."

—Luke 2:38

Mother Mary Ignatius Hayes
Founder, Missionary Franciscan Sisters
of the Immaculate Conception (1823–1894)

Elizabeth Hayes, the daughter of an Anglican priest, followed a circuitous spiritual journey. Starting out in an Anglican religious community in Oxford, she converted to Catholicism and later joined a Franciscan community in Greenwich. Aside from the traditional three religious vows, she took a fourth—to make herself available to the needs of mission. Her subsequent journey led her to Jamaica, then France, and finally to Belle Prairie, Minnesota, at that time a remote outpost. Operating out of a log cabin with a small group of sisters she formed the Missionary Franciscan Sisters of the Immaculate Conception.

They faced enormous hurdles. At one point Mother Mary Ignatius Hayes, as she was now known, traveled to Italy, hoping to find other Franciscans willing to join her in the prairie. She returned empty-handed. But eventually her community grew, and she decided it was time to spread forth—this time to serve the African American community in the South. In 1879 she established a new community in Georgia, providing education to the children of recently freed slaves.

The next year she traveled to Rome for an audience with Pope Leo XIII. He persuaded her to open a novitiate in Rome. She complied, though it meant she would never return to the United States. She died on May 6, 1894.

"The greatest miracle is myself, that I should be a Catholic, a religious, a Franciscan. Yet, I am so weak bodily, so sensitive mentally, that left to myself a moment I should not bear up against the least cross."
—Mother Mary Ignatius Hayes

St. Jutta
Widow (ca. 1200–1260)

St. Jutta was born in Thuringia, in Germany. At the age of fifteen she married a nobleman, with whom she enjoyed a happy marriage. Inspired by the example of St. Elizabeth of Hungary, a Thuringian princess who had renounced her royal station to embrace poverty as a Franciscan tertiary, Jutta attempted to conform her life, and that of her family, to the principles of the Gospel: charity, service, and a spirit of poverty.

Her husband died while on pilgrimage to the Holy Land, leaving Jutta to raise her children alone. When, over time, each one of them entered religious life, she was free to pursue her heart's desire. After giving away all her property to the poor, she donned a simple dress and became a wandering pilgrim. Though many were moved by her piety and the austerity she had exchanged for her previous estate, others greeted her conduct with derision.

Jutta liked to say there were three things that brought one nearer to God: painful illness, exile from home, and voluntary poverty. She experienced all three. Eventually she made her way to a distant corner of Prussia where she became a Third Order Franciscan and took up residence as a solitary hermit. Many visitors found a path to her home, whether seeking nursing care, consolation in their troubles, or spiritual counsel.

She died at the age of sixty and was later embraced as a patroness of Prussia.

"All my treasures are yours, and yours are mine."

—Message of Christ, as received by St. Jutta

Henry David Thoreau
Naturalist and Social Critic (1817–1862)

Henry David Thoreau, who was born in Concord, Massachusetts, subscribed to no organized religion. Yet there was in Thoreau something of the sage or Desert Father, an intense need to dispense with socially defined values and to experience life "first-hand." This desire led him in 1845 to spend two years in solitude at Walden Pond, "wishing to live deliberately, to front only the essential facts of life, and see if I could not learn what it had to teach, and not, when I came to die, discover that I had not lived." His account of this experience became a literary classic. But in a sense Thoreau was himself an American classic who embodied the spirit of nonconformity, the impulse to seek renewal in nature, and the will to stand by his convictions.

Thoreau's mystical communion with nature speaks to the concerns of an ecological age. But he was also a stern moralist and social critic. Finding it intolerable to live in a country that sanctioned slavery, he was arrested for refusing to pay a tax financing the Mexican War—a war to extend slavery. Though his overnight stay in jail was no more than a gesture, it resulted in a famous essay on civil disobedience, one of the most eloquent arguments ever written on the authority of conscience and the duty to resist injustice. It would be embraced by Tolstoy, Gandhi, and Martin Luther King Jr. and would inspire generations of peacemakers.

Thoreau died on May 6, 1862.

"If a man does not keep pace with his companions, perhaps it is because he hears a different drummer."

—Henry David Thoreau

Blessed Mary Catherine of Cairo
Missionary (1813–1887)

Constanza Troiani was born in Italy in 1813. At the age of six, following her mother's death, she was entrusted to the Franciscan Sisters of Ferentino. At sixteen, in this convent in which she was raised, she was accepted as a novice, taking the name Sr. Mary Catherine of St. Rose of Viterbo.

Many years passed. One day a visiting priest, just back from Egypt, spoke of the need for sisters in Cairo. Mary Catherine, who had always yearned to be a missionary, won permission from her convent to accept this challenge and with five other sisters departed for Cairo. Once there—the first Italian sisters in Egypt—they set about learning Arabic and embarked on care for the poor, opening an orphanage that welcomed children of all races and religious backgrounds.

Yet her convent had considered this a temporary mission, and when the sisters were instructed to return, they faced a dilemma. Choosing to sever ties with their congregation, they received permission from Rome to establish a new congregation: the Franciscan Missionary Sisters of Egypt. Along with their previous work, Mother Mary Catherine, known widely as "Mother of the Poor," fearlessly took up the antislavery cause. Asked by a sister during an outbreak of cholera whether anything frightened her, she replied, "My dear, only a lack of faith frightens me."

Her passing, on May 6, 1887, was mourned throughout Cairo by Christians and Muslims alike. She was beatified in 1985.

"The will of God is my perpetual hunger, my thirst, and my yearning."
—Blessed Mary Catherine of Cairo

Blessed Anna Rosa Gattorno
Founder, Daughters of St. Anne (1831–1900)

Benedetta Gattorno was born in Genoa to a wealthy family. Married at twenty-one, she was widowed six years later, leaving her with two young children to care for—one of them deaf and mute. Despite these challenges, she underwent what she called a "conversion" to greater love of God and her neighbors. Already a daily communicant, she took private vows of chastity and obedience, later adding poverty, when she became a Franciscan tertiary.

Her confessor urged her to establish a religious congregation, but she worried about what would happen to her children. No less than Pope Pius IX offered reassurance: God, he told her during an audience, would provide for her children. And so in 1866 she founded the Daughters of St. Anne (named for the mother of Mary) and later took the name Anna Rosa. The mission of the sisters was to be "Servants of the poor and ministers of mercy," seeking out and responding to all forms of suffering—whether among the poor, the abandoned, orphans, the sick, or elderly. She took a special interest in deaf children.

In 1878 the first sisters left Italy to establish houses in Latin America and other parts of Europe. By the time of Anna Rosa's death on May 6, 1900, there were 3,500 sisters at work in over 300 houses. She was beatified in 2000.

"Although I am in the midst of such a torrent of things to do, I am never without the union with my God."

—Blessed Anna Rosa Gattorno

St. Rosa Venerini
Founder, Venerini Sisters (1656–1728)

Rosa Venerini was born in Viterbo, Italy. Soon after she entered a Dominican convent, her father's death forced her to return home to help care for her family. By the time she felt free to pursue her vocation, she had given up thoughts of cloistered religious life. Instead, she had found a new calling, offering religious instruction to young girls. With support from her bishop and the collaboration of several associates, she started the first public school for girls in Italy. She perceived that by expanding opportunities for girls and young women, she might make the most effective contribution to the economic and moral uplift of society.

The evident success of her venture quickly put opposition to rest, and her schools spread to other cities. Though not recognized as a formal congregation until after her death, her so-called Religious Teachers became known as Venerini Sisters, operating under the motto, "Educate to Liberate." In 1716 Pope Clement XI, along with several cardinals, made a personal visit to her school in Rome. After observing the instruction, he proclaimed: "Signora Rosa, with these schools you will sanctify Rome." Tirelessly, she spent the rest of her life traveling throughout Italy to establish more schools. She died on May 7, 1728, and was canonized in 2006.

"I feel so nailed to the Will of God that nothing else matters, neither death nor life. I want what He wants; I want to serve Him as much as pleases Him and no more."
—St. Rosa Venerini

Servant of God Demetrius Gallitzin
Apostle of the Alleghenies (1770–1840)

Demetrius Gallitzin was raised in the highest circles of aristocracy. His father, a Russian prince, served as ambassador to Holland, while his mother was a German countess. She also happened to be a devout Catholic, and this faith, imparted to her son, set his life on a surprising course. While making a tour of America, he was struck by the needs of the struggling Church. Resolving to become a priest, he enrolled in the new seminary in Baltimore.

This news was not well received by his father. Nevertheless, Demetrius was ordained in 1795. He traveled widely, performing mission work in a territory that stretched from southern Pennsylvania to Maryland and Virginia. In 1799 he used his own fortune to purchase land for a new Catholic settlement in Loretto, Pennsylvania. For many years he was the sole priest west of the Alleghenies, covering a vast territory that now encompasses Pittsburgh, Erie, and parts of Harrisburg. Carving this settlement out of the wilderness was incredibly taxing. Aside from buying tracts of land for settlers, Gallitzin set up sawmills, tanneries, and other industries to support them. Though he had expected to inherit his parents' fortune, he found himself disinherited by a decree from the Russian government on account of his ordination as a Catholic priest.

Having exhausted himself physically and financially for the sake of his flock, he died on May 6, 1840.

"The ministers of Christ, in 1815, scattered over the globe, preach likewise one and the same doctrine, because Christ is still with them."
                          —Servant of God Demetrius Gallitzin

Blessed Mary Catherine of St. Augustine
Nun (1632–1668)

Mary Catherine de Longpré was a young girl in 1644 when she entered the Augustinian Hospitaller Sisters in Normandy. Four years later, still only sixteen, she volunteered for the community's mission in Quebec. After a perilous voyage, during which she nearly died of plague, she arrived in the primitive settlement. The Hôtel-Dieu, where she lived, was "more a hut than a hospital." Contending with hunger and cold, Sr. Catherine cheerfully dedicated herself to all those in need, not discriminating between French settlers and the native peoples, whose languages she studied. To all appearances, she was a faithful, if unexceptional nun. Upon her death at thirty-six on May 8, 1668, she was widely mourned.

Only with the publication of her biography three years later was the astonishing record of her inner struggles revealed. The author, a Jesuit priest who had access to her private journals, described Mary Catherine's sensation that her soul was assailed by demons as numerous "as the specks one sees in the air in daylight." Despite her outward serenity and cheerfulness, she had lived each moment on the edge of an abyss of despair. Offering herself as a victim soul on behalf of the people of Quebec, she had prayed to God, "I hope that you will grant me grace to love you for all eternity, even though I were in the depths of hell." She was beatified in 1989.

"My God, I adore Your divine perfections; I adore Your divine Justice; I abandon myself to it with my whole heart."

—Blessed Mary Catherine of St. Augustine

Blessed Miriam Teresa Demjanovich
Sister of Charity (1901–1927)

Teresa Demjanovich, who was born in 1901 to a family of Ruthenian immigrants, grew up amid the oil refineries of Bayonne, New Jersey. While attending the College of St. Elizabeth, she received a startling vision: "I was saying my Rosary here at the window seat when suddenly the grounds outside appeared bathed in a dazzling light and the Blessed Mother was clearly seen by me."

In 1925 she entered the novitiate of the Sisters of Charity. Her spiritual director quickly discerned her special gifts. Remarkably, he asked her—though a novice herself—to write his conferences for the other novices. Only after her death was she revealed as the true author. The theme was the way of holiness, compatible with every state of life: "Union with God is the spiritual height God calls everyone to achieve—anyone, not only religious but anyone, who chooses, who wills to seek this pearl of great price, who specializes in the traffic of eternal good, who says 'yes' constantly to God." Later published under the title *Greater Perfection*, her reflections found a wide following.

In November 1926 Sr. Miriam fell mortally ill. She was allowed to make her profession of religious vows a month before her death on May 8, 1927, at the age of twenty-six. Her beatification in October 2014 in the Cathedral of Newark was the first beatification celebrated on American soil.

"Keep the ways of the Lord. . . . The way of the cross is the path of self-sacrifice and denial. Only a humble soul can walk this path securely."
—Blessed Miriam Teresa Demjanovich

St. Pachomius
Abbot (ca. 292–ca. 346)

St. Pachomius is widely credited as the founder of cenobitic monasticism—the form of monasticism centered on community life rather than on solitary asceticism. Born in Egypt to pagan parents, he was drafted into the Roman army. During this service he came into contact with Christians, and upon his demobilization he sought to be baptized. For some years—like his contemporary St. Antony—he lived a solitary life of extreme asceticism in the desert. Eventually, however, he heard an angelic voice instruct him to gather other monks under a common rule, which he himself devised. He presided over the community as "Abba," or father—the origin of the monastic abbot.

Pachomius came to organize nine monasteries, including three for women. Their life combined common prayer interspersed with private recitation of the psalms and manual labor. Although he continued to practice strenuous self-denial—eating only one meal a day and never reclining to sleep—Pachomius modulated his Rule to the gifts and health of his monks. Nevertheless, his Rule stands out for its fantastically exact instructions on virtually every aspect of daily monastic life. Pachomius died of plague around 346.

"If it is stated that a brother lies or hates someone, or it is proved that he is disobedient, that he is given to telling jokes more than what is convenient . . . the father of the monastery will judge and punish him according to the gravity of the sin he has committed."

—Rule of St. Pachomius

Blessed Theresa of Jesus Gerhardinger
Founder, School Sisters of Notre Dame (1797–1879)

Caroline Gerhardinger was born in Stadtamhof, Germany, where she was educated by the Canonesses of Notre Dame. When the congregation was suppressed under Napoleon's campaign of secularization, she resumed her studies under a local priest. All the while she dreamed, when conditions might allow, of founding her own order of teaching sisters. There was no telling when this might be possible, but as she noted, "The love of Jesus sees into the future."

In 1833 Gerhardinger founded the School Sisters of Notre Dame, taking the religious name Theresa of Jesus. Mother Theresa believed that true education had a deeply religious dimension. As she taught her sisters, "For us education means enabling persons to reach the fullness of their potential as individuals created in God's image."

In 1847, after establishing many communities and schools in Germany, she sailed for America, where she established a second motherhouse in Baltimore with support from the German-speaking Bishop John Neumann. There she popularized the spread of kindergartens. Returning to Germany, she endured conflicts with Church leaders as well as the state. Many bishops wished to subject her local communities to their control, while she insisted on maintaining central government of her congregation. She also contended with anti-Catholic government measures that resulted in the state takeover of some of her schools. "All of God's works walk a path of suffering," she noted.

She died on May 9, 1879, and was beatified in 1985.

"My death will be a consolation for my whole life."

—Last words of Blessed Theresa of Jesus Gerhardinger

St. Damien of Molokai
Priest and Leper (1840–1889)

Westerners arrived in the Hawaiian Islands only late in the eighteenth century. Within a hundred years the ravages of disease had reduced the native population by 80 percent. Among the most dreaded scourges was Hansen's disease, or leprosy. By 1870 it had reached epidemic proportions. With no available treatment, the authorities established a settlement on the remote island of Molokai where those suffering from the disease were dispatched into exile. Conditions were horrific. For those put ashore on Molokai, there was no return.

Damien de Veuster, a young Belgian priest, had served nine years as a missioner in Hawaii when he requested to serve as chaplain on Molokai. Upon his arrival he set out to instill in the members of his "parish" a sense of self-worth and dignity. He established a burial society and proper sanitation, constructed a church, and helped build clean houses. Gradually the island was transformed; no longer a way station to death, it had become a proud and joyful community.

From the beginning, Damien realized he must not shrink from intimate contact with his people. After some years, he eventually recognized on his body the first symptoms of their disease. He rejoiced in the privilege to be truly one with the suffering of his people, confined as they were to the island. He died of leprosy on April 15, 1889. He was canonized in 2009.

"I make myself a leper with the lepers to gain all for Christ."

—St. Damien of Molokai

Walker Percy
Novelist (1916–1990)

Walker Percy was born in Birmingham, Alabama, on May 28, 1916. After studying medicine at Columbia, his career was sidelined when he contracted tuberculosis and was confined for five years to a series of sanitaria. While the rest of the world was plunged in war, Percy lay in bed, reading Kierkegaard and Russian novels, pondering the paradoxes and absurdities of the modern world. He decided to become a Catholic.

By the time he was released he had no further interest in medicine. Instead he settled in New Orleans, raised a family, and devoted himself to further reading. After publishing a series of dense philosophical essays, he turned to fiction. In 1961 he published *The Moviegoer*, a hugely entertaining novel in which he explored the theme that would surface in all his work: the human challenge of remaining fully *alive* while avoiding the lure of everydayness, routine, and despair.

Though all his novels were shaped by a Catholic understanding of reality, Percy believed it was no use simply to repeat pious verities. Christian language had been worn smooth from overuse. Another matter was the moral failure of Christianity—in his own region, displayed in the Church's failures in confronting racial oppression.

Percy sought to name the despair of modern life and to point toward a solution: our challenge was to recover our true humanity, to break loose from abstractions and ideologies, and "re-enter the lovely, ordinary world." He died on May 10, 1990.

"To become aware of the possibility of the search is to be onto something. Not to be onto something is to be in despair."

—Walker Percy, *The Moviegoer*

St. Magdalene of Canossa
Founder, Canossian Sisters of Charity (1774–1835)

Magdalene Gabriella di Canossa was born in Verona, Italy, to a wealthy family. Though her family counted on her to marry within her class, she was more devoted to the practice of charity: "Should the fact I was born a marquess prevent me from serving Jesus Christ in his poor?" Apart from teaching the catechism to children, she busied herself visiting the sick and distributing food and alms to the hungry. She had a special devotion to Mary—the Mother of Sorrows beneath the Cross—and this inspired her determination to see the image of Christ in all who suffered.

In 1799 she took two poor girls into her home. Soon she acquired a larger house and attracted other women who helped her establish a community that would combine a spirit of communion with God with practice of the works of mercy. This was the beginning of the Canossian Sisters of Charity. Schools for girls and eventually also boys spread across Italy and later around the world.

Magdalene was able to combine the demanding duties of her vocation with an intense life of mystical prayer. Periods of dryness were broken by moments when she felt herself "enraptured in God." One time while at prayer, she wrote, "I saw Him within me like a luminous sun and was absorbed by the Divine Presence to the point that . . . the strength of heavenly joy was almost suffocating me."

She died on April 10, 1835, and was canonized in 1988. Her feast is May 8.

"The Religious Life is only the Gospel translated into practice."

—St. Magdalene of Canossa

Horace McKenna
Jesuit Apostle to the Poor (1899–1982)

Horace McKenna was born in New York City in 1899 and entered the Jesuits in 1916. While serving in a Jesuit school in the Philippines he was first exposed to the world of the poor, and ever after, his ministry was devoted to those struggling on the margins. Back in the United States he was assigned to parishes in southern Maryland, where he stirred up trouble with his refusal to accommodate the practice of segregation. After several transfers he ended up in St. Aloysius parish in Washington, DC, where he remained for the rest of his life.

Fr. McKenna was a tireless servant of the poor, founding soup kitchens, homeless shelters, and, during the Vietnam War, offering a courageous witness for peace. A list of his activities hardly encompasses the tasks that filled his daily life: the car rides, the supplies procured, the meetings attended, all alongside his traditional parish ministry. He noted, "When God lets me into heaven, I think I'll ask to go off in a corner somewhere for half an hour and sit down and cry because the work is done and I don't have to worry any longer who's at the door, whose breadbox is empty, whose baby is sick, whose children can't read."

Fr. McKenna died on May 11, 1982.

"The poor are the critique of this generation . . . and I think that the parishes are where the waves of the poor break at our feet and come to us like a daily mission from the Creator, with a built-in mandate."
—Horace McKenna, SJ

Venerable Edel Quinn
Missionary of the Legion of Mary (1907–1944)

Edel Quinn was born in Ireland. While working as a secretary she joined the Legion of Mary, an organization of devout laypeople committed to invigorating the faith of their neighbors through loving service. Edel's particular mission was befriending and rescuing prostitutes.

Her desire to enter religious life was frustrated when she fell ill with tuberculosis and spent a year in a sanitarium. But in 1936, when her condition stabilized, she jumped at an invitation for Legion workers in East Africa. Arriving in Nairobi, she found a Church rigidly segregated between Europeans and Africans. Within weeks she had established Legion cells throughout the city which brought white and black Catholics together in worship.

Tirelessly she traveled throughout East Africa, everywhere leaving a share of her infectious faith and loving spirit. As one bishop put it, within a year of her arrival, "the atmosphere of my diocese had changed. Without any noise, she had brought a germ of life. . . . One could feel the passing of grace." People of all sorts perceived an aura of intense aliveness in her presence that drew them close and enlarged their faith.

By 1938 her health had seriously deteriorated, yet she refused any thought of leaving. She carried on until her death on May 12, 1944, at the age of thirty-six. The cause of her beatification was introduced in 1956.

"Live for the day. Life is made up of days. Our eternity is built on time. If one has given all to Jesus and Mary, one has no right to waste time."
—Venerable Edel Quinn

Vincent Donovan
Missionary (1926–2000)

Vincent Donovan, a Pittsburgh native and a Holy Ghost Father, departed as a missionary to Africa in 1955. Stationed in Masailand in Tanzania, he worked for a number of years in traditional mission work—building a hospital and schools. The Masai accepted such services, but they were not moved to convert. Eventually Donovan asked permission of his bishop to leave behind the mission compound, simply "to go to these people and do the work among them for which I came to Africa."

In a later book, *Christianity Rediscovered*, he described his experiences. He found that the Masai were happy to hear him talk about God. The challenge was to find a new language to present the Gospel in terms rooted in their own language and culture. Donovan found himself following in the footsteps of St. Paul and the early apostles, who had left behind the Jewish world to implant Christianity among the Gentiles. The Masai were the new Gentiles. The task was to help them encounter Christ in terms of their own culture, free of the "circumcision" of Western concepts. Many communities accepted the message Donovan brought them. And then, having helped give birth to a new Church, he moved on.

Returning to America in 1973, Donovan served in various parishes and as a chaplain at Duquesne University. To the end, he remained a missionary, seeking new ways to implant the Gospel in an alien culture. He died on May 13, 2000.

"Evangelization is centrifugal. It leaves Jerusalem and is on its way to the ends of the earth and the end of time."

—Fr. Vincent Donovan

St. Mary Mazzarello
Founder, Salesian Sisters (1837–1881)

Mary Mazzarello was born to a peasant family in a town near Genoa. After a bout of typhoid left her too weak to work the fields, she took up dressmaking. Over time, she began to take in other girls as apprentices, combining her training with religious education.

Don Bosco, founder of the Salesians, had been looking for a woman to take up with girls the educational work he was doing with boys. Introduced to Mary, he was convinced she was the one. Such was the beginning of the Salesian Sisters.

Mary, who was barely literate before the age of thirty, was in some ways a surprising choice for such an apostolate, yet she proved equal to the task. As she liked to say, "Wisdom is justified by her children." In keeping with the spirit of the Salesians, she combined education with vocational training and religious formation. "Laugh and play and dash about as much as you like," she said to the younger children, "but be ever so careful not to do or say anything that would be displeasing to God."

The order spread through Italy, France, and eventually South America. Mother Mary fell ill in 1881. When she asked Don Bosco whether she would recover, he replied, "No; it is the office of a superior to lead, even in death." She died on May 14. Her last words were, "I will see you in Heaven."

She was canonized in 1951.

"Have love in your hearts but repress the tendency to appear devout."

—St. Mary Mazzarello

René Voillaume
Founder, Little Brothers of Jesus (1905–2003)

In 1901, Charles de Foucauld, a French soldier-turned-monk and hermit (now Blessed), settled in the Algerian desert to implement a new model of religious life. Inspired by Jesus' hidden life as a carpenter in Nazareth, he wished to form a fraternity of "Little Brothers" who would carry on a contemplative life among their poor neighbors. He attracted no followers and died alone in 1916. And yet his vision did not die. In 1921 a biography was published. Among its first readers was a French student, René Voillaume, at the time only sixteen. It changed his life.

In 1933, Voillaume, now a priest, and four companions put on the habit of Brother Charles and went to live in the oasis of El Abiodh Sidi Cheikh in Algeria. It was the genesis of the Little Brothers of Jesus. Voillaume and his brothers followed Foucauld's model in adapting to the religious spirit of their Muslim neighbors: "We were not going primarily to the desert but to encounter a population that we would take into our life, through our witness and our intercession."

He lived to see the spread of the Little Brothers into many countries, and the extension of Foucauld's vision in the Little Sisters and to a broader family nourished by the same spirit. Voillaume died on May 13, 2003.

"Little we are before the task we have to accomplish. Little we shall be in the eyes of men also. All our lives we shall remain unprofitable servants, and we must wish to be so dealt with."

—René Voillaume

St. Matthias
Apostle (First Century)

Upon the death of the treacherous Judas, St. Peter determined that another disciple should be chosen to complete the original company of twelve apostles. Criteria for selection were that the candidate should have been among the followers of Jesus and a witness of the risen Lord. By the casting of lots, the choice fell to Matthias. On Pentecost, along with the other apostles, he received the gifts of the Holy Spirit and went on, with zeal, to advance the Gospel.

Other than this brief account from the Acts of the Apostles, little is known of St. Matthias. Clement of Alexandria includes him among the seventy-two disciples sent in mission by Jesus. Other accounts, with scant authority, describe later mission work in Cappadocia, and even among cannibals in Ethiopia. According to legend, he was eventually crucified, though nothing certain is known of the circumstances of his death. His body was believed to rest in Jerusalem, from which his remains were said to be translated to Rome by St. Helen.

"Then they prayed, 'Lord, you know everyone's heart. Show us which of these two you have chosen to take over this apostolic ministry, which Judas left to go where he belongs.' Then they cast lots, and the lot fell to Matthias; so he was added to the eleven apostles."

—Acts 1:24-26

The Syrophoenician Mother
Woman of Faith (First Century)

In numerous occasions in the Gospels, Jesus confronts his uncomprehending disciples with the liberating implications of his message. But on at least one occasion, the challenge was reversed. The story of an unnamed Gentile woman, identified only by her Syrophoenician origins, recalls an instance in which it was Jesus himself who was challenged to act upon the universal spirit of the Gospel.

According to the account in Mark, this woman accosted Jesus in a private home, begging him to cast out a demon from her sick daughter. Surely she knew her action violated the codes of Jewish society. Jesus rebuffed her: "Let the children first be fed, for it is not right to take the children's bread and throw it to the dogs." Undeterred by this blunt reproval, she replied with a logic he could not resist: "Yes, Lord, yet even the dogs under the table eat the children's crumbs."

Apparently persuaded by her skillful riposte, Jesus complied with her request: "For this saying you may go your way; the demon has left your daughter."

This unnamed woman deserves to be remembered as one of the foremothers of the Gentile Church, one who intuited, even while Jesus lived, that his Gospel was for everyone. She also represents the countless faithful throughout history who, in overcoming the pressure to be silent, have challenged the Church to comprehend and act upon the liberating logic of salvation.

"But immediately a woman, whose little daughter was possessed by an unclean spirit, heard of him, and came and fell down at his feet."

—Mark 7:25

St. Isidore
Farmer (1070–1130)

In 1622 five great saints were canonized together. They included St. Ignatius of Loyola, St. Francis Xavier, St. Teresa of Avila, and St. Philip Neri. The fifth, St. Isidore, stood apart. He founded no order; he accomplished no great deeds (apart from tilling the land). He was, in fact, a simple farmworker, born in Madrid, who spent his entire working life in the service of the same wealthy landowner. With his good wife, Maria, he bore one son, who died in childhood. He knew the hardships, the toil, and sorrows of all farmworkers then and since. And he displayed the simple though profound faith so common to *campesinos* the world over. He attended Mass daily and prayed continuously as he worked the fields. In Isidore's case, however, his faith was attended by visible signs and wonders. It was reported, for example, that angels were seen assisting him as he plowed.

Isidore was famous for his generosity toward those even poorer than himself. His table was always open to the indigent, while he lived on the scraps left over. His kindness extended to animals. One winter day he was so moved by the sorrowful noise of some hungry birds that he opened the sack of corn he was carrying and poured out half its contents. Though witnesses scoffed at his prodigal gesture, later, at the mill, the bag was found miraculously to be full.

In the list of canonized saints, his type is surprisingly rare; in heaven, presumably, less so.

"Listen! A sower went out to sow . . ."
—Matthew 13:3

Peter Maurin
Cofounder of the Catholic Worker (1877–1949)

Peter Maurin was born in the ancient Languedoc region of southern France. One of twenty-three children in his peasant family, he was educated by the Christian Brothers and took in the atmosphere of French Catholic populism before emigrating to North America in 1909. For twenty years he tramped through America, performing various kinds of manual labor. All the while he was devising an intellectual synthesis in the area of Catholic social philosophy.

Maurin believed the problems of society came from the severing of social values from the Gospel. His program was a "personalist revolution," based on the idea that one should begin at once to live by a new set of values. Nevertheless, he found it hard to translate his ideas into actions on a scale larger than himself.

This changed in 1932 when he met Dorothy Day, a Catholic convert, who had been seeking a sign as to how to combine her religious faith and her commitment to social change. In this rough-hewn Frenchman, she believed she had found her answer.

The result was the Catholic Worker—a newspaper and a movement that combined hospitality and the works of mercy with a radical social message drawn from the Gospels. Their aim: to build "the kind of society where it would be easier to be good." Maurin lived to see his ideas put in action, but his active years were limited. Disabled by a stroke, he fell silent and died on May 15, 1949, at the age of seventy-two.

"Everybody would be what he ought to be, if everybody tried to be what he wants the other fellow to be."
—Peter Maurin

St. Brendan
Abbot (ca. 486–575)

Within a generation of St. Patrick (d. 461), the Church in Ireland was firmly established, marked by a fervent zeal for the monastic life. So numerous and large were these monasteries that they soon began overflowing their native country.

One of the most popular of these wandering monks was St. Brendan, the abbot of Clonfert. The chronicles claim that his community in western Ireland included three thousand monks. They also claim that his travels took him to Scotland and Wales. But there is no historical basis for the wonderful journeys described in *The Voyage of St. Brendan*, a hugely popular work composed in the ninth century. According to this narrative, Brendan set off in a skin-covered boat with a company of followers and traversed the Atlantic Ocean on a seven-year quest for the Isle of the Blessed. They were attended along the way by birds who brought them food and joined them in reciting the psalms. In the course of their voyage they also discovered many wonderful islands, including one that turned out to be the back of a whale.

Although the story is clearly fabulous, for many centuries devotees of St. Brendan argued that the tale of his voyage merely embellished an actual journey, and there are even champions of the claim that St. Brendan was the original discoverer of America.

St. Brendan is the patron of sailors, travelers, and whales.

"Righteous Thou art, O Lord, in all Thy ways, and holy in all Thy works, who hast revealed to Thy children so many and so great wonders."
— St. Brendan

Julian of Norwich
Mystic (1342–1416)

This extraordinary English mystic prayed in her youth that she might be granted three graces: recollection of Christ's passion; bodily sickness; and the spirit of contrition, compassion, and longing for God. At thirty her prayer was answered when she fell seriously ill. While gazing on a crucifix she experienced sixteen revelations concerning Christ's passion, after which her sickness left her.

In these revelations she vividly experienced Christ's passion. Though his sufferings were terrible, she perceived that they revealed the depth of God's intimate love for humanity. This vision yielded further reflections on a range of issues, including the value of creation, the power of atonement, and the impotence of evil. Though creation amounted to no more than a hazelnut in the hand of God, its value was measured by the price God paid for it in blood. And in the end God's suffering became our joy with the realization that we are "soul and body, clad and enclosed in the goodness of God."

Julian herself was enclosed in an anchorhold—a dwelling attached to the wall of the church in Norwich—that afforded her a safe space to compose her spiritual ruminations. Her writings, composed in vernacular English, are notable among other things for her feminine images of God. Jesus, she says, is our true Mother, who bears us in the womb of his love and nourishes us with his own flesh. Julian died in 1416. Her writings only became known in the twentieth century.

"The greatest honor we can give Almighty God is to live gladly because of the knowledge of his love."
—Julian of Norwich

Jeremiah
Prophet (Seventh–Sixth Century BC)

Jeremiah received his call to be a prophet around the year 625 BC. His career played out against the final years of the southern kingdom of Judah and continued for some time after the destruction of Jerusalem in 587 and the great exile to Babylon. His message was directed against the elite, the monarchy, the priests, and the official cult prophets who clung to the false assurance that nothing could happen to Judah so long as the Ark of the Covenant was safe in the Temple. Like other prophets before him, Jeremiah was sensitive to a deeper contradiction in the heart of Israel. The people had failed to comprehend that true faithfulness to God must be reflected in mercy and justice. To Jeremiah the chasm between the rich and poor of the land was a yawning gap in the covenant between the people and God. Under these circumstances the official cult had become a form of idolatry. Destruction was inevitable.

Jeremiah's message didn't win many friends. He was imprisoned, forced underground, and narrowly escaped death. Eventually his worst fears were realized with the destruction of the Temple, the burning of Jerusalem, and the exile of the surviving population to Babylon. At this point he felt free at last to speak tenderly of hope and consolation. Israel would survive. And he prophesied the coming of a new covenant—not written on tablets but upon hearts.

"My grief is beyond healing, my heart is sick within me . . . / For the wound of the daughter of my people is my heart wounded."

—Jeremiah 8:18

Emily Dickinson
Poet (1830–1886)

Emily Dickinson was born in Amherst, Massachusetts. Though she studied at Amherst Academy in her youth and later spent a brief period at Mount Holyoke, at a certain point she effectively withdrew to her home and adopted the life of a recluse, hermit, or "stationary pilgrim." To her neighbors she was simply an eccentric, famous for her seclusion and for her habit of dressing only in white. She avoided church services: "Some keep the Sabbath going to Church / I keep it, staying at home / With a Bobolink for a Chorister / And an Orchard, for a dome."

After her death in 1886 her family discovered a collection of poems—1,775 in all—carefully organized in notebooks. She had shared them with only a few friends. They would secure her reputation as one of the most significant figures in American literature.

Though deceptively simple, her poems reflected a complex and deeply personal approach to the world. A great number addressed her effort to define her relationship with God—not according to the doctrines of Puritan religion but on her own terms, wavering frequently between doubt and faith. The natural world, carefully observed, served as a harbor, opening up to speculative musings on death and eternity.

The loss of friends and family, the vast bloody backdrop of the Civil War, all provided a sweeping panorama, surveyed from the seclusion of her room: "This is my letter to the World / That never wrote to me."

She died on May 15, 1886.

"God preaches, a noted Clergyman / And the sermon is never long. / So instead of getting to Heaven, at last, / I'm going, all along."

—Emily Dickinson

St. Dymphna
Martyr (d. ca. 650)

According to legend, Dymphna was the daughter of a pagan Irish king and a Christian princess, who, before her untimely death, passed along her faith to her young daughter. As Dymphna matured, the king, noticing that she bore a close resemblance to his departed wife, conceived an unnatural obsession with the girl. When he proposed that Dymphna should become his bride, she fled the court with a small retinue, including her confessor. Landing in Belgium, they made their way to Gheel, where they lived as hermits and tried to avoid attention.

In the meantime, the king's desire had turned to rage. He tracked down the refugees and insisted that Dymphna accompany him home. When she refused his advances, he struck her dead. She was mourned by the local people, whose love she had earned by her care for the poor and the sick.

In the thirteenth century, a sarcophagus in Gheel was found to contain the remains of St. Dymphna. This occasion was accompanied, it is said, by the miraculous healing of many local epileptics and others suffering from mental disturbances. From that time on Gheel became a refuge and center for the humane treatment of the mentally ill, and St. Dymphna was invoked as their patron. Her feast day is May 15.

"O God, we humbly beseech You through Your servant,
St. Dymphna, who sealed with her blood the love she bore You,
to grant relief to those who suffer from mental afflictions and
nervous disorders."
—Prayer to St. Dymphna

Larry Rosebaugh
Oblate Priest (1935–2009)

Fr. Larry Rosebaugh spent his life among people on the margins, those most vulnerable to the violence of the world. It was thus not surprising that this violence should eventually claim him. While driving in Guatemala with other priests on May 18, 2009, he was shot and killed by masked gunmen.

Rosebaugh was eulogized as a combination of John the Baptist and Francis of Assisi. Raised in Milwaukee, he was ordained in the Missionary Oblates of Mary Immaculate. Early on, his mission took an unusual turn: twenty months in prison for his role in destroying draft files with the "Milwaukee 14" in protest of the Vietnam War. Afterward he took up ministry among the homeless, living on the streets, scrounging in dumpsters for his daily bread. With his unkempt hair and long beard he was scarcely distinguishable from those he served. In 1975, while working with street people in Recife, Brazil, he was again arrested and subjected to brutal treatment. Yet another prison term came when he trespassed at Fort Benning to broadcast tapes of Archbishop Romero to Salvadoran troops who were training there.

In his last years he was working in Guatemala with young people battling AIDS, when his superiors told him it was time to come home to retire. He never made it.

"As I hit the road I realize that I have never really known what it is to be totally without. There is a faith dependency about which I do not know much at this point, but if two or three persons were called to such a life of poverty correctly understood, of prayer, and of quiet: WOW!"
—Fr. Larry Rosebaugh

St. Alcuin
Abbot (ca. 730–804)

Alcuin, who was born in Northumbria, studied at the cathedral church of York—at the time, a great center of learning. He excelled in scholarship, was ordained a deacon, and eventually became head of the school. While on a mission to Rome in 782 he met Charlemagne and was persuaded to join his court. There he became first among an illustrious circle of scholars, instructing both the king and his sons in the liberal arts, including Latin, poetry, mathematics, and grammar. (For what it is worth, Alcuin is credited with inventing an early form of the question mark.) He wrote numerous theological treatises, biblical commentaries, and hundreds of letters, which still survive.

As an advisor to the king, Alcuin exerted wide influence. He successfully exhorted Charlemagne to end his policy of forcing pagans to accept baptism under the threat of death, noting, "Faith is a free act of the will, not a forced act. We must appeal to the conscience, not compel it by violence. You can force people to be baptized, but you cannot force them to believe."

Alcuin spent the last ten years of his life as abbot of Marmoutier Abbey in Tours. There he wrote, "In the morning, I sowed the seed in Britain, now in the evening I am still sowing in France, hoping both will grow, by the grace of God, giving some the honey of the holy scriptures, making others drunk on the old wine of ancient learning. . . ." He died on May 19, 804.

"Remember to care for the soul more than the body, since the former remains, the latter perishes."
—St. Alcuin

St. Celestine V
Pope (ca. 1209–1296)

In April 2009 Pope Benedict XVI prayed in Aquila at the grave of Pope Celestine V, the last pope to resign his office. In a gesture that later took on greater significance, he left there his pallium, the woolen cloak he had worn at his own papal inauguration.

The reign of Pietro di Morone as Celestine V lasted only five months. An eighty-four-year-old hermit, he had been elected by a bitterly divided conclave after the papal throne lay vacant for two years. When Pietro threatened the cardinals with the wrath of God, they elected Pietro himself. He accepted the charge and arrived in Aquila riding on a donkey.

News of the selection of this holy man inspired wild enthusiasm. Some saw this as inaugurating a new age of the Holy Spirit. Others sought to manipulate the unworldly pope into favoring their interests. Bewildered by the affairs of the papal court, Celestine soon became convinced that his piety was no match for the duties of the papacy. He abdicated his office and returned to his monastic community.

His successor, Boniface VIII, a man whose character contrasted in every sense with his predecessor, feared the influence of the still-popular Celestine. He had the former pontiff arrested and imprisoned in a fortress, where, after ten months, he died on May 19, 1296. He was canonized in 1313.

Celestine's story attracted renewed interest in February 2013 when Pope Benedict announced his intention to resign.

"I wanted nothing in the world but a cell, and a cell they have given me."
—St. Celestine V

Blessed Columba of Rieti
Dominican Tertiary (1467–1501)

The life of Columba was marked by many wondrous signs. Her name itself derived from the story that a dove alighted on her head during baptism. By the time she was ten she had privately dedicated herself to God and cut off her hair to thwart any intended betrothal. At nineteen she took vows as a Dominican tertiary. She enjoyed visions of Saints Dominic and Catherine of Siena and once offered a detailed account of a spiritual pilgrimage to the Holy Land.

Such reports inspired a growing cult. To escape the attention, Columba quietly slipped away from home and made her way to Perugia. But fame had preceded her, and the city went out of its way to extend a lavish welcome, even providing her with her own convent, where she gathered other Dominican tertiaries.

When Pope Alexander VI, on a visit to Perugia, asked to meet her, she delivered secret admonitions, which were not to be revealed. She refused, however, to meet with the pope's daughter, the notorious Lucrezia Borgia, who became her bitter enemy. Despite Lucrezia's efforts to foment persecution against Columba with charges of sorcery, the city remained loyal to their local saint. As Columba lay dying at the age of thirty-four she exhorted the city fathers to practice charity and justice toward the poor. All of Perugia mourned her passing.

"No sister dead to grace can remain in a convent; for either she will repent of her sins, or she will be cast out on the cold shores of the world, or, of her own free will, she will leave the blessed retreat of the cloister."

—Blessed Columba of Rieti

St. Toribio Romo González
Priest and Martyr (1900–1928)

Toribio Romo González, a young Mexican priest, was among twenty-five martyrs of the Cristero Rebellion canonized by Pope John Paul II in 2000 with a feast day on May 21. The rebellion, which cost thousands of lives, was set off in 1926 in response to the enforcement of anticlerical laws that severely restricted practice of the Catholic faith. The rebels, who called themselves Cristeros, fought under the slogan "*Viva Cristo Rey!*"—Long Live Christ the King!

Fr. Toribio had no part in the violence. He had, however, experienced the rising tide of persecution, confined to his sacristy in Jalisco, unable to celebrate Mass in public. In the early morning of February 25, 1928, soldiers burst into his bedroom and shot him. He died in the arms of his sister, who cried out, "Courage, Father Toribio . . . merciful Christ, receive him! Long live Christ the King!"

In recent years, Fr. Toribio has become the object of a growing cult as patron of Mexicans struggling to cross the U.S. border. His grave in Jalisco has become a popular pilgrimage site, nourished by the reports of migrants who claim that a mysterious priest called Toribio Romo rescued them in the desert. Many of those who undertake the perilous journey now invoke his prayers and carry his image.

"Father Toribio's philosophy was that hunger knows no border. That's why many migrants come here and pray to him. They're putting their faith and lives in his hands."

—Rev. Gabriel González Pérez, parish priest
at the shrine of San Toribio

Blessed Franz Jägerstätter
Conscientious Objector and Martyr (1907–1943)

Franz Jägerstätter, an Austrian peasant and devout Catholic, was executed for refusing to serve in the German army. Known in his village of St. Radegund as a man of honesty and principle, devoted to his family and his faith, he was also known as a fervent opponent of the Nazis. Nevertheless, his singular act of resistance came as a surprise.

In 1943, when served with an induction notice, Franz turned himself in and announced his refusal to take a military oath. Before taking this stand he had sought counsel from his parish priest and the local bishop. They had advised him to do his duty and serve his Fatherland. But Franz believed the Nazis were a satanic movement and that any compromise represented a mortal sin.

In prison he spurned ongoing appeals to save himself, convinced that he could not prolong his life at the price of his immortal soul. Franz was beheaded on August 9, 1943. For years his story was little known beyond his family and fellow villagers. In time, however, the story of his solitary witness spread, and he was recognized as a heroic witness to conscience. His beatification in 2007 was attended by his widow and surviving children. His feast day is May 21.

"Not everything which this world considers a crime is a crime in the eyes of God. I have hope that I need not fear the stern Judge because of this crime."
—Blessed Franz Jägerstätter

Christian de Chergé and Companions
Trappist Martyrs of Algeria (d. 1996)

On May 23, 1996, Islamic fundamentalists in Algeria glee-fully announced the murder of seven Trappist monks. In their deaths these monks joined a long procession of past victims—both Christian and Muslim—sacrificed to competing conceptions of the glory of God. Many Christian martyrs of the past had offered their lives for the conversion of their non-Christian neighbors. Not so these Trappists, who sought to bear witness to the One God of all and to the ideal of friendship among all God's people.

For Fr. de Chergé, prior of the community, this cause was the repayment of an ancient debt. As a young French soldier fighting in Algeria, his life had been saved by a Muslim friend who shielded him during an ambush at the cost of his own life. This sacrifice prompted his own conversion, and ultimately his decision to become a Trappist monk in the highlands near Algiers.

There the monks lived a traditional life. But they made a point of offering a place where Christians and Muslims could pray together. To many neighbors they were trusted men of God. But to others they were foreign infidels. Eventually rebels invaded the monastery and marched them into the mountains. In a letter opened after his death, de Chergé had addressed his future murderer: "You too, my last-minute friend, you who know not what you do. . . . May we be granted to meet each other again, happy thieves, in paradise, should it please God, the Father of both of us."

"The only way for us to give witness is . . . to be what we are in the midst of banal, everyday realities."

—Fr. Christian de Chergé

The Baal Shem Tov
Founder of Hassidism (ca. 1700–1760)

The Baal Shem Tov—"Master of the Good Name"—was the title given to Rabbi Israel ben Eliezer of Mezbizk, founder of Hassidic Judaism. Rather than providing a set of teachings, the Baal Shem Tov—or the Besht, as his name is abbreviated—communicated his lessons through a certain attitude, a spirit of joy, an instinct for the holiness of existence, that would inspire a following far beyond the Hasidim, or "pious ones," as his followers came to be called.

The Besht was born in a small town in the Ukraine, a region steeped in pogroms and the birthplace of a number of messianic movements. After an uneventful early life, he began to travel the region, performing wonders and proclaiming a mysticism of the everyday. Within each task and moment, he taught, there was a spark of the divine. Our responsibility was to discover and fulfill the potential holiness embedded in our ordinary existence. He spoke of prayer as a window to heaven and called the entire world a prayer house.

The Hassidic community in Eastern Europe was largely decimated by the Nazis. But vibrant communities in the United States and Israel continue to live out the joyful and compassionate vision of the Baal Shem Tov. As he lay dying, on May 22, 1760, he said, "I am not worried at all for I know that I am leaving through one door and entering through another door."

"Whenever feeling downcast, each person should vitally remember, 'For my sake, the entire world was created.'"

—The Baal Shem Tov

St. Joachima de Vedruna
Founder, Carmelites of Charity (1783–1854)

St. Joachima was born to an aristocratic family in Catalonia. At sixteen she married a young lawyer from Barcelona whom she had met at her sister's wedding. Each of them had privately considered religious life, and soon after their marriage they both confided fears that they had missed their true vocations. They consoled themselves with the promise that if they still felt the same way after raising a family, they would each enter religious life.

Joachima and her husband went on to have nine children. Their married life was not without sufferings, including the death of two children and the need to flee before the invasion of Napoleon. But overall it was a happy life, and Joachima felt blessed. When her husband died, Joachima, then thirty-three, adopted a life of penance and mourning. After seven years, however, she felt the time had come to keep her resolution. Though she wished to join a contemplative order, her confessor persuaded her instead to found a new order, the Carmelites of Charity, dedicated to nursing the sick.

Joachima pursued this plan, eventually establishing hospitals throughout Catalonia. Two of her daughters wished to join the congregation, but she dissuaded them: "What sacrifice will you be offering to your bridegroom [Jesus Christ], if you stay with your mother?"

She died of cholera on August 28, 1854. She was canonized in 1959, with a feast on May 19.

"Joachima, your spouse on earth has died. Now I have chosen you to be my bride."

—The voice of Christ, according to St. Joachima de Vedruna

Girolamo Savonarola
Dominican Reformer (1452–1498)

Savonarola was a Dominican preacher who gained a wide following in Florence in the late fifteenth century as a result of his fiery sermons. Strongly influenced by prophetic and apocalyptic texts of the Bible, his sermons combined a strong moral appeal with sweeping condemnations of social injustice and religious corruption. Savonarola prophesied that God's judgment on Italy was at hand—a prediction that seemed to be fulfilled in 1494 when the French army closed in and laid siege to Florence.

While Savonarola successfully negotiated the surrender of the city, a popular uprising overthrew the ruling Medici family. Florence declared itself a republic. During the following year Savonarola's sermons became the guiding light of a remarkable experiment in social reform. He hoped the city would become "the watchtower of Italy." As his vision drew energy, he felt increasingly free to direct his criticism at the papal curia and the scandalous conduct of Pope Alexander VI, who epitomized the corruption of the Renaissance papacy. The pope, in turn, responded by ordering him to Rome. When he refused he was excommunicated.

By this time the rulers of Florence had tired of him as well. He was arrested and tortured. On May 23, 1498, along with two other friars, he was hanged and burned in the public square, maintaining until the end his faith in Christ and the justice of his cause.

"I want no cardinal's hats, no miters great or small. I only want the one You, O Lord, gave to your saints, death. A red hat, a hat of blood, that is what I want."

—Girolamo Savonarola

Servant of God Emil Kapaun
Chaplain (1916–1951)

Army chaplain Emil Kapaun, a priest from Wichita, Kansas, shipped out to Korea in July 1950, soon after the outbreak of war, along with the Eighth Cavalry Division, Third Battalion. From the moment he arrived he shared every danger with the troops, often rescuing wounded soldiers under fire and taking his turn digging latrines.

On November 2 the Eighth Cavalry was overrun by Chinese troops near the Yalu River. As they fought their way into retreat, Kapaun along with an army doctor volunteered to remain behind with the wounded, allowing themselves to be captured. At great risk, he intervened when their captors prepared to execute the prisoners. Instead they were marched eighty-seven miles to a North Korean prison camp.

In the camp the prisoners endured freezing cold, subsisting on starvation rations. Kapaun devoted himself to raising morale. He was also adept at scrounging or stealing contraband—serving up hot water with a few beans or grains of millet, likely saved from his own rations, and calling out, "Hot coffee!"

Much of his time was spent ministering to the sick and dying. Eventually Chaplain Kapaun, skeletally thin, his feet frozen, suffering from dysentery and pneumonia, was among them. Sometime in May 1951 the guards carried him to an empty shelter called "the hospital," where he died on May 23.

In 1993 his cause for canonization was accepted by the Vatican. In 2013 Kapaun, already the most decorated chaplain in U.S. history, received the Medal of Honor.

"Oh God, we ask of thee to give us the courage to be ever faithful."

—Servant of God Emil Kapaun

St. Joanna the Myrrhbearer
Witness to the Resurrection (First Century)

Joanna is named in the Gospel of Luke along with other women who had been healed of evil spirits and infirmities and now followed Jesus and his other disciples, providing for them "out of their means." A clue to the evil spirit from whom Joanna was rescued may lie in the remarkable information that she was "the wife of Chuza, Herod's steward." In other words, among Jesus' inner circle was the wife of a man who served at the right hand of Herod, the despot who had killed John the Baptist and who would later conspire in the death of Jesus himself. What a story is concealed in this casual reference!

But her story doesn't end there. She was surely among "the women who had followed him from Galilee," who "stood at a distance" and watched Jesus die on a cross, and who later returned to the site of his burial with "spices and ointments" to anoint his mangled body. Joanna is named among these "myrrhbearers" who found the empty tomb attended by angels who proclaimed that he had risen. Though they had borne faithful witness to Jesus, both in his life and in his passion, they were but women, and so their testimony was initially dismissed as "nonsense."

"Some of those who were with us went to the tomb, and found it just as the women had said."
—Luke 24:24

Venerable Maria of Jesus of Agreda
Abbess and Mystic (1602–1665)

aria of Jesus spent her entire life within the confines of her family castle in Agreda, Spain, which her mother—when Maria was twelve—had converted into a convent for herself and her daughters. In this Franciscan Convent of the Immaculate Conception of Agreda, Maria eventually served as abbess, renowned for her mystical writings and her ardor in prayer.

And yet, in the spiritual realm, she was anything but a stay-at-home nun. In her early twenties, she found herself repeatedly transported in prayer to the Indian settlements in New Spain, particularly to a tribe of hunter-gatherers called the Jumanos in present-day New Mexico. In the course of what she reckoned were five hundred trips she was able to communicate with the Indians in their own language, instructing them in the faith and urging them to seek baptism. This remarkable story gained credence when friars in New Spain encountered just such a tribe who requested baptism and claimed they had met frequently with a Lady in Blue (just like Maria).

These reports were taken seriously enough to justify a trip to Agreda by the Franciscan Superior for New Mexico. Maria was also subjected to two inquiries by the Inquisition, resulting in no action. (Her defenders included King Philip IV of Spain.)

She died on May 24, 1665. Ten years later she was declared venerable by Pope Clement X.

"My heart never delighted in earthly things, for they did not fill the emptiness in my spirit. For this reason, the world died for me in my youngest years, before I really came to know it."

—Venerable Maria of Jesus of Agreda

St. Mary Magdalene de' Pazzi
Mystic (1566–1607)

St. Mary Magdalene, born to one of the wealthiest families in Florence, entered the Carmelite convent at sixteen. Two years later she fell desperately ill. As she was carried into the chapel, she experienced a sense of deep ecstasy, which she described as union with the Holy Trinity. After this, she said that "Jesus, caressing me gently like a newly-wed, united me to him and hid me in his side, where I tasted sweet repose. The Lord then seemed to take away from me my will and all my desires, so that I can no longer wish or desire anything except what he wills."

Over time Mary received many such mystical experiences, some ecstatic and others accompanied by deep suffering. She witnessed the passion of Christ, exchanged hearts with Jesus, received the stigmata (the marks of Christ's passion), and felt his crown of thorns. Along with such experiences of intimacy with Christ, she also endured years of desolation and despair—at times so great that she was tempted by thoughts of suicide. While subsisting (except on Sundays) on nothing but bread and water, she constantly felt the assault of temptations to gluttony and impurity.

In the end, her sufferings only united her more deeply to Christ. "God does not germinate in sad souls," she said. "He wants a heart that is free and happy." She died on May 25, 1607.

"Those who call to mind the sufferings of Christ and who offer up their own to God through His passion find their pains sweet and pleasant."
—St. Mary Magdalene de' Pazzi

St. Madeleine Sophie Barat
Founder, Society of the Sacred Heart (1779–1865)

Madeleine Sophie Barat was born in a small town in Burgundy. In those days, following the French Revolution and the suppression of religious orders, Catholic education in France had virtually ceased. Madeleine's older brother Louis, a onetime seminarian, took over her education, schooling her not only in the classics but also biblical studies, Church history, and theology—a typical seminary program. Fortunately, she took happily to this strict regime. Later, she told her spiritual director that she wished to become a Carmelite, but he informed her that her true vocation was otherwise: to found an order dedicated to the education of young girls.

In 1801, with two other young women, Madeleine opened a small school in Amiens. The work grew, and from these seeds emerged the Society of the Sacred Heart. Though only 23, Madeleine became the first superior—an office she would occupy for 62 years.

Mother Madeleine spent much of her life traveling. She established an astonishing 111 houses, operating in 12 countries in Europe and North America. By the time of her death in 1865 there were nearly 4,000 members of the Society. While she played an enormous role in the resurgence of Catholicism in France, her contribution to the education of young women and their role in society was beyond reckoning. She was canonized in 1925.

"There is room for all in that wide wound in the Heart of Jesus, but its secret depths are for the little and lowly ones."

—St. Madeleine Sophie Barat

St. Bede the Venerable
Doctor of the Church (673–735)

St. Bede was a true product of the monastery. At the age of seven he was entrusted by his parents to a local abbot who saw to his education and upbringing. Later he transferred to the nearby monastery at Jarrow, where he remained for the rest of his days. He rarely emerged from his monastery and probably never traveled beyond his native Northumbria. And yet, from his obscure monastic perch, he took the measure of his world to an extraordinary degree.

Bede's passion for study and writing was his path to sanctity. He is especially remembered for his *History of the English Church and People*. Rather than simply recording names and events, Bede tried to compose a coherent narrative encompassing the arrival of Christianity in the British Isles, the progress of its great early saints and missionaries, and the gradual role of Christianity in pulling together the disparate tribes and races of Britain into a unified nation. Just as Luke's Acts of the Apostles related the movement of the Church from Jerusalem to Rome, so Bede continued the story from Rome to his own "fair and pleasant land." He believed that it was not only in Scripture but in the history of his own people and the stories of holy lives that the handwriting of God could be discerned.

In 735 Bede fell seriously ill. While dictating the final passages of his English translation of the Gospel of John, he expired on May 26, 735. His feast is May 25.

"I have devoted my energies to the study of the scriptures, observing monastic discipline, and singing the daily services in church; study, teaching, and writing have always been my delight."

—St. Bede

St. Philip Neri
Founder, Congregation of the Oratory (1515–1595)

Philip Neri was born in Florence in 1515. After experiencing a dramatic conversion, he spurned worldly success and set off for Rome, with no special plan aside from a general desire to serve God. The once-proud city had fallen into a state of moral and spiritual disrepair. An era of corrupt and worldly Renaissance popes had fostered a general apathy, if not cynicism, regarding the Christian message. In this atmosphere, Neri conceived his vocation: nothing less than the re-evangelization of Rome.

He began simply by standing on street corners and striking up conversations with passersby. In every conversation he introduced the topic of religion and inquired about the state of his new friend's soul. Such conversations often continued during a walk to a local church or to a hospital to visit the sick. Before long Neri's circle of friends and his reputation had spread, and all types of people sought his company.

In 1551 he became a priest. He would invite mixed groups of clergy and laymen to his quarters for prayer and spiritual reflection. They called themselves Oratorians, which ultimately became the name of a new congregation. Even while he lived, Neri was widely revered as a saint, if not the spiritual heart of Rome. His influence was remarkable, given that he wrote no books and proposed no original theology. He simply radiated a spirit of joy and holiness and so elevated the spiritual level of his time. He died on May 26, 1595.

"Let me get through today, and I shall not fear tomorrow."

—St. Philip Neri

St. Augustine of Canterbury
Missionary Bishop (ca. 604)

St. Augustine was the leader of a party of forty monks commissioned by Pope St. Gregory the Great to bring Christianity to Britain. Their mission nearly faltered before the band had departed France. Frightened by reports of the ferocity of the English, Augustine appealed to Gregory for permission to withdraw. The pope exhorted them to continue: "My very dear sons, it is better never to undertake any high enterprise than to abandon it when once begun. So with the help of God you must carry out this holy task. . . . I hope to share in your joyful reward."

Augustine continued to write back for instructions. Among his questions: What exactly are the functions of a bishop? What punishment should be awarded to those who rob churches? Is it permissible for two brothers to marry two sisters? On such matters as these, Augustine wrote, "These uncouth English require guidance."

Despite his fears and uncertainties, Augustine's mission proved a success. He converted King Ethelbert of Kent and with him his subjects. Within seven years of his arrival he had established three dioceses, including the cathedral see at Canterbury, where he was buried upon his death in 604.

"Pray in the spirit and sentiment of love, in which the royal prophet said to Him, 'Thou, O Lord, are my portion.' Let others choose to themselves portions among creatures, for my part, You are my portion, You alone I have chosen for my whole inheritance."

—St. Augustine of Canterbury

St. Melangell of Wales
Abbess (Seventh Century)

According to legend, Melangell was the daughter of an Irish king who wished her to marry. As Melangell had already bound herself by a vow to God, she chose instead to flee to Powys, a remote part of Wales, where she remained in seclusion for fifteen years. There one day in a forest clearing she was discovered in prayer by the local prince. His hunting hounds had pursued a hare, which deftly took shelter in Melangell's robes. When the prince asked Melangell to explain herself, she related her story. So moved was the prince that he offered her the land on which they stood as a "perpetual asylum and refuge"—not just for hares but for all who might flee harm.

There Melangell lived out the rest of her life, eventually attracting a community, for whom she served as abbess. The legend relates that this site did indeed become a haven for hares, who gathered without fear, along with many pilgrims drawn to the shrine of St. Melangell.

"I perceive that thou art the handmaiden of the true God. Because it hath pleased Him for thy merits to give protection to this little wild hare . . . I give and present to thee these my lands for the service of God, to be a perpetual asylum and refuge. If any men or women flee hither to seek thy protection . . . let no prince or chieftain be so rash towards God as to attempt to drag them forth."

—Prince of Powys to St. Melangell

St. Mariana of Quito
Franciscan Tertiary (1618–1645)

Mariana de Paredes, the patron saint of Ecuador, was born in Quito to aristocratic parents. As a child she dreamed of joining a convent, or even to carry the Gospel to Japan. But after her parents died she moved in with her sister and brother-in-law, and there, under the direction of a Jesuit confessor, spent the rest of her life. Upon receiving the habit of a Franciscan tertiary she took the name Mariana of Jesus.

It is painful to read of the austerities she imposed on herself: extreme fasting, long vigils, and a crown of thorns. As a reminder of death, she spent each Friday night sleeping in a coffin. In exchange for these sacrifices, she received many spiritual favors, including the gift of prophecy and the power to effect miraculous healings.

In 1645 Quito was struck by a series of earthquakes, followed by a terrible epidemic, which claimed over 1,400 lives. When a preacher proclaimed that these sufferings were a result of the people's sins, Mariana publicly offered herself as a victim. Immediately the earthquakes ceased. But Maria fell mortally ill and died on May 26, 1645, at the age of twenty-six. Hailed as the savior of her city, she was mourned by all of Quito. She was canonized in 1950.

"We are dealing with one who is, in a certain sense, like the final phrase of a symphony, which gathers up all of the themes, taking from each one something characteristic, to put together the marvelous harmony of spirit."

—Pope Pius XII

Marc Sangnier
Founder of the Sillon Movement (1873–1950)

Marc Sangnier, who was born in France to a wealthy family, determined from an early age to apply his faith to the social problems of his day. With fellow Catholic students he formed a study circle to examine social reality in the light of Catholic teaching. Entering the world of the workers, they sought to establish personal contacts and friendships. These efforts found encouragement in *Rerum Novarum*, the first great social encyclical by Pope Leo XIII in 1891.

In a newspaper called *Le Sillon* ("The Furrow"), founded in 1894, Sangnier tried to reconcile the principles of Catholicism with democracy and social justice. This became the foundation for a lay movement of the same name that attracted thousands of idealistic youth. Sangnier conceived of the movement as a kind of leaven to elevate the spiritual and social consciousness of French society.

Many of the bishops supported this endeavor. But with its growth came growing opposition. Conservative "integralists" charged that Sangnier wanted to introduce democracy even into the Church. In 1910 they successfully pressed Pope Pius X to condemn the movement.

Afterward, many of Sangnier's supporters urged him to defy the pope. But he obediently complied with the Vatican decree, believing this sacrifice was the best means to "serve the cause to which I have devoted my life . . . to give to the Republic a moral inspiration and to the democracy a Christian spirit."

Sangnier never again achieved social prominence. He died on May 28, 1950.

"The truth must be sought with all one's soul. . . . Love is stronger than hate."
—Marc Sangnier

Noah
A Righteous Man

The story of Noah and his ark requires no rehearsal. The charming spectacle of the animals proceeding two by two is one of the most beloved images from Scripture. It nearly overshadows the grislier aspect of the story: God's determination, on account of human wickedness, to "make an end of all flesh" on earth.

Among other things, Noah signifies the importance of the holy remnant. One does not "walk with God" for oneself alone. The call to righteousness carries with it a responsibility for the entire globe and its inhabitants. Thus, Noah represents an ethic and spirituality concerned with the preservation of the earth and the survival of endangered species and cultures; he might well serve as a patron of ecological stewardship.

Through Noah's faithfulness God makes an unconditional covenant with every living creature: "Never again shall all flesh be cut off by the waters of a flood . . ." This is a universal covenant that precedes the specific covenants with Abraham and Moses.

But the fact that God has vowed never to destroy the earth by means of flood offers no grounds for complacency. Today the earth is threatened, as never before, by human wickedness, greed, and carelessness. The challenge for Noah's descendants is not "survivalism" but defense of our common planet and its delicate ecology. If the earth becomes uninhabitable there will be no other lifeboats.

"Although 'the wickedness of man was great in the earth' (Gen 5) . . . nonetheless, through Noah . . . God decided to open a path of salvation. In this way he gave humanity the chance of a new beginning. All it takes is one good person to restore hope!"

—Pope Francis, *Laudato Si'*

St. Ursula Ledóchowska
Founder, Grey Ursulines (1865–1939)

Julia Ledóchowska was born into a remarkable Polish family. Her younger brother became provincial superior of the Jesuits in Poland, while a younger sister, founder of the Sodality of St. Peter Claver, was beatified in 1975. In 1886 Julia entered the Ursuline Order and assumed the religious name of the order's patron saint. She spent the next twenty-one years in the convent in Krakow. In 1907 she was among several sisters sent to St. Petersburg to run a boarding school for girls. From there, after the outbreak of World War I, she moved to Stockholm and Denmark, where she established a school for girls and helped with war refugees.

With the establishment of an independent Polish republic she and her sisters returned to Poland. There, with support from Rome, she established a separate Ursuline congregation known as the Grey Ursulines, who combined education with work among the poor. By the time of her death on May 29, 1939, she had become an important figure in the religious and cultural life of her country. In his homily at her canonization in 2003, Pope John Paul II hailed her as "an apostle of the new evangelization, demonstrating a constant timeliness, creativity, and the effectiveness of gospel love by her life and action. . . . From her we can learn how to put into practice every day the 'new' commandment of love."

"It is not enough to pray, 'Thy Kingdom come,' but to work, so that the Kingdom of God will exist among us today."

—St. Ursula Ledóchowska

St. Joan of Arc
Maid of Orleans (ca. 1412–1431)

Joan was a young peasant girl in southern France when she claimed to hear voices from a host of saints and angels. They charged her with a mission to save France by restoring the Dauphin to his rightful throne and driving the English enemy from French soil. So desperate was the Dauphin that he agreed to place her in command of his faltering army. She then inspired the French to a string of victories, paving the way for the crowning of the Dauphin as King of France.

But then fortune turned. Joan was captured by Burgundians who sold her to their English allies. After being imprisoned for a year she was tried and convicted by an ecclesiastical court on charges of witchcraft and heresy. On May 30, 1431, at the age of nineteen, she was burned at the stake. But soon her rehabilitation began. In 1456 an ecclesiastical investigation absolved her of all blame. She was canonized in 1920.

Joan of Arc is one of the most attractive and intriguing heroines of history—exemplar of an unusual brand of political holiness. Among canonized saints she enjoys the unique distinction of having been previously condemned by the Church and executed as a heretic. Thus, she may legitimately serve not only as a patron of France but of all those holy souls vilified in their own time in the hope of eventual vindication.

"If I am not, may God put me there; and if I am, may God so keep me."

—Joan of Arc, asked by the court if she was in a state of grace

Cardinal Emmanuel Suhard
Archbishop of Paris (1874–1949)

I n Paris in the 1940s a group of idealistic priests embarked on a new field of mission. Like traditional missionaries, they wished to implant the Gospel in a "foreign land"—though in this case in the midst of "Catholic" France. Leaving the Catholic ghetto, they entered the world of the working class, for so long estranged from the Church. Swapping their soutanes for overalls, they applied for factory jobs, and so began the extraordinary, though short-lived experiment of the Worker Priests.

The inspiration lay largely with Emmanuel Suhard, who was named archbishop of Paris in 1940, just before the German invasion. Initially a supporter of the Vichy government of Marshall Petain, Suhard in 1942 issued a loud protest against the deportation of Jews from Paris and broke with Vichy over its collaboration with the Nazis' racial policies.

The experience of the war had convinced him that the Church needed a new form of evangelization; rather than simply defending itself like a fortress against the inroads of secularism, the Church must go into the highways and byways to meet the world on its own terms. Suhard died on May 30, 1949. The worker-priest movement had many critics, and it was eventually suppressed. But Suhard's vision helped pave the way for a new spirit of evangelization in Vatican II.

"To be a witness does not consist in engaging in propaganda, nor even in stirring people up, but in being a living mystery. It means to live in such a way that one's life would not make sense if God did not exist."
—Cardinal Emmanuel Suhard

Saints Mary and Elizabeth
(First Century)

Today's feast of the Visitation does not commemorate one saint but a meeting between two pregnant saints: Mary, the Mother of Jesus, and her kinswoman Elizabeth, mother of John the Baptist. According to Luke, it was Mary who took the initiative for this "visitation." From the angel who announced her own miraculous conception, Mary had learned that Elizabeth—"she who was called barren"—had also conceived a son "in her old age." The story suggests that Elizabeth's miraculous conception was a kind of guarantee of the promise made to Mary: "For with God nothing will be impossible."

When Elizabeth hears Mary's greeting she feels the babe in her womb leap for joy and exclaims, "Blessed are you among women." Mary responds with an extraordinary prayer, acknowledging her own part in the unfolding of God's promises, especially as these relate to the poor and oppressed: "My soul magnifies the Lord. . . . for he has regarded the lowliness of his handmaiden. . . . He has filled the hungry with good things and the rich he has sent empty away."

In this remarkable vision the favor of God to two humble women is seen to presage a thoroughgoing process of social reversal. The joy of their encounter is unclouded by any foreshadowing that the kind of vision evinced in Mary's prayer will one day lead to the death of these two leaping babes. For now the feast of the Visitation remembers only the joy and celebrates the sisterhood of two women joined by faith in the God of the Impossible.

"In those days Mary arose and went with haste into the hill country. . ."
—Luke 1:39

St. Baptista Varano
Poor Clare (1458–1524)

Camilla Varano was the daughter of a powerful Italian prince and his mistress. Raised by her father and his wife, she was groomed for a life in the highest circles of society. For many years she embraced this world of "music, dancing, dress, and other worldly amusements." She could "not bear" the sight of monks or nuns. Then one day she heard a sermon that hit her like a thunderbolt. In response to prayer she received the gift of "three lilies": hatred of the world, a sense of unworthiness, and a willingness to suffer. Gradually she found herself attracted to religious life.

Her father did everything he could to thwart her vocation—even to the point of locking her up. But after two years, when she was twenty-three, he relented and allowed her to enter the Poor Clares, where she took the name Baptista. She likened the experience to crossing the Red Sea to escape from slavery under Pharaoh.

In the newfound freedom of the cloister, Baptista began to experience vivid mystical visions, including colloquies with St. Clare. In another case two winged angels held her aloft to contemplate the bleeding feet of Christ on the cross. She composed several books describing the inner sufferings of Christ as well as offering spiritual instructions.

Baptista died on May 31, 1524, and was canonized in 2010.

"A wonderful grace of the Holy Spirit led me into the depths of the heart of Jesus—an unfathomable sea of bitterness in which I should have been drowned had not God supported me."

—St. Baptista Varano

JUNE

1 St. Justin • Thomas Berry

2 Marguerite Porete • Anthony de Mello

3 St. Kevin • St. Charles Lwanga and Companions

4 Margaret Anna Cusack • Maurice Blondel

5 St. Boniface • André Trocmé

6 St. Philip the Deacon • Ann Manganaro

7 Blessed Anne of St. Bartholomew • Chief Seattle

8 Venerable Anne de Xainctonge • Gerard Manley Hopkins

9 St. Columba • Blessed Anne Mary Taigi

10 Antoni Gaudi • Gabrielle Bossis

11 St. Barnabas • St. Paula Frassinetti

12 Sigrid Undset • Medgar Evers

13 St. Anthony of Padua • Martin Buber

14 St. Elisha • G. K. Chesterton

15 Hagar the Egyptian • St. Germaine Cousin

16 St. Lutgardis • Evelyn Underhill

17 St. Emily de Vialar • Martyrs of "Mother Emanuel"

18 St. Elizabeth of Schonau • Blessed Osanna of Mantua

19 St. Juliana Falconieri • Lord John Acton

20 Blessed Michelina of Pesaro • Cardinal Yves Congar

21 St. Aloysius Gonzaga • James Chaney and Companions

22 St. Alban • St. Thomas More

23 St. Etheldreda • Blessed Mary of Oignies

24 Ruth and Naomi • Vincent Lebbe

25 The Hemorrhaging Woman • St. Febronia

26 Martyrs Under Nero • Hans Urs von Balthasar

27 Blessed Madeleine Fontaine and Companions • Hannah

28 St. Irenaeus • St. John Southworth

29 Saints Peter and Paul • St. Emma

30 Blessed Ramón Lull • Venerable Pierre Toussaint

JUNE

St. Justin
Philosopher and Martyr (ca. 100–165)

St. Justin was born of Gentile parents in Samaria at the turn of the first century. As a young man, he devoted himself to philosophy, exploring the major schools of Greek thought in his search for truth. After some years, he discovered the Hebrew Scriptures and the early Christian writings and through these texts found his way to the Church. In embracing Christianity Justin saw no need to renounce philosophy; he regarded Christianity as the "true philosophy" toward which Plato and other philosophers had been groping. From then on, Justin committed his talents to expounding the Christian faith and engaging in debate with other religious seekers.

In his apologetic works, Justin stressed the continuity between Christianity and the glimmerings of truth that were accessible to all people of good will: "Those who lived in accordance with Reason [Logos] are Christians, even though they were called godless." Clad in a philosopher's cloak, Justin traveled throughout the Greek world promoting the reasonableness and higher morality of Christianity. After settling in Rome, he was arrested during an outbreak of persecution. Asked what teaching he followed, he replied, "I have studied all in turn, but have given my adhesion to the teaching of the Christians, however displeasing it may be to those who follow error." He was beheaded.

"In every race of human beings God inserts an understanding of righteousness, that is, what is always and universally just."

—St. Justin

Thomas Berry
Priest and Geologian (1914–2009)

Thomas Berry was born in Greensboro, North Carolina. As a child he experienced a sense of the numinous wonder of nature, which remained a fixture of his spirituality. After entering a Passionist monastery at the age of twenty, he was later ordained a priest. In 1948 he lived in China, awakening a lifelong fascination with the religions of Asia. He returned to America and taught the history of religion at Fordham. But increasingly, through the influence of the Jesuit mystic and scientist Pierre Teilhard de Chardin, his reflections moved toward contemplation of the meaning of human culture within the wider evolutionary unfolding of the universe.

With Teilhard, he drew wonder from the emergence of human consciousness in the wide history of the cosmos. We were now living in an ecological age in which we must realize our capacity to shape and guide the evolutionary process. This sense of our place in the wider story of the universe called for a new set of values and spiritual consciousness—a project he called the Great Work of our time. It required humility and a deep sense of responsibility for the ethical care of the earth and the fostering of a sustainable future. The ecological crisis of our time was also a spiritual crisis. Rather than a theologian he called himself a "geologian."

Thomas Berry died on June 1, 2009.

"The planet Earth is something more than a natural resource to be used by humans. . . . Both our physical and spiritual survival depend on the visible world about us."
—Thomas Berry

Marguerite Porete
Beguine Martyr (d. 1310)

Of the life and teachings of Marguerite Porete, little is known apart from the records of the Inquisitorial court of Paris that condemned her. She identified herself as a Beguine, part of a loosely organized network of small communities of Christian laywomen that flourished in the fourteenth century. These women sought to live quiet lives of devotion without taking religious vows, thus basically opting out of the economic and ecclesiastical structures of their time.

She wrote a book, *The Mirror of Simple Souls*, which offers a mystical discourse on divine charity. Written as a dialogue between the Soul and Reason, it encourages the pursuit of spiritual perfection through the path of loving communion with God and one's neighbors.

The Inquisitors, who converted her poetic language into a series of propositions, condemned her work, accusing her of propagating a spirituality that dispensed with the Church in favor of direct communion with God. In 1310, judged a heretic, she was turned over to the "secular arm" to be burned. Whatever her errors, her writings suggest that she was a holy woman on fire with the love of God. Of those who condemned her, it is hard to conclude otherwise than that they loved orthodoxy more than they loved Christ.

"I beg you, those who read these words, try to understand them inwardly, in the innermost depths of your understanding, with all the subtle powers at your command, or else you run the risk of failing to understand them at all."
—Marguerite Porete

Anthony de Mello
Jesuit and Spiritual Guide (1931–1987)

Anthony de Mello, an Indian Jesuit, achieved international fame for his writings and spiritual retreats. From his reading of the Gospels he discerned that Christ was not so much concerned with imparting doctrines to his listeners as in awakening them to new life and the offer of salvation in their midst. Through parables and symbolic actions Jesus constantly startled people out of their preconceived notions of religion. "Wake up!"—that was his message. It was a challenging message, and one that led him to the cross.

De Mello's own teaching followed a similar style. Drawing, sometimes whimsically, on an eclectic fund of sources, including spiritual wisdom from both East and West—he tried to awaken his listeners to the presence of God in their midst.

For many years he was director of the Sadhana Institute of Pastoral Counseling in Poona, India. In the 1980s, however, his writings became known in the West, and he was in constant demand as a retreat leader. His playful spirit, his wisdom, and his ability to impart startling freshness to familiar Gospel lessons won him a wide following, though he had his detractors—including some who continued, long after his death, to scrutinize his writings for evidence of error. But his ministry was short-lived. While preparing to deliver a conference in New York on June 2, 1987, he died suddenly of a heart attack.

"DISCIPLE: 'What's the difference between knowledge and enlightenment?'

MASTER: 'When you have knowledge you use a torch to show the way. When you are enlightened, you become a torch.'"

—Anthony de Mello, SJ

St. Kevin
Irish Abbot (ca. 498–618)

As is the case with many early Irish saints, St. Kevin's life is steeped in legend. Born of a royal family, he was educated in a monastery near Dublin. One famous story from this period relates how, as he knelt praying with arms outstretched, a blackbird landed on his hand and proceeded to build a nest. Kevin remained thus, throughout Lent, as the bird laid its eggs, only relaxing when the young hatchlings flew away.

After his ordination, Kevin departed for a remote cave in the valley of Glendalough, where he dressed in animal skins and survived on nettles and sorrel. To alleviate his solitude, "the branches and leaves of the trees sometimes sang sweet songs to him." Eventually he was discovered by a farmer, who persuaded him to leave this austere life. The trees of the forest lay down to make a pathway as he passed.

St. Kevin established a monastery in Glendalough, which served for many centuries as a popular pilgrimage site. In the early years, the monks survived on salmon provided by a kindly otter—an arrangement that ended when one of the monks tried to make a glove from the otter's skin. To secure blessings for his monastery, Kevin undertook a journey to Rome, returning with "holy relics and mould."

St. Kevin is said to have lived to the age of 120.

"A soldier of Christ into the land of Ireland, a high name over the sea's wave: [Kevin] the pure, bright warrior, in the glen of the two broad lakes."
—From an early Life of St. Kevin

St. Charles Lwanga and Companions
Martyrs of Uganda (1886)

King Mwanga of the Baganda in Uganda was a cruel and capricious ruler. One of his first acts, after becoming king at the age of eighteen, was to order the murder of James Hannington, the newly appointed Anglican bishop. The Christian missionaries, he believed, were the advance guard of encroaching European powers; they were tempting his people to abandon their traditional ways and thus posed a threat to his own rule. What is more, they also reproached his habit of demanding sexual favors from the young men who served as his pages.

In May 1886 Mwanga summoned all his pages and ordered the Christians among them to step forward. Fifteen of them approached, including the eldest, twenty-four-year-old catechist Charles Lwanga, as well as the youngest, a boy of thirteen whom Charles had baptized only the night before. After declaring that they were Christians and intended to remain so, the king ordered them put to death.

The group was marched to an execution spot on Lake Victoria, more than sixteen miles away. There they were wrapped in reeds, stacked on a pyre, and set aflame. The martyrs offered no protest, but simply murmured their prayers. Lwanga's last words were "My God."

Reports of these deaths, and many more in succeeding weeks, spread quickly, resulting in many conversions. The martyrs were canonized in 1964 by Pope Paul VI, who made a pilgrimage to their shrine.

"Poor, foolish man . . . you are burning me, but it is as if you were pouring water on my body."
—St. Charles Lwanga

Margaret Anna Cusack
Founder, Sisters of St. Joseph of Peace (1829–1899)

Margaret Anna Cusack, a Poor Clare in Ireland, became widely known as "the Nun of Kenmore" for her prophetic writings on the issues of her day, urging women to claim their rights and dignity, criticizing the abuses of absentee landlords, and challenging laws that punished the poor. Her outspokenness won her many friends but also enemies—among them her own bishop, who instructed her convent to "put her out on the streets of Dublin." With permission of Pope Leo XIII, however, she founded a new congregation, the Sisters of St. Joseph of Peace, to serve the needs of young women.

In 1885 she traveled to America and established a center for Irish immigrant women in Newark. But troubles with Church authorities continued to dog her. She was accused of having defamed the archbishop of New York, though the particulars of her offense were never revealed. "In many cases," she said, "Roman Catholic priests and superiors put obedience to themselves in place of obedience to God." Believing that baseless charges were impeding the work of her community, she asked the pope's permission to withdraw from the congregation she had founded. She retired to England, where she died on June 5, 1899. Her congregation continues to honor the memory of their founder.

"My desire is for peace and justice. Not indeed peace at any price. . . . Nor indeed the justice, which, like the statue in front of Dublin Castle, by happy accident, turns its back toward the people and its face toward the great."

—Margaret Anna Cusack

Maurice Blondel
Philosopher (1861–1949)

Maurice Blondel was a French Catholic philosopher who initiated a fresh understanding of the relation between Christian faith and human existence. His particular concern was what he termed the "extrinsism" of traditional Catholic apologetics. The Church tended to present revelation as God's communication of "heavenly" truths. The Church certified the divine origin of this revelation by appealing to such signs and miracles as the resurrection. Thus, the credibility of revelation depended on its divine origin, rather than on its actual content or its intrinsic relevance to human existence.

Blondel believed the definition of saving truth was that it corresponded to actual questions and yearnings of the human heart. He proposed a "method of immanence" to show how the logic of human existence itself pointed toward transcendence. In all our actions, he taught, there is some reference to the infinite reality in which existence itself is grounded. Ultimately our lives are characterized by a choice—to be open to this dimension or to be closed in on ourselves. The Christian Gospel named this choice explicitly in the life, death, and resurrection of Jesus. Thus, Christianity concerns Good News that resonates with the meaning of our deepest experience.

Though his work departed from the dominant neoscholastic method of Catholic theology, his status as a layman helped him escape the attention of Vatican censors. His work left a deep impact on Karl Rahner and other architects of Vatican II. Blondel himself continued to teach and write until blindness encroached. He died on June 4, 1949.

"Action is the abundance of the heart."

—Maurice Blondel

St. Boniface
Missionary and Martyr (ca. 675–754)

St. Boniface, one of the great figures in the annals of Christian mission, spent the first half of his life as a monk in England. At about forty, he was seized by missionary fervor. An Anglo-Saxon by birth, he desired to convey the Gospel to the Saxon people, who were still outside the Church. From the pope he received a commission to go forth to Germany, "to those people who are still in the bonds of infidelity . . . to teach them the service of the kingdom of God by persuasion of the truth in the name of Christ, the Lord, our God."

Boniface traveled widely in Hesse and Thuringia and soon achieved extraordinary results. Before long he was writing back to the English people, asking for their prayers in the conversion of those who "are of one blood and bone with you."

Boniface was eventually named the archbishop of Mainz. Though a skilled administrator, his heart remained set on spreading the Gospel. Nearing eighty, he received permission to leave his cathedral in the hands of an assistant and to return to Frisia, his original mission field. There, with a group of followers, he was attacked and brutally killed on June 5, 754.

"This is that very day we have long dreamed of. That moment of freedom we have yearned for is right here. So be heroic in the Lord and suffer this royal grace of his will gladly. Keep your trust in the Lord and he will set your souls free."

—Dying words of St. Boniface

André Trocmé
Pastor of Le Chambon (1901–1971)

During the years of the Nazi occupation of France, the citizens of a small Huguenot village called Le Chambon offered a safe haven to thousands of Jewish refugees who were thus saved from certain death. Many hundreds took part in this "conspiracy of goodness," but no doubt a key role was played by the pastor André Trocmé and his wife Magda.

At the core of Trocmé's ministry was a literal commitment to the Sermon on the Mount and a conviction that the essence of the Gospel lay in the love of God and neighbor. Within a few years, he had managed to instill these principles in his flock.

In 1942, when the order came to deliver all Jews for deportation, the village undertook a dangerous form of resistance. During the years of the war it is estimated that as many as 3,500 Jews were protected in the village and surrounding farms. The risks of such a venture, operating under the eyes of the Gestapo, were evident. Trocmé himself was at one point detained and later went into hiding. Still the rescue continued. Trocmé so invigorated the faith and conscience of his flock that they risked their own lives to protect the lives of those labeled "outsiders."

Trocmé died on June 5, 1971. The following year he was honored in Israel with the "Medal of Righteousness."

"Nonviolence was not a theory superimposed upon reality; it was an itinerary that we explored day after day in communal prayer and in obedience to the commands of the Spirit."

—André Trocmé

St. Philip the Deacon
(First Century)

According to the Acts of the Apostles, St. Philip was among the first of seven men in the early Christian community to be appointed to serve at table and to attend to the needs of widows and the poor (this later was deemed by the Church to be the origin of the office of deacon). Little is known of his career, but he is associated with a critical moment in the Church's expansion.

Following the martyrdom of St. Stephen, the Church in Jerusalem scattered. Philip crossed into Samaria, where he found a surprisingly receptive audience. At that point an angel instructed him to travel south toward Gaza. On the road he encountered an Ethiopian eunuch, a servant of the queen of Ethiopia, who was reading the book of Isaiah. When Philip asked the Ethiopian whether he understood what he read, he replied, "How can I, unless someone guides me?"

The text was about the Suffering Servant, a providential entry to the story of Jesus. As the two traveled together the Ethiopian pointed out a body of water and asked to be baptized on the spot. So "they both went down into the water, Philip and the eunuch, and he baptized him. And when they came up out of the water, the Spirit of the Lord caught up Philip; and the eunuch saw him no more, and went on his way rejoicing."

This striking story foreshadows the subsequent spread of the Gospel beyond the confines of Israel. Through Philip and his convert, Africa is represented in the infancy of the universal Church.

"And the multitudes gave heed to what was said by Philip, when they heard him and saw the signs which he did."
—Acts 8:6

Ann Manganaro
Sister of Loretto (1946–1993)

Ann Manganaro—physician, Sister of Loretto, cofounder of Karen House, the Catholic Worker house in St. Louis— spent the last five years of her life in the battle zones of El Salvador.

Manganaro had joined the Sisters of Loretto when she was eighteen. Years later, after becoming a pediatrician and facing times of trial and discouragement, she asked herself what she truly believed. Reading the Gospels again she was caught by the commandments to love God with your whole heart and your neighbor as yourself. And she realized that her heart still burned to live those commandments.

She had already been diagnosed and treated for breast cancer when she made the bold decision in 1988 to trade the poverty of St. Louis for a village in El Salvador, at the heart of the country's civil war. She lived through helicopter attacks and night raids, remaining to see peace return, as well as the return of her illness. Then she returned to St. Louis to die. Near the end, she said she had come to understand the Wounds. Her own wounds, the wounds of El Salvador? No, she said, "The wounds of everyone, the wounds of us all." She died on June 6, 1993, at the age of forty-six.

"Sometimes it is only in retrospect, when you've gone through a really hard time, but you see the fruit that has continued to be born in your life and in other people's lives that makes you say, 'YES, God's grace was working here even when I didn't feel it in the moment.'"

—Sr. Ann Manganaro

Blessed Anne of St. Bartholomew
Carmelite (1549–1626)

Blessed Anne grew up near Avila, Spain, where she spent her early years as a shepherdess. At twenty she applied to enter the Carmelite convent in Avila, newly reformed under the leadership of St. Teresa. Most of the community, like Teresa herself, came from highborn families. Not so Anne, who could only sign her name with a cross and was admitted as a lay sister. Teresa, however, discerned Anne's special gifts and chose her to be her assistant and traveling companion. On one of these trips, the saintly founder died in Anne's arms.

Afterward Anne was chosen to join a group of five Discalced Carmelites in establishing a house in Paris. At first, she tried to take her place in the kitchen, but she was compelled to become a choir nun. In fact, she later became prioress of the community and founded a house in Antwerp. Reluctant to accept a position of authority, she protested that she was no more than a weak straw. But Christ spoke to her in her prayers, reminding her, "It is with straws that I light my fire."

The community in Antwerp attracted many noblewomen, and Anne came to be widely revered as a saint when her prayers were credited with thwarting a Protestant siege.

She died on June 7, 1626, and was beatified in 1917.

"Silence is precious; by keeping silence and knowing how to listen to God, the soul grows in wisdom and God teaches it what it cannot learn from men."
—Blessed Anne of St. Bartholomew

Seattle
Chief of the Suquamish (ca. 1786–1866)

Growing up in a Suquamish village along the Puget Sound, Seattle witnessed the arrival of the first whites in the Northwest. By the time he became chief of his tribe, the early forays of trappers had given way to a steady stream of settlers. It fell to Seattle to devise a strategy for dealing with these invaders. Rejecting violence, Seattle put his trust in peaceful dialogue. But as the intentions of the whites became clear, his goal focused simply on the survival of his people.

In 1830 Seattle converted to Christianity. He tried to integrate his faith with the beliefs of his ancestors. But with each year his traditional world grew smaller. He believed the struggle with the whites represented contrasting spiritual values. The whites considered the land a commodity. But as Seattle observed, "We are part of the earth and it is part of us."

In 1855 Seattle signed a treaty that transferred the Indian lands to the federal government in exchange for a reservation in the Northwest. In a letter addressed to President Pierce he wrote, "One thing we know, which the white man may one day discover—our God is the same God. You may think now that you own Him as you wish to own our land; but you cannot."

Chief Seattle died on June 7, 1866, near the city that today bears his name.

"Humankind did not weave the web of life. Whatever we do to the web we do to ourselves."
—Chief Seattle

Venerable Anne de Xainctonge
Founder, Society of the Sisters of St. Ursula
of the Blessed Virgin (1567–1621)

Anne de Xainctonge was born to a noble family in Dijon in 1567. Her home abutted a Jesuit college for boys, and from an early age she conceived the idea of founding a community for women along the lines of the Jesuits, with schools offering girls an education "given, not sold." This plan did not sit well with her father, a prominent parliamentarian. Nor were the Jesuits flattered by her vision.

Anne, however, was undeterred. Leaving her hometown, she settled in Dole, a university town (then in Spanish territory). There, with the help of a sympathetic Jesuit confessor and a group of companions, she established her first school. Still, the struggle to establish a congregation faced many challenges. Anne insisted that her sisters be uncloistered, free to move about among the people. She also rejected any religious habit, choosing instead a simple black dress in the style of a Spanish widow. Such innovations ran directly against the prevailing custom for religious women.

Eventually she overcame all obstacles. Her congregation, the Society of the Sisters of St. Ursula of the Blessed Virgin, was established (with "Our Lady as general, St. Ursula as lieutenant"). Inspired by the spirituality of St. Ignatius, Anne devised a rule that balanced action and contemplation. The Society's schools quickly spread to other cities and countries, and it remains active today on several continents. Anne died on June 8, 1621. She was declared venerable in 1900.

"The God whom I wish to serve is in all lands."

—Venerable Anne de Xainctonge

Gerard Manley Hopkins
Jesuit Priest and Poet (1844–1889)

Gerard Manley Hopkins was born in England to a prosperous Anglican family. Though he excelled at Oxford and seemed destined for a brilliant career, these expectations were dashed when he announced his decision in 1866 to become a Roman Catholic and then a Jesuit priest.

Hopkins was a gifted poet, but in becoming a Jesuit he presumed he must renounce his literary interests. In 1875, however, he read about a shipwreck off the coast of Kent. Among the victims was a group of Franciscan nuns escaping anti-Catholic persecution in Germany. When his superior casually mentioned that it would make a good subject for a poem, Hopkins felt authorized to resume his writing. It was as if a dam had burst. The result was his epic "The Wreck of the *Deutschland*," one of the most remarkable poems in the English language. In compressed, highly charged language, he used this event to describe the victory wrought by Christ through his passion and resurrection. Yet neither this nor any of his subsequent poems was published in his lifetime. His friends found his revolutionary style bizarre and incomprehensible.

Hopkins spent most of his life in obscure religious assignments, wracked by doubts regarding his abilities and accomplishments. Only toward the end of his life did he seem to resolve the identity of his vocations as priest and poet. Poetry, he came to see, was his own means of naming and replicating the sacramental character of the created world; it was his way of expressing his true being and thus returning praise to his Creator. He died of typhoid on June 8, 1889. His last words: "I am so happy."

"The world is charged with the grandeur of God."

—Gerard Manley Hopkins

329

St. Columba
Abbot of Iona (521–597)

St. Columba was born to a royal family in Donegal, Ireland. He entered monastic life as a boy and rose to become the founder of several important monasteries. His downfall came from his love of books. A full-out clan war erupted from a dispute that began when Columba copied a rare book without the permission of its owner, his former master St. Finnian. Columba's personal role in encouraging bloodshed is not clear, but the Church held him to blame and he accepted moral responsibility: "Ill have I served the heavenly kingdom, and ill have I served Ireland in that I have caused the men of Ireland to shed one another's blood." As restitution he uttered a public oath: "I will not rest till I have won for God the souls of as many men as have fallen in this battle."

So in 561 Columba and a band of twelve monks set to sea in an open boat, their destination unknown. They finally landed on Iona, a remote and barren island off the coast of Scotland. There, Columba established a monastery that would become famous throughout Europe, serving as a base for the evangelization of Scotland and northern England.

Columba lived in Iona for over thirty years. He died there on June 9, 597.

"Unto this place, small and mean though it be, great homage shall yet be paid. . . . The saints, also, of other churches shall regard it with no common reverence."
—St. Columba

Blessed Anne Mary Taigi
Laywoman (1769–1837)

At Anne Marie Taigi's beatification in 1920 Pope Benedict XV observed that she was "quite different from the virgins, nuns, and widows canonized by the church." In fact, she is the rare example in the calendar of saints of a woman who realized her path to holiness in the midst of ordinary family life.

Born in Siena, Anne moved with her family to Rome when her father's business failed. There her parents found work as domestic servants. At thirteen Anne went to work in a silk factory and later become a housemaid to a noble lady. In 1789 she married another servant, Dominic Taigi, and bore seven children during their forty-eight-year marriage. Her life was spent in work, service, and charitable activity, moving easily among the very poor and the very rich. Many recognized her goodness and piety; few, apart from her spiritual director, knew of her profound supernatural gifts. In prayer she beheld a "mystical sun" before her eyes in which she could foresee the future and read the secrets of other souls. Many, including prelates and nobles, sought her spiritual counsel. Her reputation spread and, not long after her death on June 9, 1837, her cause for beatification was introduced.

"The servant of God knew how to keep everyone in his place and she did it with a graciousness that I cannot describe. I often came home tired, moody, and cross, but she always succeeded in soothing and cheering me."

—From a deposition for the beatification
of Blessed Anne Mary by her husband

Antoni Gaudi
Architect (1852–1926)

In 1883 Antoni Gaudi, a young architect in Barcelona, was offered the task of designing and building the Church of the Holy Family, a project sponsored by a lay association and relying entirely on individual donations. Gaudi was, in some ways, a surprising choice. Though hailed as a creative genius, whose work combined an eclectic range of styles, he was also something of a dandy. Yet he took on the project with almost single-minded dedication. The church became more and more ambitious. Incorporating inlaid ceramics, wrought iron, and original sculpture, it began to grow into an astonishing work of art—a reflection of the artist's imagination but also, increasingly, a reflection of his growing faith.

As his church began to take shape, Gaudi grew closer to the One he called "the greatest master builder." He adopted an ascetic life, dressing as a workman, fasting frequently, and attending daily Mass. While also designing many other buildings, Holy Family became his central work. In the last months of his life he slept on a cot in the church. On June 7, 1926, he was struck by a streetcar. Mistaken for a beggar, he was taken to the charity ward of the local hospital, where he died on June 10.

Though work on the Church of the Holy Family continues to this day, it has long been recognized as one of the world's architectural treasures. In 1999 it was also named as a basilica. Its architect has been proposed as a candidate for canonization.

"Beauty is the image of truth."

—Antoni Gaudi

Gabrielle Bossis
Mystic (1874–1950)

As a child in France, Gabrielle Bossis enjoyed a special sense of God's presence. She liked to carry on "simple talks" with Jesus, a practice she continued all her life. When she described this practice to a priest, he urged her to become a nun. But she was certain that her vocation, instead, was to live out her dedication to God as a single woman in the world.

She trained as a nurse to serve the poor. But at sixty-two she began writing "moral comedies" for the theater and went on to become famous as a playwright and actor. After her death on June 9, 1950, her journals were published—to the astonishment of friends, who knew nothing of her rich inner life.

Christ's message, as conveyed by Bossis, is the imperative to seek his face not only in other people but in every circumstance and to respond to him joyfully and with love. "You were touched when you read that I was in the Gospels, hidden in the sacrament of the Word. But how much more I am present in the sacrament of human life!"

The God she loved was hidden in her own yearnings, sufferings, and ideals—but always wanting to be discovered. "Hunt for me everywhere! I'll let myself be captured with such joy! And when you have found me, give me to others. There are people I am waiting to reach only through you."

"Don't think that a saint must look saintly in the eyes of humans. . . . Their value is in their hearts."

—Gabrielle Bossis

St. Barnabas
Apostle (First Century)

S t. Barnabas, one of the earliest missionaries in the Church, played a vital role in spreading and translating the Gospel to a Gentile audience. Though not one of the original Twelve, St. Luke in Acts terms him an apostle on account of his having received a special commission from the Holy Spirit. One of his first and most fruitful contributions was to vouch for St. Paul, a recent convert who was still feared by the other apostles for his previous persecution of the Church. Later, Barnabas was sent on a preaching mission to Antioch. As his labors there bore fruit, he sent for Paul to join him, and together they implanted a thriving Church. It was in Antioch that "the disciples were for the first time called Christians."

Barnabas and Paul set off on the first formal overseas missionary journey, first to Cyprus and then to the mainland of Asia Minor. They initially preached to the Jews, but when they were rebuffed by their own, they reached out successfully to Gentile audiences. In Lystra they had to dissuade a Gentile crowd from worshiping them as gods and at the same time to escape from a crowd of angry Jews who wanted to stone them.

Eventually Barnabas and Paul parted ways. While Paul's story dominates the later narrative of Acts, Barnabas slips off the pages of history. According to legend he returned to Cyprus, where he was martyred in the year 61.

"And all the assembly kept silence; and they listened to Barnabas and Paul as they related what signs and wonders God had done through them among the Gentiles."
—Acts 15:12

St. Paula Frassinetti
Founder, Sisters of St. Dorothy (1809–1882)

St. Paula Frassinetti was born to a pious family in Genoa. Her four brothers all became priests. Though Paula, too poor to attend school, remained at home doing housework, her brothers would share their lessons with her, and in this way she received an education. Later, when she was nineteen, one of her brothers, by now the parish priest in the town of Quinto, invited her to join him and help manage a parochial school for poor girls. In this work she found her own vocation, eventually gathering other women to form a congregation: the Sisters of St. Dorothy. They defined as their mission "to be fully available in the hands of God to evangelize through education, with a preference for youth and the poorest."

They faced many obstacles—not least, their severe poverty, which forced them to work at night to support themselves. As Paula observed, "Those who suffer most, love most." Following an outbreak of cholera, they combined their educational work with care for the sick.

New houses were established in Genoa, Rome, and elsewhere in Italy. In 1866 the first sisters departed for Brazil. Paula exhorted them to be "burning flames that inflame with God's love all those you come in contact with." She died on June 11, 1882. She was canonized in 1984.

"Not only did the Cross not frighten her, but it was for her the powerful spring which moved her, the secret source from which sprang her tireless activity and her indomitable courage."

—Pope John Paul II on St. Paula Frassinetti

Sigrid Undset
Novelist and Nobel Laureate (1882–1949)

Sigrid Undset, who grew up in Norway, achieved early success with the publication of her first novels. But her life was marked by much struggle in the search for truth and happiness. She fell in love with a married man, and after his divorce, married him. She had two children, one of them mentally handicapped, but her marriage collapsed while she was pregnant with her third child. It was after this that she wrote her masterpiece—*Kristin Lavransdatter*—an intricate trilogy, chronicling the life and struggles of a medieval Norwegian woman. In 1928 she won the Nobel Prize in Literature.

Her own journey led her steadily to the Catholic faith. As she noted, "By degrees my knowledge of history convinced me that the only thoroughly sane people seemed to be those queer men and women the Catholic Church calls Saints. They seemed to know the true explanation of man's undying hunger for happiness—his tragically insufficient love of peace, justice, and goodwill to his fellow men, his everlasting fall from grace." In thoroughly Lutheran Norway her conversion caused a scandal. She later became a Third Order Dominican.

Undset fled the Nazi invasion in 1940 and settled in the United States. She returned after the war but never wrote again. She died on June 10, 1949.

"In a way, we do not want to find Truth—we prefer to seek and keep our illusions. But I had ventured near the abode of truth in my researches about God's friends. . . . So I had to submit. . . . I was received into the Catholic Church."

—Sigrid Undset

Medgar Evers
Civil Rights Martyr (1925–1963)

Medgar Evers was born in Decatur, Mississippi. Drafted into the army during World War II, he saw action in France and Germany. Returning to Mississippi after the war, he studied at a historically black college, married his sweetheart, and raised three children. But like many black veterans, Evers found it intolerable to return to segregation and the daily experience of humiliation and oppression. He became a full-time fieldworker for the NAACP—the premier civil rights organization and thus the object of fear and hatred by white supremacists throughout the South.

After organizing boycotts of segregated bathrooms and working to register African Americans to vote, Evers began to receive constant death threats. Though he acknowledged the risks, he refused to compromise. As his wife noted, "Medgar was a man who never wanted to be in the limelight. He saw a job that needed to be done and he answered the call and the fight for freedom, dignity, and justice, not just for his people but all people."

On June 12, 1963, shortly after President Kennedy delivered a historic speech on civil rights, Medgar Evers was shot in the back in the driveway of his home. He died in front of his wife and children.

"I grieve but I do not regret. Medgar didn't just belong to me—he belonged to so many. He was so willing to give his life that I feel his death has served a certain purpose. When I find myself in the pits of depression I remind myself that fulfilling this purpose is what he really wanted."
—Myrlie Evers-Williams

St. Anthony of Padua
Doctor of the Church (1195–1231)

St. Anthony was born in Lisbon and first entered religious life as an Augustinian canon in Coimbra. There one day he met a group of visiting Franciscans on their way to Morocco. He was greatly impressed by these courageous missionaries, the more so when news came of their subsequent martyrdom. At once, he was inspired to join the Franciscans. In 1221 he attended a great Franciscan gathering, the last held in the lifetime of St. Francis. Afterward he received a modest assignment to a small hospice for lay brothers at Monte Paolo.

But soon his star would shine. When asked to preach at an important occasion, he astonished his audience with the unexpected elegance, conviction, and profound learning of his sermon. Word quickly spread, and Anthony received a letter from Francis himself authorizing him to preach and to teach theology to the friars.

Eventually he was sent on a preaching mission that covered all of Italy. Thousands flocked to hear his open-air sermons, and his visits had the impact of a spiritual revival. He attacked the tyranny of the powerful, exhorting his listeners to compassion and charity toward the poor.

Anthony died on June 13, 1231, at the age of thirty-six. He was buried in Padua, where he had spent his last years, and his canonization followed only a year later. In 1946 Pope Pius XII declared him a Doctor of the Church. (Popularly, he is often invoked for his help in locating lost objects.)

"Attribute to God every good that you have received. If you take credit for something that does not belong to you, you will be guilty of theft."
—St. Anthony of Padua

Martin Buber
Jewish Philosopher (1878–1965)

Martin Buber, a Jewish philosopher and theologian, was one of the great religious thinkers of the twentieth century. He had a particular impact on many Christians, stimulating an appreciation for the Jewish origins of Christianity. But he also embodied the humanistic ideal of dialogue and understanding between peoples of different faiths, thus suggesting the positive role that religion might play in promoting a more human world.

Buber grew up and studied philosophy in Vienna before assuming a chair in Frankfurt. There he published his classic book *I and Thou*, whose central theme is the relational nature of human existence. Our own humanity, he taught, is diminished to the extent that we encounter others as objects rather than subjects. In 1933, with the Nazi rise to power, Buber was dismissed, though with luck he escaped Germany and settled in Jerusalem.

In later years his many books, including biblical reflections and popular treatments of Jewish spirituality and mysticism (including his collection of tales of the Hasidim), exerted great influence on Christian theology. He also wrote extensively on Jesus. While rejecting Christian claims about Christ, he extended affectionate recognition to Jesus, who, he believed, exemplified the highest ethical and spiritual ideals of Judaism.

Buber died in Jerusalem on June 13, 1965.

"Before his death, Rabbi Zusya said, 'In the coming world, they will not ask me: "Why were you not Moses?" They will ask me: "Why were you not Zusya?"'"
—Martin Buber

St. Elisha
Prophet of Israel

On instructions from God, the great prophet Elijah sought out a young man named Elisha to be his successor. Finding Elisha plowing his father's field, Elijah cast his cloak over the young man, who immediately left his home and oxen and became Elijah's loyal attendant. When, some years later, it came time for Elijah to depart this life, Elisha implored his master that he might inherit "a double portion" of his spirit. He then watched as Elijah was taken up into heaven on a chariot of fire. Donning Elijah's cloak, which fell to the ground, he immediately assumed his master's prophetic powers.

For many years Elisha wandered through Israel, performing numerous miracles. He purified a poisonous lake. He cured Naaman, the Syrian general, of leprosy. He provided an aged couple with a son, and later, when the boy suddenly died, restored him to life. He counseled kings and chastised them when they faltered. As he lay dying, King Joash wept, honoring him with the words Elisha had spoken at the death of Elijah: "My father, my father! The chariots of Israel and its horsemen."

Elijah and Elisha, who are recognized as saints of the Orthodox Church, are also revered as proto-saints of the Carmelite Order.

"Then he took the mantle of Elijah that had fallen from him, and struck the water, saying 'Where is the Lord, the God of Elijah?' and when he had struck the water, the water was parted to the one side and to the other. And Elisha went over."

—2 Kings 2:14

G. K. Chesterton
Apologist (1874–1936)

Gilbert Keith Chesterton was an imposing figure—over six feet tall, wide of girth, excitable, opinionated, and drawn to controversy. A hugely prolific writer on every conceivable topic, he was especially known for his "Father Brown" mystery stories. Eventually famous as a Catholic apologist, his formal conversion to Catholicism came only in 1922 when he was forty-eight, though he had been traveling in that direction for some time. In his book *Orthodoxy*, a defense of traditional Christianity published in 1908, he had set out to define his own religion, only to realize that a definition already existed in the creeds of Christianity. He compared this discovery to the embarrassment of an English yachtsman who miscalculated his course and "discovered England under the impression that it was a new island in the South Seas. . . . I am that man in a yacht. I discovered England."

One of the principles of orthodoxy Chesterton affirmed was the value of Tradition. Though some saw this as contrary to the spirit of democracy, he argued otherwise: "Tradition is only democracy extended through time."

Though his social and religious views set him in the minority in England, there were few literary figures of his time more widely admired, indeed beloved. He was recognized as someone able to combine gaiety and humor with a kind of deadly seriousness about the things that mattered. He died on June 14, 1936.

"The Christian ideal has not been tried and found wanting; it has been found difficult and left untried."
—G. K. Chesterton

Hagar the Egyptian
Slave and Surrogate

According to the biblical narrative of Genesis, Hagar was an Egyptian slave who belonged to Sarah, the wife of Abraham. When Sarah was unable to provide Abraham with a child, she proposed that her husband beget a child with her slave—a solution permitted under the law. Presumably Hagar had no choice in the matter. So she served as a surrogate mother for her mistress. But by the time Hagar was pregnant Sarah apparently regretted the arrangement. Sarah treated her so harshly that she tried to flee. But an angel of the Lord urged Hagar to return and bear her child. She was promised, like Abraham, descendants so numerous that "they cannot be numbered for multitude." And she was told that her child should be called Ishmael, which means "God hears." Hagar replied in wonder: "Thou art a God of seeing. . . . Have I really seen God and remained alive after seeing him?"

Ishmael was duly born. But after many years another child of God's promise was born to Sarah and Abraham. Sarah now insisted that Abraham send Hagar and her son alone into the wilderness. Therefore, Hagar and Ishmael were forced to wander into the desert, where they would have perished, had God not heard the tears of Ishmael and comforted Hagar, who at that point discovered a well.

Though not the main protagonist of the story of Abraham and Sarah, Hagar helps to characterize the Lord as a God of life who hears the voice of the oppressed and makes a way out of no way.

"Thou art a God of seeing."

—Hagar (Genesis 16:13)

St. Germaine Cousin
Shepherdess (1579–1601)

St. Germaine was a peasant girl from the village of Pibrac, near Toulouse, France. Her mother having died in childbirth, she was raised by an unloving father and a stepmother who made no effort to conceal her dislike for the girl. To keep Germaine away from her own children her stepmother forced Germaine to sleep in the stable or under the stairs, kept her busy with chores, and fed her table scraps.

Despite the drudgery and injustice of her life, Germaine accepted every insult with cheerfulness and love. She was especially glad to tend the sheep, as this afforded an opportunity for prayer and communion with God. As she stood watch in the field, God "spoke to her soul as he speaks to the humble and clean of heart, and she lived ever consciously in His presence."

In time Germaine acquired a reputation for holiness. This won her no special privileges at home. Indeed she was punished for sharing her table scraps with beggars. Even her stepmother was caught short, however, when she confronted Germaine on a winter's day and forced her to open her apron, revealing a cascade of spring flowers.

Afterward her family grudgingly invited Germaine to accept a bed in their home. But this real-life Cinderella preferred her humble place under the stairs. There one day she was found dead at the age of twenty-two. Her grave became a popular site of pilgrimage. She was canonized by Pope Pius IX in 1867.

"I have what God wished me to have, and I want no more."

—St. Germaine

St. Lutgardis
Mystic (1182–1246)

With parents too poor to provide a wedding dowry, St. Lutgardis was committed at the age of twelve to a Benedictine convent in the Lowlands. At first she had no inclination to religious life and passed her time as a kind of boarder. Then one day she received a vision of Christ and his wounds and determined at once to renounce all worldly concerns. Her devotion was intensified by frequent visions of Christ—so vivid that she would converse with him quite intimately. If called away to a task, she would say, "Wait here, Lord Jesus, and I will come back directly."

Eventually she chose to transfer to a more austere Cistercian convent in Aywieres. In the new convent only French was spoken, a language she was never able to master. Despite her sense of isolation, however, she became a much sought-after spiritual counselor, renowned for her gifts of healing and prophecy and her knowledge of Scripture.

In the last eleven years of her life she became completely blind, an affliction she accepted as an occasion for greater detachment from the visible world. When she felt herself close to death she received a vision of the Lord, advising her to praise God for the graces she had received, to pray for the conversion of sinners, and to rely on God alone.

She died on June 16, 1246.

"For every beat of Thy Heart and every act of love, for all Thy thoughts and desires, for all the silent and the uttered prayers which Thou didst offer while on earth . . . for all these I tender Thee a thousand thanks."

—St. Lutgardis

Evelyn Underhill
Spiritual Guide (1875–1941)

Through her voluminous writings, Evelyn Underhill did much to awaken modern interest in the mystical traditions of Christianity. As a popular writer she went further, showing the relevance of mysticism for ordinary people living in the modern world.

Underhill was raised as a nominal Anglican in a comfortable British home. Though attracted to Roman Catholicism, she chose, for a number of reasons (including the strong objections of her husband), not to formally convert. Her study of the Christian mystics resulted in 1911 in a landmark book, *Mysticism.* At the time neither Protestants nor Catholics took mysticism very seriously—the former regarding it as a form of Catholic neurosis, the latter believing it was something only relevant to God's chosen few.

For Underhill, mysticism was "the art of union with Reality." She showed the origins of mysticism in Scripture—in the life of Jesus, St. Paul, and the early disciples. As such, it was an essential expression of the Christian life; it was simply the experiential dimension of faith, "the soul of religion."

Over time, Underhill became a spiritual director to many people. She emphasized the practical dimension of spirituality. God "made us in order to use us, and use us in the most profitable way"—sometimes in heroic fashion, but more often in our "ordinary mixed life of every day" where we live out our religious vocation.

Underhill died on June 15, 1941.

"If God were small enough to be understood, He would not be big enough to be worshipped."
—Evelyn Underhill

St. Emily de Vialar
Founder, Congregation of Sisters of St. Joseph
of the Apparition (1797–1856)

Emily de Vialar was born to an aristocratic family in Gail-lac, France. Her widowed father, with whom she lived, opposed her yearning for religious life. As a result, she endured many stressful years. Yet, in the absence of a spiritual advisor, as she later wrote, "God became my director." She took to caring for neglected children, who soon filled the terrace of their home—provoking further furious complaints from her father.

After inheriting a substantial fortune from her grandfather, however, she was eventually freed to pursue her vocation. With support from a sympathetic priest, she bought a large house and, with several companions, formed the Congregation of Sisters of St. Joseph of the Apparition (a reference to the angel who revealed to Joseph the mystery of the incarnation). Their mission was to care for the poor, especially children. In 1835, when she was thirty-eight, the order was approved, and Mother Emily became superior.

Quite soon, Emily determined that the work of the congregation should extend to foreign mission. Their first overseas outpost was in Algeria, but it was followed by houses in Tunisia, Malta, Greece, Australia, and even in Jerusalem, where the sisters were the first modern Catholic congregation to establish a foothold. Mother Emily's energy and persistence in overcoming all obstacles was nothing less than amazing. All told, in its first twenty-two years, her congregation expanded to forty houses, many of them established by Mother Emily herself.

She died in 1856 and was canonized in 1951.

"If God did not breathe into me the spirit of zeal, my heart would cease to be quickened and then I would not be able to do anything."

—St. Emily de Vialar

Martyrs of "Mother Emanuel"
Charleston, South Carolina (2015)

In the evening hours of June 17, 2015, a prayer service at Emanuel African Methodist Episcopal Church in Charleston, South Carolina, was interrupted when a young white man drew a gun and began shooting. "Y'all want something to pray about?" he shouted. "I'll give you something to pray about." His violence took the lives of nine people, including the senior pastor, State Senator Clementa Pinckney.

"Mother Emanuel"—one of the oldest African American churches in the country—had a long and storied history of nourishing the faith of its members, sustaining them in the long struggle against racial oppression from slavery times to the present. The church's history, presumably, played a role in the killer's twisted plan to "ignite a race war."

In the days that followed, the country learned more of the faith and goodness of the nine people murdered that day, of how, in different ways, their faith had inspired them to lives of service and ordinary decency. And in the example of family members who confronted the killer in court to voice their pain, along with astonishing expressions of forgiveness, the world witnessed, as President Obama put it, the power of "amazing grace."

Guilty of nothing other than "praying while black," these martyrs highlighted the enduring stain of racism, and among many Americans their deaths prompted self-examination and new resolve to uproot the scourge of racism.

"[It was] an act that [the killer] presumed would deepen divisions that trace back to our nation's original sin. Oh, but God works in mysterious ways. God has different ideas."

—President Barack Obama, at the memorial
for Rev. Clementa Pinckney

St. Elizabeth of Schonau
Mystic (1129–1164)

At the age of twelve, St. Elizabeth entered a double monastery (housing both men and women) in Schonau, Germany. Six years later she was professed as a Benedictine nun. Though she suffered from ill health, she embraced the discipline of prayer and the austerities of religious life. At the age of twenty-three she began to receive extraordinary visions that continued throughout her life. Some of these experiences had an ecstatic quality, but others left her with a sense of diabolical persecution.

Eventually, in a series of books written on wax tablets, she recorded her visions and other prophetic utterances, chronicling her visions and dialogues with the Virgin Mary, her insights into doctrine, along with revelations regarding the life of St. Ursula. These were copied and widely circulated. Dozens of her letters survive, including several to her friend and contemporary St. Hildegard of Bingen in which she describes her mission to warn Christians, including many priests and bishops, to repent of their sins.

Though never formally canonized, upon her death on June 18, 1164, she was quickly acclaimed as a saint and her name was added to the Roman Martyrology.

"I, a poor earthen vessel, say these things not of myself but through the Living Light. Those who desire to do the works of God . . . should put on the breast-plate of Faith, and be humble and poor, living as He did, the Lamb whose trumpet sound they are."

—St. Elizabeth of Schonau

Blessed Osanna of Mantua
Mystic (1449–1505)

Blessed Osanna was born to a noble family of Mantua. As a child of five, she heard a mysterious voice calling her by name. After this she fell into a mystical rapture in which she was led by an angel to behold the company of the blessed in paradise. It was an experience that marked her forever. While her family hoped for an advantageous marriage, she persuaded them to allow her to put on the habit of a Dominican tertiary.

Though she continued to live at home, Osanna spent most of her time in church or praying silently in her room. Her reputation for holiness attracted wide attention. When not in prayer she was busy with the works of mercy, nursing the sick, visiting prisoners, and serving the poor. She used her connections to advocate for many victims of injustice.

It was a time of rampant corruption in the Church—particularly in Rome. Osanna foresaw much suffering and ruin hanging over Italy on account of the sins of Christians. In particular, she spoke frankly of the sins of Pope Alexander VI. She prayed mightily for his salvation, though she feared he was a hopeless case.

Osanna died on June 20, 1505, at the age of fifty-six.

"O my only Love! Must the thorns then be for Thee alone; for Thee alone the nails and the cross; and for me sweetness and consolation? Ah! not so. I will not share Thy glory unless Thou make me also share Thy pains."

—Blessed Osanna of Mantua

St. Juliana Falconieri
Founder, Sisters of the Third Order of Servites
(1270–1341)

Juliana, who was born to a wealthy family in Florence, was raised largely by her uncle, one of the founders of the Order of Servites. Inspired by his example, and with his consent, she was accepted at the age of fifteen as a Third Order Servite while continuing to live at home with her mother. Upon the latter's death Juliana moved into a community with a group of other women, which in time was recognized as a separate order, the Sisters of the Third Order of Servites. Following a simple rule, they dedicated themselves to prayer and charitable work among the poor and sick. Juliana served as superior until her death in 1341.

St. Juliana was greatly devoted to the Eucharist. As she was dying, unable to receive Communion, she asked that the Host be placed on her breast. At that moment she expired and the Host disappeared. Its image, it was said, was found imprinted over her heart. She was canonized in 1737.

"O faithful bride of Jesus and humble servant of Mary, Saint Juliana, thou who . . . didst merit to be fed miraculously with the Bread of Angels in thy last agony; obtain for me the grace to live a holy life in the exercise of every Christian duty and to be able to receive at the moment of death the comfort of the holy Sacraments in order to come with thee to the blessed happiness of heaven. Amen."
—Prayer to St. Juliana Falconieri

Lord John Acton
Historian (1834–1902)

L ord Acton was one of the outstanding historians of the Victorian Age. Because Catholics were not permitted in the great English universities, he studied in Germany, where he became convinced that Catholics must acquire a deeper historical consciousness and shake off the alliance between the Church and reactionary political causes. Specifically, he challenged the Church's claims to the Papal States and urged the pope to renounce temporal power. He promoted these causes through a series of liberal Catholic journals, though his tendency to sarcasm undermined potential support for his causes.

When Pope Pius IX issued the *Syllabus of Errors*, denouncing most of Acton's principles, he wrote a series of articles chronicling such stains on the Catholic conscience as the violence of the Inquisition and the St. Bartholomew's Day massacre of French Huguenots in 1572. Acton found it abominable that the Church should have allowed the faith to be defended by means of murder, and he regarded those theorists who justified such acts to be no better than the original culprits. This corruption, he believed, was the inevitable fruit of the marriage of sacred and temporal power.

After the definition of papal infallibility in 1870, Acton retired from public Catholic life, though he continued faithfully to attend Mass. He had spent his career trying to reconcile his faith with the principles of truth, liberty, and the rights of conscience, an effort that found few allies among his contemporaries, whether in or outside the Church. He died on June 19, 1902, receiving the last sacraments on his deathbed.

"Power tends to corrupt, and absolute power corrupts absolutely."

—Lord John Acton

Blessed Michelina of Pesaro
Widow and Franciscan Tertiary (1300–1356)

Blessed Michelina was born in the town of Pesaro, on the east coast of Italy. At twelve she married a wealthy member of the powerful Malatesta family, with whom she enjoyed a rich and frivolous social life. By twenty, however, she found herself widowed, to care alone for her young son, who became the center of her life. A Franciscan tertiary named Syriaca, whom she had befriended, urged her to put aside worldly occupations and devote herself to God. Michelina resisted this counsel. But when her son fell ill and died she put on the habit of a Franciscan tertiary, gave away her possessions to the poor, and took to begging alms from door to door.

Her sudden embrace of voluntary poverty did not inspire a corresponding charity on the part of her neighbors. Her family, thinking her mad, had her confined. Eventually, however, her evident sincerity won them over, and she was set free to dedicate herself to works of mercy, especially care of the sick. In imitation of St. Francis she had a special dedication to lepers, and there were stories of her effecting cures by her kiss. Toward the end of her life she went on pilgrimage to Rome, where she received a mystical share in the sufferings of Christ. She died on June 19, 1356.

"My God, so that I may be certain to find my son close to you, I will then renounce all the vanity of the world!"

—Blessed Michelina of Pesaro

Cardinal Yves Congar
Dominican Theologian (1904–1995)

Yves Congar, one of the towering figures in twentieth-century Catholic theology, was born in France in 1904. Ordained as a Dominican priest, he was called up in 1939 to serve as a military chaplain. After capture by the Germans, he spent years as a prisoner of war, an experience that confirmed his commitment to ecumenism and to the need for greater openness to the world.

In the 1950s Congar published groundbreaking books on the role of the laity and Church renewal. With his fellow Dominicans he sought to chart a fresh course apart from the rigid neo-scholasticism of the day—ironically, by "returning to the sources" of Scripture and the early Church Fathers. His work was controversial, and for some years he was forbidden to write or teach. But eventually Pope John XXIII asked him to serve on the preparatory committee for Vatican II. Ultimately he became one of the chief architects of the documents on revelation, the Church, mission, ecumenism, and the Church in the modern world. His mark is particularly reflected in the definition of the Church as "the People of God," in the emphasis on the role of the laity, and in the confession of the Church as being "at once holy and always in need of reformation."

Pope John Paul II named him a cardinal in 1994. Congar died on June 22, 1995, at the age of ninety-one.

"The future is prepared in the waiting when the seed, once deposited, puts forth a shoot and grows. What is essential is to have sown the seed."
—Cardinal Yves Congar

St. Aloysius Gonzaga
Jesuit (1568–1591)

St. Aloysius, who was born into the highest ranks of the Italian nobility, was groomed for a military career. When he announced his wish to become a Jesuit, his father tried every kind of inducement and threat to change his mind, but to no avail. Aloysius entered the novitiate of the Society of Jesus at the age of seventeen.

Even in the zealous atmosphere of a Jesuit novitiate, he set a standard of austerity and piety that provoked both wonder and irritation. He insisted on saying a full Hail Mary on every step as he ascended or descended the stairs. His superiors urged him to lighten up. But no one could doubt that he was happy in his vocation.

During his studies in Rome, an outbreak of plague hit the city. The Jesuits opened a hospital, where the father general and many of the other priests volunteered to serve. Aloysius received permission to join them. When he contracted the disease, he felt joy at the prospect of heaven. After receiving the Last Rites, he seemed to recover. But he soon died on the night of June 21, 1591. His last words were, "In thy hands."

St. Aloysius was canonized in 1726. He became the patron of youth and, more recently, of AIDS patients and their caregivers.

"There is no more evident sign that anyone is a saint and of the number of the elect, than to see him leading a good life and at the same time a prey to desolation, suffering, and trials."

—St. Aloysius Gonzaga

James Chaney and Companions
Civil Rights Martyrs (1964)

In 1964 the Congress of Racial Equality (CORE) and other civil rights organizations called for a Freedom Summer, recruiting northern activists to join local civil rights workers in the South to protest segregation and to register black voters. In retaliation, the Ku Klux Klan in Mississippi unleashed a wave of terror, burning crosses and destroying black churches across the state.

On June 21, three activists in Neshoba County, James Chaney (21), a local African American civil rights worker, Mickey Schwerner (24), a CORE field secretary from New York, and Andrew Goodman (20), a college student from New York, were lynched by the KKK in one of the most notorious crimes of that era. While returning from the site of a church burning, they were arrested by a deputy sheriff and held in the county jail until nightfall, when they were delivered to a mob of Klansmen in a forest clearing outside Philadelphia. There they were beaten, shot, and buried in an earthen dam.

Their disappearance was national news. The governor of Mississippi said it was a communist plot contrived to win sympathy. "The boys are in Cuba," he said. But within a month, following an intensive investigation, the truth was revealed. A pathologist who examined James Chaney said he had never seen a body so shattered. Their deaths were a milestone on the hard road to freedom. In July, President Johnson signed the Civil Rights Act of 1964; the Voting Rights Act was signed into law only a year later.

These brutal deaths are "an attack on the human brotherhood taught by all the great religions of mankind."

—Martin Luther King

St. Alban
Martyr (Third Century)

St. Alban was a prominent citizen—possibly a soldier—who lived in Roman-occupied Britain sometime in the third century. According to legend, as recounted in Bede's history of the English Church, Alban gave shelter to a priest fleeing persecution. Although Alban was himself a pagan, he was touched by the piety of his guest, and after several days he asked to receive instruction and to be baptized in the Christian faith. Aware that soldiers were in close pursuit, Alban contrived to assist the priest's escape by exchanging clothes. When the soldiers arrived at his house they seized Alban, dressed in the priest's cloak, and led him bound to the judge. Upon discovering this trickery, the enraged judge declared, "Since you have chosen to conceal a sacrilegious rebel rather than surrender him to my soldiers to pay the well-deserved penalty for his blasphemy against our gods, you shall undergo all the tortures due to him if you dare to abandon the practice of our religion." Alban declared himself to be a Christian and willingly submitted to the judgment of the court. He was flogged and beheaded.

Bede records that Alban's executioner was so moved by the courage of the condemned that he in turn confessed the faith and was "baptized" in the blood of his own martyrdom. Alban is remembered as the proto-martyr of Great Britain. His feast date is June 20.

"If you desire to hear the truth of my religion, be it known unto you, that I am now a Christian, and employ my time in the practice of Christian duties."
—St. Alban

St. Thomas More
Martyr (1478–1535)

Thomas More was one of the most highly respected men of his time. A successful barrister, an honest judge, a famous scholar, he rose to the highest status of any commoner in England, appointed by Henry VIII to the post of lord chancellor. He considered himself a loyal friend and servant of the king. But by this point King Henry was moving on a collision course with the authority of the Catholic Church. The issue was his desire to annul his marriage to Catherine of Aragon to marry Anne Boleyn. When the pope blocked his way, Henry divorced Catherine, married Anne, and required that all subjects repudiate "any foreign authority, prince or potentate." Rather than oppose the king, More resigned his position, but when he refused to take the oath he was arrested and imprisoned in the Tower of London.

After fifteen months More was put on trial and convicted on the basis of perjured testimony. On the day of his execution on July 6, 1535, he displayed his wit, asking for the executioner's help in ascending the scaffold: "As for my coming down, let me shift for myself." Addressing the gathered crowd, he spoke: "I die as the king's true servant, but God's first."

His feast and that of his fellow martyr, Bishop John Fisher, are celebrated on June 22.

"Little as I meddle in the conscience of others, I am certain that my conscience belongs to me alone. It is the last thing that a man can do for his salvation: to be at one with himself."

—St. Thomas More

St. Etheldreda
Abbess (ca. 636–679)

Etheldreda, one of the most popular of Anglo-Saxon saints, was the daughter of King Anna of East Anglia. Though she wished to devote herself to God, she was twice forced into political marriages—the first time to a much older man, who died "shortly after the wedding." She was happy to settle into a life of prayer on the Isle of Ely, a desolate piece of land which her husband had given her. Nevertheless, she was soon forced into another marriage—this time to a prince of fifteen. Her consort was content for some years to comply with her wish for a chaste relationship, but eventually he sought to revise the terms of their relationship. Etheldreda, insisting she had taken a vow to maintain her virginity, appealed to Bishop Wilfrid of York. The bishop sided with Etheldreda and consecrated her vocation. Returning to Ely, she established a double monastery for men and women.

In his history of the English Church, St. Bede notes with wonder that Etheldreda never dressed in linen garments but only in simple wool, that she seldom bathed in hot water, customarily ate no more than one meal per day, and regularly spent the entire night in prayer. He also relates at length the story that when her coffin was opened, sixteen years after her death in 679, she was found to be incorrupt, "as if she had died and been buried that very day."

"And this virgin began to be the mother of many, both by her example and her heavenly admonitions."

—St. Bede on St. Etheldreda

Blessed Mary of Oignies
Mystic (1175–1213)

Blessed Mary was born to a wealthy family of Brabant, in Belgium. Despite her yearning for religious life, she was forced into marriage at the age of fourteen with another well-born young man. She persuaded him not only to respect her desire for celibacy but to turn their house into a hospital for lepers. There they personally nursed the invalids under their care.

Soon Mary's reputation for holiness began to attract attention. She was particularly famous for her "gift of tears," a sign of her extraordinary sorrow over the sufferings of Christ in the world. When asked why her tears and constant fasting did not make her ill, she replied, "These tears are my feast; they are my bread day and night; they feed my mind; rather than emptying and afflicting my head they bring satiety to my soul."

When the stream of pilgrims to her door became oppressive, Mary's husband gave her permission to enter a convent at Oignies. There her mystical visions increased in number. Often in an ecstatic state she would sing or speak in verse. She said that when she received communion the host had the taste of honey.

Mary died on June 23, 1213, at the age of thirty-eight.

"To receive Christ's body was the same with her as to live."

—James de Vitry, first biographer of Mary of Oignies

Ruth and Naomi
Women of Faith

The Book of Ruth is set in an indeterminate time "when the Judges ruled." That period is better remembered for stories of warfare and lawless violence, often enacted on the bodies of women. The Book of Ruth, in contrast, highlights actions and faith of two women whose trust in God and in one another opens a way to overcome their precarious circumstances.

Naomi and her husband Elimelech escaped famine in Israel by moving to Moab, where their sons married local women. When her husband and both sons died, Naomi decided to move back to Israel, counseling her daughters-in-law to seek husbands among their own people. One of them, Ruth, refused to leave Naomi's side.

The two women returned to Israel—one of them a foreigner, with no means of support apart from gleaning the fields. Nevertheless, the story has a happy ending. With Naomi's encouragement, Ruth attracts the attention of a wealthy kinsman, who agrees to marry her and thus redeem the name of her dead husband.

And so Ruth, by her faith and love, is incorporated into the house of Israel; in fact, she becomes a grandmother of David and a foremother of Jesus. In the story of Ruth and Naomi, there are no acts of violence, no "mighty deeds." Just two women, trusting in one another, hoping in the God who watches over the weak, who fills the hungry, and restores life.

"Where you go I will go, and where you lodge I will lodge; your people shall be my people, and your God my God."

—Ruth 1:16

Vincent Lebbe
Apostle to the Chinese (1877–1940)

In 1901, Vincent Lebbe, a Vincentian priest from Belgium, arrived in China. Even before his arrival, he was fired by a passionate love for the Chinese and a desire to be one with them. This set him apart from many fellow French missionaries who did not conceal their sense of superiority, remaining ignorant of the language, culture, and history of the Chinese. They could not see how such attitudes alienated them from the people. To Lebbe their approach was incomprehensible. "I myself am a Chinese with all my heart and strength," he wrote.

Instead of traditional parish work, Lebbe propagated the Gospel by every means: public lectures, outreach to civic leaders, charitable organizations, schools, and the establishment of a Catholic press. The response was extraordinary. But he offended his superiors and Church authorities with his conviction that the Chinese Church must overcome its dependence on European culture and personnel. He was subjected to relentless harassment.

Forced to depart China, Lebbe became a tireless advocate for his cause in Rome. Eventually he won an audience with Pope Pius XI, handing him a list of Chinese priests who would be suitable bishops. The French bishops regarded this as treason. But in 1926 the pope consecrated six of Lebbe's priests.

Returning to China Lebbe became a naturalized citizen. No one could force him to leave again. Upon his death on June 24, 1940, the government of China declared a day of mourning.

"Vincent Lebbe was one of the persons who inspired the Second Vatican Council. He gave the Church the character of an organization truly and wholly open to all peoples of the world."

—Cardinal Leo Josef Suenens

The Hemorrhaging Woman
Disciple (First Century)

One day as Jesus passed through a crowd, a woman pressed her way past the protective circle of his disciples to touch his garment. Immediately he perceived that "power had gone forth from him." Facing the crowd, he asked, "Who touched my garments?" With fear and trembling the woman stepped forward, fell before him, and told her story. She had suffered for twelve years from a "flow of blood."

In making this humiliating confession she must have braced herself against the crowd's revulsion. More than a physical infirmity, such a condition would have rendered her unclean in the eyes of the law. Her very touch had the power of defilement. And yet, having heard reports of Jesus' healing miracles, she had dared to touch his garment, trusting that this alone could heal her. By this action she had understood, in a way that the disciples as yet did not, that the power of Jesus was at the service of love. And in touching his garment she had immediately felt herself to be healed.

Christ was present in that crowd in all his love and power. But it was a poor, frightened, untouchable woman whose faith recognized that power, awakened it with a touch, and brought it into full view. "Daughter," Jesus said, "it is your faith that has made you well." Unnamed and unremembered in the calendar of the saints, the Hemorrhaging Woman may well be remembered as one of the foremothers of the Church.

"If I but touch his clothes, I shall be cured."

—Mark 5:28

St. Febronia
Martyr (ca. 304)

According to legend, St. Febronia of Nisibis (in Mesopotamia), a beautiful young woman, was raised in a convent of nuns where her aunt was the abbess. Exceptionally intelligent, Febronia soon became famous for her exposition of Scripture. Important women of the town would gather to hear her commentary, though her aunt, eager to protect her from the world, made sure that she was veiled from sight.

During the persecution under the emperor Diocletian, soldiers arrived to suppress the convent. Febronia, who remained alone while the others fled, was arrested and brought to trial. Asked whether she was freeborn or a slave, she called herself a slave. Whose slave? She replied, "I am a servant of the Lord." Asked for her name, she answered, "The poor Christian woman."

The rest of the interrogation proceeded along these lines. Nevertheless, so impressed was the judge by her beauty that he offered to spare her life if she would renounce her religion and marry. In reply, Febronia insisted that she already had "an indissoluble bridal chamber in the heavens that is not made by hands, and a dowry which is the Kingdom of the heaven, and a deathless Bridegroom."

She was subsequently condemned to death. Prior to her beheading, however, she was stripped and subjected to grotesque tortures, so terrible that the crowd begged for mercy.

"Do not be deceived; neither labor to test me with flatteries and threats, for you will never defeat me."
—St. Febronia

Martyrs Under Nero
(d. 64)

The first great persecution of Christians in Rome, which occurred during the reign of Nero in the year 64, followed a great fire that lasted a week and destroyed two-thirds of the city. It is a measure of Nero's reputation that credible rumors began to circulate, accusing the emperor of having allowed the conflagration to continue for his own amusement, if he had not started it himself. To deflect such blame, according to the historian Tacitus, Nero "falsely charged with guilt and punished with the most fearful tortures the persons commonly called Christians, who were hated for their enormities."

It is not known how many Christians died during this persecution. Their cruel tortures were made into public sport. As Tacitus notes, "They were killed by dogs by having the hides of beasts attached to them, or they were nailed to crosses or set aflame, and, when the daylight passed away, they were used as nighttime lamps."

Tacitus held no special sympathy for the followers of Christ, whose teachings he believed were antisocial and pernicious. Yet on Nero, who was "corrupted by every lust, natural and unnatural," he focused special scorn. The emperor's depravities, Tacitus records, effected an increased sympathy for his victims.

"Despite their guilt as Christians and the ruthless punishment it deserved, the victims were pitied. For it was felt that they were being sacrificed to one man's brutality rather than to the national interest."

—Tacitus

Hans Urs von Balthasar
Theologian (1905–1988)

ans Urs von Balthasar, a Swiss theologian, never held an academic post. Alone among the great theologians of his generation, he was not invited to participate in Vatican II. Yet in his massive output, he played an enormous role in shifting the axis of Catholic theology.

Before joining the Jesuits in 1929 he had already earned a doctorate in literature. Bored by lectures in neoscholastic theology, he found himself engaged by his reading of the Church Fathers, and later by the Swiss Reformed theologian Karl Barth. A third great influence came from his encounters with a woman doctor and mystic, Adrienne von Speyr, whom he had received into the Church and whom he came to regard as his theological partner and, indeed, teacher. With her he wished to found a Secular Institute to bridge the gap between the religious and lay states. When his superiors would not support this project, he resigned from the Jesuits and became a diocesan priest.

His most significant work was an enormous trilogy of many volumes, tracing God's relation to creation in the converging lines of Truth, Goodness, and Beauty. He called his work a "kneeling theology," indicating its relation to contemplative prayer as opposed to a merely academic or "sitting" theology.

In 1988 Pope John Paul II asked him to become a cardinal. He died two days before the ceremony on June 26, 1988.

"In the trinitarian dogma God is one, good, true, and beautiful because he is essentially Love, and Love supposes the one, the other, and their unity."
—Hans Urs von Balthasar

Blessed Madeleine Fontaine and Companions
Martyrs (d. 1794)

Madeleine Fontaine was superior of a small community of Sisters of Charity in the town of Arras, France. The sisters maintained a dispensary and a school for girls and otherwise spent their time visiting the poor. Nevertheless, during the Terror of the Revolution, these sisters—who had, in the spirit of St. Vincent de Paul, dedicated their lives to the poor—found themselves charged as enemies of the people.

For some time they were ignored. Even after their school was seized and renamed from the House of Charity to the House of Humanity, the sisters were allowed to continue with their nursing. In 1794, however, a zealous ex-priest, Joseph Lebon, arrived in town to implement the strict decrees of the Revolution. Claiming to have found counter-revolutionary literature in their home, he had the sisters arrested. When they refused to take an oath recognizing the supremacy of the revolutionary state, they were tried and sentenced to death.

On June 27, four sisters went to the guillotine singing *Ave Maris Stella*. Mother Madeleine was the last to die. In a remarkable scene, she turned to the silent crowd and proclaimed the words cited below. Soon after, Mother Madeleine's prophecy would be fulfilled when both Joseph Lebon and Maximilien Robespierre, architect of the Terror, were arrested.

Madeleine Fontaine and her companions were beatified in 1920.

"Listen, Christians! We are the last victims. The persecution is going to stop. The gallows will be destroyed. The altars of Jesus will rise again gloriously."
—Blessed Madeleine Fontaine

Hannah
Mother of the Prophet Samuel

In the Gospel of Luke, Mary proclaims a remarkable hymn of praise, the Magnificat, in which she interprets the wonderful events overtaking her life in terms of a wholesale reversal of the social order: "My soul magnifies the Lord, and my spirit rejoices in God my Savior. . . . / He has put down the mighty from their thrones, and exalted the lowly; / he has filled the hungry with good things, and the rich he has sent empty away."

Mary's words echo a similar hymn by Hannah, mother of the prophet Samuel. Hannah, the barren wife of Elkanah, whose other wife tormented her, had prayed to God to open her womb, promising that she would dedicate her son to the service of the Lord. When her prayer was answered with the birth of Samuel, Hannah sang out: "My heart exults in the Lord; my strength is exalted in the Lord. / My mouth derides my enemies, because I rejoice in thy salvation."

Like Mary, she names the Lord as the champion of the oppressed: "He raises up the poor from the dust; he lifts the needy from the ash heap, / to make them sit with princes and inherit a seat of honor." And Hannah also shows herself to be a prophet, envisioning what will be: "The Lord will judge the ends of the earth; he will give strength to his king, and exalt the power of his anointed."

Samuel went on to serve the Lord. And Hannah bore five more children.

"Let your maidservant find favor in your eyes."

—Hannah (1 Samuel 1:18)

St. Irenaeus
Bishop and Theologian (ca. 130–ca. 200)

St. Irenaeus, one of the first systematic theologians of the Church, was born in Asia Minor. At some point he made his way to Lyons, a major Roman outpost in Gaul, where he was ordained a presbyter. In 177, while he was on a mission in Rome, a wave of savage persecution swept over the Church in Lyons. Upon his return Irenaeus found that his bishop, Pothinus, was among the martyrs. He was chosen to take his place.

In the rapid proliferation of Gnostic sects, Bishop Irenaeus came to believe the Church faced a threat even greater than persecution. One of the typical features of Gnosticism was a sharply dualistic understanding of matter and spirit. It was impossible for Gnostics to imagine any direct interaction between these two realms, either in the Christian doctrines of creation or the incarnation.

Irenaeus wrote his principal work to counter these ideas. He underscored the links between the Old and New Testaments, insisting on the identity between the God of creation and the God of salvation. There was nothing inherently corrupt in creation; it was only through the distortion of sin that human beings lost their "likeness to God." This was restored in the obedience of Christ, who corrected the story of the first Adam. Only the God who created human beings could also save us; and only that which was truly assumed (humanity in the incarnation) could also be redeemed.

Irenaeus died as a martyr sometime around the year 200.

"The glory of God is the human being fully alive."

—St. Irenaeus

St. John Southworth
Martyr (1592–1654)

John Southworth was born in the Elizabethan era to a loyal Catholic family of Lancashire. At the age of twenty-one he attended the English seminary in Douai, France, and was later ordained a priest. After spending some years in a Benedictine monastery he asked to return to England. While the penal laws outlawing Catholic ministry remained on the books, it was a time of relative toleration, as the French-born queen, Henrietta Maria, wife of King Charles I, was herself a Catholic.

Though he was arrested several times, the conditions of imprisonment were not entirely harsh. Puritan critics, who regarded him as a "dangerous seducer," complained that in prison "he had full liberty to walk abroad at his pleasure." Pardoned on the insistence of the queen, he disobeyed an order to leave the country and remained to minister to victims of the plague.

The situation, however, would soon deteriorate. After the outbreak of civil war and the execution of the king, Catholics were again regarded as dangerous subversives. Southworth was arrested in 1654 and executed in Tyburn on June 28. He was canonized by Pope Paul VI in 1970 as one of the Forty Martyrs of England and Wales.

"Hitherto I was sent to teach Christ's faith, not to meddle with any temporal affairs. Christ sent his apostles; his apostles, their successors, and their successors, me. I did what I was commanded by them who had power to command me. . . . I die for Christ's law, which no human law, by whosoever committed, ought to withstand or contradict."
—St. John Southworth

Saints Peter and Paul
Apostles (First Century)

This day commemorates the two preeminent apostles of the early Church. Of the two, St. Peter was among the twelve disciples called by Jesus. Originally named Simon, Jesus gave him an Aramaic name, Cephas, meaning "Rock." This inspired a memorable pun when Jesus told him, "You are Cephas [Peter] and upon this *rock* I will build my church." The occasion was Jesus' question to the disciples: "Who do you say I am?" which prompted Peter's reply: "You are the Christ." Peter emerges in the Gospels as a complex character, bold, impetuous, capable of fear, doubt, and childlike meekness; in short, a fully human creature. It was this "Rock" who denied Christ three times after his arrest but who later repented his betrayal and courageously assumed leadership of the early Church.

St. Paul, a devout Jew, was initially a persecutor of the Church. But after receiving a dazzling vision of the Risen Lord, he was convinced that Jesus was the Messiah. He went on to become a zealous missionary and servant of the Gospel. His letters to the early Christian communities became foundational documents for the early Church. By providing a theological rationale for the universality of the Gospel he was largely responsible for extending the Church to the wider Gentile world. He suffered persecution in many forms and was eventually martyred in Rome, where Peter, too, suffered the same fate.

"Though they all fall away because of you, I will never fall away."
—St. Peter (Matthew 26:33)

"And now these three remain: faith, hope, and love. But the greatest of these is love."
—St. Paul (1 Corinthians 13:13)

St. Emma
Widow (ca. 980–1045)

St. Emma was raised in the court of her kinsman, Henry II, the Holy Roman Emperor, and educated by his wife, St. Cunigunde. When she came of age, she was married to William, the Landgrave of Friesach. Though it was an arranged marriage, it was evidently a happy one. They had two sons, whom William put in charge of his mines. However, the young counts ruled so harshly that they provoked a rebellion among the mine workers, resulting in their deaths. Overcome with grief, Emma withdrew in prayer, while her husband threatened to kill all the miners and their families. After Emma dissuaded him from the path of vengeance, William went on pilgrimage to Rome, only to perish on the return journey.

Alone in the world, Emma resolved to devote the rest of her life to the service of God and the poor. She founded several monasteries, including a double monastery in the Austrian town of Gurk, where the monks and nuns prayed in shifts, maintaining a perpetual recitation of the office. Emma retired to this community, though it is unclear whether she herself took the veil. She died and was buried there in 1045.

*"Saint Emma, with rejoicing now the vales and skies are ringing /
Look down upon us now and hear your homeland singing!"*

—Austrian poet Guido Zernatto

Blessed Ramón Lull
Missionary and Martyr (1232–1316)

Ramón Lull was born in Majorca in 1232, the son of a Catalan military chief. His early life was spent in the frivolity of court life. At the age of thirty, however, prompted by a recurrent vision of Jesus on the cross, he underwent a dramatic and total conversion. Afterward he gave up all his property to his family and the poor and determined to devote his life to God's cause. In particular, he felt called to bring the Gospel to the Muslims—a vocation, he was sure, that would cost him his life.

He prepared with zeal. For over a decade he applied himself to his studies, mastering Latin and Arabic, and immersing himself—to a remarkable degree—in the literature of Muslim religion and philosophy. He believed that a missionary must be fully knowledgeable about the beliefs of those he wished to convert.

Lull traveled throughout Europe lobbying and seeking sponsors for his projects, including a series of missionary colleges where the best preachers of the world would study the language and culture of the non-Christian world. Such plans came to naught. He wrote several hundred major works as well as mystical poetry and allegorical romances about the Christian life.

Ramón made three trips to North Africa. On the first occasions he was quickly arrested and deported. However, on his third trip in Tunisia he was accosted by a mob on June 29, 1316, and stoned to death.

"He who loves not lives not; he who lives by the Life cannot die."

—Blessed Ramón Lull

Venerable Pierre Toussaint
Former Slave (1766–1853)

ierre Toussaint was born in slavery on a plantation in present-day Haiti. His owners, the Berard family, anticipating the revolutionary uprising that was to come, fled to New York, taking Pierre along with them. They encouraged him to train as an apprentice hairdresser—a skilled and lucrative trade. Meanwhile, Monsieur Berard, who had returned to Haiti, died there, leaving the family penniless. At this point Pierre, though still a slave, took to supporting the Berard family through his hairdressing. He continued in this service until the death of his mistress, who left instructions that he be freed.

Pierre married another former Haitian slave, Juliette, and their home became a center for charitable work. Through his earnings, Pierre secured the freedom of many other slaves, provided for orphans, cared for victims of plague, and even extended aid to French widows impoverished by the liberation of Haiti. He was widely recognized for his piety and devotion to the Church. Among other causes, he raised money for the construction of Old St. Patrick's Cathedral, where he was buried after his death on June 30, 1853.

He was declared venerable by Pope John Paul II in 1996.

"I have never felt I am a slave to any man or woman but I am a servant of the Almighty God who made us all. When one of his children is in need, I am glad to be His slave."

—Venerable Pierre Toussaint

JULY

1 St. Junipero Serra • Blessed Antonio Rosmini

2 St. Monegundis • Hrotsvitha of Gandersheim

3 St. Thomas • Bernard Haring

4 St. Elizabeth of Portugal • Blessed Catherine Jarrige

5 St. Anthony Zaccaria • Georges Bernanos

6 St. Maria Goretti • Blessed Mary Theresa Ledóchowska

7 Blessed Maria Romero Meneses • Peace Pilgrim

8 Jan Hus • Angelus Silesius

9 Servant of God Rose Hawthorne • St. Pauline of the Agonizing Heart of Jesus

10 Servant of God Augustus Tolton • Eve Lavalliere

11 St. Benedict • Desiderius Erasmus

12 St. Veronica • Saints Zélie and Louis Martin

13 Blessed Angelina of Marsciano • St. Clelia Barbieri

14 St. Kateri Tekakwitha • Cicely Saunders

15 St. Bonaventure • Blessed Anne-Marie Javouhey

16 St. Mary-Magdalen Postel • St. Elizabeth Feodorovna

17 St. Hedwig of Poland • Carmelite Martyrs of Compiègne

18 Bartolomé de Las Casas • St. Camillus de Lellis

19 St. Macrina the Younger • Rebecca Nurse

20 Elijah • Pope Leo XIII

21 St. Margaret • Lawrence Jenco

22 St. Mary Magdalene • Albert Luthuli

23 St. Bridget of Sweden • Anne Hutchinson

24 Saints Boris and Gleb • St. Christina the Astonishing

25 St. James the Great • St. Christopher

26 Saints Anne and Joachim • Blessed Andrew of Phu Yen

27 The Seven Sleepers of Ephesus • Blessed Titus Brandsma

28 William Wilberforce • Servant of God Stanley Rother

29 St. Martha of Bethany • Blessed Beatrice of Nazareth

30 Blessed Zdenka Cecilia Schelingova • Bishop James E. Walsh

31 St. Ignatius Loyola • Venerable Solanus Casey

JULY

St. Junipero Serra
Franciscan Missionary (1713–1784)

Junipero Serra is celebrated as one of the fathers of California. Born in Majorca, Serra entered the Franciscan Order at sixteen. After earning a doctorate in theology he taught as a professor for many years before volunteering for the missions in New Spain. He spent twenty years in Mexico, then traveled by foot to California, where he spent the rest of his life. From his arrival in 1769, when he founded the mission of San Diego, until his death fifteen years later, he tirelessly traveled the length of California, established nine missions, and baptized many thousands of Indians.

Serra espoused an austere, ascetic brand of Catholicism. In preaching, he was capable of demonstrating his zeal by striking his breast with a stone, or holding a lighted torch against his chest to demonstrate the fires of hell.

His canonization in 2015—the first to take place on North American soil—was not without controversy. Critics, including many Native Americans, raised questions about the mission settlements in which Indian converts were incorporated, becoming virtual prisoners or indentured servants. Others defended Serra and the Franciscan missionaries for protecting the Indians from harsher abuse by the secular authorities.

Serra died on August 28, 1784. He is buried in the sanctuary floor of the Mission de San Carlos Borromeo in Carmel.

"What I should like to be able to do is to affix to their hearts the words, 'Put you on the Lord Jesus Christ.' May the most provident Lord and heavenly Father grant that my wish be accomplished in their regard."
—St. Junipero Serra

Blessed Antonio Rosmini
Founder, Institute of Charity (1797–1855)

Antonio Rosmini was one of the preeminent Italian priests of the nineteenth century. Through his personal piety and scholarship he tried to raise the level of Catholic culture and to enhance the Church's leadership with respect to the social questions of his day. He founded the Institute of Charity, a congregation of priests committed to the pursuit of holiness in service of the Church. He also achieved renown as a philosopher, writing scores of scholarly books. One of these, *Five Wounds of the Church*, laid out an extensive critique of the Church and the self-imposed afflictions that prevented it from assuming its leadership in the world. These wounds included the division of the people from the clergy in worship, the defective education of the clergy, and the enslavement of the Church by riches.

These works, along with his patriotic support for Italian unification, aroused the ire of the Vatican, which placed his books on the Index of proscribed works. Although never charged with any error, he remained under a cloud for the rest of his life. Rosmini submitted gracefully to these restrictions, satisfied by the knowledge that if he were not in error his message would eventually be heard and received by future generations. He died on July 1, 1855. He was beatified by Pope Benedict XVI in 2007.

"The people should be actors in the liturgy as well as hearers."

—Blessed Antonio Rosmini

St. Monegundis
Contemplative and Healer (d. 570)

In the sixth century St. Gregory of Tours wrote a book on contemporary saints—mostly bishops, abbots, and ascetics. St. Monegundis, whom he knew firsthand, was the only woman among them. As Gregory relates, she had originally lived in Chartres with her husband and two beautiful daughters, who were the joy of her life. When her daughters died she fell into a depression so deep she feared that she would become "unmindful of God." With her husband's consent, she enclosed herself in a small cell, with only one window, where she slept on the floor and subsisted on bread and water. Eventually she moved to Tours to be near the shrine of St. Martin. There she began to attract other women seeking spiritual counsel, and her cell became the foundation of a convent.

By St. Gregory's account, Monegundis embodied the spirit of the desert ascetic, transposed into an urban setting. The space in her heart, created by her life of renunciation and prayer, was filled with a sacred power that gave her the ability to cure bodies and spirits. The many healings she performed in life continued after her death, as those who crossed the threshold of her tomb were able to "drink in the resurrection."

"It is not possible to list individually how many who suffered from chills, how many suffered from festering blisters and were almost dead as the poison raged and how many were ill from dysentery were healed by her."

—St. Gregory of Tours on St. Monegundis

Hrotsvitha of Gandersheim
Canoness, Writer (ca. 935–ca. 1002)

Hrotsvitha of Gandersheim—though her work has received little attention, and obscurity attends most details of her life—was undoubtedly one of the remarkable women of her age. Of the details of her origins, or even the spelling of her name, there is no consensus. Possibly born into Saxon nobility, she obviously received an extraordinary education and at some point entered the Abbey of Gandersheim—not as a nun, but as a canoness, taking vows of obedience and chastity. There she was encouraged to write and quickly won renown for her literary talents.

Writing in Latin, Hrotsvitha composed many volumes of allegorical poetry and moral dramas, often dealing with themes of conversion, the struggle against temptation, martyrdom, and the challenge of Christian discipleship. Many of her plays were set in the time of Roman persecution, featuring strong female heroines who challenged the rulers and the culture of their time by asserting their own identity in Christ.

Though her work was admired, many doubted that such works could be composed by a member of the "weaker gender." Hrotsvitha proudly affirmed her own talents, which were "gifts of God."

"Scorn he should not render at the writer's weaker gender / Who these small lines had sung with a woman's untutored tongue / But rather should he praise the Lord's celestial grace."

—Hrotsvitha of Gandersheim

St. Thomas
Apostle (First Century)

Though mentioned in only a few verses in the Gospel of John, St. Thomas emerges as one of the most vivid characters in the New Testament. When Jesus announces his intention to proceed toward Jerusalem and the peril that surely awaits, it is Thomas who boldly answers, "Let us also go, that we may die with him." Yet it is for his famous "doubt" that Thomas is chiefly remembered. After the resurrection, Thomas reacts incredulously to the report that fellow apostles have seen the Risen Lord. He will never believe, he insists, unless he can feel for himself the marks of the nails and place his hand in Christ's wounded side.

Eight days later Christ appears to all the disciples in the Upper Room where they are hiding. Addressing Thomas by name he invites the doubting disciple to touch his wounds. Thomas can do no more than exclaim, "My Lord and my God!" Jesus responds, "Have you believed because you have seen me? Blessed are those who have not seen and yet believe."

The activities of Thomas post-Pentecost are uncertain. According to early legends he engaged in a great missionary venture that took him as far as the south of India, where he was reportedly martyred. In fact, when Portuguese explorers in the sixteenth century landed on the coast of southern India they found in place a Christian community that attributed its origins to the evangelization of the doubting apostle. To this day their descendants call themselves St. Thomas Christians.

"Thomas's unbelief has benefited our faith more than the belief of the other disciples; it is because he attained faith through physical touch that we are confirmed in the faith beyond all doubt."

—St. Gregory the Great on St. Thomas

Bernard Haring
Theologian (1912–1998)

Bernard Haring, a German Redemptorist priest, was disappointed when his superiors sent him to study moral theology, a topic he found a "crushing bore." Over many centuries moral theology had become an intricate system of laws and prohibitions, a catalog of venial and mortal sins. Yet after earning his doctorate at Tübingen, Haring would fundamentally transform the field. Drawing on Scripture and personalist philosophy, Haring recast the moral life as a dynamic between God's invitation and the free choice of human beings to respond in love.

During the war he served as a medic in the German army. The experience of totalitarianism affected his later theology, convincing him that moral teaching must not rest on blind obedience but on the courage to be responsible. In 1954 he published his landmark work, *The Law of Christ*. He went on to serve as a key theological expert at Vatican II and spent the rest of his life promoting and defending the spirit of the Council. At the same time, he believed it "laughable" that most moral theology focused largely on sexual themes. "My main calling," he said, "must be that of an untiring apostle for the elimination of war . . . for a radical love that will not allow us to become enemies."

Haring died on July 3, 1998.

"God speaks in many ways to awaken, deepen and strengthen faith, hope, love and the spirit of adoration. We are believers to the extent that, in all of reality and in all events that touch us, we perceive a gift and a call from God."
—Bernard Haring

St. Elizabeth of Portugal
Queen (1271–1336)

St. Elizabeth of Portugal was the daughter of the king of Aragon. At twelve she married King Denis of Portugal, a profligate man, who tolerated his wife's piety while making no secret of his own infidelities. Elizabeth bore two children, a son and a daughter. Her son, Alfonso, would later come close to open rebellion against his neglectful father. For her role in effecting a reconciliation between father and son Elizabeth became popularly known as "the Peacemaker." But her peacemaking talents were exercised on an even greater level when she personally prevented a war between Portugal and Castile.

Elizabeth lived up to her public responsibilities as queen. But the greater part of her time was spent in prayer and a variety of charitable projects. She established hospitals, orphanages, and religious houses throughout the kingdom, as well as halfway homes for "fallen women."

When her husband died she put on the habit of a Franciscan tertiary and lived for her eleven remaining years in one of the monasteries she had helped to found. She emerged occasionally to intercede between rival monarchs—with most of whom she bore some relation. Even as she lived she was credited with miracles, and she was revered by the people of Portugal. She died in 1336 and was canonized three centuries later by Pope Urban VIII, who named her the Patroness of Peace.

"God made me queen so that I may serve others."

—St. Elizabeth of Portugal

Blessed Catherine Jarrige
Dominican Tertiary (1754–1836)

Catherine Jarrige, the youngest of seven children, was born to a peasant family in Doumis, France. As a child, on account of her sweet nature, she was called "the little nun," though according to her own recollection she could be quite mischievous. But her childhood was brief. At nine she was sent to work as a maidservant; at thirteen, upon her mother's death, she trained as a lacemaker.

When at last she was able to support herself she moved into a small room, which she shared with one of her sisters. She became a Dominican tertiary, taking a vow of chastity and praying the hours. Now, indeed, she lived like a little nun, finding ways in her free time to care for the poor, the sick, and elderly.

It was during the terror of the French Revolution, however, that Catherine's special mission emerged. Priests who refused to take an oath to the state faced death or exile. For those who went into hiding, Catherine established a network of safe havens. At great risk, she supplied them with food, vestments, and even altar wine, so they could celebrate clandestine Masses. She also brought them babies to be baptized. And when they were caught, she prayed with them at the guillotine.

When the persecution had passed she resumed her charitable services, particularly among prisoners and hospital patients, until her death on July 4, 1836. She was beatified in 1996.

"A Dominican tertiary, the spiritual daughter of St. Catherine of Siena, she preached Christ and his Gospel by her actions. Her message is a message of joy, love, and hope."

—Pope John Paul II on Blessed Catherine Jarrige

St. Anthony Zaccaria
Founder, Clerks Regular of St. Paul (1502–1539)

Between the corruptions of the Renaissance papacy and the challenge of the Protestant Reformation, the early sixteenth century was not the Church's finest hour. And yet a number of saints and reforming orders arose in this period, seeking to renew the Church from within by the power of their evangelical witness. Fr. Anthony Zaccaria was among them.

Born in the northern Italian town of Cremona, he initially trained to become a doctor before being persuaded by his Dominican spiritual director to become a priest. With two noblemen from Milan he founded a congregation of priests to "regenerate and revive the love of divine worship and a properly Christian way of life by frequent preaching and faithful ministering of the sacraments."

Their work in ministering to victims of the plague won them support and brought them to the attention of Pope Clement VII, who in 1533 approved their order, the Clerks Regular of St. Paul. Fr. Anthony's preaching drew primarily on New Testament themes, particularly the epistles of St. Paul. His spiritual teaching focused on devotion to the Blessed Sacrament and the crucifix. Nevertheless, his reforming spirit provoked the resentment of local clergy, who twice brought accusations of heresy against him. On both occasions he was vindicated.

Anthony Zaccaria died on July 5, 1539, at thirty-seven. He was canonized in 1897.

"Let us run like fools not only to God but also to our neighbor, who is the intermediary to whom we give what we cannot give to God."

—St. Anthony Zaccaria

Georges Bernanos
Novelist (1888–1948)

Georges Bernanos was one of the most ardently Catholic of modern French writers. All of his novels dealt with religious themes. But he struggled for many years before achieving success with the publication in 1937 of *The Diary of a Country Priest*. Written in the form of a diary, it tells the story of a young priest in a country parish, who serves God "in exact proportion to his belief that he has served Him badly." Painfully aware of his own limitations, the priest is unaware of his underlying sanctity. It becomes clear that he is pouring himself out for the salvation of his flock. By the end, as the priest is dying, we sense that he has offered himself as a victim soul. His dying words are, "Grace is everywhere."

After the publication of *The Diary of a Country Priest*, Bernanos moved to Spain, where he lived through the Civil War. At first sympathetic to Franco's cause, he became disillusioned with the atrocities on both sides—especially by those committed in the name of Christ. It seemed scandalous to him that the Church not only failed to denounce the bloodbath but even seemed to bless it as a Holy Crusade.

Throughout his life, Bernanos was haunted by the sense that there was only one happiness: to be a saint. Without saints, he said, the Church was a soulless institution that would be the first to crucify its Savior.

He died on July 5, 1948.

"I am between the Angel of light and the Angel of darkness, looking at them each in turn with the same hunger for the absolute."

—Georges Bernanos

St. Maria Goretti
Martyr (1890–1902)

Maria Goretti was born to a family of Italian peasants. Her father died when she was ten, and it fell to her mother to support the family. They shared a dwelling with another family, whose eighteen-year-old son, Alessandro, regularly made sexual advances toward young Maria. One day, when she was not quite twelve, he confronted her alone in their cottage and tried to force himself on her. When she resisted, he repeatedly stabbed her. She died the following day, though not before she had received the Eucharist and expressed forgiveness for her murderer (whom she hoped to meet in heaven).

Alessandro was sentenced to thirty years in prison. After some time he had a dream in which Maria appeared to him, again conveying her forgiveness and appealing to him for conversion. He awoke a changed man. Upon his release from prison he went to Maria's mother and begged her forgiveness.

In the meantime, Maria's story had spread far beyond her village. She was regularly invoked as a symbol of purity and Christian virtue. Thousands of people remembered her in their prayers, and many miracles were attributed to her intercession. Her canonization in 1950 by Pope Pius XII drew a record crowd, including her mother and siblings and, more remarkably, the man who had taken her life.

So this peasant girl, while clinging fiercely to her own truth, also bore witness to a redemptive power large enough to embrace the salvation of her assailant and to transcend all the cruel circumstances of their lives.

"No, it's a sin. God does not want it!"

—St. Maria Goretti, to her assailant

Blessed Mary Theresa Ledóchowska
Founder, Missionary Sisters of St. Peter Claver
(1863–1922)

Maria Theresia von Ledóchowska was born to a remark-able family of the Polish nobility. Her six siblings would include another saint, a future General of the Jesuits, and a martyr under the Nazis. Maria's vocation took an unlikely path, as she went to Salzburg to serve as lady-in-waiting to the grand duchess of Tuscany. There, in 1886 some Franciscan missionaries came to court to describe the missionary needs of Africa. Maria was immediately taken by the idea that she might dedicate herself to this cause.

After undertaking a serious study of Africa she began organizing groups to support the missions and the antislavery cause. This led to her own journal—for which she initially wrote anonymously—called *Echo from Africa*. Eventually she requested permission "to resign from the imperial court so as to transfer to the court of the Good Lord."

In 1893 she devised a plan for a missionary association, which in time became a religious congregation: The Missionary Sisters of St. Peter Claver. She was tireless in promoting general interest in Africa and its peoples and in seeking opportunities to promote their welfare. She was particularly active in publishing, producing Bibles, magazines, and educational materials in many African languages, while also promoting an audience for this output through the development of literacy programs. In 1900 she organized an antislavery conference in Vienna.

Mary Theresa died in Rome on July 6, 1922. She was beatified in 1975.

"The most divine of divine things is to cooperate in the saving of souls."
—Blessed Mary Theresa Ledóchowska

Blessed Maria Romero Meneses
Religious (1902–1977)

Maria Romero Meneses was born to a wealthy family in Nicaragua, where her father was a government minister. The experience of a serious childhood illness prompted a religious vocation, and at the age of eighteen, inspired by the example of Don Bosco, she joined the Salesian Sisters. In 1931 she was transferred to Costa Rica, where she spent the rest of her life.

The work of the sisters focused mainly on educating the daughters of the upper class. But they also operated schools for the poor. Sr. Maria moved between both worlds, and soon she found her special mission in forming the social conscience of her wealthy students. She called them her *misioneritas* (little missionaries) and trained them to help her work among the poor—offering both material service as well as religious instruction. In time she founded her own schools, clinics, and soup kitchens, and even founded a model village, Centro San José, for poor families.

Her work was supported by the local bishop, a strong advocate of the social apostolate. She died on July 7, 1977, and was beatified in 2002—the first beatified saint of Central America.

"Sr. Maria Romero knew how to reflect the face of Christ, which he made her recognize in the sharing of the bread. She was an exemplary religious, apostle, and mother of the poor, who were her real favorites."
—Pope John Paul II

Peace Pilgrim
Witness (d. 1981)

She called herself Peace Pilgrim. Otherwise, she had no interest in describing the particulars of her early life, her age, or even her given name. She walked back and forth across the United States for almost three decades owning nothing but the clothes she wore and a tunic bearing her chosen name on the front and on the back, the simple words, "25,000 Miles on Foot for Peace."

As far as she would reveal, her early years were conventional. But at a certain point she realized that a "self-centered" existence did not bring fulfillment. At this point she came to a "complete willingness, without any reservations, to give my life to God and to service." At that point she was overcome with peace.

After preparing for her mission, she set off on January 1, 1953. Those were years when even the word "peace" was regarded with suspicion. Nevertheless, she walked from town to town, engaging in conversation with whomever she met and spreading the message of peace. In 1964 she stopped counting the miles, but she maintained her pilgrimage until July 7, 1981, when she was killed in a car accident.

"Who am I? It matters not. This clay garment is one of a penniless pilgrim journeying in the name of peace. It is what you cannot see that is so very important. I am one who is propelled by the power of faith; I bathe in the light of eternal wisdom; I am sustained by the unending energy of the universe; this is who I really am."

—Peace Pilgrim

Jan Hus
Catholic Reformer and Martyr (ca. 1372–1415)

The life of Jan Hus, a Czech priest and reformer, was almost coterminous with one of the most serious crises in the history of Christendom—the Great Schism of the papacy (1378–1417)—which saw the Church rent between the claims of two, and ultimately three, rival pontiffs.

Hus was a master at the University of Prague and preacher at the University Chapel. There he emerged as a popular leader of the movement for Church reform. He attacked corruption among the clergy and urged the promotion of lay spirituality through knowledge of Scripture and frequent communion.

When one of the popes authorized the sale of indulgences to pay for a crusade against his rival, Hus spoke out. This commercialization of the sacrament of penance was all the more scandalous in that it served as an exhortation to bloodshed. His stand offended not only the archbishop of Prague but also the emperor, who stood to share in the proceeds of this commerce.

After receiving a promise of safe conduct to defend his views at the Council of Constance (convened to resolve the schism), Hus was immediately arrested and imprisoned. Following a shamelessly biased trial he was convicted of heresy and publicly burned. The papal schism was resolved. But in burning Hus, the Church lost a faithful reformer, one who might have helped forestall the far greater crisis of the following century.

"It is better to die well than to live wickedly. One should not sin in order to avoid the punishment of death. Truth conquers all things."

—Jan Hus

Angelus Silesius
Mystic and Poet (1624–1677)

Johann Scheffler, his given name, was born to Protestant parents in Breslau, the capital of Silesia. After earning a doctorate in medicine, he served as court physician to Count Sylvius Nimrod, an ardent Lutheran. Over time, his public questioning of Lutheran doctrine and his increasingly mystical leanings caused him to be viewed with suspicion. Resigning from his position, in 1653 he converted to Catholicism, taking the name Angelus Silesius. After joining the Franciscans, he was ordained a priest.

Silesius is best remembered for his two volumes of mystical poetry, *The Soul's Spiritual Delight* and *The Cherubic Pilgrim*. Most of his poems consist of epigrammatic rhyming couplets—many later adapted by both Catholic and Protestant hymnists. Silesius was fascinated by the relation between God and creation, the divine and the soul: "A Loaf holds many grains of corn / And many myriad drops the Sea: / So is God's Oneness Multitude / And that great Multitude are we." His ability to detect God's presence in all things caused some to accuse him of pantheism. But he did not worship nature. Instead, he saw in all creation the outflowing of divine love and energy and believed that the same energy and love was drawing all things toward final reunion with God. "The All proceedeth from the One, / And into One must All regress: / If otherwise, the All remains / Asunder-riven manyness."

Silesius died on July 9, 1677.

"All heaven's glory is within and so is hell's fierce burning. / You must yourself decide in which direction you are turning."

—Angelus Silesius

Servant of God Rose Hawthorne
Founder, Servants of Relief for Incurable Cancer
(1851–1926)

Rose Hawthorne was the third and favorite child of Nathaniel Hawthorne, the great American writer. He died when she was thirteen, a loss compounded a few years later by the death of her mother. Bereft, Rose accepted the proposal of the writer George Lathrop, whom she married in 1871 soon after her twentieth birthday. They had a son who died at the age of five. Rose's marriage gradually deteriorated, largely due to Lathrop's alcoholism. For a time their common attraction to Catholicism held promise of restoring their relationship. In 1891 they were both received into the Catholic Church, yet two years later they formally separated.

Finding herself alone in New York City, Rose felt called to some more heroic expression of her faith. In becoming aware of the plight of impoverished cancer patients, banished to die in isolation on Blackwell's Island, she found her calling.

After obtaining a nursing degree, she began visiting and then inviting cancer patients to share her own apartment. This became a full-time occupation. Following Lathrop's death, she formalized her vocation by entering religious life. In 1900 she and a companion were received into the Dominican Order. Six years later her own Dominican congregation was established, and she became known as Mother Alphonsa.

She died at seventy-five on July 9, 1926, at the motherhouse of her congregation in Hawthorne, New York. Her cause for canonization is in process.

"I am trying to serve the poor as a servant. I wish to serve the cancerous poor because they are more avoided than any other class of sufferers; and I wish to go to them as a poor creature myself."

—Servant of God Rose Hawthorne

St. Pauline of the Agonizing Heart of Jesus
Founder, Little Sisters of the Immaculate Conception
(1865–1942)

Amabile Lucia Visintainer was born in a small town in northern Italy. Poverty drove many of the townsfolk—her family among them—to emigrate. Amabile's family settled in Santa Catarina in southern Brazil, where the government was providing land to settlers. She and her friends took it upon themselves to care for the sick, and in 1890 her spiritual director encouraged her to pursue a religious vocation. This resulted in a new congregation, the Little Sisters of the Immaculate Conception. She took the name Pauline of the Agonizing Heart of Jesus and was appointed superior general "for life."

In 1903 she moved to the city of São Paulo, where she worked among the poor—many of them impoverished former slaves. (Slavery in Brazil was abolished only in 1888.) Somehow she came into conflict with the archbishop, with the result that she was removed as superior and sent to work at a remote hospice. The archbishop declared that "she should live and die as an underling." She endured this "exile" for nine years, at which point she was finally welcomed back to the motherhouse and acknowledged as the true "Mother Foundress."

Suffering from diabetes and eventual blindness, she died on July 9, 1942. She was canonized in 2002.

"Be humble. Trust always and a great deal in divine Providence; never, never must you let yourselves be discouraged, despite contrary winds. I say it again: trust in God and Mary Immaculate; be faithful and forge ahead."

—St. Pauline of the Agonizing Heart of Jesus

Servant of God Augustus Tolton
Priest (1854–1897)

Augustus Tolton was born a slave in Missouri in 1854. His mother escaped during the Civil War, taking her three children north to Quincy, Illinois. There Augustus was educated in a Catholic school and decided to become a priest, though no seminary would take him. After private tutorials with a local priest he was accepted at a small Franciscan school and eventually studied at the Urban College in Rome. Expecting to be assigned as a missionary to Africa, he was instead sent back to the United States to work among the struggling black Catholic population.

Tolton was appointed pastor of a black parish in his hometown of Quincy, where his effective preaching drew many white parishioners—a source of resentment on the part of neighboring white priests. Eventually he was assigned to a parish in Chicago, yet a sense of isolation remained, the burden of being the only black priest in America. He died on July 9, 1897, at the age of forty-three.

Tolton is remembered today as a pioneer, the first black priest in America who fully identified with and sought to represent the aspirations of African American Catholics. He exposed the presence of racism in the Church while striving to witness to an ideal of equality and reconciliation within the Body of Christ. His cause for canonization was introduced in 2011.

"America has been called the most enlightened nation in the world. We shall see whether it deserves that honor. If the United States has never before seen a black priest, it must see one now."

—Fr. Augustus Tolton

Eve Lavalliere
Penitent (1866–1929)

For years, Eve Lavalliere was the toast of Parisian society, a famous beauty and the most popular actress on the French stage. While performing for royalty across Europe, she enjoyed the favors of numerous lovers. "I had everything the world could offer," she noted, "everything I could desire. Nevertheless, I regarded myself as the unhappiest of souls." Unhappiness ran deep in life. Her abominable childhood had ended the day her father, in a drunken rage, shot her mother and then killed himself. Her later fame and wealth could not fill the void.

And yet Eve's life took a dramatic turn in 1917 when a priest gave her a biography of Mary Magdalene and challenged her to read it. At first defiantly and then with tears of remorse, she read the book, and when she had finished she resolved to make her peace with God. "My resolution is made," Eve wrote. "From now on, only Jesus has a right to my life, for He alone gave me happiness and peace."

Abandoning her glittering life, Eve first sought to enter religious life, but she was rejected by a number of convents, on account of her notoriety. Instead she became a Third Order Franciscan. For several years, until ill health overtook her, she volunteered with a lay-missionary nursing order in Tunisia. She spent her last years alone, penniless, and in great suffering. Yet she insisted she was the "happiest person in the world." She died on July 10, 1929.

"I left everything for God; He alone is enough."

—Inscription on the gravestone of Eve Lavalliere

St. Benedict
Abbot (ca. 480–550)

As a young man, St. Benedict was moved to abandon his studies in Rome to devote himself to the quest for God. This led him, at first, to the solitude of a cave at Subiaco. There, in time, after attracting followers, he was persuaded to assume leadership of a nearby monastic community. It was not an initial success; following his monks' attempt to poison him, Benedict shook the dust from his feet. With much better results, he went on to organize a group of monasteries, including the famous monastery at Monte Cassino, later renowned as the birthplace of the Benedictine Order. There he wrote his hugely influential monastic Rule and there, in time, he died.

Whereas earlier monastic experiments had stressed rigorous asceticism and self-denial, Benedict's Rule was designed for ordinary human beings. The element of discipline was shifted from externals to the interior, from the flesh to the will. In place of an emphasis on fasting and mortification, Benedict substituted the discipline of humility, obedience, and ongoing conversion to the spirit of monastic life. Rather than envisioning a collection of individuals competing in the quest for perfection, Benedict stressed the role of community as a school for holiness. His emphasis on the balance of work and prayer, his validation of community, and his regulation of monastic life eventually set the pattern for Western monasticism. For centuries his monasteries offered the witness of an alternative society governed by the Spirit of Christ. Few saints have left such a palpable impact on their world.

"In the reception of the poor and of pilgrims the greatest care and solicitude should be shown, because it is especially in them that Christ is received."
—St. Benedict

Desiderius Erasmus
Christian Humanist (1466–1536)

D esiderius Erasmus, the illegitimate son of a Dutch priest, was himself ordained a priest in an Augustinian monastery. After studying theology in Paris, he embarked on a career as a wandering scholar and author. A self-proclaimed "citizen of the world," he identified himself with the universal guild of scholars and the universal Church.

As one of the foremost champions of Christian humanism, Erasmus deeply wished to see the Church restored to the simplicity and holiness of the Gospels. A fervent believer in the power of human reason and dialogue to resolve conflicts, he strongly opposed the spirit of superstition and fanaticism. Along with his scholarly works, he employed the weapon of wit to confront hypocrisy and corruption in the Church of his day. When Martin Luther initiated his reform movement, Erasmus initially expressed sympathy. But as the reformers and their Catholic critics hardened their positions, he found himself in a difficult spot. While he prayed for reform of the Church, he recoiled from steps that would divide the Body of Christ. Sadly, he watched his longed-for goal of Christian renewal degenerate into violence and factionalism. What he had hailed as the dawn of a golden age had become the "very worst century" since the days of Christ.

He died in Basel on July 12, 1536.

"The world is full of rage, hate, and wars. What will the end be if we employ only bulls and the stake? It is no great feat to burn a little man. It is a great achievement to persuade him."

—Erasmus

St. Veronica
Woman of Mercy (First Century)

According to legend, Veronica was a woman who encountered Christ as he labored under the weight of the cross on his way to Golgotha. Moved by compassion, she wiped his face with her veil, which then, miraculously, bore the imprint of his features.

There is no scriptural basis for this story. Its earliest reference occurs in an apocryphal Gospel of the fourth century. Although various theologians have tried to identify Veronica with other unnamed women in the Gospels, it is speculated that her name is derived from the miracle itself: *vera icon* (true image).

The story of Veronica was eventually appropriated into the Stations of the Cross, a devotional exercise intended to place the penitent imaginatively within the drama of Christ's passion. Veronica is the faithful disciple who ought to have been present in the Gospel story. She performs the act of mercy we *ought* to have performed, had we been there. In fact the story contains no indication that Veronica was a disciple of Jesus. She was simply a woman who responded compassionately to a man in pain and anguish, a convicted felon on his way to death. Veronica wiped his face with her veil, and in the miraculous image left behind he revealed his true identity.

"For I was hungry and you gave me food . . . in prison and you visited me."
—Matthew 25:35-36

Saints Zélie and Louis Martin
Married Couple (d. 1877 and 1894)

Louis and Zélie Martin were canonized by Pope Francis in October 2015 during the Synod of Bishops on the Family. It was a fit setting for this occasion, as they became the first couple in the history of the Church to be recognized for having achieved holiness in the context of family life.

They were married in 1858, three months after their meeting in Alençon. Both Zélie, a lacemaker, and Louis, a watchmaker, had been attracted to religious life before concluding that their true vocation—and they meant this in the deepest sense—was to marriage and family. Together they had nine children, of whom five daughters survived. All of them became nuns, four of them in the same Carmelite convent in Lisieux. There is no question that the Martins offered a loving home and raised their children in an atmosphere of devout faith. But their own recognition undoubtedly follows the reputation of their youngest, Marie Françoise, better known to the world as St. Thérèse of Lisieux.

Thérèse was born in 1873. She lost her mother to breast cancer when she was four, an event that marked the end of her carefree childhood. As one by one her sisters left for Carmel, Louis gave his blessing, even finally to Thérèse, who stormed heaven to enter the convent at fifteen. Her sister Céline stayed behind to care for their father until he died in 1894, and she too left for Lisieux. Thérèse died in 1897 at twenty-four, leaving behind an extraordinary autobiography. Thus, the story of her loving parents became part of the Church's story.

"I used to jump on Father's knee and tell him what marks I had, and when he kissed me all my troubles were forgotten."

—St. Thérèse of Lisieux

Blessed Angelina of Marsciano
Founder, Franciscan Sisters of the Third Order Regular
(ca. 1377–1435)

Angelina, a daughter of nobility, married the count of Civitella when she was fifteen. Two years later, when her husband died, Angelina inherited his title and castle. Straightaway, she put on the habit of a Franciscan tertiary and gathered her female attendants into a religious community. Together they began to travel throughout the region, calling sinners to conversion and extolling the virtues of virginity. So effective were her paeans to virginity that she was deemed a threat to civil order. Placed under arrest, she was denounced as a witch (because of her sway over young girls) and a heretic (because of her supposed rejection of marriage). Brought before King Ladislas of Naples, who was fully prepared to have her burned, she mounted an effective defense. "If I have taught or practiced error, I am prepared to suffer the appropriate punishment," she said before revealing the burning embers hidden in her cloak. Though she escaped punishment on this occasion, she was later exiled from the kingdom.

On pilgrimage to Assisi, Angelina received a vision that she should found an enclosed monastery of the third order regular of St. Francis in Foligno. With support from the local bishop she carried out her plan. In 1397 she opened the first such enclosed convent under the Rule of the Third Order of St. Francis. Her community was recognized as a new congregation in 1428. Angelina was beatified in 1825.

"Behold the fire!"

—Blessed Angelina of Marsciano

St. Clelia Barbieri
Founder, Minims of Our Lady of Sorrows (1847–1870)

Clelia Barbieri was born in 1847 to a poor family on the outskirts of Bologna. After her father's death, when she was eight, she went to work spinning hemp. Despite her own modest circumstances Clelia sought every opportunity to serve her neighbors. She became well known in her parish for teaching catechism and encouraging other young girls in their faith. During this time she conceived the idea of gathering a household of other young women who would devote themselves to prayer and good works. With support from their parish priest, they took over an abandoned house and implemented this vision. Neighbors arrived the first night with donations of food. Clelia remarked, "I like the idea that our house resembles the crib where the shepherds bring their gifts."

Clelia and her companions endured poverty and hardship. In time their community took the form of a new congregation, the Minims of Our Lady of Sorrows, under the patronage of St. Francis of Paola. Clelia devised a rule that emphasized community, the spirit of contemplation, the practice of charity, simplicity, and joy. But her years were limited. She succumbed to tuberculosis at twenty-three, dying on July 13, 1870. She was canonized in 1989.

"O great Lord God, You see that my will is to love You and to try to avoid offending You. O Lord, open Your heart and throw out the flames of love. Enkindle my heart with these flames and burn me with love."

—St. Clelia Barbieri

St. Kateri Tekakwitha
"Lily of the Mohawks" (1656–1680)

St. Kateri was born in 1656 near present-day Auriesville, New York. Her mother, a captured Algonquin, was a Christian, while her father, a Mohawk chief, viewed the new religion with deep suspicion. Both parents died from smallpox when Kateri was four. Her own scarred face showed the marks of the disease, which also darkened her vision, causing her to stumble in the light. As a result her people called her Tekakwitha—"the one who walks groping her way." When a Jesuit missionary arrived in her village in 1674 she requested baptism. She was given the name Kateri—a Mohawk version of Katherine.

Kateri's conversion caused distress in her community, so much so that her confessor feared for her safety and urged her to flee. Under cover of darkness she set off from her village by foot and traveled two hundred miles to a Christian mission near Montreal, where on Christmas Day, 1677, she made her first communion.

Though free to practice her faith, she was still forced to grope her way in a world that supplied no clear models. She resisted the idea of marriage. She proposed founding a convent, an idea that was quickly dismissed. Nevertheless, in 1679 she made a public vow of chastity—as far as she got with her dream of religious life. Soon after she fell ill and died on April 17, 1680, at the age of twenty-three. She was beatified in 1980 and canonized in 2012.

"I am not my own; I have given myself to Jesus. He must be my only love."

—St. Kateri Tekakwitha

Cicely Saunders
Pioneer of the Hospice Movement (1918–2005)

Cicely Saunders—a nurse, social worker, and finally physician—is recognized as a founder of the modern hospice movement, a holistic approach to care for the dying that combines expert pain management with loving and compassionate care. Saunders's interest in this area was stimulated in part by the death of two very close friends. Working in hospitals, she was discouraged by the common attitude, in the face of terminal illness, that "nothing more can be done," whereas, she believed, there was always "so much more to be done." Believing that a patient was more than a collection of symptoms, she promoted an approach that addressed the full needs of her patients and their families—including social, emotional, and spiritual needs.

In 1967 she founded St. Christopher's hospice in London— the first dedicated institution of its kind. Saunders had undergone a deep religious conversion in her youth—as if "a switch had flipped." She considered founding an Anglican order to staff the hospice but decided instead that it should be a place where people of all faiths or none should feel welcome.

She received numerous national honors and humanitarian awards as well as the Templeton Prize for Progress in Religion. Dame Cicely died of breast cancer in her own hospice on July 14, 2005.

"You matter because you are you, and you matter to the end of your life. We will do all we can not only to help you die peacefully, but also to live until you die."
—Cicely Saunders

St. Bonaventure
Franciscan, Doctor of the Church (1221–1274)

Bonaventure, who was born to a wealthy family in Orvieto, joined the Franciscans around 1238 in the midst of his studies at the University of Paris. St. Francis had died only some dozen years before, but already his order was rapidly changing the face of the Church in Europe. Franciscan simplicity might not have seemed an attractive fit for a learned scholar. In fact, Francis had held learning in great esteem so long as it was subordinated to the pursuit of holiness. In this spirit, Bonaventure received support from the order to continue his studies. In 1257, along with his Dominican counterpart, St. Thomas Aquinas, he received his doctorate in theology.

Rather than pursue the life of an academic theologian, however, Bonaventure was immediately elected to serve as minister-general of the Friars Minor—a role in which he left a lasting mark. For his deft efforts to steer a middle course between contending factions within the order, he would become known as the Second Founder. Among his many works was an influential life of St. Francis.

In 1265 he respectfully declined an appointment as archbishop of York. In 1273, however, Pope Gregory X ordered him to accept the title of cardinal-bishop of Albano. When papal legates arrived to present him with his red hat and insignia of office, he kept them waiting while he finished washing the dishes.

Canonized in 1482, Bonaventure was declared a Doctor of the Church in 1588. He is known as the Seraphic Doctor.

"If you learn everything except Christ, you learn nothing. If you learn nothing except Christ, you learn everything."

—St. Bonaventure

Blessed Anne-Marie Javouhey
Founder, Sisters of St. Joseph of Cluny (1779–1851)

As a child, Anne-Marie Javouhey, the daughter of a prosperous farmer in Burgundy, felt the first stirrings of a religious vocation. At that time in revolutionary France all religious congregations had been suppressed. When the ban was lifted, she hastened to enter a convent of the Sisters of Charity but then withdrew on the eve of her final vows, swayed by a mysterious dream or vision in which she was surrounded by children of different races. A voice spoke to her: "These are the children God gives you. I am Teresa, and I will look after your congregation."

Eventually she did found a new congregation, the Sisters of St. Joseph of Cluny. Her dream came to fulfillment when she established a mission on the island of Bourbon off the coast of Madagascar. This led to other missions in other poor French colonies, from Senegal to French Guiana, home of the dreaded penal colony of Devil's Island. There she organized a community of six hundred emancipated slaves—a settlement so successful that it provoked the bitter jealousy of white farmers, whose ally, the local bishop, actually excommunicated her for two years. (This was not her first ordeal with hierarchs, nor would it be her last.)

By the end of her life Mother Javouhey was regarded not only as a holy woman but as a national hero. She died on July 15, 1851. She was beatified in 1950.

"The Cross is found wherever there are servants of God, and I rejoice to be reckoned among them."

—Blessed Anne-Marie Javouhey

St. Mary-Magdalen Postel
Founder, Sisters of the Christian Schools of Mercy
(1756–1846)

Julia Frances Catherine Postel was born in a small French town near Cherbourg. After studying in a Benedictine convent she returned home to teach school, though privately she dedicated herself to God's service. Her calling became clear, with the onset of the Revolution, when her parish priest went underground. Postel put herself at his service, setting up a secret chapel in her home, where clandestine services could be conducted. She herself undertook religious duties, such as carrying consecrated Hosts to administer to the dying. Thus, as Pope Pius X later commented, she served as a veritable "maiden priest."

As the persecution receded, Postel devoted herself to repairing the local church, offering religious instruction, organizing prayer guilds, and performing the works of mercy. In 1807 she determined that what she really wanted to do was to teach children, and for this she should organize a religious congregation.

With support from the bishop of Cherbourg, she and three others took vows as the Sisters of the Christian Schools of Mercy, and she became Mother Mary-Magdalen. Following their struggles through some years of dire poverty, the bishop urged them to disband. But Mother Mary-Magdalen persisted, and eventually their fortunes turned.

She died on July 16, 1846, at the age of eighty-nine. She was canonized in 1925.

"I want to teach the young and to inspire them with the love of God and liking for work. I want to help the poor and relieve them of some of their misery. These are the things I want to do."

—St. Mary-Magdalen Postel

St. Elizabeth Feodorovna
Orthodox Martyr (1864–1918)

Elizabeth was born for a life of luxury and opulence. A German princess, granddaughter of Queen Victoria, at twenty she married Grand Duke Sergei Alexandrovich, younger brother of Tsar Alexander III of Russia. Embracing her new homeland, she converted to the Orthodox faith—a decision apparently based on genuine conviction, not simply family obligation.

In 1894 her sister Alexandra married the new tsar Nicholas II. This put Elizabeth at the center of Russian royal society. It also put her at the center of social forces rapidly approaching a violent crisis. In 1905 her husband was killed by a bomb-throwing assassin.

Elizabeth abruptly altered her life. Withdrawing from the palace, she devoted herself to hospital work. With the sale of her jewelry, she purchased land outside Moscow to establish a women's religious community dedicated to serving the poor. Their rule was based on the words of Scripture, "I was hungry and you fed me."

With the outbreak of the Revolution, friends urged her to flee. She was determined, however, not to abandon her adopted homeland. She was arrested in April 1918. On July 17 the tsar and his family were murdered. The next day Elizabeth and other members of the royal family were hurled into an abandoned mine shaft. When their cries could still be heard they were dispatched with grenades.

Mother Elizabeth's remains were later interred in a Russian chapel in Jerusalem. In 1992 she was canonized by the Russian Orthodox Church.

"One must fix one's thoughts on the heavenly country in order to see things in their true light, and to be able to say 'Thy will be done.'"

—St. Elizabeth Feodorovna

St. Hedwig of Poland
Queen (1374–1399)

St. Hedwig was the daughter of Louis, king of Hungary and Poland. At the age of one she was betrothed to Wilhelm, the five-year-old heir to the grand duchy of Austria. When she was eight, however, her father decided, prior to his death, to appoint Hedwig his successor. This caused much political turmoil. Before accepting her as their monarch, the Polish nobles insisted that she marry Jagiello, grand duke of Lithuania and Ruthenia. Though Wilhelm protested, Hedwig and Jagiello were married, and she was declared "king" of Poland (indicating that she ruled in her own right, not simply as a consort).

The Hapsburg court did not concede graciously. Rumors were spread throughout Christendom that Hedwig and Wilhelm had consummated their marriage and that she was an adulteress and bigamist. Such calumny stung, but in time Hedwig's reputation as a Christian monarch was widely recognized. She endowed many churches, monasteries, and universities as well as a "college of psalmists" in the Cathedral at Kraków—a team of priests who took turns to sing the psalms twenty-four hours a day.

Hedwig died on July 17, 1399, four days after giving birth. Pope John Paul II oversaw her beatification in 1986 and her canonization in the Cathedral of Kraków in 1997.

"Today we wish to kneel with you, Hedwig, at the feet of the Crucified One, to hear the echo of that lesson of love which you listen to. We wish to learn from you how to put that lesson into practice in our time."

—Pope John Paul II, at the canonization of St. Hedwig

Carmelite Martyrs of Compiègne
(d. 1794)

In 1790 a decree of the revolutionary French Republic suppressed all religious communities, save those engaged in teaching and nursing. One of the affected communities was a convent of Carmelite nuns in Compiègne. They were forced to relinquish their habits, to dress in secular clothes, and to abandon their convent. Nevertheless, in July 1794 sixteen nuns were arrested on the charge of continuing their illicit way of life and imprisoned in a former Visitation convent. Two weeks later they were transported to Paris. By this time, judging that the moment for compromise had passed, they resumed their religious habits and openly recited the prayers of the Divine Office.

Their trial was brief. They were convicted of having made themselves "enemies of the people by conspiring against its sovereign rule." On July 17, 1794, they were transported by open wagons to the place of execution, all the while singing the *Salve Regina* and *Veni Creator Spiritus*—the hymn sung for the profession of vows—and reciting the prayers for the dying. They were beheaded in turn, beginning with the novice, Sr. Constance, and ending with the prioress, Mother Teresa of St. Augustine. A witness said they looked as though they were going to their wedding.

These Carmelites were beatified in 1906. Their story inspired a moving opera by François Poulenc, *Dialogues of the Carmelites*, for which Georges Bernanos provided the libretto.

"We are the victims of the age, and we ought to sacrifice ourselves to obtain its return to God."

—Carmelite Martyrs of Compiègne

Bartolomé de Las Casas
"Defender of the Indians" (1484–1566)

artolomé de Las Casas was the most distinguished of a number of Dominican friars who raised their voices against the rapacious violence inflicted on the Indians of the Americas. Serving originally as a chaplain in the Spanish conquest of Cuba (while also benefiting as the owner of a plantation), he underwent a dramatic conversion in 1514. After witnessing the genocidal cruelty inflicted on the Indians, he joined the Dominican Order and became a passionate and prophetic defender of the indigenous peoples. For more than fifty years he traveled back and forth between the New World and the court of Spain, attempting to expose the cruelties of the Conquest, whose very legitimacy, and not merely excesses, he disavowed.

Las Casas opposed the notion that the Gospel could be spread through slaughter or compulsion of any kind. While others claimed the Indians were a lesser race, he affirmed their full humanity and entitlement to human rights. But he went further. Identifying the Indians with the poor in the Gospel sense, he argued that in their sufferings they represented the crucified Christ.

In 1544 he was named bishop of Chiapas in southern Mexico, but he eventually resigned his bishopric and returned to Spain, the better, he hoped, to promote the cause of social justice. He died on July 18, 1566, at the age of eighty-two.

"I leave in the Indies Jesus Christ, our God, scourged and afflicted and beaten and crucified not once, but thousands of times."

—Bartolomé de Las Casas

410

St. Camillus de Lellis
Founder, Ministers of the Sick (1550–1614)

St. Camillus was not the type of saint whose childhood and youth were marked by precocious piety. In his early life he was an irascible soldier of fortune who signed on with the Venetian army to fight the Turks. After suffering a painful wound he was sent to the hospital of San Giacomo in Rome, where he worked as a servant while undergoing treatment.

After his discharge from the hospital he lost everything to gambling. In desperation he took a job working for a Capuchin community. The example of the friars awakened in Camillus a dormant thirst for God, such that he vowed to amend his life. Returning to San Giacomo, he dedicated himself in a spirit of religious discipline to the care of the sick.

Charity was not a virtue commonly associated with hospitals at the time, and healing was virtually as rare. Conditions were appalling. But in the spirit of his newfound faith, Camillus tried to treat each patient as another Christ. Before long, his loving ministrations, combined with his appreciation for cleanliness and good nutrition, produced miraculous results, and he was appointed superintendent of the hospital.

Eventually Camillus conceived the idea of founding an association of similarly dedicated nurses. After being ordained a priest, he received papal approval for his Ministers of the Sick. He personally founded fifteen houses of his order as well as eight hospitals. Canonized in 1746, he was named a patron of both nurses and their patients.

"To Christ, God and Man, sick in the person of the Poor— homage of love."

—St. Camillus

St. Macrina the Younger
Virgin (ca. 327–379)

St. Macrina was the eldest child in a remarkable family. Of her nine siblings, three others became canonized saints, along with her parents. According to a touching memoir by her brother St. Gregory of Nyssa, Macrina served as a spiritual fulcrum between her parents and her younger siblings, serving by her own example and exhortation to urge the rest of the family along the path to sanctity.

Macrina was born in Caesarea in Cappadocia around 327 and received an excellent education. After the death of her father she took special care for the education and upbringing of her younger brothers, especially St. Basil, St. Gregory, and St. Peter of Sebaste. She persuaded her mother to dispense with their inherited wealth and to adopt a life of prayerful simplicity. When her mother died she founded a convent on the family estate, where women of all social backgrounds were drawn to consecrate their lives to prayer and God's service.

In 379 St. Gregory returned home to find Macrina sick and dying. They enjoyed a sweet reunion, conversing on death and the future life. Gregory was amazed at his sister's profound insight into the mysteries of the faith, as she continued her discourse until her last breath. "All this," he said, "seemed to me more than human." He presided over her funeral.

"You who broke the flaming sword, and compassionately gave paradise back to the man crucified with You, remember me also in Your kingdom, for I, too, have been crucified with You, having nailed my flesh through fear of You and having feared Your judgments."
—St. Macrina

Rebecca Nurse
"Witch" of Salem (d. 1692)

The notorious events in Salem, Massachusetts, began in 1692 with a circle of young girls who liked to meet in the forest and dabble in charms. Their mischief took a darker turn when they began to identify witches and wizards among their neighbors. In Puritan New England this was taken with the utmost seriousness. For most of a year the search for and discovery of witches in Salem became a raging storm. One hundred twenty men and women were imprisoned, of whom twenty were executed, while another eight died in jail.

Some of the accused were persons of suspect character, but the charges eventually extended to men and women of pious reputation, including Rebecca Nurse, a seventy-one-year-old midwife, the mother of eight, widely known for her faith, charity, and simple goodness. Even the magistrate seemed skeptical of the charges, repeatedly asking the accusers if they were certain it was Goody Nurse who tormented them. When he asked Rebecca how she could retain her composure, she replied, "You do not know my heart." The jury at first found her not guilty, but this provoked such an uproar among the "afflicted" girls that they reconsidered and sentenced her to death.

After being excommunicated, "abandoned to the devil and eternally damned," Rebecca Nurse was hanged on July 19. Eventually the fire in Salem ran its course. In 1712 Nurse's excommunication was lifted. Poet John Greenleaf Whittier memorialized her: "O Christian Martyr who for truth could die / When all around thee owned the hideous lie!"

"I have nobody to look for but God."

—Rebecca Nurse

Elijah
Prophet (Ninth Century BC)

Elijah, a prophet who operated in the northern kingdom of Israel in the ninth century BC, is one of the most mysterious figures of Scripture. He was among the few survivors of a general persecution of prophets instigated by King Ahab and his wife Jezebel after they had introduced worship of the Canaanite god Baal. Dressing in rough camel hair and fed by ravens, Elijah survived in the desert. Eventually God impelled him to confront the king, challenging the prophets of Baal to a test of power, in which he easily triumphed. By this manner Elijah made himself a bitter enemy of the royal court. Yet God protected him. At one point, as he lamented his life, God passed before him on a mountain. In a memorable passage, Scripture records that God did not appear to Elijah in an earthquake, a strong wind, or a fire, but in "a still small voice." When it was time for Elijah to die, he bequeathed his cloak to his disciple Elisha and was then carried into heaven by a chariot of fire.

Later, the prophet Malachi wrote that Elijah would reappear to presage the Messiah, and to this day, in the Jewish observance of Passover, a place at the table is set for Elijah, in case he should choose to appear. The Gospels suggest that this Elijah role was fulfilled by John the Baptist, yet he also appeared to the disciples at the transfiguration, conversing with Moses and Christ.

"I alone am left, and they seek my life."

—Elijah (1 Kings 19:10)

Pope Leo XIII
Pope (1810–1903)

On February 20, 1878, Vincenzo Pecci, the sixty-eight-year-old archbishop of Perugia, was elected to succeed the long-reigning Pope Pius IX. Pius had done more than any other pope in modern times to enhance the image and power of the papacy. But having defined the mission of the Church largely in terms of negative opposition to the modern age, he left little opening for constructive engagement with issues of the day. The new pope, who took the name Leo XIII, was keen to overcome this defensive posture.

Without doubt, Leo's most significant contribution was in his pronouncements in the social realm. With his encyclical *Rerum Novarum* (1891) he inaugurated the modern era of Catholic social teaching. Leo was the first pope to address the problems associated with the rise of industrial capitalism and to declare the sympathies of the Church with the working class.

While rejecting socialism, Leo's encyclical implied a strong critique of unbridled capitalism. Most of all it declared the Church's vital interest in the social and material, as well as spiritual, welfare of human beings. It articulated a commitment to principles of social justice, the dignity of labor, and defense of the poor—a commitment that would undergo further elaboration in the subsequent century of Catholic social teaching.

Pope Leo died on July 20, 1903, at the age of ninety-three.

"I want to see the church so far forward that my successor will not be able to turn back."

—Pope Leo XIII

St. Margaret
Martyr (Dates Unknown)

St. Margaret is one of the most popular saints in Christian history. She was one of the Fourteen Holy Helpers, a group of saints commonly invoked in the Middle Ages for their effectiveness in warding off illness and misfortune. Two hundred fifty churches in England are dedicated to St. Margaret, and hers (along with those of St. Michael and St. Catherine of Alexandria) was one of the voices that St. Joan of Arc claimed to hear. For refusing to disavow these voices, St. Joan was put to death. And yet there is scant evidence that such a saint existed.

She was supposedly the beautiful daughter of a pagan priest in Antioch, who became a secret Christian. According to legend, she was arrested during the Diocletian persecution. After refusing to renounce her faith she was imprisoned, tortured, and subjected to numerous ordeals. In one case she was swallowed by the Devil, in the form of a dragon, who gagged on her cross and spit her out. (Even the usually credulous *Golden Legend* notes that this detail "is considered apocryphal and not to be taken seriously.") Initial efforts to slay her were fruitless (only resulting in the conversion of thousands of spectators, who in turn became martyrs). She was eventually beheaded.

The cult of St. Margaret took root in the ninth and tenth centuries. Nevertheless, for many centuries she was invoked as patroness of a wide circle of supplicants, including women in childbirth, exiles, and those falsely accused.

"Brother, take your sword and strike me!"

—Last words of St. Margaret, *The Golden Legend*

Lawrence Jenco
Priest (1934–1996)

In 1985, Fr. Lawrence Jenco, a Servite priest from Illinois and the director of Catholic Relief Services in Lebanon, was taken hostage in Beirut by a Shiite group called Islamic Holy War. He would spend 564 days in captivity before his release and return to the United States.

Days of unrelenting boredom—often blindfolded, locked in a closet, or handcuffed to a radiator—were interspersed with bursts of terror. During transport from one hiding place to another he was bound in tape from head to toe or wrapped with explosives. He endured beatings and several times expected execution.

Nevertheless, he sustained himself with prayer, reciting a homemade rosary, or celebrating a clandestine Mass—sometimes in the company of fellow American hostages. The night before he was released, one of the guards asked him if he could forgive his captors. Jenco realized his faith was being put to the test. While he would not forget his treatment, he chose the way of forgiveness in place of vindictiveness.

After his release, Jenco remained remarkably free of bitterness, sharing a message of peace and reconciliation. (He was more disturbed to learn that his freedom had been purchased by the sale of arms to Iran.) He served as a campus minister at the University of Southern California and died of cancer on July 19, 1996.

"God, give me a new heart and a new spirit. You have asked me to love unconditionally. May I forgive as you have asked me to forgive, unconditionally. Then you will be my God and I will be your son."

—A prayer by Fr. Lawrence Jenco,
composed the night of his release

417

St. Mary Magdalene
Apostle to the Apostles (First Century)

Mary Magdalene was one of the original Galilean disciples of Jesus and one of the many women who followed him in his itinerant ministry. Little can be said of her origins; she is characterized simply as a "woman from whom seven demons had gone out." There is no scriptural basis for the later tradition that depicted her as a penitent prostitute. All four Gospels name her among those women who followed Jesus to Golgotha and there witnessed his passion and death. While (according to the Synoptic Gospels) all the male disciples fled, it was these women who remained faithful to the end, and who went to his tomb on the third day, hoping to anoint his body.

They found, instead, an empty tomb, guarded by an angel who revealed that Jesus was raised from death. The women were charged to tell the disciples to meet the Lord back in Galilee. In the Gospels of John and Matthew (as well as the longer ending of Mark) Mary actually sees the Risen Lord. According to John, Mary was weeping outside the tomb when she saw Jesus. She failed at first to recognize him, until he addressed her with a single word: "Mary." "Rabboni! Teacher," she cried. He instructed her to go to the disciples and tell them, "I am ascending to my Father and your Father, to my God and your God."

It was Mary Magdalene, the faithful disciple, who first proclaimed this good news to the Twelve. Thus she has often been called the "Apostle to the Apostles."

"I have seen the Lord."

—St. Mary Magdalene

Albert Luthuli
Zulu Chief, Nobel Laureate (1898–1967)

Albert Luthuli, a member of the Zulu tribe, was raised in a Christian mission reserve in Natal, South Africa. Eventually he was elected chief in the village of Groutville, an office that enabled him to promote the rights of his poor and oppressed people. To the white-minority government, chiefs were regarded as useful intermediaries in their management and control of the black masses. Luthuli, however, had come to believe the interests of his people could best be served by the overthrow of apartheid. After he joined the African National Congress the government "dismissed" him as chief. This only freed him for a more active role in the antiapartheid struggle, and he became the national leader of the ANC.

As a result of his activities he was repeatedly arrested, "banned," and confined to house arrest. In 1955 he was arrested, along with the ANC leadership, and charged with high treason. He was eventually freed and helped bring the case against apartheid to the world. In 1960 he was awarded the Nobel Peace Prize.

Throughout his life, Luthuli held to a deep Christian faith. He disagreed with those activists who dismissed Christianity as the religion of the oppressor. But he challenged the Church to "be *with* the people, *in* their lives." Speaking for himself, he said, "I am in Congress precisely *because* I am a Christian."

Albert Luthuli died on July 21, 1967.

"It is inevitable that in working for Freedom some individuals and some families must take the lead and suffer: The Road to Freedom is via the CROSS."

—Albert Luthuli

St. Bridget of Sweden
Mystic and Prophet (1303–1373)

St. Bridget of Sweden was one of the great women of the fourteenth century: the wife of a nobleman and the mother of eight children; a nun and founder of monasteries as well as a religious order; a pilgrim who crossed continents and seas; a mystic who filled many volumes with accounts of her visions and colloquies with Christ; a prophet who called kings to justice and popes to live up to their sacred duties.

At fourteen she married a prince named Ulf. It was a happy marriage that lasted twenty-eight years. Fed up with the frivolity of court life, she and Ulf embarked on a long pilgrimage that took them all the way to Compostela in Spain. There, when Ulf died, Bridget received a vision instructing her to found a new monastery in Sweden. Accomplishing this, she went on pilgrimage to the Holy Land before settling in Rome for the last twenty years of her life. Wherever she traveled she spoke out against slavery, injustice, and threats to peace. She excoriated the pope for abandoning Rome for Avignon and for other corruptions. At one point she denounced the pope as "a murderer of souls, worse than Lucifer, more unjust than Pilate, more merciless than Judas." Despite her frankness, he approved the Rule of her new order, the Brigittines.

St. Bridget died on July 23, 1373. A triumphal procession accompanied her body back to Sweden, where she was laid to rest.

"The people of earth have need of a triple mercy: sorrow for their sins, penance to atone for them, and strength to do good."

—St. Bridget of Sweden

Anne Hutchinson
Puritan Prophet (1591–1643)

Anne Hutchinson arrived in Boston in 1634, accompanied by her husband, a prosperous businessman, and their several children. They were committed Puritans, though Anne was by far the more zealous. She was unusually independent—a skilled midwife and healer. She was also an avid student of the Bible, which she freely interpreted in the light of what she termed divine inspiration. Though she adhered to the principles of Puritan orthodoxy, she held advanced notions about the equality and rights of women.

In Boston Anne began inviting women to join her in her home for prayer and religious conversation. She would present a text from Scripture and then offer her own commentary—often departing from the learned but legalistic reading offered from the Sunday pulpit. For instance, she differed from the standard view that Eve was especially to blame for original sin.

In 1637 Anne was brought to trial for her views. Though forty-six and advanced in her fifteenth pregnancy, she was forced to stand for several days before a board of male interrogators. They accused her of fostering dissent against the fathers of the commonwealth. Condemned as a heretic, she was imprisoned during the cold winter months, then exiled to Rhode Island. After the death of her husband in 1642, Anne and six of her children departed for Long Island, where, sometime in the summer of 1643, they were massacred by Indians.

"It was never in my heart to slight any man, but only that man should be kept in his own place and not set in the room of God."

—Anne Hutchinson

Saints Boris and Gleb
Passion Bearers (ca. 1015)

Boris and Gleb were the beloved youngest sons of Prince Vladimir, who brought Christianity to Russia. When Vladimir died, his eldest son, Svyatopolk, sought to eliminate any rivals. As Prince Boris was returning from a military engagement he received word that his brother had acceded to the throne and was planning to kill him. Rather than be the cause of any bloodshed, he dismissed his guards and waited for his assassins. He spent the evening reciting the psalms and prayed, "Lord Jesus Christ, Thou didst accept Thy Passion on account of our sins; grant me also the strength to accept my passion. I receive it not from my enemies but from my brother. Lord, lay not this sin to his charge." The next morning his brother's men arrived and drove their spears into him. The same fate awaited Gleb. He was taken by surprise, his throat slit by his own cook.

Svyatopolk's reign was not long, and eventually the brothers' bodies were recovered and buried in the Church of St. Basil at Vyshgorod. Boris and Gleb were the proto-martyrs of the Russian Church, and their example had a tremendous influence in spreading the Christian faith. Though they did not conform to any of the traditional models of sainthood, they were acclaimed as "passion bearers." This term, in the tradition of Russian spirituality, refers to those who imitate the patient suffering of Christ. Their canonization in the Catholic Church was confirmed by Pope Benedict XIII in 1724.

"I am being slain; I know not what for; but thou, Lord, knowest."

—St. Gleb

St. Christina the Astonishing
Visionary (1150–1224)

Christina, a peasant girl born near Liège in Belgium, was orphaned at the age of fifteen. At twenty-two she suffered a seizure so severe that she was pronounced dead. As she was carried into church in an open coffin she suddenly sat up and flew up to the rafters "like a bird," as she later explained, to escape the smell of sin. When the priest coaxed her down she related an extraordinary story—of how she had been shown the souls suffering in purgatory, and then led into the court of heaven, where she was offered a choice. She might either remain in heaven or "return again to Earth to accomplish a mission of charity and suffering," relieving the suffering of those in purgatory and, through her example, inspiring sinners to be converted. Without hesitation, Christina chose to return, and immediately she woke up in her own funeral Mass.

Christina's subsequent way of life provoked contrasting reactions. She dressed in rags and slept out in the open; she would climb and perch on treetops; she would jump into flames, without suffering harm, or swim in the frozen River Meuse. Viewed by many as mad she was often taunted and persecuted. But others, including the respected Cardinal James de Vitry, regarded her as a holy prophet. She spent her last years in a convent, where she evidently was a model of obedience, and died at the age of seventy-four.

"O most beloved body! Why have I reviled you? O best and sweetest body, endure patiently."

—St. Christina the Astonishing

St. James the Great
Apostle (First Century)

St. James (called the Great, in distinction to another apostle) and his brother John, the sons of Zebedee, were fishermen in Galilee when they responded to a call from Jesus, left their nets, and followed. With Peter they are cited as witnesses to many of the great moments in the Gospels, including the transfiguration and Jesus' agony in the Garden of Gethsemane. Jesus called them Boanerges, or "Sons of Thunder," perhaps a comment on their temperaments. On one occasion, when a town of Samaritans failed to offer a proper reception, they suggested calling down fire from heaven to destroy it. Jesus rebuked them: "The Son of Man came not to destroy souls but to save them."

On another occasion the brothers asked Jesus for a favor— that when he should come into his glory they might be seated, one on his right hand and the other on his left. Jesus asked if they were willing to drink the cup of his suffering. They replied that they were.

James was among the first of the apostles to follow his Master in death. He was beheaded by King Herod Agrippa I. Legends later associated him with Spain, where he either preached sometime between Pentecost and his death, or where his body was later buried at the shrine of Santiago de Compostela—to this day, one of the most popular sites of Christian pilgrimage.

"Now about that time Herod the king stretched forth his hands to vex certain of the church. And he killed James the brother of John with the sword."

—Acts 12:1-2

St. Christopher
Martyr (Third Century)

Christopher, who was apparently a large man, embarked on a quest to find and serve "the greatest king that there was." His search led him to a holy hermit who instructed him in the Christian mysteries and suggested that he should provide service by carrying people across a dangerous river. One day as he performed this task, a small child appeared and asked to be ferried on his back. As they crossed the river, Christopher felt the child become impossibly heavy. Upon reaching the shore, where Christopher collapsed in exhaustion, the child revealed the secret: "You had on your shoulders not only the whole world but Him who made it. I am Christ your king, whom you are serving by this work."

This is the best-known story of St. Christopher, as popularized in *The Golden Legend*. Otherwise, more exact knowledge of the saint, who is said to have died as a martyr in the city of Lyca, is hard to come by. His name, Christophorus, which literally means "Christ-bearer," may have inspired his legend. Nevertheless, as the patron of travelers, St. Christopher became one of the most popular of all saints. Countless numbers of the faithful have worn his medal or invoked his name.

"He bore Christ in four ways, namely, on his shoulders when he carried him across the river, in his body by mortification, in his mind by devotion, and in his mouth by confessing Christ and preaching him."

—Blessed Jacobus de Voragine, *The Golden Legend*

Saints Anne and Joachim
Grandparents of the Lord

Anne and Joachim are revered as the parents of Mary, and thus the grandparents of Jesus. Their names do not appear in Scripture, and their tradition may be traced to the apocryphal Book of James, written in the mid-second century. That work describes Anne and Joachim as an older couple, who suffered in the belief that their childless condition was a sign of divine displeasure. Joachim retreated to the desert to fast and pray about the matter, while Anne remained at home. Both of them received a message from an angel, assuring them that they would conceive a child. That child, Mary, would later be acclaimed as the Mother of God.

No more is recorded of their story. However, with the rise of Marian devotion in the Middle Ages, there was a flurry of new interest in Anne and Joachim, and they were frequently depicted in icons and religious art. Their cult was officially recognized in the sixteenth century.

"Joachim, a Galilean from the town of Nazareth, took Saint Anne, a native of Bethlehem, as his wife. They were both righteous and walked without reproach in all the commandments of the Lord. . . . They lived for twenty years without offspring and made a vow to the Lord that if he granted them a child, they would dedicate it to the service of God."

—Blessed Jacobus de Voragine, *The Golden Legend*

Blessed Andrew of Phu Yen
Martyr (1624–1644)

The first successful inroads of Christianity in Vietnam occurred in 1623, following the arrival of the French Jesuit Alexandre de Rhodes. His success built on the work of native catechists, who were trained to work independently. One of these, Andrew of Phu Yen, would later become the proto-martyr of Vietnam.

Andrew was baptized by Fr. de Rhodes in 1641, when he was seventeen. After training as a catechist, he carried out his ministry in the kingdom of Annam. The king, fearing that Christianity was an instrument of foreign colonialism, issued a decree banning its spread. Soldiers were sent to Andrew's community, seeking to arrest Fr. Ignatius, another European priest, but finding him away, they instead seized Andrew and delivered him to the provincial governor's palace.

The governor tried to force Andrew to "desist from that foolish opinion of his and give up his faith," but Andrew refused. Consequently he was sentenced to death. The next day he was led outside the city. A procession, including Fr. de Rhodes and many other Christians, followed. When they reached an empty field Andrew was stabbed with a bamboo spear. Before the large crowd in attendance he cried aloud the name of Jesus. Then he was beheaded.

Though the cause for his canonization began shortly after his death, it was stalled for many centuries. Finally on March 5, 2000, he was beatified by Pope John Paul II.

"I wish I had a thousand lives to offer to God in thanksgiving for what he has done for me."
—Blessed Andrew of Phu Yen

The Seven Sleepers of Ephesus
Martyrs

According to an ancient legend, these seven young Christian men, seeking to escape persecution under the emperor Decius (d. 251), hid in a cavern, where they fell into a miraculous sleep. The emperor ordered them sealed within the cave. There they remained for two hundred years until the cave was unsealed, at which point they awoke, thinking they had only slept a day. When they sent one of their number into town to buy food, he was astonished to discover signs that Christianity—only yesterday a persecuted sect—was now the state religion. Merchants were equally astonished by his ancient coins and asked him the secret of his treasure. He led them to the cave where he and his companions related their remarkable story. They repeated their tale for the bishop, who rejoiced in this miraculous sign and called down God's blessings. At this point, the seven martyrs gave up their spirits. Their bodies were placed in golden caskets, and their cave became at last their grave.

The Seven Sleepers of Ephesus are included in the Roman martyrology. Though St. Gregory of Tours related their story in the sixth century, the most popular version appears in the medieval *Golden Legend* of Blessed Jacobus de Voragine.

"Believe us, for forsooth our Lord hath raised us before the day of the great resurrection. And to the end that thou believe firmly the resurrection of the dead people, verily we be raised as ye here see, and live."

—St. Maximian, one of the Seven Sleepers,
from *The Golden Legend*

Blessed Titus Brandsma
Martyr (1881–1942)

Titus Brandsma was a Dutch Carmelite priest. In the 1930s he was named by the bishops of Holland as spiritual advisor to the nation's several dozen Catholic newspapers. When the Nazis invaded Holland in 1940, Brandsma was at the center of an intense discussion in the Church regarding the level of resistance to be offered to the new regime. Brandsma spoke for the majority who opposed any compromise with the Nazi order.

In December 1941 an edict declared that all Dutch newspapers were obliged to run Nazi advertisements and propaganda. Brandsma met personally with the editors of each Catholic newspaper to explain why it was impossible to comply with such an edict.

He was arrested on January 19, 1942, and eventually sent to Dachau, home at the time to another 2,700 imprisoned clergy. There he endured weeks of brutal treatment, all the while maintaining his prayerful equilibrium. "We are here," he said, "in a dark tunnel. We must pass through it. Somewhere at the end shines the eternal life."

As his health deteriorated, he was dispatched to the hospital, a center for sadistic medical experimentation. There on July 26 he was killed by a lethal injection of acid. In 1985 Titus Brandsma was beatified by Pope John Paul II, the first victim of the Nazis to be officially declared a martyr.

"I see God in the work of his hands and the marks of his love in every visible thing, and it sometimes happens that I am seized by a supreme joy which is above all other joys."

—Blessed Titus Brandsma

William Wilberforce
Abolitionist (1759–1833)

William Wilberforce, an Evangelical Christian and member of the British Parliament, devoted his career single-mindedly to the abolition of slavery.

Wilberforce was convinced there was no greater moral blight on the English conscience than the slave trade. Though slave labor was not permitted in England, the trafficking in African slaves and the exploitation of their labor was a mainstay of the imperial economy, particularly in the Caribbean and the southern United States. Wilberforce would not rest until his country should recognize the hideous cruelty represented by this system.

Tirelessly he delivered speeches, circulated petitions, and introduced bills in Parliament. Despite complaints that his cause was quixotic, or a betrayal of his class interests, he would not relent. Constantly he pressed the point that what was being justified in the name of profit was the brutal commerce in human life. Finally, in 1806, after twenty years of effort, he won the argument. A bill in Parliament outlawed slave trading in the British colonies. Still he struggled for another twenty-five years to win the complete emancipation of all slaves in the empire. Such a bill was passed in 1833, weeks before his death on July 29. Seven hundred thousand slaves were immediately liberated.

"Never, never will we desist till we have wiped away this scandal from the load of guilt under which we at present labor, and until we have extinguished every trace of this bloody traffic which our posterity will scarcely believe had been suffered to exist so long, a disgrace and dishonor to our country."

—William Wilberforce

Servant of God Stanley Rother
Priest and Martyr (1935–1981)

Stanley Rother, a priest from Oklahoma, volunteered in 1968 to serve in his diocese's mission to Santiago Atitlán, a picturesque Indian town in Guatemala. After mastering the Mayan dialect of the Tzutuhil Indians, Rother won their trust and respect for his complete dedication to the needs of the community. Aside from the overwhelming demands of his pastoral work, Rother could often be found wielding a hoe in a farmer's cornfield or performing any number of unseen acts of friendship. For his part, Rother felt so inspired by the faith of the Tzutuhil people that he could not imagine a life apart from them.

By the 1980s, simmering resentment against social injustice erupted in open resistance, provoking in turn a massive wave of government repression. The violence drew ever closer to Santiago Atitlán. In January 1981, after his name appeared on a death list, Rother agreed to leave the country and return to Oklahoma. But he could not stand to be so far from his flock. By Holy Week he had returned. On July 28 masked men slipped into the parish rectory and tried to kidnap him. When he put up a fight they killed him on the spot.

After the funeral Mass Rother's body was returned to Oklahoma for burial. But his family agreed to the request of his parish and allowed his heart to be interred in the church of Santiago Atitlán. In 2015 the Holy See officially named him a martyr, opening the way to his beatification.

"Pray for us that we may be a sign of the love of Christ for our people."
—Servant of God Stanley Rother

St. Martha of Bethany
Disciple and Friend of the Lord (First Century)

Martha and her siblings, Mary and Lazarus, enjoyed a special relationship with Jesus, who frequently enjoyed the hospitality of their home in Bethany. During one of these visits, as Martha busied herself in the kitchen, her sister Mary sat at the Master's feet and "listened to his teaching." Martha grew resentful and urged Jesus to instruct her sister to lend a hand, whereupon he answered her, "Martha, Martha, you are anxious and troubled about many things; one thing is necessary. Mary has chosen the good portion, which shall not be taken away from her."

This passage has often been taken to favor the contemplative life of cloistered nuns over the ordinary life of women bustling in the world. At the same time, however, the story shows Jesus challenging the type of gender stereotypes that would restrict women to domestic work. Was Jesus rebuking Martha or sending a message to the other male disciples?

In a later story, following the death of Lazarus, Martha seems to rebuke Jesus, suggesting that if he had come earlier her brother would have lived. He replies: "I am the resurrection and the life." This inspires Martha to deliver one of the great christological confessions of Scripture: "I believe you are the Christ, the Son of God, he who is coming into the world."

Thus, both Martha and Mary, in their different ways, found the "one thing necessary"—to respond with love to the Christ in their midst.

"I know that whatever you ask of God, God will give you."

—St. Martha (John 11:22)

Blessed Beatrice of Nazareth
Mystic (1200–1268)

Beatrice was born to a prosperous family near Brussels. Following the death of her mother, when she was six, she was sent to a community of Beguines and later still entrusted as a child oblate to a Cistercian convent. Thus, virtually all her life was spent in the company of religious women.

She felt well suited to monastic life, and at fifteen she became a novice. Afterward she was sent to another abbey to learn to copy manuscripts. She also kept a journal of her spiritual experiences. The first of her mystical experiences occurred on Christmas Day in 1217. While singing prayers with the other nuns she found her heart ascending with Christ "right up to the Father's presence." She had a vision of the Holy Trinity, seen "not with eyes of the flesh but of the mind." While enjoying this vision she was suddenly returned "to the other senses" by the prodding of another nun, who had supposed her to be dozing.

Beatrice continued to receive supernatural visitations. She responded at times with tears, at other times with a "madness in her heart" that made her laugh for joy. In 1235 she moved to a new Cistercian monastery known as Nazareth. There she composed a mystical treatise describing the ways by which the devout Soul ascends to God, whom she names simply Love. She served as prioress there until her death on July 29, 1268.

"As a fish swims the length and breadth of the sea and rests in its depths, so the Soul feels her mind completely unrestrained in the height, width, and depth of love."

—Blessed Beatrice of Nazareth

Blessed Zdenka Cecilia Schelingova
Martyr (1916–1955)

Cecilia Schelingova was born in northern Slovakia. As a young girl she came into contact with the Sisters of Charity of the Holy Cross, a nursing order, and was inspired to join them. At fifteen, accompanied by her mother, she presented herself at the motherhouse of the congregation and asked to be admitted. After training as a nurse, with a specialty in radiology, she took her vows and became Sr. Zdenka.

In 1942 she was sent to a hospital in Bratislava. There she lived through the war and the subsequent Russian occupation. The postwar Communist regime imposed repressive measures against the Church. Many priests were arrested. Some of them, sick or recovering from torture, were sent to Zdenka's hospital. In 1952, learning that one of these prisoners was to be transferred to Siberia, she prayed for guidance: "Jesus, I offer my life for his. Save him." After putting sleeping pills in the guard's tea, she helped the priest escape. She later tried to repeat this ploy, but this time she was arrested. Subjected to torture and tried as an "enemy of the people's democracy," she was sentenced to twelve years in prison.

Her sufferings in prison—from cold, hunger, and untreated illness—were terrible. Finally, the state, not wanting to create a martyr, released her in April 1955. But her congregation, fearful of being associated with a convicted traitor, would not take her back. She died on July 31, 1955. She was beatified as a martyr in 2003.

"I want to do God's will without paying attention to myself, my comfort or my rest."
—Blessed Zdenka Cecilia Schelingova

Bishop James E. Walsh
Confessor to the Chinese (1891–1981)

On July 10, 1970, a frail and elderly man left the company of the Red Guards and walked across the bridge linking mainland China and the island of Hong Kong. After twelve years in prison, Bishop James E. Walsh, the last foreign missionary in Communist China, was on his way home.

Walsh had first gone to China in 1918 as part of the first overseas mission team of Maryknoll missioners, and in 1927 he was named bishop of Kongmoon. In 1936 he was recalled to the United States to serve for ten years as Maryknoll's second superior general. But in 1948 he was back in Shanghai. With the Communist victory, his activities were steadily restricted. Yet he swore he would never leave voluntarily. He believed the vocation of a priest remained the same, even if everything else was stripped away: to be a representative of God's love. This calling could be fulfilled under any circumstance.

In 1958 he was arrested and charged with espionage. He accepted his situation with remarkable serenity, believing that in prison he served the Gospel as faithfully as he could. Finally, in 1970, at the age of seventy-nine, he was released.

Walsh lived on for many years, revered by Maryknollers and others as a heroic and holy confessor. He disclaimed special recognition: "I was a Catholic priest and my people were in trouble. So I simply stayed with them as all priests should at all times."

He died on July 29, 1981.

"Prayer is so powerful. I am a living example of what prayer can do."

—Bishop James E. Walsh

St. Ignatius Loyola
Founder, Society of Jesus (1491–1556)

ñigo López de Loyola was born to a noble Basque family in Castile. He spent his youth as a courtier and later a soldier. Trained in the code of honor and chivalry, he was ready with his sword to avenge any slight against his dignity or the interests of his master.

In 1521 he was severely wounded in battle. While recovering in his family castle, he asked for something to read. All that was available was a collection of pious lives of the saints. In time he was inspired by these stories, imagining what a great honor it must be to serve the glory of God. When he had recovered he made a pilgrimage to the Catalonian shrine of Our Lady at Montserrat. There, after an all-night vigil, he laid his sword on the altar and became a soldier of Christ.

Ignatius studied in Paris to become a priest. While there he exhorted a group of fellow students to join him in forming a new religious order, dedicated to renewing and serving the Church in any way their services might be required. This was the nucleus of what became the Society of Jesus, or the Jesuits. The order was officially recognized in 1540, and Ignatius became its first superior general.

The Jesuits soon spread throughout the globe on perilous missions to Asia, New Spain, and Protestant England, renewing the vitality of the Church through Ignatius's principle of "contemplation in action." Within fifteen years the order increased from ten members to a thousand. Ignatius died on July 31, 1556. He was canonized in 1622.

"Act as if everything depended on you; trust as if everything depended on God."

—St. Ignatius Loyola

Venerable Solanus Casey
Capuchin Friar (1870–1957)

Solanus Casey, the son of Irish immigrants in Wisconsin, felt called to the priesthood after witnessing a drunken sailor stabbing a woman. Somehow, this scene of sin and suffering caused him to dedicate himself to God and to promote God's love as the answer to the world's troubles. After entering the Capuchins he was ordained a priest. But in light of academic difficulties, his superiors placed restrictions on his priestly faculties. He was not permitted to hear confessions or preach on doctrine. Instead he spent most of his life as a porter at St. Bonaventure's monastery in Detroit and worked in the friars' soup kitchen.

Despite his humble office, Solanus's extraordinary spiritual gifts were quickly recognized. A gifted reader of souls, he became particularly renowned for his ministry of healing prayer. Scores of people sought him out each day for spiritual counsel and intercession. Dutifully, he recorded their petitions in his prayer book and promised to ask God's assistance. Even in his lifetime, hundreds of miraculous cures were attributed to his prayers. In his final illness, he remarked, "I'm offering my suffering that all might be one. If only I could see the conversion of the whole world."

Since his death on July 31, 1957, at the age of eighty-six, the reports of healing miracles have continued unabated. His cause for canonization is in process.

"We must be faithful to the present moment or we will frustrate the plan of God for our lives."
—Venerable Solanus Casey

AUGUST

1 St. Alphonsus Liguori • The Martyrs of Nowogrodek

2 St. Basil the Blessed • St. Peter Faber

3 St. Lydia • Flannery O'Connor

4 St. John Vianney • Enrique Angelelli

5 St. Nonna • Metropolitan Anthony of Sourozh

6 St. Afra • Venerable Antonio Margil

7 St. Victricius • St. Bonifacia Rodríguez y Castro

8 St. Dominic • St. Mary MacKillop

9 St. Candida Maria of Jesus • St. Teresa Benedicta of the Cross
(Edith Stein)

10 St. Lawrence • St. Susanna

11 St. Clare • Eunice Shriver

12 St. Jeanne de Chantal • William Blake

13 Florence Nightingale • Blessed Otto Neururer and Jakob Gapp

14 Venerable Michael McGivney • St. Maximilian Kolbe

15 Jonathan Daniels • John Courtney Murray

16 St. Roch • Brother Roger Schutz

17 St. Jeanne Delanoue • Black Elk

18 St. Helena • Jessica Powers

19 Blaise Pascal • Venerable Mary Magdalen Bentivoglio

20 St. Bernard • St. Maria de Mattias

21 Geert Groote • Blessed Victoria Rasoamanarivo

22 Luis de Leon • Benigno "Ninoy" Aquino, Jr.

23 St. Rose of Lima • St. Joan Antide-Thouret

24 St. Bartholomew • Simone Weil

25 St. Genesius the Actor • St. Joseph Calasanz

26 St. Elizabeth Bichier des Ages • St. Mary of Jesus Crucified
(Mariam Baouardy)

27 St. Monica • Dom Helder Camara

28 St. Augustine • Blessed Edmund Rice

29 Martyrdom of St. John the Baptist • Blessed Santia Szymkowiak

30 St. Margaret Ward • St. Jeanne Jugan

31 Saints Joseph of Arimathea and Nicodemus • John Leary

AUGUST

St. Alphonsus Liguori
Doctor of the Church, Founder, Redemptorists
(1696–1787)

Alphonsus Liguori was born into a family of the Neapolitan nobility. Though his father wished him to study law, he felt a powerful attraction to the priesthood. After his ordination in 1726 he achieved local fame as a popular preacher in Naples. This led to an ever-widening circuit of mission tours. His simple, straightforward manner of preaching had an enormous influence on the moral and spiritual life of his listeners. Inspired by this experience, Liguori in 1732 founded the Congregation of the Holy Redeemer, an order of priests dedicated to preaching to the rural poor.

Liguori wrote over a hundred books, the most important being his *Moral Theology*. In this work Liguori steered a middle course between rigorism and laxity. He taught that all are called to salvation and that the means are available to every person. But the moral life was not a matter of tortured or legalistic compliance with the law. It was essentially the life of love. Other themes stressed by Liguori were the value of human liberty and the importance of an informed conscience. He was a pioneer in stressing the significance of concrete circumstances in evaluating moral conduct.

Liguori was canonized in 1839 and named a Doctor of the Church in 1871.

"Acquire the habit of speaking to God as if you were alone with Him, familiarly and with confidence and love, as to the dearest and most loving of friends."
—St. Alphonsus Liguori

The Martyrs of Nowogrodek
(d. 1943)

These eleven martyrs were members of the Sisters of the Holy Family of Nazareth, a Polish congregation, called to serve in the town of Nowogrodek in northeastern Poland (now in Belarus). Following the Nazi invasion of Poland in 1939, the sisters were for some time under Soviet control, forced to close their house and abandon their religious habits. After the Nazis occupied the town they returned to their convent, though now operating under the close gaze of the Gestapo. The entire Jewish population of the town was quickly deported. This was followed by the arrest of many priests and other public figures. Waves of executions occurred.

In July 1943, 120 factory workers were arrested and threatened with execution. After considerable prayer, the sisters decided to offer themselves to spare those with dependent families. Their prayers seemed to find an answer when the detainees were sent to work camps instead of being shot. When the sisters' chaplain was arrested they repeated their prayer. This time, on July 31, the sisters were arrested and held overnight in the basement of Gestapo headquarters. The next morning they were taken to a place in the woods where they were ordered to kneel before an open grave. There, one by one, they were shot. They were beatified in 2000.

"My God, if lives must be sacrificed, it is better that they should shoot us rather than those who have families. We pray that God may accept our offer."

—Blessed Maria Stella Mardosewicz, superior of the community

St. Basil the Blessed
"Holy Fool" (d. 1552)

While many saints have appeared eccentric to their contemporaries, the tradition of "holy fools" is nowhere so common or so revered as in the Russian Orthodox Church. These vagrant ascetics, often dressed in little or nothing at all, would wear a mask of madness, inviting ridicule and contempt with their outlandish behavior. Like the Hebrew prophets, they expressed solidarity with the poor, while calling down judgment on the rich and powerful. To the extent that their conduct suggested a divine inspiration, they might also merit cautious respect.

One of the most famous and widely revered of these Fools for Christ is the Muscovite Basil the Blessed. He used to wander naked through the streets of Moscow, praying as if in church. He would often take goods from shops to distribute to the poor. He would throw stones at the houses of people who made a display of their piety, while kneeling to kiss the pavement before houses of ill repute. "Devils lay siege to those," he would say of the former, whereas of the latter, "angels weep over these."

Not even the notorious tsar Ivan the Terrible was immune to his criticism. Yet so fearful was the tsar of this poor holy man that he ordered no harm be done to him. When Basil died in 1552 he was buried with honors beside the new cathedral in Moscow. After his canonization in 1580 the cathedral was named in his honor.

"If any one among you thinks he is wise in this age, let him become a fool so as to become wise."
—1 Corinthians 3:18

St. Peter Faber
Jesuit (1506–1546)

In an interview in *America* magazine in 2013, Pope Francis was asked to name his favorite saints. Surprisingly, he focused on Peter Faber, a roommate of Francis Xavier and Ignatius Loyola at the University of Paris and, though not yet canonized, long revered as one of the cofounders of the Society of Jesus. In explaining this choice, the pope mentioned Faber's "dialogue with all, even the most remote and even with his opponents; his simple piety, a certain naïveté perhaps, his being available straightaway, his careful interior discernment, the fact that he was a man capable of great and strong decisions, but also capable of being gentle and loving."

Faber, who was born to a peasant family in the French Alps, was the first among Ignatius's companions to be ordained a priest. While Francis Xavier undertook a great missionary expedition to Asia, Faber concentrated on Europe, then in the throes of the Reformation. Rather than answer the Protestants with debates, Faber believed the Church should concentrate on its own internal reform. To this end he crisscrossed the continent on foot, promoting spiritual renewal among the clergy and winning many new vocations for the Jesuits. He was on his way to serve as a theologian at the Council of Trent when he collapsed in Rome and died on August 2, 1546.

Though beatified in 1872, Faber had never been canonized—until 2013, when Pope Francis exercised the process of "equivalent canonization" to declare him a saint.

"Take care, take care, never to close your heart to anyone."

—St. Peter Faber

St. Lydia
"Worshiper of God" (First Century)

Sources regarding the role of women in the early Church are limited. Those women, such as St. Lydia, singled out for particular mention, provide some hint of a wider, forgotten history.

Lydia enters the story of the Church when St. Paul and his traveling companion Timothy first ventured onto European soil. In the city of Philippi in Macedonia, the missionaries went to the river where they "supposed there was a place of prayer" (a synagogue). Their audience turned out to consist entirely of women, including one named Lydia from the city of Thyatira, described as "a seller of purple goods, who was a worshiper of God." These mysterious details suggest she was a dealer in expensive purple-dyed fabric and a "God-fearer"—a Gentile who respected Jewish religious law.

Lydia immediately responded to the good news. She was baptized along with her entire household—the first Christian converts in Europe. She in turn pressed Paul to remain in her house: "If you have judged me to be faithful to the Lord, come to my house and stay." To this, the narrator of Acts replies in the first person: "And she prevailed upon us."

The Christian movement originated in such "house churches" as Lydia's. So it is reasonable to remember her as one of the founders of the Church in Europe.

"The Lord opened her heart to give heed to what was said by Paul."

—Acts 16:14

Flannery O'Connor
Catholic Writer (1925–1964)

Flannery O'Connor died of lupus on August 3, 1964, at the age of thirty-nine. Though her short life—largely confined to her mother's dairy farm in Milledgeville, Georgia—may have been lacking in external drama, she left behind a small output of novels and stories that assured her place among the greatest of American writers. But it was the posthumous publication of her letters, *The Habit of Being*, that made it clear how much the shape of her art owed to her Catholic faith. Her personal circumstances, her sharp intelligence, and her deeply held faith combined to forge a prophetic vision of extraordinary depth.

Unlike other "Catholic writers," O'Connor avoided explicitly Catholic settings for her stories. Nonetheless, her stories were set in a universe defined by the reality of sin, grace, and the drama of salvation. "All my stories," she wrote, "are about the action of grace on a character who is not very willing to support it."

She believed the Church was the only thing likely to make the world endurable. And yet, she added, "The only thing that makes the Church endurable is that it is somehow the Body of Christ and that on this we are fed."

She would have been glad to be remembered for her art. Posthumously, however, she has achieved an unexpected reputation as a Christian witness and spiritual advisor to many.

"I feel that if I were not a Catholic, I would have no reason to write, no reason to see, no reason ever to feel horrified or even to enjoy anything."
—Flannery O'Connor

St. John Vianney
Curé of Ars (1786–1859)

The early life of John Vianney contained no foreshadowing of greatness in any field. Born to a peasant family in Lyons, he desired nothing else than to be a priest. But his humble background and lack of education made it unlikely that he would ever realize such a vocation. With the help of a private tutor he secured a place in seminary but proved to be a miserable student. It was only with grave reservations that he was recommended for ordination. After a brief assignment in his home parish, he was named the parish priest of Ars-en-Dombes, a village of 250 souls, as remote and insignificant a place as his bishop could find.

Vianney's sermons were simple and unsophisticated. His theology was rudimentary. But there was one area in which he acquired a reputation for genius: his extraordinary gifts as a confessor. It was said that he had the ability to read souls. Fixed in his cramped confessional, he would sit ten, twelve, as many as eighteen hours a day. Special trains were provided to accommodate the heavy traffic of pilgrims to the famous confessional in Ars.

By the time of his death in 1859 Vianney was one of the most beloved figures in France. He was canonized in 1925 by Pope Pius XI and at the same time was named the patron saint of all parish priests.

"Prayer is to our soul what rain is to the soil. Fertilize the soil ever so richly, it will remain barren unless fed by frequent rains."

—St. John Vianney

Enrique Angelelli
Bishop and Martyr (1923–1976)

Enrique Angelelli was appointed bishop of La Rioja in Argentina in 1968. Among the largely conservative hierarchy of Argentina, he was among the few to strongly support the prophetic line of the Latin American bishops at Medellín. In his first message as bishop he said, "With one ear I listen to the gospel and with the other I listen to the people." Before long he was on a collision course with the military and other powerful interests, who complained that he was a communist who had "ruined the church of Pius XII."

In 1976 a military coup unleashed a vicious period of persecution. By and large the Church hierarchy stood silent—or worse, offered tacit blessings to the military's defense of order and "Christian values." Angelelli denounced the terror, which included the abduction and murder of his priests. He compiled documents proving government responsibility for these murders. These documents were with him on August 4 when two cars ran his truck off the road. He was found twenty-five yards away with his skull smashed in and his briefcase missing. The police labeled it an accident.

With the return of democracy, a court in 1986 reopened the case and termed it a clear homicide. In 2006 at a Mass commemorating the thirtieth anniversary of his death, Cardinal Jorge Bergoglio, now Pope Francis, became the first Argentine prelate to refer to Angelelli as a martyr.

"The thought crosses my mind that the Lord needs a bishop in jail or killed in order to make us wake up to our episcopal collegiality and live it more deeply."
                                        —Bishop Enrique Angelelli

St. Nonna
Matron (ca. 374)

St. Nonna was born to Christian parents in Cappadocia (in present-day Turkey). She married Gregory, a magistrate in Nazianzus, though he belonged to a non-Christian sect. As her son would later write, "This was something she could not calmly bear, that the one half be conjoined with God, whilst the other part itself should remain apart from God. On the contrary, she wanted that, to the fleshly union, there should also apply a spiritual union." Her prayers were answered when her husband converted. He went on to be ordained a priest and then a bishop, later venerated as St. Gregory Nazianzen the Elder. (There was at that time no prohibition against married clergy.) Nonna, for her part, became a deacon.

St. Nonna bore three children, all of them also venerated as saints: St. Gorgonia, who married and had three children; St. Caesarius, who became an illustrious physician; and St. Gregory Nazianzen the Younger, who became archbishop of Constantinople, and who went on to play a critical role in formulating the doctrine of the Trinity.

Young St. Gregory delivered a moving eulogy at his mother's funeral, noting, "While some mothers excel in the management of their households and others excel in piety, my mother excelled at both."

"She knew one thing to be truly noble: to be pious and to know from where we have come and where we are going; and that there is one innate and trusty wealth: to use one's substance on God and on the poor, especially the impoverished kin."

—St. Gregory Nazianzen the Younger

Metropolitan Anthony of Sourozh
Russian Orthodox Bishop (1914–2003)

Andrei Bloom was born of Russian parents in Lausanne, Switzerland. His father was in the Russian diplomatic corps, and after the Revolution his family joined the throng of Russian émigrés in Paris. Bloom had little interest in religion. But one day, in his teenage years, he forced himself to read the Gospel of Mark. As he read he became aware of a presence. "I saw nothing. I heard nothing. It was no hallucination. It was a simple certainty that the Lord was standing there and that I was in the presence of him whose life I had begun to read."

With the outbreak of war in 1939, Bloom, who had studied medicine, became a medic in the French army. At the same time he professed monastic vows and took the name Anthony. After the war he was ordained a priest and went to England to serve as an Orthodox chaplain. Over time his influence steadily grew, and he would become the bishop in charge of the Russian Orthodox Church in Great Britain and Ireland. Through his books, lectures, and radio broadcasts, he also became a beloved spiritual teacher, reaching far beyond the Orthodox community to a wide audience of Christians, unbelievers, and spiritual seekers. His aim was to introduce people to the living God and teach them to pray. He died on August 4, 2003.

"We should try to live in such a way that if the Gospels were lost, they could be re-written by looking at us."

—Metropolitan Anthony

St. Afra
Martyr (d. ca. 304)

St. Afra, who lived in Augsburg in the German province of the Roman Empire, was known as a prostitute. Therefore, when she was arrested and charged with being a Christian, her judge was incredulous. "I am informed that you are a prostitute," he said. "Sacrifice to the gods, therefore, as you are a stranger to the God of the Christians and cannot be accepted by Him." Afra replied, "My Lord Jesus Christ has said that He came down from Heaven to save sinners. The gospel says that a sinful woman washed His feet with her tears and obtained pardon, and that He never rejected the outcasts but welcomed them to eat with him." Though she admitted her own sin, she insisted that she would "not add new crimes" by making sacrifice to the Roman gods.

Condemned to death, Afra was bound to a post to be burned alive. As the smoke rose about her, she was heard to say: "I thank thee, Lord Jesus Christ, for thy goodness in receiving me, a burnt-offering for thy name's sake; thou didst offer thyself upon the cross as a sacrifice for the sins of the whole world; I offer myself a victim to thee, who livest and reignest with the Father and the Holy Ghost, world without end. Amen."

"Let the body which has sinned suffer; but I will not ruin my soul by false worship."

—St. Afra

Venerable Antonio Margil
Franciscan Missionary (1657–1726)

Antonio Margil was born in Valencia, Spain. At a young age he entered the Franciscans and adopted the nickname "Nothingness Itself," by which he subsequently signed his letters. At twenty-five, after distinguishing himself as a preacher and theologian, he was ordained. Immediately, he volunteered to join the mission in New Spain.

Fr. Antonio spent many years as a missionary in Yucatan, Costa Rica, and Guatemala. Always traveling on foot, he overcame the fears of the Indians by his poverty and simplicity, and his determination to dissociate himself from Spanish rule. For some time he interrupted his travels to preside over a missionary college in Zacatecas in Mexico, then traveled north to participate in a missionary expedition to Texas. There he established six missions, including the mission of San Antonio. His reputation for holiness began to grow, fed by astonishment over his ability to traverse huge distances in no time, to read people's souls, and other miraculous signs. Above all, he was renowned for his charity. As he said, "We must serve our neighbor more than ourselves, for by so doing we make Almighty God our debtor, and He will aid us in our necessities."

Eventually he returned to Mexico, where he died on August 6, 1726. In 1836 Pope Gregory XVI issued a decree of his heroic virtues, and he was declared venerable.

"To enjoy God there is an eternity given to us; but to perform some service for God and to do some good to our brethren, the time for that is very short."
—Venerable Antonio Margil

St. Victricius
Bishop of Rouen (ca. 330–ca. 407)

Like his friend St. Martin of Tours, Victricius was a Roman soldier who converted to Christianity and decided, simultaneously, that military service was incompatible with obedience to the Gospel. After laying down his weapons on the parade grounds, he was arrested and charged with desertion. Though subjected to flogging, he narrowly escaped execution.

Victricius traveled for some years as an itinerant preacher until 386, when he was named the bishop of Rouen. Little is known of his subsequent life in this remote mission outpost. He was greatly occupied in establishing the Church in northern France and made numerous preaching tours throughout Europe. He retained his reputation as a peacemaker and was even summoned to Britain at the request of the local bishops to settle a disagreement. There and in all circumstances, according to his own words, he "did all he could, even if he did not do all that wanted doing."

Victricius died sometime around 407. His feast day is August 7.

"I inspired the wise with love of peace. I taught it to the teachable. I explained it to the ignorant. I imposed it on the obstinate, insisting on it in season and out of season."
—St. Victricius

St. Bonifacia Rodríguez y Castro
Cofounder, Servants of St. Joseph (1837–1905)

onifacia Rodríguez y Castro was born in Salamanca, Spain, to a family of artisans. After receiving a rudimentary education she took up the trade of rope making, thus supporting herself and her widowed mother. Her deep spiritual leanings were recognized by a Jesuit priest of her parish. Though she expressed an interest in joining a convent, he encouraged her to develop a new form of religious life, based on the model of Jesus of Nazareth. Centered around the workshop, they would promote the dignity of work and gather a community of women to reflect on society in light of the Gospel.

Bonifacia and several other women took religious vows in 1874 and formed the Association of the Immaculate Conception and St. Joseph. For years the community thrived. But eventually a new bishop tried to take control of the order—steering them away from industrial work and toward more conventional religious life. Bonifacia herself was unceremoniously expelled from her community. In Catalonia she founded a new community, the Servants of St. Joseph, which in 1901 received papal approbation.

She died on August 8, 1905. She was canonized in October 2011.

"Bonifacia Rodríguez Castro is a simple worker who, in the midst of everyday life, opened herself to the gift of God, allowing it to grow in her heart with authentically evangelical attitudes.
Faithful to the call of God, she abandoned herself to the Father's arms, allowing him to imprint on her the features of Jesus, the worker of Nazareth, who spent the great part of his life hidden in the company of his parents."
—Pope John Paul II

St. Dominic
Founder, Order of Preachers (1170–1221)

Dominic Guzmán, a Spanish priest, found his vocation while accompanying his bishop on a mission in the Languedoc region of southern France. This region, at the time, was in the grip of Catharism, a religious cult with origins in the East. While lodging in an inn, Dominic was horrified to discover that their host was himself an adherent to these beliefs. Further probing disclosed that his heresy did not represent so much a rejection of the Catholic faith as a woeful ignorance of its tenets. After spending a long night explicating the contents of the faith, Dominic persuaded his host to renounce his unorthodox views.

From this, Dominic conceived the model for a new kind of missionary, based on the pattern of the original apostles. Trained in theology and the skills of communication, they would travel on foot and without money, preaching wherever there was an audience and exemplifying the Gospel ideals of faith and charity. This would become the foundation for a new congregation, the Order of Preachers (or Dominicans, as they came to be known). Like their contemporaries the Franciscans, the Dominicans introduced a new era in religious life—the age of the mendicants (beggars). Rather than live in a monastery, they would proclaim the Gospel on the road, open to the needs of the world.

Unlike Francis, Dominic did not inspire a rich personal legend. His legacy was the apostolic movement he inspired. He died among his brethren in 1221.

"Arm yourself with prayer rather than a sword; wear humility rather than fine clothes."
—St. Dominic

St. Mary MacKillop
Founder, Sisters of St. Joseph of the Sacred Heart
(1842–1909)

With her beatification in 1995, Mary MacKillop became the first recognized saint of Australia. She was the founder of a remarkable congregation, the Sisters of St. Joseph, who devoted themselves to providing free education and other services to the poor. The idea of her vocation, adapted to the rugged conditions of rural Australia, came to her while serving as a governess. Her congregation would adhere to a strict vow of poverty; there would be no social distinctions within the order; and the congregation would be subject to an elected mother general, rather than the local bishop. This latter provision became a source of grave tension between the congregation and the Australian bishops.

Mary's congregation was approved by Rome and quickly attracted scores of young women. At a time when almost no public services were available for the poor, the work of the sisters was widely admired. But the harassment from local bishops quickly reached extraordinary lengths. Mary was subjected to a shameless campaign of vilification and at one point was excommunicated. Nevertheless, Rome supported her constitutions and she was completely vindicated. Throughout her sufferings she remained free of bitterness. Innocent suffering, she believed, was an opportunity to shoulder the cross and grow closer to God. Those who caused this suffering were thus her "most powerful benefactors." When she died on August 8, 1909, her passing was mourned throughout Australia.

Mary was canonized in 2010.

"Find happiness in making others happy."

—St. Mary MacKillop

St. Candida Maria of Jesus
Founder, Daughters of Jesus (1845–1912)

Raised in a poor family in Salamanca, Spain, St. Candida spent her early life working as a maid. But she felt herself called to something more. When a young man asked her hand in marriage, she replied, "I am for God alone." Poor herself, she was moved by the sufferings of her neighbors and prayed for some way to be of service.

On Good Friday in 1868, while praying in church, she received a vision of Christ, with the Blessed Mother beside him, who instructed her to found a congregation for the education of young girls. She prayed the whole night through. And then with the help of a Jesuit priest, she set about putting her plan in motion. With little formal education herself, she organized a school for poor girls in the city. In 1871 she and five companions took vows in a new congregation, the Daughters of Jesus, and she became superior general. Explaining the charism of her order, Mother Candida said, "In Jesus we have everything. Without him we have nothing."

The congregation spread throughout Spain, and it was officially recognized in 1901. Eventually her sisters traveled the globe, including the United States. Candida died on August 9, 1912, and was canonized by Pope Benedict XVI in 2010.

"Where there is no room for the poor neither is there room for me."

—St. Candida Maria of Jesus

St. Teresa Benedicta of the Cross (Edith Stein)
Carmelite Martyr (1891–1942)

E dith Stein was born into an Orthodox Jewish family in Breslau, Germany. As a teenager, she rejected her family's faith and declared herself an atheist. A brilliant scholar, she completed a doctorate in philosophy at the age of twenty-three. Increasingly, however, her studies prompted a growing interest in religion. In 1921, after reading the autobiography of St. Teresa of Avila, she decided to become a Catholic. Though her conversion was a bitter blow to her mother, Stein felt that in accepting Christ she had been reunited—by a mysterious path—with her Jewish roots.

With the Nazi rise to power, Stein was dismissed from the university. Entering a Carmelite convent she took the name Sr. Teresa Benedicta of the Cross and proceeded to write many volumes on philosophy and mystical theology. But the convent was no protection from the rising tide of persecution, and her sisters arranged her transfer to the presumed safety of a convent in Holland. After the German invasion of Holland, Stein was required to wear the Yellow Star of David on her habit. In 1942 all Jewish Catholics, including members of religious orders, were arrested and deported. "Come, Rosa," she said to her sister. "We're going for our people." Edith Stein died in Auschwitz on August 9, 1942.

Stein accepted her fate in solidarity with the Jewish people, as an act of atonement for the evil of her time and a conscious identification with the cross of Christ. She was canonized as a martyr and a confessor in 1998.

"In order to be an image of God, the spirit must turn to what is eternal, hold it in spirit, keep it in memory, and by loving it, embrace it in the will."
—St. Teresa Benedicta of the Cross

St. Lawrence
Martyr (d. 258)

Though many of the facts of his life and death are uncertain, St. Lawrence remains one of the most venerated martyrs of the Church. As one of the seven deacons of the Church in Rome, he bore responsibility for managing church goods and overseeing distribution of alms to the poor. In 257 the emperor Valerian issued edicts against the Church, setting in motion a persecution that caused the martyrdom of Pope St. Sixtus II. St. Lawrence's martyrdom followed four days later.

According to legend, Lawrence was given an order by the prefect of Rome to produce in three days all the wealth of the Church. Lawrence responded by gathering a great assembly of the poor, the sick, the blind, lepers, widows, and orphans. "These *are* the treasure of the Church," he proclaimed.

Another famous legend of St. Lawrence concerns the manner of his death. He was ordered to be roasted on a gridiron. After enduring this torture for some time, he entreated the executioner with good cheer to turn his body over: "I am done on this side!" Then, having prayed for the conversion of Rome, he died.

"The flame of Christ's love could not be overcome by your flames. . . . You but served the martyr in your rage, O persecutor; you but swelled the reward in adding to the pain. Let us rejoice, dearly-beloved, with spiritual joy and make our boast over the happy end of this illustrious man in the Lord."

—St. Leo the Great, Sermon on the Feast of St. Lawrence

St. Susanna
Martyr (Third Century)

Though Susanna, a third-century martyr, surely existed, her story is steeped in legend. According to an account written centuries after her death, Susanna was the learned daughter of a priest in Rome and a niece of Pope St. Caius. Reports of her beauty reached the emperor Diocletian, who sent one of her uncles to secure her hand for his son-in-law. Susanna, however, had already pledged herself as a bride of Christ. When her uncle arrived she recoiled from his kiss of greeting. "It is not your kiss that I object to," she said, "but your mouth defiled by idolatrous sacrifices." She urged him to repent and be baptized.

Her uncle was apparently so struck by Susanna's faith that he did indeed seek instruction and was baptized as a Christian. The same thing happened to a second uncle whom the emperor entrusted with this mission. Enraged, Diocletian ordered both uncles and their families to be burned alive. As for Susanna, she was condemned to beheading. "I offer myself in sacrifice to my Lord," she cried before meeting her death.

An ancient church was built on the site of her uncles' home. In 1921 the Church of St. Susanna was entrusted to the Paulist Fathers, serving as the national church for Americans in Rome.

"Sufferings were to the martyrs the most distinguishing mercy, extraordinary graces, and sources of the greatest crowns and glory. . . . By honoring the martyrs, we pronounce our own condemnation."
—Alban Butler on St. Susanna

St. Clare
Founder, Poor Clares (1194–1253)

The story of St. Clare of Assisi is inevitably linked with her companion St. Francis. It was Francis who gave her a vision and enabled her to define a way of life apart from the options offered by her society. Her goal in life, however, was not to be a reflection of Francis but to be, like him, a reflection of Christ. "Christ is the way," she said, "and Francis showed it to me."

Clare belonged to one of the wealthy families of Assisi. In 1212, when she was eighteen, she heard Francis deliver a series of Lenten sermons and afterward arranged in stealth to meet with him and ask his help that she too might live "after the manner of the holy gospel." One night, soon after, she slipped out of town, met with Francis and his brothers, put off her fine clothes, cut her long hair, and assumed a penitential habit. In time other women joined her in a community dedicated to prayer and poverty, a counterpart to Francis's fraternity.

It has been said that of all the followers of Francis, Clare was the most faithful. Many stories reflect the loving bonds of friendship between them and the trust that Francis placed in her wisdom and counsel. She lived on for twenty-seven years after his death. Her own death came in 1253.

"Place your mind before the mirror of eternity! Place your soul in the brilliance of glory! And transform your entire being into the image of the Godhead Itself through contemplation."

—St. Clare of Assisi

Eunice Shriver
Founder, Special Olympics (1921–2009)

E unice Shriver, the fifth of nine children of Rose and Joseph Kennedy, was born into a remarkable home in which politics and privilege were joined by an urgent call to service. Her husband, Sargent Shriver, with whom she raised five children, founded the Peace Corps and ran for vice president. Her brothers included a president and two senators.

But perhaps the sibling who left the deepest impact was the least known—her sister Rosemary, whose mental disabilities, exacerbated by a lobotomy, caused her to spend most of her life in an institution. Shriver's belief in the full humanity of all those with disabilities led her to dedicate much of her life to their cause, battling for their full inclusion and the recognition of their gifts and abilities.

The result was the Special Olympics, a movement that helped change global attitudes toward those with mental disabilities. Inaugurating the first Special Olympics in Chicago in 1968, only weeks after the death of her brother Bobby, she greeted the athletes from many countries and led them in reciting the Special Olympics oath: "Let me win, but if I cannot win, let me be brave in the attempt."

The effects of her life, rooted in her deep faith, were incalculable. A statement by her family, after her death on August 11, 2009, noted, "She was a living prayer, a living advocate, a living center of power. She set out to change the world and to change us, and she did that and more."

"You are the stars and the world is watching you. By your presence you send a message to every village, every city, every nation. A message of hope. A message of victory."

—Eunice Shriver to Special Olympians

St. Jeanne de Chantal
Cofounder, Order of the Visitation of Mary
(1572–1641)

Jeanne de Chantal was born to a wealthy family in Dijon, France. Married at twenty, her life took a tragic turn eight years later when her husband was killed in an accident, leaving her on her own to raise four children. She vowed that she would never remarry.

In 1604 she heard a sermon by St. Francis de Sales, the holy bishop of Geneva, that changed her life. It was also the start of a deep spiritual partnership that would advance them both along their paths to sanctity. Francis taught that the spiritual life was for everyone, not just monks and nuns. Jeanne immediately responded to his message and submitted to his spiritual direction.

Eventually they founded the Order of the Visitation of Mary, a congregation dedicated to prayer and works of charity. Jeanne's daughters were married by this time, but her teenaged son opposed her plan to enter religious life. Laying himself on the threshold of their home, he implored her to stay. Jeanne stepped over him and proceeded on her way.

She proved a gifted superior, combining administrative skills with a profound instinct for the spiritual life. "No matter what happens," she wrote, "be gentle with yourself." Before her death in 1641, the order grew to include eighty communities in several countries.

"In prayer one must hold fast and never let go. . . . If it seems that no one is listening to you, then cry out even louder. If you are driven out of one door, go back in by the other."

—St. Jeanne de Chantal

William Blake
Poet and Visionary (1757–1827)

William Blake, the English poet and artist, trained first as an engraver. His habit of offending patrons, however, cost him much business, and he and his wife were often little removed from poverty. As an artist, he had a hard time drawing to please an audience wider than himself. For his fantastical paintings of angels and allegorical figures there was little market. The same was true for his poetry, which was either deceptively simple or maddeningly obscure. He prized the power of Imagination, by which he meant the ability to see reality in its full spiritual dimension.

For Blake, poetry and art were the expression of his own spiritual vision—a kind of protest against everything acceptable in his day. He deplored the moralism that passed for virtue, the hypocrisy and dogmatism of organized religion, the ugliness and cruelty of industrialism, the pedantry that passed for learning. In some ways he resembled a biblical prophet who looked at the world in light of the coming judgment.

Obsessed with the figure of Christ, he felt the churches had emptied Christianity of its revolutionary content. Thus, he invented a kind of Christianity of his own—idiosyncratic, to be sure, but also yielding moments of dazzling insight. According to Thomas Merton, Blake's rebellion "was fundamentally the rebellion of the saints. It was the rebellion of the lover of the living God."

He died on August 12, 1827.

"To see a World in a Grain of Sand / And a Heaven in a Wild Flower, / Hold Infinity in the palm of your hand / And Eternity in an hour."
—William Blake

Florence Nightingale
Nurse (1820–1910)

Florence Nightingale was born into the highest circles of English society—a world she found suffocating. From an early age she felt a keen sense that God was calling her for some special purpose—an imperative that drew her inexorably toward nursing, a calling that was unthinkable for someone of her class. When she expressed this interest to her father he forbade it. "It was as if I had wanted to be a kitchen maid," she said.

Defying her family, she underwent nursing training in Germany and afterward won an appointment as director of a small charity hospital in London. There she put in practice her theories on health-care reform—namely, the importance of sanitation, ventilation, and sound nutrition.

When the Crimean War broke out, Nightingale recruited a contingent of nurses to go to the front. Conditions there were disgraceful and scandalous. But through sheer force of will—and the proof of her results, reducing mortality by half—she took charge of the entire British medical service.

A veritable ministering angel, her compassion and dedication became legendary. She returned as a national hero. But her work was only beginning. She would not rest until she had spread her campaign for medical reform throughout society, a cause she pursued for fifty years until her death on August 13, 1910.

"I never pray for anything temporal . . . but when each morning comes, I kneel down before the Rising Sun, & only say, Behold the handmaid of the Lord—give me this day my work to do—no, not my work, but thine."
—Florence Nightingale

Blessed Otto Neururer and Jakob Gapp
Martyrs (d. 1940, 1943)

These two Austrian priests, both martyrs under the Nazis, were beatified by Pope John Paul II in 1996.

Otto Neururer (1882–1940) was the first Austrian priest arrested by the Nazis after the incorporation of Austria into Greater Germany in 1938. The immediate cause seems to have been his counsel to a young woman that she not marry a Nazi storm trooper, by whom she was pregnant. After his arrest in 1939, he was sent to Dachau and then Buchenwald, where he was consigned to a torture block and suspended by his feet until he died on May 30, 1940.

Jakob Gapp (1897–1943) was a Marianist priest who made no attempt to disguise his contempt for the Nazis. He protested when pictures of Hitler were placed in the school where he taught, and he instructed his students of their duty to love all people, "French people, Jews, and Communists alike." "God, not Adolf Hitler, is your God," he proclaimed. With the encouragement of his order, he fled Germany for France and then for Spain, where he worked as a chaplain. In 1942, Gestapo agents posing as catechumens spirited him across the border to France, where he was arrested and transported to Germany, to be charged with treason. During his interrogation, he boldly defended his faith—so effectively that Heinrich Himmler, who read the transcripts, is said to have voiced regret that there were not more Germans equally committed to National Socialism. He was beheaded on August 13, 1943.

"Everything passes; only heaven remains."

—Blessed Jakob Gapp

Venerable Michael McGivney
Founder, Knights of Columbus (1852–1890)

Michael McGivney, the son of Irish immigrants, was born in Connecticut to a family of thirteen children. At the age of sixteen he left for seminary. Ordained in 1877, he was assigned to St. Mary's Church in New Haven. It was a time of severe anti-Catholic prejudice. Most of his parishioners were poor working people, many of them immigrants. From his own family life he was aware of their struggles—particularly the hardship caused by the death of a breadwinner.

McGivney conceived the idea of a Catholic fraternal society to help strengthen faith and provide financial support to families in need. From this idea sprang the Knights of Columbus, founded in 1882. With support from the bishops, McGivney spread word of the Knights throughout Connecticut and elsewhere. It quickly took off, though Fr. McGivney's service as chaplain to the Knights did not last long. He contracted pneumonia and died on August 14, 1890, at the age of thirty-eight.

Today the Knights of Columbus, with almost two million member families, is the world's largest Catholic fraternal service organization. In 2008 Fr. McGivney's heroic virtues were recognized by Pope Benedict XVI, who declared him venerable.

"He was a man of the people. He was zealous of the people's welfare, and all the kindliness of his priestly soul asserted itself more strongly in his unceasing efforts for the betterment of their condition."

—Testimonial by the Knights of Columbus,
after the death of Fr. McGivney

St. Maximilian Kolbe
Franciscan Martyr (1894–1941)

On July 30, 1941, a prisoner escaped from Auschwitz, the notorious Nazi camp in Poland. In retaliation the commandant lined up inmates of Cell Block Fourteen and ordered that ten of them be selected for death. When one of the ten cried out that he would never see his family again, another prisoner stepped forward and volunteered to take his place. When the commandant asked who he was, he replied, "I am a Catholic priest." His offer was accepted, and so Fr. Maximilian Kolbe assumed his place among the condemned.

Kolbe and the other prisoners were locked in a death bunker with nothing to consume but their own urine. He passed the time leading his companions in prayer, preparing them for death, and keeping vigil with them as they gradually succumbed. When, after two weeks, Kolbe and three others were still alive, the Nazis dispatched them with injections of carbolic acid.

In 1982 Pope John Paul II, who as bishop of Krakow had often prayed at the scene of Kolbe's death, presided over his canonization in Rome. Present for the ceremony was the man whose life Kolbe had saved. The pope called Kolbe a true martyr and saint for our times whose heroic charity proved victorious over the architects of death.

"I would like to use myself completely up in the service of the Immaculata, and to disappear without leaving a trace, as the winds carry my ashes to the far corners of the world."

—St. Maximilian Kolbe

Jonathan Daniels
Civil Rights Martyr (1939–1965)

In March 1965 Jonathan Daniels, an Episcopal seminarian from New Hampshire, joined other northern students and clergy in answering Martin Luther King Jr.'s call to participate in the historic march for civil rights from Selma, Alabama, to the state capital in Montgomery. Though he had intended to remain only for the weekend, Daniels was so shocked by the system of segregation that he decided to stay on.

Lowndes County was a stronghold of the Ku Klux Klan. Though the population was mostly black, not a single African American was registered to vote. Daniels joined protests against segregated stores and facilities, worked to integrate the local churches, and tutored schoolchildren. All the while, he struggled to see his work as a form of ministry—not just to the oppressed but also to their oppressors. Freedom, he believed, must come by way of the Cross.

In August he spent six days in jail after being arrested at a protest. Upon his release on August 20, he, along with a white Catholic priest and two African American women, tried to buy a soda at a nearby store. Their way was blocked by a white man, who leveled a shotgun at one of the women, Ruby Sales. Jonathan pushed her aside just in time to take a full blast to his chest. He died instantly. He is commemorated in the Episcopal Church calendar on August 14.

"I began to discover a new freedom in the Cross: freedom to love the enemy; and in that freedom, the freedom (without hypocrisy) to will and to try to set him free."
—Jonathan Daniels

John Courtney Murray
Jesuit Theologian (1904–1967)

John Courtney Murray was one of the most significant American Catholic theologians of the twentieth century. His writings on pluralism and the "American experiment" helped overcome nativist doubts about the place of Catholics in American democracy. In the wider Church he helped overcome ancient doubts about the separation of Church and state and paved the way for a sea change in the Church's attitude toward religious freedom.

Outwardly his life lacked drama. He joined the Jesuits at the age of sixteen, earned a doctorate in theology, and taught for thirty years at a Jesuit seminary. In the late 1940s he wrote a series of groundbreaking essays arguing that the American traditions of pluralism and religious liberty were not only compatible with Catholicism but were a fitting reflection of the Catholic teaching on human dignity and freedom. The separation of Church and state was an ideal that liberated the Church to pursue its genuine religious mission. Such views departed from long-standing attitudes in the Church, and Murray was for some years silenced by the Vatican.

As an advisor to Cardinal Spellman he attended the Second Vatican Council where he was entrusted with drafting the council's historic document on religious freedom, finally released in December 1965. It is widely acknowledged that this document was the principal contribution of the American Church to Vatican II. Indeed, it was the contribution of John Courtney Murray to Catholic teaching. Thus he lived to see the vindication of his life's work. He died on August 16, 1967.

"The human person has a right to religious freedom."

—Declaration on Religious Freedom

St. Roch
Penitent (ca. 1348–ca. 1378)

For many centuries St. Roch was invoked as a protector against plague and pestilence. Little is known of his actual life. According to legend, he was born to a noble family in Montpelier. At the age of twenty, when his parents died, he renounced his fortune and took up the life of a mendicant pilgrim. While on a journey to Rome he encountered a number of plague-stricken cities. There he courageously nursed the sick and effected many cures, supposedly by making the sign of the cross.

Eventually, Roch himself was struck by the plague. Rather than seek help in a hospital, he dragged himself into the woods to die. There he was discovered by a dog who brought him food and cured him by licking his wounds. Upon recovering, he resumed his ministry, caring for the sick and curing many people, along with their livestock. Eventually he returned to Montpelier, where he died.

St. Roch is often depicted in the company of a dog—whose memory, some have argued, deserves equal veneration.

"O Jesu, my Saviour, I thank thee that thou puttest me to affliction like to thine other servants, by this odious ardour of pestilence, and most meek Lord, I beseech thee to this desert place, give the comfort of thy grace."

—St. Roch

Brother Roger Schutz
Founder, Taizé (1915–2005)

I n the years after World War II, Roger Schutz, a Swiss-born Protestant pastor, dreamed of founding an ecumenical monastic community that would help to heal the rifts among Christians. On the site of an abandoned abbey in Taizé, France, he set out to realize this vision, forming a community that would include both Catholic and Protestant brothers. Though he would never seek formal conversion, Brother Roger was warmly embraced by Catholic Church leaders, and he enjoyed the unusual privilege of receiving communion from more than one pope. As he noted, "I have found my own identity as a Christian by reconciling within myself the faith of my origins with the mystery of the Catholic faith, without breaking fellowship with anyone."

At the same time, Taizé became a spiritual refuge for the youth of the world. Tens of thousands of young people flocked to Taizé each year to imbibe the spirit of prayer and spiritual renewal. They, in turn, carried the spirit of Taizé back into the world and across the globe.

On August 16, 2005, during evening prayers at Taizé, Brother Roger was stabbed to death by a deranged woman. Rowan Williams, Archbishop of Canterbury, credited him with changing the religious climate of his time: "He changed the image of Christianity itself for countless young people; he changed the church's perception of the absolute priority of reconciliation. . . . And he did this without any position of hierarchical authority."

"For whoever knows how to love, for whoever knows how to suffer, life is filled with serene beauty."
—Brother Roger of Taizé

St. Jeanne Delanoue
Founder, Congregation of St. Anne de la Providence
(1666–1736)

As a shopkeeper in Saumur, France, Jeanne Delanoue was a notorious miser. She hoarded every cent and angrily drove beggars from her door. In this self-enclosed life, however, the influence of grace effected an extraordinary conversion.

It began when Jeanne provided lodging to a strange old woman who traveled the countryside visiting holy shrines. Over time, the presence of the old woman worked a strange influence on her landlord. Accompanying her lodger to weekly Mass, Jeanne no longer found the same pleasure in counting her savings. In fact, she came to believe that this old woman was a holy messenger sent from God to bear a warning and challenge: "I was hungry, and you did not feed me; I was a stranger, and you offered me no shelter." She decided at once to amend her life.

She began by taking in a homeless family with six children. Others followed. Her home became known as Providence House. Eventually willing helpers arrived, and she took this as a sign to found a religious congregation dedicated to service of the poor and sick. In time, they took religious vows and Jeanne became Sr. Jeanne of the Cross.

By the time she died at the age of seventy, she was the best-loved person in Saumur. St. Jeanne was canonized in 1982.

"It is the Spirit of God which animates you and prompts you to this penitential life. Henceforth, then, be without fear and follow your inspirations."

> —St. Louis de Montfort in a letter to St. Jeanne

Black Elk
Holy Man (1863–1950)

Black Elk, an Oglala of the Lakota Sioux, was born in 1863 on the Little Powder River in present-day Wyoming and grew up in a world on the verge of destruction. At the age of nine he experienced a life-altering vision in which he traveled to the center of the universe and heard a call to save his people.

Black Elk came from a long line of powerful medicine men. In 1881 he accepted his own initiation to this calling. In 1890 he survived the massacre at Wounded Knee, where over three hundred men, women, and children died after trusting in the mystical Ghost Dance to protect them from army bullets. Years later he said, "I did not know then how much was ended. . . . A people's dream died there. . . . It was a beautiful dream . . . the nation's hoop is broken and scattered. There is no center any longer, and the sacred tree is dead."

In 1892 Black Elk married a Christian woman and their three children were baptized. In 1904, after his wife's death, Black Elk himself became a Catholic, taking the name Nicholas. Eventually he became a catechist and traveled widely, spreading the Catholic faith. Opinions differ on the meaning of his story and how Black Elk reconciled the different halves of his spiritual history. Apparently he found a way to integrate his Christian faith with the great vision of his youth. At sixty-seven, he finally described that vision to a white author in the classic *Black Elk Speaks*.

He died on the reservation on August 19, 1950.

"Sometimes dreams are wiser than waking."

—Black Elk

St. Helena
Widow (d. ca. 330)

St. Helena is largely remembered as the mother of the emperor Constantine. She was born of humble origins—possibly the daughter of an innkeeper—in Asia Minor. Her husband, a Roman general, divorced her before becoming emperor. But her son, Constantine, remained loyal to his mother. When he eventually became emperor, after his victory at the Milvian Bridge in 312, he elevated Helena with the title "most noble woman" of Rome.

Constantine attributed his decisive victory to a vision of the cross. Though he did not formally become a Christian, by the Edict of Milan he granted toleration to Christianity, which quickly became the official religion of the empire. Helena embraced Christianity and used her resources to build churches and endow local shrines. In her old age she enthusiastically accepted a commission from her son to travel to the Holy Land. An avid pilgrim, she traced the steps of Christ's life and performed works of charity. Legend has it that, in a cistern near Calvary, she was able to discover three crosses, one of which was believed to be the True Cross on which Christ died. Pieces of this cross were distributed throughout Europe. As Evelyn Waugh later remarked, these relics, fully reassembled, would have been enough to assemble a battleship.

St. Helena spent her final years in a humble convent in Palestine, where she died around 330.

"She worshipped not the wood, but the King, Him who hung on the wood."
—St. Ambrose, on St. Helena

Jessica Powers
Carmelite Poet (1905–1988)

Jessica Powers was born and raised in Cattail Valley in rural Wisconsin. From an early age her spirit was marked by the beauty of nature and the long stretches of open space. But she was marked too by the austerity and loneliness of country living, especially the long winters and the painful struggle to eke out a living.

With the death of her father she bore responsibility for raising and supporting her siblings. But through her daily chores she nourished an inner life and a hope of finding her place in the world. After publishing her first book of poetry she surprised friends by entering a Carmelite convent, where she was given the name Sr. Miriam of the Holy Spirit and would spend the rest of her life. The poetry continued—the means by which she attended to signs of grace and struggled to make them visible to a wounded world. "There is a homelessness never to be clearly defined. / It is more than having no place of one's own, no bed or chair . . . / It is the pain of the mystic suddenly thrown back from the noon of God to the night of his own humanity."

She addressed God as "The great Undoer who has torn apart / the walls I built against a human heart . . . / the repairer of fences, turning my paths to rest."

Jessica Powers died on August 18, 1988, at the age of eighty-three.

"I need not go abroad / to the hills of speech or the hinterlands of music / for a crier to walk in my soul where all is still. / I have this potent prayer through good or ill: / here in the dark I clutch the garments of God."

—Jessica Powers

Blaise Pascal
Scientist and Apologist (1623–1662)

A brilliant intellectual and scientist, Blaise Pascal was an ornament of the dawning Age of Reason. Before turning twenty, he had invented the calculating machine. He went on to lay the foundation for calculus and designed the first public transportation system for Paris. But after a profound experience of conversion he turned his genius to the defense of Christianity, convinced that faith gave access to a dimension of truth beyond the reach of reason.

Pascal devoted his last years to a comprehensive case for Christianity. Published posthumously, his *Pensées* became one of the most significant works in the literature of Christian reflection. Rather than the typical argument from authority—whether of the Church or Scripture—Pascal based his defense of Christianity on the evidence of the human heart. With psychological insight, he painted a picture of human wretchedness: "inconstancy, boredom, anxiety." Yet, he argued, there is a greatness in human nature, a yearning for the infinite that points us in the direction of our true destiny. In Jesus Christ we find an explanation for this duality, for in him we learn simultaneously that God exists and that we are sinners.

In the end, Pascal believed the Gospel offers answers only to those who ask the right questions. "I condemn equally those who choose to praise man, those who choose to condemn him, and those who choose to divert themselves, and I can approve only of those who seek with groans." He died on August 19, 1662, at the age of thirty-nine.

"The heart has its reasons of which reason knows nothing."

—Blaise Pascal

Venerable Mary Magdalen Bentivoglio
Poor Clare (1834–1905)

In October 1875, Sr. Mary Magdalen Bentivoglio and her sister Constance, with whom she had entered her order, sailed from Italy to New York to establish the first contemplative community of Poor Clares in the United States. They had departed with the personal blessings of Pope Pius IX, who urged them to offer "a silent sermon accompanied by prayer and union with God, to make known to many that true happiness is not to be found in things temporal and material."

Unfortunately, they had departed with no assurance of a welcome. Not knowing a word of English, they were left to beg and rely on charity for most of a year while seeking a bishop who would accept them. The bishop of New York told them that a contemplative enclosure was out of character with the American spirit; the need was for teaching sisters. After fruitless efforts in other cities, the two sisters were finally welcomed by the bishop of Omaha, where they would make their home.

For years they suffered cold and hunger. As Mother Mary Magdalen wrote, "It is certain that on the one hand we do not want to pamper anyone, but on the other hand we do not want to kill anyone." But new postulants did arrive, and in time Mother Mary Magdalen traveled to establish a new foundation in Evansville, Indiana, where she lived until her death on August 18, 1905.

"All my life I have asked God for crosses and now that He has sent them, why should I not be glad?"

—Venerable Mary Magdalen Bentivoglio

St. Bernard
Abbot, Doctor of the Church (1090–1153)

St. Bernard, founder of the Cistercian Abbey of Clairvaux, was one of the towering figures of the twelfth century. From his austere monastery, he corresponded with popes, kings, and penitents of all stations, managing to exert his influence in many of the ecclesiastical, social, and intellectual disputes of his day. He traveled throughout Europe to attend synods and Church councils, to combat heresy, and to aid in the foundation of scores of Cistercian monasteries.

Bernard's personality is well conveyed through his extensive correspondence. To the bishop of Geneva he wrote: "The bishop's throne for which you, my dear friend, were lately chosen, demands many virtues, none of which, I grieve to say, could be discerned in you, at any rate in any strength, before your consecration." To a nun who wished to leave her convent: "If you are one of the foolish virgins, the convent is necessary for you; if you are one of the wise, you are necessary for the convent."

The light of history does not shine well on all his causes—such as his harsh dispute with the theologian Peter Abelard, or his role in preaching on behalf of the disastrous Second Crusade. But for his extensive writings, including his mystical commentaries on the Song of Songs and his treatises on the Virgin Mary, he was deemed the "Last of the Church Fathers."

"I believe though I do not comprehend, and I hold by faith what I cannot grasp with the mind."
—St. Bernard

St. Maria de Mattias
Founder, Sisters Adorers of the Blood of Christ
(1805–1866)

Maria de Mattias was born in the town of Vallecorsa in what were then the Papal States. This region was the center of political turmoil and warfare during the Napoleonic era. Italian priests were forced, under penalty, to abjure their allegiance to the pope. Civil society all but collapsed, and gangs of bandits engaged in kidnapping and robbery. Maria was confined to her home, receiving no formal education. Yet her life took a turn one day as she was admiring herself in a mirror and happened to glance at an image of the Virgin, who seemed to call her, "Come to me." From that point, she committed herself to learning to read so she could immerse herself in spiritual books.

The second turning point for Maria came when a Precious Blood priest came to her town to lead a mission. Listening to him preach, she felt she had found her true purpose. Eventually, with his encouragement, she organized a new religious institute, Sisters Adorers of the Blood of Christ.

The sisters combined a contemplative spirituality with an active apostolate—particularly through schools, religious education, and service to the poor—attempting to impart to all persons a sense of their preciousness in the eyes of God. Maria became a popular speaker, prompting one bishop to accuse her of being a "would-be-priest."

She died on August 20, 1866. She was canonized in 2003.

"Let us encourage one another to suffer willingly out of love of Jesus who with such great love shed his blood for us. Let us work hard to win souls for heaven."
—St. Maria de Mattias

Geert Groote
Master of the "Modern Devotion" (1340–1384)

Geert Groote inspired an influential movement of spiritual renewal and reform that swept the Lowlands and Germany in the fourteenth century. Called the *Devotio Moderna*, its members were called simply the Devout, or Brethren of the Common Life. Their principal innovation was to stress the possibility of ardent Christian devotion "in the world," as opposed to the monastery. (Thomas à Kempis, author of *The Imitation of Christ*, was one of the best-known fruits of this movement.)

Groote was born to a wealthy family in Deventer. At the age of thirty-four he experienced a deep conversion, renounced all worldly interests, and devoted himself to the service of Christ. Declining to seek ordination, he instead obtained a license to preach as a deacon in the diocese of Utrecht. For four years he traveled about spreading the fire of renewal, emphasizing inward piety rather than external exercises. He especially promoted meditation on Scripture and reflection on the life of Christ as the pattern of Christian virtue.

Eventually communities of followers began to spring up. Clergy and laypeople lived together in equality, supporting themselves by common labor. However, Groote's outspoken criticism of the worldliness and moral failings of the clergy won him numerous enemies in the Church. In 1383 the bishop revoked his license to preach. Before he could appeal this action, he died of plague on August 20, 1384.

"Always put more hope in eternal glory than fear in hell."

—Geert Groote

Blessed Victoria Rasoamanarivo
Defender of the Faith (1848–1894)

Blessed Victoria was born in the capital city of Madagascar. For most of her life, her island country was ruled by a powerful queen, who struggled to maintain her country's independence from foreign control and foreign religion. Victoria's mother was the daughter of the queen's chief minister, and she enjoyed other prominent connections. Though raised in the traditional religion of her people, at thirteen she enrolled in a new Catholic school run by the Sisters of the Congregation of St. Joseph of Cluny and was eventually baptized. While Anglican and other Protestant missionaries had made successful inroads in Madagascar, Catholics remained a minority.

In 1864 Victoria married the son of the chief minister and used her position to look after the Catholic population, who were subject to various forms of harassment. In 1883 a more savage persecution erupted, causing all French missionaries to be expelled from the country. Victoria became the de facto protector of the Catholic people, defending their churches and schools, and caring for the sick and poor in a time without any priests. When the missionaries returned in 1886 they found the Catholic community intact and secure in their faith— largely due to Victoria's efforts.

She died at forty-six on August 21, 1894. She was beatified by Pope John Paul II during a visit to Madagascar in 1989.

"Blessed Victoria Rasoamanarivo is 'a true missionary' and a 'model for today's laity.'"

—Pope John Paul II, declaring her beatification

Luis de Leon
Augustinian Theologian (1527–1591)

In 1561 Luis de Leon, an Augustinian priest and theologian from Castile, was elected to a chair at the University of Salamanca where he was assigned to teach the theology of Thomas Aquinas. But Leon was not satisfied to remain within the enclosed world of scholastic thought. In the spirit of Renaissance humanism, he hungrily explored all areas of human wisdom and culture, including Platonic and Arabic philosophy as well as Jewish mysticism. In pursuit of his own critical study of Scripture he mastered Hebrew. But when word circulated that he had acknowledged errors of translation in the official Vulgate Bible he was denounced to the Inquisition.

In 1572 he was arrested and imprisoned in a dark cell, where he remained for five years, deprived of the sacraments and provided with little food or fresh air. Despite interminable interrogations, he was never informed of the charges against him. Finally, he was declared innocent of heresy and released.

Despite his sufferings, he expressed no bitterness on his own account. But he became an outspoken critic of abuses of power, contrasting the arrogance of earthly princes with the humility of Jesus, Prince of Princes. Leon's genius was eventually recognized. In addition to theology, he won chairs in Scripture and moral theology and was elected provincial for the Augustinians of Castile. He died in 1591.

"In Jesus we find condensed as in a vast ocean the whole being and substance of the world."
—Luis de Leon

Benigno "Ninoy" Aquino, Jr.
Martyr for Democracy (1932–1983)

On August 21, 1983, Benigno "Ninoy" Aquino, the most prominent opponent of the dictatorship of Ferdinand Marcos in the Philippines, returned from exile in the United States. He knew the risk he was facing. Nevertheless, he had scarcely landed when soldiers rushed on board to escort him from the plane. Moments later shots rang out and Aquino lay dead on the airport tarmac.

A devout Catholic, Aquino had risen rapidly on the political stage of his country—as a mayor, governor, and senator—and he seemed destined for his country's highest office. Instead, with Marcos's declaration of martial law in 1972 he was arrested on trumped-up charges and sentenced to death. Seven years later, while still in prison, he suffered a heart attack. Marcos sent him into exile for treatment in the United States, along with the warning that he never return. But the years in prison had only intensified Aquino's commitment to freedom; he was determined to return and to offer his life, if necessary, for his people. "The Filipino," he said, "is worth dying for."

Aquino's assassination galvanized the Philippines. His sacrifice was the catalyst that inspired the People's Power Revolution of 1986, when nonviolent protestors, backed by elements of the army and the Catholic Church, took to the streets and drove Marcos from power. Aquino's widow, Corazon, was elected president.

"The message of Jesus, as I understand it, is that we must be ready to sacrifice for our fellow men at all times, and if need be, even offer our lives for them."
—Ninoy Aquino

St. Rose of Lima
First Saint of the Americas (1586–1617)

Like many another saint, St. Rose of Lima had to struggle to claim her vocation. Born in Lima, Peru, approximately fifty years after the arrival of the Spanish, she was called Rose on account of her extraordinary beauty. From a young age she was besieged by suitors, encouraging her parents' hopes of an eventual marriage that would advance the family fortune. But Rose had a different plan. She was determined to consecrate herself to God. Since her beauty posed an obstacle to her vocation, she deliberately disfigured herself by rubbing her face with pepper and lime.

Eventually her family acceded to her wishes and allowed her to join the Third Order of St. Dominic. She spent many years as a recluse, occupying a little hut in the garden and devoting herself to constant prayer. Eventually, however, she emerged to engage in works of mercy among the poor, the Indians, and African slaves. She had a strong sense of social as well as personal sin. Despite her severe penitential practices, it was said, she seemed to glow with the love of God.

Her reputation for holiness gradually won the reverence of the entire city. When Rose died in 1617 at the age of thirty-one, the dignitaries of Lima vied to pay her homage. She became the first canonized saint of the New World.

"Lord, increase my sufferings, and with them increase Thy love in my heart."
—St. Rose of Lima

St. Joan Antide-Thouret
Founder, Sisters of Charity (1765–1826)

St. Joan was born in a town near Besançon, France, the daughter of a tanner. After the death of her mother, she helped raise her many brothers and sisters. At twenty-two, however, she left home to join the Sisters of Charity of St. Vincent de Paul in Paris. When the Revolution struck, and before she had taken her vows, her congregation was dispersed. After some years of wandering, she ended up in Switzerland, where she found a home with the Sisters of the Christian Retreat. Eventually, when conditions at home relaxed, she accepted an invitation from the bishop of Besançon to return and take charge of a school. At first she doubted her capacity for such a responsibility, but the bishop reassured her. "Courage, virtue, and trust in God are what are required," he said, "and it seems to me that you have these qualities."

The school was opened in 1799. Before long it was joined with a soup kitchen and a free clinic. Joan and the women assisting her eventually formed the nucleus of a religious institute that became a new congregation: the Daughters of Charity under the protection of St. Vincent de Paul. Their work, which eventually spread to Switzerland and Italy, extended to include every form of service to the poor. Joan spent her final years in Naples, where she had been invited to administer a hospital. She died on August 24, 1826, and was canonized in 1934.

"Remember to consider only Christ in the person of the poor. Serve them always as you would serve Christ himself."

—St. Joan Antide-Thouret

St. Bartholomew
Apostle and Martyr (First Century)

Bartholomew is listed in the Synoptic Gospels as one of the Lord's twelve apostles. In Acts he is named among those apostles who gathered in an upper room and there witnessed the risen Christ. Otherwise, there is no reliable record of his life or teachings.

Some traditions have identified Bartholomew with the apostle Nathanael, otherwise named only in the Gospel of John. This is the apostle who, upon hearing Jesus described as the fulfillment of prophecy, quipped, "Can anything good come out of Nazareth?" Upon their meeting, Jesus greeted Nathanael with the words, "Behold, an Israelite indeed, in whom is no guile." But most scholars dispute this identification.

According to the history by Eusebius (fourth century), Bartholomew engaged in a missionary journey that took him as far as India, where he is said to have left a copy of the Gospel of Matthew. He is also said to have preached in Persia, Egypt, Armenia, and elsewhere. Legend has it that he died in Armenia, where he was flayed alive before being beheaded. Michelangelo, in his depiction of the Last Judgment in the Sistine Chapel, shows Bartholomew holding a curved blade in one hand, and in the other his own flayed skin.

"Hail, O blessed of the blessed, thrice blessed Bartholomew! You are the splendor of Divine light, the fisherman of holy Church, expert catcher of fish endowed with reason, sweet fruit of the blooming palm tree! . . . Rejoice in the enjoyment of inexhaustible happiness!"

—Sermon on St. Bartholomew by St. Theodore the Studite

Simone Weil
Philosopher and Mystic (1909–1943)

Simone Weil was born in France to a family of secular Jews. From early childhood she displayed a brilliant mind, a steel will, and an acutely sensitive conscience. After studying philosophy she embarked on a teaching career. But drawn to understand the working class, she took a series of leaves to experience factory work.

A series of profound experiences in the late 1930s brought her latent spiritual inclinations to the fore. While watching a religious procession in Portugal she felt the conviction that "Christianity is preeminently the religion of slaves, that slaves cannot help belonging to it, and I among others." Later in Assisi she felt the compulsion to kneel and pray. In 1938, while spending Holy Week in a Benedictine monastery, she felt that "Christ himself came down and took possession of me."

Though her thinking became increasingly Christ-centered, she believed her vocation was to remain on the "threshold of the Church"—in solidarity with all those outside. She could not bear to separate herself from "the immense and unfortunate multitude of unbelievers." In exile, following the German occupation of France, she died in England on August 24, 1943.

Weil was undoubtedly a complex figure. Her posthumously published writings, however, marked her as one of the most compelling religious figures of her century—an example of engaged mysticism, attuned to the pathos of the human condition and the particular struggles of our time.

"Today it is not enough merely to be a saint, but we must have the saintliness demanded by the present moment."

—Simone Weil

St. Genesius the Actor
Martyr (ca. 303)

According to legend, Genesius was an actor, one of a company of performers hired to entertain the emperor Diocletian in Rome. Knowing of the emperor's contempt for the cult of the Christians, Genesius thought it would be amusing to mock their ceremonies. With melodramatic effect he performed a comic impersonation of a Christian catechumen. His friends played along with the jest, reenacting the ceremony of baptism. At some point, however, the attitude of Genesius changed. Whether touched by grace or moved by the pathos of his own performance, Genesius dispensed with comic exaggeration and played the part with disturbing realism. When his fellow actors, in the part of soldiers, "arrested" him and presented him before the actual emperor, Genesius spoke with unexpected feeling and declared himself a true believer in Christ.

No longer laughing, the emperor ordered Genesius to be bound and tortured. Still, Genesius, in the performance of his life, continued to declaim: "No torments shall remove Jesus Christ from my heart and my mouth. Bitterly do I regret that I once detested His holy name, and came so late to His service." He continued to cry out in this fashion until he was beheaded.

St. Genesius is the patron of actors, clowns, and comedians.

"There is no other Lord beside Him whom I have seen. Him I worship and serve, and to Him I will cling, though I should suffer a thousand deaths."
—St. Genesius

St. Joseph Calasanz
Founder, Clerks Regular of the Religious Schools
(1556–1648)

St. Joseph Calasanz, born to an aristocratic family in Spain, was ordained a priest and settled in Rome. He took a keen interest in the education of the poor and encouraged parish schoolteachers to admit poor children without fees. When these efforts failed, he opened his own school—the first free public school in modern Europe. It was also the seed of an institute that was in time recognized by the pope as a religious congregation and eventually a network of schools in Europe and South America.

In his schools Joseph promoted a broad, humanistic curriculum. He was a friend of the scientist Galileo, whom he continued to support even after his condemnation by the Inquisition. Joseph, himself the victim of scheming and persecution, came under investigation. For some time he was deposed as superior by rivals in his own community who claimed he was senile and who spread vicious rumors about his sanity. An investigation by the Vatican led to his vindication, and he was restored to office. (A later pope referred to him as "a perpetual miracle of fortitude and another Job.") He was canonized in 1767. Pope Pius XII named him patron of Christian schools.

"I have found in Rome the definitive way to serve God in the children and youth, and I will never leave it for anything in the world."
—St. Joseph Calasanz

St. Elizabeth Bichier des Ages
Founder, Daughters of the Cross (1773–1838)

Elizabeth was born in France into a noble family, whose fortunes were to fall with the Revolution. Despite her own precarious circumstances, she turned her heart to helping the poor and sick and offering religious education to children. Both in the works of mercy and her catechetical work, she helped fill a gap left by the wide suppression of the Church.

Though her family disapproved of her activities, a friendly priest, St. Andrew Fournet, encouraged her vocation. "Your work is in the world," he assured her. "There are ruins to be rebuilt and ignorance to be remedied." He urged her to start a local religious community devoted to social service.

After a short novitiate with a Carmelite community in Poitiers, she gathered a number of other young women and founded the Daughters of the Cross, a congregation that eventually spread to sixty convents in Elizabeth's lifetime. Even the civil authorities came to admire and respect her dedication to those in need.

Elizabeth died on August 26, 1838. She was canonized in 1947.

"As you like, sir. But allow me to point out that I have only done what you would do yourself in the same circumstances. I found this unfortunate man lying ill; I took him in; and I looked after him. Now he is dead. I'm quite ready to report to the magistrate."

—St. Elizabeth Bichier des Ages, informed by a constable that she was liable to arrest for harboring a wanted felon

St. Mary of Jesus Crucified (Mariam Baouardy)
Carmelite (1846–1878)

Mariam Baouardy was born into a family of Melkite-rite Catholic Arabs near Nazareth in the Holy Land, at that time part of the Turkish Empire. After her parents died, when she was two, she was taken in and raised by an uncle. When she was twelve she discovered that her uncle had betrothed her to his wife's brother. She refused to cooperate in this marriage, even cutting off her hair in protest. In retaliation, she was subjected to terrible abuse. At that time she received a vision of a nun dressed in blue—the Blessed Mother, she believed—who restored her to life and foretold her later religious vocation.

For some years she was employed as a servant by various families in Egypt, Beirut, Jerusalem, and France. Finally, at twenty-two, she won her freedom and entered a Carmelite convent in Pau. Three years later she went on a missionary journey to India, where she felt particularly drawn to the Untouchables.

In 1872 she convinced her superiors to allow her to found a Carmelite community in Bethlehem. She had to overcome concerns about her health. Nevertheless she completed this project and immediately set out to build another house in Nazareth. Before its completion, however, she fell ill and died on August 26, 1878.

She was canonized in 2015.

"O Holy Spirit, source of peace and light, enlighten me. I am poor, make me rich. I am the most ignorant of human creatures, let me understand Jesus!"
—St. Mary of Jesus Crucified

St. Monica
Widow (ca. 323–387)

St. Monica is chiefly remembered through the loving testimony of her son, St. Augustine, who gave her special credit for his conversion: "In the flesh she brought me to birth in this world; in her heart she brought me to birth in Your eternal life."

Monica was an African, born near Carthage of Christian parents. She married and bore three children, of whom Augustine was the eldest and clearly her favorite. For years she suffered from the fact that her brilliant son did not share her faith, a suffering compounded by his amoral conduct and his immersion in the Manichean cult. Constantly she prayed for his conversion and wept over his sins, until finally a sympathetic bishop consoled her: "Go now, I beg of you; it is not possible that the son of so many tears should perish."

Her prayers were answered when Augustine was baptized. By this time, Monica's days were numbered. While awaiting a ship to return to Africa, Monica fell ill. While discussing the eternal Wisdom with her son, it seemed "for one fleeting instant" as if they had touched it. Monica confided that she had no need for further life: "There was one reason and one alone, why I wished to remain a little longer in this life," she told her son, "and that was to see you a Catholic Christian before I died. God has granted my wish. . . . What is left for me to do in this world?"

"Nothing is far from God."

—St. Monica, when asked if she feared dying far from home

Dom Helder Camara
Archbishop of Recife (1909–1999)

Dom Helder Camara, who died on August 27, 1999, was one of the great prophets and apostles of Christian nonviolence. He embodied the Church's "option for the poor" and defined through his actions the intimate relationship between love and justice.

He began his career as a conservative priest. His work in the slums of Rio de Janeiro, however, had a radicalizing influence. Charity was not sufficient, he concluded; what was needed was social justice. His appointment as archbishop of Recife in 1964 coincided with a brutal military coup. Immediately Dom Helder stepped forward as a champion of democracy and human rights, a role that earned him the nickname "the red bishop." He was repeatedly threatened with death, and for thirteen years his name was banned from any newspaper in Brazil.

Despite his anger in the face of injustice, Dom Helder conveyed an almost Franciscan spirit of interior peace and joy and a delight in Creation. He spoke frequently of the need for an "Abrahamic minority," the small community of those in each generation who keep hope alive and who are willing to risk security and comfort to seek the "promised land." From his see in Recife, Dom Helder served as an inspiration to that minority, a universal bishop to the poor, a pastor to all who struggled for peace and justice.

"When I feed the poor they call me a saint. When I ask why so many are poor they call me a communist."

—Dom Helder Camara

St. Augustine
Bishop and Doctor of the Church (354–430)

St. Augustine was born in North Africa. Despite the piety of his Christian mother, he felt no attraction to Christianity. In various religious philosophies he sought the meaning of life, but none answered his questions. Finally, while living in Milan as a professor of rhetoric he came under the influence of the saintly Bishop Ambrose and began to find in Christian doctrine a greater depth than he had realized. After much emotional struggle, he asked to be baptized.

Returning to North Africa, Augustine hoped to pursue a monastic life. Instead, after ordination, he was pressed, against his will, to become bishop of Hippo, a post he held until his death in 430 at the age of seventy-five.

Augustine became one of the great architects of Christian theology. In the vast library of his works he left his mark on virtually every aspect of Christian doctrine. Yet if he had left no other legacy than his autobiographical *Confessions* this book alone would assure his place in the history of Christian spirituality. In the *Confessions* he reflected on the meaning of his life in light of the pivotal turning point: his conversion and baptism in the Catholic Church. In this light he discerned the hand of God, caring for him and guiding him toward his eventual happiness. As he addressed God in one of his most famous lines, "You have made us for Yourself, and our hearts are restless until they rest in You."

"For what am I to myself without You, but a guide to my own downfall?"

—St. Augustine

Blessed Edmund Rice
Founder, Presentation Brothers and Christian Brothers
(1762–1844)

Edmund Rice was born to a family of tenant farmers in County Kilkenny, Ireland. Though Catholics continued to suffer discrimination, he was able to obtain an education and even achieved considerable success in business before falling in love and marrying. When his wife died in an accident, leaving him in "the dregs of misery and misfortune," he sought some greater purpose in life. At first he threw himself into public charities, while still feeling that "something else was yet wanting" of him. One option was to enter religious life. But then one day he saw some poor boys fighting in the street and wondered who was to care for such youth.

Inspired by Nano Nagle's Presentation Sisters, he resolved to dedicate himself to the rescue and education of street boys. With helpers who joined him, he founded a school organized on religious principles. Over time he founded similar schools in different cities, and he and eight followers took religious vows. Two congregations, the Presentation Brothers and the Christian Brothers, trace their origins to Rice's initiative. Their schools spread to England and eventually to North America and around the world.

Rice died on August 29, 1844. He was beatified in 1996.

"Let us do ever so little for God, we will be sure he will never forget it nor let it pass unrewarded. . . . Were we to know the merit of only going from one street to another to serve a neighbor for the love of God, we should prize it more than Gold or Silver."

—Blessed Edmund Rice

Martyrdom of St. John the Baptist
(First Century)

One of the most certain facts about the life of Jesus is that his public ministry was linked, initially, with the ministry of John the Baptist. St. Luke claims they were related, their mothers being cousins. Otherwise John appears in the Gospels as a mysterious reprise of Elijah and the prophets of old. Living in the wilderness, dining on honey and locusts, John emerges out of nowhere, warning Israel of a coming judgment and performing baptisms in the Jordan River for the forgiveness of sins. Jesus himself, according to all four Gospels, was among those who appeared among the penitents seeking baptism at John's hands.

Sin and the general need for conversion were John's principal themes. His concern was not so much ritual purity or observance of the law. The whole people, he proclaimed, stood under judgment. But he directed special scorn on those members of the privileged social and religious classes whom he called a "brood of vipers." He did not spare the ruler of Galilee, Herod Antipas, from his sharp criticism. When he challenged Herod for divorcing his first wife to marry the wife of his half brother, Herod had him arrested and ultimately beheaded.

Jesus, who could not help seeing in John's fate a foreshadowing of his own, offered this epitaph: "I tell you, among those born of women none is greater than John; yet he who is least in the kingdom of God is greater than he."

"I am the voice of one crying in the wilderness, 'Make straight the way of the Lord.'"

—St. John the Baptist

Blessed Santia Szymkowiak
Religious (1910–1942)

Blessed Santia was born to a wealthy family in Poland. On a pilgrimage to Lourdes in 1934 she dedicated herself to the Blessed Virgin and afterward joined the Congregation of the Daughters of Our Lady of Sorrows (the "Seraphic Sisters"). Her diaries of the time reflect her youthful zeal: "Jesus wants me to be a holy religious and He will not be happy with me until I use all my strength for Him and become a saint. . . . I have to become a saint at all costs. This is my constant preoccupation."

Her convent in Poznan fell in the direct path of the Nazi invasion in 1939. Her community was placed under house arrest, and the sisters were forced to care for the German garrison and later for Allied prisoners of war. Having studied languages in school, Santia was put to work as a translator. For her kindness and charity she was known by the prisoners as St. Santia.

After contracting tuberculosis she had an opportunity to escape but chose to remain with her community. "God's will is my will," she said. "Whatever he wants I want." She made her solemn vows on July 6, 1942, only to die on August 29 at the age of thirty-two. She was beatified by Pope John Paul II in 2002.

"Having embraced the religious life, she devoted herself to the service of others with greater fervor. She accepted the difficult times of the Nazi occupation as an occasion to give herself completely to the needy."
—Pope John Paul II

St. Margaret Ward
Martyr (d. 1588)

L ittle is known of the life of this English martyr under Queen Elizabeth. A gentlewoman of London, she was arrested in 1588 for her part in aiding the escape of an imprisoned priest, William Watson, whom she was in the habit of visiting. Taking advantage of lax security, she managed to smuggle a rope into the prison, which Watson used to lower himself from a tower. Once outside, he escaped with the help of Ward's servant, John Roche, with whom he also exchanged clothing.

The rope was easily traced back to Ward. She and Roche were both arrested and subjected to terrible tortures. They were promised their freedom if they would ask the queen's pardon and attend the established Church. When they refused this offer, they were hanged at Tyburn on August 30, 1588.

"She was flogged and hung up by the wrists, the tips of her toes only touching the ground, for so long a time that she was crippled and paralyzed, but these sufferings greatly strengthened the glorious martyr for her last struggle."

—Testimony of St. Robert Southwell, later a martyr

St. Jeanne Jugan
Founder, Little Sisters of the Poor (1792–1879)

Jeanne Jugan was born to a poor family in Brittany, France. She spent most of her life in menial service. Poor as she was, however, she believed that God intended her for some larger purpose. In 1837, along with two companions, she rented an attic apartment and formed an informal community of prayer. They supported themselves by doing laundry, while devoting their free time to catechizing children and assisting the poor.

Eventually, with new companions, Jeanne formed a religious association. Along with vows of poverty, chastity, and obedience, she added a fourth vow of hospitality. They called themselves Little Sisters of the Poor.

At this point, in a strange twist, Jeanne's spiritual director stepped in to claim authority over the group. By the time the community received papal approval in 1852, there were five hundred sisters in the congregation, and yet Jeanne's role as founder had been completely obscured. She spent the last twenty-seven years of her life supervising the manual work of the postulants. Only after her death was her true role recovered.

Jeanne died on August 29, 1879. Her last words were "Eternal Father, open your gates today to the most miserable of your children, but one who greatly longs to see you." She was beatified by Pope John Paul II in 1982 and canonized by Pope Benedict XVI in 2009.

"My little ones, never forget that the poor are Our Lord; in caring for the poor say to yourself: This is for my Jesus—what a great grace!"

—St. Jeanne Jugan

Saints Joseph of Arimathea and Nicodemus
Disciples (First Century)

These two saints, both perhaps members of the Sanhedrin, the supreme Jewish council, make significant appearances in the Gospels. Joseph from the town of Arimathea is described as a "good and just man" who, though apparently wealthy, came to follow Jesus. After the crucifixion he requested permission from Pilate to retrieve Jesus' body. With the help of Nicodemus, he wrapped the body in fine linen and had it placed in his own unused family tomb.

Nicodemus was a Pharisee and "a ruler of the Jews." In the Gospel of John he comes to Jesus secretly by night and engages him in theological discussion. "Rabbi," he addresses Jesus respectfully, "we know that you are a teacher come from God; for no one can do these signs that you do, unless God is with him." This prompts the reply from Jesus, "Truly, truly, I say to you, unless one is born anew he cannot see the kingdom of God." Later, John says that Nicodemus spoke on Jesus' behalf before the council, insisting that he receive a fair hearing. This incites a mocking response: "Are you from Galilee too?"

Scripture provides no more information about these two disciples, though Joseph is the subject of later florid legends involving the Holy Grail and his supposed travels to Glastonbury in England.

"Nicodemus said to him, 'How can a man be born when he is old? Can he enter a second time into his mother's womb and be born?' Jesus answered, 'Truly, truly, I say to you, unless one is born of water and the Spirit, he cannot enter the kingdom of God. That which is born of the flesh is flesh, and that which is born of the Spirit is spirit.'"

—John 3:4-5

John Leary
Peacemaker (1958–1982)

On August 31, 1982, John Leary was jogging home from his job at the Pax Christi Center in Cambridge to Haley House, the Catholic Worker community in Boston where he lived. This day he did not complete the trip. Without warning he went into cardiac arrest and died instantly. He was twenty-four. In subsequent days his friends were joined not only in sorrow at the brevity of a life cut short but in wonder for all he had accomplished and the many lives he had touched.

As many knew, John, while studying at Harvard, had divided his time between peace work and community life among the poor at Haley House. But he had also worked with prisoners, the homeless, the elderly. He had engaged in protests over the draft, capital punishment, and abortion. He regarded all these issues as joined in a "seamless garment." The turning point in his life was his discovery of Jesus' nonviolent way of the cross. Inspired by figures like Dorothy Day and Thomas Merton, he was drawn to integrate a very traditional spiritual discipline of prayer and sacrament with compassionate engagement on behalf of a suffering world. It was his custom to recite the Jesus Prayer as he jogged, and it is likely those words were on his lips when he died.

"John became in his short life the complete and total man for others, and those who knew him and loved him testify to the love of Christ that shone in and through him."

—Rev. Peter Gomes, Harvard Chaplain

SEPTEMBER

1 St. Drithelm • François Mauriac

2 Blessed Margaret of Louvain • French Martyrs of September

3 St. Phoebe • St. Gregory the Great

4 St. Rose of Viterbo • Blessed Catherine of Racconigi

5 Blessed Jean-Joseph Lataste • St. Teresa of Calcutta

6 Albert Schweitzer • E. F. Schumacher

7 St. Kassiani • Alexander Men

8 Saints Natalia and Adrian • Blessed Frederic Ozanam

9 St. Peter Claver • John Howard Griffin

10 St. Pulcheria • Blessed Louisa of Savoy

11 St. Notburga • Mychal Judge

12 Amos • Stephen Biko

13 St. John Chrysostom • Dante Alighieri

14 Venerable Marie-Therese de Lamourous • Blessed Pino Puglisi

15 St. Catherine of Genoa • Martyrs of Birmingham

16 St. Cyprian • St. Edith of Wilton

17 St. Hildegard of Bingen • Adrienne von Speyr

18 Dag Hammarskjöld • Corita Kent

19 St. Emily de Rodat • Sadhu Sundar Singh

20 St. Andrew Kim and the Korean Martyrs • Mercy Hirschboeck

21 St. Matthew • Henri Nouwen

22 St. Maurice and Companions • Daria Donnelly

23 St. Thecla • St. Pio of Pietrelcina (Padre Pio)

24 Blessed Robert of Knaresborough • Blessed Emily Tavernier

25 Mechthild of Magdeburg • St. Sergius of Radonezh

26 St. Therese Couderc • Blessed Paul VI

27 Margery Kempe • St. Vincent de Paul

28 St. Eustochium • St. Lioba

29 Saints Michael, Gabriel, Raphael • Blessed Richard Rolle

30 St. Jerome • Shusaku Endo

SEPTEMBER

St. Drithelm
Contemplative (ca. 700)

St. Drithelm was a Northumbrian householder who, sometime around the year 693, fell mortally ill and died. The next morning, however, he suddenly awoke—astonishing the mourners who had gathered at his bedside. "Be not afraid," he told his wife, "for I am now truly risen from death and allowed again to live among men." But, he added, "Hereafter I am not to live as I have been wont but rather in a very different manner." After dividing his property among his family and the poor, he departed for the monastery of Melrose, where he remained for the rest of his days.

To the merely curious, Drithelm refused to describe his experience, but to those who were filled "with the dread of Hell or delighted with the hope of heavenly joys," he willingly related his tale. After dying, he said, he was met by someone "with a shining countenance" who led him through a valley where he witnessed various scenes of fiery torment as well as sweet delight. He beheld both the gates of hell and the passage of heaven. But as his own fate was not yet decided, his guide returned him to his body "to live among men again," henceforth to direct his words and actions so as to win a place among the blessed.

His fellow monks marveled at his devotion and asceticism. Whenever anyone remarked on his ability to endure hardship, he would answer, "I have seen greater hardship."

"Thus he forwarded the salvation of many by his words and example."

—St. Bede

François Mauriac
Novelist and Nobel Laureate (1885–1970)

B orn in Bordeaux in 1885, François Mauriac was the last of the great giants of the Catholic literary revival that flourished in France between the wars. Following the death of his father when he was an infant, Mauriac was raised by his mother, a Catholic of stern tendencies, who impressed on her children a strong sense of sin. From his grandparents he learned the value of social status and respectability. The combination of these attitudes supplied the background of his later work.

In a series of dark novels he explored a world in which human beings were warped and distorted by frustrated hopes, pride, avarice, and the failure to connect with others in love. Yet ultimately he believed that in each person there was the outline of the fully realized human being, the saint, that we are called to become.

During the Occupation, Mauriac was haunted by the moral failure that allowed so many of his fellow citizens to collaborate in the deportation of the Jews or to look the other way. His writing took on a deeper concern for social issues. Increasingly he was recognized not just as an artist but as a voice of conscience. He won the Nobel Prize for Literature in 1952.

Mauriac died on September 1, 1970, at the age of nearly eighty-five.

"We cannot approve or practice publicly in the name of Caesar what the Lord condemns, disapproves, or curses, whether it be failure to honor our word, exploitation of the poor, police torture, or regimes of terror."
—François Mauriac

Blessed Margaret of Louvain
Virgin and Martyr (ca. 1207–1225)

Blessed Margaret, who was born in Louvain, was employed as a servant by a good-hearted innkeeper named Aubert. One night, while Margaret was out on an errand, some brigands visited the inn. They murdered Aubert and his wife for their money and were about to flee when Margaret made her ill-timed return. The robbers carried her away, intending to eliminate her as a witness. Though they proposed to spare her life if she would marry one of them, she refused. And so, "taking the innocent lamb like a cruel butcher," they slit her throat and cast her into a river. The presence of a supernatural light led to the discovery of her body, and Margaret was buried in a chapel in Louvain. The site was associated with miracles and attracted pilgrims and supplicants.

Margaret's story was related in a book of dialogues by a Cistercian monk, Caesarius of Heisterbach. In this book a novice asks what sort of martyrdom applies to the case of this girl. The answer is given: "Simplicity and an innocent life. . . . There are different kinds of martyrdom, namely, innocence, as in Abel; uprightness, as in the prophets and St. John the Baptist; love of the law, as in the Maccabees; confession of the faith, as in the apostles. For all these different causes Christ the Lamb is said to have been 'slain from the beginning of the world.'"

"All Christian virtues, being protestations of our faith and proofs of our fidelity to God, are a true motive for martyrdom."

—*Butler's Lives of the Saints*

French Martyrs of September
(d. 1792)

The martyrs commemorated on this day include 191 priests, bishops, seminarians, deacons, an acolyte, and a Christian Brother, all massacred in September 1792 during the Terror of the French Revolution. Two years previously the Constituent Assembly had passed a civil constitution subjecting all clergy to secular authority. These measures were accompanied by a mandatory oath, which all but four bishops and most of the French clergy refused to take. Those who refused were charged as enemies of the Revolution and scheduled for deportation.

In Paris on September 2, a riotous mob, enraged by reports that a foreign invasion was imminent, stormed the prisons in search of counterrevolutionary priests. One of their first stops was a Carmelite church where 150 bishops and priests were being held while awaiting deportation. Encountering Msgr. Jean du Lau, archbishop of Arles, they asked him, "Are you the archbishop?" When he answered yes, they cut him down with their swords and pikes. This initiated a killing frenzy that lasted many hours. The prisoners were gathered together and interrogated two by two. Upon their refusal to take the oath they were directed down a narrow stairway where executioners were waiting to hack them to pieces.

These martyrs were beatified in 1926.

"Here I am at your disposal, gentlemen, ready to die, but I cannot walk. Will you please be so kind as to carry me where you wish me to go."
—St. Francis de La Rochefoucauld Maumont, bishop of Beauvais, before his execution

St. Phoebe
Deacon (First Century)

What little is known of St. Phoebe and her part in the early Church is derived from her brief mention in St. Paul's Letter to the Romans: "And I commend to you our sister Phoebe, a deacon of the church at Cenchreae, so that you may welcome her in the Lord as is fitting for the saints, and help her in whatever she may require from you, for she has been a benefactor of many and of myself as well" (Rom 16:1-2). Cenchreae was a port city near Corinth, where Paul wrote his letter to the Romans, and it has been speculated that Phoebe was in fact entrusted with the delivery of this letter.

The more interesting speculation regards her designation as a "deacon" (*diákonos*), the same word used in Acts 6 to designate those men appointed to serve the local Church, attending particularly to the needs of the poor. In any case, she was commended by St. Paul for her help to others, including himself. She stands for many unnamed women who ministered in the Church and played an indispensable role in spreading the Gospel.

"Note how many ways Paul dignifies Phoebe. He mentions her before all the rest and even calls her his sister. It is no small thing to be called the sister of Paul! Moreover, he has mentioned her rank of deacon as well."

—St. John Chrysostom, *Homily on Romans*

St. Gregory the Great
Pope and Doctor of the Church (540–604)

St. Gregory was born to a patrician Roman family that had provided two previous popes to the Church. He first pursued a career in the civil service, achieving the office of prefect of Rome. The city was not what it had been. Sacked four times in a century, its great buildings were largely in ruins. Gregory won wide admiration for his deft administration. When his father died, Gregory put aside "worldly concerns" and turned his estate into a monastery. The years that followed were the happiest in his life. But in 579 he was called to serve the Church in a number of sensitive positions, concluding in 590 with his election as pope.

Though he accepted this duty with extreme reluctance, Gregory again proved himself a gifted leader. With Rome in a state of collapse, it fell to Gregory to meet a series of challenges, including war, famine, and plague. He left his mark on the spiritual life of the Church through regulation of the liturgy and promotion of plainsong choral music (later known as Gregorian chant). He encouraged the flowering of monasticism (writing a popular biography of St. Benedict) and sponsored the first successful mission to the British Isles.

In light of these accomplishments he was honored as Pope Gregory "Magnus"—*the Great*. He preferred to be called "Servant of the servants of God."

"The proof of love is in the works. Where love exists, it works great things. But when it ceases to act, it ceases to exist."

—St. Gregory the Great

St. Rose of Viterbo
Mystic (1235–1252)

The short life of St. Rose was set against the background of turbulent ecclesial and political conflicts in which, even as a child, she played a significant role. From her earliest years she had displayed remarkable spiritual gifts, including, at the age of eight, a vision of Our Lady.

In 1247 her hometown of Viterbo was occupied by forces of the emperor Frederick II, who was attempting to conquer the Papal States. Rose, though only twelve, took to the streets, preaching to growing crowds in defense of the pope and urging an uprising to expel the usurpers. Not surprisingly, her actions incurred the wrath of the imperial party. Though denounced as an enemy of the emperor, she escaped the punishment of death. Instead, she and her parents were merely banished. Rose responded by prophesying—correctly as it turned out—the emperor's imminent death. When, after a matter of weeks, this prophecy was fulfilled, the papal party was restored to power, and Rose and her family were able to return home.

Rose spent her remaining years in prayer and seclusion in her parents' home. Though she wished to enter religious life, she lacked a dowry and could find no convent that would accept her. She died in March 1252 at the age of seventeen and was canonized in 1457.

"If Jesus could be beaten for me, I can be beaten for Him. I do what He has told me to do, and I must not disobey Him."

—St. Rose of Viterbo

Blessed Catherine of Racconigi
Mystic (1486–1547)

Catherine was born to a peasant family in the town of Racconigi in Piedmont. Throughout her childhood she conducted regular colloquies with the saints, and at fourteen she received a vision of St. Stephen, who encouraged her in her trials and promised the assistance of the Holy Spirit. At that moment it seemed as if she were struck by three rays of light and heard a voice that said, "I am come to take up my dwelling in you, and to cleanse, enlighten, kindle, and animate your soul." Afterward she made a vow of virginity and in return received the mark of a ring that seemed to appear on her finger.

At twenty-eight Catherine became a tertiary of the Dominican Order, though she continued to live at home and assist her parents. Nevertheless, she came to be known for her special gifts, including the extraordinary ability to travel great distances to provide spiritual counsel to anyone in need. Yet her mystical experiences aroused fear as well as wonder, and she was shunned even by her fellow Dominicans. She agonized over the sufferings caused by warfare and for the many sinners who were destined for hell. For the lives and salvation of others, she offered herself as a victim. After a long illness, she died alone, without comfort of the sacraments, on September 4, 1547. After her death devotion to her memory increased. She was beatified in 1810.

"Jesus alone is my hope."
—Blessed Catherine of Racconigi

Blessed Jean-Joseph Lataste
Founder, Dominican Sisters of Bethany (1832–1869)

In September 1864 a young French Dominican priest, Jean-Joseph Lataste, conducted a retreat at the women's prison in Cadillac. He entered with the usual prejudices against "hardened" criminals. But his experience that day, and the attentive response of the retreatants, prompted his own conversion. Struck as never before by the Gospel message of forgiveness, he concluded that prisoners, among all people, have a special hunger for God's mercy. From this he conceived the idea of a new contemplative congregation, the Dominican Sisters of Bethany, in which ex-prisoners would be welcomed as equal members.

Père Lataste had a great devotion to Mary Magdalene—traditionally, if erroneously, depicted as a reformed prostitute. This was reflected in his choice of the name Bethany—based on the further misidentification of Mary Magdalene as the sister of Martha of Bethany. Thus, he believed, it was Mary Magdalene, a forgiven sinner, who sat reverently at the feet of Jesus while her sister bustled in the kitchen. She was said to have chosen "the one thing necessary."

Lataste's new congregation was founded in 1866. Some were scandalized at the prospect of ex-convicts clothed in the Dominican habit. Even some fellow Dominicans worried that they would now be mistaken for repentant sinners. But Lataste was not discouraged. The Sisters of Bethany grew and eventually spread to several countries. Jean-Joseph Lataste died on March 10, 1869. He was beatified in 2012, with his feast assigned to September 5 (also his birthday).

"God doesn't look at what we have been; he is interested only in what we are."
—Blessed Jean-Joseph Lataste

St. Teresa of Calcutta
Founder, Missionaries of Charity (1910–1997)

In her later years Mother Teresa was widely recognized as a living emblem of God's love. She received countless honors, including the Nobel Peace Prize. Yet for years she toiled in obscurity. In fact, the Albanian-born nun had spent twenty years as a Loreto Sister in her order's schools in India before receiving the "call within a call" that defined her distinctive vocation. One day in 1946, while traveling by train to Darjeeling in the Himalayas, she had suddenly sensed that God "wanted me to be poor with the poor, and love him in the distressing disguise of the poorest of the poor."

With her congregation's permission she left the convent, donned a simple white sari, and went out to seek Jesus in the desperate byways of Calcutta. Eventually others joined her, and they became the Missionaries of Charity. And she became Mother Teresa.

Though in time she established centers of service around the globe, she remained particularly identified with her original home for the dying in Calcutta. There, destitute and dying men and women, gathered off the streets, received loving care until they died. Those who had lived like "animals in the gutter" were enabled to "die like angels"—knowing they were valued and loved as children of God.

Mother Teresa died on September 5, 1997. She was beatified in 2003 by Pope John Paul II and canonized by Pope Francis in 2016.

"Not all of us can do great things. But we can do small things with great love."
—St. Teresa of Calcutta

Albert Schweitzer
Missionary, Nobel Laureate (1875–1965)

Albert Schweitzer—a German theologian, musician, minister, and missionary doctor—was one of the remarkable figures of his age. In his youth he was torn between the lure of scholarship and the impulse to serve. He ended up earning doctorates in both theology and philosophy, yet found time to serve as a village curate. His book *The Quest of the Historical Jesus* became a theological classic. A talented organist, he achieved renown as one of the world's authorities on the work of Bach. Despite all this, he felt called to something more. Inspired by an ad in a missionary magazine, he decided to leave everything behind, to train as a doctor, and depart for equatorial Africa.

This he did. He and his wife spent decades operating an outpost in Gabon. His hospital there was patterned after a typical African village; animals wandered freely among the buildings. Aside from his medical work, Schweitzer wrote many books expounding his philosophy of "Reverence for Life," a perspective that found resonance with African spirituality.

Despite his remote posting, Schweitzer's reputation circled the globe; his image—with white coat, pith helmet, and remarkable moustache—became an icon of selfless service. The recipient of the 1952 Nobel Peace Prize, he died on September 4, 1965.

"The purpose of human life is to serve, and to show compassion and the will to help others."
—Albert Schweitzer

E. F. Schumacher
Economist (1911–1977)

E. F. Schumacher was a prophet in the guise of an economist. He spent a lifetime mastering the principles of growth, savings, and the "invisible hand" of the market. Yet ultimately he became one of its most effective critics, alerting the world to the catastrophic consequences of the Western experiment in materialism. He inspired hope that it was not too late to fashion an alternative society, responsive to the moral, spiritual, and material needs of human beings.

Born in Germany, Schumacher went to England in the 1930s on a Rhodes scholarship. While detained during the war as an enemy alien, he converted to Catholicism. He served for many years as a top economist for the British Coal Board, eventually concluding that traditional economics was a kind of religion, based on a materialistic view of reality in which growth, efficiency, and production were the ultimate measures of value. Economists ignored the spiritual dimension, while promoting a civilization headed for disaster.

In 1973 Schumacher created a sensation with his book *Small Is Beautiful,* which promoted a vision of economics "as if people mattered." He believed we were approaching a time of convergence between the practical imperatives of planetary survival and the great, unheeded wisdom of our prophets and sages.

His writings had enormous influence, but he lived only to plant the seeds. He died on September 4, 1977, just four years after the appearance of his famous book.

"In the excitement over the unfolding of his scientific and technical powers, modern man has built a system that mutilates man."

—E. F. Schumacher

St. Kassiani
Abbess, Hymnographer (ca. 810–865)

Kassiani was born to a wealthy family in Constantinople. It is reported that the young emperor, smitten by her beauty, interviewed her as a potential bride. "Through a woman came the baser things," he remarked, referring to original sin. "And through a woman came the better things," she replied, referring to salvation. He decided to choose a different bride. As for Kassiani, in 843 she founded a convent outside the city and became its first abbess.

A poet and composer, Kassiani wrote hundreds of hymns, of which twenty-three remain in the Orthodox liturgical books today. Her "Hymn of the Fallen Woman" is regularly sung during Holy Week: "I will fervently embrace Thy sacred feet, and wipe them again with the tresses of the hair of my head, Thy feet at whose sound Eve hid herself for fear when she heard Thee walking in Paradise in the cool of the day."

During a period of fierce iconoclasm, Kassiani was arrested and scourged for her fervent devotion to icons. When the persecution passed she traveled to Italy and Greece, where she died on the island of Kasos.

"I hate the fool who acts like a philosopher; I hate the rich man who groans that he is poor; I hate the person who is forever changing his ways; I hate the judge who is a respecter of persons; I hate silence when it is time to speak."
—St. Kassiani

Alexander Men
Orthodox Priest and Martyr (1935–1990)

Alexander Men was born in Russia in the heart of the Stalinist era. Ordained an Orthodox priest in 1960, he spent most of his career in obscure pastoral assignments. Though subject, like all priests, to the threat of harassment and persecution, he was able to carve out a small zone of operation in the Moscow area. Through the 1970s he worked to establish small Christian communities which emphasized prayer and Bible study.

Gradually, he assumed a more visible role. Known as the "priest of the intellectuals" and a friend of dissidents, he was regularly picked up by the KGB for questioning. Yet he refused opportunities to leave the country. With the dawn of *glasnost* under Mikhail Gorbachev, Men was finally able to publish his spiritual writings and to offer public lectures on Christianity. Thus, he became a symbol of the resurgence of spiritual values. Not everyone welcomed this new era of openness. On September 9, 1990, unknown assailants struck him in the head with an ax as he was on his way to church. He died instantly.

Men had anticipated such a fate. As he wrote to a friend before his death, "Do not be worried about me. . . . I am only an instrument that God is using for the moment. Afterwards, things will be as God wants them."

"I have always wanted to be a Christian living not by candlelight, but in the direct light of the sun."
—Alexander Men

Saints Natalia and Adrian
Martyrs (ca. 304)

Natalia, a young Christian woman, and her husband Adrian, a pagan who served as an officer in the imperial court of Nicomedia, were married only a year when Adrian was forced to witness the scourging of a group of Christians. He was so horrified by their treatment, and moved by their faithfulness, that he stepped forward to proclaim, "Count me in with these men, for I also am a Christian."

When Natalia heard the news she rushed to the prison and kissed his chains. "You are blessed, Adrian, for you have found the riches which your father and mother did not leave to you." Cutting her hair and disguising herself in men's clothes, she bribed her way into the jail and remained there with her husband until the time of his execution. He and the other prisoners were condemned to have their bones broken and their hands and feet cut off. Natalia begged Adrian to pray that she should live a sinless life until their reunion in heaven.

In fact, within months, Natalia followed her husband, dying peacefully in Argyropolis, where the relics of Adrian and the other martyrs had been preserved. She was buried there and counted among their number.

"I have not lost my mind, but rather have I found it."

—St. Adrian

Blessed Frederic Ozanam
Founder, St. Vincent de Paul Society (1813–1853)

France in the nineteenth century was rent by the continuing reverberations of the Revolution. The Church hierarchy allied itself with the conservative cause, incurring the distrust of the working class and the disdain of those intellectuals who embraced the republican spirit of liberty. One man who tried to bridge this gap was a Catholic layman and scholar, Frederic Ozanam.

As a student and later professor at the Sorbonne, Ozanam was moved by the appalling squalor of the urban poor. Convinced that Christianity is not about ideas but about deeds of love, he formed a fellowship of Christian laypeople who would immerse themselves in the world of the poor, performing acts of charity at a personal sacrifice. This became the St. Vincent de Paul Society.

In entering the world of the poor, Ozanam saw the world and the Gospel from their perspective. He challenged the Church to renounce its alliance with the rich and powerful, along with nostalgia for a bygone prerevolutionary era. The poor, he believed, called Christians to conversion. They were "messengers of God to test our justice and our charity and to save us by our works." His stance earned the suspicion of fellow Catholics, leaving him isolated and discouraged. He died on September 8, 1853. Nevertheless, his Society spread across the globe. He was beatified in 1997 by Pope John Paul II.

"We are here below in order to accomplish the will of Providence."

—Blessed Frederic Ozanam

St. Peter Claver
Missioner to Slaves (1581–1654)

In 1610 Peter Claver, a Spanish Jesuit, landed in Cartagena (now in Columbia), a great port of entry for African slaves. Ten thousand arrived each year to work in the mines. The conditions of their journey were unspeakably atrocious, with perhaps a third of all who embarked from Africa failing to survive. To the wretched souls who remained Peter Claver devoted his life.

With the arrival of each fresh slave ship, Claver would make his way to the dock and talk his way past the captain to gain access to the "cargo." There he would move among the dazed and half-dead Africans, treating their wounds and distributing food and drink. With the help of interpreters and pictures, he would try to communicate something of the principles of Christianity. How this was received is difficult to imagine. Nevertheless, it is estimated that during a career of forty years he baptized over 300,000 slaves. Claver tried to instill a sense of their dignity and preciousness in the eyes of God. This in itself represented a subtle subversion of the slave trade, and his attitude often provoked angry opposition. Nevertheless, he was tireless in his efforts, calling himself "the slave of the Negroes forever."

In 1650 Claver was struck by plague. Though he survived, he was left physically helpless, virtually alone in his cell. He died on September 8, 1654. The city and the Church that had scorned him now competed to honor his memory. Canonized in 1888, he is the patron of social justice.

"Deeds come first, then the words."

—St. Peter Claver

John Howard Griffin
Writer and Witness (1920–1980)

In 1959 the writer John Howard Griffin traveled to New Orleans. There, with the help of drugs, dyes, and radiation, he darkened his skin, shaved his head, and "crossed the line into a country of hate, fear and hopelessness—the country of the American Negro." For two months he traveled through the Deep South, later publishing his observations in the classic *Black Like Me*.

Perhaps the roots of Griffin's experiment lay in his ten-year experience of blindness—the result of a war injury. This experience prompted a deep spiritual journey that included his conversion to Catholicism. When his sight later miraculously returned, he was struck by how much superficial appearances can serve as obstacles to perception—allowing us to regard certain fellow humans as "the intrinsic other." This was especially obvious in the case of racism.

Griffin's book went beyond social observation to examine an underlying disease of the soul. It was really a meditation on the effects of dehumanization, both for the persecuted and the persecutors themselves. When his story was published his body was hung in effigy in his hometown in Texas. Nevertheless he threw himself into a decade of tireless work on behalf of the civil rights movement, persevering with those who shared "the harsh and terrible understanding that somehow they must pit the quality of their love against the quantity of hate roaming the world." Griffin died on September 9, 1980.

"One hopes that if one acts from a thirst for justice and suffers the consequences, then others . . . may be spared the terror of disesteem and persecution."

—John Howard Griffin

521

St. Pulcheria
Empress (399–453)

Pulcheria was the daughter of Arcadius, emperor of the East. Her younger brother Theodosius II, still a boy, became emperor upon their father's death. Pulcheria—herself only fifteen—was named Augusta (Empress), to rule as his partner and tutor. For political as much as religious reasons Pulcheria took a vow of perpetual celibacy—thus shielding herself from the intrigue of potential suitors. She proved a very capable ruler and tutor to her brother, concerning herself equally with religious and civil affairs. Theodosius had little interest in these things (he was nicknamed "the Calligrapher," a reference to his love of painting). Under Pulcheria's management, the court took on the atmosphere of a monastery.

Eventually Theodosius married, and the new Augusta drove Pulcheria from Constantinople. But when her brother died she returned as empress. To solidify her rule she agreed to marry a widowed general, after winning his promise to respect her virginity. Her reign occurred during a time of bitter conflict in the Church. She sponsored the Council of Chalcedon, which defined orthodox teaching on the human and divine natures of Christ. She built and endowed many churches, including three devoted to the Mother of God, as well as hospitals and shelters for the poor. After her death she was widely acclaimed as a saint.

"Many troubles which would have been excited in the Church of this period by the influence of erroneous opinions were averted by her zeal and vigilance."

—A contemporary biographer of St. Pulcheria

Blessed Louisa of Savoy
Widow and Poor Clare (1461–1503)

Louisa was born into the highest circle of nobility. Her father was the duke of Savoy, while on her mother's side, she was a niece to the king of France. A pious child, she dreamed of entering religious life. But this was hardly an acceptable vocation for a child of her station. Instead, when she was seventeen, her uncle arranged her marriage to a young nobleman. Though they would have no children, the marriage proved a happy one. Her husband accepted her religious devotion, which she combined with an active role in court life. Together they set a high moral standard, requiring that anyone who cursed in their presence make a contribution to the poor. Meanwhile, Louisa engaged in a range of charitable activities, from care for widows and orphans, to nursing the sick and even victims of the plague.

When she was twenty-seven her husband died. After a period of mourning, she made preparations to leave her privileged world—putting on the habit of a Franciscan tertiary and distributing her fortune. After two years she entered a convent of Poor Clares in Orbe. There she spent the rest of her life in prayer and poverty, eventually rising to the office of abbess. She died on July 24, 1503, and was beatified in 1839. Her feast date, now on July 24, was for many years observed by the Poor Clares on September 9.

"Farewell my beloved sisters, I am going to Paradise. It is very beautiful there!"
—Last words of Blessed Louisa of Savoy

St. Notburga
Servant of God (ca. 1264–ca. 1313)

S t. Notburga, a peasant from the Austrian Tirol, was born sometime in the thirteenth century. As a young woman she was employed as a kitchen servant by Count Henry of Rattenberg and his wife. Notburga was in the habit of distributing leftover food to the poor, rather than feeding it to the pigs as she was instructed. Eventually this cost her her job. After this, she worked for a farmer at Eben. From this period comes one of the best-known stories about Notburga. One Saturday afternoon, upon hearing the bell ring for Vespers, she prepared to leave the field where she was working. When the farmer ordered her to keep working she refused. Since the weather was fine, she argued, there was no excuse not to answer the call to worship. But when the farmer protested that the weather might change, Notburga said, "Let this decide." She then tossed her sickle into the air, where it remained suspended, like the first quarter of the harvest moon.

After the death of his wife, Count Henry, apparently conscience-stricken over his treatment of Notburga (or fearing that her dismissal had brought him bad luck), sought her out and offered her employment once again as a housekeeper. Years later, when she was dying, she asked to be placed on an oxcart, to be buried wherever it stopped. The ox took her to the church of St. Rupert. There she was laid to rest, and her grave became a site of pilgrimage during the Middle Ages. In 1862 Pope Pius IX declared her the patroness of peasants and domestic workers.

"Notburga understood her life as a gift and mission. That which God had given her, she did not keep for herself, but passed it on. So she made the saving action of God visible in the world."

—Pope Francis on St. Notburga

Mychal Judge
Franciscan Chaplain (1933–2001)

On the bright fall morning of September 11, 2001, firefighters across New York were summoned to a scene of unimaginable horror: two hijacked airliners had crashed into the twin towers of the World Trade Center. As firefighters rushed into the burning buildings they were accompanied by their chaplain, Fr. Mychal Judge. Hundreds of them would die that day, among the nearly 3,000 fatalities in New York, Washington, D.C., and Pennsylvania. Fr. Judge would be among them.

In the days that followed, the story of his life and his sacrifice would become known around the world: how he had joined the Franciscans at the age of fifteen, how he had acquired a wide reputation for his ministry among the poor and homeless, alcoholics, victims of AIDS, and his outreach to the gay community and to others alienated or marginalized in the Church. There were stories about his own struggles with alcohol and his recovery with the help of Alcoholics Anonymous. And stories of his love for the firefighters, his courage in joining them on the front lines, his support as they coped with stress and sorrow. There seemed to be special meaning in the fact that Fr. Mychal was listed as the first certified casualty of 9/11. A photograph of his fellow firemen carrying his body from the wreckage to a neighboring church became an icon of that day: an image of loving service and sacrifice, a hopeful answer to messages born of fear and fanaticism.

"God is not an obligation or a burden. God is the joy of my life!"

—Fr. Mychal Judge

Amos
Prophet (Eighth Century BC)

Amos came from the southern kingdom of Judah in a village called Tekoa. There he was employed as a peasant, tending sheep and dressing trees, when he received a powerful call from God to be a prophet. He took his message to the northern kingdom, then under Jeroboam II (786–746 BC) and enjoying a complacent period of security and affluence.

In blistering language Amos heaped coals upon the rich and self-satisfied elite of Israel, who "sell the righteous for silver and the needy for a pair of shoes." He was equally scornful of their claims to piety: "Thus, says the Lord . . . I hate, I despise your feasts, and I take no delight in your solemn assemblies. . . . But let justice roll down like waters, and righteousness like an ever-flowing stream." While the elite measured their faithfulness by the volume of their prayers, Amos insisted that the proper measure was the degree of mercy toward the weak and justice for the poor.

Amos's shrill message evoked an angry response. He was denounced by the priests for conspiring against the king. Expelled from Israel, he was forced to return to Judah. Nevertheless, he persisted in delivering his unwelcome oracles: death, exile, and destruction for those who disregarded the covenant. His message was taken up by later prophets, and it continues to resonate in the preaching and witness of all who link the true worship of God with the cause of justice.

"Prepare to meet your God, O Israel!"

—The Prophet Amos (4:12)

Stephen Biko
South African Freedom Fighter (1946–1977)

Along the road to freedom in South Africa, many did not live to see the day of victory. Steve Biko is among the most honored martyrs of the struggle. Through the Black Consciousness movement that he inspired, he worked to foster a spirit of pride and self-reliance—a refusal by blacks to see themselves through white eyes. This included a challenge to the Church—to overcome the legacy of colonialism, to shed its "Western package," and discover "what the Christian faith means for our continent."

Biko was subjected to "banning"—a unique South African punishment designed to render a person invisible. Thus, most whites knew him only through the caricature drawn by his enemies. Though he struggled without weapons, the government recognized that his efforts to promote a liberation of consciousness constituted a direct threat to the system of white supremacy.

Biko was arrested in August 1977. After twenty-six days in custody the government announced his death—supposedly from self-inflicted injuries. An inquest determined that he had died of severe brain damage sustained during his incarceration. Rather than take him to a local hospital the police had driven him in a Land Rover, naked and in leg irons, to a prison hospital 750 miles away. Still, the inquest refused to assign responsibility to the government.

His vindication came seventeen years later when Nelson Mandela, the first black president of a free South Africa, was inaugurated.

"The sense of defeat is what we are fighting against. People must not give in to the hardship of life. People must develop hope."

—Steve Biko

St. John Chrysostom
Bishop and Doctor of the Church (ca. 350–407)

St. John was considered the greatest preacher of his time. Renowned for the sweetness of his speech, upon his death he received an honorific surname: Chrysostom, or "Golden Mouth."

Born in Antioch in Syria, John spent several years as a hermit before receiving ordination to the priesthood and serving as deputy to the bishop. His service to the poor made him a beloved figure—so much so that, when the emperor Arcadias nominated him to serve as archbishop of Constantinople, it was necessary to smuggle him out of Antioch to avoid a riot among his bereft admirers. In his new office he instituted numerous reforms. But he soon found enemies, not least among them the empress Eudoxia, whom he apparently called a Jezebel on account of her ostentatious vanity. A council of bishops called him to judgment on a list of trumped-up charges, and he was sent into exile.

St. John's sufferings were extensive, as he was driven from one remote backwater to another. While traveling under armed guard in the scorching heat he collapsed and uttered his last words, "Glory be to God for all things." Following his death his reputation was rehabilitated. He was quickly recognized as a saint, and in 1568 he was proclaimed a Doctor of the Church.

"It is not possible for one to be wealthy and just at the same time. Do you pay such honor to your excrements as to receive them into a silver chamber-pot when another man made in the image of God is perishing in the cold?"
—St. John Chrysostom

Dante Alighieri
Poet (1265–1321)

Dante Alighieri, one of the great literary geniuses of all time, was also a man of action, committed to social justice and the affairs of his native Florence. But he was at the same time a man of deep faith, a visionary and a prophet, who judged the world and the Church by the light of the Gospel and the radiance of eternity. All these factors combined in *The Divine Comedy* to create a literary as well as spiritual masterpiece.

Florence in Dante's time was bitterly divided between rival factions, one favoring the temporal power of the pope and the other committed to the autonomy of the city. Influenced by the radical Spiritual Franciscans, Dante opposed the papal claims to temporal power—particularly the worldly statecraft of the reigning pontiff, Boniface VIII—and urged a return to the evangelical ideals of poverty and simplicity. When the political tides turned against him, he was forced to flee Florence, spending his last twenty years in exile.

In these years Dante wrote his *Divine Comedy*, the record of an imaginative pilgrimage from the depths of hell, up the mount of purgatory, and finally to the ethereal rapture of paradise. The poet's journey involves his own progressive conversion, preparing him to endure the increasingly rarefied atmosphere along his spiritual path until he is drawn into the presence of "the Love that moves the Sun and the other stars."

Dante died in Ravenna, far from the city he loved.

"Beauty awakens the soul to act."

—Dante

Venerable Marie-Therese de Lamourous
Founder, Mother of the Lay Marianists (1754–1836)

Marie-Therese de Lamourous was raised in a noble family in Bordeaux. During the French Revolution, while in her thirties, she carried out the work of the underground Church, teaching catechism, visiting the sick as well as prisoners. Dressing as a cleaning woman, she would enter the office of the Committee of Supervision and read the lists of those scheduled for arrest and execution, thus helping many to escape. In 1794 her family moved to Pian. There, in the absence of a parish priest, she effectively served as pastor, conducting prayer services, providing religious instruction, and hearing deathbed confessions.

When the persecution lifted, Marie-Therese threw herself into new work. A friend enlisted her help with a shelter for former prostitutes. Marie-Therese eventually took over the shelter, named the House of the Mercy, where women were free to come or leave while receiving physical support and spiritual counseling. The population of the house grew to three hundred women. Eventually the staff of the house chose to become a religious institute. The first sisters took vows in 1818, with Marie-Therese as directress.

Meanwhile, with her spiritual advisor, Fr. William Joseph Chaminade, she engaged in another great work. He had launched a plan to re-Christianize France through small communities called Sodalities under the patronage of Mary. This was the origin of the Family of Mary, or the Marianists. Marie-Therese is recognized as the mother of their Lay Branch.

She died on September 14, 1836.

"Let us limit ourselves, my good friend, to doing, each of us, what God would wish us to do."

—Venerable Marie-Therese Lamourous

Blessed Pino Puglisi
Priest and Martyr (1937–1993)

On September 15, 1993, on his fifty-sixth birthday, Fr. Giuseppe "Pino" Puglisi was confronted outside his parish church in Palermo, Sicily, by a Mafia gunman who aimed a pistol at his face. "I've been expecting you," were the priest's last words.

Since his ordination in 1960, Fr. Puglisi, a native of Palermo, had set himself on a collision course with the entrenched power of the Cosa Nostra. This criminal network, sustained by patronage, violence, and the code of silence, was taken for granted by many Sicilians. Even Church officials tended to turn a blind eye. Puglisi struggled to challenge this culture. In his sermons he urged his flock to overcome their fears and stand up for the truth. He encouraged reconciliation between families torn by long-standing feuds. "Peace is like bread," he said. "It must be shared, or it loses its flavor." He established sports programs for teenagers to give them alternatives to drugs and crime. He lost no opportunity to denounce the crime families, rejecting their pretense of being "good Catholics," refusing their hypocritical offer of donations to the Church.

Still, his brazen murder raised a scandal in Italy. An aggressive investigation led to the arrest and conviction of the assassins as well as the powerful patrons who had ordered his murder. Pope Benedict XVI officially named him a martyr, who had laid down his life for the evangelical virtues of truth and justice. He was beatified in May 2013.

"And what if somebody did something?"

—Blessed Pino Puglisi's favorite rhetorical question

St. Catherine of Genoa
Mystic (1447–1510)

Born into an aristocratic family in Genoa, Catherine spent her early life in a dismal arranged marriage that left her depressed and listless. After years of chronic depression, she tried to engage in the frivolous diversions of society life. But this was no solution. Finally at the age of twenty-five, she was overcome with an infusion of divine compassion. She was impressed simultaneously with the immensity of her sins and with the goodness of God. But rather than bemoan her life, she resolved to dedicate herself to God's work. She began to volunteer in the local hospital, hardly the normal profession for a woman of her social standing. She deliberately took on the most repulsive chores. In time, she became hospital administrator, staying at her post during an outbreak of plague that killed four-fifths of the city. And as she grew in love, she grew in her capacity for happiness.

In her later years she drew a circle of devoted disciples, attracted not only by the opportunity to share in her charitable work but by the chance to benefit from her spiritual wisdom. She wrote several devotional classics, including a treatise extolling purgatory as the happiest place outside of heaven. Yet her profound "otherworldliness" and capacity for mystical rapture was combined with fastidious attention to practical detail and availability to the needs of others. Catherine died on September 15, 1510.

"If you are what you should be, you will set the whole world ablaze."

—St. Catherine of Genoa

Martyrs of Birmingham
(d. 1963)

On the morning of September 15, 1963, someone tossed a packet of dynamite through the basement window of the Sixteenth Street Baptist Church in Birmingham, Alabama. Moments later an explosion took the lives of four young girls and seriously injured twenty others. The slain children were Addie Mae Collins, Carole Robertson, and Cynthia Wesley, all fourteen, and Denise McNair, eleven. At the moment of the blast they had just finished their Sunday school lesson and were changing into their choir robes.

The bombing was a terrible rejoinder to the uplifting spectacle, only weeks before, of the March on Washington, where Martin Luther King Jr. had delivered his famous speech, "I Have a Dream." In Birmingham, it followed an intense summer of demonstrations to challenge the rigidly enforced policies of racial segregation. All this seemed to culminate in the explosion on this Sunday morning. The awful symbolism of such a massacre in church, and the innocence of the young victims, underscored the spiritual character of the forces engaged in the Birmingham struggle—literally a battle between the Children of Light and the Children of Darkness. Reverend King delivered the eulogy at the girls' funeral, calling them "martyred heroines of a holy crusade for freedom and human dignity" and expressing hope that their deaths would awaken the conscience of Birmingham and the nation and so douse the flames of hatred and division.

"These children—unoffending, innocent and beautiful—were the victims of one of the most vicious, heinous crimes ever perpetrated against humanity."
　　　　　　　　　　　　　　　　　　—Martin Luther King Jr.

St. Cyprian
Bishop of Carthage, Martyr (ca. 200–258)

Cyprian spent most of his life, until the age of forty-five, as an orator and professor of rhetoric in Carthage. Then, falling under the influence of a holy priest, he accepted baptism. Before long he was ordained a priest, and in 248 he was named bishop of Carthage. Within a year, however, he faced a terrible test when an edict of Emperor Decius unleashed a wave of persecution. Many priests were arrested, others apostatized, and when mobs cried out for Cyprian's blood, he chose to go into hiding—a decision that brought criticism from Rome as well as the North African Church.

The aftermath of the persecution left lingering scars, as bitter disagreements arose about the conditions under which apostates could return to the sacraments, or indeed, in the case of clergy, administer the sacraments. Cyprian took a moderate position. But positions hardened and resulted in actual schism. Cyprian is best remembered for his writings on the importance of unity in the Church, and particularly the role of the pope as a unifying figure: "There is one God, one Christ, and but one episcopal chair, originally founded on Peter, by the Lord's authority."

In 257 another wave of persecution was unleashed by the emperor Valerian. This time Cyprian was arrested, tried, and sent into exile. Brought back for further interrogation, he was offered the possibility of saving himself if he would betray his priests. After refusing, he was condemned to death and summarily beheaded.

"Do not let anything sleep in your coffers which could be profitable to the poor."

—St. Cyprian

St. Edith of Wilton
Nun (962–984)

Edith was the daughter of King Edgar and Wulfrida—a novice from Wilton Abbey, whom he had forcibly abducted. When Edith was a year old her mother returned with her to Wilton. There she grew up and was educated, spending the rest of her life within the abbey walls. At fifteen, as she prepared to take vows, her father reappeared. On one side of the chapel he held out gold and jewels, representing the option of taking her place in the royal court. On the other side, her mother, now the abbess of Wilton, held out a veil and psalter. "All prayed that God, who knows all things, would show to one still at so wayward an age what life she should choose." Without hesitation she chose to remain in her mother's community.

Though she spent her short life as a humble nun, some measure of her personality emerges from the story of a visiting bishop, who upbraided her for wearing luxurious garb. She answered that God's judgment could penetrate outward appearances. "For pride may exist under the garb of wretchedness," she noted, "and a mind may be as pure under these vestments as under your tattered furs."

Edith built the church of St. Denis in Wilton. Its consecration was attended by St. Dunstan, archbishop of Canterbury. Yet Edith died only six weeks later, on September 16, 984, at the age of twenty-two. She was buried in the church, and her grave became a popular site of pilgrimage.

"She did not leave the world; she never knew it."

—Roman Martyrology

St. Hildegard of Bingen
Doctor of the Church (1098–1179)

St. Hildegard was one of the great figures of her age: abbess and founder of a Benedictine convent, prophet and preacher, musician and composer, poet and artist, doctor and pharmacist. From her earliest childhood Hildegard enjoyed holy visions in which the word of God—both in Scripture and in the book of nature—was revealed to her. She later described these visions to her confessor, who bid her write them down.

With extraordinary symbolic illustrations, Hildegard presented a picture of human beings and the cosmos as emanations of God's love, "living sparks" or "rays of his splendor, just as the rays of the sun proceed from the sun itself." Within the cosmos, she wrote, human beings are the thinking heart, called to be cocreators with God in shaping the world. Both the cosmos and human beings, though estranged from God by sin, may through Christ find their way back to God's original blessing.

Hildegard made numerous preaching tours through the Rhineland, and her reputation extended far beyond her native land. Besides her religious writings, she wrote on medicine and physiology, avidly studied the use of medicinal herbs, and composed religious music of haunting beauty. Her holistic vision has found a wide audience in recent times, and in 2012, though she had never been formally canonized, Pope Benedict XVI declared her a Doctor of the Church.

"There is the Music of Heaven in all things and we have forgotten how to hear it until we sing."
—St. Hildegard of Bingen

Adrienne von Speyr
Mystic (1902–1967)

Adrienne von Speyr was raised in a solidly Protestant family in Switzerland. After marrying, she embarked on a career in medicine. The great turning point in her life occurred in 1940, after her husband's death, when she was introduced to Hans Urs von Balthasar, a Jesuit priest and university chaplain. What did it mean, she asked him, to submit to the will of God? In answering her, according to von Balthasar, "I inadvertently touched a switch that at one flick turned on all the lights in the hall." Freed from a lifetime of restraint, Adrienne "was carried away on a flood of prayer as though a dam had burst." A few weeks later she was baptized as a Catholic.

Her influence on her confessor, von Balthasar, was enormous. Though he became one of the most influential Catholic theologians of the century, he credited Adrienne with completely reordering his theological sensibility. He alone knew the extent of her mystical experiences. In the midst of her thriving medical practice, she spent much of the night in prayer, regularly enjoyed visions of Mary and the saints, and showed a remarkable gift for interpreting Scripture. In 1942 she received the stigmata—the marks of Christ's wounds—on her hands.

Long after illness left her too weak to write, she dictated thousands of pages of commentary on Scripture to von Balthasar, continuing her spiritual labors until the end. She died on September 17, 1967.

"All freedom develops through surrender and through renunciation of liberty. And from this freedom within commitment there arises every sort of fruitfulness."

—Adrienne von Speyr

Dag Hammarskjöld
Secretary General of the United Nations (1905–1961)

On September 18, 1961, a plane crash in central Africa took the life of Dag Hammarskjöld, secretary general of the United Nations, who was engaged in a peacekeeping mission in the Congo. He was universally mourned as a man who combined the roles of public servant and global leader.

It was only after his death that the world learned of the private faith that had guided his public mission. The publication of his spiritual journal, *Markings*, disclosed what he called the story "of my negotiations with myself and with God." It revealed his lifelong struggle with God, Christ, and such issues as the relation between faith and duty, self-doubt and pride, the meaning of existence, and the sense of deep isolation that accompanied his vocation. In short, lapidary phrases he wrestled with the concrete issues posed by his path in life: "Do not seek death. Death will find you. But seek the road which makes death a fulfillment."

Hammarskjöld came from a wealthy Swedish family. Yet he was drawn to public service. He was an example of that rare person for whom public service is not simply a career or a means to power but a religious vocation, a way of being faithful to God. The consummate diplomat, few of his friends had any notion of his religious preoccupations. In his death the world lost a great servant of peace. But clearly he had found a road that makes death a fulfillment.

"We are not permitted to choose the frame of our destiny. But what we put into it is ours."
—Dag Hammarskjöld

Corita Kent
Artist and Peacemaker (1918–1986)

Corita Kent achieved fame in the early 1960s as Sr. Mary Corita, the name she took upon joining the Sisters of the Immaculate Heart of Mary in Los Angeles. Her wildly colorful silkscreens and serigraphs, emblazoned with words or images from Scripture, combined a playful pop-art sensibility with a joyous celebration of faith and being in the world. As Dan Berrigan observed, "The joy in her work, its riotous color, was her gift to a good gray world. It seemed as though in her art the juices of the world were running over, inundating the world, bursting the rotten wineskins of semblance, rote and rot." Yet while she captured the hearts of a generation poised for change, some traditionalists found her art to be "weird and sinister."

Conflicts between the Archdiocese of Los Angeles and Corita's community went far beyond her art. When, like other religious communities in the wake of Vatican II, the order decided to abandon their religious habits, Cardinal McIntyre banned them from teaching in parochial schools. Ultimately three hundred members of the community dispensed their vows and became a noncanonical community. Corita, by that time, had already decided to leave. In 1968 she moved to Boston and pursued her art outside the public limelight, continuing to contribute in any way she could to the cause of peace and justice.

She died of cancer on September 18, 1986. Among her final works: the design of a U.S. postage stamp with the word "Love."

"Love the moment and the energy of that moment will spread beyond all boundaries."
                                                            —Corita Kent

St. Emily de Rodat
Founder, Congregation of the Holy Family
of Villefranche (1787–1852)

Emily de Rodat was born in Rodez, France. In her youth, she tested her vocation to religious life in a number of communities, none of which seemed to satisfy her. Then one day, while visiting the home of a sick neighbor, her mission was instantaneously revealed: she would teach poor children. With the encouragement of her spiritual director, she began at once to take children into her own small room. Eventually, with the arrival of helpers, she moved into an abandoned monastery, which became the nucleus for her Congregation of the Holy Family of Villefranche.

Sr. Emily's community grew in time with new foundations and the extension of her sisters' charitable works into nursing, the care of orphans, and prison ministry, She was determined at all times to balance the life of action and contemplation—the paths of both Martha and Mary. Along the way she endured much physical suffering as well as long periods of spiritual desolation. Nevertheless, she lived up to the exhortation she put to one of her postulants: "Keep your enthusiasm. Be brave. Put all your trust in God. And always maintain a holy cheerfulness." She was, as one of her spiritual advisors described her, "a saint, but a headstrong saint."

Emily de Rodat died on September 19, 1852. Her canonization followed in 1950.

"I was sixteen years of age when I learned to know Our Lord. This experience overwhelmed me and I wanted God and only God."

—St. Emily de Rodat

Sadhu Sundar Singh
Mystic (1889–1929)

Sadhu Sundar Singh, who wore the robes of an Indian holy man to preach the Gospel of Jesus Christ, was one of the most fascinating and enigmatic figures of modern Christianity. Born on September 3, 1889, to a wealthy Sikh family, he was strongly influenced by his mother, a deeply religious woman. His father, a rich landowner, enrolled him in a local mission school to receive a modern education. At first he rebelled against the Christian teaching of the school. But one night, as he prayed for a sign from God, he received a mystical vision of Christ. The next day he declared himself a Christian. This was not the outcome his father had intended. He banished his son, who went out to devote himself to his living master, Jesus Christ.

Though baptized in the Anglican Church, Sundar was determined to demonstrate an Indian way of following Christ. He donned the saffron robe of a sadhu, a holy man consecrated to God. Henceforth, with no fixed abode, he lived on alms while bearing witness to Christ through his life of poverty and prayer. Jesus, as he observed, had also lived like a sadhu.

After he had wandered across India on foot, Western friends invited him on a tour of England and America, where he attracted much attention. He was disturbed by the materialism of the West and the evident absence of prayer. In April 1929 he undertook a journey to Tibet. He was never seen again, and his fate remains unknown.

"Without daily intercourse with God there is no piety, no Christianity, no real life."
—Sadhu Sundar Singh

St. Andrew Kim and the Korean Martyrs
(d. 1839–1867)

The Church in Korea claims the distinction of having been founded not by foreign missionaries but by indigenous lay Catholics. In China in the eighteenth century, Korean diplomats first heard the Gospel and returned to Korea with Christian writings. In 1784 a young Korean named Yi Sung-hun traveled to China where he was baptized with the name Peter. He returned to Korea and established the first Catholic community in the country. Over time foreign priests arrived to serve the growing community, and in 1831 the vicariate apostolic of Korea was officially established. By this time, however, the Christian community had already suffered waves of bitter persecution.

In 1984 Pope John Paul II canonized 103 Catholic martyrs, including Andrew Kim, the first native-born Korean priest. These martyrs died over the course of many years, along the way suffering horrible tortures along with weeks and months in confinement. St. Andrew was himself the son of a Christian convert and martyr. Baptized at fifteen, he left for seminary training in Macau and eventual ordination in Shanghai before returning to minister in Korea. He was arrested in 1846 and spent three months in prison prior to his execution. Before his death he wrote a moving letter of encouragement to his fellow Christians.

"This is my last hour of life, listen to me attentively: if I have held communication with foreigners, it has been for my religion and for my God. It is for Him that I die. My immortal life is on the point of beginning."
—Last words of St. Andrew Kim

Mercy Hirschboeck
Maryknoll Sister (1903–1986)

During the Korean War, a woman correspondent happened upon a clinic in Pusan where she found a nun on her knees, cleaning the gangrenous sore on a man's leg. "Sister," she said, "I wouldn't do that for a million dollars." "Neither would I," the sister replied. That story, told of Sr. Mercy Hirschboeck, Maryknoll's first Sister-Doctor, made headlines around the world. Most of her life was spent out of the limelight.

Her first assignment in 1931, soon after joining the Maryknoll Sisters, was to a remote clinic in Shingishu in Japanese-occupied Korea. In 1943 she opened a clinic in Riberalta in the northern jungle of Bolivia—a place known for its stultifying heat and deadly snakes. Then in 1951, it was back to Korea to administer the clinic in Pusan, where in two years 700,000 patients were treated. Her next stop came in 1954 when she went to Kansas City to administer Queen of the World Hospital, the first fully integrated hospital in the city. She later served for twelve years as Vicaress General of the Maryknoll Sisters.

But her mission was not concluded. At the age of seventy she joined several other sisters in an experimental contemplative community in an apartment on Avenue C in Manhattan—a neighborhood known for crime, drugs, and poverty. There she remained, offering a witness of prayer and presence, until her death on September 20, 1986.

"You felt she was holy—not that she prayed a lot, but her whole demeanor."
—A Maryknoll Sister about Sr. Mercy

St. Matthew
Evangelist (First Century)

Of St. Matthew the Evangelist we have little information beyond this brief verse in the Gospel ascribed to his pen: "As Jesus passed on from there, he saw a man called Matthew sitting at the tax office; and he said to him, 'Follow me.' And he rose and followed him." Was St. Matthew a tax collector? If so he would have been despised by his fellow Jews as a collaborator with the Roman occupation. For consorting with such public sinners, Jesus himself would earn bitter scorn. But whatever Matthew's former life, he apparently recognized that in order to follow Jesus he must leave the past behind.

The author of Matthew's Gospel, which appears to date from the end of the first century, seems to have been a Greek-speaking Jewish Christian, determined to affirm in the face of rejection by his fellow Jews that Jesus was the Messiah, the fulfillment of the Scriptures, and messenger of a new life. Matthew's Gospel includes the Sermon on the Mount, which begins with the sublime litany of the Beatitudes. He also records the great parable about the Last Judgment, when God will issue blessings on the basis of charity: "I was hungry and you fed me. . . ."

St. Matthew is the patron of the Church's mission. Called in his own life to follow Jesus, he closes his Gospel with Jesus' Great Commission to his followers, "Go therefore and make disciples of all nations." He concludes with Jesus' words that speak to all times:

"And lo, I am with you always, to the close of the age."

—Matthew 28:20

Henri Nouwen
Priest and Spiritual Guide (1932–1996)

At the time of his death in 1996, Henri Nouwen, a Dutch-born priest, was one of the most popular spiritual writers of his time. Through dozens of books he invited readers to enter more deeply into the spiritual life—intimacy with Jesus and solidarity with a wounded world. Much of his impact came from his willingness to confide his own woundedness. The spiritual life, he insisted, was not intended simply for saints. Instead, the call of Jesus was addressed to the lame and halt, all of us in our brokenness and humanity. It was a call to conversion, a call to our true home.

The search for home was a constant motif in Nouwen's life. He taught at several prestigious American universities, lived for a while in a Trappist monastery, and explored the possibility of mission work in Latin America. Then in 1986 he left his Ivy League job to become a chaplain to a L'Arche community in Canada, living with mentally handicapped adults. It was the site of his deepest conversion, the discovery of what it means to be truly "beloved of God." His last books were marked by an intuition of mortality and the need to find a way of "befriending" one's death. How, he asked, can we see our dying as a "new way for us to send our own and God's spirit to those whom we loved and who have loved us?"

Nouwen died suddenly of a heart attack on September 21, 1996.

"We have been chosen to make our own limited and very conditional love the gateway for the unlimited and unconditional love of God."

—Henri Nouwen

St. Maurice and Companions
Martyrs of the Theban Legion (ca. 287)

A Roman legion recruited from Thebes in Upper Egypt consisted entirely of Christians. In 287 they were mobilized to assist in putting down an uprising among the rebellious Gauls. When they arrived at what is now Martigny near Lake Geneva, they were ordered to join with the assembled army, on the eve of battle, in offering a sacrifice to the gods. The Theban Legion refused to take part. After they persisted in their insubordination, they were sentenced to decimation: one out of every ten men, chosen by lots, was to be put to death. Still they disobeyed. A second lottery was taken. Still the survivors refused.

Was the issue simply the idolatrous oath, or did they have reservations about the justice of the cause? The latter is implied in the statement which St. Maurice, their officer, made on their behalf: "We are your soldiers, but we are also servants of the true God. We owe you military service and obedience; but we cannot renounce Him who is Our Creator and Master. . . . We readily oppose all your enemies . . . but we cannot dip our hands into the blood of innocent persons. . . . We would rather die innocent than live by any sin."

According to legend, the entire Theban Legion—a total of 6,600 men—was ultimately slaughtered.

"We have taken an oath to God before we took one to you; you can place no confidence in our second oath if we violate the first. You command us to punish the Christians; behold, we are such."

—St. Maurice

Daria Donnelly
Laywoman (1959–2004)

The calendar of saints offers scant attention to those who lived out their faith in the context of ordinary family life. Daria Donnelly, a young laywoman from Cambridge, a wife and mother of two children whose life was cut short by multiple myeloma, represents a kind of faithful witness—lived out, as she put it, amid "the noise, the joy, the distraction" of family life—that leaves no great monument in the world. And yet who can say that she did not exemplify as much as any "great saint" the real vocation of the Christian: to embrace God's love and reflect it back to the world.

Daria grew up in Pittsburgh in a large, loving, and devoutly Catholic family. Later, while working as an editor of *Commonweal* magazine, she engaged in many quiet ministries. When she was struck with a terminal illness she accommodated herself to her circumstances with a calm, unselfish, and benevolent balance that was the mark of her personality. As her pastor noted, "she was to her core a woman of symbol, of story, of sacrament." She was determined to make each day a witness to life and to make this her legacy to those she loved. As she wrote from her deathbed—"The only thing that matters is showing love and compassion in the time that is given us." She died on September 21, 2004.

"My getting sick increased my attention to the everyday heroism of refugees, the depressed, the arthritic, the mourning, the lonely, all those who know how good it is simply to get through a day."

—Daria Donnelly

St. Thecla
Evangelist (First Century)

Though steeped in legend, the witness of St. Thecla, one of many saintly virgins of the early Church, has exerted a powerful influence in Christian history. Her story is preserved in *The Acts of Paul and Thecla*, a second-century text that found a warm reception from many Church Fathers, including Augustine and Ambrose.

According to her *Acts*, Thecla was a beautiful young woman whose life was transformed when she heard St. Paul preaching in the street beneath her window and found herself "subdued by the doctrines of faith." Under this influence, she announced her intention to break off her engagement and to embrace a life of chastity. Her family, scandalized by this behavior, denounced her to the governor and caused her arrest. Sentenced to death, she twice found miraculous deliverance from her fate and went on to enjoy a long life.

Seeking out St. Paul, she revealed that she had been commissioned by Christ to baptize and preach in his name. According to this story, Paul recognized her as a fellow apostle and authorized her to spread the Gospel. Wherever she went, "a bright cloud conducted her in her journey."

Eventually, Thecla retired to a cave and later formed a monastic community of women, whose members she instructed "in the oracles of God."

"I am a servant of the living God. . . . He is a refuge to those who are in distress, a support of the afflicted, a hope and defense to those who are hopeless."
—St. Thecla

St. Pio of Pietrelcina (Padre Pio)
Capuchin Friar and Mystic (1887–1968)

Padre Pio, a Capuchin friar of peasant background, spent virtually his entire life in a monastery in southern Italy. In most respects he was indistinguishable from his fellow friars. But for some mysterious purpose Padre Pio was set apart. For the thousands of pilgrims who flocked to hear him say Mass, or to have him hear their confessions, or simply to rest their gaze on his bandaged hands, he was living proof for the existence of God.

Like St. Francis, Pio was a stigmatic; he bore on his hands, feet, and side the wounds of Christ. These mysterious open wounds, for which there was no natural explanation, appeared on his body in 1910 and remained until some months before his death. He was credited with thousands of miracles and enjoyed other extraordinary gifts, including the ability to "read the hearts" of penitents.

He regarded his celebrity as a terrible cross. Many denounced him as a charlatan or a neurotic. To discourage his popularity, Church officials for many years instructed him not to say Mass. Eventually his faith and sufferings were vindicated by the Church. In 2002, thirty-four years after his death, he was canonized by Pope John Paul II—formerly a Polish priest, Fr. Karol Wojtyla—whose papal election Padre Pio had prophesied in 1947 after hearing his confession.

"Pray, hope, and don't worry. Worry is useless. God is merciful and will hear your prayer."
—St. Pio of Pietrelcina

Blessed Robert of Knaresborough
Hermit (ca. 1160–1218)

Robert Flower was born in York to a family of means and distinction. As a youth he desired to enter the priesthood but left off his studies to join a Cistercian monastery. After only four months there he determined that God was calling him to something else. Leaving everything he had, he retired to a cave near Knaresborough, some distance from York, where he devoted himself to prayer.

He was not, however, left undisturbed. His solitude was frequently invaded by bandits and eventually by the local constable who, after charging him with harboring outlaws, destroyed his humble dwelling. Afterward he settled on a small piece of land, on which he supported himself and provided for any poor person in need. One of his charitable practices was the ransom of prisoners. According to an epic poem that describes his deeds, "To beg and bring poor men of bail, this was his purpose principale."

His reputation for holiness eventually spread. According to the poet, he was a "devout, debonair, and discreet man than whom a milder could not be met." Robert's brother, by this time the mayor of York, tried to persuade him to adopt a more conventional monastic life, but he refused. So his brother built him a little chapel in his original cave, where Robert happily retired and later died on September 24, 1218.

"Here is my resting place forever; here will I dwell, for I have chosen it."
—Blessed Robert of Knaresborough

Blessed Emily Tavernier
Founder, Sisters of Providence (1800–1851)

Emily Tavernier, who was born in Montreal, was orphaned at an early age and raised by her aunt. At the age of twenty-three she married a wealthy farmer and bore three children, though within four years they had all died, leaving her alone in the world. Turning to Mary, Mother of Sorrows, she vowed to make the poor her new family. She began by taking in a young mentally handicapped child and his mother. But gradually she opened her home to all those in need—orphans, abandoned children, the sick and mentally ill. She named her home the House of Providence. With her inheritance she opened other houses and sought volunteers to assist her.

In 1843, with support from the bishop of Montreal, Emily and her companions established a new congregation, the Sisters of Providence. Emily took her first vows in 1844 and became the first mother superior.

Lack of clean water at the time led to regular outbreaks of cholera and typhus. The sisters responded heroically in their care for the sick. But eight years after the founding of the congregation, Emily herself was struck with cholera and died on September 23, 1851. She was beatified in 2001.

"Blessed Emily's spiritual life gave her strength for her charitable mission; she emptied herself of all things and found the energy to comfort everyone. Taking her as your model, I urge you to put yourselves at the service of the poor and of society's most underprivileged, who are God's beloved, to alleviate their sufferings and thus make their dignity shine out."

—Pope John Paul II

Mechthild of Magdeburg
Mystic (ca. 1210–ca. 1282)

Mechthild of Magdeburg, a German mystic of the thirteenth century, is known to us entirely through *The Flowing Light of the Godhead*, a kind of spiritual journal, written in her own hand, which she continuously amended over the course of her life.

At the age of twenty she left her wealthy family near Magdeburg in Saxony to join a house of Beguines—a movement of women who fashioned an independent religious life, free of rules, enclosure, or ecclesiastical approval. Mechthild's life of intimacy with God brought with it much loneliness and estrangement from the world. She accepted the price along with the rewards of her vocation.

In her writings, which were copied and widely circulated, she offered a vivid account of her dialogues with Christ, along with unsparing criticism of ecclesial worldliness and corruption: "Alas! Crown of holy Church, how tarnished you have become. . . . Alas crown of holy priesthood, you have disappeared, and you have nothing left but your external shape—namely, priestly power—with this you do battle against God and His chosen friends." Not surprisingly, such sentiments attracted negative attention, so that she described herself as "a post or target at which people throw stones." At the age of sixty she left the Beguines for the safe haven of the Cistercian convent in Helfta. There, almost blind, she was welcomed and cared for until her death.

"I cannot dance, Lord, unless you lead me. / If you want me to leap with abandon, / You must intone the song. / Then I shall leap into love."
—Mechthild of Magdeburg

St. Sergius of Radonezh
Russian Abbot (1314–1392)

St. Sergius, a fourteenth-century monk and abbot, is one of the most popular saints of the Russian Orthodox Church. He is also one of a few Russian saints who appears on the Catholic calendar. He epitomizes the ideal of the Russian monk who, through his transparent holiness, illuminates an entire age.

Though Sergius was born to noble parents, his family was impoverished by civil war, and they were forced to live as peasants. Eventually feeling the call to a life of prayer, Sergius retreated to a hermitage in the forest. There fellow seekers were drawn to him, and he received permission to establish a monastery, for which he served as abbot.

The story of St. Sergius and his brothers recalls the joyfulness and poverty of St. Francis, replete with accounts of his communion with nature and its wild beasts. Gradually the fame of the Monastery of the Holy Trinity spread far and wide, and a well-worn path brought a constant flow of penitents and spiritual seekers. Sergius received all visitors with courtesy, but for the poor he felt a special affection. His reputation for charity endeared him far beyond the monastery walls. To this was added his reputation as a national liberator after he encouraged Prince Dimitry of Moscow in his successful resistance to Tartar invaders.

Sergius performed many miraculous healings, and it was said that he enjoyed mystical visions of the Holy Mother. He died on September 25, 1392.

"He uttered few words, but gave the brethren a far greater example by his works."
—First biography of St. Sergius of Radonezh

St. Therese Couderc
Founder, Religious of the Cenacle (1805–1885)

Marie-Victoire Couderc was born to a poor farming family in France. At twenty she joined a community of teaching sisters in the town of Aps and took the name Therese. Three years later the founder of this community, Fr. Jean Terme, appointed her as superior of a community operating a hospice for women pilgrims at a popular local shrine. Later still, Fr. Terme determined that the sisters should concentrate on giving retreats for women—a novel idea at the time. This was the origin of a new order, the Religious of the Cenacle—a reference to the "upper room" where Mary stayed with the disciples awaiting the Holy Spirit.

Fr. Terme's death in 1834 marked a sad turn for Mother Therese. His successor replaced her as superior with a wealthy novice. Therese was relegated to manual labor, her role as foundress of the community effectively effaced. She embraced her obscurity without complaint. "Have confidence in God," she said. "The tree of the Cross bears fruit in every season and in every land." In later years her role as foundress was reestablished, and she was recognized for her deep spiritual gifts. Before dying she received a vision in which the word "Goodness" was stamped in gold letters on every creature.

She died on September 26, 1885, and was canonized in 1970.

"Love of the Holy Spirit, be the origin of all the workings of my soul, so that all may be in harmony with the divine good pleasure! Amen!"
—St. Therese Couderc

Blessed Paul VI
Pope (1897–1978)

Giovanni Battista Montini, archbishop of Milan, was elected pope in the conclave of June 1963. He chose to be called Paul VI. Shy and somewhat ascetic in appearance, he faced a difficult challenge in succeeding the jovial and universally beloved Pope John XXIII. But he faced still greater challenges. It fell to Pope Paul to implement the revolutionary vision that John XXIII had unleashed with the Second Vatican Council (1962–1965). To this task Montini brought considerable diplomatic skills, gained during a lifetime of service in the Vatican Secretariat of State. He steered the Church through one of the most turbulent decades in history, buffeted by criticism from all sides, both from those who felt the Church was changing too quickly as well as from those who felt the pace was not fast enough.

Pope Paul's pontificate was clouded by divisive controversy over his renewal of Church teaching on birth control. His social teaching, however, marked him as one of the most radical pontiffs in history. His encyclical *Populorum Progressio* was the first Church document to deal with the problems of the Third World, particularly the growing gap between rich and poor. He firmly committed the Church to the project of authentic development, "The transition from less than human conditions to truly human ones." In this and other documents he strongly identified the Church with the hopes and struggles of the poor. He died on August 6, 1978, and was beatified by Pope Francis in 2014. His feast day is September 26.

"The Church looks at the world with profound understanding, admiration, and with the sincere intention not of dominating it but of serving it."
—Blessed Paul VI

Margery Kempe
Mystic and Pilgrim (ca. 1373–1438)

The Book of Margery Kempe offers a vivid self-portrait of a remarkable religious seeker from fourteenth-century England. Margery was the wife of a beer brewer, with whom she bore fourteen children. Upon receiving a vision of the merriment in heaven, she underwent a deep conversion, renouncing her previous worldly interests. Afterward she dedicated herself to a life of prayer, penance, and service of God.

Margery wandered widely in England, visiting shrines and seeking audiences with spiritual guides. She was conspicuous for her "gift of tears," weeping loudly throughout the day, especially in church or anywhere that reminded her of the sufferings of Christ. Her "gift" inspired wonder but also much ridicule and contempt.

At forty she undertook a pilgrimage all the way to the Holy Land. Her fellow pilgrims quickly tired of her incessant weeping and tried to lose her along the way. But she completed the journey and returned with vivid descriptions of the settings of Christ's life and passion. Among the clergy there were those who recognized the genuineness of her vocation, including willing scribes who transcribed her autobiography. In one of her mystical colloquies, the Lord told her: "I have ordained you to be a mirror amongst your fellow Christians, to have great sorrow, so that they should take example from you to have some little sorrow in their hearts for their sins, so that they might through that be saved."

"Patience is more worthy than miracle-working."

—Margery Kempe

St. Vincent de Paul
Founder, Vincentians (1580–1660)

Vincent de Paul was born to a peasant family in Gascony. Though he later achieved fame for his dedication to the poor, his early life was spent in a determined struggle to escape his humble roots. For this goal, he chose a career in the priesthood. After ordination, his charm and social skills gained him entry into the highest levels of society. A turning point came in midlife, when he was summoned to hear the dying confession of a peasant. He was struck as never before by the seriousness of his vocation and determined afterward that his priesthood would be dedicated to service of the poor.

Eventually he established a mission congregation—later known as the Vincentians—and, with St. Louise de Marillac, founded the Daughters of Charity to serve the poor and sick. There were few charitable projects in which Vincent was not engaged. He founded hospitals and orphanages as well as homes for the humane care of the mentally infirm. He ministered to prisoners and galley slaves and became, already in his lifetime, something of a legend. The rich and powerful vied to endow his projects, while the poor accepted him as one of their own. His spirituality was based on the encounter with Christ in the needs of one's neighbors. As he instructed his priests and sisters, "The poor are your masters and you are their servants."

He died on September 27, 1660, at the age of eighty. He was later named patron of all charitable societies.

"I am for God and the poor."

—St. Vincent de Paul

St. Eustochium
Virgin (ca. 367–419)

Eustochium was the third of four daughters of St. Paula, a Roman matron who experienced a deep conversion after the death of her husband. Joining a community with St. Marcella and other widowed Christian women, Paula devoted herself to prayer and the works of mercy. Eustochium was the only one of Paula's daughters to join her in this new life, and she soon took a vow of perpetual virginity.

Their lives took a new direction under the influence of St. Jerome, a learned scholar, who became a chaplain to the community. Jerome's detractors spread scurrilous rumors about his devotion to these women, prompting his departure for the Holy Land. Paula and Eustochium followed. Establishing a community in Bethlehem, mother and daughter learned Greek and Hebrew to assist Jerome in his ambitious translation of the Scriptures into Latin.

Paula's death in 404 left her disconsolate daughter like "a baby weaned from her nurse." Paula had wished to be so poor as not to leave a penny, and Jerome notes approvingly that she far exceeded this aim, leaving her daughter with a mountain of unpaid bills. Nevertheless, Eustochium assumed responsibility for her mother's community, and with help from the bishop of Jerusalem, she was able to put her affairs in order by the time of her own death in 419. She was buried beside her mother in the cave of the Nativity.

"Set before your eyes the blessed Virgin Mary, whose purity was such that she earned the reward of being the mother of the Lord."

—St. Jerome's counsel to St. Eustochium

St. Lioba
Nun and Missionary (ca. 700–780)

St. Lioba, an English nun, was a distant relative of St. Boniface, an English monk who had embarked on a bold and perilous missionary journey to Germany. After following accounts of his exploits, Lioba wrote him a charming letter: "To the most reverend Boniface, bearer of the highest dignity and well-beloved in Christ, Lioba, to whom he is related by blood, the least of Christ's handmaids, sends greetings for eternal salvation."

This was the start of beautiful friendship. After corresponding for a full twenty years, Boniface invited Lioba and a group of other nuns to join him in his mission and establish monastic centers for women in Germany. She was delighted to accept this invitation. Along with a group of thirty nuns she traveled to Germany and established a community in Mainz.

Lioba was renowned for her wisdom, piety, and pleasant disposition, and many sought her out for spiritual counsel. After Boniface died as a martyr in Frisia, Lioba lived on for over twenty-five years, and with her monastery she continued to advance the steady evangelization of Germany. When she died in 780 her body was buried in the abbey church of Fulda, according to their common wishes, a short distance from the bones of Boniface.

"I send you this little gift, not because it is worth your consideration but simply so that you may have something to remind you of my humble self; may it draw tighter the bond of true love between us forever."
—St. Lioba to St. Boniface

Saints Michael, Gabriel, Raphael
Archangels

Of the many angels—messengers of God—who appear throughout the Scriptures, only three are named. These archangels, so-called because they deliver messages of supreme importance, are celebrated on this day. Unlike human saints, the very existence of these incorporeal beings is a matter of faith. And yet their deeds are assigned a special place in the history of salvation.

Michael, a warrior, appears in the Book of Revelation, where he leads the armies of God in battle against the forces of evil. The angel Gabriel appears to Zechariah to prophesy the birth of his son John the Baptist, and later he is "sent from God to a city of Galilee named Nazareth, to a virgin betrothed to a man whose name was Joseph, of the house of David; and the virgin's name was Mary." His greeting to Mary resonates to this day: "Hail, O favored one, the Lord is with you." The angel Raphael appears in the Book of Tobit, where he serves as a guide to the young Tobias.

We may not aspire to emulate these holy beings in the same way we do other saints. But we may invoke their aid and invite their assistance in resisting evil, in bearing witness to the good news, in navigating our way through the challenges that beset us, and in finding our way to those we are intended to meet.

"For with God nothing shall be impossible."

—St. Gabriel (Luke 1:37)

Blessed Richard Rolle
Mystic (1300–1349)

Richard Rolle, one of the great mystics who thrived in fourteenth-century England, was born to a prominent family in Yorkshire. At the age of nineteen he left his studies and adopted a solitary life of prayer and devotion. Though his parents thought him mad, he found patrons who set him up in a simple hermitage that remained his home.

Rolle wrote a number of books describing his mystical rapture, an experience of ardent love characterized in terms of "warmth, song, and sweetness." Yet he was capable of acerbic criticism of conditions in the Church and society, challenging the worldliness of many clergy and espousing an ideal of apostolic poverty. Though this caused him difficulties with his bishop, he said, "The more men have raved against me with words of backbiting, so much the more I have grown in spiritual profit."

Despite his solitary life, he was no gloomy misanthrope. He exemplified that "mirth in the love of God" that he attributed to the saints. Having perfected his capacity for contemplation, he found himself equally capable of encountering God among other people or in nature as in solitude. He wrote, "If our love be pure and perfect, whatever our heart loves, it is God."

He died on September 29, 1349, a victim of the Black Death.

"In the beginning . . . I thought I would be like the little bird that for love of its lover longs; but in her longing she is gladdened when he comes that she loves. And joying she sings, and singing she longs, but in sweetness and heat."

—Blessed Richard Rolle

St. Jerome
Monk and Doctor of the Church (331–420)

St. Jerome was one of the great scholars of the Christian Church. Learning, indeed, was his first passion, as later it would be his path to sanctity. In his youth he cared far more for classical poetry than he did for the vulgar Greek of the Gospels. However, after a powerful dream in which God accused him of being more Ciceronian than Christian, he resolved to make a break with the world and devote himself strictly to God's books.

He retreated (with his library) to the wilderness and with the aid of a rabbi undertook the study of Hebrew. With this knowledge, along with his mastery of Greek, he undertook to translate the entire Bible into Latin, the common language of the time. It was an overwhelming project, which occupied most of his life. Disgusted with the luxury of Rome, and the enemies he had incurred through his sarcastic tongue, Jerome embarked for the Holy Land, where he established a monastery in Bethlehem and a free hospice for pilgrims (so that it might never again be said that the Mother of God had to sleep in a stable). For himself he preferred to live in a cave, in which he continued his work of translation and engaged in theological disputation until his death in 420.

His great work, the Vulgate Bible, was the official text of the Church for over 1,500 years.

"Ignorance of scripture is ignorance of Christ."
—St. Jerome

Shusaku Endo
Novelist (1923–1996)

The novelist Shusaku Endo, who was baptized as a child following his parents' divorce, spent much of his life pondering the ambivalence and tension implied in his identity as a Japanese and a Catholic. He later likened his faith to an arranged marriage; he tried several times to leave, but something always held him close.

After a trip to the Holy Land, Endo developed a deep love for the image of the Suffering Servant, despised and rejected. He believed this image of the Christ who made himself nothing, an image of maternal compassion in place of an image of power and judgment, was the image that might touch the Japanese heart. He expanded these reflections in a popular *Life of Jesus*.

Endo is best known for his novel *Silence*, which tells the story of a Portuguese Jesuit in Japan during the time of fiercest persecution. After his own arrest and torture, he is forced to watch a parade of faithful Christians go to their deaths. To spare their lives, he is finally induced to recant and trample on a holy image, after hearing the voice of Christ tell him, "Trample! Trample! I more than anyone know of the pain in your foot. Trample! It was to be trampled on by men that I was born into this world. It was to share men's pain that I carried my cross."

Endo died on September 29, 1996.

"God is not a punishing God, but a God who asks that children be forgiven."

—Shusaku Endo

OCTOBER

1 St. Thérèse of Lisieux • Romano Guardini

2 Agneta Chang • Carlo Carretto

3 St. Theodore Guerin • Blessed Columba Marmion

4 St. Francis of Assisi • Blessed Bartholomew Longo

5 Blessed Francis Xavier Seelos • St. Mary Faustina Kowalska

6 St. Bruno • Blessed Mary Rose Durocher

7 John Woolman • Eileen Egan

8 St. Pelagia the Penitent • Penny Lernoux

9 Blessed John Henry Newman • Mollie Rogers

10 Blessed Angela Truszkowska • Oskar Schindler

11 St. John XXIII • João Bosco Bournier

12 Elizabeth Fry • Caryll Houselander

13 Rabbi Nachman of Breslau • Madeleine Delbrêl

14 St. Callistus • Servant of God Julius Nyerere

15 St. Teresa of Avila • Jules Monchanin

16 St. Hedwig • St. Margaret Mary Alacoque

17 St. Ignatius of Antioch • Ursuline Martyrs of France

18 St. Luke • Mother Antonia Brenner

19 St. Isaac Jogues • Blessed Jerzy Popieluszko

20 Blessed Mary Teresa de Soubiran • St. Mary Bertilla Boscardin

21 St. Ursula and Companions • St. Margaret Clitherow

22 Mother Janet Erskine Stuart • St. John Paul II

23 Maura O'Halloran • Adorers of the Blood of Christ

24 St. Anthony Mary Claret • Rosa Parks

25 Saints Daria and Chrysanthus • The Forty Martyrs of England and Wales

26 Blessed Contardo Ferrini • Sarah and Angelina Grimké

27 St. Severinus Boethius • Henri Perrin

28 St. Simon and St. Jude • Clarence Jordan

29 St. Marcellus • Blessed Restituta Kafka

30 Hadewijch of Brabant • St. Dorothy of Montau

31 St. Alphonsus Rodriguez • Louis Massignon

OCTOBER

St. Thérèse of Lisieux
Carmelite, Doctor of the Church (1873–1897)

Thérèse Martin, a young French nun, seemed driven from her childhood to spiritual greatness. "I would like to perform the most heroic deeds," she wrote. "I feel the courage of a Crusader. I should like to die on the battlefield in defense of the church. If only I were a priest!" This was not to be. In fact, she died of tuberculosis at the age of twenty-four, only nine years after joining an obscure Carmelite convent in Normandy. Ultimately, she came to believe her vocation was nothing less than Charity itself. "In the heart of the Church, who is my Mother, *I will be love.*"

Thérèse translated this mission into a science of sanctification—what she called "The Little Way." This involved performing all her daily actions in the presence and love of God. By this means one could turn any situation into a profound arena for holiness; each moment could become an occasion for heroism and a potential step along the path to sanctity.

She shared her spiritual teachings in an autobiography, composed under obedience. The final chapters were written from her deathbed as she experienced terrible anguish of body and spirit. Toward the end she said, "After my death I will let fall a shower of roses. I will spend my heaven in doing good upon earth."

In 1925, only twenty-eight years after her death, Thérèse was canonized and named the patron of mission. In 1997 she was named a Doctor of the Church.

"Holiness consists simply in doing God's will, and being just what God wants us to be."
—St. Thérèse of Lisieux

Romano Guardini
Priest and Philosopher (1885–1968)

Romano Guardini, who was born in Italy and raised in Germany, experienced a period of spiritual questioning in his youth. When at last his doubts were resolved, he determined to become a priest. But he never lost touch with his own quest for meaning, and he was determined to devise a religious language that took seriously the questions of the modern age.

As a professor in Berlin, Guardini attracted enormous crowds for his lectures, which drew on Scripture, literature, and psychology. Many other theologians and Church officials were disturbed by his disregard for the prescribed neo-Scholastic theology. In its place he proposed a form of Christian humanism, relating the mystery of God to the mysteries of the human heart.

In 1939 Guardini was dismissed by the Nazis for making anti-Hitler statements. He used this "forced retirement" to write books that later spoke to the spiritual hungers of the postwar world. Pope Paul and many of the later Council Fathers were influenced by Guardini's work, and he thus contributed to opening the Church to a new style of Christian teaching. As Cardinal Joseph Ratzinger later put it, "As we are taught by Guardini, the essence of Christianity is not an idea, not a system of thought. . . . The essence of Christianity is a Person: Jesus Christ himself. . . . To become truly real means to come to know Jesus Christ and to learn from him what it means to be human." (Among those he influenced was the future Pope Francis, whose unfinished dissertation focused on the work of Guardini.) He died on October 1, 1968.

"The most important things in human life originate not in the mind alone, but in the heart and its love."

—Romano Guardini

Agneta Chang
Maryknoll Sister and Martyr (1910–1950)

Agneta Chang, who came from a prominent and devoutly Catholic family of Korea, was among the first Koreans to join the American-based Maryknoll Sisters in 1922. In describing the reason for her application, she wrote, "In order to become holy and then to help my country and people." After spending her novitiate in the motherhouse in New York, she was assigned to return to Korea, where she spent a number of peaceful years in parish and catechetical work. This was interrupted by the outbreak of World War II, when the American-born sisters were first imprisoned by the Japanese and then repatriated. Sr. Agneta remained behind, cut off from the outside, as she helped to develop the first Korean women's congregation, the Sisters of Our Lady of Perpetual Help.

Upon the conclusion of the war, with Korea divided at the 38th Parallel, Sr. Agneta and her novices found themselves trapped in the Communist North. Though bedridden as a result of an old injury, Sr. Agneta was ordered to report for mandatory civil defense work. When she could not comply, soldiers loaded her on an oxcart and she was carried away. She was last seen on October 4, 1950. Her last words were, "Lord, have mercy on us." Word later arrived that Sr. Agneta was shot and buried in a nearby ditch.

"Oh miserable night! My heart seemed to shatter and break into a thousand pieces and it seemed pitiless to me that the ground did not cleave open."

—A fellow sister, describing Sr. Agneta's arrest

Carlo Carretto
Little Brother (1910–1988)

Carlo Carretto spent his early life as a leader in Catholic Action, a dynamic lay movement in Italy that sought to advance the religious and social message of the Church. At the age of forty-four, however, he surprised his friends by dispensing with activism and joining the Little Brothers of Jesus, a community of desert contemplatives inspired by the spirituality of Charles de Foucauld. As he explained, he felt summoned by a call from God: "Leave everything and come with me into the desert. It is not your acts and deeds that I want. I want your prayer, your love."

Carretto remained for ten years in the Saharan desert of Algeria before returning to Italy. The publication of his book *Letters from the Desert* established his reputation as one of the most popular spiritual teachers of his time. His writings offered an ascetic, yet joy-filled spirituality available to laypeople in the midst of pressing obligations, the noise of the city, poverty, and even suffering. (He was no stranger to loss. An accident during his novitiate had left him crippled for life.)

Essentially, he showed how to live a contemplative life in the midst of the world, in the desert that is ultimately everywhere. The challenge of the Gospel, according to Carretto, was to create in this desert an oasis of love. He died on the feast of St. Francis, October 4, 1988.

"Love is the synthesis of contemplation and action, the meeting-point between heaven and earth, between God and humanity."

—Carlo Carretto

St. Theodore Guerin
Founder, Sisters of Providence (1798–1856)

In 1840 Mother Theodore Guerin and five fellow Sisters of Providence embarked on a long journey that would take them from their motherhouse in France to "St. Mary-of-the Woods"— at the time, merely a log cabin in the middle of the woods in Indiana. Building on these inauspicious beginnings, the sisters established a thriving community, attracting postulants and drawing eager students from the scattered pioneer families.

Along with cold, hunger, and illness, the greatest trial confronting Mother Guerin turned out to be the campaign of harassment waged by her local bishop. He regarded the community as his personal possession and tried to control its affairs in every detail. She tried at first to regard him charitably as "an excellent father." Never, she said, had she found "a heart more compassionate under an exterior so cold."

Tensions reached the point that Mother Guerin offered to resign as superior. "I love Indiana with my whole soul," she wrote the bishop. "To do good there was my whole ambition; the good God has permitted that you did not wish it. May his will be done." The bishop was not content; he declared she was no longer even a Sister of Providence. He ordered her to leave his diocese and "go elsewhere to hide her disgrace." He furthermore threatened to excommunicate any sister who followed her. Hearing this, the entire community began to pack their bags. But at this point surprising news arrived: the Vatican had appointed a new bishop. Mother Guerin was restored to office, and under her leadership the community prospered.

Mother Guerin was canonized in 2006.

"Let us never forget that if we wish to die like the Saints we must live like them."
—St. Theodore Guerin

Blessed Columba Marmion
Monk and Spiritual Writer (1858–1923)

Columba Marmion, the son of an Irish farmer, was ordained at the age of twenty-three. After passing four years as a parish priest, his bishop allowed him to pursue a calling to monastic life, and he entered the Benedictine Abbey of Maredsous in Belgium. There he flourished in a range of offices, including abbot, but it was for his skills as a preacher, retreat master, and spiritual director that he gradually won renown far beyond the abbey.

With the publication of his book *Christ, the Life of the Soul*, Dom Marmion became one of the most influential spiritual teachers in the Church of his time. Drawing on Scripture, the Church Fathers, and other sources, his writing, which was marked by a lucid and inviting style, endeared him to a wide audience. He taught that the center of spiritual life was simply Christ, whom we know by spending time with him in prayer and by following him in charity toward our neighbor. The aim was holiness, a goal accessible to anyone, not just monks and religious. As he noted, "It is not our PERFECTION (i.e. Good Deeds) which DAZZLE God, since He is surrounded by shining Angels. No! It is our MISERY, our POVERTY, our avowed UNWORTHINESS, which draws down his Mercy upon us, and brings us his ATTENTION."

Dom Marmion died on January 30, 1923. He was beatified in 2000, with a feast on October 3.

"When we consider the Mysteries of the life of Jesus, which of His perfections do we see especially shine out? It is LOVE."

—Blessed Columba Marmion

St. Francis of Assisi
Founder, Friars Minor (1182–1226)

Francis of Assisi was the son of a wealthy cloth merchant. His early life was spent in frivolous enjoyment. But a series of harsh experiences, including war, captivity, and sickness, turned his heart from worldly ambitions. A breakthrough in his life came when he kissed a leper whom he met on the road. Afterward he took to emptying his father's warehouse to give to the poor. When his father publicly upbraided him, he stripped off his fine clothes and vowed henceforth to recognize no other father but God in heaven.

While praying before a crucifix in a ruined chapel, Francis heard a voice commanding him to "repair" the Church. At first he took this quite literally, setting about to rebuild old church ruins. But in time he repaired the Church in a more profound way. Attracting followers, he launched a new order, the Friars Minor, who, in their strict faithfulness to the Gospel—seeking out the poor, the sick, the marginalized, embracing poverty and nonviolence—turned the values of their society upside down.

The stories of his life reflect the joy and freedom that were hallmarks of his spirituality. In his life and in his relationship with the poor, with women, outcasts, and all of creation, Francis represented the emergence of a new model of human and cosmic community. His last years were marked by terrible suffering, including the wounds of the cross that marked his hands and feet. He died on October 3, 1226. His feast day is observed on October 4.

"All praise be yours, my Lord, through those who grant pardon for love of you."
—St. Francis

Blessed Bartholomew Longo
Dominican Tertiary (1841–1926)

Bartholomew Longo studied law at the University of Naples and dabbled in spiritualism before embracing Catholicism. In 1871 he became a Dominican tertiary, receiving the name "Brother Rosary" in recognition of his heartfelt commitment to this devotion. The next year, on a business trip to Pompeii, he was appalled by the level of destitution and the impoverished state of the Church. Describing conditions, he wrote, "In the same dog-hole where the donkey, cow, and pig were, not a few families passed their lives, lying and sleeping on the same dirty litter." He determined to help repair the soul of Pompeii.

His chief method was to promote devotion to the rosary, to this end visiting every home and hovel. He purchased a dilapidated painting of Our Lady of the Rosary, which he restored and installed in a special Marian shrine. This became the headquarters of his campaign. Longo was assisted by a noblewoman, Countess Mariana de Fusco, whom he later married. She commented that the painting was so ugly it appeared to be designed to counter devotion to the rosary. But Longo was undeterred. In fact, the shrine became the site of miraculous healings, and it was later designated a pontifical basilica.

Meanwhile, Longo also established orphanages, schools, housing projects, and other charitable works. And in time he was able to measure the effects of his efforts in the social and spiritual renewal of the city.

Longo died on October 5, 1926. He was beatified in 1980.

"My only desire is to see Mary."

—Final words of Blessed Bartholomew Longo

Blessed Francis Xavier Seelos
Redemptorist (1819–1867)

Soon after joining the Redemptorists in Bavaria, Francis Xavier Seelos was sent in mission to the United States, where his order largely ministered to the German population. After completing his novitiate in Baltimore he was ordained in 1844. His first assignment was to a parish in Pittsburgh where the pastor was St. John Neumann. The parishioners included French, German, and English speakers, both white and black. Fr. Seelos became a popular confessor and preacher. Despite the many demands upon him, he exclaimed, "I cannot thank God enough for my vocation."

In 1860, when the bishop of Pittsburgh was due to retire, he recommended Fr. Seelos as his successor. This proposal ran contrary to Seelos' personal desires. When he subsequently learned that he had been passed over (largely because of anti-German sentiment among Irish-American Catholics) he organized a celebration for the Redemptorist seminarians, declaring, "I would rather be bishop of my students than bishop of Pittsburgh."

During the Civil War he worried that only priests, and not seminarians, were exempt from the draft. When his personal appeal to President Lincoln proved unsuccessful, he persuaded the bishop to protect the seminarians from the draft by ordaining them immediately.

In 1863 he was appointed superior of the Redemptorist "mission band" and traveled throughout the country leading retreats. He died in New Orleans of yellow fever on October 4, 1867. He was beatified in 2000.

"To the abandoned and lost Fr. Francis Xavier preached the message of Jesus Christ . . . and in the long hours spent in the confessional he convinced many to return to God."

—Pope John Paul II

St. Mary Faustina Kowalska
Mystic (1905–1938)

St. Mary Faustina, who was born to a large family in rural Poland, entered a convent of the Sisters of Our Lady of Mercy in Warsaw. Although outwardly there was little to distinguish her from her sisters, privately she enjoyed an extraordinary series of conversations with Jesus, recorded in a diary known only to her confessor. In one vision, she saw Jesus pointing to two bright rays that emanated from his heart—one white and one red. He told her: "These beams signify water and blood. The water that purifies souls; the blood that is the life of the soul. They spring from My heart which was opened on the Cross."

Devotion to God's mercy became the central theme of her spirituality; her central mission, to remind Christians of this mercy. Her superiors, however, doubted her visions, believing she was delusional. Only after her death from tuberculosis did they discover her diary and submit it for examination in Rome. There it was viewed with suspicion and eventually placed on the Index of Forbidden Books. Restoration of her reputation began when Karol Wojtyla became archbishop of Krakow. He initiated an investigation of her holiness and later, as Pope John Paul II, presided over her canonization. At the same time, he proclaimed that the Second Sunday of Easter would be celebrated as "Divine Mercy Sunday."

"Jesus loves hidden souls. A hidden flower is the most fragrant. I must strive to make the interior of my soul a resting place for the Heart of Jesus."
—St. Mary Faustina Kowalska

St. Bruno
Founder, Carthusian Order (ca. 1030–1101)

After achieving early success as a scholar, St. Bruno rose to occupy a number of important Church offices, including chancellor of the diocese of Rheims. At that point, however, he felt called to a new life of prayer, poverty, and withdrawal from the world. With several companions, he applied to one of his former pupils, St. Hugh, bishop of Grenoble, for permission to settle in his diocese. There, in a remote valley called "La Chartreuse," they built an oratory and some cells that became the motherhouse—La Grande Chartreuse—for a new religious order known as the Carthusians.

Though following loosely the Rule of St. Benedict, the Carthusians adopted a more hermit-like style of contemplative life, living alone in their cells, supporting themselves largely by copying books, and gathering for Mass only on Sundays and feast days. Bruno would happily have lived out his days in this manner. But he was eventually summoned by another former pupil, now Pope Urban II, to come to Rome and serve as his councilor. He complied reluctantly, spending the rest of his life in or close to Rome, where he tried to adhere to a spirit of poverty and solitude while assisting the pope in various tasks. He died on October 6, 1101.

The Carthusian Order, it has been said, is the only religious order that has never undergone reform since its founding—so faithfully have its members observed the spirit of their founder.

"Here we strive for that vision by whose clear gaze the bridegroom is wounded with love, and by whose cleanness and purity God is discerned."
—St. Bruno

Blessed Mary Rose Durocher

Founder, Sisters of the Holy Names of Jesus and Mary
(1811–1849)

Eulalie Durocher was born in a village in Quebec on October 6, 1811. Three of her nine siblings became priests. Though she wished to enter religious life she was thwarted by ill health. Instead she spent twelve years assisting one of her brothers in the administration of his parish, organizing efforts to help the poor and providing religious education to children. Over time she became increasingly aware of the lack of educational opportunities in the vast territories beyond Montreal. Having failed in efforts to attract teaching orders from Europe, Durocher eventually won support from her bishop to establish a congregation devoted to the education of the poor.

Durocher, whose own spirituality was based on the imitation of Christ and Mary, named her congregation the Sisters of the Holy Names of Jesus and Mary. The order was formally approved in 1844. Taking the name Mary Rose, Durocher became the superior—an office she held until her death, only five years later. She died on her birthday in 1849 at the age of thirty-eight, after uttering her last words: "Jesus, Mary, Joseph! Sweet Jesus, I love you. Jesus, be to me Jesus!" By that time her congregation had expanded widely in Canada, and later it continued to spread to many other countries. She was beatified in 1982.

"Marie Rose Durocher acted with simplicity, prudence, humility, and serenity. She refused to be halted by her personal problems of health or the initial difficulties of her new-born work. Her secret lay in prayer and self-forgetfulness."
—Pope John Paul II

John Woolman
Quaker (1720–1772)

John Woolman, an American Quaker born in Rancocas, New Jersey, dedicated himself to a continuous effort to heed the dictates of Christ and to apply them in all areas of his life. Above all, he took it as his personal mission to oppose the institution of slavery. He was particularly offended by the knowledge that many fellow Quakers saw no harm in this evil institution. To Woolman's mind, "The only Christian way to treat a slave is to set him free."

Traveling by foot, Woolman undertook a series of ever-widening journeys to admonish slave-owning Quakers. Believing that "conduct is more convincing than language," he would not accept hospitality in the home of a slave owner. Not only was he determined to avoid direct oppression of fellow human beings, but he tried as well to root out indirect enjoyment of exploited labor. He would not eat anything made with sugar or molasses or wear dyed clothes, thus disdaining the products of slave labor in the West Indies.

In 1772 he extended his mission to England, witnessing to Quakers there about the evils of slavery. He caught smallpox and died on October 7, 1772. His journal, published posthumously, became a classic expression of Quaker spirituality, highlighting the practice of simplicity, the obligation to heed the inner voice and to recognize "that which is of God" in each person.

"May we look upon our treasures and the furniture of our houses and the garments in which we array ourselves and try whether the seeds of war have any nourishment in these our possessions, or not."

—John Woolman

Eileen Egan
Peacemaker (1912–2000)

Though never so well known as her friends Dorothy Day or Mother Teresa of Calcutta, Eileen Egan, in her own quiet way, was a remarkably effective force for peace. Her abhorrence of war came through firsthand experience. In 1943 she joined the newly formed Catholic Relief Services. Her experience with refugees and desperate human need led to her conclusion that war—no matter the cause—was a diabolical force, contrary to the spirit of the Gospel. Her mission was based on the essential insight that each suffering person is "Jesus in disguise."

At Vatican II she lobbied for a condemnation of nuclear war, which came to pass in the final session of the Council. As a representative for CRS at the United Nations in 1969, she first introduced a resolution to recognize conscientious objection as a universal right. She was alive in 1987 to see this resolution adopted. As one of the founders of Pax Christi USA, she pushed the U.S. bishops to take a stand against the Vietnam War. She was a key advisor to the American bishops in preparing their 1983 pastoral letter on peace, which recognized Gospel nonviolence as an authentic Catholic tradition. It was she who coined the term "seamless garment" to refer to a consistent ethic of life—a phrase later adopted by Cardinal Joseph Bernardin.

Egan spent her life behind the scenes, talking, listening, attending meetings, fostering channels of dialogue that ultimately yielded unexpected fruits. At the age of eighty she was violently mugged and suffered a broken hip. Her only concern was for the poor young man who had attacked her. She died on October 7, 2000, at the age of eighty-eight.

"My life has had a single strain: to see Jesus in every human being."

—Eileen Egan

St. Pelagia the Penitent
(ca. Fourth Century)

The original Pelagia was a young Christian girl in Antioch who died in the fourth century. Her name was gradually attached to another saint, whose story has far less basis in history. According to legend, Pelagia was a beautiful courtesan in Antioch. One day she happened to be riding on a white donkey, bedecked in lavish jewels, when she passed a church synod where one of the bishops, Nonnus, was holding forth. Pointing her out to his fellow bishops he said she bore a significant lesson: "She goes to an infinity of trouble to keep herself beautiful and to perfect her dancing, to please men, but we are considerably less zealous in the care of our dioceses and of our own souls."

Whatever effect these words had on the bishops, they touched Pelagia deeply. The next day she sought out Nonnus in the basilica and asked for baptism and forgiveness of her sins. After distributing all her property to the poor, she departed from the city. The legend relates that she made her way to Jerusalem, where she dressed in men's clothes, retired to a cave on the Mount of Olives, and was revered by the people as Pelagius, a "beardless monk," until her death.

"I have heard that your God came down to earth not for the sake of the righteous but to save sinners. . . . If you really are a true disciple of Christ do not turn your face away from me, for through you I long to see the Savior and get a glimpse of his holy face."

—St. Pelagia

Penny Lernoux
Journalist (1940–1989)

In the 1970s Christians around the world became aware of two related stories in Latin America. One was about the spread of terror under brutal military dictatorships. The other concerned the transformation of the Latin American Church, traditionally an ally of the rich, now emerging as a prophetic champion of human rights and the cause of the poor. These stories converged in the repression and martyrdom of countless Christians.

Penny Lernoux, an American journalist based in Latin America, was among those who helped to tell these stories. She had drifted away from the Catholicism of her childhood. But her encounter in the early 1970s with priests, nuns, and missioners living in solidarity with the poor had renewed her faith and determined the form of her vocation as a journalist.

While other journalists pursued a Cold War narrative of the battle against communism, Lernoux told the story of Latin America from the standpoint of the poor. Her writings became a critical link between the churches and peoples of North and South America. She herself became a witness, a voice for the voiceless, and a hero to many who depended on her courage in reporting the truth.

Lernoux died on October 8, 1989, soon after receiving a diagnosis of cancer. Walking this final path, she said, was a new chance to experience the helplessness of the poor and "the ultimate powerlessness of Christ."

"You can look at a slum or peasant village, but it is only by entering into that world—by living in it—that you begin to understand what it is like to be powerless, to be like Christ."

—Penny Lernoux

Blessed John Henry Newman
Theologian (1801–1890)

John Henry Newman spent the first half of his life as a distinguished Anglican priest. A leader of the High-Church Oxford movement, his research on the development of doctrine led him to a famous conversion to Catholicism. After studies in Rome he was ordained as a Catholic priest and returned to England to establish an Oratory of St. Philip Neri in working-class Birmingham. His writings were enormously influential in combating anti-Catholic prejudice in England.

At the same time he found himself embroiled in controversies in his own Church. Although he was deeply conservative in his temperament, Newman's writings on such topics as the primacy of conscience, the role of the laity, his nonscholastic approach to theology, and his spirit of tolerance contrasted with the reactionary mood of the Church in his time. He was scorned by many Catholic contemporaries as a dangerous liberal, and negative reports of his work were frequently sent to Rome. Nevertheless, he received some vindication in his own lifetime, when a new pope, Leo XIII, made it one of his first acts to name Newman a cardinal. He chose as his motto, "Heart speaks to heart."

Newman is remembered as one of the most attractive figures of his age and as someone who embodied values consonant with the modern Catholic sensibility—particularly his appreciation for the spiritual integrity of the intellectual life. Pope Paul VI said that Vatican II was "Newman's Council." He was beatified in 2010.

"Lead Kindly Light . . . I do not ask to see the distant scene, one step enough for me."
—Blessed John Henry Newman

Mollie Rogers
Founder, Maryknoll Sisters (1882–1955)

Mollie Rogers, founder of the Maryknoll Sisters, dated the beginning of her vocation to a summer evening at Smith College when a crowd of her fellow students rushed outdoors singing "Onward Christian Soldiers." They had just signed the Student Volunteer pledge to go to China as Protestant missionaries. Mollie shared their exhilaration, mixed with regret that there was no similar Catholic mission group.

Her prayers were answered several years later when she met Fr. James A. Walsh, who, along with Fr. Thomas Price, planned to establish a mission seminary—Maryknoll. Mollie volunteered to help launch this project. Eventually, she and a small group of women who joined her won approval to found a new religious congregation—the Maryknoll Sisters—with Mollie, now Mother Mary Joseph, as superior. Their aim was not simply to serve as helpers to the priests but to engage in their own overseas work of evangelization and service. It was a radical departure from traditional, enclosed religious life. Mother Mary Joseph stressed the importance of flexibility and individuality. She didn't want the sisters' work "to be hampered by an over-regimented and parceled-out prayer life."

From mission work among Japanese immigrants in California, to China, Korea, and eventually throughout the world, the work of the Maryknoll Sisters spread. At the time of Rogers's death on October 9, 1955, there were 1,100 Maryknoll Sisters serving worldwide. They marked their centenary in 2012.

"Love, work, prayer, and suffering will sustain us in the future as they have in the past. All who are here now, all who will come after us, will have no other tools than these with which to build."

—Mollie Rogers

Blessed Angela Truszkowska
Founder, Felician Sisters (1825–1899)

Camille Sophia Truszkowska, who later took the religious name Mother Angela, was born in Poland to an educated, middle-class family. Her father was a juvenile court judge, and he encouraged Camille's acute social conscience and her interest in the causes of poverty and injustice. At the age of twenty-three she underwent what she called her "conversion," the beginning of an intense life of prayer and devotion. Though she considered entering a contemplative order, she perceived that her vocation was to be of service to the suffering poor. Joining the St. Vincent de Paul Society, she spent her time visiting and befriending those on the margins.

In 1855 she and a companion took a vow before the icon of Our Lady, pledging themselves to the will of God in all things. This became the foundation of the Sisters of St. Felix, a name inspired by a local Franciscan shrine. The works of the congregation, the first in Poland to combine action and contemplation, were wide ranging, involving care for orphans, social centers, and hospitals.

At the age of forty-four, Mother Angela retired from leadership and devoted herself quietly to prayer. She lived on for thirty years, much of the time suffering in poor health. Her community, meanwhile, continued to grow, even sending sisters to North America. She died on October 10, 1899. She was beatified by Pope John Paul II in 1993.

"Do not discriminate among the sick. Give aid to all without exception; your vocation obliges you not to exclude anyone, for everybody is your neighbor."
—Blessed Angela Truszkowska

Oskar Schindler
"Righteous Gentile" (1908–1974)

Among the heroes of the Holocaust, the German industrialist Oskar Schindler is a curious case. Not a man of evident faith or even conventional virtue, he was in fact an opportunist, a philanderer, and a member of the Nazi Party who made a fortune employing Jewish slave labor in occupied Poland. But at some point his moral compass shifted. His factory became a haven; the rescue and preservation of "his Jews" became, in fact, his only real business.

To this end he used his considerable wiles, desperately widening the tenuous circle of life. The personal dangers he faced only emboldened him in his audacious mission. As the Jewish population in Poland was steadily decimated, Schindler transferred his arms factory and his entire workforce of 1,100 to Czechoslovakia. The factory was a con game. Though guarded by SS troops and run with apparent efficiency, it produced nothing. Schindler spent his entire fortune to keep the operation running until May 1945 when the war ended. He shamed the guards into disobeying their orders to exterminate the surviving workers.

No one, least of all "Schindler's Jews," doubts that what he did was good. But *why* did he do it? His Catholic upbringing supplies no clear explanation. He lived the rest of his life in obscurity. But as his story became known he was inducted into the list of Righteous Gentiles. After his death in 1974 he was buried, by his request, in Jerusalem.

"He who saves one life saves the entire world."

—Words from the Talmud, inscribed in a gold ring
presented to Schindler by his Jewish workers

St. John XXIII
Pope (1881–1963)

On October 28, 1958, a new pope greeted the Church from the balcony overlooking St. Peter's Square. There stood the smiling, rotund figure of Angelo Giuseppe Roncalli, the son of peasants and recently the patriarch of Venice. "I am called John," he said.

In appearance and in almost every other respect Pope John XXIII stood in contrast with his gaunt and otherworldly predecessor. Gregarious and open, John exuded an enthusiasm for life that in itself set a positive tone for his pontificate and raised hopes for a season of change. These hopes were answered by the astonishing announcement that he intended to convene an ecumenical council, the first in almost a hundred years. He spoke of the need to "open the windows" of the Church and to let in fresh air. It was the signal of an extraordinary renewal, an era of openness and positive dialogue between the Church and the modern world.

Having launched Vatican II, Pope John did not live to see it completed. Dying of cancer, he retained his humor and humility. "My bags are packed," he said, "and I am ready to go." He died on June 3, 1963. In a few brief years he had won the hearts of the world, and his passing was universally mourned. He was canonized in April 2014.

"In convening the Second Vatican Council, Saint John XXIII showed an exquisite openness to the Holy Spirit. *He let himself be led and he was for the Church a pastor, a servant-leader. This was his great service to the Church; he was* the pope of openness to the Holy Spirit."

—Pope Francis, at the canonization of St. John XXIII

João Bosco Bournier
Jesuit Martyr of Brazil (1917–1976)

João Bosco Bournier entered the Jesuits with dreams of serving in the overseas mission. Instead he was assigned for nearly thirty years to administrative duties that brought little sense of fulfillment. He prayed for some deliverance. At last in 1966 he was assigned to be a missionary—not overseas, but in the frontier region of Mato Grosso, a newly created region carved out of the Amazon jungle. For wealthy cattle barons there were fortunes to be made. But for landless peasants who provided the labor, existence was little removed from bondage.

In this context Bournier had to rethink everything he had learned about theology. He concluded that his task was not just to administer the sacraments but to advance the cause of human dignity and justice. He was fortunate to find in his bishop, Pedro Casaldáliga, one of the true prophets of Latin America. Together they visited the most remote villages in the diocese. On October 11, 1976, they set off to a local jail to intercede for two peasant women who were incarcerated.

Outside the jail they confronted the police, who responded contemptuously, calling them "commies." When one of them struck Bournier with his gun, it discharged, shooting the priest in the head. "I've finished my course," he whispered. "Dom Pedro, we've come to the end of the job together."

"In this place was assassinated Father João Bosco Bournier, for defending the liberty of the poor. He died, like Jesus Christ, offering his life for our liberation."

—Inscription on a cross erected on the site of Fr. Bournier's death

Elizabeth Fry
Quaker Reformer (1780–1845)

Elizabeth Fry was born into a prosperous English Quaker family. At seventeen she encountered a Quaker abolitionist from the United States who stimulated her desire to pursue a path of godly service. Afterward, she wrote, "I wish the state of enthusiasm I am now in may last, for today I have felt there is a God."

After marriage her life was absorbed in the responsibilities of a growing family. She bore eleven children. But after twelve years she felt that she was missing out on her true vocation, noting, "I fear that my life is slipping away to little purpose."

Soon after this she made her first visit to Newgate Prison, where the horrid conditions filled her with shame and indignation: women and children crowded into fetid cells, in rags and filth, sleeping on the floor. This was the beginning of a cause that would occupy Fry for the rest of her life. With the support of a committee of other Quaker women, she launched a campaign for prison reform. Her efforts were criticized by those who felt that by humanizing prisons she was undermining their deterrent value. But Fry was motivated by the conviction that prisoners, regardless of their crimes, were human beings who bore within them the spark of the divine image. It was sacrilege to treat them with no more than punitive cruelty.

She pursued her cause tirelessly until her death on October 12, 1845.

"Oh Lord, may I be directed what to do and what to leave undone."

—Elizabeth Fry

Caryll Houselander
Mystic (1901–1954)

Caryll Houselander, an English laywoman, had a very definite sense of her vocation: to awaken others to the presence of Christ in the world. This conviction was implanted from her childhood by a series of mystical experiences that continued throughout her life. The most striking of these visions occurred as an adult, while she stood on a crowded underground train in London. As she looked at the people around her, "quite suddenly I saw with my mind, but as vividly as a wonderful picture, Christ in them all . . . living in them, dying in them, rejoicing in them, sorrowing in them." When she left the train "it was the same here, on every side, in every passerby, everywhere—Christ." This vision lasted intensely for several days and altered her life completely.

Houselander supported herself by woodcarving and decorating churches. Later she wrote poetry and children's books. Her true mission, however, consisted in her relationships with others—not just friends, but strangers, neurotics, friendless people whom others avoided. Simply through attention and friendship, she sought to awaken them to a sense of their own divine spark. Eventually her writing mission took over. During the Second World War she offered a message of consolation to those struggling with their faith, sharing the good news that Christ was truly present in the sufferings of the world. She died of breast cancer on October 12, 1954.

"Christ asks for a home in your soul . . . where you and he, alone together, can laugh and be silent and be delighted with one another."

—Caryll Houselander

Rabbi Nachman of Breslau
Hasidic Master (1772–1810)

Rabbi Nachman of Breslau was the great-grandson of the Baal Shem Tov, founder of Hasidic Judaism. The Hasidim, or "pious ones," celebrated the holiness of everyday life in the belief that each moment contains a spark of the divine awaiting discovery.

Rabbi Nachman was born in a village in Ukraine. From his earliest childhood he exhibited a deep thirst for the divine, and by the time he married, at the age of thirteen, he had already begun to attract followers. Traveling from village to village, he spread his teachings through stories and parables that reflected the mystical wisdom of Scripture and its application in daily life. He stressed the importance of joy in the spiritual life and encouraged his followers to spend an hour a day conversing with God, "as you would with your close friend." Each person, he taught, has the potential to become a *tzaddik* (a saintly/righteous person).

In 1802 he settled in the town of Breslau. Thousands would travel to hear him preach, his reflections often enlivened by poetry and song "to arouse people from their slumber." He died of tuberculosis on October 16, 1810. The line of his followers never selected a successor but continue to this day to look to him as their rabbi.

"God, I stand beaten and battered by the countless manifestations of my own inadequacies. Yet we must live with joy. . . . Aid me in this quest, O God. Help me find satisfaction and a deep, abiding pleasure in all that I have, in all that I do, in all that I am."

—Rabbi Nachman of Breslau

Madeleine Delbrêl
Missionary and Activist (1904–1964)

Madeleine Delbrêl was the daughter of a French railroad worker. In her youth she considered becoming a nun but decided her vocation was in the world, among "ordinary" people. "We, the ordinary people of the streets, believe that this street, this world, where God has placed us, is our place of holiness." In the secularized world of the working class she conceived the need for a new type of missionary—a "missionary without a boat"—not traveling overseas, but crossing the borders of faith to bear witness to the Gospel in friendship and solidarity.

With several friends she established a small lay community in Ivry, a working-class city near Paris and a stronghold of the Communist Party. Over time they won many friends. During World War II the city government even asked Delbrêl to oversee social services. Later, she served as lay advisor to a new movement of "worker priests" who worked in factories alongside the poor. (The movement was eventually suppressed.)

She called her spiritual discipline the "Prayer of the Agenda"— a heightened awareness of the presence of God in all the ordinary activities of life, whether meeting people or answering the phone. In this awareness, a person could experience the deepest spiritual dimension of life.

She embraced Vatican II and its affirmation of the vocation of the laity but did not live to see its conclusion. She died on October 13, 1964.

"Each tiny act is an extraordinary event, in which heaven is given to us, in which we are able to give heaven to others."

—Madeleine Delbrêl

St. Callistus
Pope and Martyr (d. 222)

St. Callistus began life as the slave of a Christian. He fled his master, following the failure of a financial enterprise with which he had been entrusted. After being quickly apprehended he was sent to the Sardinian mines, where he languished for some years. After his release he found a position with Pope St. Zephyrinus as superintendent of a Christian cemetery on the Appian Way. Zephyrinus ordained him a deacon and made him a trusted advisor.

In 217 when the pope died, Callistus, remarkably, was elected to replace him. His election prompted bitter opposition from Hippolytus, a priest of Rome and a rival candidate. His opposition only stiffened in the face of what he deemed the overlaxity and mercifulness of Callistus's approach to sinners. The pope admitted murderers and adulterers back to communion after they had performed public penance. He allowed priests to marry and ordained twice- and even thrice-married men to the clergy. He recognized marriages between free women and slaves, a violation of Roman law. He welcomed converts from heretical or schismatic sects into the Church. All this offended Hippolytus's image of the Church as the ark of the saints.

Despite these attacks, Callistus never tried to silence Hippolytus—even when he had himself consecrated as a rival pope. But the reign of Callistus was short—only five years. He was apparently killed in a riot and so was included in the list of papal martyrs.

"We should not do unto others what we would not that they should do unto us."
—Motto of St. Callistus

Servant of God Julius Nyerere
President of Tanzania (1922–1999)

In 2005 the Catholic diocese of Musoma initiated the cause for canonization of Julius Nyerere, who served as president of Tanzania from its independence in 1961 until his retirement in 1985. Politics and "heroic virtue" are a rare combination. But Nyerere was an unusual man. Born the son of a chief (one of twenty-six children), he was educated in Catholic schools and converted to Catholicism when he was twenty. Originally a schoolteacher, he entered politics and helped lead his country to independence without bloodshed.

As president of Tanzania, he maintained a simple lifestyle, attended daily Mass, and strived to create a model of development for his country based on African cultural values—*ujaama*, or "familyhood." Widely admired for his integrity and commitment to social justice, he was called the "conscience" of Africa, and he challenged the Church to assume greater leadership in the struggle for justice. Upon leaving office—the rare African leader to relinquish office voluntarily—he retired to his family farm. He continued to work for peace in Africa and debt relief for impoverished countries until his death in 1999.

"We, the people of Tanganyika, would like to light a candle and put it on the top of Mount Kilimanjaro which would shine beyond our borders giving hope where there was despair, love where there was hate and dignity where before there was only humiliation. . . . We cannot, unlike other countries, send rockets to the moon, but we can send rockets of love and hope to all our fellow men wherever they may be."
—Julius Nyerere

St. Teresa of Avila
Mystic, Doctor of the Church (1515–1582)

Teresa was the daughter of a wealthy Spanish merchant. Though she became a nun at twenty, her vocation initially had little to do with the love of God. The Carmelite convent in Avila was quite lax—more a boardinghouse for wealthy maidens than a house of prayer. At the age of thirty-nine, however, Teresa experienced a powerful conversion. Filled with loathing for her spiritual mediocrity, she determined to devote herself more seriously to prayer—and more, to establish a new reformed Carmelite community.

Her campaign of reform became the foundation for the Discalced (shoeless) Carmelites—a reference to their strict poverty. Given that she was a woman and a reformer who based her authority on private visions, Teresa's activities entailed considerable risk. In fact, she was subjected to investigation by the Inquisition. Nevertheless, she surmounted all obstacles, including sickness, hunger, and poverty, sustained by an extraordinarily intense communion with God.

Teresa could be at turns charming, imperious, irreverent, and impossible, depending on the circumstances and the provocation. But there was little doubt among any she encountered that her courage and wisdom were rooted in a special relationship with God. Apart from the communities she established, she produced several classic volumes of mystical theology. By any standard she was one of the towering figures of her age and of all Christian history. She died in 1582 and was canonized forty years later. In 1970 she was the first woman named a Doctor of the Church.

"Prayer is nothing but friendly intercourse, and frequent solitary converse, with Him who we know loves us."

—St. Teresa of Avila

Jules Monchanin
Monk (1895–1957)

Jules Monchanin, a French priest, was one of the great twentieth-century pioneers in Hindu-Christian dialogue. His interest in Eastern religion began in seminary, when he happened upon a book on Buddhism. Later, while serving as a parish priest, he began to study Hinduism. But it was many years later, and only after a near-fatal illness, that he resolved to continue his exploration in India. In 1939, with the blessing of his bishop, and an invitation from the bishop of Tamil Nadu, he departed for India. While living a contemplative life, he immersed himself in the study of Sanskrit and dreamed of founding a Christian ashram that would integrate Christianity with elements of Indian culture—hoping that "what is deepest in Christianity may be grafted into what is deepest in India."

In 1948 he was joined by Henri Le Saux, a French Benedictine, who later took the name Swami Abhishiktananda. Together they founded Saccidananda Ashram at Shantivanam. Dressed in the ochre robes of Indian holy men, they adopted a vegetarian diet and incorporated Sanskrit prayers in their worship. Monchanin's initial goal was to "grasp the authentic Hindu search for God in order to Christianize it, starting with ourselves first of all, from within."

Their efforts had little impact on their Hindu neighbors, but Monchanin felt that in the deep spiritual wells of India he was able to connect more deeply with the true mystical sources of Christianity. Monchanin died on October 10, 1957.

"May India take me and bury me within itself—in God."

—Jules Monchanin

St. Hedwig
Widow (ca. 1174–1243)

S t. Hedwig, who was born in Bavaria to a noble family, was betrothed at the age of twelve to Henry, duke of Silesia, then eighteen. Though he did not approach his wife's piety, he supported Hedwig's efforts to establish a number of hospitals and monasteries in Silesia, including the first convent for women. Despite her elevated status, Hedwig adopted an austere and ascetic life, wearing a hair shirt beneath her fine clothing and walking barefoot to church, regardless of snow and ice.

Hedwig and Henry had seven children, the source of many worries. A dispute between two of their sons resulted in a major battle. Henry too was often called away by military engagements. As for Hedwig, she tried at all times to promote peace; in at least one case she successfully averted a war. In 1238 she suffered the loss of both her husband and her eldest son. Despite her sorrow, she shed no tears on the occasion of this or any other loss.

Soon after, while not taking formal vows, she put on a religious habit. In this manner she continued to administer her property on behalf of the poor. In her later years she was gifted with prophecy and credited with many miracles. She died in October 1243.

"Would you oppose the will of God? Our lives are His. Our will is whatever He is pleased to ordain, whether our own death or that of our friends."

—St. Hedwig, upon learning of the death of her husband and son

St. Margaret Mary Alacoque
Nun and Mystic (1647–1690)

St. Margaret Mary, a Visitation nun who lived in seventeenth-century France, was largely responsible for popularizing devotion to the Sacred Heart of Jesus. It was soon after her entry into the Visitation convent at Paray-le-Monial that she received the first of a series of revelations from Jesus. He told her that she would be the instrument for spreading the love of his Sacred Heart—an emblem of God's love and compassion for humanity—and making it known in the world.

The young nun's superiors were not persuaded by her reports of these visions. Instead, they treated her with disdain. A panel of theologians determined she was delusional. Eventually, however, she won the support of a new confessor, St. Claude La Colombière, who fully embraced her message and encouraged her to continue with her mission. Nevertheless, her presence in the community continued to provoke mixed feelings, with many of the sisters believing the worst about her.

St. Margaret Mary died on October 17, 1690. The Feast of the Sacred Heart of Jesus was established in 1856 by Pope Pius IX. Margaret Mary was canonized in 1920, and in a 1928 encyclical, Pope Pius XI affirmed the credibility of her visions.

"The divine heart is an ocean full of all good things wherein poor souls can cast all their needs; it is an ocean full of joy to drown all our sadness . . . an ocean of love in which to submerge our poverty."
—St. Margaret Mary Alacoque

St. Ignatius of Antioch
Bishop and Martyr (d. ca. 107)

St. Ignatius became bishop of Antioch in Syria toward the end of the first century. Arrested during the persecution of Christians under the emperor Trajan, he was condemned to fight with wild beasts in Rome. This required his transport in chains by an overland route that took him through Asia Minor. During this journey he was able to meet with representatives from the local churches, some of whom traveled great distances to pray with him.

Ignatius also wrote seven letters, which provide an unusually intimate portrait of his faith and of his struggle to interpret his impending martyrdom in the light of Christ's passion and death. "Let me be fodder for wild beasts. . . . Then I shall be a real disciple of Jesus Christ when the world sees my body no more." Rather than boasting in his courage, Ignatius's letters show him steeling himself against his fears. He believed that his life and death did not belong to himself alone. It was his responsibility as a bishop to strengthen the faith of his flock, and his ultimate concern was that he not give scandal by doubting the teaching of the resurrection. "We have not only to be called Christians," he wrote, "but to *be* Christians." He died in the amphitheater in Rome.

"If what our Lord did is a sham, so is my being in chains. Why, then, have I given myself up completely to death, fire, sword, and wild beasts? For the simple reason that near the sword means near God."
—St. Ignatius of Antioch

Ursuline Martyrs of France
(1794)

For over a hundred years the Ursuline Sisters maintained a convent and religious school in Valenciennes in northeast France. When the Revolution of 1789 suppressed religious houses the sisters moved to a sister house across the border in Austrian Netherlands (now Belgium). After the Austrians occupied Valenciennes, the sisters felt it was safe to return and resume their life. But when the French retook the town, they charged the Ursulines as illegal émigrés who were running religious schools without permission. The sisters were arrested and imprisoned. In their trial they openly admitted that they had returned to practice and share the Catholic religion with their neighbors, and they were sentenced to death.

Eleven sisters were beheaded in the public square. Whereas the execution of counterrevolutionaries was often greeted with jeering, in this case the crowd was silent. The only sound, interrupted by the falling blade of the guillotine, was from the sisters themselves, who sang the Litany of Our Lady. Eleven Ursuline nuns were beatified as martyrs in 1920. They included a lay sister, Cordule Barré, who had escaped arrest but who stepped out of the crowd to join her sisters on the tumbril and was executed along with the rest. They were among the last victims of the Terror.

"We die for the faith of the Catholic, Apostolic, and Roman Church."
—Blessed Mary Clotilde Paillot, Mother Superior

St. Luke
Evangelist (First Century)

S t. Luke was the author of one of the four Gospels as well as the Acts of the Apostles. From references in the letters of St. Paul it is supposed that he was a Gentile Christian who accompanied Paul on many of his journeys and who attended him faithfully during his final days of imprisonment. In one letter Paul refers to "Luke, the beloved physician," a phrase that has prompted the traditional depiction of Luke as a doctor.

Luke's Gospel is marked by a special concern for the poor, the marginalized, women, and social outcasts. His account of the nativity, with its stress on the faith of Mary, emphasizes the humbleness of Jesus' birth and its significance in fulfilling the hopes of the poor. It is in Luke's Gospel that Jesus preaches, "Blessed are the poor," and where we find the parable of the rich man and the poor beggar Lazarus, offering such a striking image of the relation between mercy and justice in this life and in the life to come.

Of all the evangelists, Luke had the most vital sense of God's presence in ongoing history. That is why his story does not end with the resurrection of Jesus but continues with Pentecost, the missionary journeys of Paul, and the ongoing story of Christ's presence in the life of the Church and in the midst of the world.

"It seemed good to me also . . . to write an orderly account for you, most excellent Theophilus, that you may know the truth concerning the things of which you have been informed."

—St. Luke (1:3-4)

Mother Antonia Brenner
"Prison Angel" (1926–2013)

Mother Antonia Brenner, who died on October 17, 2013, spent nearly thirty years in prison, though she had committed no crime. Instead, responding to a call from God, she had abandoned her life in Beverly Hills, taken religious vows, and voluntarily entered the La Mesa prison in Tijuana, Mexico, to live there as an inmate and to minister to those behind bars.

She was born Mary Clarke to a very different life. Twice married and divorced, she raised seven children. In 1969, after Jesus appeared to her in a dream, she determined to devote her life to his service. While going through her second divorce a priest had invited her to help in his prison ministry at La Mesa—an overcrowded prison that housed eight thousand inmates.

After years of visiting the prison and performing small acts of charity she felt that God was calling her to something more. As no religious order would accept a fifty-year-old divorced woman, she sewed her own habit and took private religious vows. Eventually she received permission to move into a cell in the women's section of the prison. "I felt as if I'd come home," she said. In the prison she walked freely among murderers, gang members, and other desperate criminals. Her loving presence often quelled violence. She was known as the "Prison Angel," or simply Mama.

"Happiness does not depend on where you are. I live in prison. And I have not had a day of depression in 25 years. I have been upset, angry. I have been sad. But never depressed. I have a reason for my being."
—Mother Antonia Brenner

St. Isaac Jogues
Jesuit Martyr (1607–1646)

Fr. Isaac Jogues arrived in New France in 1636, one of a company of French Jesuits who volunteered for a perilous mission among the Indians. Apart from the difficulties of language, the harsh environment, and the Indians' natural distrust of Europeans, these Jesuit "Blackrobes," as they were called, also had to contend with the state of perpetual warfare among the tribes of the region. In 1642 Jogues was captured by a war party of Mohawks. He was subjected to terrible tortures and kept as a slave for many months before escaping and making his way back to France.

In Paris, where he was acclaimed as a national hero, Jogues experienced a second ordeal. He begged permission to return to the Mohawks, to carry on the work of evangelization and to offer his life, if necessary, for their salvation. The Jesuits acceded to his wish and obtained for him a special gift: a papal dispensation from the canonical rubrics, allowing him to celebrate Mass despite his mutilated fingers.

Eventually Jogues returned to the very village where he had been held captive. At first he was received respectfully. But when crop failures were followed by a deadly epidemic, suspicion fell on the Blackrobe, and he was beaten to death.

Jogues and several companions are commemorated as the first North American Martyrs.

"We begged God to accept our lives and our blood and unite them to His life and His blood for the salvation of these tribes."

—St. Isaac Jogues

Blessed Jerzy Popieluszko
Priest and Martyr (1947–1984)

The end of the communist era in Eastern Europe began in June 1979 when John Paul II, the newly elected pope from Poland, returned to his homeland for the first of three visits. As communist authorities stood by helplessly, millions turned out to hear the pontiff's message: "Do not be afraid to insist on your rights. Refuse a life based on lies and double thinking. Do not be afraid to suffer with Christ." Within a year of his visit the militant Solidarity trade union movement was born.

Fr. Jerzy Popieluszko had not previously taken an active part in politics. But when steelworkers in Warsaw chose to support the striking ship workers in Gdansk he volunteered to celebrate Mass at their factory. It was a turning point in his life. The workers' struggle for justice, he realized, was truly a spiritual struggle. He became their chaplain.

Fr. Jerzy accompanied the Solidarity struggle through martial law and persecution. Though he himself was repeatedly interrogated and threatened with arrest, he refused to seek asylum abroad. "The priest is called to bear witness to the truth," he said, "to suffer for the truth, and if need be to give up his life for it."

On October 19, 1984, he was abducted by security police, beaten, and drowned in a reservoir. Five years later, in the first free elections in Poland, a Solidarity government was elected. Fr. Jerzy was beatified in 2010.

"It is not enough for a Christian to condemn evil, cowardice, lies, and use of force, hatred, and oppression. He must at all times be a witness to and defender of justice, goodness, truth, freedom, and love. He must never tire of claiming these values as a right both for himself and others."
—Blessed Jerzy Popieluszko

Blessed Mary Teresa de Soubiran
Founder, Society of St. Mary the Helper (1835–1889)

Sophia Thérèse de Soubiran felt an early attraction to religious life. In 1864, after spending years in a community of laywomen who took temporary vows, she founded a new congregation—the Society of St. Mary the Helper, dedicated to saving souls through practical work. Houses sprang up in France and then in England, with work that ranged from the care of orphans to teaching the poor and establishing hostels for young working women.

As Mother Mary Teresa, she spent over twenty-five happy years as superior of her community. But then her story took a bizarre turn. In 1871 the congregation elected an assistant mother general, Mother Mary Frances, whose charisma masked a disturbing will to power. She managed to wrest control of the congregation, deposed Mother Mary Teresa, and ultimately succeeded in having her expelled from her own congregation. She was forced to relinquish her habit and forbidden any contact with her sisters.

And so, in 1874, Mother Mary Teresa was suddenly a laywoman, forced to begin life over again. Eventually she found another congregation willing to take her in. But she suffered terribly from her dejection and from reports of the steady decline, under the usurper, of the congregation she had founded. She died of tuberculosis in 1889. Soon after this, in another strange twist, Mother Mary Frances herself abandoned the congregation. Under her successor the memory of Mother Mary Teresa was restored to a place of honor. She was beatified in 1946.

"I love God's plans and I am as nothing before His holy and incomprehensible will."
—Blessed Mary Teresa de Soubiran

St. Mary Bertilla Boscardin
Nun (1888–1922)

St. Mary Bertilla Boscardin was raised in a poor peasant family in northern Italy. Slightly built and without any distinctive qualities, she attracted little attention; among her companions she was known as "the goose." At fifteen, after deciding to enter religious life, she finally found a community willing to accept her: the Sisters of St. Dorothy at Vicenza, who deemed her well-enough suited to peel potatoes. She spent many years working in the laundry and the kitchen until finally, during an emergency, she was permitted to nurse the sick in the order's hospital. There her true gifts were allowed to flourish.

During the war in 1915 the hospital was taken over by the military. Bertilla remained by the wounded throughout bombardment. "Here I am, Lord," she wrote, "to do your will whatever comes, be it life, death, or terror." After the war, when she was put in charge of a children's ward, she wrote, "Dear Mother, I do not ask you for visions or revelations, or favors, even spiritual ones. . . . In this life I want only what you want; just to believe, without any proof or enjoyment, and to suffer joyfully without any consolation . . . to work hard for you until I die."

By the time of her death on October 20, 1922, Mary Bertilla was recognized by her community and by many who experienced her care as a woman of rare spiritual depth and heroic goodness. She was canonized in 1961.

"I'm a poor thing, a goose. Teach me. I want to become a saint."

—St. Mary Bertilla Boscardin, to her first novice mistress

St. Ursula and Companions
Martyrs (ca. Fourth or Fifth Century)

An inscription from the fourth or fifth century on the Church of St. Ursula in Cologne records the site of a massacre of holy virgins. Upon this text, several centuries later, the legend of St. Ursula began to take shape. It was related that St. Ursula was the daughter of a Christian king in Roman Britain. When told she must marry a pagan king, she asked that she might have a delay of three years to sail the seas with eleven noble ladies, each accompanied by a thousand handmaidens. Their ship landed in Gaul, from whence they embarked on a pilgrimage to Rome. On the way back they were waylaid by marauding Huns, who slaughtered them all.

Quite apart from certain extravagant details, there is scant historical basis for the cult of St. Ursula. Her feast was omitted from the revised calendar of saints in 1969 (though it remains in the Roman martyrology). Nevertheless, the story of St. Ursula and her companions was revered by many saints, including Hildegard of Bingen and Elisabeth of Schönau. Eventually, her story inspired St. Angela Merici to found the Order of Ursulines, devoted to the education of young women.

"They came at last to blessed Ursula. Their chief was dazzled by her wondrous beauty. He tried to console her over the death of her companions and promised that he would make her his wife. But she scorned his offer, and he, seeing that she despised him, transfixed her with an arrow and so consummated her martyrdom."

—*The Golden Legend*

St. Margaret Clitherow
English Martyr (d. 1586)

Margaret Clitherow was the first English woman martyr for the Catholic faith during the reign of Queen Elizabeth. Born to a wealthy merchant in York, at sixteen she married a butcher named John Clitherow. Though raised as a Protestant, she converted to the Catholic faith some years after her marriage, apparently inspired by the sufferings of so many Catholics under the penal laws of the time.

Despite the risks, she offered a safe haven in her home for fugitive priests. Her devoted husband turned a blind eye to these actions, though she made little secret of her faith. At one point she was imprisoned for two years, a time she set to good use by learning to read. On March 10, 1586, she was arrested again. Charged this time with sponsoring illegal religious services, she refused to enter a plea, thereby hoping to spare her family the risks of testifying at her trial. She understood that this would automatically incur a judgment against her and the terrible penalty of death by pressing.

When she was urged to beg the queen's forgiveness and also that of her husband, she replied, "If ever I have offended him, I do ask him for forgiveness from the bottom of my heart." John Clitherow cried out that she was the best wife in the kingdom.

Margaret was laid on a sharp stone while increasingly heavy weights were placed upon her. She died after fifteen minutes. Canonized in 1970, she is included among the Forty Martyrs of England and Wales commemorated on October 21.

"Jesu, have mercy on me."

—Last words of St. Margaret Clitherow

Mother Janet Erskine Stuart
Religious of the Sacred Heart (1857–1914)

J anet Erskine Stuart, the daughter of an Anglican minister, was born in Cottesmore, England. At the age of twenty-one she converted to Catholicism and the next year entered the Society of the Sacred Heart in Roehampton, where she remained for the next thirty years. Eventually, after serving as superior of her community, she became the superior general of the worldwide order (founded by St. Madeleine Sophie Barat), with its network of schools for girls.

She exerted a wide influence through her writings on spirituality and the education of girls. She considered education—"fitting citizens for the Kingdom of Heaven"—as a deeply religious calling. But it also suited her interests. "I would not have minded what I taught, so long as I could have caught someone and taught them something." As she reminded her sisters, "It is not so much what we say or do that educates; what really educates is who we are."

In books and talks she offered a positive spiritual message that spoke to an audience far beyond the convent: "Remember that the source of happiness is within ourselves. Nothing outside can give it, even if you make your circumstances ideal. Nothing can take it away."

She died on October 21, 1914, at the age of fifty-six.

"Your life is a sacred journey. It is about change, growth, discovery, movement and transformation. . . . It is continuously expanding your vision of what is possible, stretching your soul, teaching you to see clearly and deeply, helping you to listen to your intuition."

—Mother Janet Erskine Stuart

St. John Paul II
Pope (1920–2005)

Karol Wojtyla, archbishop of Krakow, was elected pope in 1978, taking the name John Paul II. Growing up in Poland he had experienced firsthand the realities of war, genocide, and totalitarian ideology. All this deeply marked his faith and his vision of the Church's role in defending human dignity and the life of the spirit. During his twenty-six-year reign, he in turn left a profound mark on the Church and the world.

His appearances in his homeland soon after his election set in motion a moral-political resurgence that fostered the dissident Solidarity labor movement. A first crack in the edifice of communism, this ultimately spelled the demise of the communist regime in Poland, setting in motion a chain reaction that presaged the collapse of the communist bloc in Eastern Europe and the end of the Cold War.

An actor in his youth, John Paul was a master of the dramatic gesture. In 1981 he was nearly killed by a Turkish assassin in St. Peter's Square. He survived to visit his assailant in prison and offer his forgiveness. In his final years, overtaken by the effects of Parkinson's disease, he humbly offered a different kind of witness to the power of the spirit.

Upon his death on April 2, 2005, a cry of *Santo Subito!* ("sainthood immediately") arose among mourners in St. Peter's Square. He was beatified six years later and canonized in April 2014.

"Do not be afraid. Do not be satisfied with mediocrity. Put out into the deep and let down your nets for a catch."

—St. John Paul II

Maura O'Halloran
Christian Zen Monk (1955–1982)

Born in Boston and raised in Ireland in a large Catholic family, Maura O'Halloran graduated from Trinity College, Dublin. From a young age, she displayed a deep compassion for human suffering. After college she worked in soup kitchens and traveled widely in Latin America. Her concern for social justice was accompanied by a serious attraction to the spiritual life. After experimenting with various methods of prayer, she decided to explore the wisdom of the East.

In 1979 she flew to Japan and applied for admission to a Zen Buddhist monastery in Tokyo. Her journals record her experience—sustained periods of meditation, manual labor, and an ascetic discipline of mind and body. After six months she experienced an ecstatic breakthrough, which her Master recognized as enlightenment. So impressed was he by her progress that he made an extraordinary offer—to entrust his monastery to her. But Maura did not believe this was her vocation. "I'm twenty-six and I feel as if I've lived my life," she wrote. "Strange sensation, almost as if I'm close to death. . . . I'm totally content. Of course I want to get deeper, see clearer. . . . If I have another fifty or sixty years (who knows?) of time, I want to live it for other people."

After leaving the monastery she was killed in a bus accident on October 22, 1982. Today a small statue of her in the monastery in Japan is revered by many pilgrims, both Christians and Buddhists.

"Suddenly I understood that we must take care of things just because they exist."
—Maura O'Halloran

Adorers of the Blood of Christ
Martyrs in Liberia (d. 1992)

The Adorers of the Blood of Christ, a congregation founded in Italy in 1834 by St. Maria de Mattias, is dedicated to providing a reconciling presence among the poor. To be an Adorer of the Blood of Christ, according to their constitution, one must become "a living image of that divine charity with which [Christ's] blood was shed, and of which it was and is sign, expression, measure and pledge." In October 1992 five American sisters, Barbara Ann Muttra, Shirley Kolmer and her cousin Mary Joel Kolmer, Agnes Mueller, and Kathleen McGuire, were engaged in such loving service when they were called to shed their own blood.

The West African nation of Liberia, where the congregation had served since 1971, had been rent for years by almost constant civil war and brutal military governments. Though violence in 1990 forced the sisters to leave the country, they returned the following year. In 1992 an ethnically charged civil war resumed. The question of whether to leave or stay was constantly present. But this time, despite the risks, the sisters chose to remain with their people. On October 20, 1992, two of the sisters were shot in an ambush while transporting one of their workers. Three days later, rebels invaded the convent in Gardnersville, shot the remaining sisters, and mutilated their bodies. In commemorating their deaths, Pope John Paul II called the sisters "Martyrs of Charity."

"Believing in Jesus is believing in humanity, and that is, I believe, the great challenge of our time."
—Sr. Shirley Kolmer

St. Anthony Mary Claret
Founder, Claretians (1807–1870)

St. Anthony was the son of a Spanish weaver. His dream following ordination to the priesthood was to serve in the foreign missions. Ill health thwarted this plan, and he was persuaded to remain a missionary in his own country. To this end he spent many years giving missions and retreats in Spain and founded a congregation, the Missionary Sons of the Immaculate Heart of Mary, popularly known as the Claretians, which would become internationally renowned for its catechetical work and publishing ministries. (In the United States, they are the publishers of *U.S. Catholic* and other media.)

In 1850 Anthony was appointed archbishop of Santiago in Cuba. There his reforming spirit aroused the opposition of powerful interests, so much that on several occasions he narrowly escaped assassination. In 1857 he was called back to Spain to serve as confessor to Queen Isabella II, an office he found most uncongenial. ("The palace is a continuous martyrdom for me," he wrote.) In Spain he established many educational and cultural projects, including a science laboratory and a museum of natural history. Meanwhile the Claretian Order circled the globe. In 1868 a liberal revolution in Spain forced Queen Isabella along with Anthony, her confessor, into exile in Rome. He died in France on October 24, 1870. His canonization followed in 1950.

"I live, but my life is that of Christ. And in possessing me, my poor Lord possesses nothing. And I, in possessing Him, possess everything."
—St. Anthony Mary Claret

Rosa Parks
"Mother of the Freedom Movement" (1913–2005)

On December 1, 1955, Rosa Parks, a forty-two-year-old African American seamstress, boarded a city bus in Montgomery, Alabama, on her way home from work. According to the Jim Crow ordinances common throughout the South, black passengers were supposed to sit at the back of the bus. When the bus driver ordered Parks to give up her seat to a white man, she refused. She was arrested and jailed.

In later years, when asked what caused her defiance, Parks denied the story that she was tired. "I was not tired physically," she said. "No, the only tired I was, was tired of giving in." Though she had not planned to face arrest that day, in fact Parks had long been active in the local NAACP, had attended workshops on civil rights, and was well prepared to affirm her human dignity. As she was being arrested, she later said, "I knew that it was the very last time that I would ever ride in humiliation of this kind."

In fact, Rosa Parks's action would be the decisive spark to the modern civil rights struggle. Outraged by her arrest, the black churches of Montgomery, under the leadership of a young minister, Martin Luther King Jr., organized a boycott of the city's buses that lasted over a year until the city repealed the segregation ordinance.

Though an icon of the movement, Parks and her husband could no longer find work in Montgomery and eventually moved to Detroit, where she lived until her death at ninety-two on October 24, 2005.

"It was just time."

—Rosa Parks

Saints Daria and Chrysanthus
Martyrs (ca. Third Century)

According to legend, Chrysanthus was the son of a Roman patrician. After converting to Christianity, he refused his father's demand that he marry. Nevertheless, his father somehow contrived for him to marry Daria, one of the Vestal Virgins, consecrated to the service of Minerva. But the story did not end as the father had planned. Chrysanthus converted Daria, and the two agreed to embrace a chaste union.

After the couple began preaching and winning converts, they were denounced and brought before a tribune who tried, by force, to make them worship the pagan gods. When, even after torture, Chrysanthus refused these entreaties, he was put in prison. Daria, for her part, was consigned to a brothel, where she was fortunate to receive the protection of a lion, which had escaped from the arena. Eventually Daria and Chrysanthus were stoned and cast alive into a sand pit, which was sealed behind them.

Over the centuries, there have been many reports of the discovery of their remains. The most recent came in 2008, when scientists working on the Italian cathedral of Reggio uncovered an ancient crypt. It contained the skeletons of a young man and woman, transferred to this site centuries before. It was announced that these might be the remains of Saints Daria and Chrysanthus.

"O Chrysanthus, in the sweet fragrance of holiness / thou didst draw Daria to saving knowledge. / Together in contest you routed the serpent, the author of all evil, / and were worthily taken up to the heavenly realms."
                                              —Orthodox hymn

The Forty Martyrs of England and Wales
(1535–1679)

The religious persecutions that accompanied the period of the English Reformation claimed many victims on both sides. For Catholics, the period of martyrdom began in 1535, following the Act of Supremacy, which declared Henry VIII the "Supreme Head of the Church in England." The forty martyrs commemorated on this date—canonized in 1970 by Pope Paul VI—are but a small number of the Catholics who died in this era. They include thirteen secular priests, ten Jesuits (including the famous Edmund Campion, Henry Walpole, and Robert Southwell), ten other religious priests, and seven laypeople.

An act of 1585 forbade the presence in England of any priest ordained abroad (a law directed against the Jesuits and other priests ordained at the English seminary in Douai, France, and smuggled into the country). After that, any priest caught in the country or any layperson harboring him could be convicted of treason.

Behind the list of martyrs are many stories of heroic faith. Any of these Catholics might have been spared if they had abjured their faith. Most of them endured grotesque tortures—subjection to intolerably cramped confinement, deprivation of sleep, waterboarding—before execution.

The final victims in this group were killed in 1679, which concluded the era of martyrdom.

"In condemning us, you condemn all your own ancestors, all our ancient bishops and kings, all that was once the glory of England—the island of saints, and the most devoted child of the See of Peter."
—St. Edmund Campion, Martyr

Blessed Contardo Ferrini
Scholar and Layman (1859–1902)

Among the great majority of official saints drawn from traditional "religious life," Contardo Ferrini stands out as a layman who expressed his holiness in the world of scholarship and public service. From early youth he had felt a deep attraction to prayer. Rather than enter the priesthood, however, he elected to pursue a religious vocation in the secular world. Through studies in Pavia in Italy and later in Berlin he became one of the world's authorities on Roman law. He taught at a number of universities and published hundreds of scholarly articles and several textbooks. In 1895 he was elected to the municipal council of Milan. Apart from this work he had a passion for nature and mountaineering.

Although he was a Franciscan tertiary, he was not the type of saint famous for prodigious acts of charity or mystical visions. What seems to have impressed those who came in contact with him was an overwhelming goodness and thirst for life—the evidence that it is possible to lead a holy life amid the ordinary duties of work and life in the world. In pronouncing his beatification in 1947, Pope Pius XII referred to him as a man who "gave an emphatic 'Yes' to the possibility of holiness in these days."

Ferrini died of typhus on October 17, 1902, at the age of forty-three. His feast is October 26.

"Nature lives by the breath of God's omnipotence, smiles in its joy of him, hides from his wrath—yet greets him, eternally young, with the smile of its own youth."
—Blessed Contardo Ferrini

Sarah and Angelina Grimké
Abolitionists and Feminists (d. 1873, 1879)

These sisters were raised on a South Carolina plantation that employed many slaves. Sarah, the elder, chafed against the hypocrisy of such injustice in a "Christian society." Fleeing to Philadelphia, she embraced Quakerism. Angelina soon joined her there, and together they threw themselves into the abolitionist cause. Writing "An Appeal to the Christian Women of the Southern States," Angelina set out a warning of the violence to come if slavery was not peacefully abolished. Before long the Grimké sisters were prominent speakers on the abolitionist circuit.

In time they began to see connections between the bondage of black Americans and the overt and subtle measures used to keep women silent and *in their place.* As Angelina put it, "The rights of the slave and the women blend like the colors of the rainbow." Sarah penned the first feminist manifesto in American history, "Letters on the Equality of the Sexes and the Condition of Women."

In 1838 the sisters were invited to present their views before the Massachusetts state legislature. Sarah delivered a blistering speech: "I stand before you as a repentant slaveholder . . . to do all I can to overturn a system of complicated crimes built upon the broken hearts and the prostrate bodies of my countrymen in chains."

Sarah and Angelina lived to see the end of slavery and the rise of the women's movement.

"I ask for no favors for my sex. . . . All I ask of our brethren is that they take their feet off our necks, and permit us to stand upright on the ground which God has designed us to occupy."

—Sarah Grimké

St. Severinus Boethius
Philosopher (480–524)

Boethius was born to one of the most prominent families of Rome. A consul of Rome and Master of the King's Offices, he seemed to be a man on whom fortune smiled. But his fortunes changed when he interceded on behalf of an innocent man accused of conspiring against the emperor. Boethius himself was arrested, charged not only with treason but with the impious study of philosophy and astronomy. Stripped of his honor and possessions, he was imprisoned for nine months before being tortured and executed.

During his imprisonment he wrote *The Consolation of Philosophy*, an imagined conversation with Lady Philosophy, who attempts to comfort her disciple in his present sufferings. Philosophy counsels him to become detached from worldly cares and to focus his attention on God, the Creator of all things. In such a mind his peace and equilibrium will not be determined by outward circumstances.

Though his death was not the product of his faith so much as a miscarriage of justice, Boethius's piety and the courage with which he endured his fate were widely recognized by the Church in Rome, and he was quickly acclaimed as a saint and martyr. His book became one of the most influential works of the Middle Ages.

"We men are so small a part of Your great work, yet we wallow here in the stormy sea of fortune. Ruler of all things, calm the roiling waves and, as You rule the immense heavens, rule also the earth in stable concord."
—St. Boethius

Henri Perrin
Worker Priest (1914–1954)

In Paris in the 1940s a group of idealistic priests embarked on a new field of mission. Rather than travel to foreign lands, they aimed to cross the threshold of the Catholic enclave and enter the world of the working class, so long estranged from the Church. Swapping their soutanes for overalls, they applied for factory jobs, and so began the extraordinary, though sadly short-lived, experiment of the worker priests.

Henri Perrin was one of these pioneers. During World War II he and a number of priests volunteered to accompany French workers conscripted for factory work in Germany. From this experience they dreamed of an apostolate aimed at breaking down barriers between the Church and poor. In 1947, with support from their bishops, they implemented this program. Perrin found work in a plastics factory. When his identity was discovered, he was rewarded with an experience of respect and fellowship he had never known in parish life.

Though the French bishops were initially pleased with the experiment, in 1954, under pressure from Rome, they called it to a halt. For the worker priests it was a devastating blow. Perrin struggled over his response. "It is impossible that I should return to the ghetto," he wrote. But his choices were bleak. With his dilemma still unresolved he was killed in a motorbike accident on October 25, 1954.

"With us, or without us, or in spite of us, God will fill that gulf— if only we don't put too many spokes in the wheels."

—Fr. Henri Perrin

Saints Simon and Jude
Apostles (First Century)

Among all the original twelve apostles, St. Jude is perhaps the most commonly invoked in prayer. He enjoys widespread popularity as the "patron of hopeless causes." The origins of this designation are obscure. Possibly owing to the similarity of his name to the traitor Judas Iscariot, petitioners would not appeal for his help until they had unsuccessfully exhausted other options. In any case, his popularity in this role is an ironic compensation for his obscurity in the Gospels. Aside from the citation of his name in listings of the Twelve, St. Jude is quoted only once. In the Gospel of John, he asks Jesus at the Last Supper why he does not manifest himself to the whole world. This Jude is also the supposed author of the shortest book of the New Testament, "The Letter of Jude," which in its twenty-five verses warns against the danger of false teachers who divide the Church and lead many astray.

Information about St. Simon is even more limited. Though he is listed among the twelve apostles, he is never quoted, and there is no reliable record of his activities after Pentecost.

Both these saints have long been celebrated together—possibly owing to the legend that they were martyred in Persia on the same day.

"Jude, a bondservant of Jesus Christ, and brother of James, to those who are called, sanctified by God the Father, and preserved in Jesus Christ: Mercy, peace, and love be multiplied to you."

—Epistle of Jude

Clarence Jordan
Founder, Koinonia Farm (1912–1969)

Clarence Jordan, who was born in rural Georgia, earned ministerial credentials as well as a doctorate in New Testament studies from Southern Baptist Theological Seminary in Louisville. But rather than a career in ministry or academe, he chose the less common vocation of discipleship to Jesus Christ. In 1942, with his wife Florence and a couple of other families, he founded Koinonia Farm, an experiment in communal Christian living, near Americus, Georgia. Koinonia was the Greek word used in Acts to describe the early Church community and its atmosphere of reconciliation and partnership. Jordan believed the most vital need for reconciliation in the South was between blacks and whites. At a time in the South when such talk was considered dangerously radical, Jordan's views drew a wedge between Koinonia and its neighbors. He was expelled from the local Baptist church.

Troubles truly began in the 1950s after the Supreme Court ruling on school desegregation. Koinonia was subjected to a campaign of terrorism—shootings, bombings, and vandalism, along with an economic boycott of the community. (Dorothy Day, visiting the community, was a survivor of one of these terrorist attacks.)

Jordan published a vernacular translation of the New Testament called his "Cotton Patch version," setting the story of Jesus "along the dusty rows of cotton, corn, and peanuts" in rural Georgia. He believed the problems with Christianity stemmed from the fact that most Christians pictured Jesus enthroned in heaven or safely confined to "Bible Times," thus missing the challenge of the incarnation. By glorifying Christ, he wrote, "we more effectively rid ourselves of him" than did those who crucified him. Jordan died on October 29, 1969.

"The resurrection places Jesus on this side of the grave, here and now, in the midst of life."   —Clarence Jordan

St. Marcellus
Martyr (d. 298)

Marcellus was a centurion in the Roman army, serving in the city of Tangier in North Africa. During a feast in honor of the emperor's birthday, he suddenly threw down his soldier's belt, his sword, and his military insignia and proclaimed, "I serve Jesus Christ the eternal king. I will no longer serve your emperors, and I scorn to worship your gods of wood and stone, which are deaf and dumb idols."

Nothing is known of Marcellus's earlier life, of what prompted his conversion or his conviction that military service was incompatible with profession of the Christian faith. Both his fellow soldiers and the authorities who hastened to arrest him evidently thought him "insane." Nevertheless, he repeated his statements in court. Asked if it was true that he had cast away his arms, he stated: "I did. For it was not right for a Christian man, who serves the Lord Christ, to serve in the armies of the world." He was henceforth sentenced to death by the sword. As he was led away to execution he addressed his last words to his judge: "May God be good to you."

"On July 21, in the presence of the standards of your legion, when you celebrated the festival of the emperor I made answer openly and clearly that I was a Christian and that I could not accept this allegiance, but could serve only Jesus Christ, the Son of God the Father Almighty."

—St. Marcellus

Blessed Restituta Kafka
Martyr (1894–1943)

Restituta Kafka was raised in Vienna. When she was nineteen years old she entered a nursing order, the Franciscan Sisters of Christian Charity, taking her religious name from a third-century martyr beheaded under the Roman emperor Aurelian. She served faithfully for many years in the district hospital in Mödling, near Vienna, where she was put in charge of the operating room.

After the *Anschluss* in 1938, the Nazis forbade any religious symbol in hospitals. Sr. Restituta not only refused to comply with this order, but she defiantly installed crucifixes in every room in a new ward of the hospital.

After being denounced to the Gestapo by a hospital surgeon, a fanatical Nazi, she was arrested on Ash Wednesday in 1942. Martin Bormann, Hitler's secretary, wished to make a special example of her and personally ordered her execution. After a year in prison, she was beheaded on March 30, 1943. Her body was thrown into a mass grave.

Restituta was beatified by Pope John Paul II in 1998.

"I have lived for Christ; I want to die for Christ."

—Last words of Blessed Restituta Kafka

Hadewijch of Brabant
Beguine Mystic (Thirteenth Century)

Almost nothing is known of the life of Hadewijch, a Flemish mystic who lived in the thirteenth century. Although a prolific author, she inspired no biography. All that is known of her story must be inferred from her writings. She was apparently a Beguine, part of a movement in the Low Countries that attracted women to a new form of community-based religious life, distinct from traditional enclosure. The Beguines stressed prayer, the works of mercy, simplicity of life, and a devotion to the humanity of Jesus.

Hadewijch's central theme is Love. Everywhere she turned—in creation, in community, or in her inner depths—she encountered the love of God. Not just a warm feeling, this love was a burning fire. In her letters of spiritual direction she emphasized love as the essential key to the knowledge and service of God: "Let us live in sweet love. Live for God; let his life be yours, and let yours be ours."

The Beguines were subjected to all kinds of pressure and persecution. Eventually Hadewijch was expelled from her community—under what circumstances we cannot know. In one of her last letters she writes, "What happens to me, whether I am wandering in the country or put in prison—however it turns out, it is the work of Love." Thus, she vanished from history, leaving behind only a final exhortation: "Farewell and live a beautiful life."

"Once on Pentecost Sunday I received the Holy Spirit in such a manner that I understood all the will of Love in all."

—Hadewijch of Brabant

St. Dorothy of Montau
Widow and Anchoress (1347–1394)

St. Dorothy was born to a peasant family in Prussia. At the age of seventeen she married a wealthy swordsmith, with whom she bore nine children—only one of whom survived. It was an unhappy marriage. Her husband, Albert, was an angry and abusive man who had little tolerance for her charity or her mystical visions. One time he beat her so badly that he thought he had killed her. Upon her recovery, he agreed, in penance, to accompany her on a pilgrimage to Aachen. Afterward, they undertook numerous pilgrimages together. In the Holy Year of 1390, as Albert lay ill, she traveled alone to Rome. Upon her return, she learned that her husband had died. Thus, a widow at the age of forty-three, and with her daughter a Benedictine nun, she was free to pursue her own vocation.

In 1393 Dorothy received permission to be walled up in a cell attached to a church in Marienwerder. Her cell had three windows, one opening to the street, where she could receive visitors and bestow spiritual counsel; one to the cemetery, where she could contemplate her earthly fate; and one to the high altar of the church, where she could feast her eyes on the Blessed Sacrament. In this small, unheated cell, she lived on for only a year before her death in 1394. She was canonized in 1976.

"I have never seen anyone work so hard in this life as she did for the afterlife."

—From the original life of St. Dorothy of Montau

St. Alphonsus Rodriguez
Jesuit Lay Brother (1533–1617)

The early life of Alphonsus Rodriguez was marked by a number of tragedies, including the death of his wife in childbirth, followed by the death of his two children. Shattered by these misfortunes, Alphonsus chose to devote the rest of his life to God. Though he was turned away by the Jesuits on account of his age and lack of education, he was eventually admitted as a lay brother in 1571. For the next forty years he served as a porter at the Jesuit College in Majorca. He embraced this humble job as seriously as any mission assignment, determined to welcome each caller as if he were Christ himself. So deeply did the porter's faith and love shine through his daily occupation that many of the students who passed through his doorway ended up applying for his spiritual direction.

No great events marked the rest of his life. But the impact of his personality was felt by countless people. He had responded to tragedy by opening his heart to God. Henceforth he encountered God in each person who passed through his open door.

Alphonsus died on October 31, 1617, at the age of eighty-four. His funeral was attended by the Spanish viceroy and crowds of the poor and sick among whom his holiness and reputation for miracles were well known. Canonized in 1888, his feast is October 31.

"To try to know oneself is the foundation of everything. He who knows himself despises himself, while he who does not know himself is puffed up."
—St. Alphonsus Rodriguez

Louis Massignon
Prophet of Dialogue (1883–1962)

Louis Massignon, a French scholar, played a key role in promoting the cause of Catholic-Muslim dialogue. The seeds of his vocation were planted in his youth and his avid interest in Arab culture. While conducting research in Mesopotamia he was arrested and charged as a spy. During his captivity he received a profound mystical experience, which brought him to an overwhelming sense of God. This prompted an ardent return to his Catholic roots. But he was also deeply affected by the experience of Muslim piety and vowed to devote his life to increasing understanding between these two religious traditions, both heirs of the faith of Abraham. (He was also deeply influenced by his friendship with the desert hermit, Blessed Charles de Foucauld.) In 1930 he became a Franciscan tertiary, taking the name "Ibrahim." He also made a vow, offering his life for the Muslims, "not so they would be converted, but so that the will of God might be accomplished in them and through them."

Later in life Massignon became a Melkite Greek Catholic and was ordained as a priest, permitting him to celebrate the Mass in Arabic according to the Byzantine Rite Liturgy. A follower of Gandhian nonviolence, he supported efforts to promote peace in the Middle East and for a peaceful resolution of the war in Algeria.

He died on October 31, 1962.

"Man is not made for works of external mercy, but first of all to worship the divine Guest in his heart, in the present moment."

—Louis Massignon

NOVEMBER

1 Feast of All Saints

2 Léon Bloy • Mother Mary Walsh

3 St. Malachy • St. Martin de Porres

4 St. Charles Borromeo • Raissa Maritain

5 Saints Zechariah and Elizabeth • Blessed Bernard Lichtenberg

6 Blessed Joan Mary de Maille • Little Sister Magdeleine of Jesus

7 Alexander de Rhodes • John Kavanaugh

8 Blessed John Duns Scotus • Søren Kierkegaard

9 Blessed Elizabeth of the Trinity • Kristallnacht Martyrs

10 St. Leo the Great • The Lübeck Martyrs

11 St. Martin of Tours • Venerable Catherine McAuley

12 St. Josaphat • Lucretia Mott

13 St. Agnes of Assisi • St. Frances Xavier Cabrini

14 St. Gregory Palamas • Joseph Cardinal Bernardin

15 St. Gertrude the Great • Blessed Mary of the Passion

16 St. Margaret of Scotland • Ignacio Ellacuría and Companions

17 St. Hilda of Whitby • St. Elizabeth of Hungary

18 St. Roque Gonzalez • St. Rose Philippine Duchesne

19 St. Mechtild of Hackeborn • Venerable Henriette DeLille

20 Henri Dominique Lacordaire • Frank Sheed

21 Blessed Mary Frances Siedliska • C. S. Lewis

22 St. Cecilia • Jeanne Fontbonne

23 St. Columbanus • Blessed Miguel Pro

24 St. Andrew Dung-Lac and Companions • St. Joseph Pignatelli

25 St. Catherine of Alexandria • Venerable Margaret Sinclair

26 Sojourner Truth • Blessed James Alberione

27 Saints Barlaam and Josaphat • Dom Virgil Michel

28 Isaiah • St. Catherine Labouré

29 Mother Jones • Servant of God Dorothy Day

30 St. Andrew • Etty Hillesum

NOVEMBER

Feast of All Saints

Since the early centuries, the Church has reserved one day to remember, collectively, all the saints, both those officially named as well as the vast number—surely the greater part—known only to God.

The official process of canonization involves a prolonged investigation that can take centuries to complete. The formality of this process, the emphasis on certified miracles, and the fact that those officially named are invariably exceptional figures, can serve to emphasize the gap between "real saints" and "people like us." In that sense, the process can hinder, rather than help us realize a crucial fact: that all Christians, not just a select few, are called to holiness.

That doesn't mean we should aspire to canonization. It simply reflects the fact that in calling ourselves followers of Christ we have pledged to conform our hearts and minds to the pattern of *his* holiness. This holiness is not necessarily expressed in writing learned tomes, performing fantastic feats of asceticism, founding religious congregations, or performing miracles. If we want to see the face of holiness we can recognize it in the qualities Jesus enumerates in the Beatitudes: Blessed are the poor in spirit . . . the meek . . . the merciful . . . the peacemakers . . . the pure of heart.

In this litany Jesus summarizes the virtues and attitudes implied by faithful discipleship. It is good to recall that these blessings are not directed to abstract qualities (poverty of spirit, meekness, purity of heart) but to the people who embody them, doubtless fully human, with all the faults and weaknesses that implies. Though these "blessings" do not exactly describe the traditional criteria for sanctity, we know that when we stand in the presence of such people or read their stories we feel closer to Jesus, with a renewed sense of possibility. Such was the experience of Ignatius Loyola, while recovering from war wounds, when he read a book of lives of the saints. He found himself excited by the thought, "What if I should do what St. Francis did, what St. Dominic did?"

It is easy to think of holy people from our time who embody these qualities: Mother Teresa (the merciful), Dorothy Day (the peacemaker), Oscar Romero (hungering and thirsting for righteousness). But it is also possible to recognize people of our own acquaintance who embody these qualities. It may be someone who stands out for her gentleness or forgiveness; someone who retains a spirit of joy in the midst of sorrows; someone who risks disapproval or looking foolish for taking an unpopular stand; someone whom we always count on to provide an example that is loving, brave, and true. Such people also represent the face of holiness in our time. It is not likely they will be canonized. Churches will not be named in their honor. And yet they too may be counted among the great "cloud of witnesses" recognized on the feast of All Saints.

Léon Bloy
Novelist (1846–1917)

The novelist Léon Bloy was more than a man of letters. To his friends he was a prophet, a "pilgrim of the Absolute," a man on fire with zeal for the justice and love of God. To his critics he was a man blinded from staring too long at the sun. In any case, he played a key role in stimulating the extraordinary revival of French Catholic literature in the early twentieth century.

Bloy's life was marked by affliction. Sales of his books were dismal, and two of his children died in infancy from the effects of deprivation. Still, Bloy was driven by an unshakeable sense of vocation—not just as a writer but as a witness to the beatitude of poverty and the spiritual value of suffering. The other side of Bloy's pathos was a capacity for holy rage over the materialism of bourgeois civilization, and he erupted in prophetic wrath when he detected such values in the Church. For the sins of the world, especially injustice and anti-Semitism, he predicted a coming cataclysm.

He received little recognition from the Church, while in the literary world he was dismissed as a Catholic fanatic. Yet he inspired the faith of many artists and thinkers, including the converts Jacques and Raissa Maritain, for whom he served as godfather.

In melancholy over the First World War, he died on November 3, 1917.

"There is only one sadness—not to be a saint."

—Léon Bloy

Mother Mary Walsh
Founder, Dominican Sisters of the Sick Poor
(1850–1922)

Mary Walsh, a young Irish woman whose parents died when she was an infant, immigrated to New York in 1869. There she found work as a laundress and, under the influence of the Dominican pastor of her parish, joined the Third Order of St. Dominic.

One day in 1876, while on her way to work, Mary heard a young girl crying. Following the child to her apartment she found the girl's mother lying sick on a mattress on the floor with a dead newborn baby at her side and three other hungry children with no one to care for them. Their father was in jail. Mary decided to drop all else while she cared for the family, nursing the mother, even finding a job for the father when he got out of jail. Though in the meantime she had lost her own job, Mary had found her vocation.

With the support of her parish, Mary gathered a group of coworkers who supported themselves doing laundry while visiting the sick poor in their homes. Although the women barely scraped by themselves, these women, who called themselves Friends of the Sick Poor, devoted themselves in every way to those in need—regardless of race, religion, or lack thereof.

In 1910 they were recognized as a Dominican congregation, and Mary became mother superior—though not before she had submitted humbly to training as a novice. She died on November 6, 1922.

"What a privilege it is to work for the sick poor!"

—Mother Mary Walsh

St. Malachy
Bishop (1094–1148)

St. Malachy was born in Armagh in the north of Ireland. Early in life, his special gifts were recognized by the archbishop of Armagh, St. Celsus, who sent him to be trained and ordained as a priest. After serving briefly as the abbot of an abbey in Bangor, he was chosen bishop of Connor. There he contributed to a great renewal of religious fervor, until forced by an invasion to flee.

In 1129 Archbishop Celsus died. From his deathbed he decreed that Malachy should replace him. This caused a furor among the bishop's family. Over many generations the see of Armagh had become a hereditary position, and Celsus's kinsmen set about to install one of their own, thus setting up a bitter rivalry with Malachy and his supporters, among them, the papal legate. Malachy, so far as possible, governed the diocese, but he would not enter the city as long as there was danger of bloodshed. For years he had to travel with an armed bodyguard.

Eventually Malachy's authority was recognized, whereupon, having restored discipline and peace to the diocese, he promptly resigned. In 1137 he returned to his former see. Two years later he traveled to Rome, where the pope confirmed all his actions and named him papal legate. In the course of his travels he visited the Cistercian abbey of Clairvaux, where he found an instant friend in the illustrious abbot, St. Bernard. It was during a subsequent visit to Clairvaux that Malachy fell ill and died in 1148.

"May he protect us by his merits, whom he has instructed by his example and confirmed by his miracles."

—St. Bernard on St. Malachy

St. Martin de Porres
Dominican Lay Brother (1579–1639)

Martin de Porres was born in Lima, Peru, the illegitimate son of a Spanish nobleman and a free black woman. His father refused to recognize his "mulatto" child. When Martin was fifteen he applied to enter a Dominican monastery as a lay helper and was assigned such menial tasks as sweeping the cloister and cleaning the latrines. Despite his extreme humility, Martin could not long disguise his talents and abilities, particularly in the field of medicine and nursing. Soon he was put in charge of the monastery infirmary, where his knowledge of herbal remedies was apparently supplemented by miraculous powers to heal by his mere touch or presence.

Martin's charity toward the poor and homeless was legendary. He cared for the sick and injured wherever he found them. He had a special ministry to African slaves. But he treated sick animals with the same devotion he extended to humans. Innumerable legends describe his service and communion with creatures of every kind.

On both the natural and moral planes, Martin seemed to exceed the limits of the possible. This included his extreme asceticism. He took on himself the sins of his age—slavery, the scorn heaped on Indians, the oppression of the poor. Once when the monastery was in debt he offered himself to be sold as a slave. The prior ordered him back to the monastery: "You are not for sale," he told him. In declaring him a saint, Pope John XXIII named Martin patron of all who work for justice.

"He was a man of great charity . . . who also assisted in the larger duty of spreading the Great Love of the world."

—A contemporary witness

St. Charles Borromeo
Bishop (1538–1584)

Charles Borromeo, one of the eminent heroes of the Catholic Reformation, was born in 1538 to an aristocratic Italian family. His life took a sudden turn when his uncle became Pope Pius IV and immediately appointed Charles as a cardinal, and then as administrator of the see of Milan, followed by a string of other official offices, including papal secretary of state, which required that he remain in Rome. All this was a remarkable challenge for a young man, not yet twenty-two—and not yet ordained.

Among Charles's contributions was to assist in the final session of the Council of Trent, where he helped to draft the Catechism. In 1563 he was finally ordained a priest, followed by consecration as a bishop. Upon the death of his uncle, he won permission from the new pope to travel to his long-neglected see in Milan. Finding the diocese in a deplorable state, Charles dedicated himself to reform and renewal, regularizing the condition of the clergy, establishing seminaries, and overseeing the training of catechists. He won popular devotion through his charity in time of famine and, during an outbreak of plague, for his courage in caring for the sick. Exhausted by his labors, Charles died on November 4, 1584, at the age of forty-six.

"If we wish to make any progress in the service of God we must begin every day of our life with new eagerness. We must keep ourselves in the presence of God as much as possible and have no other view or end in all our actions but the divine honor."

—St. Charles Borromeo

Raissa Maritain
Poet and Contemplative (1883–1960)

The life of Raissa Maritain was inextricably intertwined with that of her husband, Jacques, the renowned Catholic philosopher. Born in Russia to Orthodox Jewish parents, Raissa had immigrated to France as a girl and enrolled at the Sorbonne at sixteen. There she met Jacques Maritain when he solicited her signature on a petition against repression in Tsarist Russia. Soon they were inseparable, and they married in 1904. Apart from their love of art, poetry, and social justice, they shared a passion for truth. They pledged together to seek the meaning of life—a quest that led them eventually to Catholicism.

Both Raissa and Jacques conceived of their lives in religious terms. Though they took vows as oblates of St. Benedict, they believed they were called to live out their faith in the midst of the intellectual and artistic circles in which they were immersed.

Although she published several volumes of poetry, Raissa tended to remain in the background. Only after her death on November 4, 1960, and the discovery of her private journals, did Jacques realize the depth of spirituality that had remained hidden even from him. Her journals reflected an intense life of prayer and her understanding of her vocation as a contemplative "on the roads of the world."

"I love the saints because they are lovable; and the sinners because they are like me."
—Raissa Maritain

Saints Zechariah and Elizabeth
Parents of John the Baptist (First Century)

The first chapter of the Gospel of Luke relates the story of Zechariah and Elizabeth, an elderly and childless couple who would become the parents of St. John the Baptist. Elizabeth was a kinswoman of Mary, while Zechariah was a priest. One day while serving in the Temple, Zechariah was astonished by the appearance of an angel who announced that he and his wife would have a son named John, who would be filled with the Holy Spirit, even in his mother's womb. Zechariah questioned how this could be, whereupon the angel struck him dumb.

Later, when Mary was told by the same angel that she would bear a son by the Holy Spirit, she too asked how this could be and was told, by way of a sign, that her kinswoman Elizabeth was at that very moment with child. Mary hastened to visit Elizabeth. Upon Mary's arrival, Elizabeth felt her child leap within her womb.

In time Elizabeth did indeed bear a son, and Zechariah—still speechless—wrote on a tablet: "His name is John." At that moment his tongue was loosed, and he praised God, exclaiming, "And you, my child, will be called a prophet of the Most High; for you will go on before the Lord to prepare the way for him."

"Most blessed are you among women, and blessed is the fruit of your womb."
—St. Elizabeth (Luke 1:42)

Blessed Bernard Lichtenberg
Priest and Confessor (1875–1943)

I n November 1938 the Kristallnacht pogrom in Germany offered the world a brazen display of the Nazi persecution of the Jews. Many Church officials turned a blind eye, but not Bernard Lichtenberg, provost of St. Hedwig's Cathedral. He condemned the attack and from then on regularly prayed publicly for the Jews and other victims of persecution. He later denounced the Nazi policy of "euthanasia." In a letter to the Chief Physician of the state he wrote, "As a human being, a Christian, a priest, and a German, I demand of you that you answer for the crimes that have been perpetrated at your bidding, and with your consent, and which will call forth the vengeance of the Lord on the heads of the German people."

In October 1941 the Gestapo raided his home. They found a sermon he had planned to deliver, denouncing the Reich Minister of Propaganda's claim that anyone greeting a Jew on the street was guilty of treason. He had intended to remind his flock of Christ's commandment, "You shall love your neighbor as yourself."

He was arrested and served two years in Tegel Prison. When the Gestapo offered to free him if he would refrain from preaching, he asked instead to be deported to Poland with the Jews. He was remanded to Dachau concentration camp but fell ill and died in transit on November 5, 1943. He was beatified in 1996.

"Outside, the Temple is burning, and this too is a house of God. . . . The Jews are my brothers and sisters, also created with an immortal soul by God!"
—Blessed Bernard Lichtenberg

Blessed Joan Mary de Maille
Franciscan Tertiary (1332–1414)

Blessed Joan was born to a noble family in France. It was said that, as a child, her prayers had saved a neighbor boy, Robert de Sillé, from drowning after he fell into a pond. When Joan turned sixteen, she married him. Although they elected to maintain a celibate relationship, she and Robert were apparently a devoted couple, who adopted and raised three orphans. During an invasion by the English, Robert was taken captive and held for ransom. Though he escaped, this experience inspired Joan and Robert to devote themselves to the ransom of other prisoners.

This charity infuriated Robert's family. Upon his death in 1362 they expelled Joan from her house. For several years she supported herself as best she could, eventually learning to prepare medicines and becoming a Franciscan tertiary. But for a while she was reduced to living in pigsties and dog kennels. When her in-laws eventually restored her property she gave it all to the Carthusians, and at the age of fifty-seven retired to a small room in Tours where she devoted herself to prayer and works of mercy. Though to some she appeared quite mad, many others recognized her evident holiness. She was known for her gift of prophecy and for her special dedication to prisoners— whether criminals or captives of war. At one time she even persuaded the king to release all the prisoners of Tours. She died on March 28, 1414, and was beatified in 1871. Her feast is November 6.

"I was a prisoner, and you visited me."

—Matthew 25:36

Little Sister Magdeleine of Jesus
Founder, Little Sisters of Jesus (1898–1989)

Growing up in France, Madeleine Hutin felt a powerful devotion to Jesus but could find no religious congregation corresponding to her sense of vocation. Then, in her twenties, she came upon a biography of Charles de Foucauld, the modern desert hermit who died in North Africa in 1916. Foucauld had envisioned a new kind of contemplative life, rooted in the world of the poor, based on the "hidden years" that Jesus spent as a carpenter in Nazareth. Madeleine determined to make him her spiritual guide.

In 1936 she set sail for Algeria, where she met René Voillaume, a priest who had been similarly inspired by the witness of Foucauld to found the Little Brothers of Jesus. With his help and encouragement, she eventually won approval for a new congregation, the Little Sisters of Jesus. She became Little Sister Magdeleine.

The mission of the Little Sisters was to bear witness to God's love among the poorest and most powerless of the world. Living in small "fraternities," they maintained an intense commitment to contemplative prayer while entering fully into the life of their neighbors. The Little Sisters eventually spread around the globe, from urban slums to pygmy villages in Cameroon, among boat people in Southeast Asia and gypsy caravans in Europe. In every setting they sought to provide a spiritual leaven in the midst of the world. Little Sister Magdeleine died at ninety-one on November 6, 1989.

"The Lord Jesus suffered and died for all. In the name of his love, all, without exception, have a right to your love."

—Little Sister Magdeleine

Alexander de Rhodes
Jesuit "Apostle of Vietnam" (1591–1660)

Alexander de Rhodes, a French Jesuit, arrived in Hanoi in 1619. Though missionaries had been active in Indochina for several years, their accomplishments were limited, largely owing to their failure to master the difficult language. De Rhodes, in contrast, not only learned Vietnamese but composed a Vietnamese dictionary and catechism. More importantly, he devised a Vietnamese alphabet based on romanized script that remains in use. After ten years, by his own account, he had overseen six thousand conversions.

Part of his success reflected his skill in using words and concepts from Vietnamese culture to communicate the Gospel. In preaching he claimed to possess a pearl of great value, which he was willing to sell at a cheap price. When asked what this was, he said it was the true *tao* (way) that leads to everlasting light.

In 1630, Vietnamese rulers, wary of European influence, expelled de Rhodes from Vietnam. When he returned ten years later he was arrested and sentenced to death, though instead he was sent into exile. Back in France he was instrumental in founding the Paris Foreign Missions Society. Though he longed to return to Vietnam, his next assignment was to Persia, where he died on November 5, 1660.

"I left Cochinchina in my body, but certainly not in my heart; and so it is with Tonkin. My heart is in both countries and I don't think it will ever be able to leave them."

—Alexander de Rhodes, SJ

John Kavanaugh
Jesuit (1941–2012)

As a young Jesuit priest, John Kavanaugh went to work with Mother Teresa at her home for the dying in Calcutta. It was a transformative experience. "The most indelible thing about Mother Teresa was her insistence that the greatest need in life is greater trust, that the absence of love is the greatest poverty, and that the Eucharist is not only the center of our worship, but also the center of our concern for the poor." Those lessons, he later said, were the "three sustaining things in my life."

A quest for the value and meaning of human life became the central theme in his career as a philosopher and ethicist at St. Louis University, where he taught for thirty-six years. He was a particularly sharp critic of the accommodation of Christian faith to the idols of culture. His book *Following Christ in a Consumer Society* contrasted the soul-destroying aspects of a materialistic society with the personalism of the Gospel. The implications of this perspective caused him to challenge the comfortable pieties of both the left and the right. What was needed, he taught, was to recover in Christ the model of what it means to be a human person, fully alive, and to recognize in others the image of God. This was "revolutionary holiness."

He died after a long illness on November 5, 2012.

"It is only when we let go and turn to God in total trust that our searching hands are at last open to a final embrace of Love who is our Risen Lord."

—John Kavanaugh, SJ

Blessed John Duns Scotus
Franciscan Theologian (ca. 1266–1308)

John Duns, later known as the Subtle Doctor, was called Scotus on account of his birth in Scotland. He entered the Franciscans at the age of fifteen and was later ordained a priest. After studies in Oxford and Paris, he went on to hold teaching positions in Paris and Cologne. He was acclaimed as one of the greatest of the scholastic theologians. His mystically charged theology held particular charm for the Franciscans, rendering in philosophical terms the creation-centered spirituality of their holy founder.

Duns Scotus defined God as infinite love. He taught that the incarnation was not required as payment for sin; it was willed through eternity as an expression of God's love, and hence God's desire for consummated union with creation. Our redemption by the cross was likewise an expression of God's love and compassion rather than an appeasement of God's anger or a form of compensation for God's injured majesty. He believed that knowledge of God's love should evoke a loving response on the part of humanity. He wrote, "I am of the opinion that God wished to redeem us in this fashion principally in order to draw us to his love." Through our own loving self-gift, he argued, we join with Christ in becoming "co-lovers" of the Holy Trinity.

Duns Scotus died on November 8, 1308. He was beatified in 1993.

"O Lord, our God . . . Teach your servant to show by reason what he holds with faith most certain, that you are the most eminent, the first efficient cause and the last end."

—Blessed John Duns Scotus

Søren Kierkegaard
Philosopher (1813–1855)

Søren Kierkegaard made no pretense of being a saint. He hardly dared to call himself a Christian. But he claimed to know what it *means* to be a Christian. This knowledge imposed the thankless but nevertheless sacred duty of exposing official Christianity for what he believed it to be: a counterfeit and a fraud. Thus, indirectly, he hoped to bear witness to the truth.

He was born in Copenhagen. With the support of an inheritance he devoted himself to writing, and in a few short years produced a library of works on philosophy, ethics, and theology. Though this secured his later reputation, such acclaim came many generations after his death. In his life he was regarded more as a nuisance and a fool.

The thrust of his work was to show what it means to become and to be a Christian—an ironic task for one living in an officially Christian country. He believed this was the problem: people believed that being a Christian was no more than a matter of being born in a Christian state. Thus, nobody was challenged to *become* a Christian, to make a decisive leap of faith. The result was Christendom: a species of baptized paganism in which every respectable citizen could pass for a disciple. The harm was compounded by theologians who turned Christianity into a system of ideas.

A month after collapsing on the street, Kierkegaard died on November 11, 1855, at the age of forty-two.

"What the age needs is not a genius but a martyr."

—Søren Kierkegaard

Blessed Elizabeth of the Trinity
Carmelite Mystic (1880–1906)

Though as a child she wished for nothing more than to become a Carmelite nun, Elizabeth Catez acceded to her mother's condition—that she await her twenty-first birthday. On that day she entered the convent in Dijon and became Sr. Elizabeth of the Trinity. The next two years passed happily. "I find Him everywhere," she wrote, "while doing the wash as well as while praying." But then, soon after taking her vows, she was diagnosed with an incurable disease of the adrenal glands. Elizabeth welcomed her condition as an opportunity to "conform herself to the Crucified in love."

In increasing agony, she lived on for three years. Under obedience she recorded her spiritual thoughts in notebooks published after her death. Her teaching was reflected in a letter she wrote to a friend: "We carry our heaven within ourselves, because he who satisfies the saints with the light of vision gives himself to us in faith and in mystery. It's the same thing. I feel I have found heaven on earth, because heaven is God and God is in my soul. The day I understood this a light went on inside me, and I want to whisper this secret to all those I love, so that they too, in whatever circumstances, will cling increasingly to God."

Elizabeth died on November 9, 1906, and was beatified by Pope John Paul II in 1984.

"A soul united to Jesus is a living smile."

—Blessed Elizabeth of the Trinity

Kristallnacht Martyrs
(1938)

Before implementing their plan to exterminate the Jewish people, the Nazis advertised their intentions through a number of public spectacles. The most dramatic of these occurred on the night of November 9, 1938, when Nazi storm troopers throughout Germany mounted a coordinated assault on the Jewish community. Hundreds of synagogues were burned to the ground, particular care being taken to destroy prayer books, scrolls, and religious books. Jewish tombstones were overturned and the graves desecrated. Seventy-five hundred Jewish-owned shops were destroyed. Because of the many shattered windows the pogrom became known as the *Kristallnacht*, or Crystal Night. Throughout the pogrom police merely watched, while firefighters stood by to make sure no non-Jewish property was threatened. In addition, twenty thousand Jewish men were arbitrarily arrested and placed in "protective custody," with half of them shipped to the Buchenwald concentration camp. Nearly one hundred Jews were killed.

The following day there was little protest in Germany. There was no general expression of outrage from the Churches or public expressions of solidarity. Notes from a meeting of the top-ranking Nazi officials indicate that they considered the night's activities a tremendous success.

"Mob law ruled in Berlin throughout the afternoon and evening. . . . Racial hatred and hysteria seemed to have taken complete hold of otherwise decent people. I saw fashionably dressed women clapping their hands and screaming with glee, while respectable middle-class mothers held up their babies to see the 'fun.'"
—Report in the London *Daily Telegraph*

St. Leo the Great
Pope and Doctor of the Church (ca. 400–461)

St. Leo was elected pope in 440. His pontificate coincided with a period of crisis. The once glorious Roman Empire was in a state of collapse; heretical doctrines were circulating freely; barbarian armies were pressing at the gates. Under such circumstances the Church might well have disintegrated had it not been for Leo's forceful leadership.

Among other achievements, Leo proposed language at the Council of Chalcedon (451) that settled the long-protracted dispute over the dual natures of Christ. Leo taught that Christ is one Person, the Divine Word, in whom two natures, human and divine, are permanently united without confusion or mixture. When his letter was read to the council the bishops cried, "Peter has spoken by Leo."

Soon after, he intervened with the armies of Attila the Hun to spare Rome. His efforts were less successful with the Vandal Gaiseric, who later ransacked the city. Much of his energy in succeeding years was spent in ministering to the broken victims left behind. Nevertheless, thanks to Leo, the Church not only survived the collapse of Rome but was able to emerge as one of the strongest institutions of the medieval world. Thus he earned the title "the Great" (one of only three popes to be so honored). He died in 461.

"It is one and the same Son of God who exists in both natures, taking what is ours to Himself without losing what is His own."

—St. Leo the Great

The Lübeck Martyrs
(1943)

On November 10, 1943, four Christians were executed by the Nazis in a prison in Hamburg. They were Fathers Johannes Prassek, Eduard Müller, and Hermann Lange, all Catholic priests who worked at the Sacred Heart Church in Lübeck, and Karl-Friedrich Stellbrink, an Evangelical Lutheran minister. Beheaded within minutes of one another, their blood literally ran together.

Although ecumenical dialogue was unusual at the time, these four men had formed a deep friendship some years before, having delicately discovered their shared opposition to the ideology of National Socialism and the regime's policies of euthanasia, anti-Semitism, and other crimes. The authorities had for some time suspected their loyalty and employed informants to gather evidence against them. A specific trigger came after the Palm Sunday service when Pastor Stellbrink gave a sermon interpreting an air raid as a judgment of God. He was arrested the next day, with the priests following soon after.

Charged with defeatism, malice, favoring the enemy, and listening to enemy broadcasts, they were convicted and sentenced to death. Their bond was strengthened in the months they spent awaiting death. "We are like brothers," Lange wrote. "Personally, I am quite calm and await firmly what is to come. Once one really has achieved complete devotion to the will of God, then there is a wonderful peace and the consciousness of absolute security."

The three priests were beatified in 2011 in a service that made special note of the witness of their Protestant brother.

"The ecumenism of the martyrs and the witnesses to the faith is the most convincing ecumenism."
—Pope John Paul II

St. Martin of Tours
Bishop (d. 397)

St. Martin, bishop of Tours, is particularly remembered for the circumstances of his conversion. This occurred, one cold winter day in Gaul, where he served as an officer in the Roman army, when Martin came upon a shivering beggar, dressed in rags. Having no money to offer, Martin removed his cloak, which he divided into two pieces with his sword, giving one piece to the beggar and wrapping himself in the remnant. That night he dreamed he saw Jesus wearing that part of the cloak he had given away. The next morning he resolved to be baptized.

His conversion was striking for its combination of two themes: the encounter with Jesus in the face of the poor, and the conviction that the way of Christ was the way of nonviolence. This insight prompted Martin to present himself to his superiors to request discharge from the army. When he was accused of cowardice he volunteered to go into battle the next day at the front of the line, unarmed, to meet the enemy in the name of Christ.

Instead, Martin was imprisoned—though not executed. After being released, he, along with others who joined him, founded the first monastery in Gaul. Ten years later he was called out of solitude to become bishop of Tours, an office he held for twenty-five years, until his death in 397. As bishop he continued his commitment to peacemaking, opposing the use of violence against heretics.

"I am a soldier of Christ and it is not lawful for me to fight."

—St. Martin of Tours

Venerable Catherine McAuley
Founder, Sisters of Mercy (1778–1841)

When she established a house in Dublin for the care of destitute women and orphans, Catherine McAuley had no intention of founding a religious institution. Orphaned herself and raised by kindly guardians, she had long felt a strong desire to be of service to the poor. When she came into a sizeable inheritance she saw her opportunity.

A number of other women joined her in her work, and they received the blessing of the archbishop. He authorized them to wear a distinctive garb, to visit the sick, and to call themselves Sisters of Mercy. Still, it was some time before they began to consider forming a religious congregation. Catherine wished the sisters to combine a commitment to contemplative prayer with active service in the world. Their mission quickly extended to all the works of mercy—managing schools, hospitals, and orphanages, caring for the hungry and homeless, and visiting prisoners.

In 1831 the first Sisters of Mercy took their vows, and Catherine became Mother Mary Catherine, the first superior of the new congregation. In her lifetime she established twelve communities in Ireland and two in England, though later the sisters would spread to North America and around the world. She died in her original House of Mercy in Dublin on November 11, 1841. In 1990 she was declared venerable in the process of canonization.

"Prayer is a plant, the seed of which is sown in the heart of every Christian, but its growth entirely depends on the care we take to nourish it."
—Venerable Catherine McAuley

St. Josaphat
Bishop and Martyr (1580–1623)

St. Josaphat Kuncewycz was born in Ukraine to Orthodox parents. After learning about the Union of Brest (1596), which brought about union between the Ruthenian Orthodox and Catholic Churches, he became an enthusiastic champion of Church unity and converted to the Byzantine rite.

In 1604 Josaphat entered the Basilian Holy Trinity monastery in Vilnius. Eventually he was ordained and became the bishop of Polatsk in Belarus. In this position he continued to preach and speak out for Church union, though his mission provoked increasingly angry opposition from Orthodox opponents.

In 1623 he preached a series of sermons on Church unity in Vitebsk Cathedral. There, on November 12, an angry mob attacked and killed him on the cathedral steps and afterward threw his body in the River Dvina.

Josaphat was canonized in 1867, the first Eastern-rite saint recognized by the Church. He might also be recognized as an avant-garde witness to the spirit of ecumenism.

"If you have anything against me, here I am!"

—Last words of St. Josaphat

Lucretia Mott
Abolitionist and Feminist (1793–1880)

Lucretia Coffin, the daughter of a whaling captain, was educated in Quaker schools in New York before settling in Pennsylvania. In 1811 she married James Mott, in whom she found a loving companion and loyal ally in all her causes. She bore six children, but the death of her first son prompted a period of deep religious introspection. Afterward she was formally recognized as a Quaker minister.

The Motts were ardent abolitionists, forswearing cotton or any commerce in the fruits of slavery. These sentiments soon found their way into Lucretia's preaching, drawing complaints from Quaker elders. After creating a stir when she rose to speak at an antislavery convention in Philadelphia, she founded the Philadelphia Female Anti-Slavery Society. This work provoked an especially violent backlash. In one case a hall where she was speaking was burned to the ground by a riotous mob.

When she was denied a chance to speak at an antislavery convention in London, her efforts shifted toward the feminist cause. The religion of Jesus, she insisted, was founded on a spirit of liberation, justice, and equality. In 1848 she helped organize the Women's Rights Convention in Seneca Falls, New York, and read aloud its revolutionary manifesto, which began, "We hold these truths to be self-evident: that all men *and women* are created equal."

She continued in the struggle for justice and equality for all until her death on November 11, 1880.

"We deem it our duty, as professing Christians, to manifest our abhorrence of the flagrant injustice and deep sin of slavery by united and vigorous actions."

—Lucretia Mott

St. Agnes of Assisi
Poor Clare (1197–1253)

The conversion of Francesco di Bernardone, the son of a wealthy merchant, caused scandal and wonder in the town of Assisi. This increased as a procession of other prominent young men joined him in embracing radical poverty. Together they formed a new order of Friars Minor. Soon they were followed by Clare, daughter of another wealthy family of Assisi. Stealing from home, she put off her fine clothes and cut off her long hair as a sign of espousal to Christ. Francis welcomed her as the founder of a female branch of the Franciscan family known as the Poor Clares. One of the first to join her was her younger sister Catherine, whom Francis renamed Agnes.

Though the young women's family tried to force them to return home, they relented in the face of their adamant conviction. Francis set them up in a chapel in San Damiano, which became their convent. Agnes went on to become the abbess of a new convent in Florence—she wrote a touching letter on the heartbreak of separation from her sister—and later established communities in Mantua, Venice, and Padua.

In August 1253 Agnes was summoned to San Damiano to be with Clare in her dying hours. Clare predicted that her sister would soon follow, as indeed she did on November 16. Their bodies eventually rested in adjacent tombs in the church of Santa Chiara in Assisi.

"After a few days, Agnes, called to the wedding feast of the Lamb, followed her sister Clare to the eternal delights."

—From the Chronicle of Clare of Assisi

St. Frances Xavier Cabrini
Founder, Missionary Sisters of the Sacred Heart
(1850–1917)

Frances Xavier Cabrini was born in a small village south of Milan. Trained as a schoolteacher, she dreamed of becoming a missionary in China. But after being rejected by two congregations that deemed her too frail for the rigors of convent life, she resolved to form a new congregation, the Missionary Sisters of the Sacred Heart. Though she managed by sheer strength of will to attract a band of companions, still the exact mission of her congregation remained in question. Her bishop urged her to consider the United States, where masses of poor Italian immigrants crowded the city slums with no one to tend to them. The matter was decided in an audience with Pope Leo XIII, who counseled her, "My daughter, your field awaits you not in the East but in the West." And so in 1889 Mother Cabrini and six sisters sailed for America.

In the following years Mother Cabrini and her sisters established schools, orphanages, and eventually hospitals across the United States and later in Latin America. Prepared to face any challenge, she personally established more than fifty foundations. In an audience with the pope he told her to "hurry all over the earth if possible, in order to take the holy name of Jesus everywhere."

Mother Cabrini died on December 22, 1917. She was canonized in 1946, with a feast day of November 13. Having become a naturalized American citizen, she enjoyed the distinction of being the "first citizen saint" of the United States.

"Money we have not, but from our faith will spring forth miracles."

—St. Frances Xavier Cabrini

St. Gregory Palamas
Monk and Mystical Theologian (1296–1359)

St. Gregory Palamas spent most of his life as a monk on Mount Athos, a virtual republic of Eastern monasticism, situated on a peninsula in Thessalonica. There, in a network of independent communities and hundreds of hermitages, the monks and hermits practiced a form of "hesychastic" spirituality, of which St. Gregory was the most famous advocate. "Hesychia," the Greek word for quietude, was here applied to a spiritual discipline of interior prayer and rest in God. The hesychasts took to heart St. Paul's exhortation to "pray without ceasing." By constantly repeating the name of Jesus, sometimes coordinated with the rhythm of their breathing, the monks entered into a state of extreme concentration on spiritual reality. In such a state they liked to say that the Holy Spirit was praying through them. By such means the Christian might latch on to the divine nature, much like a rope flung over a rock, and so pull free of worldly attachments.

Gregory spent many years as a hermit. His later preeminence is due to his role in defending hesychastic spirituality against the attacks of a Calabrian monk named Barlaam, who called the hesychasts "navel-gazers." This battle was bitter and protracted, though it was resolved in Gregory's favor by a synod in 1351. He spent his last years as archbishop of Thessalonica and died in 1359. He was canonized by the Byzantine Church in 1368.

"This is the very nature of prayer, that it raises one from earth to heaven, higher than every heavenly name and dignity, and brings one before the very God of all."
—St. Gregory Palamas

Joseph Cardinal Bernardin
Bishop (1928–1996)

With his appointment in 1982 as archbishop of Chicago, followed by his elevation to the College of Cardinals, Joseph Bernardin achieved the pinnacle of success in a distinguished episcopal career. But inwardly, he had embarked on a different journey. Some years before, he had faced the realization that his life was focused more on the Church than on Christ. That insight began a process of conversion that transformed a successful churchman into a man of God and prepared him for the trials that were to come.

First came the humiliating accusation from a former seminarian that Bernardin had once molested him. After the troubled young man, who was dying of AIDS, abruptly withdrew the charges, Bernardin met with him and forgave him. Soon after, Bernardin announced that he himself was suffering from pancreatic cancer. In a moving statement he announced, "I can say in all sincerity that I am at peace. As a person of faith, I see death as a friend, as the transition from earthly life to life eternal."

In his last weeks, as his candle burned visibly shorter, Bernardin received a great outpouring of affection and admiration. By the manner of his dying, he offered a powerful public witness to his faith in God, and his passing, on November 14, 1996, was mourned by people of all faiths.

"As my life ebbs away, I am not anxious, but rather reconfirmed in my conviction about the wonder of human life, a gift that flows from the very being of God."
—Joseph Cardinal Bernardin

St. Gertrude the Great
Mystic (1256–1302)

At the age of five, St. Gertrude was given over by her parents to the nuns of Helfta in Saxony, where she remained for the rest of her life. This monastery was one of the great religious communities of its time, distinguished by women of great learning as well as a number of mystics, including St. Mechtild of Hackeborn, who was put in charge of the young girl and who oversaw her education.

The religious life was all Gertrude had ever known. Nevertheless, she truly owned her vocation only at the age of twenty-five. The turning point came one evening when she experienced a vision of Christ in the form of a young man. "Fear not," he said, "I will save and deliver you." He was bathed in a dazzling light that emanated from his five wounds. "You have licked the dust with my enemies and sucked honey from thorns. Now come back to me and my divine delights shall be as wine to you."

For the rest of her life Gertrude enjoyed frequent mystical revelations, often couched in dialogues with Christ. These she recorded in a book, which touched on nearly all the themes of Catholic theology. She had a special devotion to the Sacred Heart of Jesus, the point where human and divine love are most intimately joined.

Gertrude served her community as a spiritual director and often led the community in prayer. She died in 1302.

"Let my heart be united with Yours. Let my will be conformed to Yours in all things. May Your Will be the rule of all my desires and actions. Amen."
—St. Gertrude

Blessed Mary of the Passion
Founder, Franciscan Missionaries of Mary (1839–1904)

Hélène Marie Philippine was born in France to a noble family. After a short stint with the Poor Clares she joined a contemplative community in Toulouse, the Society of Mary Reparatrix, where she took the name Mary of the Passion. In 1865 she was sent to Madurai in southern India, where her order was helping to establish a congregation of Indian sisters. There she proved so adept in leadership that she was named provincial superior. In 1876, however, long-simmering divisions in the community erupted to the point that Mary and nineteen other sisters withdrew and established a community under the aegis of the Paris Foreign Missions Society.

At this point Mary conceived of a new congregation that would combine contemplation with active mission work. After becoming a Third Order Franciscan, she received permission from Rome to establish the Franciscan Missionaries of Mary. Her community grew with impressive speed. In India, she directed her sisters to provide medical care for women, whose health was compromised by their unwillingness to be seen by male doctors.

Mary's sisters spread across the world, often in perilous situations. Seven of them (later canonized) were killed in China during the Boxer Rebellion. Mary remained the superior general until her death on November 15, 1904, at which time there were over 2,000 Franciscan Missionaries of Mary working in 86 countries. She was beatified in 2002.

"Combining a mystical and an active vocation, passionate and intrepid, she gave herself with an intuitive and bold readiness to the universal mission of the Church."
—Pope John Paul II

St. Margaret of Scotland
Queen (1046–1093)

St. Margaret was one of the last members of the Anglo-Saxon royal family. After the Norman Conquest in 1066 she and her family took refuge in Scotland, where she found favor with her host, King Malcolm. They married three years later and enjoyed a happy marriage—happy as well for the nation, for the queen used her influence to promote the virtues of faith, charity, and justice. Malcolm honored her piety and gave her free rein to promote the practice of Christianity in his kingdom. Together they founded churches, monasteries, hospices, and almshouses throughout the land.

Aside from works of charity, Margaret attended to the institutional life of the Church. At her instigation the Church in Scotland convened its first synod. Margaret played an important role in the discussions, sharing her interpretation of Scripture as well as the principles of faith.

Margaret worked to curb the feuding and warlike proclivities of her people. But she could not prevent the frequent recurrence of conflict between Scotland and England. In 1093 Malcolm and their eldest son were killed in battle. Margaret, already on her deathbed, cried out: "I thank thee, Almighty God, that in sending me so great an affliction in the last hour of my life, thou wouldst purify me from my sins, as I hope, by thy mercy."

She died on November 16, 1093.

"So thoroughly did her outward bearing correspond with the staidness of her character that it seems as if she had been born the pattern of a virtuous life."

—Bishop Turgot, St. Margaret's biographer

Ignacio Ellacuría and Companions
Jesuit Martyrs of El Salvador (d. 1989)

I n the early morning hours of November 16, 1989, army commandos invaded the University of Central America in San Salvador, roused the sleeping Jesuit community, and sprayed them with machine-gun fire on the garden lawn. The victims included six Jesuit priests along with their housekeeper and her teenaged daughter.

For years the Jesuits had angered the ruling elite by siding with the oppressed in the bitter social conflict that divided the country. Spanish-born Ignacio Ellacuría, rector of the university, had emerged as a particularly effective advocate of national dialogue and a critic of injustice. For his efforts he was derided in right-wing propaganda as the "brains" of the "communist" movement. The Jesuits were no communists. They were priests who struggled to live out the Church's preferential option for the poor and who had committed themselves to the Jesuit mission: "service of faith and promotion of justice." They had committed the university to this same mission, believing that in a world of conflict a Christian university must stand with the victims of violence.

During a rebel offensive that spread to the capital city, top military commanders issued an order to eliminate all suspected leftist sympathizers. The Jesuit-run university was among the targets. The massacre of the UCA martyrs was the grim conclusion of a decade that began with the death of Archbishop Oscar Romero. Peace negotiations, begun the next year, were concluded in 1992.

"Always remember that there is no conversion to God if there is no conversion to the oppressed."
—Ignacio Ellacuría, SJ

St. Hilda of Whitby
Abbess (ca. 610–680)

St. Hilda was one of the great lights of the early Anglo-Saxon Church. The great niece of St. Edwin, king of Northumbria, she was baptized by the missionary St. Paulinus when she was thirteen. While her early life was spent in secular activities, she eventually decided to "serve God alone." After spending time in a number of monasteries in East Anglia she returned home to found a new monastery at Whitby. This would remain her home for the rest of her life; under her leadership it would become an important center for the spread of the Christian faith in England.

Whitby was a "double monastery," including both men and women who lived separately, gathering together to chant the office. Hilda set a standard for holiness, wisdom, and scholarship. She served as a gifted spiritual director, and five of her monks went on to become bishops. Through her example, as her biographer St. Bede wrote, Hilda promoted "the observance of righteousness, mercy, purity, and other virtues, but especially in peace and charity." In her monastery "no one was rich or poor."

Whitby was chosen in 664 as the site of an important Church synod to resolve tensions between the Roman model of episcopal authority and the more monastic model characteristic of the Celtic Church. Hilda favored the latter, but the synod decided otherwise. Her last counsel to her community was to "maintain the gospel peace among yourselves and with others." She died on November 17, 680.

"All that knew her called her mother."

—St. Bede

St. Elizabeth of Hungary
Queen (1207–1231)

St. Elizabeth, the daughter of Hungarian royalty, was betrothed as a child of four to Ludwig, the nine-year-old prince of Thuringia in southern Germany. Despite this arrangement, the two children established a close friendship that eventually blossomed into a loving marriage. Elizabeth bore three children. But Ludwig's family disapproved of her piety (she had become a Franciscan tertiary) and especially her "excessive" charity toward the poor and sick. Ignoring their wishes, she opened the royal granaries during a time of famine. This won her the people's devotion, though such generosity made her an object of scorn among the elite members of the court.

In 1227 Ludwig embarked on a Crusade and died on his journey. In a paroxysm of grief, Elizabeth cried, "The world is dead to me, and all that was joyous in the world." Without her husband's protection, she was at the mercy of her in-laws. They banished her from the court, forcing her to leave the palace on a winter night, carrying nothing but her newborn child. She accepted shelter in a pig shed.

Eventually, to avoid scandal, she was provided with a simple cottage, where she supported herself by spinning and fishing. Otherwise, she visited the sick in their homes or in the hospices she had endowed. Over time, her reputation for holiness spread, and she earned the grudging respect of those who had persecuted her. She died on November 17, 1231, at the age of twenty-four. She was canonized less than four years later.

"We must give God what we have, gladly and with joy."

—St. Elizabeth of Hungary

St. Roque Gonzalez
Jesuit Martyr of Paraguay (1576–1628)

Roque Gonzalez, the son of a Spanish nobleman, was a second-generation Paraguayan. Ordained at twenty-three, he later entered the Society of Jesus, attracted by the Jesuits' missionary work among the Indians. Leaving the security of the colonial enclaves, Gonzalez and his fellow Jesuits set out for unexplored territories, braving hunger, disease, and the threat of death in each fresh encounter with one of the scattered Indian communities along the Parana and Uruguay Rivers. While endeavoring to convey the Christian faith, they also encouraged the Indians to abandon their nomadic existence in favor of farming in organized settlements. These efforts met with surprising success. Between 1610 and 1624 twenty-three of these settlements, or "reductions," were established, with a combined population of 100,000.

Many colonists were furious at the Jesuits for closing off a vast pool of exploitable labor, and the reductions were frequently attacked by marauding slave traders. But while the priests won the devotion of many Indians, to others they represented nothing but a more benign form of foreign incursion.

In the fall of 1628 one of the hostile chiefs gave an order to kill the white fathers. Roque Gonzalez was killed with a stone hatchet on November 15. In 1934 he became the first American-born martyr to be beatified. He was canonized in 1988.

"God does not command the Gospel of Our Lord Jesus Christ to be preached with the noise of arms and with pillage. What he rather commands is the example of a good life and holy teaching."

—St. Roque Gonzalez

St. Rose Philippine Duchesne
Missionary Nun (1769–1852)

R ose Philippine Duchesne was born in Grenoble. Her desire to enter religious life was complicated for many years by the French Revolution and the suppression of religious orders. But eventually, in 1804, she joined the new Society of the Sacred Heart, founded by Madeleine Sophie Barat. Her true vocation began fourteen years later when she embarked with several sisters for North America, responding to a plea from the bishop of New Orleans for nuns to serve in the huge diocese of Louisiana.

The first foundation of Sacred Heart sisters outside of France was in a log cabin in St. Charles, on the Missouri River near St. Louis. Conditions were primitive, and the winters were especially harsh. While the sisters endured every challenge of frontier life, the community grew, building schools and orphanages, including a school for Indians. Eventually additional houses were opened near New Orleans, St. Louis, and elsewhere. When she retired as superior, Philippine set up a school in Kansas for the Potawatomi Indians, who gave her the name "Woman-Who-Prays-Always."

Philippine died on November 18, 1852, at the age of eighty-three. She was canonized by Pope John Paul II in 1988.

"We cultivate a very small field for Christ, but we love it, knowing that God does not require great achievements but a heart that holds back nothing for self."
                                        —St. Rose Philippine Duchesne

St. Mechtild of Hackeborn
Mystic (ca. 1241–1298)

St. Mechtild was one of a trio of extraordinary mystics, including St. Gertrude the Great and St. Mechthild of Magdeburg, who inhabited the same Benedictine convent in Saxony in the late thirteenth century. She entered the convent of Helfta when she was seven. Her first mystical vision occurred while receiving communion. Christ appeared to her, held her hands, and left his imprint on her heart "like a seal in wax." Christ furthermore presented his own heart to her in the form of a cup and said, "By my heart you will praise me always; go, offer to all the saints the drink of life from my heart that they may be happily inebriated with it."

Mechtild had a great devotion to the humanity of Christ, the "door" by which human beings and all creation entered into union with divinity. In one vision she perceived that "the smallest details of creation are reflected in the Holy Trinity by means of the humanity of Christ, because it is from the same earth that produced them that Christ drew his humanity."

As a result of her visions, Mechtild wielded tremendous authority within her community and beyond. She was regarded as a prophet, teacher, and counselor, "a tender mother of the unfortunate by her continual prayers, her zealous instruction, and her consolations."

She died on November 19, 1298.

"She gave teaching with such abundance that such a one has never been seen in the monastery and we fear, alas, will never be seen again."
— St. Gertrude, on her teacher St. Mechtild

Venerable Henriette DeLille
Founder, Sisters of the Holy Family (1812–1862)

enriette DeLille was born in New Orleans in 1812 to a white father and a Creole woman of Spanish and African ancestry. Though it was illegal for her parents to marry there was in New Orleans at that time a culture of relative freedom for persons of "mixed race." Nevertheless, at a time when slavery was still the law of the land in the southern United States, Henriette DeLille would manage to found a congregation for "free women of color."

As a teenager she taught in the local Catholic school and dreamed of entering religious life. But there was no congregation that would take her. And so, in 1836, she formed her own religious community, Sisters of the Presentation, consisting of herself and seven other young Creole women. Her brother—who was able to pass for white—objected to her activities, fearful of her calling attention to their Creole roots. But Henriette paid him no mind. She and her sisters dedicated themselves to the care of the old and sick, with special ministry to slaves and those of African descent.

In 1837 DeLille's congregation was recognized by the Vatican. In 1842 its name was changed to Sisters of the Holy Family. Mother DeLille died on November 17, 1862. She was declared venerable in 2010.

"I believe in God. I hope in God. I love God. I want to live and die for God."
— Mother DeLille's only recorded writing

Henri Dominique Lacordaire
Dominican (1802–1861)

Henri Lacordaire devoted his life to the spiritual renewal of France, a task, he believed, that could not be achieved without overcoming the mutual hostility between the Church and the forces of liberty. As a young priest he was disturbed that the Church seemed sadly out of touch with the times, still traumatized by the Revolution but stuck in pious nostalgia for a bygone era.

He started a journal dedicated to reconciling Catholicism and the positive features of the Revolution—the principles of liberty, democracy, and the separation of Church and state. The journal lasted only a year before it was suppressed by the bishops, a move followed by a general papal condemnation of liberalism.

Nevertheless, a series of Lenten sermons he delivered at Notre Dame Cathedral in 1835 caused a sensation, indicating that the times were ready for a renewed presentation of the faith. Soon after, Lacordaire announced that he was joining the Dominicans. After training in Rome he returned to Paris in 1840 wearing his Dominican habit—the first time this garb had been seen in France in fifty years. He was in constant demand as a preacher, though his commitment to political and religious liberty continued to generate controversy. He remained content to exist on the margins of toleration, scorned by most of the hierarchy, while continuing to serve his dual project: to maintain a space for liberty in the Church and a space for religion in the Republic. He died on November 21, 1861.

"I am a citizen of the future."

—Henri Dominique Lacordaire, OP

Frank Sheed
Catholic Publisher and Apologist (1897–1981)

Frank Sheed was one of the most eminent Catholic evange-lists of the twentieth century. Through a stream of books, lectures, and the great publishing house he founded with his wife, Maisie Ward, he did much to elevate the level of Catholic culture in England and America.

Sheed was born in Sydney, Australia, but immigrated to England after completing a law degree. Having ardently embraced the Catholicism of his Irish mother, he took seriously the imperative to spread the faith. In London he took up with the Catholic Evidence Guild, a group of laypeople who literally stood on soapboxes in Hyde Park to defend the Catholic faith. Its members had to be steeped in theology, philosophy, and Catholic history, and prepared to answer any possible challenge. The best of them were also equipped with wit and grace in deflecting hostile hecklers. Sheed was one of the best. It was there that he met his wife, the scion of a distinguished Catholic family. Soon after their marriage they founded Sheed & Ward, inaugurating a golden age of Catholic publishing with authors such as Ronald Knox, G. K. Chesterton, Evelyn Waugh, and Caryll Houselander. They later brought their publishing house to America.

In writing on theology, Sheed was skilled at making the truths of faith seem clear, reasonable, and ultimately necessary for happiness. "We can never attain a maximum love of God with only a minimum knowledge of God," he wrote. He died on November 20, 1981.

"Each new thing learned and meditated about God is a new reason for loving him."
—Frank Sheed

Blessed Mary Frances Siedliska
Founder, Congregation of the Holy Family of Nazareth
(1842–1902)

Franciszka Siedliska was born to a noble family in Poland in 1842. After she expressed an attraction to religious life, her father, hoping to nip her vocation in the bud, took the family on a grand tour of Europe. When this failed to dissuade her, her father gave his reluctant consent. Yet she did not feel drawn to any existing congregation; instead, with the support of her spiritual director, she believed she was called to initiate something new. In 1873, with the support of Pope Pius IX, she founded the Congregation of the Holy Family of Nazareth. Its members would "offer their prayers, works and their entire life for the Church and the Holy Father, and imitate the hidden life and the virtues of the Holy Family."

From their motherhouse in Rome, the sisters focused their care on abandoned children and on providing religious education to the poor. Mother Mary encouraged independent thinking among her sisters. Though most religious congregations stressed conformity to a certain pattern of religious life, Mother Mary believed that "in Nazareth there should be freedom of conscience, the liberty of the children of God, regard for the psyche of the sisters, their temperament, and their natural disposition."

By 1884 five houses were established in Poland. These were followed by houses in the United States, France, and England. Mother Mary died on November 21, 1902. She was beatified in 1989.

"Thus I envisioned our life in Nazareth as a life of love externally given to work, service, performance of whatever Our Lord may require."
—Blessed Mary Frances Siedliska

C. S. Lewis
Christian Apologist (1898–1963)

Clive Staples Lewis, who was born in Belfast in Northern Ireland, spent most of his life in Oxford, where he served as a scholar of medieval literature. Though in his youth he had spurned religious faith, at the age of thirty-two he found his way back to Christianity. Afterward, through books and radio broadcasts, Lewis came to be recognized as one of the most popular exponents and defenders of Christianity in the English language—a reputation that continues to the present.

While he remained comfortably settled in the Anglican Church, Lewis espoused what he called "Mere Christianity"— an expression of the essential elements of the Gospel—that appealed to readers across denominational boundaries. His arguments, rooted in reason and everyday experience, were leavened by aphoristic wit. For example: "Christianity, if false, is of no importance, and if true, of infinite importance. The only thing it cannot be is moderately important." Or: "I believe in Christianity as I believe that the sun has risen: not only because I see it, but because by it I see everything else."

Late in life, Lewis married an American woman, Joy Davidman. Her death from cancer four years later was a devastating blow, an experience he described in one of his most personal works, *A Grief Observed*. Lewis himself died three years later on November 22, 1963.

"The Christian does not think God will love us because we are good, but that God will make us good because He loves us."

—C. S. Lewis

St. Cecilia
Martyr (ca. Third Century)

Though St. Cecilia has long enjoyed a popular cult, the first account of her life dates only from the fifth century. According to this story she was born to a patrician family in Rome and raised as a Christian. Although she wished to consecrate her life to God, she was betrothed to marry a young man named Valerian. On their wedding night she related to her husband that an angel watched over her and that if he "touched her in the way of marriage" the angel would be angry and cause him suffering. When Valerian asked to see this angel, Cecilia told him that if he received baptism he too would see the angel. Remarkably, Valerian consented.

The couple dedicated themselves to good works, particularly the perilous task of burying the bodies of martyrs. As a result they were eventually arrested and ordered to make sacrifices to the gods. Upon their refusal they were both executed. The soldier assigned to behead Cecilia botched the job. Left for dead, she lingered for three days.

Cecilia is depicted in art with a musical instrument. Her designation as patron of music apparently owes itself to a line in her biography that describes her on her wedding day "singing to the Lord in her heart."

"Blessed Cecilia, appear in visions. / To all musicians, appear and inspire: / Translated Daughter, come down and startle / Composing mortals with immortal fire."

—W. H. Auden, "Anthem for St. Cecilia's Day"

Jeanne Fontbonne
Sister of St. Joseph (1759–1843)

Jeanne Fontbonne was born in the area of Le Puy in France. In 1779 she was received in a community of Sisters of St. Joseph in Monistrol founded by Bishop de Gallard. Six years later, upon becoming superior, she became known as Mother St. John. She devoted herself to overseeing the sisters' work in operating a hospital and educating the poor. But with the outbreak of the Revolution, the sisters' fate became increasingly tenuous. The clergy were required to sign an Oath of the Civil Constitution of the Clergy, rejecting the authority of Rome. When Bishop de Gallard refused to sign, Mother St. John chose to stand beside him.

She remained in her house as long as she could. But eventually she was forcibly evicted by a mob, and the community was dispersed. Though she returned to her father's home, her life remained at risk. In fact, her arrest and imprisonment followed shortly, and she was sentenced to death. Surprising news, however, came on the day before her scheduled execution: Maximilien Robespierre, architect of the Terror, had been arrested. Mother St. John was summarily released.

Though it was still many years before she was able to resume religious life, in 1807 Mother St. John was summoned to Lyons to become the superior of a community of women who had been dispersed from their congregations. In 1812 they were officially restored as the Sisters of St. Joseph. Mother St. John went on to establish over two hundred communities. She died on November 22, 1843.

"In everybody she could discern something good; so that it might be said she was something like the bee, which sucks honey from even the bitterest plants."

—From *The Life of Rev. Mother St. John Fontbonne*

St. Columbanus
Abbot (ca. 540–615)

Within a generation of St. Patrick's work in establishing the Church in Ireland, a wave of Irish missionaries began to overflow their native country, spreading the Christian faith across the British Isles and the Continent. In the course of their travels they established an impressive network of monasteries, havens of learning and culture that played an important part in stabilizing and unifying the primitive civilization of Europe.

Among these intrepid missionaries, St. Columbanus was one of the greatest. After many years in a remote monastery in Bangor he set off with a dozen companions for Gaul, where he established a monastery in Burgundy that quickly attracted such large numbers that he was forced to found several other monasteries in the area.

Despite his growing popularity, he came in for criticism from the local bishops, who objected to his severe Celtic spirituality. He also ran afoul of the royal family and was forced to leave Burgundy along with all his Irish monks. He made his way to Austria and Switzerland, everywhere establishing new monasteries. Finally he crossed the Alps and settled in Milan, where he founded yet another monastery, as well as becoming embroiled in controversy surrounding the Arian heresy.

Columbanus did much to extend and popularize the monastic movement in Europe. He also devised an influential monastic rule, notable for its heavy emphasis on discipline (eventually eclipsed by the more clement Rule of St. Benedict).

"Nothing is sweeter than the calm of conscience, nothing safer than purity of soul—yet no one can bestow this on himself because it is properly the gift of God's grace."

—St. Columbanus

Blessed Miguel Pro
Jesuit Martyr (1891–1927)

I n 1926 Mexico was passing through a period of violent anti-Catholic repression. As a Jesuit novice Fr. Miguel Pro had fled the country in 1914. Now he returned in disguise; to be identified as a priest would mean instant arrest. His mission was simple: to serve the Catholic people, strengthen their faith, celebrate the sacraments, and elude arrest as long as possible.

Making his way to the capital, Fr. Pro managed to survive several close calls. He spent his days hearing confessions, performing clandestine baptisms, saying Mass. There were spies everywhere but also, it seemed, an inexhaustible supply of loyal Catholics prepared to undergo terrible risks to assist a priest on the run.

Eventually he was captured. After Pro was charged with participation in a plot against the government, President Calles personally ordered his execution. On the morning of November 23, 1927, he was taken to the police firing range, where a crowd of reporters had been summoned. After praying, Pro stood and held out his arms in the form of a cross. As the firing squad took aim, he called out, *"Viva Cristo Rey!"*—Long Live Christ the King!

The president had surely not reckoned on the power of martyrdom. Photographs of Fr. Pro's execution became holy cards, eagerly distributed among the faithful. He was beatified in 1988.

"We ought to speak, shout out against injustices, with confidence and without fear. We proclaim the principles of the Church, the reign of love, without forgetting that it is also a reign of justice."

—Blessed Miguel Pro

St. Andrew Dung-Lac and Companions
Martyrs of Vietnam

In 1988 Pope John Paul II dedicated this day to the vast number of Vietnamese martyrs (more than 100,000), both named and unnamed, including Andrew Dung-Lac, a Vietnamese priest, who was among the first group of 117 to be canonized in 1900.

The first martyrs of Indochina were Spanish missionaries in 1580. The local rulers, regarding Christianity as a foreign incursion, responded with waves of savage persecution. The tortures inflicted on Christians in Vietnam are among the worst in recorded history. Many of the victims were suffocated, burned alive, had their limbs hacked off joint by joint, or their flesh torn from their bones. The martyrs included foreign bishops and priests as well as countless laypeople.

Andrew Dung-Lac, a diocesan priest, was born in 1795. He grew up in Hanoi, where he met a catechist and decided to be baptized. His own dedication as a catechist led to his being selected for theological training and eventual ordination in 1823. In 1832 the emperor Minh-Mang expelled all foreign priests and ordered Vietnamese Christians to renounce Christianity. Churches were destroyed, and the teaching of Christianity was forbidden. Andrew was twice arrested but managed to win his release. After being arrested a third time he was beheaded on December 21, 1839.

"In the midst of these torments, which usually terrify others, I am, by the grace of God, full of joy and gladness, because I am not alone—Christ is with me. Our Master bears the whole weight of the cross, leaving me only the tiniest, last bit."

—St. Paul Le-Bao-Tinh, Martyr, 1843

St. Joseph Pignatelli
Jesuit (1737–1811)

After midnight on April 2, 1767, Jesuit houses throughout Spain were roused by the delivery of an astonishing edict from King Charles—that "for grave reasons," which "by their nature must remain unrevealed in our royal bosom," the king had ordered the immediate expulsion from Spain of all members of the Society of Jesus.

Thus began the most terrible ordeal in the history of the Jesuits—a concerted effort by Bourbon princes throughout Europe to suppress the Society in order to assert their control over the Church. Their efforts failed—in no small part due to the Spaniard Joseph Pignatelli, credited as a "Second Founder" of the Jesuits.

The expulsion from Spain and Portugal was bad enough, but worse was to come. In 1773 Pope Clement XIV suppressed the Society altogether. At once 23,000 Jesuits were dispensed from their vows. There was a peculiar catch. Empress Catherine the Great refused to allow the bishops in Russia to deliver the brief. Thus, at least in this corner of Europe, the Jesuits survived.

Learning of this anomaly, Pignatelli affiliated with this province, and so without ever setting foot in Russia he renewed his vows and quietly became the only Jesuit in Italy. In 1804 Pope Pius VII restored the Society in Naples, and Pignatelli became provincial.

Eventually the Society was fully restored, but Pignatelli did not live to see it. He died on November 11, 1811, and was canonized in 1954. His feast day is November 24.

"The time will come when they will cry out for these Fathers to return."
—St. Joseph Pignatelli

St. Catherine of Alexandria
Martyr (Dates Unknown)

St. Catherine of Alexandria was for many centuries one of the most popular of all saints, the patron of maidens and women students, of philosophers, preachers, and many others. Her voice was one of those that inspired St. Joan of Arc to maintain her mission against all odds.

According to legend, Catherine was the daughter of a patrician family in Alexandria, Egypt, sometime in the Roman era. Through her study of philosophy she became convinced of the truth of Christianity and converted to the illicit faith. After she tried to convert the emperor himself, he had her examined by fifty of the leading philosophers of the court, resulting in their own conversion (and subsequent martyrdom). Catherine preferred prison to the emperor's invitation to be his consort. Even in prison, however, she managed to convert the emperor's wife, her jailer, and two hundred of the imperial guards. Enraged, the emperor condemned her to be tortured on a spiked wheel (her famous emblem), but the machine broke apart. Finally, she was put to the sword.

In 1969 Catherine's feast day was removed from the Roman calendar (on the basis of doubts that such a saint truly existed), but it was restored in 2002 as an optional memorial.

"Lord Jesus Christ, my God, I thank Thee for having firmly set my feet on the rock of the Faith and directed my steps on the pathway of salvation. Open now Thy arms wounded on the cross to receive my soul, which I offer in sacrifice to the glory of Thy Name."

—St. Catherine of Alexandria

Venerable Margaret Sinclair
Poor Clare (1900–1925)

Margaret Sinclair was born in Edinburgh to a poor family. She left school at fourteen to work in a series of factories, helping to support her family. An eventual marriage proposal served as the catalyst for deeper reflection on her vocation, resulting in her decision to enter the Poor Clares. As the community in Edinburgh had no room for her she was accepted into a community in Notting Hill in London.

Her working-class roots set her apart from the educated and upper-class backgrounds of the other sisters. Margaret stood out as much for her practical knowledge of the working world as she did for her Scottish brogue. One time, noticing that Margaret was having too much fun whitewashing an outhouse, a nun upbraided her, "You'll never be a saint." Margaret replied, "Dinna fash yerself" (don't let that trouble you).

Her time in the convent was limited. She died of tuberculosis on November 24, 1925, at the age of twenty-five. Despite her obscure life, her reputation soon spread, especially in Scotland, where she was celebrated as a saint of "ordinary life." She was declared venerable in 1978. Pope John Paul II described her as "one of God's little ones who, through her very simplicity, was touched by God with a real holiness of life."

"O, God . . . I desire to . . . rejoice when I feel the pinch of poverty, and always remain modest and prudent, thinking of this in our Blessed Lady, and how she would like it in her child."

—Venerable Margaret Sinclair

Sojourner Truth
Abolitionist (1797–1883)

Sojourner Truth was born a slave in Hurley, New York. Her parents named her Isabella, a name she abandoned at forty-six when she took up her calling as a prophet and preacher. In her youth she was bought and sold many times. Yet throughout these years she carried on a conversation with God, to whom she poured out her sufferings. And God told her that she would be free.

As a young woman she had been given in marriage to an older slave, with whom she bore five children. But early one morning in 1826 she walked away from her master's farm and stole herself from slavery, taking only her infant daughter with her. For some years she worked as a servant in New York City. But by 1843 she became convinced that God was calling her to a greater mission. Taking the name Sojourner Truth, she commenced an itinerant ministry of the word, preaching from the Scriptures and delivering God's judgment against the evils of slavery. In time she joined this theme with commitment to women's rights.

At times she faced violent mobs. Yet she never doubted that the end of slavery would come. In fact, she was present in the capital in 1865 when Congress ratified the constitutional amendment abolishing slavery. She continued to struggle for freedom and equality until the day she died on November 26, 1883, at the age of eighty-six. A few days before she had told a friend, "I'm not going to die, honey. I'm going home like a shining star."

"What we give to the poor we lend to the Lord."

—Sojourner Truth

Blessed James Alberione
Founder, Society of St. Paul (1884–1971)

James Alberione was born to a farming family in northern Italy. After attending seminary in Alba he was ordained in 1907, from which he went on to earn a doctorate in theology and to direct pastoral work at the seminary. On the last night of 1900 he had spent the evening in prayer, trying to discern how he might find a way of serving the Church in a new way, appropriate to a new century.

The answer came in 1913 when he took over a weekly Catholic magazine, *Gazzetta d'Alba*, thus beginning his lifelong work in the field of mass communication. In the following year he founded the Society of St. Paul (the Paulines), which was joined later by the Daughters of St. Paul, cofounded with Mother Thecla Merlo. Other congregations followed. Altogether the mission of the Pauline family focused on the apostolate of the Word—through bookstores, newspapers, magazines, and other publications.

In 1969 Pope Paul VI, receiving a delegation of Pauline priests and sisters in an audience, recognized and greeted the founder: "Here he is, humble, silent, tireless, always vigilant, recollected in his thoughts, which run from prayer to action; always intent on scrutinizing the 'signs of the times,' that is, the most creative way to reach souls. Our Fr. Alberione has given the Church new instruments with which to express herself."

Fr. Alberione died on November 26, 1971. He was beatified in 2003. The work of his Pauline family continues in thirty countries around the globe.

"The first concern of the Pauline family should be holiness of life; the second, holiness of doctrine."
—Blessed James Alberione

Saints Barlaam and Josaphat
Monks (Dates Unknown)

According to legend, St. Josaphat was the son of an Indian king who had persecuted his Christian subjects. When a seer foretold that Josaphat himself would one day become a Christian, the king had him locked up in seclusion. Eventually, however, the young man was converted by Barlaam, a wandering monk of Mt. Sinai, who approached him in the guise of a merchant offering to sell "a pearl of great price." Josaphat gladly received baptism, afterward renouncing his throne and all worldly wealth. He went on to retire to the desert with Barlaam to pursue his ongoing quest for moral and spiritual truth.

The story had a long and influential life in the Christian East and West. In recent times it has been traced to a Georgian monk on Mt. Athos in the eleventh century, whereupon it circulated in many languages. The story is clearly legendary. But it has a complicated history. Scholars have shown that the Christian legend was an Islamic story taken from Manichean sources in Western Asia. Going back further it can be traced to Siddhartha Gautama, the Hindu prince who renounced his family, wealth, and worldly power to seek the path of enlightenment, eventually becoming the Buddha. In the transmigration of the story the word *Bodhisattva* became Bodisaf (Manichee), Yudasaf (Arabic), Lodasaph (Georgian), Ioasaph (Greek), and finally Josaphat (Latin).

So by a curious route the Buddha became a Christian saint who inspired later generations of Christians (including the Russian novelist Leo Tolstoy) to pursue the path of enlightenment. It is a fascinating parable for an era of interreligious dialogue.

"By the hands of the poor we can store up riches in eternity."

—St. Barlaam

Dom Virgil Michel
Benedictine, Liturgical Reformer (1890–1938)

Virgil Michel, a Benedictine monk from St. John's Abbey in Collegeville, Minnesota, was the pioneer of the liturgical movement in the United States. Through his writings, he struggled to promote a proper understanding of the Mass in the life of the Church and, by extension, the place of the Church in the life of the world.

In the 1920s, when Michel initiated these efforts, most lay Catholics tended to be passive spectators at Mass. Michel felt it was vitally important to recover a sense of the Mass as the central expression of the living Church. This required a reform of the liturgy to restore the participation of the people.

Ultimately, Michel regarded the purpose of liturgical renewal as a means of advancing the penetration of Christian values into the world. If Christians were passive before the altar, "how can we expect them to be active Christians in their daily life out in the world?" A "clericalized" view of the Church contributed to the gap between the religious realm and the everyday world, and this, he believed, contributed to the materialism, secularism, and social problems of the age.

In all these concerns Michel anticipated by decades the reforms of Vatican II. A pioneer in promoting lay spirituality, he wished to see the liturgical spirit "radiate forth from the altar of Christ into every aspect of the daily life of the Christian."

"The liturgy . . . sets supreme value on human life by properly aligning it with the source of all life."
—Dom Virgil Michel

Isaiah
Prophet (Eighth Century BC)

Isaiah received his prophetic call in the Temple in Jerusalem, where he probably served as a priest. It began with a vision of the Lord sitting upon a throne. When the prophet bewailed his "unclean lips," an angel touched his mouth with a burning coal. He heard the Lord saying, "Whom shall I send?" and he answered, "Here am I! Send me!"

His career as a prophet took place against a bewildering backdrop of international intrigue. Caught between empires, the rulers of Jerusalem sought to maintain their independence through military alliances. Isaiah believed that by trusting such alliances Israel was losing sight of its dependence on God.

His oracles are filled with references to disobedience and hypocrisy: The poor are oppressed; the nation bows down to idols of security and affluence. All the fine sacrifices in the Temple are an abomination. Rather than offer prayers with bloody hands, the people must "cease to do evil, learn to do good; seek justice, correct oppression . . ."

Yet along with these warnings, Isaiah's message was marked by hope. He leavened his oracles with the promise of a future Messiah and the vision of a peaceable kingdom to come. His active mission lasted forty years, but it inspired a tradition of reflection in his name that would last for two centuries. The book of Isaiah ends with a vision of cosmic fulfillment: "a new heaven and a new earth," wherein justice and peace shall dwell.

"They shall beat their swords into plowshares. . . . One nation shall not raise the sword against another, nor shall they train for war again."
—Isaiah 2:4

St. Catherine Labouré
Visionary (1806–1876)

St. Catherine spent most of her life as a humble member of the Daughters of Charity of St. Vincent de Paul in convents in Paris and later Enghien-Reuilly. Her superiors described her as "insignificant, cold, almost apathetic." She spent the last forty-five years of her life working in and eventually directing all operations of a nursing home for elderly men run by her order. But it is for the first year of her religious life, in 1830, and the extraordinary series of visions she experienced that year, that Catherine is remembered.

In one vision she saw the Blessed Mother standing on a globe with shafts of light emanating from her hands. Surrounding the image were the words, "O Mary, conceived without sin, pray for us who have recourse to thee." When the Blessed Mother turned about, Catherine saw the letter M with a cross above and two hearts below. She heard a voice instruct her to have this image struck as a medal with the promise that those who wore it would receive favors through Mary's intercession.

Her confessor secured permission from the archbishop of Paris to strike such a medal. The "miraculous medal" became vastly popular, worn by millions. Catherine, however, refused to speak publicly of her visions to anyone but her confessor, and she rejected any special attention. Only after her death, on December 31, 1876, did the world learn of her role in promoting the famous medal. She was canonized in 1947.

"One must see God in everyone."

—St. Catherine Labouré

Mother Jones
Labor Activist (ca. 1830–1930)

Mary Harris Jones bore four children. But it was her activities in the second half of her life, as a tireless agitator and advocate for the oppressed, that earned her the affectionate title Mother Jones. Among those who owned the mills and mines, her name was spoken with contempt. But to the great masses who labored in the darkness of the coal pits or coughed out their youth working sixty-five hours a week in the mills, she was indeed a mother and ministering angel.

Born in Ireland, she immigrated to the United States, where she married and raised a family—all cut down by yellow fever in 1867. After moving to Chicago she discovered the Knights of Labor and devoted herself to the cause of labor.

She achieved her first fame in the 1890s as an agitator for the United Mine Workers, covering a territory from Virginia to Colorado. Her fiery oratory, steeped in the language of the prophets, emboldened workers to action, while her white hair shamed armed deputies to lower their rifles. She was repeatedly and illegally jailed by company guards and federal troops. She remained indomitable.

She died on November 30, 1930.

"Pray for the dead and fight like hell for the living."

—Mother Jones

Servant of God Dorothy Day
Cofounder of the Catholic Worker (1897–1980)

Dorothy Day, who died on November 29, 1980, was widely regarded as the radical conscience of the American Catholic Church. A convert to Catholicism, she had spent her youth engaged in the struggle for social change and a restless search for love and community. The great turning point in her life came in 1926, as she was living on Staten Island with a man she deeply loved, when she discovered that she was pregnant. Her daughter's birth was the catalyst for a profound conversion. She decided to have her child baptized—a step she followed in 1927, though it meant a painful separation from the father of her child, who would have nothing to do with marriage.

In 1932, after meeting a Frenchman, Peter Maurin, she found a way to integrate her faith with her passion for justice and the cause of the poor. Together they launched *The Catholic Worker*, a paper that promoted the social message of the Gospel. This gave birth to a lay movement, combining voluntary poverty, hospitality, and the works of mercy. While offering a prophetic witness for peace and nonviolence, Day and her companions were repeatedly arrested for acts of civil disobedience. All the while her activism was rooted in a disciplined life of prayer and sacrament.

Her cause for canonization was initiated in 2000, and she was named a Servant of God. In his speech before Congress in 2015, Pope Francis, citing her among four "great Americans" who "offer us a way of seeing and interpreting reality," praised her commitment to justice and the cause of the oppressed.

"But there was another question. Why was so much done in remedying the evil instead of avoiding it in the first place? . . . Where were the saints to try to change the social order, not just to minister to the slaves but to do away with slavery?"

—Dorothy Day

St. Andrew
Apostle (First Century)

Andrew, the brother of Simon Peter, was one of the twelve apostles appointed by Jesus. The Gospels provide two versions of his first encounter with the Lord. In the Gospel of John, Andrew is described as a disciple of John the Baptist. He and another disciple were present when the Baptist referred to Jesus as "the Lamb of God." As a result, they decided to follow Jesus. When he asked them, "What do you seek?" they answered, "Rabbi, where are you staying?" "Come and see," he replied. After they had spent some hours with Jesus, Andrew sought out his brother Simon and said, "We have found the Messiah!"

In the other three Gospels, Jesus finds Andrew and Simon casting their nets in the Sea of Galilee and says to them, "Follow me and I will make you become fishers of men." Immediately they drop their nets and follow.

Whatever the circumstances of the first encounter, Andrew would become one of the principal apostles. Though the details of his later life remain obscure, according to ancient legend he died in Patras in Achaia, where he was bound to a cross, from which he continued to preach for two days until he finally expired.

St. Andrew is deemed a patron of Scotland, due to an ancient claim that his relics were carried there in the fourth century. His emblem is an X-shaped cross.

"Another of his disciples, Andrew, Simon Peter's brother, spoke up, 'Here is a boy with five small barley loaves and two small fish, but how far will they go among so many?'"
—John 6:8

Etty Hillesum
Mystic of the Holocaust (1914–1943)

Etty Hillesum, a young Jewish woman who lived in Amsterdam during the Nazi occupation, became one of the millions of victims of the Holocaust. Though in her public life she left little trace, her diary, published many years after her death, offered a meticulous record of her inner life. From the day Dutch Jews were ordered to wear a yellow star up to the day she boarded a cattle car for Poland, Etty consecrated herself to an ambitious task: to bear witness to the inviolable power of love and to reconcile her keen sensitivity to suffering with her appreciation for the beauty of existence.

Though she identified with no particular religious tradition, Etty's spirituality drew on eclectic sources—the Bible, Christian mystics, Rilke, Dostoevsky. She believed the most important task was to hold fast to the encounter with God in her soul and other people, to affirm the meaning of life in the face of all evidence to the contrary. Gradually, as the net of persecution drew tighter, her diary became a prayer to God. When she knew she would be deported she accepted her fate and her calling: to be present at the heart of suffering, to be "the thinking heart of the concentration camp."

She was deported to Auschwitz on September 7, 1943. There she died on November 30 at the age of twenty-nine.

"That is why I must try to live a good and faithful life to my last breath; so that those who come after me do not have to start all over again."

—Etty Hillesum

DECEMBER

1 St. Edmund Campion • Blessed Charles de Foucauld

2 Blessed Liduina Meneguzzi • Maura Clarke and Companions

3 St. Francis Xavier • St. Anuarite Nengapeta

4 Clement of Alexandria • St. John Damascene

5 St. Crispina • St. Christina of Markyate

6 St. Nicholas • Wolfgang Amadeus Mozart

7 St. Ambrose • St. Maria Josepha Rossello

8 Swami Abhishiktananda (Henri Le Saux) • Servant of God Walter Ciszek

9 Servant of God Bernard of Quintavalle • Venerable Fulton J. Sheen

10 Karl Barth • Thomas Merton

11 Martyrs of El Mozote • Walter F. Sullivan

12 Our Lady of Guadalupe • Cardinal Avery Dulles

13 St. Lucy • St. Odilia

14 St. John of the Cross • Servant of God Catherine de Hueck Doherty

15 St. Virginia Centurione Bracelli • St. Mary di Rosa

16 Blessed Frances Schervier • Maude Dominica Petre

17 St. Lazarus • St. Olympias

18 The Samaritan Woman • Alicia Domon

19 Rahab • Meister Eckhart

20 The Anointer of Bethany • Origen

21 St. Peter Canisius • Mothers of the Disappeared

22 Servant of God Isaac Hecker • Martyrs of Acteal

23 St. Marguerite d'Youville • Rabbi Abraham Heschel

24 John Muir • Chico Mendes

25 Holy Shepherds • Blessed Jacopone of Todi

26 St. Stephen • The Pilgrim

27 St. John • St. Fabiola

28 Holy Innocents • Blessed Sara Salkahazi

29 St. Thomas Becket • Sebastian Castellio

30 Blessed Eugenia Ravasco • John Main

31 St. Melania the Younger • St. John Francis Regis

DECEMBER

St. Edmund Campion
Jesuit Martyr (1540–1581)

From the time he arrived at Oxford at the age of fifteen, Edmund Campion showed signs of extraordinary promise. But there was an impediment to his ambition—namely, his growing conviction that he should become a Catholic. Such a move, in Elizabethan England, meant professional ruin, if not the risk of life. Nevertheless, in 1571, his doubts resolved, he crossed the Channel and entered the English College at Douai. Two years later he moved to Rome and entered the Society of Jesus. In 1580, following his ordination, he was assigned the perilous mission of returning to his native land. As he described his mission: "Of free cost to preach the Gospel, to minister the Sacraments, to instruct the simple, to reform sinners, to confute errors—in brief, to cry alarm spiritual against foul vice and proud ignorance, wherewith many of my dear Countrymen are abused."

He was eventually captured and confined to the Tower of London. After four days of confinement in a tiny cell, which permitted room neither to stand nor lie down, he was brought directly before Queen Elizabeth, whom he had once met in Oxford under happier circumstances. While he acknowledged her temporal authority he refused to recognize her authority in matters of religion. After the semblance of a trial, he was charged with sedition and put to the rack. On December 1, 1581, he was drawn and quartered at the gallows at Tyburn.

"God lives. Posterity will live. Their judgment is not so liable to corruption as that of those who now sentence us to death."

—St. Edmund Campion

Blessed Charles de Foucauld
Desert Hermit (1858–1916)

Charles de Foucauld, a French aristocrat, spent his early years as a party-loving playboy and military officer. At the age of twenty-eight, however, he underwent an astonishing conversion. "As soon as I believed that there was a God," he wrote, "I understood that I could not do anything other than live for him." On a pilgrimage to the Holy Land—following the actual footsteps of Jesus—he was struck by the fact that Jesus, the Son of God, had spent most of his life as a poor carpenter in Nazareth. This insight inspired the theme of his vocation: to imitate the "hidden life" of Jesus by living among the poor in a spirit of service and solidarity.

Eventually he moved to the Algerian desert to set in motion the dream of a new type of contemplative religious life. "The whole of our existence, the whole of our lives should cry the Gospel from the rooftops . . . not by our words but by our lives."

Foucauld spent fifteen years in the desert preparing for followers who never came. On December 1, 1916, he was murdered by Tuareg rebels. Despite his seeming failure in life, Foucauld would become one of the most influential spiritual figures of the twentieth century. Several religious communities were inspired by his example. He was beatified in 2005.

"Father, I abandon myself in Your hands, do with me what You will . . . I am ready for all, I accept all, let only Your will be done in me, as in all Your creatures."

—Blessed Charles de Foucauld

Blessed Liduina Meneguzzi
Missionary Sister (1901–1941)

Elisa Angela Meneguzzi, who took the name Liduina in religious life, was born to a peasant family in northern Italy. At fourteen she entered domestic service, working for the next ten years in hotels and for wealthy families until she quit and joined the Sisters of the Congregation of St. Francis de Sales.

In 1937 she was sent to the Ethiopian town of Dire Dawa—at the time under Italian rule. For the next two years she served as a nurse in the city hospital. With the outbreak of World War II the hospital was taken over by the military. Liduina cared for wounded soldiers of all colors and creeds, including Catholics, Copts, and Muslims. She spoke to them all of the goodness of God and the promise of heaven. In turn she was treasured as an "angel of charity."

After enduring bombing raids and every kind of violence, Liduina was diagnosed with cancer. She died on December 2, 1941. Her ecumenical witness, courage, and spirit of charity were remembered by all who had known her. She was beatified in 2002. The decree on her heroic virtue noted, "The message that Bd. Liduina Meneguzzi brings to the Church and the world is that of hope and love. A kind of love that is a spur to solidarity, to sharing, and to service."

"In the course of her brief but intense life, Sr. Liduina poured herself out for her poorer and suffering brothers."

—Pope John Paul II

Maura Clarke and Companions
Martyrs of El Salvador (d. 1980)

On a December morning in 1980 a small assembly gathered in a cow pasture in El Salvador to witness the exhumation of four North American women. One by one their broken bodies were dragged from the shallow grave: Maura Clarke and Ita Ford, both Maryknoll Sisters; Dorothy Kazel, an Ursuline Sister; and Jean Donovan, a lay missioner from Cleveland. On December 2, Salvadoran soldiers, acting under orders from superior officers, had taken them to a secluded spot, raped two of them, and then shot them in the head.

Each woman had followed a different path: Maura and Ita, with many years in mission in Nicaragua and Chile; Dorothy, the longest in El Salvador; Jean Donovan, only twenty-seven, who had wrestled with the possibility of marriage and a lucrative career before choosing, instead, to remain in El Salvador. But for each one, called by Christ to live out her faith in solidarity with the poor, the path had led to the same cow pasture.

In these nightmare years in El Salvador, thousands of civilians were killed by security forces on suspicion of "subversion." Representatives of the Church who embraced the "option for the poor," including these women, shared the same fate. Witnesses to the cross, they joined a long line of witnesses to the resurrection.

"One cries out, 'Lord, how long?' and then too what creeps into my mind is the little fear or big, that when it touches me very personally, will I be faithful?"
—Sr. Maura Clarke

St. Francis Xavier
Jesuit Missionary (1506–1552)

Francis Xavier was one of the original six companions of St. Ignatius Loyola who took vows in the Society of Jesus. In 1541, armed with a papal decree naming him apostolic nuncio to Asia, he embarked on a perilous journey to Portuguese Goa—the beginning of one of the greatest of all missionary journeys, one that would last eleven years, and from which he would never return.

In 1549 Francis arrived in Japan, a highly advanced kingdom as yet unknown to Westerners. In light of the sophistication of Japanese culture, Francis changed his approach to mission. Previously he had seen himself building on barren ground. Now he felt a need to comprehend the local culture, to discover its latent strengths and virtues, and to find ways of connecting these with the Gospel message.

After two years in Japan, long enough to implant a small Christian community, Francis set his sights on a new frontier. While sailing to China in 1552 he became seriously ill. On an island off the coast he was taken off his ship. There he died on December 3 at the age of forty-six. Canonized in 1622, in 1927 he was named a patron of foreign mission.

"It is not the actual physical exertion that counts towards one's progress, nor the nature of the task, but the spirit of faith with which it is undertaken."
—St. Francis Xavier

St. Anuarite Nengapeta
Congolese Nun and Martyr (1939–1964)

Anuarite Nengapeta was born in 1939 in a village in the then-Belgian Congo (now the Democratic Republic of the Congo). Though her parents were non-Christians, she attended a mission school and was baptized in 1945. Admiring the sisters in her school, she wished to enter religious life, a choice her parents opposed. Nevertheless, they yielded to her wishes when she stowed away on a truck carrying postulants to the convent of the Holy Family Sisters. In 1959 they witnessed her first vows and even presented the nuns with two goats. Anuarite, who took the religious name Sr. Marie-Clementine, adapted easily to religious life, gladly performing any work assigned to her. She said her mission was to do her duty and to make others happy.

In 1964 civil war erupted. On November 29 soldiers invaded the convent and forced all the sisters into a truck for transport. On December 1, Sr. Marie-Clementine was separated from the rest and presented to an officer. When she resisted his increasingly forceful advances, he ordered his soldiers to beat her and stab her with bayonets. "I forgive you for you know not what you are doing," she said, before he shot her.

Anuarite was beatified in 1985 by Pope John Paul II, who said that in her faithfulness unto death she demonstrated the transfiguration that occurs in the soul united with God. She was canonized in 1999, becoming the first Congolese woman saint.

"The Lord Jesus, when He calls us, demands sacrifice: the sacrifice of the things of this world, the sacrifice of human love, the sacrifice of our selves."
—St. Anuarite Nengapeta

697

Clement of Alexandria
Christian Apologist (ca. 150–ca. 215)

Clement was the director of a Christian school in Alexandria, Egypt, at that time the center of Hellenistic culture. Little is known of his life. Apparently he was born in Athens and traveled widely in a quest for wisdom before converting to Christianity. As a Christian philosopher he strenuously opposed the anti-intellectual bias of many Christians. "What has Jerusalem to do with Athens?" asked his contemporary Tertullian. Clement's answer was that "Greek philosophy provides for the soul the preliminary cleansing and training required for the reception of the faith." He believed that God's wisdom had been communicated in some form to every people. The task of the Christian apologist was to seek out that primordial wisdom in the culture of a people—Greek philosophy in his case—and to build on that foundation in expounding the Gospel.

While Clement pioneered the adaptation of the Gospel to the positive features of his culture, he was adamant in opposing those gnostic Christians for whom the Gospel was entirely subordinated to Greek philosophy. In contrast he affirmed the value of the created world, defended the role of free will, and expounded the virtues of Christian marriage.

For many centuries Clement was venerated as a Catholic saint. He was dropped from the Roman martyrology in the sixteenth century.

"There is but one river of truth, but many streams pour into it from this side and from that."
—Clement of Alexandria

St. John Damascene
Doctor of the Church (ca. 657–749)

John Damascene grew up in the Muslim city of Damascus, inheriting his father's office as collector of revenue. In time he resigned this post and entered the monastery of St. Sabas in Jerusalem, where he aroused resentment from more strait-laced monks on account of his theological creativity and his enthusiasm for composing hymns.

It was his defense of icons, however, that assured his lasting reputation. The controversy over icons was as bitter as any dispute over the Trinity. Critics charged that the veneration of icons was idolatrous. Their defenders responded that it was not the icon that was venerated but the spiritual reality it represented. According to St. John, what was at stake was the capacity of material things to serve as a vehicle for divine grace. This, he argued, was the very basis of the incarnation—the question of whether Christ, a true man, was truly the image (icon) of the invisible God.

The status of icons was not resolved until the Second Council of Nicaea (787), long after John's death. In the meantime, he was denounced by critics as an idol worshiper. Ironically, it was only his residence in Jerusalem—a city under Muslim control and thus beyond the power of the Christian emperor—that assured his safety.

St. John was proclaimed a Doctor of the Church in 1890.

"I do not worship matter, I worship the God of matter, who became matter for my sake, and deigned to inhabit matter, who worked out my salvation through matter."

—St. John Damascene

St. Crispina
Martyr (d. 304)

Crispina, a Christian noblewoman from North Africa, was married and the mother of several children. During a period of anti-Christian persecution in 304 she was arrested and brought before the proconsul. In the transcript of her trial she emerges as a woman of exceptional courage and self-possession. Clearly unimpressed by the power of her judge, she confronted his threats with stern patience and uncompromising dignity.

When the proconsul proclaimed that she must be stupid not to worship the gods of Rome she replied that she worshiped none other than the true and living God: "A religion that inflicts torture on those who do not adhere to it is not a religion. . . . I have remained a stranger to your rites, and as long as I live I shall never honor them."

When her judge asked whether she wanted to live a long time or die in torment, Crispina replied: "If I wanted to die and deliver my soul to the ravages of eternal fire, I would put my faith in your demons." Upon hearing the sentence of death, she proclaimed: "I bless my God and thank him for the grace he accords me in thus freeing me from your hands. Thanks be to him."

After marking herself with the sign of the cross, she knelt and offered her neck to the executioner.

"I sacrifice to the eternal God who made the sea, the green fields, the sand of the desert. What have I to fear from those who are only his creatures?"

—St. Crispina

St. Christina of Markyate
Maiden of Christ (1097–1161)

Christina was the daughter of a noble Anglo-Saxon family. At the age of nine she made a private vow offering herself to God in perpetual virginity. Unfortunately, her desires ran counter to her parents' plans. The chronicle of her subsequent struggle to pursue her vocation involves an extraordinary cast of characters: bishops, noblemen, merchants, abbots, and holy hermits. The effort of one young woman to claim her own spiritual identity seems to have shaken her society to its roots.

The story has many shocking twists and turns, including her escape from the lecherous advances of a visiting bishop; her forced betrothal to a young nobleman; her parents' encouragement of the young man to take their daughter by force; an ecclesiastical court that ordered her to marry; and finally a daring escape. Finding help from a network of monks, she eventually found refuge with a hermit, huddling for four years in a cramped hole in the ground. In the end her family and her fiancé relented and freed her to pursue her vocation.

Christina was consecrated as a nun and became the abbess of a convent in Markyate. Famous for her visions and healing powers, she was sought out by abbots, bishops, and even kings for her counsel. She died in 1161.

"I am free to love Christ above all."

—St. Christina of Markyate

St. Nicholas
Bishop of Myra (Fourth Century)

St. Nicholas is one of the most popular of all saints: patron of Russia and Greece and of many classes of people, from children to prostitutes. Many hundreds of churches are named after him, and his feast day is an occasion for ardent celebration in many parts of the globe. But as for his biography, it may be summarized in the simple statement that he served as bishop of Myra, a provincial capital in Asia Minor sometime in the fourth century.

The most curious development in his cult has been the amalgamation of this fourth-century bishop with the features of a Scandinavian elf. The transfiguration of St. Nicholas into Santa Claus has been traced to Dutch Protestants living in New Amsterdam. As the story made its way back to England the familiar features of Father Christmas gradually took shape until he had achieved iconographic status.

In this role there are at least echoes of certain ancient legends. In one story Nicholas rescued three young girls whose father, for want of a dowry, was about to sell them into prostitution. Nicholas tossed three bags of gold through their window, enough to pay the dowry for each sister. In another story he restored three little boys to life after they were murdered by an evil maniac.

Well does he deserve to be remembered as the patron of children, honored not just as the purveyor of toys but as a protector of the innocent.

"The Giver of every good and perfect gift has called upon us to mimic His giving, by grace, through faith, and this is not of ourselves."

—Attributed to St. Nicholas

Wolfgang Amadeus Mozart
Composer (1756–1791)

Wolfgang Amadeus Mozart, arguably the greatest classical composer of all time, was born in Salzburg, Austria, in 1756. His prodigious musical talent was evident from early childhood. By the age of six he was performing in the royal courts of Europe, and his fame as a composer quickly followed. His compositions ranged across every genre, from Masses and oratorios to symphonies and secular operas. Still, he spent much of his life in financial insecurity, depending on the fickle support of patrons in the Church and various royal courts. His short life ended in poverty and protracted illness. In 1791 he worked feverishly on a requiem, convinced he was composing for his own funeral Mass. He died before its completion, on December 5, 1791, and was buried in a pauper's grave.

Mozart is widely regarded as a great religious artist—and not only on account of his liturgical compositions. In all his work there is a delight in creation, a balance, an affirmation of the final triumph of light and life over death and darkness. George Bernard Shaw wrote that Mozart's music is "the only music that would not sound out of place in the mouth of God."

"I never lie down at night without reflecting I may not live to see another day. . . . For this blessing I daily thank my Creator and wish with all my heart that each one of my fellow-creatures could enjoy it."

—Wolfgang Amadeus Mozart

St. Ambrose
Bishop and Doctor of the Church (339–397)

I n 374, the death of the bishop of Milan left the local Church bitterly divided. With violent tempers threatening to erupt, Ambrose, the provincial governor, went to the basilica and exhorted the assembly to find a peaceful solution. Suddenly a voice rose up: "Ambrose for bishop." The cry was quickly taken up by the entire assembly. Ambrose was horrified. Not only was he a layman; he was not even baptized. Nevertheless, he acquiesced. Within one week he was baptized, confirmed, ordained, and consecrated bishop of Milan.

Despite his lack of preparation, Ambrose made up for lost time. He gave away all his property, adopted an austere and strenuous habit of prayer, and immersed himself in the study of Scripture and theology. He became the protector of the poor and oversaw the preparation of catechumens and the training of clergy. He was responsible for innumerable conversions, most famously that of St. Augustine, whom he personally instructed and baptized.

Though Ambrose wrote many books, he is best remembered for his deft leadership of the Church in a tumultuous era. The Arian heresy, which denied the full divinity of Christ, had divided the Church into rival factions. When the emperor tried to impose civic harmony by ordering Ambrose to cede one of his churches for use by the Arians, Ambrose refused. "The emperor is *in* the church," he said, "not *over* it." The emperor backed down.

"No one is good but God alone. What is good is therefore divine, what is divine is therefore good."
—St. Ambrose

St. Maria Josepha Rossello
Founder, Daughters of Our Lady of Mercy (1811–1880)

Benedetta Rossello was born to a large, poor family on the Ligurian coast of Italy. Lack of a dowry frustrated her desire to enter religious life. Instead she became a Third Order Franciscan and entered domestic service to a wealthy family, sending all her earnings to her family.

When she heard that the bishop of Savona wished to do something for girls and young women at risk of abuse, she volunteered her services. The bishop recognized her gifts and readily agreed to set her up with three companions in a run-down house. They took the name Daughters of Our Lady of Mercy, and Benedetta, who would serve as superior for the rest of her life, became Maria Josepha.

Despite their poverty, they quickly attracted new recruits. Remembering her own sad experience, Mother Maria decreed that no worthy woman would be turned away for lack of a dowry. At first the sisters founded a series of homes—Houses of Divine Providence—for girls in trouble. But schools and hospitals followed, and in 1875 the first foundation was established in Argentina.

Mother Maria never scorned the most humble tasks. But when illness left her unable to walk she could do no more than oversee the work of her sisters. "There are God, the soul, eternity," she said, "the rest is nothing." She died on December 7, 1880. She was canonized in 1949.

"The hands are made for work, and the heart for God."

—St. Maria Josepha Rossello

Swami Abhishiktananda (Henri Le Saux)
Monk (1910–1973)

Swami Abhishiktananda, who would become one of the great spiritual pilgrims of his day, was born Henri Le Saux into a traditional Catholic family in a small town in Brittany. After entering the Benedictine monastery of Kergonan in 1929 he was ordained a priest. Though happy in this life, he found himself drawn by an inexplicable desire to go to India. In 1948, with the permission of his community, he left for India, never to return. Together with another French Benedictine he founded an ashram in Tamil Nadu called Shantivanam and took on a new name: Abhishiktananda ("the bliss of the Anointed One").

Though his initial mission was to Christianize India along Benedictine lines, his journey soon took a more personal turn— a quest to experience the way of Christ by way of Hindu wisdom. After meeting Ramana Maharshi, a holy Hindu sage, he assumed the life of a sadhu, or wandering monk. Embracing total renunciation, he spent some years in a cave on Mount Arunachala, seeking a breakthrough to *advaita*, or non-duality. He described his journey in many books. Still, the struggle to realize his goal and to reconcile the different dimensions of his soul caused great and ongoing tension. After spending his final years as a hermit in the Himalayas, he died on December 7, 1973.

"I am like someone who has one foot on one side of the gulf, the other on the other side. I would like to throw a bridge across, but do not know where to fasten it, the walls are so smooth."

—Swami Abhishiktananda

Servant of God Walter Ciszek
Jesuit Confessor (1904–1984)

In 1939 the Soviets invaded eastern Poland. Among the thousands of refugees swept up and transported back to labor camps in Russia was Walter Ciszek, a young American Jesuit. In 1941, his identity discovered, he was charged with espionage. Thus began his long journey through the Soviet Gulag.

Ciszek spent the next five years in solitary confinement in the Lubianka prison in Moscow. To keep his wits intact he practiced a routine of spiritual exercises remembered from his Jesuit formation. Later, he could say, "Lubianka was a school of prayer for me."

Eventually he was sentenced to fifteen years in Siberia. In everything that befell him, Ciszek believed he could discern the will of God. To the extent that he abandoned himself to Providence, convinced that he was exactly where God wanted him to be, he experienced peace and freedom. He believed this was a lesson with relevance for all people under any circumstances. Thus he found the grace to carry on.

After surviving his entire sentence, he was able to write home, and his astonished family learned that he was still alive. In 1963 he was suddenly returned to America in exchange for a Soviet spy. He lived on for another twenty years, dying on December 8, 1984.

"For each of us, salvation means no more and no less than taking up daily the same cross of Christ, accepting each day what it brings as the will of God, offering back to God each morning all the joys, works and sufferings of that day."

—Walter Ciszek, SJ

Servant of God Bernard of Quintavalle
Franciscan (d. ca. 1241)

Bernard, one of the wealthiest young men of Assisi, was intrigued by reports that another young man of the town—Francis, previously known as something of a dandy and carouser—had recently drawn contempt and ridicule for his ostentatious embrace of poverty. Bernard thought he should invite Francis to dine with him and spend the night in his home. During the course of the night, Bernard overheard his guest's ardent prayers and was so moved that the next day he asked Francis to help him discern God's will. Opening the missal at random, Francis alighted on the text, "If you wish to be perfect, go and sell all you own, and give it to the poor." A second time he opened the book and found, "Take nothing for your journey." On a third attempt, he found, "If anyone would follow me, let him deny himself." "This is the advice that the Lord has given us," said Francis. "Go and do as you have heard." Following these instructions, Bernard disposed of his property and adopted Francis's way of life.

Bernard became one of Francis's most trusted companions, accompanying him on many journeys and undertaking a special mission to Santiago de Compostela. From his deathbed in 1226 Francis bestowed on him a special blessing. Bernard himself died around 1241 and was buried near his spiritual father in the Basilica of St. Francis.

"Of Bernard, St. Francis said that he was worthy of all reverence, and that he had founded this Order, because he was the first who had left the world, keeping back nothing for himself, but giving everything to Christ's poor."

—From *The Little Flowers of St. Francis*

Venerable Fulton J. Sheen
Archbishop and Evangelist (1895–1979)

Fulton J. Sheen served as a parish priest, a professor of philosophy and theology (he held doctorates in both), and as bishop of Rochester, New York. But he was best known, as *Time* magazine described him, as "U.S. Catholicism's famed proselytizer," the "golden-voiced" host of a series of popular radio and television shows that brought the Catholic message to a wide audience.

His radio ministry began in 1930 when he hosted *The Catholic Hour*. In 1951 he made the switch to television in *Life Is Worth Living*, speaking to the camera without notes and with no props aside from a blackboard and a statue of the Blessed Mother. Combining inspirational stories with the teachings of Thomas Aquinas, Sheen showed how the teachings of the Church answered the deepest longings of the human heart. With the advent of color TV he cut a particularly striking figure in his red cape and gold pectoral cross. The show was watched by millions and won two Emmys, though Sheen was careful to credit his writers: "Matthew, Mark, Luke, and John." He signed off each show with "God love you."

In 1969 Sheen was named titular Archbishop of Newport, Wales, which freed him to focus on his writing, preaching, and public ministry. He died on December 9, 1979. His cause for canonization was introduced in 2002.

"Show me your hands. Do they have scars from giving? Show me your feet. Are they wounded in service? Show me your heart. Have you left a place for divine love?"

—Venerable Fulton J. Sheen

Karl Barth
Protestant Theologian (1886–1968)

Karl Barth, a theologian whose work, in its scope, has been compared to that of Augustine, Calvin, and Aquinas, began his career as the pastor of a Reformed church in Switzerland. He had studied with some of the great names of liberal Protestant theology, whose work reflected the optimistic spirit of the age. For such thinkers the outbreak of World War I came as a terrible blow. But Barth was particularly scandalized to read a manifesto signed by his theology professors supporting the Kaiser's war efforts.

Shocked by this ethical collapse, Barth went back to the Bible and became convinced that liberal theology had lost sight of its true object—God—opting instead to talk about "man in a loud voice." In 1919 he published his commentary on the Epistle to the Romans, a work that single-handedly changed the theological landscape of the Church and academy. He then commenced on his multivolume *Church Dogmatics*, a work that would dominate the rest of his life.

With the rise of Adolf Hitler and his efforts to co-opt the churches, Barth saw the apotheosis of the manipulation of God that he detested. As the prime author of the Barmen Declaration, he helped to launch what became the "Confessing Church." Dismissed from his teaching chair in Bonn for refusing to sign an oath to Hitler, he was deported to Switzerland.

He died on December 10, 1968.

"Jesus Christ, such as Scripture bears witness of Him for us, is the one word of God that we must hear, that we must trust, and that we must obey in life and death."

—Karl Barth

Thomas Merton
Trappist Monk (1915–1968)

With the publication of his best-selling autobiography, *The Seven Storey Mountain*, Thomas Merton became the most famous monk in America. Merton, who described himself as "the complete twentieth century man," had tasted a life of freedom, excitement, and pleasure, only to reject it all as an illusion. After becoming a Catholic and finally, on the eve of World War II, joining the Trappist Abbey of Gethsemani in Kentucky, Merton had sought to escape the claims of ego, the anxious desire to "be somebody." Ironically, his book won him countless readers, and his superiors ordered him to keep writing.

Despite his call to solitude, Merton became increasingly concerned with drawing connections between the monastery and the wider world. One day in downtown Louisville he had a mystical experience in which he seemed to "wake from a dream of separateness" from the rest of humanity. Rather than an "escape" from the world, he now saw his vocation more in terms of compassion and solidarity. Along with books on traditional spiritual topics, he began to write on nuclear war, racism, and other issues of the day, while engaging in dialogue with artists, writers, and people of other faiths.

In 1968 his abbot allowed him to attend a conference of Christian monks in Bangkok. There, on December 10, he was accidentally electrocuted in his room.

"Merton was above all a man of prayer, a thinker who challenged the certitudes of his time and opened new horizons for souls and for the Church. He was also a man of dialogue, a promoter of peace between peoples and religions."

—Pope Francis, addressing a Joint Session of Congress in 2015

Martyrs of El Mozote
(d. 1981)

On December 11, 1981, scores of Salvadoran troops entered the small hamlet of El Mozote. Their mission, code-named "Rescue," was to pursue guerrilla troops and eliminate subversives. No one had ever accused the people of El Mozote of being subversives. More than half of them were born-again Evangelicals, a fact that may have accounted for their determination to remain neutral in the ongoing civil war. On the day of Operation Rescue the town was swollen with refugees, drawn by their belief that El Mozote would offer a safe haven.

On the first day the soldiers gathered the townspeople and interrogated them about the guerrillas. At some point the decision was made simply to destroy the town. For the next two days the soldiers systematically gathered the people into small groups and massacred the lot of them. One peasant woman, Rufina Amaya, managed to hide among some bushes. There she remained for days, watching and listening as the soldiers completed their mission, biting her tongue to keep from screaming as she witnessed the death of her own husband and children. One night she overheard some of the soldiers talking in fear and wonder of a young girl who had continued singing hymns even as she was raped, shot, and finally hacked with machetes.

Rufina survived to tell the world what happened at El Mozote, where as many as a thousand people were killed. As a later U.N. forensic investigation confirmed, it was the largest massacre in modern Latin American history.

"They did not die, they are with us, with you, and with all humanity."
—Memorial at El Mozote

Walter F. Sullivan
Bishop of Richmond, Virginia (1928–2012)

When, in 1974, Walter F. Sullivan became the eleventh bishop of Richmond, he spurned a formal dinner, instead hosting a cookout with hot dogs, to which all, including the homeless, were welcome. It was a telling start to his episcopal service of twenty-nine years. In the 1980s he acquired a national reputation for his outspoken opposition to the nuclear arms race. His stance provoked controversy, but it was in keeping with the character of Bishop Sullivan, who tried in every way he could to be a devoted pastor, especially for those who were poor and marginalized. The range of his ministries was truly staggering.

Early on, Sullivan became known for his commitment to prisoners, especially those on death row. In a similar way he instituted ministries to serve migrant workers, championed the poor of Appalachia, worked to overcome racial prejudice, reached out to gays and lesbians, and helped endow retirement homes for the elderly. He was a leader in ecumenical and interreligious dialogue, and endeared himself to the Jewish population by erecting—at his own expense—a memorial to the Holocaust on the cathedral grounds.

Taking to heart the teachings of Vatican II, he promoted the role of laypeople and especially encouraged the leadership of women. Rumors about liturgical and doctrinal abuses reached Rome, leading in the 1980s to a formal investigation, which ended with no disciplinary action.

Sullivan retired in 2003 and died on December 11, 2012.

"The word Catholic means there's room for everyone. We are united in our different cultures by our common faith."

—Bishop Walter F. Sullivan

Our Lady of Guadalupe

On the morning of December 9, 1531, a Christian Indian named Juan Diego passed a hill at Tepeyac, not far from present-day Mexico City. Hearing a voice calling him by name, he looked up to see a young Indian maiden. She instructed him to tell the bishop to construct a church on this hill, the site of an ancient shrine to the mother goddess. The bishop paid Juan no attention. In subsequent showings the maiden identified herself as the Mother of God and told Juan to gather roses that grew, unseasonably, at her feet. When he returned to the bishop and opened his cape, Juan revealed a full-color image of the Lady mysteriously imprinted on the rough fabric.

So was born the cult of Our Lady of Guadalupe (as the Indian name of the Lady was rendered in Spanish). But the apparition truly marked the birth of the Mexican people—a fusion of the Spanish and Indian races and cultures. With her dark skin and Indian features, the Lady offered an image of divine compassion for a demoralized people. At the same time, she called the Church to heed the voice of the poor, to serve as a vehicle for their cultural and spiritual survival.

The image, enshrined in Mexico City, attracts millions of pilgrims each year. Juan Diego was canonized in 2002.

"My dearest son, I am the eternal Virgin Mary, Mother of the true God, Author of Life, Creator of all and Lord of the Heavens and of the Earth."
—Apparition of Our Lady to Juan Diego

Cardinal Avery Dulles
Theologian (1918–2008)

Avery Dulles was born into a distinguished family. His father, John Foster Dulles, became the U.S. secretary of state. Though raised as a Presbyterian, he converted to Catholicism while an undergraduate at Harvard. "The more I examined," he wrote, "the more I was impressed with the consistency and sublimity of Catholic doctrine." After serving in the Navy during World War II, he entered the Jesuits and was ordained a priest in 1956. He spent his career teaching in numerous universities, ultimately at Fordham University in the Bronx.

The author of many books, Dulles became one of the most influential Catholic theologians in the United States. His book *Models of the Church*, a modern classic, outlined a fresh approach to theology. In clear language he outlined a range of models of the Church, each with its own warrants, strengths, and potential limitations. Thus he showed how many theological disputes and conflicts in the Church might be traced to differing ecclesiological models.

Despite tensions and polarization in the post–Vatican II Church, Dulles retained a capacity to dialogue with all sides. Unfailingly courteous, he was widely respected for his wisdom, his humility, and his deep love for the Church. In 2001 he was named a Cardinal—an unprecedented honor for an American academic theologian. In his last years, a recurrence of polio left him paralyzed and unable to speak. Yet his mind was unaffected, and he continued to write until his death on December 12, 2008.

"A theologian who does not pray could hardly be a good theologian."

—Avery Dulles, SJ

St. Lucy
Martyr (d. 304)

Despite the paucity of reliable information about her life, St. Lucy is one of the most famous of the so-called virgin martyrs of the early Church. According to legend, she was a young woman from Sicily, raised as a Christian by her wealthy parents. At a young age she privately dedicated herself to Christ. When she refused the proposal of a prospective suitor, he angrily denounced her as a Christian. Subsequently she faced a series of ordeals and futile punishments—commitment to a brothel, death by fire—until at last she was put to the sword.

Because of associations between her name (Lucia) and the Latin word for light (*lux*), as well as certain gruesome tortures that adorn her legend, Lucy has been invoked as a patron of those who suffer from eye troubles. Her feast day in Sweden is a festival of light, celebrated by a procession of young girls wearing crowns of lighted candles.

The stories of Lucy and similar female martyrs have often been used to exalt the "virgin" state. In fact, like the stories of Perpetua and Felicity (both young mothers), her story describes a woman's power in Christ to claim her own identity and a kind of integrity her persecutors were powerless to defile.

"If now, against my will, you cause me to be polluted, a twofold purity will be gloriously imputed to me. You cannot bend my will to your purpose; whatever you do to my body, that cannot happen to me."

—St. Lucy

St. Odilia
Abbess (d. 720)

Odilia's father, a Frankish nobleman in Alsace who had wanted a son, was appalled at the birth of a daughter—the more so when she was found to be blind. In his fury he was ready to have the infant killed but only relented on the condition that she be sent away and her origins kept a secret. Her mother entrusted Odilia to a peasant woman, who later delivered her to a convent, where she was raised and educated. When she was twelve, a bishop received a dream instructing him to find and baptize a young blind girl in the local monastery. Finding Odilia, as he had been told, he baptized her and anointed her eyes with sacred oil. Immediately her sight was restored.

Word of this miracle reached Odilia's father, yet he still refused to receive his daughter. When her brother Hugh defied his wishes and sent for Odilia, his father struck him dead. Curiously, this final outrage prompted a sudden change of heart, and her father at last received Odilia with great tenderness. She lived happily at home for some years, dedicating herself to prayer and works of charity. Eventually her father offered his castle in Hohenburg as a monastery. There Odilia established a community, over which she presided as abbess.

Odilia died on December 13, 720. Her grave became a popular pilgrimage site, and she became the patron saint of the blind and those with eye diseases.

"In the name of Jesus Christ, may the eyes of your body and the eyes of your soul receive light."

—Prayer of Bishop Erhard of Regensburg as he anointed St. Odilia

717

St. John of the Cross
Mystic and Doctor of the Church (1542–1591)

Juan de Yepes became a Carmelite friar at the age of twenty-one, taking the name Juan de la Cruz. The Spanish Carmelites were renowned for their tradition of interior prayer, but by John's day their practice had become lax. A turning point in John's life came in 1567 when he met Teresa of Avila, leader of a Carmelite reform movement and one of the great figures of her age. Despite the gap of twenty-seven years between them, Teresa recognized in John a kindred spirit. She asked him to be her confessor and to initiate a parallel reform to her female Discalced ("shoeless") Carmelites.

In this era of the Inquisition spiritual innovation was a dangerous matter, and John's own brothers recoiled from his reforming efforts. They kidnapped him and imprisoned him for nine months in a Carmelite dungeon, forcing him to live on bread and water. Eventually, on a dark night, he made a miraculous escape (an incident that supplied one of his potent metaphors for the spiritual life), yet he endured ill treatment until his death at forty-nine.

All the while John composed mystical treatises of astonishing psychological insight and poetic power. His subject: the path by which the soul is united in love with God—a journey that is marked by stripping and desolation as much as by periods of joy. For these writings, especially his classic reflections on the "Dark Night of the Soul," he was not only canonized but proclaimed a Doctor of the Church.

"Where there is no love, put love, and you will draw love out."

—St. John of the Cross

Servant of God Catherine de Hueck Doherty
Founder of Madonna House (1896–1985)

Catherine Kolyschkine, born in Russia to a wealthy Catholic diplomat, married a baron at the age of fifteen. No sooner had she entered the Russian aristocracy than war and revolution stripped her of everything. Eventually, close to starvation, she escaped with her newborn son and made her way to New York. Her marriage had collapsed, but Catherine soon found a lucrative career giving lectures on her experiences in Russia.

At the peak of her success she felt a powerful impulse to give up her new wealth to serve Christ and the poor. In Toronto she established Friendship House, a center for the works of mercy. In 1937 she established a similar house in Harlem as a sign of interracial justice and reconciliation.

Later still, remarried to the journalist Eddie Doherty, she returned to Ontario and established Madonna House, a place of prayer and retreat. In *Poustinia* and other books, she drew on her Russian roots to promote the values of silence and prayer. Through her writings and the work of Madonna House she continued to promote the two principles by which she lived: a commitment to the social apostolate in the world and the need to root such a commitment in a life of prayer and the spirit of Christ. She died on December 14, 1985.

"What you do matters—but not much. What you are matters tremendously."

—Catherine de Hueck Doherty

St. Virginia Centurione Bracelli
Laywoman (1587–1651)

Virginia Centurione was born to a noble family of Genoa. Though she was attracted to religious life, her parents arranged her marriage at fifteen to Caspar Bracelli. While he matched her noble lineage, he differed from his wife in every other way, and their marriage was unhappy. Virginia tried in vain to curb his dissolute ways. When after five years he died, leaving her with two young daughters, she refused her family's efforts to arrange a second marriage and took a vow of celibacy.

While raising her daughters, she began to undertake the charitable work that would increasingly occupy her. This began with the rescue of an abandoned girl, whom she found lying in the street and brought into her own home. Eventually she founded a school for orphans. When her daughters married, she devoted all her time and resources to the school and founded an order of teachers to maintain it. During an outbreak of plague she purchased a building that housed as many as three hundred patients.

Virginia died on December 15, 1651. She was canonized in 2003.

"St. Virginia Centurione Bracelli leaves the Church the witness of a simple and active saint. Her example of courageous fidelity to the Gospel also continues to exert a powerful influence on people in our time. She used to say: when God is one's only goal, 'all disagreements are smoothed out, all difficulties overcome.'"

—Pope John Paul II

St. Mary di Rosa
Founder, Handmaids of Charity of Brescia (1813–1855)

Paula di Rosa was born to a noble family in Brescia. Although she felt called to some work for God, it was many years before she founded her own congregation and entered religious life as Sr. Mary of the Crucified. In the meantime, as a laywoman, she found abundant opportunities for service. She cared for the sick during an outbreak of cholera; she operated a house for poor and abandoned girls; she started a school for deaf-mute girls; she helped to found a religious society dedicated to the care of the sick—not as nurses, offering only medical care, but serving the whole person, body and soul.

Her life of service was rooted in an intense discipline of prayer. She rose each day two hours before dawn, attended the first Mass of the day, and then prayed for another two hours. Thus she prepared for whatever the day might offer.

In 1850, in an audience with Pope Pius IX, she received approval of her plan for the Congregation of the Handmaids of Charity. She lived for five years to see her congregation well established, in the meantime responding to outbreaks of cholera and ministering to victims of civil war. She died in 1855 at the age of forty-two and was canonized in 1954.

"I can't go to bed with a quiet conscience if during the day I've missed any chance, however slight, of preventing wrong-doing or of helping to bring about some good."
—St. Mary di Rosa

Blessed Frances Schervier
Founder, Sisters of the Poor of St. Francis (1819–1876)

Frances Schervier, the daughter of a wealthy industrialist, was born in Aachen, Germany. Upon the death of her mother, when Frances was thirteen, she assumed responsibility for the household and the care of her younger siblings. With other women in Aachen she engaged in various charitable projects, visiting prisoners, caring for the sick in their homes, and rescuing prostitutes. In 1844 she entered the Third Order of St. Francis.

In 1845, following the death of her father, she joined with several other women to form a religious community, the Sisters of the Poor of St. Francis. They established soup kitchens and fearlessly cared for those suffering from typhoid, cholera, and smallpox. Eventually Frances sent sisters to America, where she visited in 1863 and offered her services as a nurse during the Civil War. Returning to Germany she joined her sisters in nursing soldiers and staffing ambulances during the Franco-Prussian War. She died on December 14, 1876. Her beatification followed in 1974.

"If we do this [follow Jesus' command to love one another] faithfully and zealously, we will experience the truth of the words of our father St. Francis who says that love lightens all difficulties and sweetens all bitterness. We will likewise partake of the blessing which St. Francis promised to all his children, both present and future, after having admonished them to love one another even as he had loved them and continues to love them."

—Blessed Frances Schervier

Maude Dominica Petre
Theologian (1863–1942)

Maude Petre was raised in a Catholic household in England. After pursuing theological studies in Rome, she became one of the first Catholic women theologians in modern times. The great turning point in her life came in 1900 when she met Fr. George Tyrrell, a charismatic Jesuit theologian. A deep intellectual and spiritual bond developed between them. Tyrrell's work challenged the rationalistic mode of Catholic teaching. Instead of appealing to dogmatic authority, he emphasized the affective and mystical dimension of Christianity and its appeal to human experience. In her own books Petre did not so much address theological matters as defend the principle of freedom within the Church to raise the kinds of questions posed by Tyrrell and his friends. She later compared her efforts with the famous motivation for World War I: to make the world—in this case the Church—safe for democracy.

The response of the Vatican was furious. Following the 1907 condemnation of Modernism, Tyrrell and several others were excommunicated. He died soon after, and Petre became his literary executor. When her bishop insisted she also take the "anti-Modernist oath," Petre refused, arguing that such an oath would accord equal weight to these papal documents and the Nicene Creed. Excommunicated in her diocese, she moved to a different diocese, where she remained a daily communicant.

Petre died on December 16, 1942.

"If I am wrong, then I am so deeply fundamentally wrong that only God can prove it to me. If I am right, then He will make good to me what I have forfeited before men."

—Maude Dominica Petre

St. Lazarus
Jesus' Friend (First Century)

Lazarus and his sisters Martha and Mary were friends, as well as followers, of the Lord, who often enjoyed the hospitality of their home in Bethany. When Lazarus fell ill his sisters hastened to notify Jesus. But he did not immediately come. After deliberately dawdling, he arrived some days later to find Lazarus already dead and buried. The sisters' greeting carried a reproach: "If you had been here our brother would not have died." Nevertheless, Jesus proclaimed: "I am the resurrection and the life. He who believes in me shall live even though he dies."

After instructing that the stone be rolled away from Lazarus's tomb, Jesus called out, "Lazarus, come forth!" From deep in the darkness there was an unmistakable movement, and a moment later Lazarus emerged, alive again.

How Lazarus made use of this new gift is unknown. John reports that this extraordinary sign simply added fuel to the hatred of Jesus' enemies; they began to plot not only his death but that of Lazarus as well. Various legends describe the later post-Easter adventures of Lazarus—whether preaching in Cyprus or, according to more fanciful accounts, escaping with Mary Magdalene to the south of France.

The Gospels record no words of Lazarus. He serves silently as a powerful witness to Christ's power over death and as the first to respond to Christ's call—addressed to all believers—to leave behind the ways of deadness, to embrace the Risen Life.

"Our friend Lazarus has fallen asleep; but I am going there to wake him up."
—John 11:11

St. Olympias
Deaconess (ca. 361–408)

St. Olympias is revered as one of the great women of the Eastern Church. One contemporary saint described her as a "precious vase filled with the Holy Spirit." Raised in a noble family in Constantinople, Olympias was well educated and extremely devout. In 384 she married a former prefect of the city. Upon his death she refused entreaties by her family as well as the emperor that she remarry. "Had my King wished me to live with a husband," she said, "he would not have taken my first one away."

Instead, she devoted her life and her fortune to the Church and the care of the poor. St. Nectarius, bishop of Constantinople, ordained her as a deaconess. Aside from founding a hospital and orphanage, she established an enclosed convent attached to the church of Santa Sophia, where she lived with as many as 250 women.

Her close friendship with St. John Chrysostom, who became bishop of Constantinople, would cause a change in her fortunes. When St. John's enemies drove him from his see, Olympias too was forced into exile. A voluminous collection of his letters is testimony of the deep bonds of respect and affection between them.

Olympias died in Nicomedia in 408.

"I cannot cease to call you blessed. The patience and dignity with which you have borne your sorrows have won you a glory and a reward which hereafter will make all your sufferings seem light and passing in the presence of eternal joy."

—Letter of St. John Chrysostom to St. Olympias

The Samaritan Woman
Evangelist (First Century)

The story of the Samaritan woman at the well is one of several occasions in the Gospels in which an "outsider" became an important witness to the Good News. In this story Jesus, as he passed through the land of the Samaritans, took rest beside a village well, where he asked a woman to give him a drink. At first she was astonished. As a woman and a Samaritan—a people despised by the Jews for their unorthodox religious practice—she anticipated scorn. But Jesus spoke in a puzzling way, saying that if she knew who was asking for a drink, "You would have asked him and he would have given you living water."

A conversation about water turned to the woman's own existential thirst for a deeper life: "Sir," she said, "give me this water, that I may not thirst." Then, touching on intimate matters, Jesus asked her to call her husband. "I have no husband," she said. This is true, he said, "for you have had five husbands, and he whom you now have is not your husband." This prompted her to interview him about religious matters, including the coming of the Messiah. He replied, "I who speak to you am he."

Suddenly an ordinary well in the heat of the day had become holy ground. A woman burdened by shame had become a different person. Immediately she went to tell everyone what had happened: "Can this be the Christ?" And many Samaritans from that day believed "on the strength of her witness."

"He told me everything I ever did."

—John 4:39

Alicia Domon
Martyr (1937–1977)

During the period of 1976 to 1983 a military dictatorship in Argentina conducted a "dirty war" against "subversives" and dissidents. Thousands of civilians were killed; many more were "disappeared"—abducted by the military, never to be seen again. Two French nuns, Sisters Alicia Domon and Léonie Duquet, were among them.

Both members of the Toulouse Institute of the Sisters of Foreign Mission, these women were among the many foreign missioners who came to work in Latin America in the 1960s. While at first they engaged in traditional ministries, by 1969, like many other religious of the time, they had moved out of their convent and into an urban shantytown to share the life of the poor.

Sr. Alicia became involved with the "Mothers of the Disappeared," who gathered in the central plaza each day, holding photographs of their missing children, offering a silent rebuke to the military regime. On December 8, 1977, she and eleven other women were seized. Her housemate Sr. Léonie was also picked up. Though neither of them was ever seen again, later reports confirmed that they had been tortured and then tossed from an airplane over the Atlantic Ocean.

Several months before her death Alicia had written to the archbishop of Toulouse: "I would ask you not to do anything to save me which could endanger others. I have already made the sacrifice of my life."

"I didn't come here [to the shantytown] to tell people what they had to do but in order that we could help each other and share life's joys and sorrows."
—Sr. Alicia Domon

Rahab
Faithful Prostitute

The name of Rahab, a Canaanite prostitute, is an unlikely addition to the list of biblical saints and heroes. Yet St. James singles her out with Abraham as a model of faith in action. The author of Hebrews includes Rahab among the "mighty cloud of witnesses." St. Matthew even includes her name in the genealogy of Jesus.

Rahab's story appears in the book of Joshua in connection with the siege of Jericho. When Joshua sent spies into the city to survey its defenses, they sought shelter in the house of "a harlot whose name was Rahab." The king's informants quickly discovered their arrival, but Rahab helped them escape. Before doing so she struck a bargain. She had heard of the deliverance of Israel from Egypt and confessed her belief that "the Lord your God is he who is God in heaven above and on earth below." In exchange for sheltering these spies she exacted their promise to protect her and her family's lives. Joshua made sure that this promise was kept. And so Rahab escaped the destruction of Jericho and lived out the rest of her life among the people of Israel.

The authors of Scripture drew various meanings from this story. But there are other lessons. Rahab's is the story of a marginalized "outsider" who, by her courageous deeds and faith in the Lord of history, was raised to a place of honor among God's special servants.

"And Rahab dwelt in Israel to this day because she hid the messengers whom Joshua sent to spy out Jericho."

—Joshua 6:25

Meister Eckhart
Dominican Theologian and Mystic (ca. 1260–ca. 1329)

Meister Eckhart, a Dominican theologian of the early fourteenth century, was the greatest of the Rhineland mystics. Though he twice held the prestigious Dominican chair at the University of Paris, he spent most of his career in positions of service within his order. In 1326, on the basis of twenty-eight propositions supposedly derived from his work, he was accused of heresy by the archbishop of Cologne. Though he disputed the accusation, he died before learning that the pope had confirmed his condemnation.

Modern examination of Eckhart's writings has left little doubt of his sincere faith and loyalty to the Church. At the same time, it is no wonder that his mystical and poetic formulations aroused suspicion. Eckhart tried by means of paradoxical language to describe the ineffable union of the soul with God. He taught the need to let go of our concepts of God, all of the illusions and finite objects onto which we project our longing for the Absolute. "Do not cling to the symbols, but get to the inner truth!" he urged. Unfortunately, it seemed to Church authorities that what he dismissed as symbols were what they preferred to call sound doctrine and authority.

The date of Eckhart's death remains unknown. Before dying, however, he apparently issued a statement in which he "revoked and also deplored" the condemned articles "*insofar* as they could generate in the minds of the faithful a heretical opinion."

"We are all meant to be mothers of God, for God is always needing to be born."

—Meister Eckhart

The Anointer of Bethany
Faithful Disciple (First Century)

One of the great women of the Gospels is remembered by her deed alone; her name is totally lost. St. Mark relates that as Jesus sat at table in Bethany an anonymous woman proceeded to anoint his head with precious oil. The extraordinary value of the oil—virtually the equivalent of a year's wages—gave rise to grumbling. Could not the money have been spent on the poor?

Jesus silences the complainers and accepts the woman's gesture. In fact he does more. He underscores the prophetic timeliness of her deed and so names it as one of the exceptional and defining moments of the Gospel. Her deed is comparable to Peter's famous confession: "You are the Christ [the Messiah/Anointed One]." In that case, however, the disciples had recoiled from Jesus' elaboration of what it meant to be God's Anointed: that he would have to suffer and die.

In this case, Jesus accepts without qualification the woman's symbolic acclamation and once again interprets his messiahship—his mission—in terms of suffering and death. "She has done what she could; she has anointed my body beforehand for my burial." Thus, in her wordless act of compassion, this woman recognized in Jesus the Anointed One (the Christ) who was about to die. Though her name would be forgotten, Jesus held her forth as the faithful disciple whose deed should be remembered wherever the Gospel is preached.

"Truly, I say to you, wherever the gospel is preached in the whole world, what she has done will be told in memory of her."

—Mark 14:9

Origen
Theologian (ca. 184–253)

Origen, the greatest theologian of the early Greek Church, was born to Christian parents in Alexandria, Egypt. He had a penchant for extreme asceticism, reflected famously in his literal response to the text of Matthew 19:12, which extols those who have made themselves eunuchs for the sake of the kingdom of heaven. His self-mutilation was considered grounds to prevent his ordination. Origen is said to have written 6,000 works, though only a small number survived. Later, his teachings on universal salvation—even for the devil—and the preexistence of souls also generated controversy, resulting in the condemnation of "Origenism" in the sixth century.

Nonetheless, in the area of biblical studies Origen left a huge legacy. In one of his works he assembled the entire Old Testament in six parallel columns, including variant Hebrew and Greek versions. More importantly, he devised a method of interpreting Scripture that laid the foundation for all medieval exegesis. He believed the text could be read on several levels, corresponding to body, soul, and spirit. Beyond the literal, historical meaning, one could uncover additional symbolic meanings, to which Christ supplied the interpretive key. Thus, virtually any text in the Old Testament could be seen as a foreshadowing of the New Testament and of our heavenly destination.

During a wave of persecution in 250 Origen was subjected to torture. He survived but lived on for only a few short years.

"The physical voice we use in prayer need not be great nor startling; even should we not lift up any great cry or shout, God will yet hear us."

—Origen

St. Peter Canisius
Doctor of the Church (1521–1597)

Peter Canisius was among the earliest Jesuits to make a solemn profession of vows. Afterward he became a nearly ubiquitous figure in the campaign of Catholic renewal in Europe. He served in Sicily, Rome, Bavaria, and Vienna, before being named the first Jesuit provincial of South Germany. For his successful service in this post he was later called "the second apostle of Germany." In 1580 he was assigned to the Catholic city of Fribourg, where he founded a famous university (one of many he would establish in Europe) and almost single-handedly preserved the Catholic presence in Switzerland.

At a time when vicious defamation was commonly traded between opposing sides of the Reformation, Canisius maintained a tone of charity and generosity toward his opponents. He believed the Church's best response to the Protestant challenge was to cleanse its own house, present the faith in a clear and attractive form, and offer the living witness of evangelical piety.

The author of a fantastically successful *Catechism*, Canisius was exceptional among Catholic reformers (in contrast to Luther and other Protestants) in appreciating the power of printed media. In every city where he worked he was active in promoting Catholic printers and publishers. This contribution was especially emphasized by Pope Pius XI, in 1925, when he canonized Peter Canisius and named him a Doctor of the Church.

"If you have too much to do, with God's help you will find time to do it all."

—St. Peter Canisius

Mothers of the Disappeared
Argentina (1977–1983)

Following a period of economic crisis and political instability in Argentina, many members of the middle class, including Church leaders, openly welcomed the military coup of March 24, 1976, hoping it would presage a return to stability and order. Few anticipated the savage repression that would follow.

In their "war against subversion" the military unleashed a reign of terror. But rather than fill stadiums and prisons with political prisoners, they perfected the tactic of kidnapping their victims, murdering them in secret, and disposing of their bodies. In this manner 20,000 men and women joined the *desaparecidos*—the "disappeared."

The aim of this repression was to silence all protest, and it was largely successful. It fell to a group of women—the so-called Mothers of the Disappeared—to break this silence. In their grief they found each other. They began to offer a silent vigil in the Plaza de Mayo, the public square of Buenos Aires. They were called "crazy." They were subjected to arrest and bullying. But they carried on. What gave them such courage? As one said, "When a woman gives birth to a child, she gives life and then at the same time, when they cut the cord, she gives freedom. We were fighting for life and for freedom."

At a time when truth was everywhere suppressed, the Mothers became the conscience of the nation. But their missing children never returned, even when the discredited military was swept from power in 1983.

"When everyone was terrorized we didn't stay at home crying— we went to the streets. We were mad, but it was the only way to stay sane."
                                        —One of the Mothers of the Disappeared

Servant of God Isaac Hecker
Founder, Paulist Fathers (1819–1888)

Born to a family of German immigrants in New York City, Isaac Hecker spent his youth in a wide-ranging spiritual journey—from the Methodist Church to experiments with Unitarianism, Mormonism, and the Transcendentalist community at Brook Farm—before he finally ended up, at the age of twenty-five, in the Roman Catholic Church. This was hardly the typical destination for religious seekers of his day. Anti-Catholicism in America was at an all-time high. Hecker, however, believed that Catholicism and Americanism were complementary. If the Catholic Church could divest itself of its European appearance, he believed, it could fulfill its ultimate mission: the conversion of America to Catholicism.

Hecker was ordained in the missionary Redemptorist order. Eventually, however, he won support from Rome to establish a community in the United States devoted to the conversion of Protestants: the Congregation of St. Paul the Apostle. Hecker and his Paulist Fathers traveled throughout the country lecturing on the compatibility between Catholic faith and the principles of American democracy. In the end he did not convert America to Catholicism. But his work led indirectly, by the time of Vatican II, to the contribution of the American bishops in securing wider respect in the Church for the principles of democracy, the separation of Church and state, and religious pluralism. Hecker died on December 22, 1888.

"One may be right, and by contradiction and condemnation, open the way to the success of the truth."
—Isaac Hecker

Martyrs of Acteal
Mexico (d. 1997)

On the morning of December 22, 1997, a prayer gathering in the church of Acteal in the highlands of Chiapas, Mexico, was disturbed by the sound of gunfire. The church was surrounded by paramilitary troops who proceeded over the next six hours to massacre forty-five indigenous civilians, mostly women and children, including infants. The victims were members of a remarkable organization called Las Abejas —"the bees"—founded in 1992 and drawing from the local indigenous communities.

Based on their reflection on Scripture and with a strict commitment to nonviolence, the Abejas had formed to promote social justice and human rights, promoting their cause through prayer, fasting, and demonstrations. They chose their name because, "Like the bees, we want to build our houses together, to collectively work and enjoy the fruit of our work. We want to produce 'honey' but also to share with anyone who needs it. . . . We know that, like the little bees, the work is slow but the result is sure because it is collective."

In 1994 the Zapatista Army launched an insurrection in Chiapas to promote justice for the indigenous people. The Abejas sympathized with the goals, but not the means, of the Zapatistas. Nevertheless, they were tarred as subversives.

After the massacre, the Abejas, who now included fifty-four orphans, continued to pray and press for justice.

"We want to say to you we are keeping you company on this Christmas Day, the saddest Christmas Day of our lives."

—Bishop Samuel Ruiz, at the funeral in Acteal

St. Marguerite d'Youville
Founder, "Grey Nuns" (1701–1771)

St. Marguerite, the first native-born saint of Canada, grew up in poverty and spent her early life in an unhappy marriage. Her husband, a fur trader who also supplied alcohol to the Indians, was frequently absent. She bore six children, of whom only two survived. Despite her hard and lonely life, she devoted herself to prayer and works of mercy among the poor and sick.

With the death of her husband in 1730, the range of her charitable works increased. When her elder son entered the seminary, Marguerite and three companions rented a house in Montreal where they took in sick and impoverished women. They were disdained by their neighbors, who sneeringly referred to them as "Grey Nuns," a name Marguerite embraced.

Other women joined in, and eventually they were recognized as a congregation, the Sisters of Charity of the General Hospital (though Marguerite liked to keep the old name, to "remind us of the insults of the beginnings, and to keep us humble"). The wide scope of their charitable works came to include hospitals, schools, orphanages, as well as service among prisoners, Indians, African slaves, prostitutes, and mentally handicapped persons.

Marguerite suffered many setbacks and trials. She embraced them all. As she commented, "We need crosses in order to reach heaven." She died on December 23, 1771, and was canonized in 1990.

"All the wealth in the world cannot be compared with the happiness of living together happily united."

—St. Marguerite d'Youville

Rabbi Abraham Heschel
Teacher and Prophet (1907–1972)

Abraham Heschel was born in Warsaw in 1907. Though descended from a long line of Hasidic rabbis, he chose to study philosophy in Warsaw and Berlin. He believed it was his vocation to connect two worlds: the mystical world of Hasidic Judaism and the modern world of "man in search of meaning."

Expelled as a Jew from his teaching position in Frankfurt in 1938, he barely escaped from Warsaw just weeks before the Nazi invasion in 1939. After making his way to the United States he spent the rest of his life teaching in Jewish as well as Christian seminaries. Through a series of books in the 1950s Heschel emerged as one of the most significant religious voices of his time. While contributing to the spiritual renewal of Judaism, he exerted an almost equal influence on Christians— so much that he was called another "apostle to the gentiles." His writings, including his classic studies on the prophets, recalled Christians to their Jewish roots and their common faith in the God of Israel.

Heschel was a passionate champion of interfaith dialogue, and he played an important role in challenging the Catholic Church to overcome the harmful legacy of anti-Semitism. A courageous champion of peace and civil rights, he marched in Selma with Dr. Martin Luther King Jr., believing, with the prophets, that religion involved a deep responsibility to this world and its questions and needs. "To speak about God and remain silent on Vietnam is blasphemous," he said. Faithful to his Hasidic roots, he communicated to a largely secular world a sense of the "holy dimension of all existence." He died on December 23, 1972.

"To pray is to dream in league with God, to envision His holy visions."
—Rabbi Abraham Heschel

John Muir
Naturalist (1838–1914)

John Muir, who has been called "the patron saint of the American wilderness," was born in Scotland and immigrated to America in 1849. Though he was raised in a strict Protestant sect, he eventually abandoned church affiliation, embracing instead "the Book of Nature." Yet he remained a deeply spiritual man—indeed a kind of mystic. After recovering from an accident that nearly blinded him, he "saw the world"—and his purpose—"in a new light." As he wrote, "This affliction has driven me to the sweet fields. God has to nearly kill us sometimes, to teach us lessons." From that point he dedicated his life to the study of nature and "the godful wilderness."

In 1867, he walked 1,000 miles from Indiana to Florida, then traveled to California, drawn by stories of Yosemite. Returning there again and again, he spent months alone communing with the "Divine Soul" he encountered in the rocks, cliffs, and trees. Eventually he built a cabin where he lived for two years. His hero Ralph Waldo Emerson came to visit and offered him a chair at Harvard. Muir scoffed: "I never for a moment thought of giving up God's big show for a mere profship!"

Muir dedicated himself to the preservation of the wilderness. He helped establish Yosemite and Yellowstone as national parks, and through the Sierra Club he became a forerunner of the modern environmental movement.

He died on December 24, 1914.

"Rocks and waters, etc., are words of God and so are men. We all flow from one fountain Soul. All are expressions of one Love."

—John Muir

Chico Mendes
Rubber Worker and Martyr (1944–1988)

Chico Mendes, who was assassinated in 1988, was the leader of a movement linking the defense of the Amazon region with justice for the poor who lived there. Living in the state of Acre in the Amazonian region of Northwest Brazil, he organized a union of the region's rubber tappers and other poor families who earned their meager living by extracting the renewable resource of the rain forest. Mendes was himself the son of tappers who arrived in the Amazon in the 1940s to take advantage of the rubber boom. In subsequent years the fate of such workers had been threatened by giant landowners and ranchers who preferred to burn and clear the forests to make way for cattle.

When Mendes began organizing the rubber workers in 1977, his initial aim was simply to protect their livelihood. But he gradually expanded his concerns to encompass a wider ecological vision. The burning of the forest threatened the survival of the planet. Thus "the cry of the earth" was connected to the "cry of the poor." Though the owners resorted to threats and violence to break the union, the workers' nonviolent tactics gradually attracted international attention. But it was not enough to protect Mendes. He was shot and killed on December 22, 1988.

"Chico had a lot of faith. When he died I was filled with despair. But God comforted me and inspired me to work alongside others to carry on Chico's work. They killed him but they didn't kill his ideals or crush the struggle."

—Ilza Mendes, widow of Chico Mendes

Holy Shepherds
Witnesses to the Nativity (First Century)

In many religious traditions, the birth of a divine king is attended by wondrous signs from heaven. The same is true of the nativity stories of Jesus. But in the Gospel of Luke, the announcement of Christ's birth is not delivered first to kings, priests, or anyone of importance, but to nameless shepherds in the countryside outside Bethlehem, keeping watch over their flocks by night.

While the image of the shepherd in Hebrew Scripture carries a dignified status, actual shepherds in the time of Jesus were among the poor and marginal class of people—what one scholar has called "the expendables." Nevertheless, these shepherds are greeted by an angel who proclaims, "I bring you good news of great joy that will be for all the people. For unto you is born this day in the city of David a Savior, who is Christ the Lord." As a sign, they are told to look for an infant wrapped in swaddling clothes and lying in a manger—a feed trough for animals.

Following these instructions, the shepherds find Jesus and his parents, just as they had been told. And then they "spread the word concerning what had been told them about this child, and all who heard it were amazed at what the shepherds said to them."

In future years this Child would be called many things—Good Shepherd, as well as Lamb of God. His identity would be announced to important people, who would torture and kill him. But in the beginning, it was to certain poor shepherds, tired from keeping watch, rank with the smell of their sheep, that the Gospel of great joy was first revealed.

"The shepherds returned, glorifying and praising God for all the things they had heard and seen, which were just as they had been told."

—Luke 2:20

Blessed Jacopone of Todi
Franciscan Poet (1230–1306)

Jacopone Benedetti was a prosperous lawyer in the Umbrian town of Todi. His life took a tragic turn one day when his young wife was killed in an accident. His world in ruins and his ambitions laid bare, Jacopone quit his profession, gave away all his belongings, and became a public penitent—to all appearances, a kind of wandering fool. For ten years he maintained this life of aimless poverty and penance. Then, at the age of forty-eight, he knocked on the door of the Franciscans and applied for admission.

Remarkably, in joining the Franciscans he also found a new voice as a poet, indeed one of the great lyric poets of the Middle Ages. In the passionate language of love, his mystical poems described the soul's yearning for Christ. But they retained a mournful undertone, the accent of a faith born in loss. Among his most famous poems is the *Stabat Mater Dolorosa*, a heartbreaking meditation on the sorrows of Mary at the foot of the cross.

Jacopone was a leader of the Spirituals, a Franciscan party dedicated to the most radical form of apostolic poverty. The Spirituals ran into conflict with the worldly Pope Boniface VIII, whose legitimacy they challenged. After addressing a bitter manifesto to the pope, Jacopone was imprisoned for five years. Only after Boniface's death was he freed to live out the rest of his life as a hermit. He died on Christmas Day in 1306.

"Here lie the bones of Jacopone of Todi, Friar Minor, who, having gone mad with love of Christ, by a new artifice deceived the world and took heaven by violence."

—Inscription on the tomb of Blessed Jacopone of Todi

St. Stephen
Martyr (ca. 34)

S t. Stephen, whose story is recounted in the Acts of the Apostles (chapters 6 and 7), is remembered as the Proto-Martyr of the Church, the first disciple to shed his blood in witness to Christ. As such, his example became a model for subsequent accounts of Christian martyrdom.

A Hellenistic Jew, described as "a man full of faith and the Holy Spirit," Stephen was one of the first seven men selected by the Church in Jerusalem to distribute food to the poor (an office that later inspired the order of deacons). Nothing is told of his early life or conversion, but evidently he liked to engage his fellow Jews in public disputations about the teachings of Christ. For this he was denounced before the Jewish Sanhedrin. Charged with blasphemy, he delivered a long sermon chronicling the history of God's covenant with his servants Abraham and Moses before rising to a shocking climax in which he turned the accusation of blasphemy against his accusers. His audience responded with predictable outrage. Stephen was driven from the city and stoned to death.

His death marked a new turn for the early Church; Jesus' proclamation of the reign of God had given way to the proclamation of Jesus himself. But the continuity was underlined in the fact that the disciple met the same fate as his Master.

"While they were stoning him, Stephen prayed, 'Lord Jesus, receive my spirit.' Then he fell on his knees and cried out, 'Lord, do not hold this sin against them.' When he had said this, he fell asleep."

—Acts 7:59-60

The Pilgrim
(Nineteenth Century)

he Way of a Pilgrim, an extraordinary narrative published in Moscow in 1884, is the story of an anonymous man of peasant origins, who, following the death of his wife, abandoned his village and assumed the life of a wanderer. Carrying only his Bible and a sack of dried bread, he undertook a fantastic journey, traversing the whole of Russia and Siberia on foot.

One day in church he was struck by the text of St. Paul: "Pray without ceasing." Obsessed with discovering the meaning of these words, he finally found a holy monk who introduced him to the Jesus Prayer, instructing him to repeat the words, "Lord Jesus Christ, have mercy upon me." The Pilgrim set out to recite this prayer 3,000 times a day. Within weeks he had advanced to 12,000. Gradually, these words became his constant companion, to the point that the prayer moved from his lips to the beating of his heart.

Nothing else is known of his identity. The rest of the book describes his wanderings and his encounters with a rich assortment of characters. For the Pilgrim, good fortune and bad are alike. Every encounter is an opportunity to extol the power of prayer and the beauty of the Gospel. Through his prayer, the whole world is transformed; whether other people or the natural world, everything becomes his kinsfolk. "I found on all of them the magic of the Name of Jesus."

"I spent the whole day in a state of the greatest contentment. . . .
I lived as though in another world."
—The Pilgrim

St. John
Apostle (First Century)

St. John, one of the earliest of the twelve apostles, plays a prominent role in all four Gospels. He and his brother James, both Galilean fishermen, were called by Jesus "sons of thunder." John was a privileged witness to many significant moments in Jesus' life, including the transfiguration and the agony in the garden. By tradition, John is also identified as the author of the Fourth Gospel. If not actually written by his hand, this text is certainly the product of a community that traced its identity and spirituality to the apostle John, referred to throughout as "the disciple whom Jesus loved." He alone, among the Twelve, is described in this Gospel as a witness to the crucifixion. There, Jesus, in his parting moments, takes care to entrust the disciple and his mother to each other's care. For the community that honored the "Beloved Disciple," the Gospel message was succinctly summarized in the charge to love one another as Jesus loved us.

According to tradition, John outlived the rest of the Twelve. He escaped martyrdom and was sent into exile on the island of Patmos. Later he retired to Ephesus, where he presided over the local Church until the end of his days.

"For God so loved the world that he gave his only Son, that whosoever believes in him should not perish but have eternal life."

—John 3:16

St. Fabiola
Widow (d. 399)

St. Fabiola was one of a number of patrician women in Rome, including St. Paula and St. Marcella, who were inspired by St. Jerome to dedicate themselves to God. In Fabiola's case, her course was more roundabout. Her first husband was a vicious man, from whom, with Jerome's approval, she obtained a civil divorce. She incurred excommunication, however, when she violated Church law by remarrying. Upon the death of this second husband she presented herself for public penance and was readmitted to communion by Pope Siricius.

At this point Fabiola's life greatly changed. She devoted her great wealth to works of charity, endowing churches and establishing the first Christian public hospital in the West. There, as Jerome observed, "She often carried on her own shoulders persons infected with jaundice or covered with filth. She also often cleansed the revolting discharge of wounds which others could not bear to look at." In 395 she traveled to the Holy Land to visit Jerome and Paula, who were now living in Bethlehem. She might have remained, but the austerity of consecrated life was not for her. Instead she returned to Rome where she continued her charitable work until her death in 399. All of Rome mourned her passing.

"Today I take as my theme Fabiola. . . . Whatever point in her character I choose to treat of first, pales into insignificance compared with those that follow after. Shall I praise her fasts? Her alms are greater still. Shall I commend her lowliness? The glow of her faith is yet brighter."
—St. Jerome

Holy Innocents
Martyrs (First Century)

The Gospel of Matthew relates the story of wandering wise men from the East who, in pursuit of a star, were led to Jerusalem. There they met King Herod and asked him—unwisely—where they might find the newborn king of the Jews. Herod responded with the fear familiar to any despot that somewhere, perhaps in an obscure village, a child is living who will one day signal the end of his power. Rather than wait for the day of reckoning, he ordered his troops to Bethlehem to kill every male child under the age of two. But the massacre was fruitless. Joseph, forewarned in a dream, had already taken his family into exile in Egypt.

This terrible story, omitted from the typical Christmas pageant, is a vivid reminder of the violent world into which Jesus was born. From the early centuries, the Church has commemorated the feast of these Holy Innocents. Unlike traditional martyrs who would later die bearing witness to Christ, these little ones died unwittingly in the place of Christ. They were killed by the same interests that would later conspire in his death and for the same reasons—to stifle from birth any hope that the world might be changed. They represent all those who die in the dream of a different future, hoping but never knowing that their redeemer lives. In remembering these victims of Herod's rage, the Church also celebrates his failure. His power is doomed. The child lives.

"A voice was heard in Ramah, sobbing and loud lamentations: Rachel weeping for her children, and she would not be consoled, since they were no more."
—Matthew 2:18

Blessed Sara Salkahazi
Martyr (1899–1944)

As a young woman growing up in Hungary, Sara Salkahazi described herself as a "light-hearted reveler." She explored various careers, including teaching and journalism. For some months she was engaged to marry but ultimately felt the irresistible lure of a different calling. In 1929 she astonished her friends by entering the Sisters of Social Service. Though she had never given the impression of deep piety, her diaries reveal the passion with which she embraced her vocation: "Oh, my Lord, my God, how have I become worthy of your goodness? How have I deserved that you have granted me such a beautiful, a deep, a blissful and a meaningful life?"

With Hungary's alliance with Nazi Germany, Sara watched in horror the rise of race hatred. In a hostel for working women, which she directed in Budapest, she hid hundreds of Jews. In 1943 she took a vow before her superiors, offering her life to spare the other members of her Society, should persecution arrive.

On December 27, 1944, the house was raided. Four Jews along with a religion teacher were arrested. After turning herself in, Sara, along with the others, was marched to the banks of the Danube, where they were stripped and shot. Before dying she knelt in the snow and signed herself with the cross. She was beatified in 2006.

"Burning love is like a burning lamp; only burning love can enlighten the dark of the road; only the warmth of burning love can turn the cold of this journey friendly, and burning love can make its ruggedness surpassable."
—Blessed Sara Salkahazi

St. Thomas Becket
Archbishop and Martyr (1118–1170)

The murder of Archbishop Thomas Becket in Canterbury Cathedral in 1170 is one of the most celebrated episodes in medieval history. Within days of his death, there were reports of miracles at his grave, and his canonization followed only two years later.

The circumstances of Becket's death were rooted in his long and complicated relationship with King Henry II. For years they were close friends. Henry appointed Becket as his chancellor, the second most powerful office in the realm. Later he also appointed him to the vacant see of Canterbury. The king's intentions were not terribly subtle. But Thomas disappointed him by taking his new office seriously. He resigned his post as chancellor and adopted a new regime of prayer and fasting. More significantly, he began to resist the king's encroachments on the independence and prerogatives of the Church. Relations between the former friends soured to the point that Thomas was forced to flee England for six years of exile in France.

Eventually, a fragile reconciliation allowed Thomas to return. But further provocation caused Henry to utter a fateful curse: "Who will rid me of this troublesome priest?" Four knights, understanding the king's meaning, departed for Canterbury and slew the archbishop at his altar. All Europe was horrified, and Henry fasted in penance for forty days. Thomas was immediately acclaimed a saint by the common people, and his tomb became one of the most frequented pilgrimage sites in Europe.

"I commit myself and my cause to the Judge of all men. Your swords are less ready to strike than is my spirit for martyrdom."

—St. Thomas Becket

Sebastian Castellio
Prophet of Religious Freedom (1515–1563)

As a young man in Lyons in 1540 Sebastian Castellio witnessed the execution of three Lutheran heretics. Profoundly shaken, he forsook his country and his Catholic faith. Declaring himself a Protestant, he traveled to Geneva, where John Calvin appointed him a schoolmaster. Nevertheless, because he rejected Calvin's notion that some people were predestined to damnation, he was denied ordination. Discouraged, he moved to Basel and taught Greek.

In 1553, at Calvin's instigation, an amateur theologian named Michael Servetus was burned at the stake for denying the Trinity. For Castellio, this was a defining moment. The message of Jesus was mercy; he believed there could be no greater blasphemy than to kill a human being in the name of God. He set forth his views in a major work. How could one love one's neighbors, he asked, while killing them over differences in "sound doctrine"? "How God will despise these theologians on the Day of Judgment for this sound doctrine!"

His views on toleration and respect for the rights of conscience were exceptional for his time and, indeed, for many centuries. "To force conscience is worse than cruelly to kill a man," he wrote, "because I must be saved by my own faith and not by that of another. . . . The Church can no more be constructed by persecution and violence than walls can be built by cannon blasts."

Though he published under a pseudonym, Castellio's identity was easily discovered and he was charged with heresy. He died on December 29, 1563, before his case could be concluded.

"To kill a man is not to defend a doctrine, but to kill a man."

—Sebastian Castellio

749

Blessed Eugenia Ravasco
Founder, Congregation of the Sacred Hearts
of Jesus and Mary (1845–1900)

Eugenia Ravasco, who lost both her parents before the age of ten, was raised by loving relatives in Genoa. A pious child, she developed a deep devotion to the Sacred Heart of Jesus and the Immaculate Heart of Mary. When, in 1863, she attended a retreat by a missionary of the Sacred Heart, she was deeply stirred by his words: "Is there no one out there who feels called to dedicate themselves to doing good for love of the Heart of Jesus?" She felt that his words were directed personally to her.

It was a time in Italy of widespread hostility to the Church. Her own brother had joined the anticlerical Freemasons. Eugenia wished to dedicate herself to providing religious education to poor young girls, many of them abandoned and living on the streets. Friends joined her and from this small beginning Eugenia—at the age of only twenty-three—founded a new religious community, the Congregation of the Sacred Hearts of Jesus and Mary. Their goal, as she put it, was to form "honest citizens in society and saints in Heaven."

The congregation won diocesan approval in 1882. Eugenia traveled widely, spreading houses and extending the congregation's work from the education of young girls to caring for prisoners, the dying, and people estranged from the faith.

She died on December 30, 1900, and was beatified in 2003.

"With foresight, she was able to open herself to the pressing needs of the mission, with special concern for those who had 'fallen away' from the Church."
—Pope John Paul II

John Main
Monk (1926–1982)

John Main spent his early life in a range of occupations as soldier, lawyer, and British civil servant in Malaya before becoming a Benedictine monk at the age of thirty-three. He had felt called to a life of prayer and dedication to God. But in becoming a monk he had only opened the door on another search: to find the relevance of monastic life to the spiritual hunger afflicting the modern world. What was needed, he believed, was a form of prayer adapted to the demands of life in the world. Returning to the spiritual practice of the Desert Fathers, he remembered their practice of meditating on certain words or mantras, such as *maranatha*—the Aramaic prayer, "Come, Lord Jesus."

In 1975 Main organized a small prayer group at Ealing Abbey in England to experiment with this new form of Christian meditation. Through imageless prayer and the repetition of a mantra, he taught that one might move from the surface of consciousness to the silent place where Jesus lives and prays within us. "To meditate," he wrote, "means to live out of the center of our being."

Many people were drawn to his prayer circle. In 1977 the bishop of Montreal invited Main to launch an experimental monastic community including both monks and laypeople. This new priory became the center for a worldwide network of Christian meditation, which continues today. John Main died of lung cancer on December 30, 1982.

"All Christian prayer is a growing awareness of God in Jesus."

—John Main, OSB

St. Melania the Younger
Widow (383–439)

St. Melania was one of the great women of the early Church. In a life of unusually varied experiences she assumed many roles—as wife and mother, monk and hermit, pilgrim and spiritual director—all united in an underlying call to the spiritual life.

Born to a wealthy Christian family in Rome, she was forced to marry at the age of fourteen. After the death of her children, however, she won the consent of her husband and widowed mother to consecrate herself to God. What is more, she convinced them both to join her in giving up all their property and adopting a life of prayer and good works.

She and her husband fled the sack of Rome and settled in North Africa, where they established a pair of monasteries. Later they moved to the Holy Land, settling in Jerusalem, where they lived for fourteen years until her husband's death. At that point, Melania retired to a nearby cell, which became in time the center of a large convent of women.

While spending the Christmas of 439 in Bethlehem she became ill and died on December 31. Her final words: "As the Lord willed, so it is done."

"The Lord knows that I am unworthy, and I would not dare compare myself with any good woman, even of those living in the world. Yet I think the Enemy himself will not at the Last Judgment accuse me of ever having gone to sleep with bitterness in my heart."

—St. Melania the Younger

St. John Francis Regis
Jesuit (1597–1640)

John Francis Regis, who was born in the Languedoc region of France, entered the Jesuits at the age of eighteen and was ordained in 1631. Though his greatest desire was to join the mission to New France and there to offer his life, his superiors assigned him instead to labor in Huguenot country in the south of France, where the Church was scorned and priests were few. In 1633 he went to the diocese of Viviers, spending some years trudging through mountains, across winter snowdrifts and raging rivers, to conduct his mission retreats. He was tireless in visiting prisoners, the sick, and the poor. Though he often encountered hostile crowds, he disarmed them with his humility and compassion. His preaching skills and his dedication as a confessor won him a devoted following and a growing reputation for holiness.

In Montpelier he established a group to help women escape from prostitution. When told that certain aristocrats didn't care for his spending so much attention on those at the margins, he replied, "So much the better: we are doubly blest if we relieve a poor brother at the expense of our dignity."

In the winter of 1640 he fell ill and died on December 31 at the age of forty-three. His last words were, "Into thy hands I commend my spirit." He was canonized in 1737.

"If I can keep a person from committing one sin that except for my efforts they would have committed, it's worth all my effort."

—St. John Francis Regis

INDEX

ThisDay^{Give Us}